Challenging Sonority

Studies in Phonetics and Phonology
Edited by Martin J. Ball, Linköping University, and Pascal van Lieshout, University of Toronto

The aim of this series is to provide both accessible and relevant texts to students of linguistics, phonetics and speech sciences, and to publish more advanced texts and edited collections. The textbooks aim to cover a wide variety of topics relevant for such an audience, and to introduce these topics in a practical way to enable students to undertake a range of analysis procedures. The more advanced books will present state-of-the-art research in the topic concerned.

While we intend to cover a wide range of topics in phonetics and phonology, there will be an emphasis on phonetic studies of under-reported languages, or the bringing of new data to explore phonetic characteristics on the one hand, and on phonological studies that employ more psycholinguistic, cognitive and functional approaches on the other (and, of course, on the interaction between phonetics and phonology). The recent increase in interest in laboratory phonology we see as particularly to be welcomed. Each volume will be authored by leading authorities in the field, who have a grasp of both the theoretical issues and the practical requirements of the area and, further, are at the forefront of current research and practice.

Forthcoming:
Romance-Germanic Bilingual Phonology
Edited by Mehmet Yavaş, Margaret Kehoe and Walcir Cardoso

Challenging Sonority
Cross-Linguistic Evidence

Edited by
Martin J. Ball and Nicole Müller

SHEFFIELD UK   BRISTOL CT

Published by Equinox Publishing Ltd.
UK: Office 415, The Workstation, 15 Paternoster Row, Sheffield, South Yorkshire S1 2BX
USA: ISD, 70 Enterprise Drive, Bristol, CT 06010

www.equinoxpub.com

First published 2016

British Library Cataloguing-in-Publication Data
A catalogue record for this book is available from the British Library.
ISBN 978 1 781792 27 8 (hardback)

Library of Congress Cataloging-in-Publication Data
Names: Ball, Martin J. (Martin John) editor. | Müller, Nicole, 1963-editor.
Title: Challenging sonority : cross-linguistic evidence / edited by Martin J. Ball and Nicole Müller.
Description: Sheffield, UK ; Bristol, CT : Equinox Publishing Ltd, [2016] | Series: Studies in Phonetics and Phonology | Includes bibliographical references and index.
Identifiers: LCCN 2016007368| ISBN 9781781792278 (hb) | ISBN 9781781794548 (e-epub)
Subjects: LCSH: Sonorants (Phonetics)
Classification: LCC P221.7.C53 2016 | DDC 414—dc23
LC record available at https://lccn.loc.gov/2016007368

Typeset by S.J.I. Services, New Delhi
Printed and bound by Lightning Source Inc. (La Vergne, TN), Lightning Source UK Ltd. (Milton Keynes), Lightning Source AU Pty. (Scoresby, Victoria)

Contents

Introduction

Martin J. Ball and Nicole Müller

Sonority has been of interest to phoneticians and phonologists for over a century. In recent years there has been a renewed interest in the topic – as shown, for example, in Steve Parker's important collection (Parker 2012). The impetus for the present collection came from investigations of under-reported languages and from normal and disordered speech development, and speech disorders in aphasia. It seemed to us that many of these studies presented a challenge to sonority, a challenge that a new collection in sonority might highlight.

A more personal renewal of interest in sonority came from the editors' recent move to Sweden. Swedish phonology (see, for example, Riad 2014) shows at least two interesting features as far as sonority is concerned. One is a series of phonological changes (some quite recent) whereby /Cj-/ clusters have undergone cluster reduction. However, the changes are not those predicted by the Sonority Sequencing Principle (SSP, see Clements 1990), whereby syllable onsets and codas are lower in sonority than the vocalic nucleus of the syllable, and whereby onset and coda clusters show increasing and decreasing sonority profiles respectively with no reversals of sonority part way through. The SSP would predict the deletion of /j/; however, in many cases we see the reduction of the first, less sonorous, consonant. This occurs with plosives (/dj-/ → /j-/, /gj-/ → /j-/), a fricative (/hj-/ → /j-/), and a liquid (/lj-/ → /j-/), though other combinations have resulted in a blend of the stop and glide into a fricative (e.g., /tj-/ → /ɕ-/), and others again are so far unaffected (e.g., /fj-/).

Another phonological characteristic of interest in Swedish is the complex word-final clusters that are possible through the addition of inflectional suffixes. Riad (2014: 295) gives the following examples of 4, 5 and 6 consonant clusters (where a hyphen represents the boundary between morphemes): /rm-st/ *närmst* 'nearest'; /lm-sk-t/ *skälmskt* 'roguish'; /lm-sk-t-s/ *skälmskts* 'roguish [genitive]'. While the first two examples adhere to the SSP (albeit being very complex), the last breaks the SSP by producing a fall-rise in sonority values. Garlén (1988) provides an example of a

5 consonant word-final cluster with a sonority reversal: /st-sk-t/ *väst-kustskt* 'west-coastly'. Of course, as with complex final clusters in English, such clusters are simplified in normal connected speech. Indeed, such simplifications have often been used as evidence for the power of sonority and the SSP. Nevertheless, such claims do have implications for models of phonology where sonority is deemed to be an innate or integral part of a speaker's competence.

Phonotactic simplification is a synchronic pattern. That is, if we say that clusters are simplified in colloquial, connected, speech, we still recognize that they are not in careful speech. For example, Welsh final consonant clusters such as /-vn/ and /-bl/ (*ovn* 'fear'; *pobl* 'people') are often realized in colloquial speech with an epenthetic vowel between the obstruent and the sonorant (see Awbery 1984). However, there are enough contexts for formal speech in Wales such that a good number of speakers will use the realizations without the epenthetic vowel, which thus produce sonority reversals.

Therefore, if SSP breaching syllable shapes can be used by speakers of certain languages, but these syllable shapes may be simplified (in line with the SSP) in some speech modes, where is sonority situated (assuming that it is an in-built part of a speaker's competence)? Arguably, not in the phonology, as speakers do use the non-simplified forms. Perhaps, following the arguments of Ball, Müller and Code (this volume), it would be in a phonetic planning component, intermediate between the phonology and a motor implementation component. Of course, an alternative view is that sonority is an artifact, emergent from other factors such as articulatory or perceptual constraints.

These and other arguments are made in several of the chapters in this collection. The book starts with a survey of sonority in natural language by Joan Rahilly, followed by two cross-linguistic chapters: Heather Goad examines /s/-clusters across languages and Ioana Chitoran investigates articulatory timing as related to sonority. The next eleven chapters look at sonority (and problems for sonority theory) in a range of different languages. Brent Archer and Matthew Faytak look at languages in South Africa and Cameroon respectively; Li Qiang presents a study of syllable shapes in Mandarin Chinese, and Anastasia Karlsson and Jan-Olof Svantesson look at casual and formal speech in Mongolian. Samira Farwaneh presents data on codas and coda clusters in Palestinian Arabic. Three chapters are devoted to sonority in North American languages: Marie Klopfenstein looks at Ottawa, Sonya Bird and Ewa Czaykowska-Higgins examine Salish languages, and Jason Brown's focus is on Gitskan. Yolanda Rivera-Castillo's study is of syllable structure in the Creole language Papiamentu spoken in the Caribbean islands of Curaçao, Aruba, Bonaire and Saba. Two chapters look at European languages: Chiara Meluzzi who describes a new degree of sonority in the Italian dialect of Bozen (South Tyrol), and Martin Ball and Nicole Müller who examine the effect of initial consonant mutation in Celtic languages.

The next five chapters deal with language development and with disordered language. Jessica Barlow provides a comprehensive review of sonority in relation to this topic, and is followed by chapters on a Greek-English bilingual child (Mehmet Yavaş and Elena Babatsouli), and cluster acquisition in Egyptian Arabic (Mona Maamoun) and in Farsi (Froogh Shooshtaryzadeh). Martin Ball, Nicole Müller and Chris Code conclude this topic by investigating the role of sonority in explaining speech disorders in aphasia and related acquired neurogenic speech disorders.

The final chapter by Mark Jones presents a review of the problems encountered when applying sonority to natural languages, and proposes an alternative explanation, a synthesis of approaches to acoustic-auditory recoverability. Thus, this collection covers data from a range of languages and from language acquisition and breakdown, but also a range of theoretical alternatives to phonological models of sonority. We feel the book offers a challenge to sonority, and look forward to more studies that test it further.

References

Awbery, G.M. (1984). Phonotactic constraints in Welsh. In M.J. Ball and G.E. Jones (eds.), *Welsh phonology: Selected readings* (pp. 65–104). Cardiff: University of Wales Press.

Clements, G.N. (1990). The role of the sonority cycle in core syllabification. In J. Kingston and M. Beckman (eds.), *Papers in laboratory phonology I* (pp. 283–333). Cambridge: Cambridge University Press.

Garlén, C. (1988). *Svenskans fonologi*. Lund: Studenlitteratur.

Parker, S. (ed.) (2012). *The sonority controversy*. Berlin: de Gruyter.

Riad, T. (2014). *The phonology of Swedish*. Oxford: Oxford University Press.

Martin J. Ball is Professor of Speech-Language Pathology (Clinical Linguistics and Phonetics) at Linköping University, Sweden. He is co-editor of the journal *Clinical Linguistics and Phonetics* (Taylor & Francis), and of the book series *Communication Disorders Across Languages* (Multilingual Matters). His main research interests include sociolinguistics, clinical phonetics and phonology, and the Celtic languages. He is an honorary Fellow of the Royal College of

Speech and Language Therapists, and a Fellow of the Learned Society of Wales.

Nicole Müller is Professor of Speech-Language Pathology at Linköping University, Sweden; she will be taking up the position of Professor of Speech and Hearing Sciences at University College Cork, Ireland, early in 2017. Her areas of research interest include clinical linguistics, clinical discourse studies and pragmatics, age-related disorders of communication and cognition, multilingualism, and systemic functional linguistics. She is co-editor of the journal *Clinical Linguistics and Phonetics* and of the book series *Communication Disorders across Languages*.

1
Sonority in Natural Language: A Review

Joan Rahilly

1.1 Broad Themes in Sonority

This chapter offers a critical overview of the core principles in sonority theory and analysis, and considers a range of influential studies, past and present, which draw upon sonority as the central means for explaining phonological behaviour. We also refer to work which is not explicitly focused on sonority and which, in some instances, does not mention sonority at all, but whose findings are strongly anchored in sonority frameworks. The underlying position in the present chapter is that sonority-driven accounts have tended to oversimplify explanations of phonological patterning, by dividing sequences of sounds into those which observe a sonority hierarchy and those which do not, and by offering a general categorization of markedness to capture the apparent violations which constitute the latter category. It should be noted, of course, that the terms 'marked' and 'markedness' are wide-ranging: they indicate not just relative articulatory complexity and common versus less common occurrences (see Reimers 2006, for a comprehensive taxonomy of markedness), but also invoke a more formal and specific framework within Optimality Theory (OT). Neither is the existence of markedness uncontroversial in itself, whether in its traditional or OT sense, with Ohala (1990: 159), for instance, referring to the 'circularity' inherent in traditional explanations and accounts which offer markedness as an explanation of relative frequencies of particular sound types.

With reference to natural language varieties, including speech acquisition and disorder, the relative strengths and shortcomings of a sonority-based approach will be considered here. It will be shown that, on the basis of available evidence, there is a need to problematize various approaches to sonority, given their inability to account in a consistent fashion for unusual or irregular patterns in speech, whether in normal or non-normal varieties.

The present chapter concludes by highlighting analytic frameworks within which traditional aspects of sonority have been accommodated alongside more revelatory approaches, with a focus on insights from OT.

1.2 Core Controversies in Sonority Analysis

The central contribution of sonority analysis to phonology has been its role in highlighting widespread patterns of segment combinations and sequences, where 'widespread' refers to: cross-language effects, common patterns in language acquisition irrespective of the ambient language, and typical trends in diachronic and synchronic language change. In these areas, existing research on sonority in natural language is particularly indebted to Clements' (1988) work on syllabification wherein, amongst other insights, it is noted that adherence to sonority principles underlie 'cross-linguistic preferences' (p. 1) for particular syllable structures. As a brief but facilitative working definition, and notwithstanding the variety of taxonomical approaches taken by researchers, 'sonority' denotes the relative resonance of speech sounds which, in turn, derives from their degree of constriction: within syllables, segments rise in sonority or become less constricted as they reach the nucleus, and fall in sonority thereafter within the syllable. Clements notes that this 'Sonority Sequencing Principle' (SSP) which is shared amongst languages offers 'one of the highest-order explanatory principles of modern phonological theory' (1988: 2). Along similar lines, Parker (2011) states that sonority patterns are sufficiently widespread across languages to warrant a place in Universal Grammar.

However, in spite of the overwhelming tendency for segments within clusters and syllables to adhere to the SSP, it is clear that not all examples from natural language do observe the principle. Where an apparent violation occurs (for cross-linguistic examples, see Parker 2011, for instance, and contributions to this volume), questions arise regarding whether to treat the distribution merely as an anomaly without further scrutiny, or to find alternative and more enlightening analyses. Smith (2010), for instance, in an account of phonological acquisition, moves beyond the sort of approach which labels sonority breaches as exceptions to the general rule, and invokes a so-called 'differential ranking of constraints' within an OT context, albeit with 'no way of accounting for how [the differential ranking] is acquired' (p. 15).

Whilst investigations since Clements' work of the late 1980s and early 1990s have provided broadly consistent and convincing evidence in support of the SSP, less attention has been paid to cases which appear to be at odds with the stated norms. Recent and current research, on the other hand, is making considerable progress in charting instances where languages or varieties of language, including disordered types, do not conform to expected sonority patterns. Admittedly, though, the rigorous attention paid to typologizing exceptions to established patterns falls somewhat short of explaining precisely why those exceptions occur. Nonetheless, current work aims to recalibrate relevant thinking both on the structure of the variety under investigation and of natural language more generally. We now move on to consider available contexts for theorizing and analysing sonority.

1.3 Trends in Sonority Analysis

It seems fair to suggest, on the basis of emerging accounts of sonority, that researchers are willing to adopt a broad-church approach where it enables them to benefit from various phonetic and phonological insights. We should note, though, that assumed principles of sonority ranking and ordering within syllables have been far from universally agreed upon, with Ohala's interventions offering the most notably strident claim that 'sonority has never been satisfactorily defined' (1990: 160), that contemporary accounts are circular (1990; 1992), and that traditional approaches 'should be abandoned' (1992: 334). Ohala also states that 'there are no prospects that anyone is getting even close to solving this problem – except, perhaps by abandoning it and invoking an entirely new notion to explain segment sequences' (1990: 160). His own response to the issue of capturing phonological regularity (Ohala 1992) recommends a phonotoactic approach in which segment sequences and their 'predicted survival' in the world's languages (p. 329) are defined by their relative acoustic salience, with the effect that 'rapid modulations would be better than slow' (p. 327) and without recourse to their role in syllable structure. Here, 'modulations' refers to the speed of change of acoustic parameters: [ta] is more salient than [ma], for instance, because the former requires a more rapid articulatory inter-segment adjustment. In the context of a study on children's lexical development and with reference to clinical varieties of speech, Gierut, Morrisette and Brown (2015) note that focusing on teaching marked structures, such as those involving greater sonority distances, is more productive than treating unmarked examples. It is clear that the concerns raised by Ohala have been responsible, at least in part, for moving matters regarding sonority beyond the traditionally syllable-specific domain, whilst maintaining the insights afforded by the SSP.

Current approaches which maintain a segment sequencing framework for sonority-based accounts tend to do so in a modified form within the framework of OT. Notwithstanding the OT focus, though, significant research effort continues to be expended on physiological patterns within syllables, and relevant studies underscore the importance of charting articulatory organization as a means for explaining syllable structure. The majority of such studies, however, tend not to invoke sonority per se as an overarching principle (for a summary, see Krakow 1999). Indications are that the most propitious model for analysing sonority will be a salience-based one, drawing upon insights both from OT and articulatory and perceptual phonetics and phonology.

1.4 Sonority Domains and Definitions

Sonority analysts have tended to adopt either a localized phonetic approach to individual segments with a view to establishing whether given segments are sonorous or not, or have used a higher level phonological approach for examining how aspects of sonority are distributed across segment strings and how the sonority of individual segments might be altered by adjacent segments.

The phonetic approach focuses on aspects of vocal tract constriction or resonance, and follows either a strict binary feature system in which segments are classed as sonorant or not sonorant, or a ranked system in which all speech sounds are placed in a hierarchy according to their manner of articulation. The manner of articulation parameter may be taken as synonymous with resonance and intensity (see McCarthy 2008), although Heselwood (1998) warns that assuming correlations between sonority and vocal tract configuration is far from straightforward. He indicates that two prerequisites must be in place before the existence of sonority can be identified: 'perceptually salient periodicity, and vocal tract resonance with no supralaryngeal sound source superimposed on it' (p. 75). The binary system combines aspects of the early model offered by Jakobson and colleagues (see Jakobson, Fant and Halle 1963, for instance) which emphasized the acoustic identification of linguistically significant elements of speech sounds. Those acoustic parameters are then mapped onto articulatory, perceptual and phonological correlates (for a summary of how relevant trends in binary approaches have filtered into current work on phonological representation in sonority see Lahiri and Reetz 2010). Within the distinctive feature context, plosives, affricates and fricatives are not sonorant ([−son]), whilst other consonants and all vowels are sonorant ([+son]), leading to natural classes of sonorants and non-sonorants.

Proctor and Walker (2012) have provided an innovative strand to the investigation of sonority, namely an MRI-focused study, and their findings indicate clearly that constriction must be considered more finely, i.e. not just in overall terms, but with reference to the detail of particular configurations in carefully defined articulatory regions. They state, for instance, that laterals and rhotics have 'intrinsic articulatory differences' (p. 308), irrespective of some underlying similarities in their respective sonority profiles. Similarly, Gordon, Ghushchyan, McDonnell, Rosenblum and Shaw (2012) present findings from their acoustic measurement of prominence in central vowels for five languages and conclude that a single dimension for differentiating sonorants from non-sonorants is insufficient. They note that 'there is no single parameter that predicted sonority distinctions across all languages' in their data (p. 33) and report and underscore the counterintuitive finding that schwa often emerged with a greater sonority profile than the peripheral vowels which they investigated.

The growing evidence that sonority cannot be adequately captured with reference to the mere presence or absence of constriction of segments is echoed by Green (2003) for Icelandic data. In addition to the constriction-based profiling system, phonetic approaches have equated sonority with loudness, either as perceived auditorily or manifest in acoustic terms. Flipsen (2006), for instance, refers to sonority as 'relative loudness' (p. 305) and underscores the importance of loudness in the acoustic signal by stating that it enables analysts to identify syllable nuclei even in the absence of familiarity with the language under investigation.

Whilst the phonetic approaches outlined above focus on individual segments and the binary presence or absence of sonority, phonological accounts assume a scalar distribution of sonority aspects and consider how that distribution maps onto higher levels of language structure. The scalar system (popularized by Foley 1972, for example) assigns degrees of resonance to all segment types based on their relative constriction and provides a ranked hierarchy of segments ranging from vowels to stops. Within the scalar system, it is not the case that segments are merely sonorant or not: fricatives, for example, are placed on the sonority scale but they are ranked lower than nasals and above plosives, and vowels tend to be subdivided based on their particular configurations. The sonority scale progresses, therefore, from low vowels as the most sonorous segments through to the least sonorous category of voiceless plosives, as follows (where '>' indicates 'has higher sonority than'): low vowels > mid vowels > high vowels > flaps > laterals > nasals > voiced fricatives > voiceless fricatives > voiced plosives > voiceless plosives. The precise details of the sonority scale are not uniform for all authors, largely due to the extent to which each segment category is subdivided, but established, influential and representative scales are available in Gierut (1999); Steriade (1990); Prince and Smolensky (2004).

With specific regard to higher level domains, i.e. those which go beyond the individual segment, the core role of sonority analysis is its contribution to the understanding of phonological patterning within syllables. Howard and Heselwood's (2013) account of vowel development and disorder, for instance, states that 'syllables can be conceptualized as a sonority profile' and the authors summarize the role of vowels, in their capacity as sonority peaks, as having 'a key organizational role in syllables' (p. 95). In a comment which recalls the salience and modulations arguments advanced by Ohala (1992), they go on to note how a CV syllable structure, entailing a low followed by a high sonority segment, facilitates listeners' ability to perceive and understand linguistic structure because they can 'more easily keep track of events through time if successive events are maximally different' (p. 95). The idea that the SSP facilitates perceptual categorization is further underscored by Ohala (1992) who, referring to Kawasaki's (1982) earlier acoustic work on sound sequences, notes that sounds with 'similar trajectories' would be 'subject to confusion and thus merger' (pp. 327–8). Along similar lines, Prince and Smolensky (2004) draw on work by Dell and Elmedlaoui on Imdlawn Tashlhiyt, a North African dialect of Berber (see, for example, Dell and Elmedlaoui 1985) to illustrate the legitimacy of determining the nucleus of a syllable by means of relative rather than inherent sonority so that, in fact, the nucleus need not be realized by a vowel at all. In the examples given by Prince and Smolensky (2004), stops, fricatives, nasals and liquids are shown to occupy syllable nucleus position. The Dell-Elmedlaoui Algorithm (DEA) is a method which predicts syllable nuclei and syllabification based on sonority: in this model, the optimal or most harmonic syllable nuclei are those which are most sonorous, but Prince and Smolensky note that '[s]egments of high sonority are not intrinsically more harmonic than those of lower sonority. It is only when sonority is contemplated in a structural context that the issue of well-formedness arises' (p. 21).

1.5 Sonority Sequencing

The phonological approach aims to account for the ways in which segments combine with one another in terms of their type and frequency within syllable structure. This aspect of sonority forms the basis of the SSP, the investigative trend which has dominated work in the field since the late 20th century (see Clements 1988). The SSP indicates a tendency, shared across languages but not universal, for syllables to be structured internally in particular ways, i.e., with the most sonorous element constituting the syllable peak and the less sonorous portions occurring to the right and left of the peak. According to the SSP, the directional distribution of sonority across syllables is such that rightward movement rises towards the peak, and post-peak segments decline in sonority. Ettlinger, Finn and Hudson Kam (2011) provide evidence for the relevance of the SSP for perceptual categorization, in the case of segmentation in word learning tasks. According to Clements (1988), syllables which do not observe the SSP are 'relatively infrequent' (p. 4).

In addition to offering a means for accounting for language-wide patterns in syllable structure, and as a trend which facilitates listeners' processing and comprehension as indicated above, there is also evidence that the SSP offers an enlightening means for explaining sound change (see Foley 1972). The value of the SSP, however, has been questioned by Carnie (1994) who, for modern Irish, suggests that what matters are linear relationships between adjacent segments and not longer-term or 'hierarchical' or 'long distance' (p. 82) relationships spanning a number of segments.

The SSP presupposes a rank order numeric scale which places segments according to their relative sonority profile, although analysts vary in terms of whether the scale rises or falls to reflect increasing sonority. Roca (1994), for instance, assigns a value of 1 to plosives and 6 to vowels, employing lower numbers to indicate less sonorous sounds. Between 1 and 6 for Roca, a score of 2 corresponds to fricatives, 3 to nasals, 4 to liquids, and 5 to glides. Furthermore, the number of ranked positions on the sonority scale varies according to the number of subcategories identified for consonants and vowels. As an illustration of both a reversed and expanded scale, in comparison with Roca, the clinical study by Morrisette, Farris and Gierut (2006) is instructive. The authors examine the effect of targeting syllable structure complexity, measured partly in terms of sonority distance, upon learnability in a clinical context. They adopt Steriade's (1990) system in which the following values are assigned: 7 for voiceless stops and 6 for voiced stops; 5 for voiceless fricatives and 4 for voiced fricatives; 3 for nasals; 2 for liquids; 1 for glides; and 0 for vowels. The values allow sonority distance between cluster members to be captured, so that [pl], for example, has a value of 5 (7 – 2) and is therefore less sonorous than [bl] which has a value of 4 (6 – 2). According to this scale, clusters with negative values signal combinations in which relatively sonorous segments are followed by less sonorant varieties: in [sp], for example, the sonority distance is –2 (i.e., 5 – 7). Morrisette et al. (2006) highlight that, for clinical contexts, it is this distance aspect of sonority profiling which has particular relevance. They state, for instance, that although a child's substitute of [bw-] for /bl-, br-/ introduces a non-permissible combination for English, its sonority distance of 5 is identical to that of other clusters in English (e.g., /pl/) and, thus, it is 'adult-like in its organization as a well-formed onset of a syllable' (p. 211).

When considering segment sequencing in the particular context of consonant clusters such as those mentioned above, it is evident that the SSP has guided analysts' investigations even where it is not specifically cited as being an organizing principle. It is also the case that such investigations have enhanced our understanding of phonological naturalness. Tobin's (2002; 2009) accounts of phonology as human behaviour (PHB), for example, attribute certain phonological processes at syllable level to the minimum effort or economy of effort criterion (after Martinet 1955 and Diver 1979) and it is this so-called 'human factor' which underlies what Tobin refers to as the 'non-random distribution of phonemes in the structure of language' (2009: 327). Clements (1988) underscores the fact that particular syllable structures predominate across languages, and draws on earlier research to note that 'certain syllable types are less complex or less *marked* than others across languages' (p. 1; italics original). Tobin (2002) considers C_1C_2 clusters in 42 languages and concludes that these clusters are possible with the following caveats: C_1 may be a mobile or a stable phoneme, and C_2 may be either a mobile trill /r/ or a stable lateral /l/. In Tobin's terms, a 'mobile phoneme' is one that requires movement of the articulators, such as in a stop, whereas a 'stable phoneme', such as a fricative, requires no intra-segment articulatory movement. Such 'favoured' clusters fulfil the minimum effort criterion in relation to articulation, in addition to satisfying SSP requirements.

1.6 Breaches of the SSP

Given what has been said above about the SSP, it will be clear that not all sequences in all languages observe graduated patterns of sonority distribution either at syllable level or within clusters. Where apparent violations occur, various attempts have been made to explain the divergence between expectations arising from the SSP and the phonological patterns in question. As indicated above, some investigators have simply written off exceptions to the SSP as being inexplicable, whilst others have attempted to offer more productive ways of understanding relevant segment sequences. A straightforward example is /spɪt/ and other syllables beginning with /sp-/, in which the sonority progress of segments in the onset cluster represents a decrease rather than a rise in sonority in the approach to the syllable nucleus; an apparent breach, therefore, of the SSP. Parker (2011) states that clusters with an initial /s/ followed by a plosive are '[c]ross linguistically, the most frequent exceptions to the SSP' (p. 1164), but goes on to note that what might appear to be exceptions to the SSP are not necessarily so. He suggests, for instance, that judgements of adherence to the SSP should not be made on the basis of syllables which occur at word-edge only without reference to word-internal occurrences, since syllables in the former category cannot be considered as belonging to the so-called 'canonical syllable type' (p. 1163) but may be influenced by preceding consonants across word and syllable boundaries. In this respect, Parker echoes Hooper's (1976) observation for Spanish that sonority of a syllable-final consonant must exceed that of a following syllable-initial consonant, a tendency also observed for Latin by Cser (2012) and formulated as the Syllable Contact Law. It is misleading, therefore, to isolate word-initial clusters and syllables from their preceding environment. In such instances, Parker (2012) notes that 'factors other than sonority' are responsible for what appear to be SSP violations (p. 1163). He goes on to offer a range of examples which appear to violate the SSP but which, when analysed according to appropriate frameworks 'cannot withstand further scrutiny' and are best analysed as a 'degenerate syllable or an extra syllabic appendix licensed by the prosodic word' (p. 1163). Other authors, along with Parker, lend support to the position that what look like failures of the SSP should be viewed as having special status. Morelli (2003) for example, summarizes a range of studies which argue that apparent exceptions to the SSP should be seen as, in fact, 'immune' (p. 357) to expectations arising from the SSP, although she herself adopts an OT-led analysis to the investigation of /s/ plus stop onsets.

As noted above, Tobin's (2009) work on PHB invokes sonority principles albeit without explicit mention of the term, and in spite of PHB's helpfulness in uncovering the aspects of naturalness which underlie the SSP, it has less to say regarding instances where speakers do not observe sequencing norms implied by the SSP. Nonetheless, there is a recognition that certain disfavoured clusters, meaning those which are not entirely compatible with PHB, are motivated by communicative ends, or what Tobin refers to as a 'mini-max struggle', i.e., 'the desire to create maximum communication with minimal effort' (p. 331), by way of allowing articulatory progressions which are within the speaker's control. The 'mini-max struggle' reference here seems to echo Ohala's (1992) salience model summarized above. Where speech errors from clinical and developmental data diverge from expected patterns, Tobin states that they are the result of 'either extreme minimal effort or a lack of control over the articulatory tract or mechanisms' (2009: 344).

The relationship of communicative context to sonority patterns is considered in detail by Moreton, Feng and Smith (2008) with specific reference to perceptibility theory. They use a language 'sounding out' game to investigate listeners' preferences for CV or VC productions and find, for example, that voiced fricatives are preferred over nasals as onsets, and that nasals are preferred over liquids, also as onsets. They note that their game experiment allows them to uncover aspects of communicative salience which are not always derivable within the traditional sonority approaches and 'not evident in the ordinary language' (p. 51).

1.7 The Place of Optimality Theory and Markedness

One of the most fruitful methods of accounting for patterns which cannot be explained with reference to the SSP is to adopt the analytic context and theoretical frameworks of OT and Markedness. It will be clear from what has been said above that, in OT, the formalization of markedness moves beyond the definition of the term which predominated in the last decade of the 20th century. It is no longer a general designation of the sort criticized by Ohala (1990) for any phonological occurrence or pattern which simply does not observe given strictures such as SSP norms. Markedness is the framework which has been proposed to help explain aspects of naturalness in languages, where 'naturalness' in turn refers to degrees of phonological complexity. For example, a fricative is more complex in terms of articulatory gestures than a plosive consonant, and because of this relative complexity, the fricative is the marked example, whilst the stop is unmarked. For clinical speech, Anderson (1987) points out that greater generalization effects pertain in therapy when the marked version is treated and taught: the ability to produce marked variants implies the ability to produce unmarked examples, whereas targeting the unmarked version leads to improvements only in the specific unmarked class. For Barlow (2001), markedness applies to '... structures that are more difficult to perceive or produce, or that have limited occurrence cross-linguistically, ... structures [which] typically are acquired late by children and pose difficulty for second language learners' (p. 242). Barlow also notes that certain segment types are innately unmarked (vowels, glides, nasals and stops) whilst others (fricatives, affricates, liquids and consonant clusters) are innately marked.

Within OT, markedness acquires added significance insofar as it captures one type of relationship between possible input and output forms. Whilst the so-called generator or 'GEN' creates a variety of realizations of the input, the evaluator or 'EVAL' assesses the validity of those realizations with reference to particular constraints, and those constraints, in turn take one of two forms: Faithfulness constraints, in which the input and output forms are the same as one another, and Markedness constraints, in which some difference occurs between the input and output form. For example, one Faithfulness constraint 'MAX' indicates that no deletion should occur: if /tɒp/ is realized as [tɒp], then MAX is observed but, if it is produced as [tɒ] then MAX is violated and the realization is a marked one. The particular relationship of OT to sonority has been examined by Smith and Moreton (2012), for example, who refer to a 'markedness hierarchy involving sonority' (p. 169), a hierarchy which entails peak sonority at syllable nucleus and comparatively low sonority at onsets. Within the peak category, they note that low vowels have the highest sonority, followed by mid and then high vowels. Where sonority preferences are not observed, the OT explanation is that the Faithfulness and Markedness constraints have been reordered or ranked differently: Baertsch (2012), for example discusses a variety of language-specific differences in constraint hierarchies (see also Kiparsky 2003, for constraints in Arabic, in particular). On the one hand, violations of Faithfulness constraints lead automatically to markedness, but specific Markedness conditions also exist independently: examples are *COMPLEX and *CODA which indicate that there should be no realization of clusters and no codas, respectively. Where /flai/ is an input and [flai] is an output, for instance, the Markedness constraint *COMPLEX is violated. For Morelli (2003) the OT treatment of sonority violations in the initial consonant clusters in examples such as /rta/ and /sta/ can be accounted for with reference to two separate constraints, i.e. *REVERSAL and *PLATEAU, which disallow sonority reversals and plateaux, respectively. For /rta/, the *REVERSAL constraint is uppermost whilst, for /sta/, the *PLATEAU constraint takes precedence. The clusters in question are, therefore, marked in some respects and unmarked in others.

Morelli (2003) notes that all constraints suggested by the SSP are 'in principle violable' (p. 359), just as all other instances of exceptions to phonological patterns may be considered possible. What matters of course, is not so much the recognition that violation exists, but the methodology for explaining the series of events which lead to it. In broad terms, the shifting of sonority issues from the SSP to the OT domain requires the sonorant feature to be cast as a constraint which can be reordered where appropriate in order to allow patterns which would otherwise be illegal. A core advantage of the OT approach is that it enables analyses which recognize universal constraints, and is not limited, therefore, to probing language- or other variety-specific phonological properties and behaviours. It is tempting to argue that, in some senses, OT statements of Markedness may be just as vulnerable to the accusation of circularity levelled by Ohala at sonority: by simply creating constraints which reflect available realizations, we create a set of descriptors which offer an alternative statement rather than explanation of those realizations.

1.8 Revisiting the SSP

Whilst the OT framework has offered a productive interpretation of and facility for representing segment sequences which are otherwise difficult to capture, the SSP continues to drive much current work in the area of sonority analysis. The case of schwa epenthesis in a number of language varieties (see Sell 2012, for example, for Irish and Irish English in the west of Ireland) is typically accounted for by means of a resyllabification process designed to break up 'heavy coda clusters' (ibid.: 48) and avoid the lack of sonority distance between the original coda segments. For Modern Irish, there is some superficial difference of opinion concerning the environments which trigger epenthetic schwa: whilst the insertion is common between sonorant consonants followed by voiced stops (Sell cites Carnie's 1994 example of 'bolb' ['boləb] for *caterpillar*), there is less agreement regarding its prevalence where sonorant consonants are followed by voiceless stops. Carnie (1994), however, notes that epenthesis does take place in the latter environment but that it is specific to certain positions within syllables. So, for example, it is possible within coda clusters ([doɹəxə] for *dorcha*, i.e., dark) but not onset clusters. For Welsh, Hannahs (2013) refers to 'a significant number of words which, from their dictionary entries, appear to violate sonority sequencing' (p. 87) in coda clusters, such as *pobl* (people) and *cwbl* (all), but notes the problem has been circumvented by a vowel insertion between the coda consonants, and Lodge (2009) offers similar examples of sonorant 'interlude' (p. 53) for Scottish Gaelic. These apparent exceptions to the SSP tend to be merely noted as such, but no further justification of their status as exceptional cases is provided. Carnie's (1994) account adopts a feature geometry approach to explain how epenthesis is licensed only by the combination of some nodes and not others. Whilst the examples from Irish, Welsh and Scottish Gaelic provide an illustration of the ways in which the SSP continues to underlie general patterns of phonological production behaviour regarding epenthesis, Berent, Steriade, Lennertz and Vaknin (2007) and Berent, Lennertz, Smolensky and Vaknin (2009) approach the issue from a listener perspective. They offer an experimental basis for listener sensitivity to and preference for certain clusters. Their suggestion that 'sonority-related knowledge' (Berent et al. 2007: 624), acquired developmentally, underpins listener responses in these areas leads them to confirm 'the repeated emergence of the sonority hierarchy across languages and its convergence with the preferences of individual speakers' (p. 625).

1.9 Synthesis

This chapter has provided an overview of the core methods used by analysts to uncover aspects of sonority in natural speech, and given a sense of the theoretical innovations which have characterized sonority accounts in recent years. Nonetheless, some fundamental gaps in our knowledge remain, particularly regarding explanations for exceptions to general sonority patterns. Whilst earlier accounts, particularly the SSP, offer a clear basis for explaining and understanding common patterns of phonological patterning within syllables, they are less successful in accounting for unusual patterns. On the other hand, OT and Markedness offer a rich methodology for charting and calibrating universal constraints in natural language, but they are less concerned with accounting for why patterns in question come about. It seems clear that available models will continue to be used in tandem, as analysts pursue not just fuller descriptions of language-specific and universal phonological behaviours, but also explanations for those behaviours.

References

Anderson, J. (1987). The markedness differential hypothesis and syllable structure difficulty. In G. Ioup and S. Weinberger (eds.), *Interlanguage phonology: The acquisition of a second language sound system* (pp. 279–91). New York: Harper & Row.

Baertsch, K. (2012). Sonority and sonority-based relationships within American English monosyllabic words. In S. Parker (ed.), *The sonority controversy* (pp. 3–37). Amsterdam: Mouton de Gruyter.

Barlow, J.A. (2001). Case study: Optimality theory and the assessment and treatment of phonological disorders. *Language, Speech and Hearing Services in Schools*, 32, 242–56.

Berent, I., Steriade, D., Lennertz, T. and Vaknin, V. (2007). What we know about what we have never heard: Evidence from perceptual illusions. *Cognition*, 104, 591–630.

Berent, I., Lennertz, T., Smolensky, P. and Vaknin, V. (2009). Listeners' knowledge of phonological universals: Evidence from nasal clusters. *Phonology*, 26, 75–108.

Carnie, A. (1994). Whence sonority? Evidence from epenthesis in Modern Irish. *MIT Working Papers in Linguistics*, 21, 81–108.

Cser, A. (2012). The role of sonority in the phonology of Latin. In S. Parker (ed.), *The sonority controversy* (pp. 39–63). Amsterdam: Mouton de Gruyter.

Clements, G.N. (1988). The role of the sonority cycle in core syllabification. *Working Papers of the Cornell Phonetics Laboratory*, 2, 1–68. Reprinted in J. Kingston and M.E. Beckman (eds.) (1990). *Papers in laboratory phonology 1: Between the grammar and the physics of speech* (pp. 283–333). Cambridge: Cambridge University Press.

Dell, F. and Elmedlaoui, M. (1985). Syllabic consonants and syllabification in Imdlawn Tashlhiyt Berber. *Journal of African Languages and Linguistics*, 7, 105–30.

Diver, W. (1979). Phonology as human behavior. In D. Aaronson and R. Rieber (eds.), *Psycholinguistic research: Implications and applications* (pp. 161–86). Hillsdale, NJ: Lawrence Erlbaum.

Ettlinger, M., Finn, A.S. and Hudson Kam, C. (2011). The effect of sonority on word segmentation: Evidence for use of a phonological universal. *Cognitive Science*, 36, 655–73.

Flipsen, P. (2006). Measuring the intelligibility of conversational speech in children. *Clinical Linguistics and Phonetics*, 20, 303–12.

Foley, J. (1972). Rule precursors and phonological change by meta-rule. In R.P. Stockwell and R.K.S. Macacauley (eds.), *Linguistic change and generative theory* (pp. 96–100). Bloomington: Indiana University Press.

Gierut, J. A. (1999). Syllable onsets: clusters and adjuncts in acquisition. *Journal of Speech, Language, and Hearing Research*, 42, 708–26.

Gierut, J.A., Morrisette, M.L. and Brown, K.M. (2015). Sonority principles meet probabilistic phonotactics in lexical development. In M. Yavaş (ed.), *Unusual productions in phonology* (pp. 10–27). London: Psychology Press.

Gordon, M., Ghushchyan, E., McDonnell, B., Rosenblum, D. and Shaw, P.A. (2012). Sonority and central vowels: A cross-linguistic study. In S. Parker (ed.), *The sonority controversy* (pp. 219–57). Amsterdam: Mouton de Gruyter.

Green, A.D. (2003). Extrasyllabic consonants and onset well-formedness. In C. Féry and R. Van de Vijver (eds.), *The syllable in optimality theory* (pp. 238–53). Cambridge: Cambridge University Press.

Hannahs, S. J. (2013). *The phonology of Welsh*. Oxford: Oxford University Press.

Heselwood, B. C. (1998). An unusual kind of sonority and its implications for phonetic theory. *Leeds Working Papers in Linguistics and Phonetics*, 6, 68–80.

Hooper, J. (1976). *An introduction to natural generative phonology*. New York: Academic Press.

Howard, S.J. and Heselwood, B. (2013). The contribution of phonetics to the study of vowel development and disorders. In M.J. Ball and F. Gibbon (eds.), *Handbook of vowels and vowel disorders* (pp. 61–112). London: Psychology Press.

Jakobson, R., Fant, G. and Halle, M. (1963). *Preliminaries to speech analysis: The distinctive features and their correlates*. Michigan: MIT Press.

Kawasaki, H. (1982). *An acoustical basis for universal constraints on sound sequences*. Doctoral dissertation, University of California, Berkeley.

Kiparsky, P. (2003). Syllables and moras in Arabic. In C. Féry and R. van de Vijver (eds.), *The syllable in optimality theory* (pp. 147–82). Cambridge: Cambridge University Press.

Krakow, R.A. (1999). Physiological organization of syllables: A review. *Journal of Phonetics*, 27, 23–54.

Lahiri, A. and Reetz, H. (2010). Distinctive features: Phonological underspecification in representation and processing. *Journal of Phonetics*, 38, 44–59.

Lodge, K. (2009). *Fundamental concepts in phonology: Sameness and difference*. Edinburgh: Edinburgh University Press.

Martinet, A. (1955). *Economie des changements phonétiques traité de phonologie diachronique*. Berne: Francke.

McCarthy, J. J. (2008). *Doing optimality theory: Applying theory to data*. Oxford: Blackwell.

Morelli, F. (2003). The relative harmony of /s+stop/ onsets: Obstruent clusters and the sonority sequencing principle. In C. Féry and R. van de Vijver (eds.), *The syllable in optimality theory* (pp. 356–71). Cambridge: Cambridge University Press.

Moreton, E., Feng, G. and Smith, J.L. (2008). Syllabification, sonority, and perception: New evidence from a language game. *Papers from the Annual Regional Meeting, Chicago Linguistic Society*, 41, 341–55.

Morrisette, M.L., Farris, A.W. and Gierut, J.A. (2006). Applications of learnability theory to clinical phonology. *Advances in Speech-Language Pathology*, 8, 207–19.

Ohala, J.J. (1990). There is no interface between phonology and phonetics: A personal view. *Journal of Phonetics*, 18, 153–71.

Ohala, J.J. (1992). Alternatives to the sonority hierarchy for explaining segmental sequential constraints. *Papers from the Parasession on the Syllable: Chicago Linguistics Society, 1992*, 319–38.

Parker, S. (2011). Sonority. In M. van Oostendorp (Ed.), *The Blackwell companion to phonology* (pp. 1160–84). Oxford: Blackwell.

Parker, S. (ed.) (2012). *The sonority controversy*. Berlin: de Gruyter.

Prince, A. and Smolensky, P. (2004). *Optimality theory: Constraint interaction in generative grammar*. Oxford: Blackwell.

Proctor, M. and Walker, R. (2012). Articulatory bases of sonority in English liquids. In S. Parker (ed.), *The sonority controversy* (pp. 289–316). Amsterdam: Mouton de Gruyter.

Reimers, P.M. (2006). *The role of markedness in the acquisition of phonology*. PhD dissertation, University of Essex.

Roca, I. (1994). *Generative phonology*. London: Routledge.

Sell, K. (2012). ['fɪləm] and ['faɹəm]? Sociolinguistic findings on schwa epenthesis in Galway English. In B. Migge and M. Ní Chiosáin (eds.), *New Perspectives in Irish English* (pp. 47–65). Amsterdam: John Benjamins.

Smith, J.L. and Moreton, E. (2012). Sonority variation in stochastic optimality theory: Implications for markedness hierarchies. In S. Parker (ed.), *The sonority controversy* (pp. 167–94). Amsterdam: Mouton de Gruyter.

Smith, N. (2010). *Acquiring phonology: A cross-generational case-study*. Cambridge: Cambridge University Press.

Steriade, D. (1990). *Greek prosodies and the nature of syllabification*. New York: Garland Press.

Tobin, Y. (2002). Phonology as human behavior. In E. Fava (ed.), *Clinical linguistics: Theory and applications in speech pathology and therapy* (pp. 3–22). Amsterdam: John Benjamins.

Tobin, Y. (2009). Phonology as human behavior: Clinical phonetics, phonology and prosody. *Poznán Studies in Contemporary Linguistics*, 45, 327–52.

Joan Rahilly is Senior Lecturer in Linguistics and Phonetics at Queen's University, Belfast. Her research focuses on phonetic and phonological manifestations of speech and language disorders, but she is also pursuing work on literacy acquisition amongst young people in the Northern Irish context.

2
Sonority and the Unusual Behaviour of /s/

Heather Goad

2.1 Introduction

A cross-linguistic examination of phonological behaviour generally supports the position that stops and fricatives form a single sonority class of obstruents (e.g., Clements 1990). Among obstruents, however, /s/ stands out as exceptional. It often defies the phonotactic constraints that hold off other obstruents. It also commonly resists participating in processes that target or yield voiceless fricatives. From an acoustic perspective, /s/ differs from other obstruents in containing robust internal cues for place and manner of articulation (Wright 2004). This ensures that it can be appropriately identified, regardless of where it appears in a string of segments, and makes it resistant to participating in change.

Most of the literature on the unusual behaviour of /s/ has focused on Indo-European languages. One unexpected construction that many of these languages share is word-initial /s/+consonant (sC) clusters, so much of the literature has motivated analyses for /s/ in this context. However, sC clusters are sometimes considered to be an Indo-European anomaly, which leads us to question whether non-Indo-European languages have sC clusters displaying similar properties; and, more generally, whether /s/ behaves in unusual ways outside of Indo-European and, if so, how this should be formally expressed.

These questions will be addressed by examining /s/ in the syllabification systems of three unrelated languages: Acoma (Keres) (Miller 1965), Blackfoot (Algonquian) (Frantz 2009) and Ōgami (Ryukyuan) (Pellard 2009). In all three, /s/ functions unusually, but the patterns it displays differ from language to language and are, to a great extent, unlike what has been observed for Indo-European. We will thus conclude that /s/ patterns outside of its sonority class in typologically diverse languages, although the behaviour that it displays is not necessarily the same in all languages. This leads to the difficult challenge of finding a unified representation for /s/. Although we will conclude that this is not possible, we will nevertheless show that the diverse phonotactic behaviour that /s/ displays can be analysed in terms of ordinary syllable constituents if an abstract view of the syllable is adopted.

2.2 /s/ in Indo-European

We first demonstrate some of the ways that /s/ patterns outside the sonority class of obstruents in Indo-European languages, beginning with phonotactics.

2.2.1 A Preliminary Look at Phonotactics

A cross-linguistic examination of the constraints holding of word-initial clusters reveals that obstruents must typically be followed by segments of higher sonority, while /s/ is not restricted in this way.[1] Table 2.1 illustrates this for English and Italian respectively: stops and fricatives must be followed by approximants in English and by liquids in Italian, while /s/ can additionally be followed by stops and nasals in both languages, as well as by fricatives in Italian.[2,3]

The observation that obstruent-initial clusters must rise in sonority is consistent with the view that stops and fricatives are optimally located in positions that maximize their perceptibility (Wright 2004): they are identified most reliably when followed by sonorants. By contrast, /s/ is not bound to the segment that follows it in the same way. It contains robust cues for place and manner, which ensures that it can be appropriately identified regardless of where it appears. Perceptibility, then, is one element required

1 Henceforth, the terms 'obstruent' and 'fricative' will be used to refer to obstruents and fricatives other than /s/, unless otherwise noted.

2 English [ʃr] is typically assumed to be derived from /sr/ (Clements and Keyser 1983; Goldsmith 1990); hence its inclusion in Table 2.1.

3 Italian [zr] is absent from Table 2.1 because it is restricted to forms where a prefix boundary interrupts the cluster.

Table 2.1. Word-initial clusters in English and Italian.

English:			Italian:		
Stop-initial:			Stop-initial:		
[pl]/[bl]		[kl]/[gl]	[pl]/[bl]		[kl]/[gl]
[pr]/br]	[tr]/[dr]	[kr]/[gr]	[pr]/[br]	[tr]/[dr]	[kr]/[gr]
	[tw]/[dw]	[kw]			
Fricative-initial:			Fricative-initial:		
[fl]			[fl]		
[fr]	[θr]		[fr]		
	[θw]				
/s/-initial:			/s/-initial:		
[sp]	[st]	[sk]	[sp]/[zb]	[st]/[zd]	[sk]/[zg]
			[sf]/[zv]		
[sm]	[sn]		[zm]	[zn]	
	[sl]			[zl]	
	[ʃr]				
[sw]					

to explain why /s/ falls outside its sonority class and seemingly has a freer distribution than other obstruents in initial clusters.

2.2.2 The Behaviour of /s/ in Phonological Processes

If the acoustic properties of /s/ are partly responsible for its behaviour, the same cues which ensure that it can be appropriately identified should also make it resistant to participating in change. Specifically, there should be languages where alternations between stops and fricatives leave /s/ untouched. Such processes are attested in Indo-European. Consider, for example, Grimm's Law, which describes several systematic changes in consonants that took place between Proto-Indo-European and Proto-Germanic. The change of concern is that where Proto-Indo-European voiceless stops weakened to voiceless fricatives: *p* > *ɸ*, *t* > *θ*, *k* > *x*. Notably, *t* weakened to *θ*, not to *s*.

Surprisingly, though, weakening does commonly target /s/ in Indo-European, as observed in the historical development of Greek, Sanskrit and Armenian, and in the synchronic grammars of Gaelic and Ibero-Romance languages. For example, Andalusian Spanish as well as Caribbean and coastal dialects of Latin American Spanish all exhibit lenition in word-final position, where /s/ is realized as [s]~[h]~Ø (e.g., Alcina Franch and Blecua 1975; Lipski 1994). /s/ lenition is unexpected, as the place and manner (i.e., stridency) of /s/ should be readily recoverable from the acoustic signal, such that /s/ is reliably perceived as distinct from zero. In searching for an explanation of this unexpected behaviour, we probe the phonetic properties of /s/ in leniting varieties of European Spanish.

Experimental work undertaken by Romero (1995) shows that Andalusian /s/ is articulated differently from Castilian /s/. In the latter variety, /s/ is a strident apico-alveolar fricative, which contrasts with non-strident lamino-dental /θ/. Andalusian has neutralized this contrast in favour of laminal /s/, which has a variable constriction location. Romero shows that, when compared to Castilian, Andalusian laminal /s/ involves a reduction of gestural magnitude, which he further proposes was the trigger for lenition in this dialect. When this is coupled with Shadle (1991), who observes that apico-alveolar tongue posture is optimal for achieving the narrow constriction required for strident /s/, we can conclude that Andalusian /s/ is low in stridency, thereby approaching [θ].

Thus far, we have seen that the perceptual properties of /s/ enable it to pattern differently from other consonants in its sonority class. On one hand, high strident /s/ can have an unusual phonotactic distribution: in initial position, for example, it does not depend on the presence of a following sonorant to be reliably identified. Low strident /s/, on the other hand, can be singled out for lenition. At this point, we must address whether the unique behaviour of /s/ can be explained solely by its perceptual properties or whether these work in concert with structural properties. To address this question, we return to the phonotactic constraints that hold of initial sC clusters. As we will see, although the perceptual properties of strident /s/ can account for why /s/ can appear before stops in such clusters, it cannot account for the distributional constraints that hold of sC clusters across Indo-European.

2.2.3 Phonotactics Revisited

In Section 2.2.1, we observed that although the phonotactic constraints holding of word-initial clusters reveal that obstruents must typically be followed by segments of higher sonority, data from Indo-European demonstrate that /s/-initial clusters need not respect this constraint. Table 2.1 showed that sC clusters are quite free in English and Italian in terms of the range of sonority profiles they exhibit. Indeed, when viewed from the perspective of obstruent-initial clusters, the patterns in these two languages suggest that it is before stops, as well as before nasals, that /s/ is unusual, as these are the only clusters with a flat or shallow rise in sonority.[4] In English, for example, /s/+liquid (*sly, shrill*) would appear to mirror obstruent+liquid (*fly, trill*). However, an examination of the patterns from French in Table 2.2 indicates otherwise: the only sC clusters it natively permits are /s/+stop.[5]

Table 2.2. Word-initial clusters in French.

Stop-initial:		
[pl]/[bl]		[kl]/[gl]
[pʀ]/[bʀ]	[tʀ]/[dʀ]	[kʀ]/[gʀ]
Fricative-initial:		
[fl]	[fʀ]/[vʀ]	
/s/-initial:		
[sp]	[st]	[sk]
	*[s]+sonorant	

A comparison of Tables 2.1 and 2.2 suggests that English and French fall at opposite ends of the spectrum regarding the range of profiles attested for sC clusters. Table 2.3 reveals that this is indeed the case: Indo-European languages that allow sC fall on a continuum such that languages that permit /s/+rhotic also permit /s/+lateral; languages that permit /s/+lateral also permit /s/+nasal; etc.[6,7] In short, as the sonority of the consonant following /s/ rises, the well-formedness of the cluster deteriorates (Goad 2011, 2012).

4 Recall that Italian also permits /s/+fricative. I have ignored this here as the presence or absence of /s/+fricative does not follow the sonority continuum observed for sC in Table 2.3: languages with /s/+sonorant do not necessarily have /s/+fricative. Wright (2004: 51) proposes that /s/+fricative is disfavoured across languages as there is not enough perceptual distance between the two consonants.

5 French also permits /s/+glide, but the glide is located in the nucleus (e.g., Kaye and Lowenstamm 1984; Schane 1989). Indeed, in Table 2.3 here, we have excluded /s/+glide because glides in CGV strings can be syllabified in various ways across languages, each of which is subject to different constraints.

6 Information on Picard was provided by Julie Auger (personal communication).

7 /s/+nasal is only marginally acceptable in Greek.

Table 2.3. Word-initial sC clusters in Indo-European.

	Spanish, Brazilian Portuguese	French, Picard	Greek, Romansch	Italian, Dutch	English, Russian
/s/+stop	*	✓	✓	✓	✓
/s/+nasal	*	*	✓	✓	✓
/s/+lateral	*	*	*	✓	✓
/s/+rhotic	*	*	*	*	✓

Can the typology in Table 2.3 be predicted from the perceptual properties of /s/? To some extent, yes. First, the low stridency of /s/ in dialects of Spanish, as well as in Brazilian Portuguese (see Goad, forthcoming), could in part account for the absence of sC clusters in these languages. Since all languages with sC clusters allow /s/+stop, reliably identifying weak /s/ in such clusters would be compromised by the absence of a sonorant following /s/. Not surprisingly, then, in both languages, sC-initial roots are repaired through prothesis when they surface word-initially, which enhances the perceptibility of weak /s/ (e.g., Spanish: [e̲spirar] 'to exhale,' cf. [a-spirar] 'to inhale, aspire to'; Brazilian Portuguese: [i̲stavɛw] 'stable,' cf. [ĩ-stavɛw] 'unstable').

Second, the perceptual properties of strident /s/ can explain why /s/+stop is permitted in languages with sC clusters: as discussed earlier, /s/ has strong internal cues to place and manner, which means that it need not rely on an adjacent sonorant to be well-perceived.

In view of results like these, we may be tempted to conclude that a purely perceptual approach to the behaviour of /s/ can be provided. Indeed, in research that departs from the view that syllables are structurally represented, differences between /s/ and other obstruents are attibuted entirely to perceptual considerations (e.g., Fleischhacker 2001): consonants are ordered to maximize their perceptibility and the acoustic properties of /s/ versus other obstruents account for their divergent behaviour (e.g., Wright 2004). Such an approach, however, cannot explain why no language that allows sC forbids /s/+stop, nor can it explain why the well-formedness of sC worsens as the sonority of C increases (Goad 2016). Answers to these questions emerge when perceptual considerations are coupled with structural considerations, as discussed below.

2.2.4 Representations

In research that assumes a structured view of the syllable, the different phonotactic generalizations of /s/- versus obstruent-initial clusters, as well as differences in their phonological behaviour, have led to the proposal that obstruent-initial clusters form branching onsets while sC clusters have /s/ located outside the onset constituent containing the following C, as shown in (1) (see Goad 2011, for a recent review).

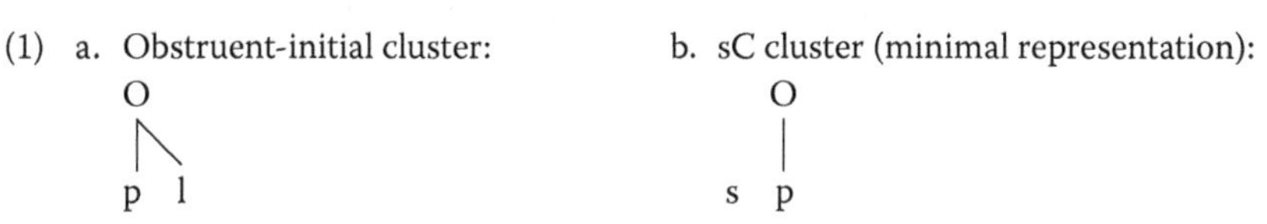

The representation in 1b is the minimal one that holds for sC clusters. Various proposals for the organization of /s/ have been forwarded in the literature, most commonly: that /s/ is extraprosodic (e.g., Steriade 1982), i.e., it does not belong to higher structure but is nevertheless protected from deletion; that /s/ is organized directly by the syllable (e.g., van der Hulst 1984) or prosodic word (e.g., Goldsmith 1990); or that /s/ is the coda (rhymal dependent) of an empty-headed syllable (following Kaye 1992). Each of these options is sketched in (2). (The representation in (2d) is slightly simplified.)

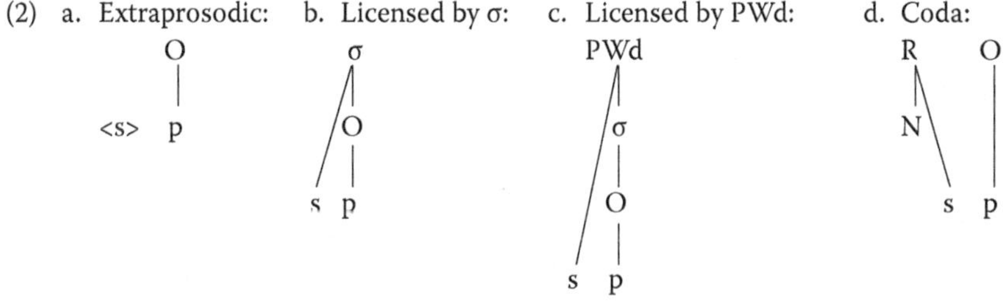

Of the options in (2), only (2d) correctly captures the phonotactic observations in Table 2.3 (Goad 2012, forthcoming b), specifically, that sC clusters should respect the constraints observed of coda+onset clusters, as detailed below. By contrast, the options in (2a–c), where /s/ is not organized by any type of sub-syllabic constituent, predict that /s/ and the consonant that follows it should not observe the same constraints that hold of other cluster types (branching onset, coda+onset etc.).

We have shown that sC cluster well-formedness is tied to the relative sonority of the consonant following /s/. To examine how this mirrors the constraints that hold of word-medial coda+onset clusters, we turn to the Syllable Contact Law (SCL) in (3).

(3) Syllable Contact Law (Murray and Vennemann 1983: 520):
The preference for a syllabic structure *A$B*, where *A* and *B* are marginal segments and *a* and *b* are the Consonantal Strength values of *A* and *B* respectively, increases with the value of *b* minus *a*.

Assuming the sonority scale in (4), higher consonantal strength values are assigned for consonants that are progressively lower in sonority.[8]

(4)

Sonority scale:	obstruent (incl. /s/) <	nasal <	lateral <	rhotic
Consonantal strength:	4	3	2	1

If we examine word-medial heterosyllabic clusters with an obstruent in coda, the SCL correctly predicts that clusters with an increasingly steeper rise in sonority are more costly due to poor syllable contact:

(5) Word-medial position:

Segmental profile:	Vp.tV >	Vp.nV >	Vp.lV >	Vp.rV
	Vs.tV >	Vs.nV >	Vs.lV >	Vs.rV
Syllable contact (*b*–*a*):	0	–1	–2	–3

In fact, word-medial clusters that steeply rise in sonority are optimally syllabified as complex onsets (✓V.plV/✓V.prV). If, however, this representation is never available for corresponding sC clusters (*V.slV/*V.srV), the coda+onset parse (Vs.lV/Vs.rV) will be the only option available (Goad 2012).[9] In many languages, the steep rise in sonority observed for such

8 The sonority scale in (4) is that most commonly accepted in the literature (e.g., Clements 1990), aside from the division drawn been types of liquids. The higher sonority of rhotics over laterals has been proposed by, for example, Selkirk (1984), Hall (1992) and Smith (2005) and is consistent with the relative well-formedness of /s/+rhotic versus /s/+lateral in Table 2.3.

9 Ashley Farris-Trimble has informed me that a handful of understudied languages permit /s/+liquid as their only sC cluster. As the optimal branching onset across languages is obstruent+liquid (Clements 1990), these /s/+liquid clusters may form branching onsets, counter to the proposal forwarded here. If this analysis can be supported, we speculate that /s/ may be low in stridency in these languages and, thus, unsuitable for involvement in true sC (coda+onset) clusters. /s/+liquid would thus be more akin to branching onset /θ/+liquid in these languages. Another possibility is that the liquid in /s/+liquid is nuclear in these languages, as proposed by Kaye (1985) for Vata. We leave detailed exploration of these languages to future research.

clusters will not be permitted, excluding word-medial sC clusters of these shapes altogether. In French, for example, while steeply rising medial clusters are well-formed when they can form branching onsets (e.g., [a.tʀɛ] 'attraction', [ta.kle] 'to tackle'), parallel /s/-initial clusters are illicit (*[as.ʀɛ], *[tas.le]). When the sonority profile is flat, by contrast, the first consonant can be an obstruent or /s/, as the cluster will be represented as coda+onset ([ɔk.tav] 'octave', [kɔs.tal] 'coastal').

If sC clusters in initial position are similarly heterosyllabic, the same effect will be observed: while obstruent-initial clusters that rise in sonority will form branching onsets (e.g., [.tʀɛ] 'very', [.kle] 'key'), sC clusters will form coda+onset clusters and, therefore, their well-formedness will be sensitive to whether and how steeply the cluster rises in sonority. In French, only flat sonority sC is permitted ([s.taʒ] 'internship'; *[s.ʀɛ], *[s.le]), paralleling what is observed in medial position.

In short, languages draw the boundary between well- and ill-formed sC clusters at different points, depending on sonority slope. Although the poor syllable contact in steeply rising /s/-initial clusters is licit in some languages, like English (e.g., [s.lɛd] 'sled', [ʃ.rɛd] 'shred'), as the sonority profile of sC increases, the heterosyllabic parse worsens, making such clusters illicit in others, like French.

Unlike what has been discussed for French, though, the same language may draw the boundary at different places for initial and medial sC clusters. In English, for example, initial sC with C of all sonority profiles is observed (Table 2.3). Word-medially, however, /s/+sonorant is essentially unattested, as in French. In spite of this, the cross-linguistic options for medial sC reflect the typology in Table 2.3 for initial position: medial sC deteriorates as the sonority of C increases.

Because the sonority profiles for initial and medial sC may not perfectly align in any given language, one may question whether they should truly be analysed in the same manner, as coda+onset. In view of this concern, we briefly examine differences in the voicing patterns of sC versus obstruent-initial clusters when sonority slope is held constant. Because voicing in coda is often dependent on the voicing value of following onsets, we should expect to find languages where /s/ in /s/+liquid clusters is voiced to [z], while voiceless obstruents in obstruent+liquid clusters are not, whether the cluster is located in initial or medial position. Consider Spanish. Although initial sC is not permitted in Spanish, in medial position, Spanish has the same profile as Dutch and Italian in Table 2.3. As demonstrated in (6a), voicing agreement targets /s/ but not voiceless obstruents. This supports a coda+onset analysis for /sl/. Turning to Italian, recall that in initial position, sC clusters other than /s/+rhotic are permitted. (In medial position, Italian has the same profile as French.) As in Spanish, the Italian data in (6b) show that voicing agreement targets initial /s/ but not voiceless obstruents.

(6) a. Spanish: medial position:

/sl/	[izla]		'island'
/fl/	[ʧifla],	*[ʧivla]	'whistle'
/kl/	[ʧikle],	*[ʧigle]	'chewing gum'

b. Italian: initial position:

/sl/	[zlanʧo]		'dash, leap'
/fl/	[flanʤa],	*[vlanʤa]	'flange'
/pl/	[planʧa],	*[blanʧa]	'console'-N

These two languages support the view that /s/- and obstruent-initial clusters are syllabified differently and that sC form coda+onset clusters in both initial and medial position. If the coda+onset parse is the only one available for sC, these clusters will be sensitive both to the SCL, where clusters with a (steeply) rising sonority profile are disfavoured, as well as to coda voicing constraints.

2.3 Beyond Indo-European

As mentioned earlier, the literature on the unexpected distribution of /s/ has concentrated on Indo-European languages, with most attention focusing on sC clusters. Because such clusters are sometimes viewed as an Indo-European accident, we turn now to look beyond Indo-European to examine whether /s/ patterns unusually in languages from other language families.

We consider the behaviour of /s/ clusters in the syllabification systems of three unrelated languages: Acoma (Keres) (Miller 1965), Blackfoot (Algonquian) (Frantz 2009) and Ōgami (Ryukyuan) (Pellard 2009). As we will see, /s/ functions unexpectedly when compared with other obstruents, but the patterns it displays differ from language to language and are unlike what has been discussed for Indo-European. While /s/ patterns outside its sonority class in genetically unrelated languages, because the behaviour it displays differs across languages, we are led to the difficult challenge of finding a unified representation for /s/. Although we will conclude that this is not possible, we will nevertheless show that the diverse phonotactic behaviour that /s/ displays can be analysed in terms of ordinary syllable constituents if an abstract view of the syllable is adopted: /s/ functions as the coda of an empty-headed syllable in Indo-European, as an onset followed by an empty nucleus in Acoma, and as nuclear in Blackfoot and Ōgami.

2.3.1 Acoma

We begin with Acoma, a Keres language spoken in New Mexico (Miller 1965). As in Indo-European, /s/ patterns differently from other obstruents. At first glance, Acoma resembles French in that sC clusters are limited to /s/+occlusive. A closer look, however, reveals that a coda+onset analysis of sC is unwarranted, as there are no codas elsewhere in the language (in native words) (ibid.). Coupled with other patterns of behaviour, namely the presence of a laryngeal contrast on the C following /s/ and an unusual type of allophony on the /s/ preceding C, we argue that sC clusters are not true clusters in Acoma but, instead, that an empty nucleus intervenes between /s/ and the following consonant (Goad 2012). Consequently, unlike in Indo-European sC, where /s/ functions as a coda preceded by an empty nucleus, in Acoma, /s/ functions as an onset followed by an empty nucleus.

The data in (7) show that sC clusters, which are realized as [s̺C] or [ʃC] (see below), occur both initially and medially in Acoma (transcriptions have been converted into IPA).[10] Medial clusters occur after both short (7b) and long vowels (7c). Although the former context might suggest a coda analysis for /s/, the latter casts doubt on this, as three position rhymes (i.e., VVs) in non-final position are cross-linguistically highly marked (e.g., Harris 1994). Combined with the lack of codas in Acoma, an alternative solution for sC must be sought.

(7)	a. #sC		b. VsC		c. VVsC	
	[s̺púuná]	'pottery'	[ʝút͡s̓is̺p'ə́tʰini]	'backbone'	[w̓ì̓ iʃp'i]	'cigarette'
	[ʃt͡ʃȁit͡sʰi]	'it is muddy'	[suʃt̓á]	'I took water'	[ʔúuʃt͡ʃúut͡sʰi]	'drum'
	[s̺kút͡s̺úw̓a]	'tadpole'	[ʔés̺ká]	'rawhide'	[s̓úuʃkʰì̓ it͡sʰi]	'I am brave'

In searching for an appropriate analysis for Acoma, we provide two pieces of evidence that sC cannot form clusters in Acoma, that is, that /s/ and C are not truly adjacent in this language. The first piece of evidence is that the three-way laryngeal contrast present in the language is maintained after /s/, as shown in (8).

(8)				
	[ʔiʃtûwá]	'arrow'	[s̺kủitʰaaʔa]	'he asked me'
	[m̓ȁaʃtʰu]	'silver fox'	[s̺kʰúuʝu]	'giant'
	[nȁaʃt̓ém̓i]	'starry eyes'	[s̺k'ət͡s̺ə́əná]	'crumbs'

10 Transcriptions such as [m̓], [s̓], etc. represent glottalized consonants.

Languages where /s/+stop truly form clusters typically display one of two patterns: (i) such clusters are uniformly voiceless unaspirated, even if the language otherwise exhibits aspiration of voiceless stops (e.g., English); (ii) laryngeal contrasts are maintained after /s/, but /s/ itself undergoes assimilation to the following stop (e.g., European Portuguese), as observed in (6) for /s/+liquid in Spanish and Italian. Illustrative data from English and European Portuguese appear in (9) and (10), respectively.

(9) English:

a.	[tʰɪl]	'till'	[dɪl]	'dill'	b.	[stɪl], *[stʰɪl]	'still'
	[əkʰórd]	'accord'	[rəgάrd]	'regard'		[əskórt], *[əskʰórt]	'escort'-v

(10) European Portuguese (Mateus and d'Andrade 2000: 43):

a.	[ʃpásu]	'space'	b.	[ʒbíʀu]	'constable'
	[ʃtaɾ]	'to be'		[ʒdrúʃulɐ]	'dactyl'
	[ʃkútɐ]	'listening'		[ʒgɐ́nɐ]	'strangulation'

To explain how the Acoma data in (8) cast doubt on a coda+onset analysis for sC, we must address why stops are uniformly unaspirated after /s/ in languages like English. We follow Iverson and Salmons' (1995) analysis which, itself, builds on Kim (1970). Kim proposes that aspiration is a consequence of the glottal width present in voiceless stops: in singleton stops, the vocal folds do not reach the adducted state required for voicing until after the release of the closure, which results in aspiration. As the glottis is open for the same interval of time in /s/+stop clusters as in singleton voiceless stops, it will have narrowed by the point when the stop closure is released and, consequently, the onset of voicing will align with the release. To formally capture Kim's observations, Iverson and Salmons posit a single [spread glottis] feature shared between /s/ and the following stop. See (11a), which is adapted to the representation for sC clusters proposed here for Indo-European.

In view of this articulatorily-grounded account for the lack of aspiration after /s/ in English-like languages, it is surprising to find a language like Acoma with contrastive aspiration after /s/, if /s/ and the following stop are truly adjacent. If, by contrast, an empty position interrupts the two consonants, this pattern is as expected, as each consonant would bear its own [SG] specification. Compare the representation for Acoma in (11b) with that for English in (11a).

(11) a. English:
[skai] 'sky'

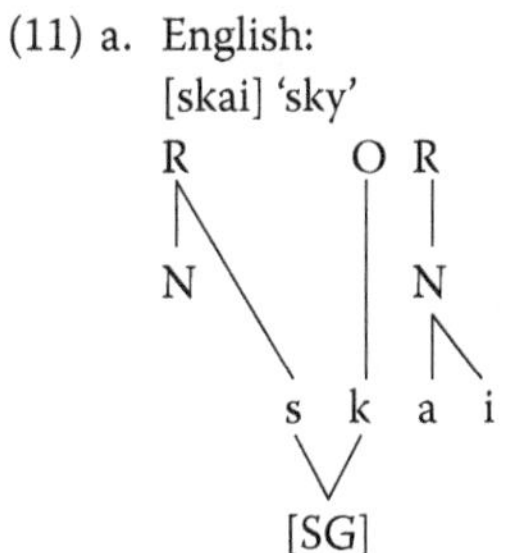

b. Acoma:
[ʂkʰúuju] 'giant'

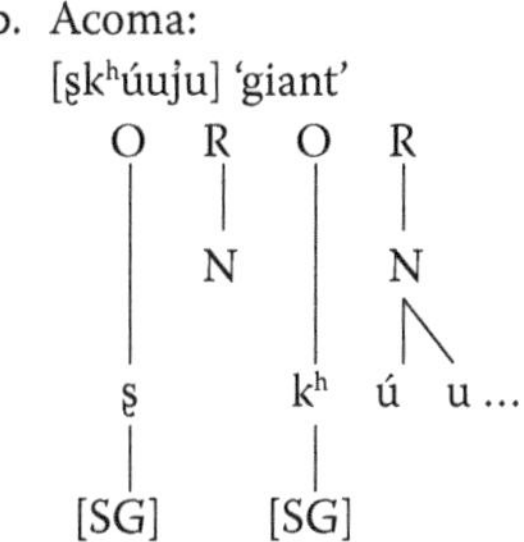

Further support that sC clusters in Acoma are interrupted by an empty nucleus comes from an unusual pattern of /s/ allophony in the language, as mentioned earlier. Acoma exhibits a three-way contrast amongst sibilants before vowels: /s, ʃ, ʂ/. In sC clusters, however, sibilants are not contrastive: /s/ surfaces as [ʂ] before labial and velar stops followed by /u, ə, a/ and as [ʃ] before dental and palato-alveolar occlusives and before labial and velar stops followed by /i, e/.

In earlier work, I argued that [ʃ] and [ʂ] are derived from /s/ in sC clusters in Acoma, due to the low stridency of /s/ in this language (Goad 2012). In Section 2.2.3 above, I suggested that the absence of sC clusters in Spanish and Brazilian Portuguese could, in part, be attributed to the weakly strident /s/ in these languages. Another pattern that occurs in languages with low strident /s/ is that sC clusters are well-formed but a posterior sibilant replaces /s/. This occurs in German, for example, where the sibilant in sC clusters is realized as [ʃ]. German /s/ is quite [θ]-like: it involves greater constriction width, which results in a lowered spectral mean, than English /s/, more akin to English /θ/ (Fuchs and Toda 2010). Given that all languages with sC clusters require /s/+stop, precisely the context where the perceptibilty of /s/ is most compromised, Goad (2012) proposes that German selects [ʃ] over [s] in such clusters, because of the [θ]-like quality of /s/ in this language.

Returning to Acoma, /s/ is described by Miller (1965) as dental (p. 7) and as followed by a 'theta offglide' (p. 13). This is consistent with /s/ being weakly strident in this language, like /s/ in German and in dialects of Spanish and Brazilian Portuguese. If /s/ were to surface as [s] in sC clusters, its perceptibility would be compromised, especially in Acoma where the only type of sC cluster permitted is /s/+occlusive. /s/ is thus realized as fully strident [ʂ] or [ʃ]. Which posterior sibilant surfaces depends on the context: I suggest that [ʃ] results from assimilation and that [ʂ] appears in contexts where assimilation cannot apply. The two contexts where assimilation takes place, (i) before dental and palato-alveolar occlusives and (ii) before labial and velar stops followed by /i, e/, are exemplified in (12). We consider the feature involved to be [coronal] although, clearly, this needs to be examined further.

(12) a. Context (i):
[ʔiʃtûwá] 'arrow'
[ʃt͡ʃ̓aits͡ʰi] 'it is muddy'

b. Context (ii):
[hîuʃpéj̓u] 'cry baby'
[s̓úuʃkʰi̓ its͡ʰi] 'I am brave'

Each of the assimilation contexts in (12), however, presents challenges. The challenge arising for assimilation context (i) is the following: if an empty nucleus interrupts /s/ and the consonant that follows, how can the feature involved spread from this consonant back to the preceding /s/? In other languages, place assimilation between consonants applies locally, that is, between string-adjacent consonants; indeed, it normally involves a coda assimilating to an immediately following onset, which may suggest that Acoma instead warrants a coda+onset analysis of sC clusters, as in Indo-European. However, even if a coda+onset analysis were proposed for sC in Acoma, the assimilation would apply non-locally in context (ii): the process is triggered by /i, e/, but it applies over top of labial and velar stops, as seen in (12b). Indeed, the pattern in (12b) would appear to pose a problem for any analysis of sC.

I suggest that an answer to the challenges posed by both assimilation contexts emerges from the representation for sC clusters I have provided for Acoma. Assimilation does not target /s/; rather, it targets the empty nucleus that follows /s/. Since the empty nucleus lacks all other features, however, the outcome of the spreading of [coronal] is perceived on the preceding sibilant. Importantly, the operation applies locally in both assimilation contexts. In context (i), it applies between string adjacent segments: the trigger is the coronal C in sC and the target is the empty nucleus that immediately precedes the trigger; see (13a). In context (ii), the trigger is the coronal vowel following the /s/+labial or /s/+velar cluster and the target is the empty nucleus that interrupts the cluster; the process thus applies locally, from vowel-to-vowel; see (13b).

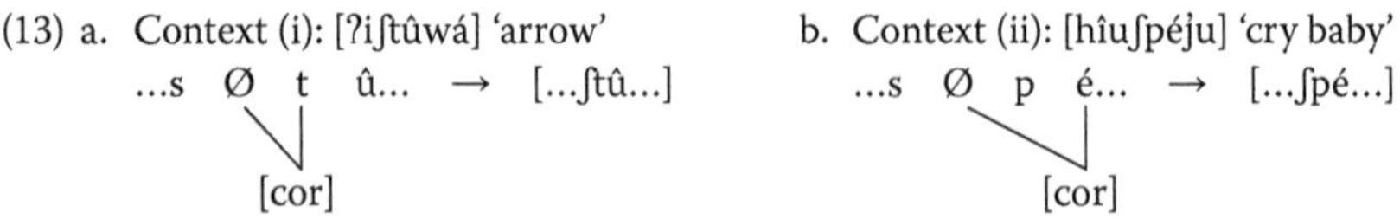

To summarize, the patterns of behaviour observed in Acoma – the absence of codas, the presence of a laryngeal contrast after /s/, and the pattern of allophony observed for /s/ – reveal that an analysis where sC strings are treated as clusters is spurious; instead, an empty nucleus interrupts /s/

and the following C. Thus, in spite of some parallels between Acoma and French, the coda+onset analysis of sC clusters is not warranted for Acoma. Moving outside of Indo-European has led to an alternative representation for sC clusters; clearly, they are not always entities of the same type.

One question that arises now is whether an empty nucleus between /s/ and the following consonant is ever warranted for sC in Indo-European. The answer is yes. /s/+fricative loanwords in English are a case in support of this. Recall from note 4 that Wright (2004: 51) proposes that /s/+fricative is disfavoured across languages because there is not enough perceptual distance between the two members of the cluster to ensure appropriate identification of both consonants. This may suggest that, in some languages where such clusters exist, an empty nucleus interrupts the consonants. Indeed, in English, an alternative to the coda+onset analysis that otherwise holds for sC clusters in this language would reflect the fact that /s/+fricative is tolerated but not productive. Empirical support for an intervening empty nucleus in clusters of this shape comes from the observation that /s/+fricative loanwords display a voicing contrast: compare *[sf]ere* and *[sv]elte* (Goad 2012). The latter example, where sharing of [voice] is not observed, in contrast to European Portuguese seen earlier in (10), is consistent with the presence of an empty nucleus between the two consonants.[11]

Thus far, we have seen that /s/ in sC clusters requires two different analyses: /s/ can be a coda preceded by empty nucleus; and /s/ can be an onset followed by empty nucleus. Although this approach to the analysis of sC requires an abstract view of the syllable – empty nuclei must be admitted – the result is that these clusters can be analysed using independently motivated syllable constituents (onset, coda), without recourse to additional machinery such as syllable appendices; see (2a–c).

2.3.2 Blackfoot

We turn now to Blackfoot, an Algonquian language spoken in Alberta and Montana (Frantz 2009). Like French and Acoma, word-initial sC clusters are limited to /s/+occlusive; see (14a). However, the forms in (14b), where

11 In Sanskrit, a plain-aspirated contrast is found after /s/ (e.g., /stan/ 'thunder', /sthā/ 'to stand'). This may suggest the presence of an empty nucleus between the two consonants in this language as well. However, the phonology of Sanskrit sC is complex (see, e.g., Steriade 1982, 1988); it would be premature to conclude that this contrast supports such an analysis at this time.

sC clusters can begin with long /s/, already make this language appear unusual.[12]

(14) a. [spát͡siko] 'sand' (D220)
[st͡síki] 'another' (D232)
b. [sstamat͡sisa] 'Tether him to the stake!' (D229)
[sskánatsskiniwa] 'She has nice hair' (D22)

An appropriate analysis for Blackfoot becomes even more challenging when we consider the other contexts in which /s/ clusters can occur. The data in (15a) show that short and long /s/ can be flanked by consonants, while those in (15b) and (15c) show that long and overlong /s/ can follow or precede a consonant, respectively:

(15) a. [áakokstakiwa] 'She will count' (G79)
[itápsskonakiwaik͡si] '(My friend) shot at them' (G50)
b. [kitssoká?pssi] 'You are nice' (G23)
[ááhsssapiwa] 'He enjoyed watching' (D258)
c. [ínikáto?katsiiwa anníísska óssska] 'he imitated his son-in-law' (D61)

A common element in works that have examined the unusual distribution of /s/ cross-linguistically is that none of them contest the position that /s/ is an obstruent. Like a vowel, however, and unlike other members of its sonority class, /s/ has strong internal cues, which ensure its perceptibility and identifiability, independent of context, as discussed earlier. We argue that the unusual distribution of /s/ in Blackfoot demonstrates that it functions as a strident vowel in this language (Goad and Shimada, 2014; building on earlier work by Derrick 2006 and Denzer-King 2009).[13] In short, then, in sC clusters in Indo-European languages, /s/ functions as a coda; in sC strings in Acoma, it functions as an onset; and in Blackfoot /s/ clusters, it functions as a vowel.

Syllabification: When 'unusual' /s/, exemplified in (14) and (15), is excluded from consideration, an examination of Blackfoot forms reveals

12 Data are drawn from Frantz's (2009) grammar (G) and Frantz and Russell's (1995) dictionary (D). Numbers following G and D refer to page numbers in these sources. Transcriptions depart from these sources as follows: the addition of a ligature on what we consider to be affricates and the use of [?] for glottal stop.

13 Derrick (2006) states that Blackfoot /s/ 'sometimes acts like a vowel'; Denzer-King (2009: 51), proposes that '/s/ is inherently moraic, and can act as a syllable nucleus'. Differences between our proposal and that of Denzer-King are spelt out in Goad and Shimada (2014).

that syllabification in this language is relatively straightforward, reflecting what is commonly observed in other languages: word-medial syllables generally require onsets, branching onsets are forbidden and coda+onset phonotactics are governed by constraints on sonority and place (Goad and Shimada 2014; building on Elfner 2006; Denzer-King 2009; and Frantz 2009). Forms containing unusual /s/, by contrast, seem to freely violate these constraints. Contrary to appearance, it will be shown that if /s/ is analysed as a vocoid, we can arrive at an analysis of these complex patterns that respects the language's syllable structure constraints, that is, without treating /s/ as an appendix in any context (cf. Denzer-King 2009) and without relaxing constraints on the structure of onsets (cf. Elfner 2006).

Although unusual /s/ patterns as nuclear in Blackfoot, we espouse moraic theory (Hayes 1989), as it appears to be the only theory of syllabification that yields the flexibility needed for the various parses of /s/. We contend that unusual /s/ differs from other consonants, including 'ordinary' /s/, in moraicity and syllabification. Ordinary /s/ can be underlyingly non-moraic or monomoraic: non-moraic /s/ is syllabified in onset (e.g., [póósa] 'cat' (G9)) or coda (e.g., [míínist͡si] 'berries' (G94)); monomoraic /s/, when intervocalic, yields a geminate (e.g., [ik͡síssiwa] 'he is tough' (G5)). Unusual /s/ can also be underlyingly monomoraic, or bimoraic, but unlike intervocalic geminate /s/, it projects its own syllable, like a vowel. As we will see, this need not be stipulated: the context alone regulates the syllabification.

Monomoraic unusual /s/ in medial position: Monomoraic unusual /s/ yields syllables with short nuclear /s/. The data in (16) show the four ways that $/s_\mu/$ can be parsed into syllable structure, depending on the quality of adjacent segments and, thus, constraints on their syllabification.

(16) Syllabification:

a. nuc: áa.ko.ks.ta.ki.wa 'She will count.' (G79)
b. nuc+ons: a.nis.tá.ps.sí.wa 'be-3:nonaffirmative' (G133)
c. ons+nuc: í.ss.ka 'pail' (G14)
d. ons+nuc+ons: áh.ss.sa.pi.wa 'He enjoyed watching' (D258)

Truncated structures are provided in (17). In all cases, $/s_\mu/$ projects a syllable node, minimally yielding nuclear [s]. In (17a), we see that $/s_\mu/$ is realized as nuclear [s] alone when surrounded by consonants that must form onsets, in respect of syllabification constraints on place. When preceded by an onset consonant and followed by a vowel, as in (17b), $/s_\mu/$ is realized as nucleus+onset [ss]; the additional link creating an onset is forced by the requirement that medial syllables have onsets in Blackfoot. In (17c), where a vowel immediately precedes $/s_\mu/$, $/s_\mu/$ must become the onset of its own syllable, yielding an onset+nucleus parse, again due to the constraint against medial onsetless syllables. The structure in (17d) additionally has a vowel following /s_{μ}/. Thus, the constraint against onsetless syllables comes into play twice, requiring /s_{μ}/ to be syllabified as the onset of its own syllable as well as onset of the following syllable. (Note that [h] cannot be parsed in onset in Blackfoot.)

(17) a. /s_{μ}/ as nucleus:
[áa.ko.ks.ta.ki.wa] (16a)

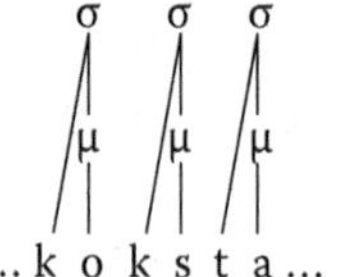

b. /s_{μ}/ as nucleus+onset:
[a.nis.tá.ps.sí.wa] (16b)

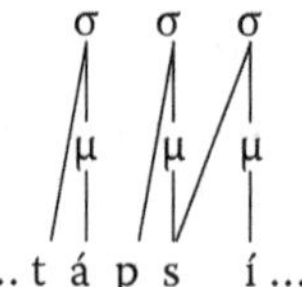

c. /s_{μ}/ as onset+nucleus:
[í.ss.ka] (16c)

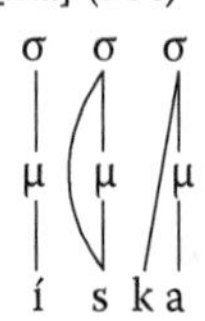

d. /s_{μ}/ as onset+nucleus+onset:
[áh.ss.sa.pi.wa] (16d)

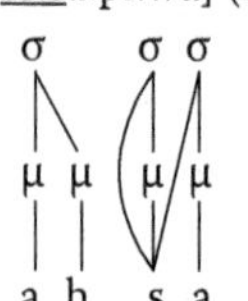

Bimoraic unusual /s/ in medial position: Bimoraic unusual /s/ yields syllables with long nuclear /s/. The data in (18) illustrate the three manners in which /$s_{\mu\mu}$/ can be parsed into syllables.

(18) Syllabification:

a.	nuc:	i.tá.pss.ko.na.ki.wai.k͡si	'(My friend) shot at them' (G50)
b.	nuc+ons:	s.tá.mss.sáa.ko.noo.sa	'Try to recognize her!' (D166)
c.	ons+nuc:	ínikáto?katsiiwa anníisska ó.sss.ka	'He imitated his son-in-law' (D61)

Structures for these forms are provided below. In (19a), /$s_{\mu\mu}$/ is syllabified as nuclear [ss], parallel to (17a), as the immediately adjacent consonants must be parsed as onsets. The form in (19b) similarly parallels that in (17b): in addition to being parsed as a long nucleus, bimoraic /s/ must become the onset of the following syllable, to avoid a word-internal onsetless syllable. Finally, in (19c), this same constraint ensures that bimoraic /s/ is parsed as the onset of its own syllable, parallel to (17c).

(19) a. $/s_{\mu\mu}/$ as nucleus:
[i.tá.pss.ko.na.ki.wai.t͡si] (18a)

b. $/s_{\mu\mu}/$ as nucleus+onset:
[s.tá.mss.sáa.ko.noo.sa] (18b)

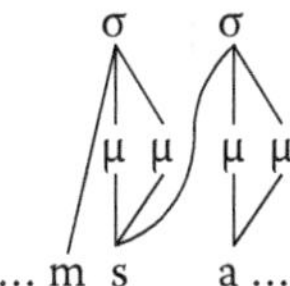

c. $/s_{\mu}/$ as onset+nucleus:
[ó.sss.ka] (18c)

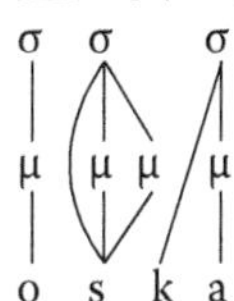

Unusual /s/ in initial position: We turn finally to sC and ssC clusters in word-initial position. The forms below expand on those provided earlier. Note that initial sC (20a) and ssC (20b) respect the same constraints; this suggests that the same analysis should hold for both.

(20) a. [spát͡siko] 'sand' (D220)
[stámitapoot] 'just go there!' (D232)
[st͡síki] 'another' (D232)
[skiim] 'female animal' (D214)
b. [sspitááwa] 'He is tall' (G23)
[sstamat͡sisa] 'Tether him to the stake!' (D229)
[sst͡sipísoohsit] 'Punish (whip) yourself!' (G105)
[sskánatsskiniwa] 'She has nice hair' (D22)
[ssk͡só?sat͡sisa] 'Flesh a hide!' (D225)

The first option to consider is whether initial sC and ssC clusters could be treated as coda+onset, as in Indo-European. This analysis is suspect, as medial sC clusters that are indisputably coda+onset are required to share place in Blackfoot (e.g., [istópiit] 'Sit there!' (F94)), while word-initial sC clusters are not (20a). More importantly, this analysis cannot be extended to initial ssC clusters in a principled way. Another option is Elfner's (2006) proposal that initial sC clusters form complex onsets. This proposal is challenged by the observation that Blackfoot does not permit typical rising sonority complex onsets. In addition, we denied this possiblity for sC clusters in all languages (Section 2.2.4). A third option is Denzer-King's (2009) proposal that sC clusters are appendix-initial. This analysis cannot be extended to ssC, as appendices can only occur at the edges of morphological domains (Hayes 1981; Harris 1983), which would not hold of the medial consonant in ssC. Perhaps because of this, Denzer-King analyses ssC in a different manner, as bimoraic, an analysis we adopt.

Because we consider it important that the same analysis hold for both sC and ssC, we propose that [s] in initial sC is underlyingly monomoraic and [ss] in ssC underlyingly bimoraic, parallel to our analysis of word-internal unusual clusters. /s_{μ}/ and /$s_{\mu\mu}$/ both project a syllable, as the cluster cannot otherwise be syllabified:

(21) a. Initial /s_{μ}/ as short nucleus: [st͡síki] (20a)

σ σ σ
μ μ μ
s t͡s í k i

b. Initial /$s_{\mu\mu}$/ as long nucleus: [sspák͡siʔk͡saahkoist͡si] (20b)

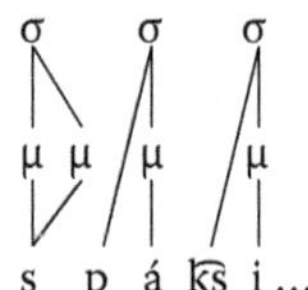

In sum, the account forwarded here, where Blackfoot /s/ is analysed as a vocoid, can straightforwardly capture a range of patterns that the language exhibits, in both initial and medial position. Importantly, allowing /s/ to be underlyingly (bi)moraic, thereby requiring it to project a syllable node, leads to the observed patterns without violating the language's constraints on syllabification: the context alone determines the parse.

2.3.3 Ōgami

Before concluding, we briefly address whether there are other languages like Blackfoot, where /s/ is fruitfully analysed as a vocoid. Ōgami (Southern Ryukyuan) appears to be such a language (Pellard 2009). The forms in (22) show that fricatives, including /f/, can be syllabic in this language, but similar to Blackfoot, it seems that only /s/, which can be short or long, can appear between consonants (22b).

(22) Ōgami (Pellard 2009: 80):

a.	[s̩tɑ]	'underneath'	b.	[ps̩tu]	'person'
	[f̩tɑi]	'forehead'		[ps̩:mɑ]	'day'

Beyond the parallels that hold with Blackfoot, Ōgami also draws attention to the fact that obstruents other than /s/ can function as vowels. Ōgami is not alone in this respect. In Imdlawm Tashlhiyt Berber (Dell and Elmedlaoui 1985), both stops and fricatives can function as nuclear; in Niger-Congo and Sino-Tibetan languages, voiced coronal and labio-dental fricatives can function in this way (Faytak 2012 and this volume). We have seen, however, that /s/ is particularly conspicuous. Indeed, the comparison across languages has revealed that /s/ is atypical in several ways when judged against other members of its sonority class.

2.4 Conclusion

We have demonstrated some of the ways in which strident /s/ stands apart phonotactically from other members of its sonority class. This behaviour is grounded in the perceptual properties of /s/: its place and manner are readily recoverable from the acoustic signal, which ensures that it can be identified as distinct from other segments, regardless of the context in which it appears. At the same time, we have shown that the phonological patterning of /s/ cannot be reduced to perception. Indeed, perceptual considerations can be trumped by structural constraints. For example, the SCL favours /s/+stop over sC clusters with rising sonority in Indo-European.

Determining the appropriate representation for /s/ in cluster contexts has proven to be challenging, as the patterns it displays differ across languages, which became apparent once we moved outside of Indo-European to examine typologically diverse languages. Nevertheless, although the range of behaviour that /s/ displays is diverse, we have shown that it can be analysed using ordinary syllable constituents if an abstract view of the syllable is adopted, one which admits both empty nuclei and strident nuclei: in cluster contexts, /s/ functions as the coda of an empty-headed syllable (Indo-European), as an onset followed by an empty nucleus (Acoma), and as nuclear (Blackfoot, Ōgami).

The possibility that sC clusters form branching onsets was rejected. We observed, though, that some languages admit /s/+liquid only, suggesting precisely this analysis. We leave examination of these languages, which we hypothesized contain non-strident /s/, to future research.

References

Alcina Franch, J. and Blecua, J.M. (1975). *Gramática española.* Barcelona: Ariel.

Clements, G.N. (1990). The role of the sonority cycle in core syllabification. In J. Kingston and M. Beckman (eds.), *Papers in laboratory phonology I* (pp. 283–333). Cambridge: Cambridge University Press.

Clements, G.N. and Keyser, S.J. (1983). *CV phonology: A generative theory of the syllable*. Cambridge, MA: MIT Press.

Dell, F. and Elmedlaoui, M. (1985). Syllabic consonants and syllabification in Imdlawn Tashlhiyt Berber. *Journal of African Languages and Linguistics*, 1, 105–30.

Denzer-King, R. (2009). *The distribution of /s/ in Blackfoot: An optimality theory account.* Master's thesis, University of Montana, Missoula, MT.

Derrick, D. (2006). Syllabification and Blackfoot 's'. Paper presented at the 38th Algonquian Conference, University of British Columbia, October.

Elfner, E. (2006). *The mora in Blackfoot.* Master's thesis, University of Calgary, Calgary, Canada.

Faytak, M. (2012). Logical sonority scales and turbulence in fricative-vowel languages. Paper presented at the 38th Annual Meeting of the Berkeley Linguistics Society, University of California, Berkeley, February.

Fleischhacker, H. (2001). Cluster-dependent epenthesis asymmetries. *UCLA Working Papers in Linguistics*, 7, 71–116.

Frantz, D. (2009). *Blackfoot grammar* (2nd edition). Toronto: University of Toronto Press.

Frantz, D.G. and Russell, N.J. (1995). *Blackfoot dictionary of stems, roots and affixes* (2nd edition). Toronto: University of Toronto Press.

Fuchs, S. and Toda, M. (2010). Do differences in male versus female /s/ reflect biological or sociophonetic factors? In S. Fuchs, M. Toda and M. Zygis (eds.), *Turbulent sounds: An interdisciplinary guide* (pp. 281–302). Berlin: Mouton de Gruyter.

Goad, H. (2011). The representation of sC clusters. In M. van Oostendorp, C. Ewen, E. Hume and K. Rice (eds.), *The Blackwell Companion to Phonology* (pp. 898–923). Oxford: Wiley-Blackwell.

Goad, H. (2012). sC clusters are (almost always) coda-initial. *The Linguistic Review*, 29, 335–73.

Goad, H. (2016). Phonotactic evidence from typology and acquisition for a coda+onset analysis of initial sC clusters. In K.-m. Kim, P. Umbal, T. Block, Q. Chan, T. Cheng, K. Finney, M. Katz, S. Nickel-Thompson, L. and Shorten (eds.), *Proceedings of the 33rd West Coast Conference on Formal Linguistics* (pp. 17–28). Somerville, Mass: Cascadilla Press.

Goad, H. (forthcoming). Superset and subset grammars in second language acquisition: The role of sonority in the representation of sC clusters. In P. Guijarro-Fuentes, M. Juan-Garau and P. Larrañaga (eds.), *The acquisition of Romance languages from a generative perspective: New challenges and approaches.* Berlin: De Gruyter Mouton.

Goad, H. and Shimada, A. (2014). /s/ can be a vocoid. In J. Iyer and L. Kusmer, L. (eds.), *NELS 44: Proceedings of the Forty-Fourth Annual Meeting of the North East Linguistic Society* (pp. 135–48). Amherst, MA: GLSA.

Goldsmith, J. (1990). *Autosegmental and metrical phonology.* Oxford: Blackwell.

Hall, T.A. (1992). *Syllable structure and syllable-related processes in German.* Tübingen: Max Niemeyer.

Harris, J. (1983). *Syllable structure and stress in Spanish.* Cambridge, MA: MIT Press.

Harris, J. (1994). *English sound structure.* Oxford: Blackwell.

Hayes, B. (1981). *A metrical theory of stress rules.* Doctoral thesis, MIT, Cambridge, MA.

Hayes, B. (1989). Compensatory lengthening in moraic phonology. *Linguistic Inquiry*, 20, 253–306.

Iverson, G. and Salmons, J. (1995). Aspiration and laryngeal representation in Germanic. *Phonology*, 12, 369–96.

Kaye, J. (1985). On the syllable structure of certain West African languages. In D. Goyvaerts (ed.), *African linguistics: Essays in memory of M.W.K. Semikenke* (pp. 285–308). Amsterdam: Benjamins.

Kaye, J. (1992). Do you believe in magic? The story of s+C sequences. In *SOAS Working Papers in Linguistics*, 2, 293–313. London: SOAS, Department of Linguistics.

Kaye, J. and Lowenstamm, J. (1984). De la syllabicité. In F. Dell, D. Hirst and J.-R. Vergnaud (eds.), *Forme sonore du langage* (pp. 123–61). Paris: Hermann.

Kim, C.-W. (1970). A theory of aspiration. *Phonetica*, 21, 107–16.

Lipski, J. (1994). *Latin American Spanish.* London: Longman.

Mateus, M.H. and d'Andrade, E. (2000). *The phonology of Portuguese.* Oxford: Oxford University Press.

Miller, W. (1965). *Acoma grammar and texts.* Berkeley and Los Angeles: University of California Press.

Murray, R. and Vennemann, T. (1983). Sound change and syllable structure in Germanic phonology. *Language*, 59, 514–28.

Pellard, T. (2009). *Ōgami: éléments de description d'un parler du sud des Ryūkyū.* Doctoral thesis, CNRS, Paris.

Romero, J. (1995). An articulatory view of historical s-aspiration in Spanish. *Rivista di Linguistica*, 7, 113–20.

Schane, S. (1989). Diphthongs and monophthongs in early Romance. In C. Kirschner and J. De Cesaris (eds.), *Studies in Romance linguistics* (pp. 365–76). Amsterdam: Benjamins.

Selkirk, E. (1984). On the major class features and syllable theory. In M. Aronoff and R. Oehrle, (eds.), *Language sound structure* (pp. 107–36). Cambridge, MA: MIT Press.

Shadle, C. H. (1991). Source parameters for the fricative consonants /s, ʃ, ç, x/. *Journal of the Acoustical Society of America*, 89(4B), 1893.

Smith, J. (2005). *Phonological augmentation in prominent positions.* New York: Routledge.

Steriade, D. (1982). *Greek prosodies and the nature of syllabification.* Doctoral thesis, MIT, Cambridge, MA.

Steriade, D. (1988). Reduplication and syllable transfer in Sanskrit and elsewhere. *Phonology*, 5, 73–155.

van der Hulst, H. (1984). *Syllable structure and stress in Dutch.* Dordrecht: Foris.

Wright, R. (2004). A review of perceptual cues and cue robustness. In B. Hayes, R. Kirchner and D. Steriade (eds.), *Phonetically based phonology* (pp. 34–57). Cambridge: Cambridge University Press.

Heather Goad completed her PhD in Linguistics at the University of Southern California. She is currently an Associate Professor in the Department of Linguistics at McGill University, Montreal. Her research focuses on phonology and language acquisition. She is principally concerned with motivating articulated representations for phonological behaviour and examining how these representations can inform our understanding of patterns observed in the productions of first and second language learners. Dr Goad was formerly an Associate Editor of *Language Acquisition* and Co-editor of the *Canadian Journal of Linguistics*. She is currently on the editorial board for *Language Acquisition*, for John Benjamins' Language Acquisition & Language Disorders series and for Oxford Studies in Phonology.

3
Relating the Sonority Hierarchy to Articulatory Timing Patterns: A Cross-Linguistic Perspective

Ioana Chitoran

3.1 Introduction

The sonority hierarchy is a central concept in phonology, one that is, arguably, not theory-dependent. It captures a robust typological generalization about preferred syllable structures cross-linguistically. This generalization is present, in slightly different formulations, in every phonological model of the major theoretical approaches – structuralist, functionalist, generativist.[1] Equally robust, however, are the exceptions to this generalization, which are often hard to interpret and consequently hard to account for. Famous 'troublemakers' in this category are, for example, Tashlhiyt Berber (see Dell and Elmedlaoui 2002, for theoretical implications) or Salish (Bagemihl 1991; Shahin and Blake 2004; Bird and Czaykowska-Higgins, this volume). Consonant sequences in these languages defy syllabification algorithms and principles of syllable organization based on sonority. Such data have challenged and catalysed research, and depending on their accessibility, they have inspired new directions of study, improving our understanding of the syllable as a unit of information, processing, and production.

The goal of this chapter is to consider what sonority-based syllabic organization may mean when examined from an articulatory perspective. I propose that we have good reason to believe, based on results of experimental

1 The strict CV model of phonology (Lowenstamm 1996), derived from Government Phonology (Kaye, Lowenstamm and Vergnaud 1990; Kaye 1990), may be considered an exception, because sonority relations are rendered superfluous by the canonical CVCV syllable structure. However, Scheer (1996) proposed a theory of consonantal interactions, needed to account for restrictions on word-initial consonant clusters.

studies of consonant sequences in a variety of languages, that the sonority hierarchy can be best understood in its relation to articulatory timing. I will argue that the organizational role that has been attributed to the sonority hierarchy follows from language-specific properties of articulatory timing. The idea of the link between sonority and articulatory timing is not new. It is explicitly formulated by Mattingly (1981, 1998) in the concept of 'parallel transmission' of information. Parallel transmission captures the essential coarticulatory properties of the speech signal that are crucial for maximum intelligibility and maximum speed in communication. We have now gained sufficient empirical knowledge to evaluate whether timing patterns of articulatory gestures can be related to syllabic organization via the concept of parallel transmission. The sonority hierarchy, as we know it, may have limited predictive power. It certainly captures one way of maximizing parallel transmission. But other options are attested in the world's languages, and are predicted by aspects of articulatory timing. From a slightly different perspective, based on the articulatory study of liquids in American-English, Proctor and Walker (2012) have also proposed that understanding the relative sonority of segments can gain from considering their articulatory properties beyond degree of constriction.

The view expressed here assumes that the syllable exists and is an indispensable unit of linguistic organization (see Blevins 1995; Goldsmith 2011, for comprehensive reviews). Recent neurophysiological studies have inspired models that reinforce the role of syllable-sized units in speech processing (Doelling, Arnal, Ghitza and Poeppel 2014; Ghitza 2011, 2013; Giraud and Poeppel 2012; Howard and Poeppel 2012). The role of signal modulations is highlighted in a particularly relevant way in Ghitza's (2011) Tempo model, where syllable-sized units with prominent energy peaks are tracked by the peripheral auditory system in the decoding process. Speech production models (Guenther 1995; Guenther, Ghosh and Tourville 2006; Bohland, Bullock and Guenther 2010; MacNeilage and Davis 2000; Nam, Goldstein and Saltzman 2009; Tilsen 2013) all include a model of the syllable. In terms of phonological representations, the proposal made here is consistent with the main tenets of Articulatory Phonology, henceforth AP (Browman and Goldstein 1992; Goldstein and Fowler 2003), and is related to the representation of syllabic organization in AP.

The chapter is organized as follows: in Section 3.2 I introduce the sonority hierarchy as a phonological organizational principle of syllable structure. Section 3.3 presents three case studies of syllabification (Georgian, Slovak, Tashlhiyt) in terms of the traditional sonority hierarchy. In Section 3.4 I discuss the same patterns with respect to properties of their articulatory timing. In Section 3.5 I propose the connection between the sonority hierarchy and parallel transmission in articulatory terms. Section 3.6 contains a final discussion and conclusions.

3.2 Sonority – Phonology and Phonetics

All definitions of the sonority hierarchy (from Jespersen 1897–99, to Clements 1990, to subsequent work) consider that an alternation of peaks and troughs corresponds to the preferred cross-linguistic ordering of manner classes by degree of constriction (see Parker 2002, for a full chronological review of this concept). The preferred order is one of rising sonority in a syllable onset (obstruent < nasal < liquid < glide < vowel), and the opposite in a syllable rhyme. This generalization captures the fact that *kla* is preferred over *kta*, which is in turn preferred over *lka*.

The acoustic correlates of the peak/trough alternation are understood as maximal modulations in multiple parameters that vary simultaneously: amplitude, periodicity, spectral shape, F0 (Ohala and Kawasaki-Fukumori 1984; Ohala 1992; Parker 2002; Clements 2009). These acoustic correlates underlie speech intelligibility; however, they are not sufficient for characterizing the syllable as a unit of linguistic organization. They do predict the typologically common patterns of rising and falling sonority relative to the nucleus (e.g., *kla*). At the same time, there is an inconsistency between the generalization and the acoustic correlate of maximal modulation because the latter also predicts the less common sonority reversals such as *lka*. These are also alternations of troughs and peaks, whether the liquid is syllabic or not, therefore *kla, lka* should both be preferred over a sonority plateau *kta*. Sonority plateaus are not predicted, and yet, they are cross-linguistically more common than reversals.

Syllabic organization involves two related questions. One is quantitative, and concerns the number of elements that can be contained in a syllable onset, while the second one concerns the ordering of these elements. Cross-linguistically, an ordering that follows the sonority hierarchy results in a larger number of elements accommodated in a syllable onset. Many languages allow only one element in a syllable onset. Languages that allow more than one element usually follow the sonority hierarchy. Others, however, also allow sonority plateaus and reversals. In current phonological models the latter are treated as exceptions, and it is not clear that they need to be. I propose that a careful consideration of the articulatory timing patterns in some of the languages that have been experimentally studied reveal new, more efficient generalizations regarding syllabic organization.

I argue that articulatory correlates relating to timing patterns between gestures can provide a deeper insight into organizational principles underlying the syllable because they can predict both common and uncommon patterns. The different acoustic consequences of these timing patterns help refine these predictions on a language-specific basis. For example, variation in timing lag between adjacent consonantal gestures can affect the way in which information about these consonants is maintained in the acoustic signal, and consequently perceived by the listener. Thus, a given, short lag duration may have different effects on stop-liquid and stop-stop sequences. For a given lag duration, a stop-liquid sequence such as /kl/ will consist of a constriction with an acoustic release and formant transitions into an open constriction. But for the same short lag duration, a stop-stop sequence such as /kt/ may lose information about C1 /k/. If the tongue tip gesture for /t/ begins before the release of /k/, then /k/ will be partly hidden by /t/. It will not have an acoustic release. Unless the /kt/ cluster is intervocalic, acoustic information about /k/ is only present in its release burst. The absence of an acoustic release may thus lead to misperception. At the same time, if the lag is too long in either a stop-liquid or a stop-stop sequence, in the presence of voicing, a vocalic transition can emerge between the two consonantal gestures. In this case the percept of a consonant sequence may be lost and replaced with a CV alternation.

As already mentioned, the generalizations that I propose are consistent with a phonological analysis of syllabic organization in the framework of AP. Therefore, before considering the three case studies in the next section, I first introduce the two main tenets of AP:

(1) articulatory gestures are at once discrete, combinatorial units of representation and units of continuous action in space and time;
(2) gestures have a temporal dimension. The discrete specifications of gestures are dynamic, and pairs of gestures are dynamically coupled. The coupling accounts for contextual variation. Common processes such as assimilation, insertion, deletion, are accounted for by variable relative timing between gestures.

Finally, in its current form (Goldstein and Fowler 2003) AP is compatible with, but does not crucially assume, the view that articulatory, rather than acoustic events, are the objects of speech perception.

My proposal is based on patterns of syllable structure in three languages – Georgian, Slovak, Tashlhiyt – and the articulatory timing patterns that characterize them. The relevant data are presented in Section 3.3, and the experimental results in Section 3.4.

3.3 Sonority – Three Representative Patterns

Syllable organization is compared in three languages: Georgian (Chitoran, Goldstein and Byrd 2002; Chitoran and Goldstein 2006), Slovak (Pouplier and Beňuš 2011), and Tashlhiyt (Ridouane 2008; Ridouane and Fougeron 2011). All three languages allow sequences of consonants, but their organization into syllables differs in terms of their behavior as syllable nuclei versus syllable margins. Thus, Georgian allows only vowels as nuclei, Slovak allows vowels and liquids, and in Tashlhiyt vowels and all consonants can be syllabic. The three syllabification patterns are illustrated below:

(1) Syllabification patterns according to the nature of the nucleus (nuclei are in bold):

a. Georgian – vowels only:	rb**e**.n**a**	'to run'
	mtkn**a**.r**e**.b**a**	'yawn'
	t'k'b**i**.l**i**	'sweet'
b. Slovak – vowels, liquids:	mr**a**k	'darkness'
	m**r**k	'wink'
	sm**r**k	'sniff'
	b**l**b	'stupid guy'
c. Tashlhiyt – vowels, all consonants:	**s**.m**u**n	'accompany' causative
	t**s**.m**u**n	'accompany' 3rd feminine singular causative

Considering the data in terms of the traditional definition of the sonority hierarchy, it follows that the relative sonority of consonantal segments is language-specific. Thus, in Georgian all consonantal segments are equivalent to one another in terms of sonority and all are equally distant from the vowels, because they can appear in any order in a syllable/word onset. This is not true of Slovak or Tashlhiyt, where sonority reversals are disallowed. In these languages, instead, we find a more fine-grained organization. The Slovak pattern suggests that liquids share the high sonority of vowels, so that when an actual vowel is missing, they can take over as nuclei. By the same criteria, in Tashlhiyt all consonants share the sonority of vowels.

The three languages consequently differ in their tolerance for complex onsets. Tashlhiyt is the most restricted, allowing only one segment in a syllable onset. Georgian is the most liberal, as it not only allows complex onsets, but it allows many combinations within an onset, whether they observe or violate the sonority hierarchy. The three patterns are summarized in (2). We see that an increase in the number of elements that can occupy a syllable nucleus implies a decrease in the complexity of the onset.

Thus, Tashlhiyt strictly disallows complex onsets, but allows any segment in nucleus position. Georgian shows exactly the reverse pattern, with high onset complexity but only one type of segment (vowels) in nucleus position.

(2) A typology of nuclei and phonotactic (onset) complexity:

	Georgian	Slovak	Tashlhiyt
Nuclei	vowels	vowels	vowels
		syllabic liquids	syllabic liquids
			syllabic nasals
			syllabic obstruents
Onsets	complex onsets	complex onsets	no complex onsets
	sonority plateaus	sonority plateaus	
	sonority reversals		
	k-	*k-*	*t-*
	kr-	*kr-*	
	rb-, mtkn-, t'k'b-	*mr-*	

Such generalizations, however, cease to be useful beyond a purely descriptive level. They require further explanation as to why a segment can be more or less sonorous relative to another, on a language-specific basis. Why do we see in (2) an inverse relation between the nature of the elements that can fill a syllable nucleus (increasing from left to right in row 1) and the combinatorial complexity in a syllable onset (decreasing from left to right in row 2)?

I propose to examine the same data by comparing the syllabification patterns to the articulatory timing patterns characterizing sequences of consonants in the three languages. I turn to this comparison in the next section.

3.4 Articulatory Timing – Three Representative Patterns

I present in this section the relevant results from previous articulometer (EMA) studies on timing coordination in Georgian, Slovak, and Tashlhiyt. I begin by defining the four landmarks of an articulatory gesture, on which EMA measures of relative timing are based.

(3) Landmarks of an articulatory gesture:
 1 – gesture onset
 2 – target onset = the point where the target constriction is reached
 3 – target offset = the point where the constriction is released
 4 – gesture offset

The particular context that interests us is the sequencing of consonantal gestures. The relative timing of these gestures has been shown to vary as a function of segmental, prosodic, speech style factors. Syllable position is a major factor that determines whether gestures are more or less overlapped in speech. For example, in a complex onset, as consonants are added to an onset (CV versus CCV versus CCCV), the rightmost consonant is expected to shift progressively closer to the nucleus vowel. The timing lag between the rightmost consonant and the vowel is expected to shorten. This rightward shift is interpreted as resulting from the multiple coordination patterns characterizing a complex onset: it is specifically hypothesized that the consonants in an onset are coupled to each other in *anti-phase* mode (moving away from each other), as well as being each coupled *in-phase* (moving closer) to the following vowel (Browman and Goldstein 2000). A rightward shift is thus predicted in an onset if such a compromise exists between competing targets. Regardless of how many consonants are in an onset, the onset as a whole maintains a stable coordination relationship with the nucleus vowel. This hypothesis has been confirmed for a number of languages. The in-phase coupling is interpreted as characterizing a syllable onset.

In what follows I will review against this background the characteristic timing patterns for each of the three languages examined.

3.4.1 Georgian

Kinematic studies of Georgian consonant sequences revealed several patterns that are relevant for syllabic organization. The data were obtained with an electromagnetic articulometer (EMA) system (Perkell, Cohen, Svirsky, Matthies, Garabieta and Jackson 1992). It was found that Georgian has a timing pattern sensitive to the order of constriction location (Chitoran, Goldstein and Byrd 2002; Chitoran and Goldstein 2006). Thus, front-to-back sequences (e.g., *bg, dg, rk, pl*), where the release of an anterior constriction is followed by a posterior constriction in the vocal tract, are systematically more overlapped, more co-produced, than back-to-front sequences (e.g., *gb, gd, rb, kl*). In the latter, a posterior constriction is released into a vocal tract that is still closed by an anterior constriction.

Such back-to-front sequences were found to have a longer lag between the two C gestures. They are less overlapped, and in sequences where at least one consonant is voiced, a vocalic transition is visible in the acoustic signal. The vocalic transition is present predominantly in back-to-front stop-stop sequences (58 per cent) such as *gd-eba* 'to be thrown', *g-ber-av-s* 'is inflating you', *k'bil-i* 'tooth', *a-gd-eb-a* 'throw in the air', *da-gb-er-a* 'inflate', those with minimal overlap. Only 23 per cent of front-to-back stop-stop sequences show a similar vocalic transition, in the forms: *bgera* 'sound', *dg-eb-a* 'stands up', *abga* 'saddle bag', *a-dg-eb-a* 'will stand up'. Figure 3.1 shows an example of a back-to-front stop-stop sequence with a long lag and a vocalic transition.

A subsequent study (Goldstein, Chitoran and Selkirk 2007) has shown that, when such a vocalic transition is present, there is no rightward shift, as mentioned above, indicative of a complex onset. This suggests that, in Georgian, a consonant that is part of a complex onset may be timed as a single onset relative to this vocalic transition. In *ts'k'ᵛriala* 'shiny' a vocalic transition can occur between [k'] and [r], and when it does, the three consonants in the sequence do not show the coordination pattern of an onset

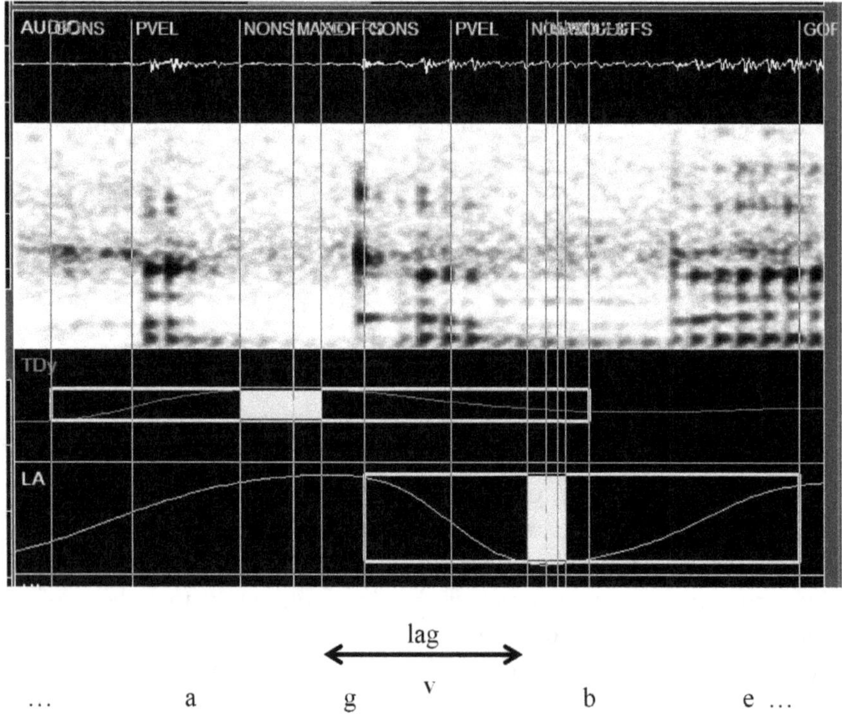

Figure 3.1. Example of long lag and vocalic transition in Georgian #gb in g-ber-av-s.

cluster. The relevant measure considered is the distance between the time when the tongue tip reaches the constriction for [r] and the time when the tongue body reaches the target for the vowel [i]. This distance is compared in three forms: *riali* 'commotion', *k'riali* 'glitter', *ts'k'riala* 'shiny'. If [k'r] and [ts'k'r] were complex onsets, it would be expected that the target onset of [r] would move progressively closer to the target onset of [i], as more consonants are added to the onset.

For one of the two Georgian speakers in this study, a rightward shift was not found between [k'riali] and [ts'k'riala]. This suggests that the mode of coordination in [ts'k'riala] is not that of a complex onset. Since these cases also show a vocalic transition, the absence of a rightward shift suggests that the vocalic transition is acting as a syllable nucleus itself. This is not a systematic result, and a definitive conclusion is premature. We also do not know yet whether the vocalic transitions are due to long timing lags or to characteristics of a voiced C1 release when C1 is a stop, or to both. Nevertheless, it is interesting to speculate about the possible phonologization of vocalic transitions. If vocalic transitions are generalized, are actively perceived by native speakers, and are associated with the specific timing pattern of Georgian CC sequences, it is conceivable that over time an active vowel gesture may be produced, that acts as a syllable nucleus. Thus, a particular coordination mode, one that favours long lags (a low degree of overlap), would have an acoustic consequence that corresponds to the signal modulation preferred in a sonority profile.

3.4.2 Slovak

The main difference between Slovak and Georgian is that in Slovak the liquids /l/ and /r/ can be syllabic. The relevant results for Slovak (Pouplier and Beňuš 2011) show consistent differences in timing patterns between syllables with consonantal nuclei and those with vocalic nuclei. Articulatory (EMA) coordination measures were taken for the following comparisons:

Onset-nucleus coordination:	**CV** (*bib*) versus **CL** (*blb, brm*)
Complex onset coordination:	CV (*lak, raky, mog*) versus
	CCV (*vlak, braky, smog*)
	CL (*bl.kol, mrk*) versus
	CCL (*zbl.kol, smrk*)
CC coordination:	**CC**V (*klak, mrak*) versus
	CL**C** / **C**L**C** (*klk, krk*) versus
	V**CC** (*kalk, park*)

Degree of overlap is measured by the duration of the plateau lag, given by the distance from the target offset (release) of C1 to the target onset (achievement of the target constriction) for C2. A longer lag indicates less overlap between the target plateaus of the two consonants. The relevant results are summarized below.

In terms of onset-nucleus coordination, the authors compared the peak velocity lag of the closing movement in ***bib*** versus ***blb***, ***brm***. Peak velocity is the time point of maximum articulator velocity before the articulator reaches its target. No difference was found between ***bib*** with a vocalic nucleus and ***blb*** with a consonantal nucleus, but there was a significant difference between ***blb*** and ***brm***: syllabic /r/ has the longest peak velocity lag, differing significantly from syllabic /l/.

With respect to complex onset coordination, both vocalic (CV, CCV) and consonantal (CL, CCL) nuclei behave the same way. Neither shows the rightward shift expected as consonants are added to the onset. Although this result is surprising, two additional measures did show the expected difference in timing between simple and complex onsets. A significant difference was found between vocalic and consonantal nuclei in terms of the size of the effect. Syllables with vocalic nuclei showed a significantly greater change between simple and complex onset than syllables with syllabic consonants. Slovak stop-liquid sequences show generally little overlap. With respect to CC coordination, onset-nucleus stop-liquid sequences as in ***krb***, ***klk*** were found to be less overlapped than the same stop-liquid sequences in onset-onset (***kr**ab*, ***kl**ak*) or coda-coda cases (*pa**rk***, *ka**lk***). Onset-nucleus CL sequences (***kr**b*, ***kl**k*) were less overlapped than nucleus-coda LC sequences (*k**rk***, *k**lk***).

The authors note that in both the onset-nucleus (*krb*) and the onset-onset (*krab*) cases, the reduced overlap often results in open transitions with vocoids emerging between the release of the stop and the tongue tip gesture of the liquid. The vocoid is attributed to the tongue body retraction gesture that is characteristic of liquids. In Slovak, /l/ is dark, having both an apical raising gesture and a tongue body retraction gesture. The apical trill /r/ also shows an apical gesture and a retraction of the tongue dorsum. The vocalic transition is the acoustic consequence of the long timing lag between the onset consonant and the tongue tip gesture of the liquid, whether the liquid is in nucleus or onset position. It is therefore not the transitional vocoid itself that provides a sonority peak, but rather the substantial timing lag favouring it. The authors conclude that in a syllabic liquid the vocalic retraction gesture does not simply act as a vowel. Instead, both the consonantal tongue tip gesture and the vocalic retraction gesture together belong to the nucleus, and timing between onset and nucleus is such that it results in an acoustic vocalic element intervening between two consonants.

Once again, similarly to the case of Georgian, a language-specific pattern of articulatory timing results in open transitions. In Slovak, this timing pattern is found for obstruents and liquids, whether they coordinate as onset-onset or onset-nucleus, in a way that is consistent with a rising sonority profile in syllable onsets.

3.4.3 Tashlhiyt

Tashlhiyt is radically different. In Tashlhiyt all consonants, not just liquids, can be syllabic. Complex onsets do not exist. A sequence of two different consonants is produced as an onset-nucleus sequence, even when a complex onset would actually be consistent with the sonority hierarchy. Thus, a form such as *gli* 'guide' is obligatorily disyllabic (*g.li*). A timing pattern consistent with this phonotactic generalization is thus expected. Tashlhiyt has been experimentally studied by Fougeron and Ridouane (2008), Ridouane and Fougeron (2011), Hermes, Ridouane, Mücke and Grice (2011), and Ridouane, Hermes and Hallé (2014).

Fougeron and Ridouane (2008) use electropalatography (EPG) data (Hardcastle and Roach 1979) from one native speaker to study the kinematic properties of syllabic consonants and their timing relationships with surrounding segments as a function of syllable position. Their findings indicate that consonants in nucleus position are less variable than in onset or coda. They are less overlapped by a following non-coda consonant, and relatively more overlapped by a preceding onset consonant. There is more EPG contact in nucleus than in onset or coda position.

In a detailed acoustic study of data from five more speakers, Ridouane and Fougeron (2011) focus on the vocalic transitions that characterize the Tashlhiyt timing pattern. The data examined consist of word-initial CC sequences. A vocalic transition is present if at least one of the consonants is voiced (especially the second one), and if the vocal tract is sufficiently open in the transition between the two consonants. They are found most frequently at C1 release, in sequences with minimal overlap. The presence or absence of a vocalic transition does not affect the acoustic duration of the onset cluster, proving that they are intrusive (excrescent) schwas rather than full phonologically inserted vowels.

Finally, the analysis of EMA data (Hermes et al. 2011) confirms the timing of simple onsets in a CC sequence, based on the absence of rightward shift in data such as *fik* 'give yourself' versus *kfik* 'give yourself', versus *tkfik* 'she gave you'. The results are therefore consistent with those of Goldstein, et al. (2007). The rightmost consonant remains stable in its timing relation to the nucleus /i/, as more consonants are added to its left. The exact same pattern is found for consonantal nuclei, as in *fnk* 'they gave you' versus *kfnk* 'they gave you' versus *tkfnk* 'she buried you'.

The three language-specific timing patterns examined here all share the presence of minimal gestural overlap, which may be accompanied by vocalic transitions. These occur in back-to-front sequences in Georgian (*g*^{v}*beravs*), before liquids with a retraction gesture in Slovak (*k*^{v}*rb, k*^{v}*rab*) and possibly in Georgian as well (*ts'k*^{w}*riala*). In Tashlhiyt the vocalic transitions are the most frequent among the three languages, and are primarily related to voicing. I argue that this common characteristic that emerges from the cross-linguistic comparison is worth considering and subjecting to further testing because it can be highly informative with respect to phonotactic typology.

The sonority hierarchy falls short of explaining the combinatorial possibilities encountered in all three languages. Descriptively, the three languages differ with respect to the sonority hierarchy: many of the Georgian complex onsets violate the sonority profile, while the ones in Slovak do not. Tashlhiyt does not violate sonority because it does not have complex onsets. But Tashlhiyt challenges the sonority hierarchy with the following question: why is an obstruent-liquid sequence such as *gli*, with a perfect rising sonority profile, not parsed as a complex onset? The sonority hierarchy alone cannot account for this.

In the following section I argue that a valid organizational principle underlying the syllable is one that simultaneously enhances signal modulation and coarticulation as parallel transmission, in ways that include, but are not limited to, the sonority hierarchy.

3.5 Sonority and Parallel Transmission

'The overlapping of multiple gestures in speech makes possible parallel, hence rapid, transmission of information' (Mattingly 1998: 276). Mattingly explicitly proposes that the syllable organization based on sonority ranking can be interpreted as corresponding to the requirement for efficient speech communication. Parallel transmission is maximized 'if less open constrictions are being released or applied in the presence of more open constrictions' (Mattingly 1981: 418). The ordering of constriction degrees corresponds to the preferred ordering of manner classes in a syllable onset:

obstruent > nasal > liquid > glide > vowel. But it also corresponds more generally to other ways in which information can be encoded during constrictions and constriction releases, if variation in timing patterns is considered. Parallel transmission is ensured by coarticulation. Coarticulation is maximized when gestures are most co-produced, provided they do not obscure one other. Thus, releasing less open constrictions into more open ones favours maximum coarticulation with minimal loss of information as to the identity of the gestures.

I propose that the attested cross-linguistic diversity of combinatorial restrictions, including the sonority hierarchy, follows from any possible coordination pattern that allows gestures to be maximally co-produced, and that also allows maximal modulation of the signal. Such a view covers the very common patterns that are in agreement with the sonority hierarchy, but it explains in addition why other linguistic patterns can also develop in some of the world's languages, where sonority reversals and plateaus are well-formed. The preferred sequencing of applied constrictions is a sequencing that allows tighter intergestural coordination and faster transmission. This is the case of sequences like *pla* or *kra*, and it corresponds to the order of the sonority hierarchy, where more closed constrictions are released into gradually more open ones, allowing more gestural overlap. But if the order of constriction degree is reversed (as for *mpa*, *rka*), for example by the addition of consonantal prefixes, in this case some languages can parse the signal differently, preferring longer lags. When a C1 constriction is not released into a more open C2 constriction, a low degree of overlap allows the first constriction to have a release, which in and of itself contributes to the modulation of the signal. In this respect it is worth considering whether the presence of additional morpho-syntactic information may lead to changes in encoding. One hypothesis that emerges is that languages with uncommon phonotactic patterns are also languages whose morphologies are characterized by multiple consonantal prefixes attached to a root. If the ranking of faster versus accurate information transmission is encoded in patterns of articulatory organization, then in such languages longer timing lags would be predicted to be preferred, because they minimize loss of information.

The vocalic transitions, or excrescent vowels, that sometimes accompany these longer lags, provide peaks of energy and are potentially phonologizable properties of the signal. The resulting signal still has a clear acoustic modulation, with sonority peaks and troughs. Longer lags can therefore be exploited in those languages that allow sonority reversals or plateaus in word onsets.

3.6 Discussion and Conclusion

The question raised in this chapter concerns both the segmentation of the speech stream into syllables and the internal organization of a syllable. The brief comparison of timing coordination in three languages suggests the following interpretation of a general principle of syllable organization: what goes into a syllable onset is whatever can be maximally co-produced without minimizing signal modulation and without losing intelligiblity. This can be achieved by an ordering of constrictions as the one captured by the sonority hierarchy, or by other types of ordering. In the latter case, longer lags maintain the alternations in the modulation of the signal.

Syllable-sized portions of the acoustic signal are known to play an important part in speech perception and comprehension. The studies of neural envelope tracking mentioned in the introduction have shown that the auditory cortical representations of the speech signal are sensitive to syllable-sized windows. An important piece of evidence comes from experimental studies of speech intelligibility in which the temporal speech envelope was manipulated. An experiment carried out by Ghitza and Greenberg (2009) involved time-compressed speech. The authors showed that the reduced intelligibility induced by a high compression factor can be overturned if the speech is 'repackaged' by inserting silent gaps in-between successive intervals of compressed speech. Intelligibility increased when silent gaps of 20–120 ms were inserted, then decreased again for longer silent intervals (160 ms). Intelligibility was optimal when the distribution of the acoustic information in the time-compressed signal matched (was aligned with) that in the original, uncompressed signal.

In the authors' interpretation, the resulting U-shaped performance implies that the auditory channel capacity is determined by the syllable-sized theta-frequency of neural rhythms, and that the appropriate unit to express speech information transfer rate is theta-syllables/s. MEG studies (Doelling et al. 2014) support this interpretation, showing that stimulus intelligibility is affected by the presence or absence of temporal fluctuations that occur at the syllabic (theta) rate. The role of temporal speech envelope information and entrainment to the input speech rhythm is supported by several experiments. It is a necessary component of speech comprehension. The importance of parsing the signal in syllable-sized chunks is reinforced, at least for recognizing syllables in speech without context.

If the temporal organization of the speech stream is indeed driven by the theta/syllable-rate, then it can be hypothesized that temporal properties of spoken language concur with this general property. It has been proposed by Pouplier and Beňuš (2011) that longer lags provide a favourable environment for syllabic consonants to emerge. I would add that they provide, more generally, an environment for energy peaks to emerge. What counts as an energy peak further depends on details of the language-specific timing patterns, as well as on the lexical and morpho-syntactic makeup of a linguistic system. For example, the long lags in Georgian and Tashlhiyt may be related to the specific morphologies of these languages. Typologically they are quite different, but both morphological systems are rich in consonantal affixes stacked up, primarily preceding the root. Many of the ideas expressed here clearly await further verification. As a preliminary conclusion, successful encoding, transmission and decoding of linguistic information crucially depend on intergestural timing patterns.

References

Bagemihl, B. (1991). Syllable structure in Bella Coola. *Linguistic Inquiry*, 22, 589–646.

Blevins, J. (1995). The syllable in phonological theory. In J.A. Goldsmith (ed.), *The handbook of phonological theory* (pp. 206–44). Oxford: Blackwell.

Bohland, J.W., Bullock, D. and Guenther, F.H. (2010). Neural representations and mechanisms for the performance of simple speech sequences. *Journal of Cognitive Neuroscience*, 22, 1504–29.

Browman, C.P. and Goldstein, L. (1992). Articulatory phonology: An overview. *Phonetica*, 49, 155–80.

Browman, C.P. and Goldstein, L. (2000). Competing constraints on intergestural coordination and self-organization of phonological structures. *Les Cahiers de l'ICP, Bulletin de la Communication Parlée*, 5, 25–34.

Chitoran, I. and Goldstein, L. (2006). Testing the phonological status of perceptual recoverability: Articulatory evidence from Georgian. Poster presented at Laboratory Phonology 10, Paris, June 2006.

Chitoran, I., Goldstein, L. and Byrd, D. (2002). Gestural overlap and recoverability: articulatory evidence from Georgian. In C. Gussenhoven and N. Warner (eds.), *Laboratory phonology 7* (pp. 419–47). Berlin, New York: Mouton de Gruyter.

Clements, G.N. (1990). The role of the sonority cycle in core syllabification. In J. Kingston and M.E. Beckman (eds.), *Papers in laboratory phonology I. Between the grammar and physics of speech* (pp. 283–333). Cambridge: Cambridge University Press.

Clements, G. N. (2009). Does sonority have a phonetic basis? In E. Raimy and C. Cairns (eds.), *Contemporary views on architecture and representations in phonological theory* (pp. 165–75). Cambridge, MA: MIT Press.

Dell, F. and Elmedlaoui, M. (2002). *Syllables in Tashlhiyt Berber and in Moroccan Arabic.* Dordrecht: Kluwer Academic Publishers.

Doelling, K.B., Arnal, L.H., Ghitza, O. and Poeppel, D. (2014). Acoustic landmarks drive delta-theta oscillations to enable speech comprehension by facilitating perceptual parsing. *NeuroImage*, 85, 761–68.

Fougeron, C. and Ridouane, R. (2008). On the phonetic implementation of syllabic consonants and vowel-less syllables in Tashlhiyt. *Estudios de Fonética Experimental*, 18, 139–75.

Ghitza, O. (2011). Linking speech perception and neurophysiology: speech decoding guided by cascaded oscillators locked to the input rhythm. *Frontiers in Psychology*, 2, 1–13.

Ghitza, O. (2013). The theta-syllable: a unit of speech information defined by cortical function. *Frontiers in Psychology*, 4, 138.

Ghitza, O. and Greenberg, S. (2009). On the possible role of brain rhythms in speech perception: Intelligibility of time-compressed speech with periodic and aperiodic insertions of silence. *Phonetica*, 66, 113–26.

Giraud, A.-L. and Poeppel, D. (2012). Cortical oscillations and speech processing: emerging computational principles and operations. *Nature Neuroscience*, 15, 511–17.

Goldsmith, J.A. (2011). The syllable. In J.A. Goldsmith, J. Riggle and A.C.L. Yu (eds.), *The handbook of phonological theory*, 2nd edition (pp. 164–96). Chichester: Wiley Blackwell.

Goldstein, L., Chitoran, I. and Selkirk, E. (2007). Syllable structure as coupled oscillator modes: Evidence from Georgian and Tashlhiyt Berber. *Proceedings of ICPhS XVI*, Saarbrücken (pp. 241–44), 6–10 August 2007.

Goldstein, L. and Fowler, C.A. (2003). Articulatory phonology: A phonology for public language use. In N.O. Schiller and A.S. Meyer (eds.), *Phonetics and phonology in language comprehension and production* (pp. 159–207). Berlin: Mouton de Gruyter.

Guenther, F.H. (1995). Speech sound acquisition, coarticulation, and rate effects in a neural network model of speech production. *Psychological Review*, 102, 594–621.

Guenther, F.H., Ghosh, S.S. and Tourville, J.A. (2006). Neural modeling and imaging of the cortical interactions underlying syllable production. *Brain and Language*, 96, 280–301.

Hardcastle, W.J. and Roach, P.J. (1979). An instrumental investigation of coarticulation in stop consonant sequences. In H.H. Hollien and P. Hollien (eds.), *Current issues in the phonetic sciences* (pp. 533–50). Amsterdam: John Benjamins.

Hermes, A., Ridouane, R., Mücke, D. and Grice, M. (2011). Kinematics of syllable structure in Tashlhiyt Berber: The case of vocalic and consonantal nuclei. *Proceedings of ISSP 9* (pp. 401–8), Montréal, Canada.

Howard, M.F. and Poeppel, D. (2012). The neuromagnetic response to spoken sentences: Co-modulation of theta band amplitude and phase. *NeuroImage*, 60, 2118–27.

Jespersen, O. (1897–99). *Fonetik en systematisk fremstilling af laeren om sproglyd.* Copenhagen: Det Schuboteske Forlag.

Kaye, A. (1990). 'Coda' licensing. *Phonology*, 7, 301–30.

Kaye, A., Lowenstamm, J. and Vergnaud, J.-R. (1990). Constituent structure and government in phonology. *Phonology*, 7, 305–28.

Lowenstamm, J. (1996). CV as the only syllable type. In J. Durand and B. Laks (eds.), *Current trends in phonology, models and methods* (pp. 419–42). University of Salford, Manchester: ESRI.

MacNeilage, P. and Davis, B. (2000). Origin of the internal structure of words. *Science*, 288, 527–31.

Mattingly, I.G. (1981). Phonetic representation and speech synthesis by rule. In T. Myers, J. Laver and J. Anderson (eds.), *The cognitive representation of speech* (pp. 415–19). Amsterdam: North-Holland Publishing Company.

Mattingly, I. G. (1998). Why did coarticulation evolve? *Behavioral and Brain Sciences*, 21, 275–6.

Nam, H., Goldstein, L. and Saltzman, E. (2009). Self-organization of syllable structure: A coupled oscillator model. In F. Pellegrino, E. Marsico, I. Chitoran and C. Coupé (eds.), *Approaches to phonological complexity* (pp. 299–328). Berlin: Mouton de Gruyter.

Ohala, J.J. (1992). Alternatives to the sonority hierarchy. *Papers from the Parasession on the Syllable* (pp. 319–38). Chicago Linguistic Society.

Ohala, J.J. and Kawasaki-Fukumori, H. (1997). Alternatives to the sonority hierarchy for explaining segmental sequential constraints. In S. Eliasson and E.H. Jahr (eds.), *Language and its ecology: Essays in memory of Einar Haugen* (pp. 343–65). Berlin: Mouton de Gruyter.

Parker, S. (2002). *Quantifying the sonority hierarchy.* PhD dissertation, University of Massachusetts, Amherst.

Perkell, J., Cohen, M., Svirsky, M., Matthies, M., Garabieta, I. and Jackson, M. (1992). Electromagnetic midsagittal articulometer (EMMA) systems for transducing speech articulatory movements. *Journal of the Acoustical Society of America*, 92, 3078–96.

Pouplier, M. and Beňuš, S. (2011). On the phonetic status of syllabic consonants: Evidence from Slovak. *Laboratory Phonology*, 2, 243–73.

Proctor, M., and Walker, R. (2012). Articulatory bases of sonority in English liquids. In S. Parker (ed.), *The sonority controversy* (pp. 289–316). Berlin: de Gruyter.

Ridouane, R. (2008). Syllables without vowels: Phonetic and phonological evidence from Tashlhiyt Berber. *Phonology*, 25, 321–59.

Ridouane, R. and Fougeron, C. (2011). Schwa elements in Tashlhiyt word-initial clusters. *Laboratory Phonology*, 2, 275–300.

Ridouane, R., Hermes, A. and Hallé, P. (2014). Tashlhiyt's ban of complex syllable onsets: Phonetic and perceptual evidence. *STUF – Language Typology and Universals*, 67, 7–20.

Scheer, T. (1996). *A theory of direct consonantal interaction.* PhD dissertation. Université Paris 7.

Shahin, K. and Blake, S. (2004). A phonetic study of schwa in St'at'imcets (Lillooet Salish). In D.B. Gerdts and L. Matthewson (eds.), *Studies in Salish linguistics in honor of M. Dale Kinkade* (pp. 311–27). Missoula: University of Montana.
Tilsen, S. (2013). A dynamical model of hierarchical selection and coordination in speech planning. *PLoS ONE*, 8(4): e62800. doi:10.1371/journal.pone.0062800

Ioana Chitoran is professor of linguistics at Université Paris Diderot. Her research lies at the phonetics-phonology interface, and focuses on the relationship between temporal variability and the emergence of phonological structure and phonotactic complexity. Her work examines data from Romance languages and some languages of the Caucasus.

4
Sonority in Zulu

Brent Ernest Archer

4.1 Introduction

Over the last 200 years, many authors have noted that words are inclined to display specific sonority patterns; the edge sounds of syllables usually have lower sonority than the center sounds. Clement's Sonority Sequencing Principle (SSP) (Clements 1992) is the latest, most formal statements of this general notion.

This chapter attempts to use statistical methods to determine whether or not the SSP accurately predicts the results of a corpus analysis of data from a language which is unrelated to those usually cited in this respect. Such an investigation can contribute to debates concerning the universality of sonority patterns and associated claims about the nature of the psycholinguistic architecture thought to support phonological aspects of language.

4.2 Transition Scores

How to measure sonority in an exact and non-arbitrary way has been the subject of some debate (Ohala 1990). A full resolution of these questions need not concern us here. The purpose of this study is to evaluate the merits of the SSP, as stated by its proponents. Accordingly, I will use the sonority rankings provided in Ball, Müller and Rutter (2010) which appear representative of the majority of scales available:

Vowels: 6
Glides: 5
Liquids: 4
Nasals: 3

Fricatives: 2
Stops: 1

Based on this hierarchy, it is possible to calculate transition scores for syllables. Here, I will operationalize a syllable's transition score as the difference in sonority ranking between the onset and the nucleus.[1] Zulu features 43 consonants and 5 vowels and syllables must conform to a V or CV structure. Thus 216 possible syllables exist. Table 4.1 provides transition scores for a few of these. Syllables which consist of a single vowel would receive a score of 0, since no sonority transition occurs during their production.

Table 4.1. Transition scores for four syllables.

Syllable	Calculation	Transition score
be-	1–6	–5
zi-	2–6	–4
nu-	3–6	–3
wa-	5–6	–1

Maximum sonority differences between onsets and nuclei are viewed as optimal under traditional sonority-based theories of phonotactics. As can be seen from Table 4.1, the smaller the transition score, the closer the transition is to the ideal form postulated by Clements (i.e., a difference of –5 is preferable, under this model, to one of –1). Given the phonemes (and categories of phonemes) used in Zulu, the lowest possible transition score is –5, while the highest is –1 (see Section 4.4, More about Transition Scores: Some Special Cases and Exclusions, for further information on how sonority values for various Zulu phonemes were arrived at).

4.3 The Corpus

Zulu was chosen as the language of focus in this study for a number of reasons.

Firstly, authors investigating the SSP have tended to focus their efforts on Indo-European languages. If linguists are to claim the SSP has universal

1 Since the corpus to be analysed in this study is a Zulu one, and Zulu is a typical Bantu language that does not permit CVC syllables, we can confine our discussion to onsets and nuclei.

validity (as they do e.g., Jany, Gordon, Nash and Takara 2007), its implications should be measured against data obtained from a wide range of languages. Zulu, as a language that has no topological or historical relation to the Indo-European family, is a prime candidate for study.

Secondly, Zulu orthography is entirely regular (Ziervogel, Louw and Taljaard 1985). Corpora in Zulu would thus lend themselves to ready analysis, since by examining the written forms, we are simultaneously examining the spoken forms of the language. The resources and procedures needed to study a language like Zulu are minimal in comparison to those that might be required for an analysis of a language such as English, whose spelling system is distantly and tangentially related to speech.

Thirdly, syllables in Zulu are formed according to a set of rules, shared by many other Southern Bantu languages. In essence, the vast majority of syllables follow a CV pattern, with a smaller number of syllables consisting of a single vowel (Canonici 1989). Codas and clusters are rarer. Analysing large amounts of Zulu data is thus much more straightforward than a similar exercise in a language like English. If a nonsense word such as *amata* is to be sequenced according to the parameters of these two languages, English allows a variety of options: *a-ma-ta, am-a-ta, am-at-a.* Zulu conversely licenses *a-ma-ta* only. Thus when searching a database of Zulu forms, if a CV structure is identified as occurring a certain number of times, the analyst can be assured that both the C and V were part of the same syllable, and not constituents of different syllables.

Finally, a large and accessible corpus of Zulu data is available online. 'Ukwabelana' is an open source corpus of Zulu words developed by the University of Bristol and contains over 15,000 lexical items (Spiegler, van der Spuy and Flach 2010). This would appear to be the largest, most user-friendly electronic corpus of any indigenous African language spoken in South Africa in existence.

4.3.1 Tendency: A Working Definition

Clements has stated that languages have a tendency to sequence phonemes such that there is maximum difference between the onset and nucleus (e.g., using Clements' gradings of sonority, a transition between a voiceless stop and a vowel, whereby a phoneme with the lowest sonority is followed by a phoneme with the highest sonority, is preferable to a glide followed by a vowel, whereby a phoneme with a relatively high sonority is followed by another phoneme with high sonority) (Clements 1992).

A first step in this direction might be to devise a more precise definition for 'tendency'. To do so, we could turn to the discipline of statistics which furnishes us with the cognitive tools we need to turn the above suppositions into objectively falsifiable claims. For the statistician, the term 'tendency' has a very specific meaning.

Consider the statement: 'Goldfish who live for a decade tend to die within a year of their tenth birthdays'. A statistical interpretation of this statement would entail three elements.

Firstly, if such a statement is to be judged true, a standard way of measuring goldfish lifespan is needed. Keeping track of the number of days that pass between the fishes' births and deaths would suffice.

Secondly, in order to adjudicate how well the hypothesis (most goldfish die shortly after turning 10) matches with real world data, it may be necessary to conduct statistical tests of various kinds. The selection of tests is always determined by the type of data under examination. In this case, we are interested in a time period (the number of days beyond ten years the fish are still alive). Since quantities of time can be divided up into meaningful units whose size can be compared (i.e., two minutes is demonstrably twice as long as one minute), the data is interval in nature. Because the data is interval, we can calculate measures of central tendency and related constructs (means, variances, standard deviation) that are essential for hypothesis testing.

Thirdly, implicit in the above statement (and in all statements about tendencies) is the notion that data should be distributed in some pattern that approximates 'normality'. In this case, we would expect some sort of distinct downward progression. Though a few anomalous events may be encountered, we would reasonably expect to find fewer and fewer survivors with the overall trend being a decrease in the number of living fish with the passage of time.

Figure 4.1 provides a statistically-oriented visualization of the statement that goldfish who live for a decade are inclined to die within a year of their tenth birthdays. The rate of deaths is geometrically configured (50 per cent of the fish die in the first year, 25 per cent in the second, 12.5 per cent in the third and so on) in order to meet the criterion of 'normality'. This progression ensures that the first year features the largest number of deaths, and that subsequent years taper off, with no anomalous years noted.

We can readily apply the same concepts to arrive at a more precise and testable claim about sonority sequences.

Firstly, since we are concerned with transitions between onsets and nuclei in syllables, we could operationalize a syllable's transition score as

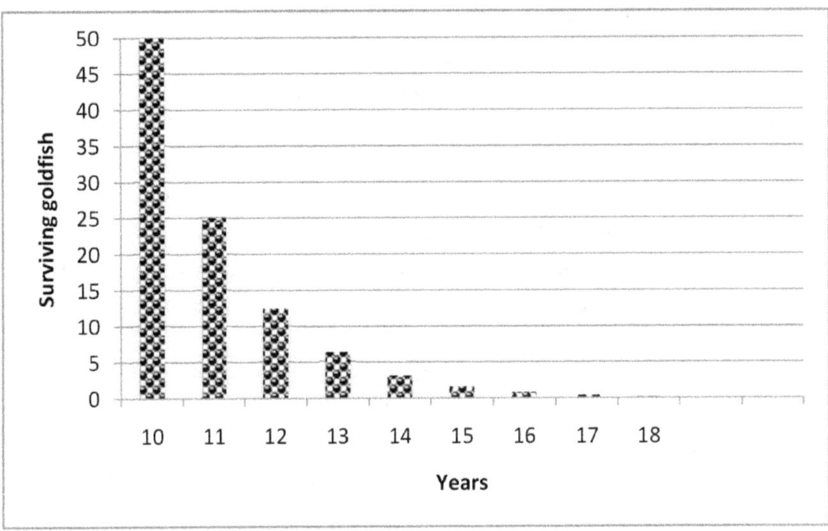

Figure 4.1. Goldfish survival distribution.

the difference in sonority ranking between the onset and the nucleus. Doing so would provide a standard method for deriving measures of transition.

Secondly, the level of measurement of transition measures should be determined. Most authors describe sonority in terms that would seem to indicate this trait can be best understood as an ordinal variable. Words like 'hierachy' and 'ranking' both seem to suggest that phonemes (or large classes of phonemes) can be arranged on a ladder stretching from the most to least sonorous. Most texts remain silent as to the relationship between steps on the ladder, offering no indication that vowels are six times as sonorous as stops. However, more detailed analyses such as those appearing in Clements (2009) and Price (1980) describe sonority by invoking acoustic concepts which themselves can be measured using interval scales. For example, Clements (2009: 168) argues that:

> Sounds perceived as sonorant tend to be characterized by a relatively low degree of resistance or acoustic loss, leading to a slow decay of formant oscillation, manifested in the spectrum as a reduction in formant bandwidth (i.e., as more sharply peaked formants). In contrast, sounds perceived as having low sonority have a relatively high degree of resistance or loss, leading to a faster decay of formant oscillation and a consequent increase in formant bandwidth (in the limit case, a flat spectrum).

Since all of the properties (resistance, formant oscillation, bandwidth) are themselves measured on interval scales, there is no compelling reason to treat sonority itself as an ordinal concept. As regards transition scores derived to provide an indication of the degrees of difference between different sets of onsets and nuclei, since the components used to make these calculations are interval, I will proceed under the assumption that transition scores are also interval quantities.

Thirdly, since a maximum difference in sonority between onsets and nuclei is the ideal, we would expect most syllables to display this characteristic. Normal distribution would ensure that syllables that deviate from the ideal are less common, with the number of any one type of syllable being indirectly proportional to the deviance noted.

It is now possible to restate claims about sonority tendencies in a way that allows us to test these ideas. If we obtain sonority transition scores for a large number of syllables in an as yet unstudied language, the mode score (i.e., most popular score) will be the ideal (following Clements, maximum sonority difference between onset and nucleus). All non-ideal transition scores should be ranked below the mode; as transition scores move further and further away from the mode, fewer and fewer syllables should display these scores.[2]

We can adapt the figure used to represent the goldfish longevity hypothesis to provide a visual analogue of claims about sonority inclinations. The x-axis scale in Figure 4.2 stretches from –5 (i.e., a score obtained by syllables in which there is a maximal difference between the onset and the nucleus; an ideal syllable) to –1 (i.e., a score obtained by syllables in which there is a minimal difference between the onset and the nucleus; the least ideal syllable). The transition scores described in Figure 4.2 are the only ones permissible, given most sonority hierarchies. The y-axis in Figure 4.2 lists the number of syllables that should be categorized under each transition score if SSP-based predictions are valid.[3]

2 While syllables will generally be constructed according to this ideal, variety in syllable form allows the imperative of constrastivity to be met (i.e., if every syllable in a language consisted of a voiceless stop followed by a vowel, the lexicon would feature an unworkably large number of homophones, making the language a singularly poor system for efficiently communicating about the large number of entities and actions that require verbal labels). A normal distribution represents a good balance between optimal syllable shapes and the need for languages to feature an array of syllable forms.

3 The number of syllables placed in each category does not align perfectly with the percentages presented in Figure 4.1. For example, the number of syllables allocated to the –5 portion of the x-axis is 141,880, slightly more than 50 per cent of the 280,258 syllables available for analysis. This adjustment was made so that all of the data could be placed into one of the x-axis categories; since

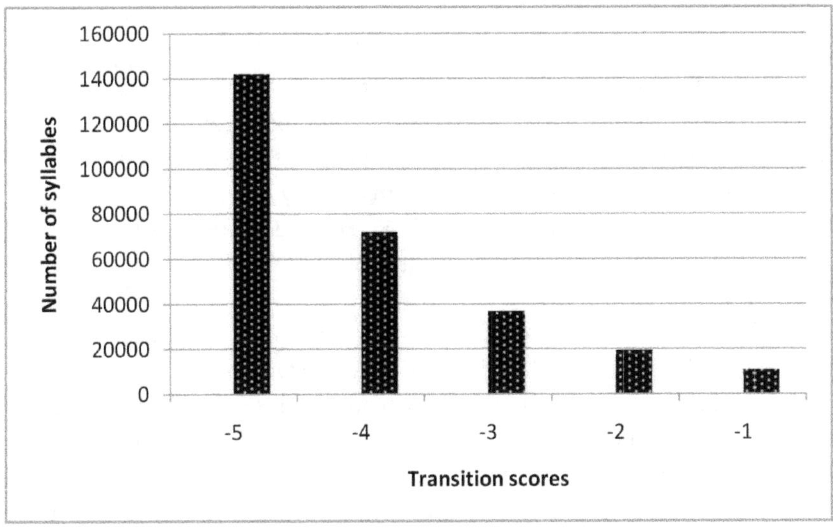

Figure 4.2. Predicted transition score distribution.

One way of testing claims about goldfish mortality and sonority sequencing tendencies is by simply comparing the predicted distribution to the actual distribution. Various statistical tests can be used to ascertain the degree to which the two distributions differ.

4.4 More about Transition Scores: Some Special Cases and Exclusions

Zulu features certain categories of phonemes (ejectives, implosives and clicks) which have not received a great deal of attention in the phonetics literature. There is therefore scant guidance on how best to quantify the sonority of these sounds. In order to complete this study, it was necessary for me to consult publications on the perceptual aspects these sounds, and infer how best to calculate the transition scores of the syllables in which they occur.

---

there are fewer categories in Figure 4.1 than in Figure 4.2, it was necessary to increase the number of syllables carried by each category in Figure 4.2. As can be seen from Figure 4.2, this minor alteration does not drastically effect the normal nature of the distribution.

Phonologically speaking, ejectives may pattern with stops, fricatives or affricates (Campbell 1973). In the case of Zulu, there do not appear to be any formal linguistic studies about how to classify the voiceless bilabial, alveolar and velar ejectives. However, introductory grammars often state that homorganic unaspirated stops can be substituted for the ejectives, and that the pronunciation of these stops is very close to the native ejective forms (e.g., Wilkes and Nkosi 1996). For the purposes of this analysis, I will therefore treat ejectives as unaspirated voiceless stops (sonority ranking of 1).

Implosives present more of a conundrum, with the consensus being they cannot be readily replaced by any English sounds. Again, works specific to Zulu could not be obtained. Instead, studies of implosives in other languages had to be consulted, and the appropriate calculation had to be devised. According to Clements and Osu (2002), most implosives are to be considered stops; as the total constriction at a point in the vocal tract needed to produce a stop is taking place, the glottis moves downwards, rarefying the airstream. The phoneme is then released, but because of this rarefication, it has an imploded character. Following these authors' view that implosives are non-obstruent stops, I will afford them the same sonority status as stops (sonority ranking of 1).

Zulu features a number of clicks. Coding of clicks was, again, based on the literature within phonetics concerning these phonemes. Clicks are produced by the adoption of a complex tongue gesture. The back of the tongue makes total contact with the oral cavity surface of the vellum while the tip or blade of the tongue makes closed contact with the dental ridge, alveolus or hard palate (depending on the click). The body of the tongue then moves downwards, rarefying the air in the oral cavity. The final stage of click production occurs when the tongue tip or body is released, followed by release of the back of the tongue. These actions give rise to the very perceptually marked class of sounds known as clicks. The glottis does not participate in the production of clicks.

Since no definitive statement about click sonority exists, it is difficult to know how to classify clicks in the sonority hierarchy. What little acoustic and articulatory data is available seems to indicate that clicks are more or less equivalent to plosives in terms of amplitude, intensity and airflow (after Cruttenden 1992). However, as Cruttenden points out, some qualifications to this general schema are needed. Following his recommendation, all nasal clicks were assigned nasal sonority scores, dental, lateral or aspirated clicks (alveolar aspirated) were coded as fricatives, while the remainder were awarded plosive ratings.

4.5 Analysis and Results

The 15,000 words of the 'Ukwabelana' corpus were fed into a text analysis program, and sequenced into syllables. For the sake of simplicity, a small number of syllables were removed from the data. Unlike other Bantu languages, Zulu phonotactics does permit the production of certain CCV clusters. Consultation of the corpus showed that the total number of CCV clusters found in the data was 8,507. Thus the percentage of syllables in the corpus which featured clusters was 3 per cent. Given the size of the corpus, and the smallness of this proportion, excluding clusters would not exert any noticeable impact on the overall integrity of the study. Clusters were thus not considered during analysis.

Similarly, how to encode affricates or syllables consisting of two vowels in terms of sonority is still the subject of some debate. To simplify analysis here, all items containing /ʧ/, /ʤ/ or two vowels (fewer than 50 items in total) were excluded.

Zulu orthography is regular, making this language an ideal candidate for corpus studies, since data does not need to be transformed before it can be analysed (linguists can simply consult standard orthographic forms to gain insights into the sound patterns of the language). During my analysis, however, I discovered that Zulu spelling does conflate two phonetic values into a single symbol; the voiced velar implosive and voiced velar stop are both rendered with the <g> symbol. Again, the total number of syllables featuring both these sounds are small, 271 in total. Since these syllables account for 0.14 per cent of those used, the impact on the overall findings is negligible.

A total of 280,258 CV syllables were analysed. Each syllable was awarded a transition score as per the guidelines laid out in Section 4.2. The number of each type of score (−5, −4, −3, −2, −1) was then tallied. The distribution of the corpus scores can be seen in Figure 4.3.

As stated earlier, the simplest way to compare the expectations concerning phonotactic patterns that follow from the SSP with actual data gathered from a given language, is to compare the distributions associated with the model set up by the SSP, and the model derived from a corpus. Figure 4.4 provides an overlay of the predicted and corpus distributions.

As can be seen from Figure 4.4, the predictions of the SSP do not appear to align well with the findings flowing from examinations of the corpus data. To determine if this impression was supported by more impartial analysis procedures, a chi squared test was conducted. Because the number of data points used in this study was large, transformed data (all

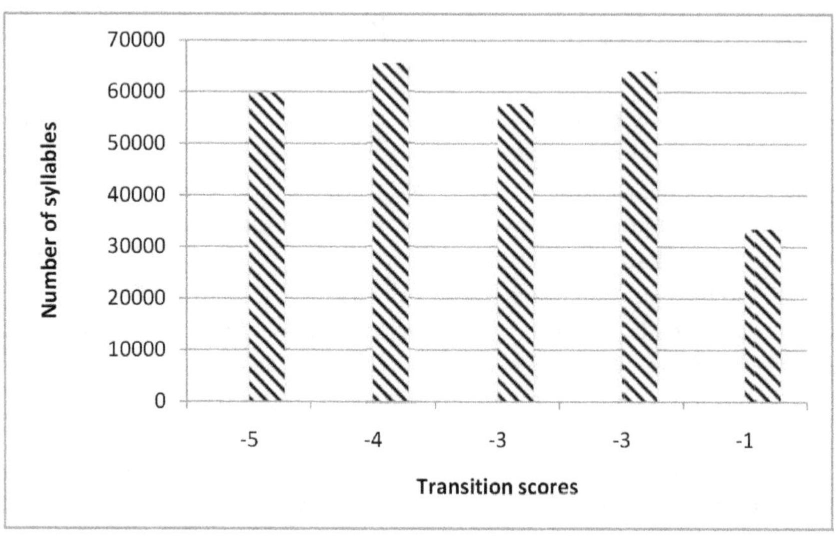

Figure 4.3. Observed transition score distribution.

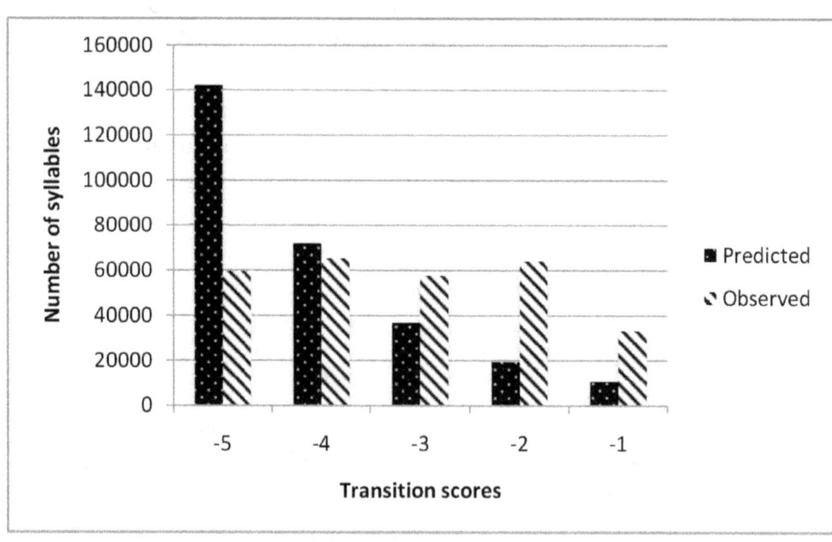

Figure 4.4. Predicted and observed transition score distributions.

figures were divided by 10,000), was used for this purpose. The results of this process yielded the following result: χ^2 (4, 280,258) = 214, $p < 0.001$. Accordingly, the probability that the two distributions in question (predicted and observed) are drawn from the same population is exceptionally small.

Taken in concert, a visual inspection of Figure 4.4 (which charts the degree of overlap between the two distributions) and the results of the chi squared test would strongly suggest that there is very little commonality between the predictions of SSP-based theories and this natural language corpus.

4.6 Discussion

The tendency of languages (or, at very least, the language of Zulu) to sequence syllables such that maximal sonority differences exist between onsets and nuclei would appear to be a very minor one. Clearly, if some universal pattern of syllable formation does indeed exist, it is the product of an organizing principle other than sonority sequencing.

Claims that rigid sonority patterning tendencies are 'hardwired' into the brain (Christman 1992; Sussman 1984) seem much less defensible when the regularities predicted by SSP are almost entirely absent from corpus data. Arguments for a neurological basis for strict sonority sequences need to be amended in light of this data. At best, innatists can claim that the human nervous system seems to be minimally geared towards arranging maximal differences between syllable onsets and nuclei.

If the dictates of the SSP do not play a significant role in shaping the form of syllables, Ohala's (1990) contention that acoustic peaks and valleys at the borders between syllables help listeners to comprehend speech signal seems to deserve less credence. Given the wide divergence between the dictates of the SSP and an analysis of real-world data, linguists should take recourse to other concepts to explain how auditory comprehension takes place. Other mechanisms (semantic and syntactic forms of utterances, minimal features as drivers of differences in acoustic signals, etc.) need to be invoked before an accurate picture of how speech sounds are decoded can emerge.

4.7 Conclusions and Future Research

The analysis conducted in this study would seem to suggest that the SSP is not a universally valid description of syllable formation in human languages. The results of this study imply that the credence which sonority oriented approaches have been given in phonology is misplaced. Large-scale corpus investigations of non-Indo-European languages would help to assess the assumption that sonority theories play a significant role in shaping syllables in regularly studied languages. Moreover, future research should clarify whether Clements' and others' postulations reflect the nature of these specific languages, or more general natural language phenomena.

References

Ball, M.J., Müller, N. and Rutter, B. (2010). *Phonology for communication disorders.* New York: Psychology Press.

Campbell, L. (1973). On glottalic consonants. *International Journal of American Linguistics*, 39, 44–6.

Canonici, N.N. (1989). *Imisindo Yesizulu: A simple introduction to Zulu phonology.* Durban: Department of Zulu Language and literature, University of Natal.

Christman, S.S. (1992). Uncovering phonological regularity in neologisms: Contributions of sonority theory. *Clinical Linguistics and Phonetics*, 6, 219–47.

Clements, G.N. (1992). The sonority cycle and syllable organization. In W.U. Dressler, H.C. Luschützky, O. Pfeiffer and J. Rennison (eds.), *Phonologica 1988* (pp. 63–76). Cambridge: Cambridge University Press.

Clements, G.N. (2009). Does sonority have a phonetic basis. In E. Raimy and C. Cairns (eds.), *Contemporary views on architecture and representations in phonological theory* (pp. 165–75). Boston, MA: MIT Press.

Clements, G.N. and Osu, S. (2002). Explosives, implosives and nonexplosives: The linguistic function of air pressure differences in stops. In C. Gussenhoven and N. Warner (eds.), *Laboratory Phonology*, 7 (pp. 299–350). Berlin: Mouton de Gruyter

Cruttenden, A. (1992). Clicks and syllables in the phonology of Dama. *Lingua*, 86, 101–17.

Jany, C., Gordon, M., Nash, C.M. and Takara, N. (2007). How universal is the sonority hierarchy?: A cross-linguistic acoustic study. In *Proceedings of the International Congress of Phonetic Sciences* (Vol. 16, pp. 1401–4). Saarbrucken, Germany.

Ohala, J. (1990). Alternatives to the sonority hireachy for explaining segmental sequential constraints. In *The Parasession on the Syllable in Phonetics and*

Phonology, 26th Regional Meeting of the Chicago Linguistics Society (pp. 319–38). Chicago.

Price, P.J. (1980). Sonority and syllabicity: Acoustic correlates of perception. *Phonetica*, 37, 327–43.

Spiegler, S., van der Spuy, A. and Flach, P.A. (2010). Ukwabelana: An open-source morphological Zulu corpus. In *Proceedings of the 23rd International Conference on Computational Linguistics* (pp. 1020–8). Beijing: Association for Computational Linguistics.

Sussman, H.M. (1984). A neuronal model for syllable representation. *Brain and Language*, 22, 167–77.

Wilkes, A. and Nkosi, N. (1996). *Teach yourself Zulu*. Pretoria: NTC Publishing Group.

Ziervogel, D., Louw, J.A. and Taljaard, P.C. (1985). *A handbook of the Zulu language*. Pretoria: van Schaik.

Brent Ernest Archer is Assistant Professor in Communication Sciences and Disorders at Bowling Green State University, Ohio, USA, and hails from Johannesburg, South Africa. After graduating from the University of the Witwatersrand in 2006, he worked as a speech pathologist in a small rural hospital in South Africa. In 2012, he moved to Lafayette to pursue a PhD in Applied Speech and Language Sciences. His research interests include fluency disorders, aphasiology and service provision for bilingual clients.

5
Sonority in Some Languages of the Cameroon Grassfields

Matthew Faytak

5.1 Introduction

In this chapter, I describe the unusual phonotactics of languages representative of an area in northwestern Cameroon known as the Cameroon Grassfields. I aim to highlight here how underdocumented languages – and the underdocumented phonotactics of these languages – provide some interesting challenges to sonority as an analytical construct. In Kom and Limbum, two languages of the Cameroon Grassfields, a set of obstruents I refer to as *fricativized vowels* is licensed for syllabicity to the exclusion of all or nearly all sonorant consonants. Tautosyllabic combinations of sonorant onset or coda consonants and obstruent syllable nuclei also result in sonority troughs, rather than peaks, that coincide with prominence peaks. These phonotactic phenomena either call for reconsidering the phonetic substance that corresponds to sonority or reconsidering the use of sonority as the driving principle behind syllabification and sequencing in the first place. Data from languages with fricativised vowels suggest a need to move beyond a sonority loosely organized around constriction degree or 'openness' alone to a more complex set of segment sequencing principles that take multiple acoustic parameters into account.

This chapter proceeds as follows: in Section 5.2, I introduce the reader to Kom and Limbum as representatives of their linguistic area in Cameroon, and Section 5.3 introduces fricativized vowels and the current understanding of their acoustics and typological distribution. In Section 5.4, I highlight problems posed by fricativized vowels for theoretical accounts of prominence licensing, using Kom and Limbum as case studies. In Section 5.5 I similarly highlight some general problems posed by fricativized vowels for sequencing phenomena. Finally, in Section 5.6, I attempt to provide an alternative account of Kom and Limbum phonotactics starting from the notion of modulation of multiple acoustic parameters (cf. Ohala and Kawasaki-Fukumori 1997; Harris 2006), including the presence or absence of continuous high frequency aperiodic noise typical of fricative noise sources.

5.2 Kom, Limbum and Their Linguistic Area

Kom and Limbum are Grassfields Bantu languages, spoken in south-western Cameroon not far from the Nigerian border (Figure 5.1, see also Hammerström, Forkel, Haspelmath and Bank 2015). Kom is spoken by about 230,000 people and Limbum by about 130,000 (Lewis, Simons and Fennig 2015). The two languages are geographically close to one another, both being spoken along the same major ring road in Cameroon's Northwest Region. However, they belong to two fairly separated genetic subgroups (Piron 1995; cf. Grollemund 2012): Limbum to the Eastern Grassfields or Mbam-Nkam subgroup of Grassfields Bantu, and Kom to the Ring subgroup of Grassfields Bantu, sometimes counted as part of a larger Western Grassfields group (Hyman 1980).

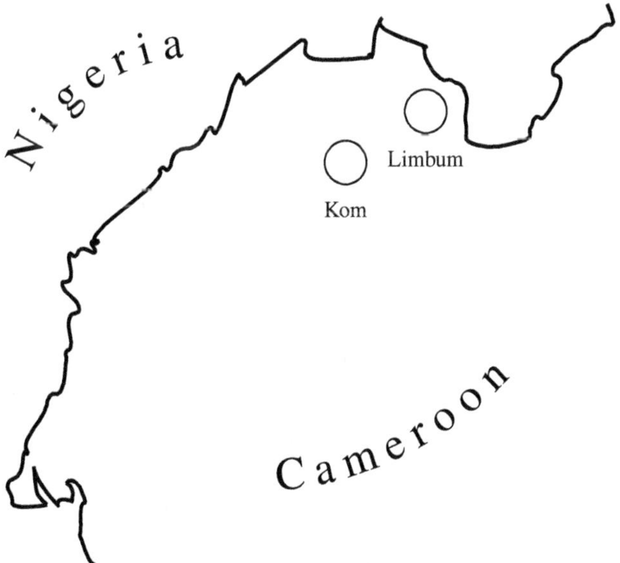

Figure 5.1. Kom- and Limbum-speaking areas in the southern portion of Cameroon.

Detailed linguistic description of the two languages is somewhat limited. Limbum is the subject of a grammar with an attached lexicon (Fransen 1995) that is the source of Limbum lexical data in this chapter unless otherwise indicated. Several shorter descriptive works also exist, including descriptions of its noun class system (van Reenen and Voorhoeve 1980) and a phonology sketch that includes considerable phonetic detail (Fiore 1977). Less work of a comprehensive nature has been carried out on Kom. Descriptive works include a dissertation on the tense-aspect system (Chia 1976), a provisional lexicon (Jones 2001), a detailed discussion of nominal tone and the noun class system (Hyman 2005) and some phonological and grammatical sketches (Shultz 1993, 1997). I have carried out fieldwork on Kom since 2013 in the United States and Cameroon; the Kom data used here comes directly from my own notes. A segmental phonemic inventory

Table 5.1. Kom and Limbum phonological inventories.

Limbum consonant phonemes*					Kom consonant phonemes**				
	Lab.	Alv.	Pal.	Vel.		Lab.	Alv.	Pal.	Vel.
Stop	b	t d	ʧ ʤ	k g	Stop	b	t d	ʧ ʤ	k g
Nasal	m	n	ɲ	ŋ	Nasal	m	n	ɲ	ŋ
Fric.	f	s	ʃ ʒ		Fric.	f	s		
Approx.	w	l	j	ɰ	Approx.	w	l	j	ɰ
Tap		ɾ							

Limbum vowel phonemes				Kom vowel phonemes			
Fric.	z zː	v vː		Fric.	z	v	
	Front	Central	Back		Front	Central	Back
High	i iː		u uː ɯ ɯː	High	i (y)		u ɯ
Mid	e eː		o oː	Mid	e ~ ə		o
Low		a aː		Low	ɛ (œ)	a	

Notes:
The Kom vowels in parentheses /y/ and /œ/ are in apparent free variation with sequences [wi] and [wɛ], respectively. Kom /e/ is realized as [ə] in closed syllables. Limbum data modified from Fransen (1995).

* Coda /b/ in Limbum is realized as [p] and coda /k/ as [ʔ]. The tap /ɾ/ is devoiced [ɾ̥] in coda position.

** Coda /n/ in Kom conditions a regular palatal glide insertion or, alternately, diphthongization of the preceding vowel, for instance /an/ > [ajn], /un/ > [ujn]. The fricativized vowels exhibit analogous changes, transitioning briefly to a high front vocoid free of frication before the /n/ closure. Coda /k/ is realized as [k] after the fricativized vowels and /ɯ/ but is realized as [ʔ] elsewhere.

of both languages is given in Table 5.1. Both languages also have fairly complex tonal systems that I do not analyse here.[1]

5.3 Description of Fricativized Vowels

Both Kom and Limbum are notable for having in their phonemic inventory obligatorily syllabic obstruent segments that I refer to as *fricativized vowels*. These are produced with fricative noise similar to [z] or [v], respectively. Throughout this chapter I transcribe them simply as [z] and [v] given that there are no consonantal, nonsyllabified versions for them to be confused with; these segments are syllabified in all forms in which they appear below. The fricativized vowels have been the subject of some analytical debate. Fransen (1995: 35–6) analyses the labiodental fricativized vowel in Limbum as the surface realization of a 'labiodentalizing' high vowel /ɨ/ or a sequence /wɨ/, depending on the initial; the coronal fricativized vowel is described as the surface realization of /jɨ/. Shultz (1993) similarly analyses the fricativized vowels in Kom as underlying sequences /vɨ/, /zɨ/. An analysis of these vowels as some type of CV sequence is implicit in both languages' orthographies (Chia and Kimbi 1984; Jones 2001; Fransen 1995: 60–72).

Fricativized vowels as phonological entities have also been remarked upon by some researchers. Van Reenen and Voorhoeve (1980) and Fiore (1977) adopt analyses substantially similar to my own, describing fricativized vowels as single syllabified obstruent segments. Connell (2007: 16–17) adopts a similar analysis for Len Mambila, another language spoken near Limbum but outside of the Grassfields proper, and refers to two vowels with associated fricative noise as *fricative vowels*. While apparently common in the northern section of the Cameroon Grassfields discussed here, fricativized vowels are also common in the Chinese languages and Tibeto-Burman languages of southwestern China; in the descriptive literature for these areas, they are referred to as *apical vowels* or *fricative vowels* (Duanmu 2002: 36–7; Ling 2009: 13–69).

Acoustically, fricativized vowels are produced with the voicing source and relatively intense and well defined formants typical of a vowel, but with

1 Note that throughout this chapter, I use Chao tone letters (Chao 1930) to transcribe tone in both languages, given the lack of other suitable IPA transcriptions for some surface contours (for instance, the Kom high-mid falling contour, as in [i˧bi˥˧] 'kola nut').

an additional fricative noise source (figure 5.2). This fricative noise source is produced at one of two major places of articulation: labial, most often as a labiodental constriction, and coronal, most often as an alveolar or postalveolar constriction. Phonation quality is typically modal, barring the presence of contrastive phonation on fricativized vowels, as occurs in the Wu Chinese dialects (Cao and Maddieson 1989; Qian 1994), such that the aperiodic component of these sounds' spectra cannot be attributed to non-modal phonation alone. Although the vowel quality conveyed by the formants in the signal is auditorily central and high, formant-cavity affiliations unusual for vowels produce these formant patterns (Ling 2009: 55–9); the similar auditory impression can obscure the fact that fricativized vowels' tongue position is quite different from those employed for canonical high vowels.

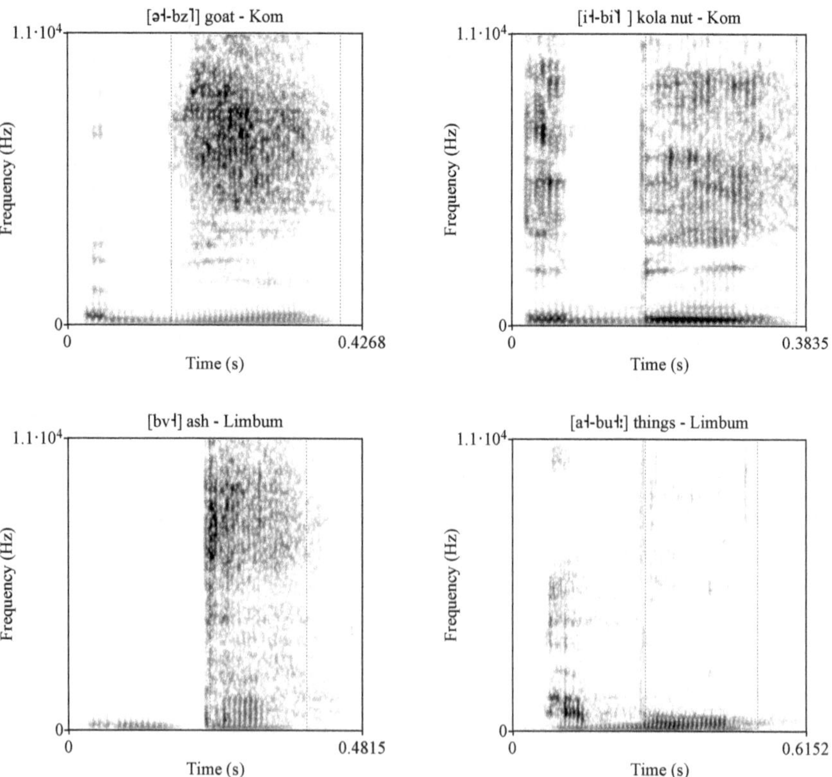

Figure 5.2. Spectrograms of fricativized vowels (left) and similar high vowels (right). Note: Compare Kom [ə˧-bz˥] 'goat' to [i˧bi˥˩] 'kola nut' and Limbum [bv˧] 'ash' to [a˧-buː˧] 'things'. Vowels at issue are marked off with vertical dotted lines. Recordings are drawn from my own fieldwork.

Although fricative noise is consistently associated with fricativized vowels, the temporal organization of this noise over the course of the vowel tends to vary, and the voicing of adjacent segments tends to affect the voicing of the vowel. A fricative noise source is expected to be relatively difficult to maintain under conditions of prolonged voicing (Ohala 1983), and as might be expected, a brief portion of less noisy acoustic quality more similar to a vowel occasionally occurs towards the end of fricativized vowels as a result. There is interspeaker variation in the frequency and extent of this frictionless portion, but the default state appears to be little to no loss of frication, particularly in Limbum. Connell (2007: 10–11) describes a similar state of affairs in Len Mambila. An additional permutation (albeit a phonologically regular one) occurs in both Kom and Limbum, voiceless

Table 5.2. Minimal or near minimal pair data for Kom (left) and Limbum (right).

Kom		Limbum	
/i/ : /z/		/i/ : /z/	
bi˥ 'to be ripe'	a˧-bz˥ 'ashes'	ɾ-biː˧ 'breast'	bzː˧ 'dance (n.)'
ndi˧ 'to insult'	i˧-dz˧ 'termite sp.'	ɾ-liː˧ 'tongue'	ɾ-lzː˧ 'name'
/u/ : /v/		/u/ : /v/	
ndu˨ 'to go'	ndv˨ 'most'	tuː˥ 'to cross'	tvː˥ 'to knit'
ku˨ 'to take'	ŋkv˨ 'rope'	buʔ˥ 'to beat (eggs)'	bvʔ˥ 'to crack'
/ɯ/ : /z/			
ə˧-bɯ˥ 'dog'	a˧-bz˥ 'ashes'		
ə˧-fɯ˥ 'hoe (n.)'	fz˥ 'to take'		
/ɯ/ : /v/		/ɯ/ : /v/	
a˧-kɯ˥ 'mortar'	a˧-kv˥ 'dead one'	ʒɯ˥ 'to know'	ʒv˥ 'to kill'
ə˧-ŋgɯ˩ 'gourd sp.'	ə˧-ngv˨ 'chicken'	ʃɯʔ˨ 'to shake'	ʃvʔ˨ 'to light (tr.)'
/v/ : /z/		/v/ : /z/	/v/ : /z/
ndv˨ 'most'	a˧-dz˩ 'sore (n.)'	bz˥ 'to give birth'	bv˥ 'to disappear'
z˥ 'to enter'	i˧-v˥ 'rain'	n-dzː˩ 'back'	dvː˩ 'to be dull'

Note: Noun class prefixes are separated from stems by a dash. Note that in Limbum, the contrast /ɯ/ : /z/ cannot be demonstrated, given that /ɯ/ has a restricted distribution (following /s ʃ ʒ ɾ/) that /z/ does not occur in. One could coerce /ɯ/ and /z/ to a single phoneme, but such an analysis is not possible for /v/ and any other vowel.

onsets partially devoice fricativized vowels, for instance, Limbum /tv:˥/ 'to knit' produced as [tfv:˥] and Kom /ŋkv˧/ 'rope' produced as [ŋkfv˧].

Kom and Limbum, much like Len Mambila, have two surface fricativized vowels, one with a labiodental fricative noise source and an alveolar or postalveolar fricative noise source. Northern dialects of Limbum tend to lack the vowel with the alveolar noise source, instead having [i] in the appropriate lexical items (Fiore 1977: 33–5). In both Kom and Limbum, the fricativized vowels contrast with high vowels, including the high central or back vowels they most closely resemble auditorily (Table 5.2, see also Connell 2007: 10). Unlike in Len Mambila, where the fricativized vowels do not contrast with one another, the choice of /v/ or /z/ being entirely predictable from initial consonant place (Connell 2007: 10), the two fricativized vowels in Kom and Limbum also contrast with one another.

In spite of their associated fricative noise, fricativized vowels pattern phonologically as vowels in languages that have them. Evidence is strongest for this alignment in Kom, where low vowels assimilate in frontness to preceding vowels and fricativized vowels but not consonants (Table 5.3). This also suggests a distinction in some feature [±back] between /z/ and /v/. In Len Mambila, Connell (2007: 16–17) provides evidence from a word game for a similar interpretation of the segments as vowels. In addition, in

Table 5.3. Kom -/a/ 'IMPF' assimilates in backness to [+high] stem vowels if in hiatus with them.

	Unmarked	Imperfective (-/a/)
Coda C: -a	tum˥ 'to send'	tu˧ma˥ 'sending'
	bəf˥ 'to be bad'	bə˧fa˥ 'being bad'
	jəs˩ 'to sweep'	jə˧sa˩ 'sweeping'
Hiatus, high back V: -a	ʒɯ˧ 'to eat'	ʒɯa˧˥ 'eating'
	fu˥ 'to give'	fua˧˥ 'giving'
	ɲv˧ 'to drink'	ɲva˧˥ 'drinking'
Hiatus, high front V: -æ	si˩ 'to sift'	siæ˥˩ 'sifting'
	ʒy˥ 'to kill'	ʒyæ˧˥ 'killing'
	bz˥ 'to give birth'	bzæ˥˩ 'giving birth'
Hiatus, nonhigh V: complete assim.	fœ˩ 'to rot'	fœ:˥˩ 'rotting'
	bo˧ 'to weave'	bo:˧˥ 'weaving'
	fe˧ 'to fall'	fe:˥˩ 'falling'

Note: Fricativized vowels appear to behave as [+high] vowels of different [±back] values. Consonant /s/, with similar place features to /z/, does not condition the front allophone of /a/: note 'sweeping'.

both Kom and Limbum, fricativized vowels function as tone bearing units, and can license any of the languages' complex tonal contours. Kom in particular has at least seven contrastive surface tones (Hyman 2005: 315–16) and Limbum eight (Fransen 1995: 73), that may be realized on nominal stems; there are no apparent combinatorial restrictions on tone and fricativized vowels in either language.

5.4 Syllabification

Regardless of the extent to which fricativized vowels can be identified with vowels or consonants, we can minimally establish from the previous section that they are syllabic obstruents of *some* sort. In this and the following section, I consider the implications of this finding for the phonotactics of languages like Kom and Limbum.

Licensing syllabicity to obstruents is an unusual but attested phonotactic pattern in the world's languages, with language-specific phonological evidence for their presence in Blackfoot (Goad, this volume), some Ryukyuan languages (Pellard 2009: 80–106; Goad, this volume) and Imdlawn Tashlhiyt Berber (Dell and Elmedlaoui 1985), among other languages (Bell 1978). Licensing syllabicity to obstruents on its own is not of interest here, however. Assuming a canonical sonority scale like the one shown in Table 5.4 (Clements 1990: 292; Parker 2002: 64), the aforementioned languages fit neatly into a generalization that a language will syllabify all segment classes higher in sonority than the least sonorous syllabified segment class (Blevins 1995: 220). Put another way, a single span of segment classes arranged along a sonority scale will be licensed for syllabicity; the inclusion of segments of unusually low sonority in this single span is not problematic.

Kom and Limbum exhibit phonotactics that present an exception to the generalization in Table 5.4: some sonorant segment classes are not licensed for syllabicity in spite of the syllabification of obstruent fricativized vowels in these languages. This results in syllabicity being licensed to two discontinuous stretches of the sonority scale. These two languages are not alone in exhibiting the 'skipping' phonotactics discussed above. A review of other languages with fricativized vowels shows that similar syllabification phonotactics can be found (see Faytak 2014b); in other words, this is not a fluke but rather a reasonably common pattern present in several linguistic areas.

Table 5.4. Cross-linguistic tendency to license syllabicity to a single 'span' of segment classes; Kom and Limbum as an exception.

	Highest ←			→ Lowest		
	V	R	L	N	S	T
Hawai'ian	yes	*no* →				
Sanskrit	yes	yes	*no* →			
Lendu	yes	yes	yes	*no* →		
English	yes	yes	yes	yes	*no* →	
Yi (Li and Ma 1983)	yes	–	yes	yes	yes	*no*
Imdlawn Tashlhiyt Berber	yes	yes	yes	yes	yes	yes
Kom, Limbum	yes	*no*	*no*	(yes)	yes	*no*

Note: Data from Blevins (1995) except where indicated. Segment classes from Blevins (1995): V stands for vowel; R, L for rhotic and lateral approximants, respectively; N for nasal, S for fricatives and T for affricates and plosives.

In Kom, neither nasals nor liquids are syllabified, but the fricativized vowels /z/ and /v/ are. Kom does exhibit nasal prefixes that Hyman (2005) describes as tone bearing; however, these are accompanied by an additional prefixal [ə], implying a process of epenthesis. In Limbum, liquids are not syllabified, but /m/ is marginally syllabified, occurring only in two limited, morphologically derived environments. Multiples of ten take a prefix [m̩˧] (e.g., [taːr˥] 'three'; [m̩˧-taːr˥] 'thirty,' Fransen 1995: 42) and the 1sg subject agreement prefix is realized as [m̩˨] in several verbal constructions, for instance in sequential constructions (e.g., [m̩˨-ʃa˥ŋi˩] '1sg.seq-run,' ibid.: 182). Syllabified /v/ and /z/, on the other hand, are prominent in most parts of speech and occur in nonderived environments, in spite of the fact that available liquids and nasals are not syllabified. This suggests that the syllabified obstruents in Kom and Limbum are part of a system where potentially syllabifiable segment classes are either entirely or for the most part 'passed over,' and the generalization from Blevins (1995) does not hold. The sonority hierarchy that this minimally suggests is given in Table 5.5, in which a subset of the obstruents is ranked above liquids and nasals for purposes of syllabification.

The syllabification phonotactics discussed above present a complication for existing theories of sonority: either an unnatural reversal of ranks on the sonority scale must be proposed for a subset of the world's languages, including Kom and Limbum, or the aforementioned 'passing over' of sufficiently sonorous segment classes must be accepted. Although there has traditionally been some room for language-specific reordering of sonority

Table 5.5. The sonority scale, modified from Table 5.4, suggested by Kom and Limbum phonotactics.

	Highest ←			→ Lowest		
	V+S1	R	L	N	S2	T
Kom, Limbum	yes	*no* →		(yes)		
	where S1 contains fricativized vowels and S2 contains other obstruents					

Note the reversal between obstruent class S1 and sonorant classes R, L and N.

scales, such that one could conceivably argue that Kom and Limbum simply have unusually ranked obstruents, the specific reversal of obstruents and any sonorant class is not proposed in the literature. Parker (2002) provides an extensive overview of sonority scales posited based on the phonological patterns of individual languages. The ranking of all sonorants over all obstruents is never called into question, and sonorant segments appear to universally have higher sonority than obstruent segments.

I do not wish to propose such a reversal here, in part due to concerns over naturalness of the construct that would result. Even assuming a phonetic property that aligns with sonority, such as intensity, which may be unexpectedly low or high for obstruents in certain languages, cross-linguistic acoustic studies show that sonorants consistently have greater intensity or overall sound level than obstruents (Jany, Gordon, Nash and Takara 2007; Parker 2008). It appears to be a safe assumption that high intensity, or equally some more abstract phonological index of high sonority, does not appear to be characteristic of obstruents such that they can possibly outrank – or should be made to outrank in some abstract sense – sonorants in languages such as Kom and Limbum, and that the prominence licensing puzzle remains.

5.5 Sequencing and Sonority Troughs

Fricativized vowels similarly present exceptions to the Sonority Sequencing Hierarchy (e.g., Clements 1990). Assuming the typical sonority scale as in Table 5.4, syllables in Kom and Limbum may have nuclei that are not also peaks in sonority within their respective syllables. This results in a surprising number of syllables in which obstruent nuclei are *less* sonorous than one or multiple adjacent tautosyllabic consonants.

Sequencing of fricativized vowels and consonants in Kom and Limbum is relatively unrestricted, and similar sequencing phonotactics generally apply to the broader set of languages discussed in Faytak (2014b). Within the CVC stems typical of Kom and Limbum a number of unusual CV (in a syllable-based account, onset-nucleus) and VC (nucleus-coda) *biphones*, or sequences of two phones, are attested. The patterns of segmental sequencing in the CV biphones of CV stems do not differ from those in the CV biphones of CVC stems.[2] The full inventory of possible CV and VC biphones for Kom and Limbum (Table 5.6) includes a number of cases where a nasal or lateral precedes (as a stem-initial consonant) or a nasal or lateral follows (as a stem-final consonant) a fricativized vowel. In all cases in both languages, the nasals and laterals are fairly canonical examples of their respective segment classes, and are produced fully voiced and free of fricative noise. In Limbum, the alveolar tap /ɾ/ is attested preceding /v/ and following both fricativized vowels. In Kom, the palatal approximant /j/ may

Table 5.6. Attested biphones in Kom and Limbum CV(C) stems, with the first segment implying the possible sequential occurrence of (→) the other.

Kom CV biphones				Kom VC biphones		
	t → v, z	ʧ → v	k → v			v → k
b → v, z	d → v, z	ʤ → v	g → v	v → m	v, z → n [jn]	v → ŋ
m → z	n	ɲ → v	ŋ	v → f	v, z → s	
f → v, z	s [ʃ] → v				v → l	
w	l → v	j [ʒ] → v	ɥ			
Limbum CV biphones				**Limbum VC biphones**		
	t → v, z	ʧ	k → v			v,z → k [ʔ]
b → v, z	d → v, z	ʤ	g → v	v,z → b [p]		
m → v	n	ɲ → v	ŋ			z → ŋ
f → v	s → v	ʃ → v				
		ʒ → v			v,z → ɾ [ɾ̥]	
w	l → v, z	j	ɥ			
	ɾ → v					

Note: Positional surface allophones are indicated in square brackets.

2 Monomorphemic CV_1CV_2 stems are also fairly common in both languages, with the V_1C sequences generally similar to the VC biphones in CVC stems. CV_2 biphones are sharply restricted due to reduced vowel inventory in V_2 position, and I opt not to discuss them here.

also precede the fricativized vowel /v/, but in this position (and additionally before /ɯ/) it is realized as a fricative [ʒ].

The difficulty for theories of segment sequencing based on sonority comes in the form of troughs of sonority that coincide with peaks in phonological prominence. In slightly different terms, there is a misalignment of what would canonically be deemed the peak of sonority (in the syllable onset and/or coda) and the peak of prominence within the same syllable (the nucleus). Clements (1990: 288–9) observes that sonority troughs or plateaus within a syllable are exhibited by a large number of languages other than the ones investigated here, but none of the troughs discussed there involve an obstruent flanked by two sonorants, which is reasonably frequent in both Kom and Limbum (Table 5.7). In this case, prominence is evident from which segment bears the tonal contrast of the stem.

In this section I have made reference to syllable structure by evaluating peak prominence assignment with respect to each segment within the boundaries of a syllable. It is not clear that a syllable-oriented approach to the discussion here is the best one, given that there are other approaches that remove the need for the syllable in analysis, working solely from (speakers' knowledge of) surface sequences (cf. Heinz 2007). I further discuss whether syllables are required to model Kom and Limbum phonotactics at the end of Section 5.6. In this case, modelling segment sequencing using canonical sonority fails to predict reality whether or not syllables are invoked: regardless, obstruents are expected to support many fewer robust cues to the place (or existence) of other segments (Wright 2004), but fricativized vowels do not support an especially small number of biphones when compared to more canonical vowels in Kom or Limbum. As illustrated for Kom /v/ and /u/ in Figure 5.3, attested coda biphones are identical for the two vowels, and only four onsets occur before /u/ and not /v/.

Table 5.7. Words with sonority troughs in Kom and Limbum.

Kom	Limbum
ɲv˧ 'to drink'	ɾvː˧ 'to age'
mz˩ 'to swallow'	mvː˧ 'middle'
lvjn˧ 'immediately'	lzp˧ 'to beat'
i˧-vm˥ 'ten'	lvɾ̥˥ 'fool'
ə˧-gvl˥ 'maggot'	ɾ-lzɾ̥˧ 'eye'
i˧-zjn˥ 'name'	ɾ-dzŋ˥ m-buː˩ 'buttock'

Note: Tone bearing segments appear to have peak prominence in the stem. Noun class morphology is separated from stems by hyphens as appropriate.

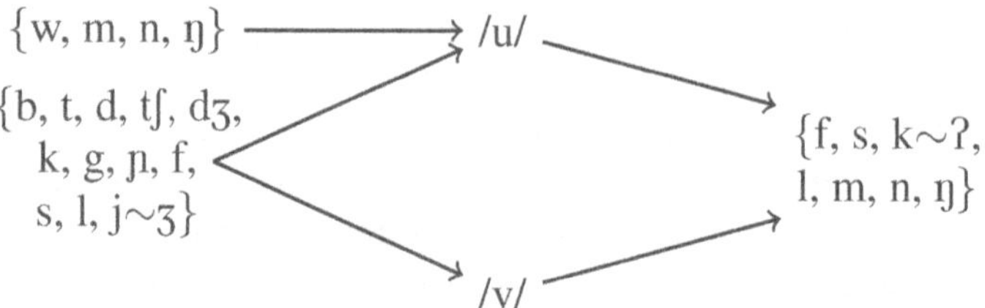

Figure 5.3. A comparison of biphones involving /v/ and /u/ in Kom.

5.6 Improving Phonotactic Models

In the preceding descriptive sections, I have explored the phonological systems and phonotactic phenomena of Kom and Limbum with a focus on the shared phenomenon of fricativized vowels: segments produced with obstruent noise acting as if they have unexpectedly high sonority. In this section, I explore two possibilities for modelling this phenomenon. First, connecting fricativized vowels to their historical origins, which have not yet been discussed, presents one way to make sense of the phonotactic systems that contain them. Given that fricativized vowels are always historically derivable from high vowels, it seems reasonable to suppose that fricativized vowels simply behave as if they are still normal high vowels in spite of their phonetic realization. However, this analytic decision has the undesirable side-effect of introducing circularity into the definition of sonority.

Fricativized vowels, as they are currently understood, arise historically from plain high vowels (e.g., [i], [u]) over time through regular sound change. On the one hand, fricativized vowels may result from complete assimilation of a high vowel to a fricative onset (e.g., *si > sz), resulting in a fricativized vowel as a contextually predictable allophone of a more typical high vowel, as occurred with *i in Middle Chinese and as is reflected in many Chinese dialects today (Chen 1976). Just as frequently, however, an intracategorical change I refer to as *high vowel fricativization* results in an entire high vowel category coming to be produced with fricative noise regardless of consonantal context. Subsequent to this, a lower vowel category often rises to occupy the original high vowel's phonetic position in a series of changes resembling a chain shift (e.g. o > u > v, Faytak 2014a). Comparative work on Kom and Limbum's genetic subgroups shows that the fricativized vowels in these languages are the endpoints of the latter type of change.

The Ring subfamily of Grassfields Bantu (Hyman 1980) can be divided into four subgroups, one of which, the Central Ring group, contains Kom. Comparison of back vowels among Central Ring languages reveals the changes shown in Table 5.8. Proto Central Ring (PCR) *u is maintained as a distinct category in Kom due to fricativization (*u > v). Reflexes of lower vowels *ʊ and *o vary, but generally raise in Kom and its close relative Babanki; Bum appears to reflect a more conservative phonological system in retaining *ʊ as [u].

Analogous changes have occurred for Limbum relative to its immediate ancestor Proto Nkambe (PN), a subgroup of Eastern Grassfields (Elias, Leroy, Voorhoeve, Sadembouo, Domche and Breton 1984), as shown in Table 5.9. From a vowel system very similar to PCR – which reflects shared inheritance from a common ancestor language – Limbum maintains a conrast between PN *u and *ʊ by fricativizing *u, resulting in present-day /v/. PN *ʊ has raised reflexes in the more innovative languages of the subgroup (Limbum, Mbat) but a very similar reflex in the more phonologically conservative Adere.

Based on their historical connection to plain high vowels, one could reasonably produce an abstract phonological account of fricativized vowel phonotactics that entirely sidesteps the problems raised in Sections 5.4 and 5.5. Fricativized vowels' behaviour as obstruents anomalously high in sonority can be explained away as a *retention* of their phonological status as vowels in some abstract sense. This retention comes in spite of a radical change in the realization of the phonological categories at issue: fricativization converts phonetically sonorous sounds to sounds that are

Table 5.8. Central Ring comparative data and reconstructed Proto Central Ring (PCR).

	PCR	Kom	Babanki	Bum
water	*-mo	ə˧-mu˥	mu˥	m˧-mo˥
to leave	*lo	lu˩	lu˩	lo˩
to stab	*so	su˩	su˩˥	so˩
head	*-tʊ	a˧-tu˥	kə˩-tʉ˥	a˧-to˥˩
honey	*-lʊ	ə˧-lu˥˩	ə˩-lʉ˩	u˧-lo˥˩
to wash	*sʊ	su˩	ʃʉ˩˥	so˩
chicken	*-ŋgu	ə˧-ŋgv˧	m˩-bvʉ˥	a˧-ŋgu˥˩
to drink	*ɲu	ɲv˧	ɲʉ˥	ɲu˧
fish	*-su	ə˧-ʃv˥	ə˩-ʃʉ˧	–

Note the fricativized reflex of PCR *u in Kom and raised reflexes of PCR *ʊ and *o in Babanki and Kom.

Table 5.9. Nkambe group comparative data and reconstructed Proto Nkambe (PN).

	PN	Limbum	Mbat	Adere
hand	*bo	bo˧	bo	bɔ
pumpkin	*-(m)bok	ɾ-boʔ˨	mboʔ	li-bok
intestines	*(n)ton	to˧	nton	tɔ
mouth	*tʃʊ	ʃuː˩	tsu	tso
head	*tʊ	tu˧	tu	to
bean	*-(ŋ)kʊn	ɾ-kuː˧	ŋkpən	fi-ŋkon
ashes	*bu	bv˧	vɨ	bu
night	*tuk	tvʔ˧	–	tuk
cadaver	*(ŋ)gun	gvː˨	mvən	gun

Note: Limbum data from Fransen (1995); other data from Elias (n.d.); the latter does not contain reliable tone data.

considerably less so. Converting this portion of the phonological grammar to fossilized layers of historical happenstance, however, ignores the substantive factors that guide linguistic systems to these ends: a good model of language should contain information on the constraints on change that led it to its present state. Furthermore, if sonority is defined in a diachronic sense and not based on some present-day phonetic substance, the entire concept threatens to become circular: sonorous segments are in some sense those that were sonorous at some point in the past.

In order to better account for fricativized vowel phonotactics, I adopt a spectral modulation account of segment sequencing restrictions. Such an account models restrictions on segments in sequence as due to the need for *perceptible acoustic modulations* between segments in order for them to be perceived as distinct (Ohala and Kawasaki-Fukumori 1997; Harris 2006). Arising from the difficulty of finding a single parameter (acoustic or otherwise) that corresponds to sonority and of making one parameter predict certain problematic phenomena of phonotactics, these multiple parameters may be in one or more of several spectral dimensions, including those identifiable with voicing, continuancy and some place features (cf. Stevens and Blumstein 1981).

A notion of sonority as tightly corresponding to a *single* relatively invariant acoustic parameter is not without defenders, but the single parameters that have been proposed do not predict the phonotactic behaviour of fricativized vowels. The predictions of a sonority based on constriction degree or intraoral pressure (Vennemann 1988; Ladefoged 1997: 615) on the one hand, or received intensity (Parker 2002, 2008) on the other hand, are at odds with fricativized vowels' apparently high sonority: they exhibit a high degree of constriction and relatively low acoustic intensity. On the latter point, experimental evidence has confirmed that voiced fricatives generally do not have intensity greater than that of sonorants in surveyed languages (Jany et al. 2007; Parker 2008). This does not rule out variation in language-specific intensity of voiced fricatives. However, it does suggest that such hypothetical variation in acoustic properties is unlikely to explain the recurring phonotactic position of fricativized vowels in Cameroon and other linguistic areas.

I find two crucial advantages to using a modulation account with multiple acoustic parameters for the specific case of fricativized vowel phonotactics in the two languages at issue. First, a modulation account stands to explain *why* fricativized vowels are able to exhibit phonotactic behaviour similar to that of vowels in spite of developing acoustic qualities that are decidedly not like those of vowels: they have consistently presented a perceptible modulation for learners throughout their history, including in the present day as syllabic obstruents, and as such retain their production characteristics (in this case, fricative noise) through intergenerational transmission. Secondly, spectral modulation accounts allow for *additional* dimensions of modulation that may improve modelling of fricativized vowels' characteristic phonotactics. The identity of these additional dimensions of modulation is the subject of the remainder of this section. I consider here only how the modulation account relates to sequencing phonotactics, given that modulations say nothing per se about prominence assignment, a notion that will be discussed more at the end of this section.

The first and most important dimension of perceptible modulation I propose here is the relative presence or absence of high frequency aperiodic energy, which in nonspectral terms is identifiable with fricative noise from the anterior part of the vocal tract (Table 5.10, a). Fricativized vowels, which do exhibit this type of fricative noise source, are most frequently preceded or followed by a consonant that is not produced with sustained fricative noise; the biphones contained within this set present a sharp contrast between the two segments contained therein. This set contains a large number of the more unexpected sequences in Kom and Limbum that violate the canonical SSH (liquids, taps or nasals in sequence with fricativized vowels) in addition to many that do not (stops and affricates in sequence with fricativized vowels).

Another dimension of perceptible spectral modulation is the presence or absence of voicing. Presence of voicing can be characterized spectrally as the presence of very low frequency periodic energy (Stevens and Blumstein 1981: 29), although numerous other spectral properties could instead be recruited by the auditory system to distinguish voiced and voiceless phones in sequence (cf. Atal and Rabiner 1976). Some of the biphones characterized by a change in the amount of aperiodic energy also happen to be characterized by a switch in voicing as well (Table 5.10, b). This set is rather small in Kom and more elaborated in Limbum, partly due to the latter's tendency to have devoiced or voiceless stem-final consonants. However, a number of other sequences are only differentiated by voicing in both Kom and Limbum, particularly when a fricative onset precedes a fricativized vowel (Table 5.10, c). Kom has somewhat more of these sequences, given the presence of voiceless fricatives /f s/ as codas. The overarching tendency is for fricative consonants preceding or following fricativized vowels to be voiceless.

The Kom biphone /jv/, which is realized as [ʒv], and the comparable Limbum biphone /ʒv/ present a complication in that both biphones have a relatively static value for both high frequency aperiodic energy and voicing (Table 5.10, d). Other changes in spectral shape, such as a general lowering of formant values and other spectral prominences due to labial constriction, may present an additional type of sufficient modulation, but how this would be characterized in spectral terms is not precisely known. Whatever its character, a modulation account predicts that this biphone is among the least likely to be robustly perceptible among those discussed here. This is borne out by data from the field: a sound change involving the /jv/ biphone is in progress for young Kom speakers, some of whom consistently produce lexemes usually containing /jv/ sequences as if they contained /v/ alone (e.g. /a˧-vs˥/ instead of /a˧-jvs˥/ 'spirit, soul'), the [ʒv] sequence presumably having been among the biphones least likely to be perceived correctly during acquisition.

I remain agnostic on whether syllable structure and other prominence assignments are required to model the phonotactics described here. In part, this is because 'syllables are logically subsequent, not antecedent, in

Table 5.10. Dimensions of perceptible modulation for Kom and Limbum biphones, and the biphones that modulate along each dimension.

Dimension	Kom biphones	Limbum biphones
a. HF energy	bv, bz, dv, dz, ʤv, gv, mz, ɲv, lv, vm, vn, zn, vŋ, vl	bv, bz, dv, dz, gv, mz, ɲv, lv, lz, ɾv, vŋ, zŋ
b. Voicing and HF energy	tv, tz, ʧv, kv, vk	tv, tz, kv, vp, zp, vɾ [vɾ̥], zɾ [zɾ̥], vk [vʔ], zk [zʔ]
c. Voicing energy	fv, fz, sv, vf, vs, zs	fv, sv, ʃv
d. Spectral lowering	jv [ʒv]	ʒv

constructing the optimal segmental stream itself' (Ohala and Kawasaki-Fukumori 1997: 355); that is, prominence can be construed of as epiphenomenal to sequencing restrictions (ibid.: 355–8; see also Blevins 2003; Ohala, 2008). There is a tight correlation between continuous noise in a single range of the acoustic spectrum, be it low frequency and periodic (prototypically sonorous) or high frequency and aperiodic (like a fricativized vowel), such that one might argue for a direct line to be drawn between these acoustic parameters and suitability for prominence licensing. However, further discussion is beyond the scope of this chapter.

5.7 Conclusions and Further Work

Languages of a portion of the Cameroon Grassfields are notable for aspects of their unusual phonotactic systems; with Kom and Limbum as representative example languages, I have examined fricativized vowels and the problems they present for models of phonotactics in these two languages and others. On the one hand, canonical sonority is effectively based on a single parameter (abstracted constriction degree, intensity); on the other hand, accounts based on sonority carry the expectation of regular, alternating peaks and troughs in this one parameter. Neither of these expectations is borne out in the data from Kom and Limbum, and the data instead suggest an organizing principle for segment sequencing that is based in multiple spectral parameters that are not necessarily dependent on or covarying with one another and which modulate but do not organize into regular peaks and troughs.

Some details and implications of the phonotactic accounts I advance here demand exploration. The most significant of the spectral parameters put forward here is continuous high-frequency aperiodic energy. However, broader phonotactic and perceptual research is required to confirm the perceptual relevance of this and other spectral parameters along which modulation might occur in the segmental stream. Also yet to be explored is the possible cross-linguistic variation in recruitment of certain spectral dimensions for segment demarcation. It is clear that there is a set of parameters commonly recruited that form a basis for canonical descriptive accounts of sonority. However, the data presented here suggest that some languages diverge from this norm more extremely than has been appreciated, including languages with fricativized vowels. If modulations in certain spectral dimensions are recruited to signal segment boundaries in Kom, Limbum and other languages with fricativized vowels, *but not other languages*, the possibility of language-specific segment and biphone frequencies and other structural considerations influencing what counts as a sufficiently perceptual or salient modulation must be taken into account in future research.

References

Atal, B.S. and Rabiner, L.R. (1976). A pattern recognition approach to voiced-unvoiced-silence classification with applications to speech recognition. *IEEE Transactions on Acoustics, Speech, and Signal Processing*, 24, 201–12.

Bell, A. (1978). Syllabic consonants. *Universals of human language*, 2, 153–201.

Blevins, J. (1995). The syllable in phonological theory. In J.A. Goldsmith (ed.), *The handbook of phonological theory* (pp. 206–44). Oxford: Blackwell.

Blevins, J. (2003). The independent nature of phonotactic constraints: an alternative to syllable-based approaches. In C. Féry and R. van de Vijver (eds.), *The syllable in optimality theory* (pp. 375–403). Cambridge: Cambridge University Press.

Cao, J. and Maddieson, I. (1989). An exploration of phonation types in Wu dialects of Chinese. *UCLA Working Papers in Phonetics*, 72, 139–60.

Chao, Y.R. (1930). A system of tone letters. *Le Maître Phonétique*, 45, 25–27.

Chen, M.Y. (1976). From Middle Chinese to Modern Peking. *Journal of Chinese Linguistics*, 4 (2/3), 113–277.

Chia, E.N. (1976). *Kom aspects and tenses.* PhD thesis, Georgetown University.

Chia, E.N. and Kimbi, J.C. (1984). *Guide to Kom orthography*. Yaoundé: SIL.

Clements, G.N. (1990). The role of the sonority cycle in core syllabification. In J. Kingston and M. Beckmann (eds.) *Papers in laboratory phonology I: Between the grammar and the physics of speech* (pp. 283–333). Cambridge: Cambridge University Press.

Connell, B. (2007). Mambila fricative vowels and Bantu spirantization. *Africana Linguistica*, 13, 7–31.

Dell, F. and Elmedlaoui, M. (1985). Syllabic consonants and syllabification in Imdlawn Tashlhiyt Berber. *Journal of African Languages and Linguistics*, 7 (2), 105–30.

Duanmu, S. (2002). *The phonology of Standard Chinese.* New York: Oxford University Press.

Elias, P. (n.d.). Nkambe group comparative wordlist. Unpublished manuscript.

Elias, P., Leroy, J., Voorhoeve, J., Sadembouo, E., Domche, E. and Breton, R. (1984). Mbam-Nkam or Eastern Grassfields. *Afrika und Übersee: Sprachen, Kulturen*, 67 (1), 31–107.

Faytak, M. (2014a). Chain shifts, strident vowels, and expanded vowel spaces. *LSA Annual Meeting Extended Abstracts.* Linguistic Society of America. Available at http://journals.linguisticsociety.org/proceedings/index.php/ExtendedAbs/article/view/2400.

Faytak, M. (2014b). Compiling sonority scales with obstruent vowels. In K. Carpenter, O. David, F. Lionnet, C. Sheil, T. Stark and V. Wauters (eds.), *Proceedings of the 38th Annual Meeting of the Berkeley Linguistics Society* (pp. 151–62). Berkeley, CA: Berkeley Linguistics Society.

Fiore, L.E. (1977). *A phonology of Limbum (Nsungli).* Cameroon: SIL.

Fransen, M.A.E. (1995). *A grammar of Limbum: A Grassfields Bantu language spoken in the North-West Province of Cameroon.* PhD thesis, Vrije Universiteit te Amsterdam.

Grollemund, R. (2012). *Nouvelles approches en classification: Application aux langues bantu du Nord-Ouest.* PhD thesis, Université Lumière Lyon II.

Hammerström, H., Forkel, R., Haspelmath, M. and Bank, S. (2015). Glottolog 2.5. Leipzig: Max Planck Institute for Evolutionary Anthropology. Available online at http://glottolog.org.

Harris, J. (2006). The phonology of being understood: Further arguments against sonority. *Lingua*, 116, 1483–94.

Heinz, J.N. (2007). *Inductive learning of phonotactic patterns.* PhD thesis, University of California, Los Angeles.

Hyman, L.M. (1980). Babanki and the Ring Group. In L. Bouquiaux, L.M. Hyman and J. Voorhoeve (eds.), *L'expansion bantoue: Actes du Colloque International du CNRS, Viviers (France), 5–16 avr. 1977 (I)* (pp. 225–58). Paris: Société d'Etudes Linguistiques et Anthropologiques de France.

Hyman, L.M. (2005). Initial vowel and prefix tone in Kom: Related to the Bantu augment? In K. Bostoen and J. Maniacky (eds.), *Studies in African comparative linguistics with special focus on Bantu and Mande: Essays in honour of Y. Bastin and C. Grégoire* (pp. 313–41). Tervuren: Royal Museum for Central Africa.

Jany, C., Gordon, M., Nash, C.M. and Takara, N. (2007). How universal is the sonority hierarchy? A cross-linguistic acoustic study. *Proceedings of ICPhS 16*, 1401–4.

Jones, R. (2001). *Provisional Kom-English Lexicon.* Yaoundé: SIL.

Ladefoged, P. (1997). Linguistic phonetic descriptions. In W.J. Hardcastle and J. Laver (eds.), *The handbook of phonetic sciences* (pp. 589–618). Oxford: Blackwell.

Lewis, M.P., Simons, G.F. and Fennig, C.D. (eds.) (2015). *Ethnologue: Languages of the World, 18th edition.* Dallas: SIL International. Online version: http://www.ethnologue.com.

Li, Min 李民 and Ma, Ming 马明 (1983). *Liangshan yiyu yuyin gailun* 凉山彝语语音概论 (*Introduction to the sounds of Liangshan Yi*). Chengdu: Sichuan Nationalities Press.

Ling, F. (2009). *A phonetic study of the vowel system in Suzhou Chinese.* PhD thesis, City University of Hong Kong.

Ohala, J.J. (1983). The origin of sound patterns in vocal tract constraints. In P.F. MacNeilage (ed.), *The production of speech* (pp. 189–216). New York: Springer-Verlag.

Ohala, J. J. (2008). The emergent syllable. In B.L. Davis and K. Zajdó (eds.), *The syllable in speech production* (pp. 179–86). New York: Taylor and Francis.

Ohala, J. J. & Kawasaki-Fukumori, H. (1997). Alternatives to the sonority hierarchy for explaining segmental sequential constraints. In S. Eliasson and E.H. Jahr (eds.), *Language and its ecology: Essays in memory of Einar Haugen* (pp. 343–65). Berlin: Mouton de Gruyter.

Parker, S.G. (2002). *Quantifying the sonority hierarchy.* PhD thesis, University of Massachusetts, Amherst.

Parker, S.G. (2008). Sound level protrusions as physical correlates of sonority. *Journal of Phonetics*, 36, 55–90.

Pellard, T. (2009). *Ōgami – Éléments de description d'un parler du sud des Ryūkyū.* PhD thesis, Ecole des hauts études en sciences sociales, Paris.

Piron, P. (1995). Identification lexicostatistique des groupes Bantoïdes stables. *Journal of West African Languages*, 25 (2), 3–39.

Qian, N. 钱乃荣 (1994). *Dangdai wuyu yanjiu* 当代吴语研究 *(Studies in Modern Wu languages).* Shanghai: Shanghai Education Press.

Shultz, G. (1993). *Notes on the phonology of the Kom language.* Yaoundé: SIL.

Shultz, G. (1997). *Kom language grammar sketch: Part 1.* Yaoundé: SIL.

Stevens, K.N. and Blumstein, S.E. (1981). The search for invariant acoustic correlates of phonetic features. In P.D. Eimas and J.L. Miller (eds.), *Perspectives on the study of speech* (pp. 1–38). Hillsdale, NJ: Lawrence Erlbaum Associates.

van Reenen, P. and Voorhoeve, J. (1980). Gender in Limbum. In D.J. van Alkemade, A. Feitsma, W.J. Meys, P. van Reenen and J.J. Spa (eds.), *Linguistic studies offered to Berthe Siertsema* (pp. 217–28). Amsterdam: Editions Rodopi N. V.

Vennemann, T. (1988). *Preference laws for syllable structure and the explanation of sound change: With special reference to German, Germanic, Italian, and Latin.* New York: Mouton de Gruyter.

Wright, R. (2004). A review of perceptual cues and cue robustness. In B. Hayes, R. Kirchner and D. Steriade (eds.), *Phonetically based phonology* (pp. 35–57). Cambridge: Cambridge University Press.

Matthew Faytak is a doctoral candidate in Linguistics at the University of California, Berkeley. His research centres on the complex relationships between phonological encoding, phonetic implementation, and sound change, with a particular focus on the actuation of intracategorical change and its possible outcomes. He has written on phonotactics and cross-linguistically unusual vowel articulations of languages of Cameroon and China.

6 An Investigation of Sonority Theory in Mandarin Chinese

Li Qiang

6.1 Introduction

Sonority refers to the acoustic and aerodynamic characteristics of individual speech sounds (Ball, Müller and Rutter 2010). Ever since Sievers (1876), who believed that sonority was the relative loudness of speech sounds, linguists have tried to apply different parameters to define sonority, such as perceptual prominence (Ladefoged 1982; Clements 1990), the amount of airflow in the resonance chamber (Goldsmith 1995), acoustic energy (Price 1980; Goldsmith 1990; Keating 1988; Wright 2004), force (Bloch and Trager 1942; Bloomfield 1933; Jakobson and Halle 1968), and intensity (Parker 2002, 2008). Some phoneticians believed that sonority should be interpreted in a comprehensive way with multiple phonetic parameters (Ohala and Kawasaki 1984; Ohala 1990).

Although there is no widely agreed-upon method of measuring sonority, it is possible to form a sonority scale of all the consonants and vowels concerned because each individual sound segment in any given language has a sonority ranking (Ball, Müller and Rutter 2010). For instance, the Sonority Sequencing Principle (SSP) is the tendency of syllables to exhibit an alternating pattern of sonority crests and troughs (Parker 2002). Clements (1990) proposed a simple sonority hierarchy: Vowels > Glides > Liquids > Nasals > Obstruents. Vowels (V) are the most sonorous group of sounds, with low vowels more sonorous than high vowels. Following the vowels, in descending order of sonority are the glides, liquids, nasals and obstruents (including stops, fricatives and affricates) (Clements 1988, 1990). Three requirements need to be met for the SSP: (a) in every syllable there is exactly one peak of sonority, contained in the nucleus; (b) syllable margins exhibit a unidirectional sonority slope, rising towards the nucleus; (c) the more oblique the onset slope, the better-formed the syllable, and the less oblique the coda slope, the better-formed the syllable in terms of the SSP (Ren, Gao and Morgan 2010). Nevertheless, it is still debatable as to how to produce these groupings because different groupings will lead to divergent subsequent analyses.

It is believed that cross-linguistically the maximum difference in sonority is preferred between the onset of a syllable and its nucleus, presumably in order to increase the perceptual salience of segments within the syllable (Clements 1990). In fact, the Sonority Sequencing Principle states 'not only that the onset and/or coda segments in a syllable should be of less sonority value than the peak, but also that they should be ordered so as to yield an increase in sonority from the left-most periphery of the syllable inward toward the peak, and a decrease in sonority from the peak out toward the right-most periphery' (Christman 1992: 67).

There have been studies which either examine sonority theory itself, or apply the theory to disordered speech. For example, Ohala (1999) tested children aged between 1;2 and 3;2 with normal language development. She found that the children reduced the consonant clusters to whichever consonant would result in the least complex syllable as defined by sonority. The children also reduced initial clusters to whichever consonant produced the greatest rise in sonority and final clusters to whichever produced a minimal sonority descent. Christman (1992) studied abstruse neologism formation and argued that sonority is a component of normal and abnormal language processing.

Very few studies to date have applied sonority theory to Chinese. Chung, Code and Ball (2004) investigated Cantonese-speaking aphasic clients, and by comparison with Code and Ball's (1994) results, they suggested that phoneme frequency may well derive from sonority patterns of syllabification, and in turn these may reflect the historical survival of perceptually strong distinctions, motorically simple combinations, and/or phonological patterns hardwired neurologically (see also Ball, Müller and Code, this volume).

The current study will investigate the most frequently used Chinese characters, and analyse the syllable shapes they represent to test the frequency method proposed by Code and Ball (1994) in relation to sonority theory.

6.2 The Phonological Inventory of Mandarin Chinese

6.2.1 Vowels

According to Duanmu (2007), Mandarin Chinese has 5 vowels as in Table 6.1. /i/ and /u/ are ordinary high unrounded vowels. /y/ is a front high rounded vowel. Both /i/ and /u/ can serve as the second part in a diphthong, but not /y/. For example, /mai/ in tone 3 means 'buying', and /kau/ in tone 3 means 'grilling' (for the Mandarin Chinese tone system, please refer to Yip 2002).

Table 6.1. Mandarin Chinese vowel phonemes.

High	i	y	u
Mid	ə		
Low	a		

The mid vowel has 5 variants (Duanmu 2007: 37) including [o], [ᴇ], [ɤ], [e] and [ə]. [o] occurs in open syllables (also called free syllables) after labials such as [wo] in tone 3 meaning 'I'. [ᴇ] denotes a vowel that is higher than [ɛ] but lower than [e]. It is used in open syllables after palatals ([j], [ɥ], [Cʲ] or [Cᶣ]). For example, [jᴇ] in tone 4 means 'leaf'; and [lʲᴇ] in tone 4 means 'crack'. [ɤ] occurs in open syllables but not after a labial or a palatal, such as [kɤ] in tone 1 meaning 'song'. [e] is used before [-i] like [fei] in tone 1 meaning 'fly'. And [ə] is used before [-u, -n, -ŋ] such as [kəu] in tone 3 meaning 'dog', [mən] in tone 2 meaning 'door', and [məŋ] in tone 4 meaning 'dream'.

The low vowel also has 5 variants (Duanmu 2007: 39) including [ᴀ], [ɑ], [a], [æ] and [ɐ]. [ᴀ] as in [pᴀ] in tone 1 meaning 'eight' is used in open syllables. [ɑ] is used in diphthongs and closed syllables before [u] or [ŋ], such as [tʰɑu] in tone 2 meaning 'peach', and [tʰɑŋ] in tone 2 meaning 'sugar'. [a] occurs in diphthongs and closed syllables before [n] or [i] but not after a palatal, such as [kʰai] in tone 1 meaning 'to open', and [san] in tone 1 meaning 'three'. [æ] occurs in closed syllables before [n] and after [j] or [Cʲ]. For instance, [jæn] in tone 2 means 'salt'; [pʲæn] in tone 1 means 'side'. [ɐ] also occurs in closed syllables before [n] but after [ɥ] or [Cᶣ], such as [ɥɐn] in tone 2 meaning 'round', and [ɕʷan] in tone 3 meaning 'to select'.

Besides these, there is a retroflex vowel, transcribed as [ɚ] by Duanmu (2007) or [r] elsewhere. It occurs either in words without a suffix, or as a suffix replacing the coda of the syllable it attaches to. For instance, [ɚ] in tone 2 meaning 'son' is a word without suffix; and [kan] in tone 1 means 'dried food', which also occurs as [kaɚ] in the Beijing dialect. It is worth noting that in written form, the former is a single character '儿' (son) and the latter is a two-character word '干儿' (dried food).

6.2.2 Consonants

There are 19 consonant phonemes in Mandarin Chinese, which are listed in Table 6.2 (Duanmu 2007: 24). All the consonants except [ŋ] can be the onset of a syllable, but codas are restricted to [n] and [ŋ] only (often with incomplete oral closure); they are represented in Pinyin (the official alphabetic spelling system for Mandarin) <-n> and <-ng> respectively.

Table 6.2. Mandarin Chinese consonant phonemes.

	Labial	Dental	Retroflex	Velar
Stop	p, pʰ	t, tʰ		k, kʰ
Affricate		ts, tsʰ	tʂʰ, tʂ	
Fricative	f	s	ʂ, ʐ	x
Nasal	m	n		(ŋ)
Liquid		l		

6.2.3 Glide and Consonant-Glide Combination

Glides and consonant-glide combinations are two special groups of consonants. In Mandarin Chinese glides are found when the high vowels occur before another vowel, and they are realized as [j, ɥ, w] (Duanmu 2007: 23). For instance, Pinyin <yan> in tone 1 meaning 'smoke' represents the sound sequence [jan]; <yuan> in tone 1 meaning 'grievance' represents [ɥan], and <wan> in tone 1 meaning 'curve' represents [wan]. However, the glides do not contrast with the corresponding high vowels [i, u, y], and the two sets can be treated as variants of each other.

Consonant-glide combinations occur before the nuclear vowels. In many studies, they are treated as two sounds. But Duanmu (2007), following Chao (1934: 42), believes that phonetically a consonant-glide combination is a single sound in Mandarin Chinese. This is partly because it is argued that there is only one phonological slot in the onset, which the consonant and the glide must share. For example, Pinyin <suan> in tone 1 means 'sour'. Its phonetic onset is a consonant-glide combination [sʷan], where [s] and [ʷ] are articulated at the same time (i.e., a labialized fricative). In comparison, in the English word 'sway,' [w] occurs after [s], which are thus two separate sounds (for details, see Duanmu 2007: 79–81; Parker 2012: 101). The current study analyses the consonant-glide combination as a singleton, but to show clearly the sonority sequencing patterns, they are denoted as CG (and thus differentiated from the other singleton consonants) when we examine detailed consonant ordering.

Phonetically, there are three palatals [tɕ], [tɕʰ], and [ɕ], as in [tɕi] in tone 1 meaning 'chicken,' [tɕʰi] in tone 1 meaning 'seven,' and [ɕi] in tone 1 meaning 'west.' Duanmu (2007: 31) states that these 3 palatals occur with the pre-nuclear glides [j, ɥ] or the high vowels [i, y], and thus that they can be considered consonant-glide combinations. These three palatals are synchronically in complementary distribution with the velars [k, kʰ, x], the dentals [ts, tsʰ, s], and the retroflexes [tʂʰ, tʂ, ʂ]. Duanmu (2007) notes the debate over which phoneme to assign these palatals to. Here, we assume they are allophones of the dental consonants, consequently, the six palatalized dentals are deemed to be realized by the palatals [tɕ, tɕʰ, ɕ] and [tɕʷ, tɕʰʷ, ɕʷ]. Altogether, there are 29 consonant-glide combinations, as shown in Table 6.3.

Table 6.3. Consonants and consonant-glide combinations in Mandarin Chinese.

	Labial	Dental	Retroflex	Velar
C	p, pʰ, m, f	t, tʰ, n, l, ts, tsʰ, s	tʂ, tʂʰ, ʂ, ʐ	k, kʰ, x
Cʲ	pʲ, pʰʲ, mʲ	tʲ, tʰʲ, nʲ, lʲ, tɕ, tɕʰ,ɕ		
Cʷ		tʷ, tʰʷ, nʷ, lʷ, tsʷ, tsʰʷ, sʷ	tʂʷ, tʂʰʷ, ʂʷ, ʐʷ	kʷ, kʰʷ, xʷ
Cᶣ		nᶣ, lᶣ, tɕʷ, tɕʰʷ,ɕʷ		

6.3 The Syllable of Mandarin Chinese

Duanmu (2007: 71) argues that the syllable of Mandarin Chinese could be CGVV or CGVC maximally, where C is a consonant, G a glide, VV either a long vowel or a diphthong. The current study treats CG as a single consonant. The syllable structure of Mandarin Chinese could be simply depicted as $(C_1)V(C_2)$, where C_1 represents a consonant or a consonant-glide combination; V represents a vowel, a long vowel, or a diphthong; and C_2 represents [n] or [ŋ]. The bracket means the position could be empty. There are no segmental prefixes, but one suffix [ɚ] mentioned above, which will not be discussed further in this study.

6.4 Methodology

To examine the sonority hierarchy, especially the SSP, in Mandarin Chinese, 2,500 Chinese characters were analysed, which were transcribed from the List of commonly used characters in Modern Chinese (Ministry of Education 1988). There were altogether 2,842 items, 342 more than the 2,500 selected characters due to the polyphonic feature, which means that one Chinese character can represent more than one specific syllable. For example, '还' represents two pronunciations, <hai> ([xai]) in tone 2 meaning 'also', and <huan> ([x^{w}an]) in tone 2 meaning 'return'.

The syllables representing the selected characters were transcribed. The syllable shapes were categorized and the number of items in each category was counted. Further, the distribution of consonants, focusing on onset consonants, was analysed in terms of sonority theory.

6.5 Results

6.5.1 Syllable Shapes

The syllables represented by the 2,500 most frequently used Chinese characters (2,842 items with polyphones), follow 6 basic syllable shapes. As shown in Table 6.4, CV is the most common pattern with 1,160 items, or 41 per cent; followed by 1,098 (39 per cent) CVC syllables; and 546 (19 per cent) CVV syllables. The patterns V, VV and VC have no onset and account for 1 per cent altogether among the most frequently used characters.

Table 6.4. Basic phoneme ordering patterns and their distribution.

	CV	CVC	CVV	V	VV	VC
#	1160	1098	546	17	14	7
%	41	39	19	0.5	0.4	0.1

In further analysis, glides and CGs are listed separately to demonstrate the sonority change and distribution. This results in the 12 syllable shapes listed in Table 6.5. The most frequent pattern is still CV, with 671 items, or 24 per cent; CVC accounts for 621 items, or 22 per cent. The distribution of the patterns CVV, CGV and CGVC are very similar, with 395, 361 and 356

Table 6.5. Detailed segment ordering patterns and their distributions.

	CV	CVC	CVV	CGV	CGVC	GV
#	671	621	395	361	356	128
%	24	22	14	13	13	4
	GVC	CGVV	GVV	V	VV	VC
#	121	99	52	17	14	7
%	4	3	2	0.5	0.4	0.1

items, or 14, 13 and 13 per cent respectively; then there are 128 instances of GV (4 per cent), 121 of GVC (4 per cent), 99 of CGVV (3 per cent) and 52 of GVV (2 per cent).

6.5.2 Syllable Nuclei

In Mandarin Chinese, vowels are syllable nuclei, and most are also assigned tone. The distribution of high, mid and low vowels is listed in Table 6.6. High vowels occur more frequently than others, at 34 per cent; low vowels account for 27 per cent, and mid vowels and diphthongs for 19.5 per cent each.

Table 6.6. Distribution of Mandarin Chinese vowels.

High	i = 545, y = 87, u = 332	964	34%
Mid	o = 148, ᴇ = 105, ɤ = 94, e = 0, ə = 201	552	19.5%
Low	ᴀ = 178, ɑ = 212, a = 278, æ = 71, ɐ = 34	773	27%
Diphthong	ei = 68, ou = 3, əu = 91, ai = 109, ɑu = 226, uo = 56	553	19.5%

6.5.3 Syllable Onsets

The distribution of syllable onsets is shown in Table 6.7, with frequency counts for each segment and its corresponding Pinyin symbol(s), as well as total number of occurrences and percentage for each consonant class. The frequency ordering is different from what would be predicted by the SSP: CG > Stop > Fricative > Affricate > Glide > Nasal > Liquid.

Table 6.7. Distribution of Mandarin Chinese consonants.

Consonant	Phoneme	Pinyin	Total amount	Percentage
Stop	p, p^{h};	<b> = 125, <p> = 87;	583	21%
	t, t^{h};	<d> = 118, <t> = 98;		
	k, k^{h}	<g> = 102, <k> = 53		
Affricate	ts, ts^{h};	<z> = 66, <c> = 52;	395	14%
	tʂ^{h}, tʂ	<ch> = 111, <zh> = 166		
Fricative	f;	<f> = 96;	433	15%
	s;	<s> = 54;		
	ʂ, ʐ;	<sh> = 148, <r> = 37;		
	x	<h> = 98		
Nasal	m;	<m> = 102;	142	5%
	n	<n> = 40		
Liquid	l	<l> = 134	134	5%
Glide	j;	<y> = 199;	301	11%
	ɥ;	<yu> = 21;		
	w	<w> = 81		
Consonant-Glide combination	p^{j}, p^{hj}, m^{j};	<bi> = 14, <pi> = 15, <mi> = 13;	816	29%
	t^{j}, t^{hj}, n^{j}, l^{j};	<di> = 19, <ti> = 15, <ni> = 11, <li> = 34;		
	tɕ, tɕ^{h},ɕ;	<j> = 216, <q> = 98, <x> = 157;		
	t^{w}, t^{hw}, n^{w}, l^{w};	<du> = 9, <tu> = 4, <nu> = 2, <lu> = 2;		
	ts^{w}, ts^{hw}, s^{w};	<zu> = 6, <cu> = 6, <su> = 13;		
	k^{w}, k^{hw}, x^{w};	<gu> = 29, <ku> = 18, <hu> = 46;		
	tʂ^{w}, tʂ^{hw}, ʂ^{w}, ʐ^{w};	<zhu> = 15, <chu>=16, <shu> = 15, <ru> = 3;		
	l^{ɥ}, tɕ^{w}, tɕ^{hw},ɕ^{w}	<lü> = 2; <ju> = 14; <qu> = 13; <xu> = 11		

6.5.4 Syllable Codas

As mentioned above, syllable codas in Chinese are simple. Among the 2,842 items analysed here, syllables ending in vowels (empty coda slot) account for 61 per cent (1,737), while syllables ending in [n] or [ŋ] make up 21 per cent (583) and 18 per cent (522) respectively.

6.6 Discussion

The current study has analysed the frequency distribution of consonants and vowels, and the shapes of syllables in Mandarin Chinese, in order to examine whether sonority theory, and specifically the SSP, is a good predictor of syllable preferences in this language. Code and Ball (1994), in their study of nonlexical speech automatisms in English and German aphasic speakers, found preferences for the syllable shapes predicted by the SSP, which suggests that phoneme frequency might well reflect sonority patterns in syllabification. That being true, a high occurrence of vowels and stops would be expected because the former are the most sonorant and occur as the syllable nuclei, while the latter are the least sonorant forming an ideal sharp slope in the onset position at least. The distribution of other consonants should rank between the vowels and the stops accordingly.

The Sonority Sequencing Principle includes a constraint that syllables tend to universally abide by: Every syllable exhibits exactly one peak of sonority, contained in the nucleus (Parker 2012: 102). Vowels, the most sonorant segments in the sonority hierarchy, are the nuclei in all Mandarin Chinese syllables. Clements (2009) formulates the sonority ranking for English vowels as follows: low vowels > mid vowels > high vowels ('>' represents 'more sonorant'). A more sonorant nucleus vowel will lead to a sharper slope on the margins. Consequently, if the SSP were a good predictor of preferred syllable shapes in Mandarin Chinese, a higher proportion of low vowels would be expected as the ideal nucleus, than that of mid vowels, while high vowels should occur as the least preferred. Yet, in the current study the distribution ranking is: high vowels > low vowels > mid vowels. The least sonorant, high vowels occur most frequently, and are more preferable as the syllable nucleus in Chinese. One possible explanation is that the articulation of high vowels is easier, which requires the least movement of the lips, the tongue and the jaw, while the articulation of mid vowels might be claimed to be the most difficult, possibly because of more effort needed to control the lips, the tongue and the jaw.

Compared to other languages such as English, the syllabic structure of Chinese is simple, (C_1)V(C_2). Consonant clusters are not permitted in a Chinese syllable, thus making the onsets and the codas of Chinese less complex. Among the 6 syllable shapes, 3 do not have onsets, and 4 do not have codas. Among the 2 patterns with codas, 583 out of 1,105 items end with [n], while the rest (522 items) end with [ŋ]. Clements (1990) states that syllable codas do not share the preference for a sharp change in sonority, and that there is a greater preference for codas that fall less sharply. When the coda slot is empty, there is of course no fall at all in sonority level. It is possible that such a tendency to have a less sharp fall in sonority at the coda position enables the initial segment of the following syllable or word to be lower in sonority than the final segment of the previous syllable or word. The codas in Mandarin Chinese seem to follow this pattern, with a less sharp sonority fall, thus allowing the onset of a following word, potentially at least, to be lower in sonority than the coda of the preceding word.

Although the ideal preference order of the consonants in onsets according to the SSP is: Stop > Affricate > Fricative > Nasal > Liquid > Glide, their distribution in Mandarin Chinese is different. Mandarin Chinese gives preference to CGs as Onsets, which occur even more frequently than Stops. Also, Fricatives are preferred to Affricates. Glides are the most sonorant consonants according to the SSP, yet receive higher distribution than Nasals and Liquids in this study. The above preferred distribution could be described by Parker's Minimal Sonority Distance (MSD), where the sonority index 5, 4, 3, 2, 1 is assigned to vowels, glides, liquids, nasals and obstruents, respectively. Then the minimal distance between two segments in a given onset is calculated as 0, 1, 2 or 3 (Parker 2012: 103, 110). This MSD can be applied to any two neighboring segments in a given Chinese syllable with the result that the distance can be 0, 1, 2, 3 and 4. If so, in the current study certain distances between a consonant and a vowel are more preferable than others. For instance, the distance between fricatives and vowels is more popular than that between affricates and vowels; and the distance between glides and vowels is more preferable to that between nasals and vowels. Naturally, these distances are not those predicted by Parker (2012) for typical syllables of English.

Sonority does not appear to predict the frequency distribution of segments in syllables in Mandarin very well. On the one hand, phoneme frequency may not be a suitable metric to judge the effectiveness of the sonority hierarchy. As suggested by Code and Ball (1994), phoneme frequency may only reflect the historical survival of perceptually strong distinctions, while other delicate sonority differences between consonants are not distinguished in some versions of the hierarchy, such as between fricatives and affricates. On the other hand, it is also possible that sonority theory is problematic in itself and not universal at all. The cluster pattern /s+stop/ represents a pattern of sonority falling towards the peak of the syllable, but it occurs in many languages as an onset cluster: Morelli (2003: 357) listed 16 languages that possess /s+stop/. There are studies on English that show patterns contradicting the SSP. For example, Wyllie-Smith, McLeod and Ball (2006) compared 16 normally developing children and 40 children with impaired speech. They investigated whether children's word-initial clusters reductions adhered to sonority theory, and found that when both groups reduced word-initial clusters to a target consonant, the realization was as predicted by sonority theory; but when the clusters were reduced to a non-target consonant, the theory was violated. Thus it is concluded that although sonority may be a valuable concept, it does not account for all patterns of cluster reduction evident in children's speech.

Meanwhile, the Chinese characters analysed in the current study may not be sufficient to give a good account of frequency distributions in syllable patterns. According to Leng and Wei (1994), there are 87,019 Chinese characters. If more characters than the 2,500 mostly commonly used ones were taken into consideration, then segment frequency might change, as well as the distribution of syllabic patterns.

6.7 Conclusion

By analysing the 2,500 most commonly used Mandarin Chinese characters, the segment frequency and their distribution were obtained to compare with the predictions of the sonority hierarchy, especially the SSP. Although not perfectly matched, there is still some similarity between the frequency patterns and the sonority ranking, such as obstruent > nasals > liquids. But consonant-glide combinations and glides themselves are an area that needs further study. It would be desirable to investigate Mandarin Chinese syllable patterns and their frequency based on all the Chinese characters, to further reveal the relationship of phoneme frequency and the sonority hierarchy.

References

Ball, M.J., Müller, N. and Rutter, B. (2010). *Phonology for communication disorders*. Hove: Psychology Press.

Bloch, B. and Trager, G.L. (1942). *Outline of linguistic analysis* (Special publications of the Linguistic Society of America). Baltimore: Linguistic Society of America.

Bloomfield, L. (1933). *Language*. New York: Holt.

Chao, Y.R. (1934). The non-uniqueness of phonemic solutions of phonetic systems. *Bulletin of the Institute of History and Philology, Academia Sinica*, IV(4), 363–97.

Christman, S.S. (1992). Abstruse neologism formation: Parallel processing revisited. *Clinical Linguistics and Phonetics*, 6, 65–76.

Chung, K., Code, C. and Ball, M.J. (2004). Speech automatisms and recurring utterances from aphasic Cantonese speakers. *Journal of Multilingual Communication Disorders*, 2, 32–42.

Code, C. and Ball, M.J. (1994). Syllabification in aphasic recurring utterances: Contributions of sonority theory. *Journal of Neurolinguistics*, 8, 257–65.

Clements, G.N. (1988). The sonority cycle and syllable organization. In W. Dresher, S. Luschützky, O. Pfeiffer and J. Rennison (eds.), *Phonologica 1988* (pp. 63–76). Cambridge: Cambridge University Press.

Clements, G.N. (1990). The role of the sonority cycle in core syllabification. In J. Kingston and M. Beckman (eds.), *Papers in laboratory phonology I: Between the grammar and physics of speech* (pp. 282–333). Cambridge: Cambridge University Press.

Clements, G.N. (2009). Does sonority have a phonetic basis? In E. Raimy and C. Cairns (eds.), *Contemporary views on architecture and representations in phonology* (pp. 165–75). Cambridge, MA: MIT Press.

Duanmu S. (2007). *The phonology of Standard Chinese*, 2nd edition. Oxford: Oxford University Press.

Goldsmith, J. (1990). *Autosegmental phonology*. New York: Garland Press.

Goldsmith, J. (1995). Introduction: Phonotactics, alternations, contrasts: representations, rules, levels. In J. Goldsmith (ed.), *Handbook of phonological theory* (pp. 1–23). Oxford: Blackwells.

Jakobson, R. and Halle, M. (1968). Phonology in relation to phonetics. In B. Malmberg (eds.), *Manual of phonetics* (pp. 411–49). Amsterdam: North Holland.

Keating, P. (1988). Comments on the jaw and syllable structure. *Journal of Phonetics*, 11, 401–6.

Ladefoged, P. (1982). *A course in phonetics*. Orlando: Harcourt Brace Jovanovich.

Leng, Y. and Wei, Y. (1994). *Zhonghua zihai*. Beijing: Zhonghua Book Co.

Ministry of Education (1988). 现代汉语通用字表 *Xiàndài hànyǔ tōngyòngzì biǎo* (List of commonly used characters in Modern Chinese). Beijing: Ministry of Education.

Morelli, F. (2003). The relative harmony of /s+stop/ onsets: Obstruent clusters and the sonority sequencing principle. In C. Fery and R. van de Vijver (eds.), *The syllable in optimality theory* (pp. 356–72). Cambridge: Cambridge University Press.

Ohala, D. (1999). The influence of sonority on children's cluster reductions. *Journal of Communication Disorders*, 32, 397–422.

Ohala, J. (1990). Alternatives to the sonority hierarchy for explaining segmental sequential constraints. *CLS 26: Papers from the 26th Regional Meeting of the Chicago Linguistic Society, Volume 2: The parasession on the syllable in phonetics and phonology* (pp. 9–38). Chicago: Chicago Linguistic Society.

Ohala, J. and Kawasaki, H. (1984). Prosodic phonology and phonetics. *Phonology Yearbook*, 1, 113–27.

Parker, S. (2002). *Quantifying the sonority hierarchy*. PhD dissertation, University of Massachusetts Amherst.

Parker, S. (2008). Sound level protrusions as physical correlates of sonority. *Journal of Phonetics*, 36, 55–90.

Parker, S. (2012). *The sonority controversy*. Berlin: De Gruyter Mouton.

Price, P.J. (1980). Sonority and syllabicity: acoustic correlates of perception. *Phonetica*, 37, 327–43.

Ren, J., Gao, L., and Morgan, J.L. (2010). Mandarin speakers' knowledge of the sonority sequencing principle. Presented at 20th Colloquium of Generative Grammar, University of Pompeu Fabra, Barcelona.

Sievers, E. (1876). *Grundzüge der Lautphysiologie zur Einführung in das Studium der Lautlehre der indogermanischen Sprachen* (Reprint 1980). Hildesheim/New York: Olms.

Wright, R. (2004). A review of perceptual cues and cue robustness. In B. Hayes, R. Kirchner and D. Steriade (eds.), *Phonetically based phonology* (pp. 34–57). Cambridge: Cambridge University Press.

Wyllie-Smith, L., McLeod, S. and Ball, M.J. (2006). Typically developing and speech-impaired children's adherence to the sonority hypothesis. *Clinical Linguistics and Phonetics*, 20, 271–91.

Yip, M. (2002). *Tone*. Cambridge: Cambridge University Press.

Qiang Li is associate professor at the School of Foreign Languages, Dalian University of Technology, China. He is currently working towards his PhD in the Department of Communicative Disorders, University of Louisiana, Lafayette, USA. His research interests are focused on language perception, especially on how people with language disorders perceive a language, in order to explore more general patterns of language perception in human beings. Currently he is studying tone perception at the phonetic and phonological levels in Chinese speakers with aphasia, together with relative clause comprehension at the syntactic and semantic levels, in order to investigate patterns of perception in Chinese.

7
Sonority and Syllabification in Casual and Formal Mongolian Speech

Anastasia Karlsson and Jan-Olof Svantesson

7.1 Background

Mongolian belongs to the Mongolic language group and is spoken by about 2.5 million people in Mongolia, and by approximately 2.7 million in Inner Mongolia in China. The subject of the present description is Standard Mongolian, the Halh (Khalkha) dialect spoken in Ulaanbaatar, the capital of Mongolia. Halh Mongolian is written with the Cyrillic script, and for words exemplified here, their orthographic form is given as well.

The sonority principle governs the syllabification of Mongolian formal speech fairly well. However, syllabification in everyday speech deviates to a high degree and violates a number of principles established on the basis of studies of formal speech. Within the same speaker we find variations in the realization of the same word from well-formed according to the rules for formal speech, to syllabification that violates one or more of these rules. This might stand out as trivial since phonetic variation is frequent in languages like English, German, Russian or Swedish. However, a major difference between these languages and Mongolian is that in addition to phonemic vowels, Mongolian also has non-phonemic vowels. In formal speech, underlying consonant strings are syllabified by epenthesis of schwa vowels, following the Sonority Principle. However, epenthesis often fails in everyday casual speech, leading to violations of the Sonority Principle. For example, underlying /carcʰʊɮ-gt-sn-ig/ зарцуулагдсаныг 'to use-PASS-PST-ACC' is pronounced [car.cʰʊ.ɮəgt.sə.nig] in formal speech, but can be pronounced [car.cʰʊɬxts.nig] in casual speech. The second form is not due to vowel reduction, but rather a result of failed epenthesis.

The following phenomena in Mongolian speech are described here in connection with syllabification: epenthesis, assimilation, stability of consonantal strings, devoicing of phonemic vowels and whispering. The description is based on recordings of read and spontaneous speech from 15 speakers, recorded at different occasions and for different purposes.

7.2 Phoneme System

The description of the Mongolian phoneme system is based on Svantesson, Tsendina, Karlsson and Franzén (2005). The Mongolian consonant phonemes are given in Table 7.1. Some consonants found only in loanwords are excluded.

Mongolian does not use the feature [voice] phonemically and our investigation shows that dental and alveopalatal stops and affricates contrast by the feature [aspirated], manifested as pre- or postaspiration depending on the position of the segment within the word. Contrasting pairs are /t^h/ ~ /t/, /t^{jh}/ ~ /t^j/, /c^h/ ~ /c/ and /$\check{c}^h$/ ~ /č/. Aspirated stops and affricates are postaspirated word-initially and preaspirated in all other positions, so that preaspiration is the main distinctive feature. If the preceding word ends in a vowel or a sonorant, preaspiration occurs even in word-initial position.

Table 7.1. Mongolian consonant phonemes.

	Labial	Palatalized labial	Dental	Alveo-palatal	Palatal	Velar	Uvular
Voiceless aspirated stops			t^h	t^{jh}			
Voiceless unaspirated stops	p	p^j	t	t^j			
Voiced stops					g^j	g	ɢ
Voiceless aspirated affricates			c^h	$\check{c}^h$			
Voiceless unaspirated affricates			c	č			
Voiceless fricatives			s	š	x^j	x	
Nasals	m	m^j	n	n^j		ŋ	
Voiced lateral fricatives			ɮ	$ɮ^j$			
Rhotics			r	r^j			
Glides	w	w^j			j		

The consonants /g/, /r/, and especially /ʒ/, are often devoiced and /p/ is often produced as a semivowel with no occlusion. /s/ is strongly aspirated.

There are seven basic vowels: *i, e, a, u, ʊ, o, ɔ*. There is an opposition between long vowels (here written with double vowel symbols) and short vowels, but this opposition occurs only in initial syllables, for example: /aaw/ аав 'father' ~ /aw/ ав 'battue'. In addition to the monophthongs, there are four diphthongs /ai, ɔi, ʊi, ui/.

There are also non-phonemic epenthetic vowels, here denoted *ə*, which occur only in non-initial syllables. They are inserted at the surface level to form syllables and their occurrence is predictable in formal speech. In traditional descriptions of Mongolian, the epenthetic vowels are analysed as short phonemic ('reduced') vowels, and non-initial full vowels are regarded as long vowels (Poppe 1970). This analysis is reflected in the Cyrillic script of Mongolian, but not in that of Kalmuck (another Mongolic language), in which epenthetic/reduced vowels are not represented graphically.

Mongolian has vowel harmony of two types: pharyngeal (ATR) and rounding. The vowel of the initial syllable governs the quality of the other vowels of the word. The quality of the epenthetic vowels follows vowel harmony to some extent (see Svantesson et al. 2005: 5–7), but we also found some evidence that their quality is more influenced by the consonantal surrounding than by the harmony class (Karlsson 2005).

7.3 Syllabification in Mongolian Formal Speech

In Mongolian formal speech, syllabification can be derived by rules based on the Sonority Principle. This was established using citation forms obtained from words read in isolation or in focused position in a sentence frame (Svantesson et al. 2005). We also found this type of syllabification in our most formal speaker (a teacher of Mongolian) when she read texts.

The Mongolian sonority scale is simple: voiceless consonants < voiced consonants (< vowels). Only one-consonant onsets are allowed (the Complex Onset Constraint), and only those syllable codas that have strictly decreasing sonority are possible. This means that only clusters of voiced+voiceless consonants are allowed as codas, while other combinations trigger epenthesis. For example, /pugt/ бүгд 'all' is syllabified as [pugt], without schwa insertion, while /xamr/ хамар 'nose', /pʊst/ бусад 'other' and /atg/ адаг 'end' require a schwa and are syllabified as [xa.mər], [pʊ.sət] and [a.təg]. The only exceptions are clusters of a fricative followed by an aspirated stop or affricate (except /c^h/), which do not trigger epenthesis: /t^{h}uux-t^h/ түүхт [t^{h}uuxt^h] 'historical', /c^{h}axč^h/ цахч [c^{h}aχč^h] 'magpie'. There are also three-consonant codas consisting of a voiced consonant followed by one of these permitted clusters, for example /iɮst^h/ элст [iɮst^h] 'sandy'.

Since Mongolian has a rich suffix-based morphology, underlying forms can contain long consonant strings. Syllabification is governed by three principles: the Sonority Law, Right-to-Left Syllabification (the Directionality Principle) and the Principle of Cyclicity. The surface syllable structure in formal Mongolian is (C){V(V)/ə}(C)(C)(C), with VV, V and *ə* as possible nuclei. Onsetless syllables are allowed only word-initially; in case of vowel hiatus within a word, /g/, /ɢ/ or /j/ is inserted to build an onset. In accordance with the Onset Satisfaction Principle, a consonant followed by a vowel becomes an onset, so that the syllable division of for example /xʊʊšʊr/ хуушуур 'dumpling' is [χʊʊ.šʊr].

The direction of syllabification is important for predicting the correct place of schwa insertion. In Mongolian formal speech, epenthesis proceeds from right to left, so that a maximal coda is formed at the right edge of the word and combines with the preceding vowel to a rhyme. When a consonant cluster cannot form a coda, a schwa is inserted. For example, /šitms/ шидэмс 'rope' is syllabified as [ši.təms] – not as [*šit.məs], as would be the case if syllabification proceeds from left to right.

Mongolian is an agglutinative language where derivations and inflections are formed by suffixation. The syllabification of affixed words is cyclic, so that words are syllabified at each addition of a new affix, that is, at each morphological cycle. Derived or inflected words are syllabified in the same way as monomorphemic words until a new suffix requires the insertion of a schwa in the already-syllabified part of a word, in which case the insertion is blocked by the Resyllabification Constraint (Svantesson et al. 2005: 74):

> *Resyllabification Constraint:* On each morphological cycle, an epenthetic vowel cannot be inserted into the already syllabified part of a word. For example, /t^{h}ogrg/ төгрөг 'round' is syllabified as [t^{h}og.rəg]. If the derived verb /t^{h}ogrg-ɮ/ төгрөглө 'to circulate' were a monomorphemic word, its syllabification would be *[t^{h}o.gər.gəɮ], but since this introduces a new schwa between *g* and *r* in [t^{h}og.rəg], it is forbidden by the Resyllabification Constraint, and the actual syllabification is [t^{h}og.rə.gəɮ]. This creates open syllables with a schwa nucleus, not occurring otherwise.

7.4 Syllabification in Mongolian Casual Speech

Mongolian casual speech is characterized by frequent reductions and assimilations. The description of the phoneme system above shows that Mongolian does not use the feature [voice] contrastively. Except for the nasals, voiced consonants are often devoiced by assimilation in casual speech, where the voiceless material is rich and often dominating. In general, phonemic vowels can be reduced (or even deleted) while consonants are seldom deleted.

Consonant combinations are split by schwa epenthesis less frequently in casual speech than in formal speech, resulting in long strings of consonants, without any intervening schwa vowel. When schwa epenthesis occurs in casual speech it is often as late as possible in the word. Thus, syllabification in casual speech is often not predicted by the syllabification rules that apply to formal speech. We will still use the term 'syllabification' for casual speech even though it is sometimes unclear where the syllable boundaries should be placed.

7.4.1 Vowel Reduction

Phonemic vowels are often devoiced (i.e., lose the feature [voice]) or even completely deleted (i.e., the vowel segment is acoustically missing), independent of their quality. For instance /t^{h}aɮ-t/ талд 'side-DAT' is frequently realized as [t^{h}ɬt^{h}], with no voicing, in our spontaneous material. This is common for short vowels in initial syllables and sometimes occurs even for long initial vowels in words that have been mentioned previously in a conversation, e.g., /t^{h}iiše-ge/ тийшээгээ 'direction-REFL' is realized as [tš^{h}ege]. Phonemic vowels in non-initial syllables are usually not reduced. Thus the initial syllable seems to be the most unstable position for vowel realization, although it is phonologically strong: vowels contrast in length only in this position and the initial vowel decides the vowel harmony class of the following vowels. Devoicing and deletion of vowels are triggered by voiceless environments, so that vowels are devoiced between two voiceless consonants. As shown below, assimilatory devoicing is common in casual Mongolian, creating many devoiced consonants, which in their turn create voiceless environments in which phonemic vowels are prone to be devoiced or deleted. For instance, /ciwsgɮɮ/ зэвсэглэл 'armament' can be realized as [cfs^{h}əgɬɮ] instead of formal [ciw.s^{h}əg.ɮəɮ], with complete

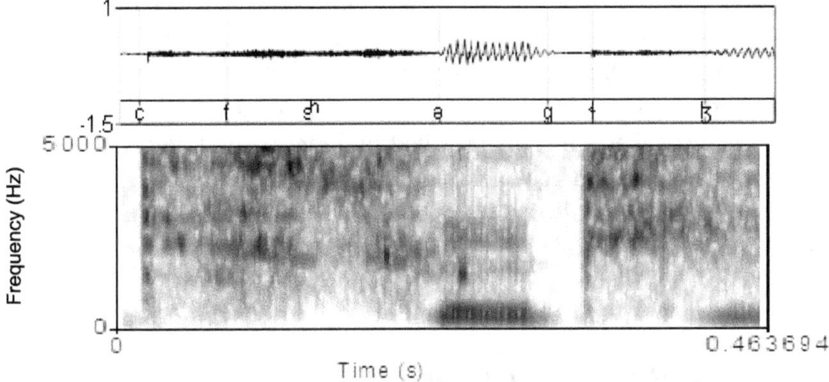

Figure 7.1. Oscillogram and spectrogram of the word /ciwsgɮɮ/ realized with complete reduction of the first phonemic /i/ and devoicing of /w/ and /ɮ/: [cfs^{h}əgɬɮ].

reduction of the phonemic /i/ and devoicing of /w/ and /ɮ/, see Figure 7.1. The occurrence of devoicing or deletion of all phonemic vowels of a word can be taken as an argument for the analysis that there is no lexical stress in Mongolian (Karlsson 2005), since stress normally needs a voiced vowel for its phonetic realization.

Mongolian speakers often whisper in casual speech. The difference between devoicing and whispering is that devoicing is a local event with the word as its domain (sometimes it applies over a word boundary if the following word begins with a preaspirated consonant), while whispering spreads over several words towards the end of the utterance, see Figure 7.2. Whispering is found in our spontaneous material, but since this material

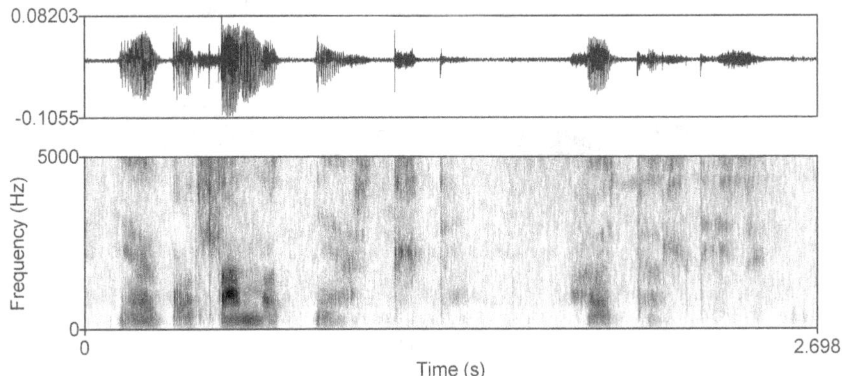

Figure 7.2. Illustration of whisper during a map task.

was spoken only by female speakers we cannot judge whether it is gender dependent or not. Whispering does not trigger vowel deletion and thus does not affect syllable structure. It is not clear if whispering and devoicing, which are the results of separate events, can occur simultaneously.

A female speaker whispers (marked by braces annotated with 'W' for whisper; see Ball, Esling and Dickson 1995, for details of the VoQS transcription system) in: /jag ʊɮaŋ mɔt-ni {W art t^{h}al-t bai-n W}, xɔit {W t^{h}al-t xisg W} .../ яг улаан модны ард талд байна, хойд талд хэсэг ... 'just red tree-GEN back side-DAT COP-PRS, back side-DAT a.bit ...'

7.4.2 Consonant Devoicing

Except for the nasals, voiced consonants are often devoiced by assimilation, and /g, g^{j}, ɢ/ are often fricativized as well, being pronounced [x, x^{j}, χ]. Regressive devoicing is very frequent in casual speech and is almost obligatory before aspirated stops and optional but frequent before voiceless fricatives and unaspirated stops. Assimilatory voicing occurs occasionally in Mongolian. Nasals and /ɮ, ɮ^{j}/ can be syllabic, forming a syllable nucleus, in casual speech.

Word internal clusters of voiced and voiceless consonants tend to keep the same sonority profile by devoicing of voiced consonants and we have found combinations of up to five voiceless consonants without intervening schwa, as in /sɔɮ^{j}-gt-č^{h}x-sŋ/ солигдчихсон 'change-PASS-INTENSIVE-PST' [sɔɬ^{j}xtč^{h}sŋ]. When devoicing does not take place, the resulting combination

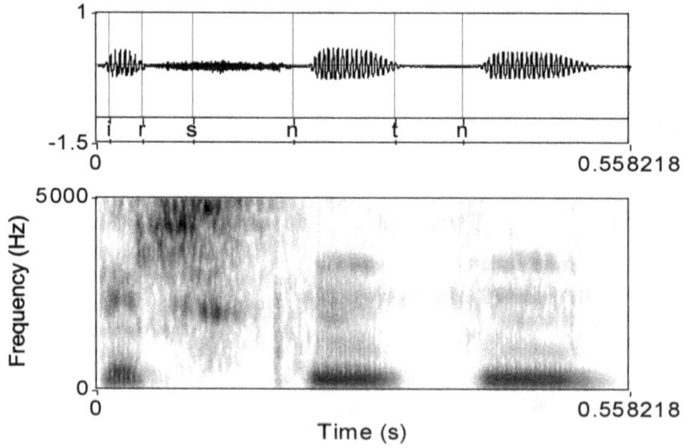

Figure 7.3. Oscillogram and spectrogram showing the realization of /ir-sn-t=n/ as [ir.sn̩.tn̩] with the two last syllables having syllabic nasals as nuclei.

of a voiceless+voiced consonant triggers epenthesis. Thus, /paacɮ-tg-ar/ баазаллдагаар 'team up-HAB-INS' was realized either as [paa.cəɮt.gar] or as [paacɬt.gar] by the same speaker. The nasals and laterals can form syllable nuclei in casual speech, so that schwa epenthesis does not take place. For example, /ir-sn-t=n/ ирсэнд нь 'come-PST-DAT=TOP' can be realized as [ir.sn̩.tn̩] instead of the formal [ir.sən.tən], see Figure 7.3.

7.4.3 Cyclic Syllabification

Open syllables with an epenthetic schwa vowel as nucleus, resulting from cyclic syllabification in formal speech, are not frequent in casual speech. Instead, closed syllables are built by epenthesis which might indicate that the cyclic syllabification rule does not apply in casual speech. However, since we found both cyclic and non-cyclic forms said by the same speaker, it is unclear to what extent cyclicity is applied in casual speech. For instance, one speaker pronounced /xʊwʲsɢɮ-iŋ/ хувьсгалын 'revolution-GEN' in two different ways: either using cyclic syllabification leading to an open syllable: [χʊwʲs.ɢə.ɮiŋ], or using non-cyclic syllabification with only closed syllables: [χʊwʲ.səɢ.ɮiŋ].

7.4.4 Preservation of Consonants

While many languages with complex codas, such as Russian and Swedish, tend to reduce some consonant clusters, Mongolian prefers not to. The reason for this seems to be the necessity to preserve the identity of the morphological suffixes, many of which consist only of consonants. Multiple suffixation often results in long consonant clusters, which usually are fully realized. In formal speech, the insertion of epenthetic schwas based on the Sonority Law creates well-formed syllables, but in casual speech the Sonority Law is relaxed, allowing long clusters of voiceless consonants, partly created by assimilation, without intervening schwas. Both strategies preserve the consonants and consequently the identities of morphological suffixes.

One example from our material is the words /caaɮt-tg/ заалддаг 'to sue-HAB', /caaɮt-tg-ar/ заалддагаар 'to sue-HAB-INS' and /caaɮt-tg-ar-a/ заалддагаараа 'to sue-HAB-INS-REFL', spoken in the frame sentence /pii ___ gisŋ/ Би___гэсэн 'I said ___'. In 14 of 23 occurrences, both consonants in the sequence /tt/ were realized with both occlusion and release, and no epenthesis occurred. The other occurrences of /tt/ were reduced to one [t]. An example is given in Figure 7.4, where the word /caaɮt-tg-ar/

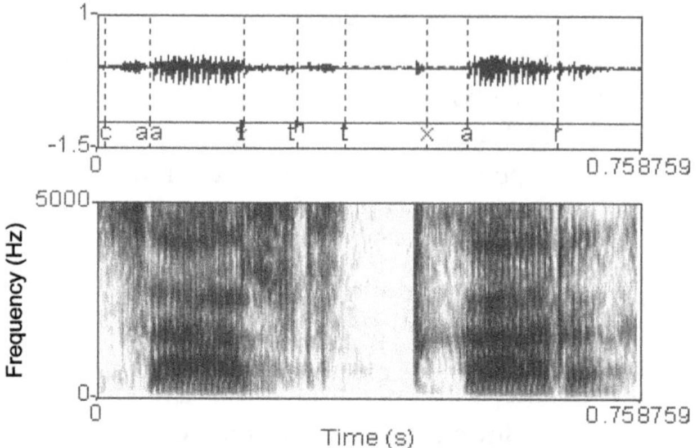

Figure 7.4. Oscillogram and spectrogram of /caaɮt-tg-ar/ realized as [caaɬtʰtxar].

is not realized as formal [caaɮt.tə.gar], but as [caaɬtʰtxar]. The two adjacent occurrences of the stop /t/ are fully realized with two occlusions and releases.

/ɮɮ/ clusters are very stable and not reduced. They can result from non-insertion of schwa in words like /tʰimtgɮɮ/ тэмдэглэл 'note', which can be pronounced as [tʰimtgɮɮ], [tʰimtgɬɮ] or [tʰimtgɮɬ] instead of formal [tʰim.təg.ɮəɮ]. The addition of the enclitic focal particle /ɮ/ л also results in this cluster in words as /mantɮ=ɮ/ мандаал л 'rise-FOC', which occurred as [mantɬɮ] or [mantɮɬ], see Figure 7.5. Duration data suggest that the final /ɮɮ/ cluster is not simplified to one segment but includes two consonants (Karlsson and Svantesson 2007).

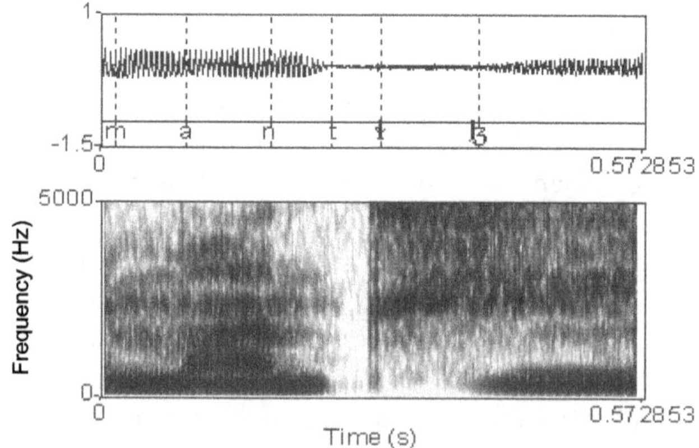

Figure 7.5. Oscillogram and spectrogram of /mantɮ=ɮ/ realized as [mantɬɮ].

When clusters of two identical or similar consonants go across word boundaries, they are often reduced to one consonant, presumably since there are no morphological requirements in this case. Thus, with very few exceptions, clusters of stops with the same place of articulation occurring across word boundaries are reduced to one stop. For example, /c^{h}ai-t t^{h}ɔs-t^{h}ɔi/ цайд тостой 'tea-DAT butter-COM' is realized as [c^{h}ait^{h}ɔst^{h}ɔi].

In contrast to Mongolian, clusters of identical stops are produced in many languages with only one release, but with longer occlusion phase. This is the case in Russian where we find minimal pairs as /podt^{j}a'nut^{j}/ подтянуть 'to pull up' versus /pot^{j}a'nut^{j}/ потянуть 'to pull' or /podto'čit^{j}/ подточить 'to sharpen a little' versus /poto'čit^{j}/ поточить 'to sharpen', realized as [pət^{j}ːɪ'nut^{j}] versus [pət^{j}ɪ'nut^{j}] and [pətːɐ'čit^{j}] versus [pətɐ'čit^{j}]. Here, the pronunciation of the cluster with two stops is simplified to only one occlusion and release, but the different durations of the occlusions in each pair carry the contrastive function (based on our informal observations). In other languages, clusters of identical consonants may be simplified to single consonants at least in some positions. Thus, Swedish pairs such as *avvisa* 'reject' versus *avisa* 'de-ice' or *uttrycka* 'express' versus *utrycka* 'pull out' are pronounced in the same way (as ['ɑːˌviːsa] and ['ʉːˌtʁʏka] in the Southern Swedish pronunciation of the second author), although the morphological and phonological structures of the words in each pair are different (/aːv-viːsa/ versus /aːv-iːsa/ and /ʉːt-tryka/ versus /ʉːt-ryka/).

7.4.5 Positional Dependencies of Epenthesis

Combinations of fricatives seem to be preferred consonant clusters in speech. Fricatives are frequently formed by lenition and devoicing of /g ɢ/, and wc find forms as [šxɮʒč̥] for underlying /ošgl-ž/ өшиглөж 'kick-CV', where the phonemic vowel is deleted. In connection with this, there are two interrelated problems that need to be investigated. First, is speech syllabified over word boundaries? If this is the case, we should analyse the above-mentioned word /ošgl-ž/ in its context, in this case following the word /pompg/ бөмбөг 'ball'. This seems reasonable as the final /g/ in /pompg/ is lenited to [x], which may be due to influence from the following [š]. We also find almost complete reduction of some words. For example, /ɢaxai/ is reduced to [qχ] in /xar ɢaxai xɔjr-iŋ/ хар гахай хоёрын 'black pig two-GEN' realized as [χarqχɔjriŋ]. Assuming that syllabification takes place over word boundaries, we propose that the phrase is syllabified as [χarq.χɔj.riŋ]. Second, it is unclear how (and if) such forms should be divided into syllables.

Syllabification over word boundaries might also explain why epenthesis is more frequent in word-final clusters than in other positions. Word-finally we often find epenthesis in two-consonant clusters which are not split by epenthesis word-internally. The position within the phrase also influences the occurrence of epenthesis: for the same word we find epenthesis more often in utterance-final than in medial position. For instance, /patŋ/ Бадан 'Badan (proper name)' is realized as [patm] in the sentence /t^{h}iim in patŋ pain/ Тийм, энэ Бадан байна 'Yes, this is Badan' and as [pa.təŋ] with epenthesis when said utterance-finally in /t^{h}iim in patŋ/ Тийм, энэ Бадан 'Yes, this is Badan.' The lower rate of epenthesis internally in words and phrases can be due to the existence of another alternative for articulatory chunking: in final position, uncomfortable consonant clusters are split by schwa, but internally, the last segment(s) of such a cluster can be joined with the following consonant to form an articulatorily homogeneous onset, eliminating the need for epenthesis.

7.5 Conclusion

Syllabification in formal Mongolian speech is governed by sonority, using a very simple sonority scale (voiceless consonants < voiced consonants < vowels) and a directional rule that inserts schwa vowels as syllable nuclei when necessary. Furthermore, morphologically complex words are syllabified cyclically, taking the morphological structure into account. In casual speech, syllabification is much more complicated and variable. Devoicing of both vowels and consonants is common, sometimes creating long strings of voiceless consonants that are pronounced without any intervening schwas. It appears that the strict interpretation of the sonority scale in formal speech, which allows only strings of a voiced and a voiceless consonant as syllable codas, is relaxed to a 'less or equal' interpretation of the scale in casual speech, allowing strings of voiceless consonants of (at least in theory) any length without intervening schwas. Furthermore, cyclic syllabification, which occurs in formal speech and differentiates words with different morphological structure, is not present, or is at least relaxed, in casual speech.

The two speech varieties differ in several respects from each other, but both tend to preserve the morphological structure of words by keeping consonant reduction to a minimum, although they employ different strategies to reach this goal. This allows a unified explanation of syllabification in Mongolian speech along the axis casual > formal speech. In casual speech, the preferred way of preserving consonant strings is to use voice assimilation and stop lenition to achieve pronounceable consonant strings, and schwa insertion is avoided as long as articulation allows this. In more formal speech, the degree of assimilation decreases and schwa epenthesis is used more frequently for making consonant clusters pronounceable without consonant loss by breaking them up into syllables. This poses the question of what constitutes a syllable in Mongolian, and whether the establishment of an inventory of syllable types is relevant for this language.

References

Ball, M.J., Esling, J. and Dickson, C. (1995). The VoQS System for the transcription of voice quality. *Journal of the International Phonetic Association*, 25, 61–70.

Karlsson, A.M. (2005). *Rhythm and intonation in Halh Mongolian*. PhD thesis, Lund University. Lund: Studentlitteratur.

Karlsson, A.M. and Svantesson, J.-O. (2007). What happens to consonant clusters in Mongolian speech? In P.O. Rykin (ed.), *Проблемы исторического развития монгольских языков. [Proceedings of international conference on Mongolian languages: Problems of historical development]* (pp. 74–81). St Petersburg, Russia: Nestor-Istorija.

Poppe, N. (1970). *Mongolian language handbook*. Washington, DC: Center for Applied Linguistics.

Svantesson, J.-O., Tsendina, A., Karlsson A.M. and Franzén, V. (2005). *The phonology of Mongolian*. Oxford: Oxford University Press.

Anastasia Karlsson is an Associate Professor in Phonetics at Centre for Languages and Literature, Lund University, Sweden. Her research interests focus on the interplay between prosody and information structure in spoken discourse, interplay between intonation and lexical tones, realization of lexical tones in singing, and aspiration in Mongolic and Turkic languages. She mainly works with Mongolian, Kammu (Mon-Khmer) and Formosan (Puyuma, Bunun and Seediq) languages.

Jan-Olof Svantesson is Emeritus Professor of General Linguistics at Lund University, Sweden. His main research interests are the phonology and morphology of Mongolic and Austroasiatic languages.

8
Sequential Constraints on Codas in Palestinian Arabic

Samira Farwaneh

The basic syllable inventory in Palestinian Arabic, as in many Eastern Arabic dialects, allows open CV and CVV, and closed CVC and CVVC syllables. In addition, Palestinian allows, unlike many dialects, complex syllables with complex onsets (CCVC) and complex codas (CVCC). While complex onsets are for the most part qualitatively unrestricted, complex codas are subject to markedness constraints governing the quality of coda sequences. Sequencing constraints on codas have frequently been claimed to be derivable from the Sonority Sequencing Principle (Itô 1986, 1989; Kenstowicz 1986). The Sonority Sequencing Principle, henceforth the SSP, stipulates that every syllable contains a segment constituting a sonority peak preceded and or followed by segments with decreasing sonority values. Hence, rhyme sequences such as [Vwl], [Vlm], [Vmp], are permitted under the SSP whereas the reverse sequences *[Vlw], *[Vml], *[Vpm], are not (see various formulations of this principle in Hooper 1976; Selkirk 1984; Clements 1990; among others).

In this chapter I show, through an examination of permissible and impermissible coda sequences in Palestinian Arabic (henceforth PA) that the SSP is a necessary but not sufficient constraint on syllable melody in that it overgenerates impermissible sequences and fails to account for some permissible ones. The data which consist of monosyllabic deverbal and lexicalized nominals of the shape CVCC (traditionally termed superheavy syllables) reveal that in order to properly characterize the phonotactic properties of PA rhymes three universal principles are needed: the SSP, the Obligatory Contour Principle (OCP), and markedness constraints on segmental features, none of which is reducible to any of the others. Section 8.1 gives an outline of the syllable structure of PA. The role of sonority in well-formed complex codas is taken up in Section 8.2 which favours a general Sonority Scale as in Clements (1990) over a scale with obstruent subdivisions as in Jespersen (1904, cited by Clements 1990) and his followers. I further argue in this chapter for the SSP as a negative condition on syllable templates thereby excluding sequences with rising sonority value only. Sections 8.3 and 8.4 discuss the role of the OCP and markedness respectively. Section 8.5 concludes the chapter by showing that OCP and markedness effects do not involve a minimum sonority difference requirement between adjacent syllable positions, Hence, both principles cannot be reduced to the SSP.

8.1 Syllable Structure in PA

Core syllabification in PA allows no more than two moras per syllable, hence a nucleus and one post nuclear position. Underlying syllables may then be monomoraic (light) syllables, or bimoraic (heavy) syllables: CVC-CVV. The representation of these two basic types is shown in (1).

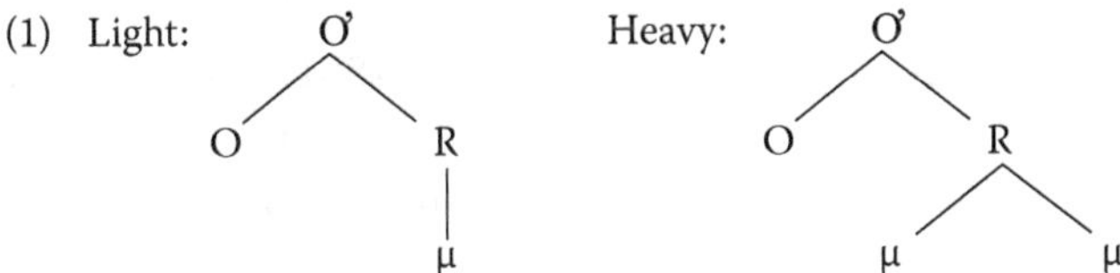

In addition to the basic light and heavy syllables, PA recognizes a surface superheavy syllable type with three rhyme positions CVCC/CVVC derivable by adjunction of an unsyllabified segment into one of the core syllable types: CVV+C or CVC+C. Such syllables often occur in word-final and sometimes word-medial positions,[1] e.g., *mak.tuub#* 'letter', *ka.tabt#* 'I wrote', *šaaf.ha* 'he saw her', *šuft.ha* 'I saw her'.

8.2 Superheavy Syllables and the Sonority Sequencing Principle

In this section I show the inadequacy of the traditional sonority scale proposed in Jespersen and Sievers and in more recent works of Hooper (1976)

1 In standard Arabic and some modern dialects referred to as Onset dialects (Broselow 1992; Farwaneh 1995; Kiparsky 2003), e.g., Egyptian and Saudi, superheavy syllables occur only word-finally, as adjunction to syllable applies only to extrasyllabic segments.

and Selkirk (1984) whereby the sonority scale comprises subdivisional classes of obstruents, nasals and liquids. A detailed scale as such fails to restrict the range of possible segment sequences and wrongly predicts the permissibility of unattested sequences. Instead I opt for a more general scale such as that of Clements (1990) which discriminates between major classes but not between members of the same class thus avoiding overgeneralization. I then discuss the role of the Sonority Sequencing Principle (SSP) as a well-formedness condition on syllable melody in PA. In doing so, it will be shown that the SSP, though a necessary condition on syllable codas, is not sufficient to account for all cases of well-formed coda sequences in PA. Consequently, I propose a negative rather than positive formulation of the SSP, banning sonority rise rather than requiring sonority decline at the right edge of the syllable.

8.2.1 The Sonority Scale

In the early works of Jespersen (1904) and Sievers (1881) discussed in Clements (1990), it has been observed that there is a cross-linguistic preference to certain tautosyllabic clusters while other clusters are rare or non-existent. Based on this observation, it has been proposed that segments have inherent degrees of sonority according to which they are ranked on a sonority scale. The highest point on the scale is occupied by low vowels, and the lowest by voiceless stops. Other segments are ranked between these two poles. Jespersen's version of the sonority scale recognizing subdivisions within each major natural class is given in (2).

(2) Jespersen's Sonority Scale (Clements 1990: 285)
1. (a) voiceless stops, (b) voiceless fricatives
2. voiced stops
3. voiced fricatives
4. (a) voiced nasals, (b) voiced laterals
5. voiced r-sounds
6. voiced high vowels
7. voiced mid vowels
8. voiced low vowels

Several variations of the sonority scale were proposed in the works of Hooper (1972, 1976); Selkirk (1982, 1984); Haddad (1984) and many others. This variation stems from debates over issues involving sonority of segments or segment classes. Three issues will be discussed briefly here and will be dealt with when further constraints are proposed in later sections: (a) subdivision of obstruents; (b) sonority of /r/; (c) sonority of gutturals.

The subdivision of obstruents is drawn along one of the two features of voicing or continuancy. If continuancy is taken to be the decisive feature, obstruents will then be divided into fricatives and stops, after which each class will be divided into voiced and voiceless, yielding the sonority ranking found in (3).

(3) Obstruents
Fricative-Voiced > Fricative-Voiceless > Stops-Voiced > Stops-Voiceless
4 3 2 1

On the other hand, taking voicing as the major subdividing feature and continuancy as the secondary subdividing feature will yield the sonority ranking in (4).

(4) Obstruents
Voiced-Fricatives > Voiced-Stops > Voiceless-Fricatives > Voiceless-Stops
4 3 2 1

The partial sonority scale in (3) predicts that voiceless fricatives may precede voiced stops, whereas the sonority scale in (4) predicts the reverse. The first sequence [voiceless fricative, voiced stop] is unattested due to the constraint which prohibits voiced obstruents from following voiceless obstruents, at the right edge of a syllable, morpheme or word (Harms 1973). Such sequences generally undergo an obligatory voiceless assimilation rule to keep syllables in accord with the constraint. The reverse sequence [voiced stop, voiceless fricative] is attested only if the second segment is a coronal (Haddad 1984). Hence, non-coronal voiceless fricatives may not follow voiced stops. Thus, both scales (3) and (4) predict that non-existing clusters are permissible.

Another issue still subject to debate is the sonority status of /r/ and its position with respect to /l/. /r/ exhibits different articulatory features in different languages. Its articulation ranges from a retroflex in many varieties of English to an alveolar flap in Arabic and Spanish to an alveolar trill in Spanish to a uvular trill in French and Modern Hebrew (Ashkenazi pronunciation). Do all varieties of /r/ have the same sonority value? In German and English, /r/ is evidently more sonorous than /l/ (Rubach 1990) as can be detected from words like 'girl' and 'snarl'. However, Haddad argues that in Lebanese Arabic, /r/ is less sonorous than /l/, because, unlike /l/, it may follow nasals; e.g., [tamr] 'dates' but *[ħiml]_'load' (1984: 35). /r/ is also less sonorous than /m/ because it may follow but not precede it; e, g., [tamr] 'dates' but *[barm] 'turning'. Haddad's data hence argue for the partial Sonority Scale seen in (5).

(5) Vowel > Glide > l > Nasal > r > Obstruent

The third issue involves the position of gutturals on the sonority scale. McCarthy (1991, 1994) following Haddad (1984) considers gutturals to be sonorous compared to other fricatives. /ʕ/ is the most sonorous of all gutturals, almost vocalic, while /X/ and /ġ/ are the least sonorous, ranking with true fricatives. The PA data discussed below show that sequencing of gutturals with respect to other segments indicates their higher sonority index compared to other fricatives, suggesting a sonority rank parallel to nasals.

In contrast with Jespersen's sonority scale in (2), the scale adopted in Clements (1990) is defined in terms of four independently motivated binary class features: syllabic, vocoid, approximant and sonorant. The sonority scale for nonsyllabic elements is derived by taking the sum of the plus-specifications for each feature (Clements 1990: 290). The scale does not involve subdivision of obstruents into stops and fricatives or voiced and voiceless. Nor does it concern itself with the order of the liquids /r/ and /l/ with respect to each other. This is because although there is a cross-linguistic tendency to order segments within syllables according to the sonority scale in (6) below, the distribution among members of the same class is subject to linguistic variation. If the sonority scale is to be complicated to derive all possible segment ordering in all languages, its explanatory value will be weakened considerably. The available evidence is that a single scale, perhaps O < N < L < G < V or a simple variant of this, defines the unmarked order of segments within the syllable across languages, and that apparent deviations from this scale have independent explanations. Moreover, distributional regularities among same class segments can be attributed to independent principles as will be shown.

(6) Sonority Scale (Clements 1990: 292)

O	<	N	<	L	<	G	
–		–		–		–	'Syllabic'
–		–		–		+	Vocoid
–		–		+		+	Approximant
–		+		+		+	Sonorant
0		1		2		3	Rank (relative sonority)

The feature Syllabic marks the distinction between the two skeletal positions C and V. The feature Vocoid is the converse of the feature Consonantal thus it groups vowels and glides under one class. The feature Approximant, first proposed by Ladefoged (1982), combines vowels, liquids and glides. The feature Sonorant designates the traditional distinction between sonorant and obstruent consonants. According to the sonority scale in (6) obstruents have the lowest sonority value, 0, whereas vowels have the highest, 4. I will show in later sections that while the general formulation of the sonority scale serves as a constraint on across-class distribution in codas, other principles, e.g., OCP and markedness, are responsible for within-class distribution in a single rhyme.

8.2.2 The Sonority Sequencing Principle

The Sonority Sequencing Principle is a locality constraint on syllabification which requires a well-formed syllable to exhibit a rise in sonority at its left edge and a decline in sonority at its right edge. The decline at the right edge requirement implies that the SSP is viewed as a positive constraint requiring a certain sonority distance between the postvocalic coda consonant and the peripheral one; hence, the postvocalic coda consonant must be more sonorant than the peripheral consonant; otherwise, violation ensues. The SSP as a positive condition is defined in (7).

(7) The Sonority Sequencing Principle: Positive Constraint (Clements 1990: 285)
Between any member of a syllable and the syllable peak, only sounds of higher sonority rank are permitted.

English words with sonorant-obstruent sequences like 'tent', 'bird' or 'film' exemplify optimal codas that conform to the SSP. The following forms from PA likewise consist of sonorant-obstruent sequences and are a perfect exemplification of the SSP as defined in (7).[2]

(8) Sonorant+Obstruent:

dars	'lesson'	bint	'girl'
bard	'cold'	ʔalb	'heart'
ʕamd	'premeditation'	milk	'property'

This interpretation of the SSP rules out two possible violations, sonority reversals, rarely occurring in languages, and sonority plateaus which are quite common.

2 The following phonetic symbols are used throughout this chapter: ʔ – glottal stop; ʕ – voiced pharyngeal sonorant (previously labelled fricative); ħ – voiceless pharyngeal fricative; ġ – voiced uvular fricative; š – voiceless alveopalatal fricative; ž – voiced alveopalatal fricative; ŋ – velar nasal; ṭ/ḍ/ṣ/ẓ – t/d/s/z with emphatic articulation.

Concerning sonority reversals, if the syllable ends in a sonority reversal with the more sonorous segment ordered after the less sonorous one, such SSP violation would block the incorporation of the second postvocalic consonant from sharing the same coda node with the first postvocalic consonant. Three repair mechanisms to unsyllabifiability are theoretically available: epenthesis which creates an additional syllable to incorporate the offending segment as its onset or coda; stray erasure which deletes unsyllabified segments; and assimilation which spreads a feature or features from one segment to a neighbouring one thereby facilitating the clustering of both under one rhyme node. Arabic dialects opt for the first and third responses. The second response is ruled out due to the structure preservation of root consonants.[3] The forms in (9) below are all repaired by obligatory epenthesis as assimilation is not a viable option:

(9) Sonority Reversal: Obstruent+Sonorant:

*žisr	žisir	'bridge'	*ʔabl	ʔabil	'before'
*baṭn	baṭin	'abdomen'	*ʕaḍm	ʕaḍim	'bones'
*badr	badir	'full moon'	*ʔakl	ʔakil	'food'

The second type of violation to the SSP in its positive formulation requiring sonority distance between first and second coda consonants is brought about by syllables ending in sonority plateaus, i.e., segments bearing the same sonority value. However, as the forms featuring obstruent clusters in (10) illustrate, sonority plateaus are quite tolerated in PA and epenthesis here is optional.

(10) Sonority Plateaus: Obstruent+Obstruent:

mažd	mažid	'glory'	ʕabd	ʕabid	'slave'
fuzt	fuzit	'I won'	naħt	naħit	'sculpture'
darast	darasit	'I studied'	ʔuXt	ʔuXut	'sister'

The forms in (9) and (10) would be true violations of the SSP as a positive condition on syllabification. However, this restrictive formulation would lead to undergeneration as it fails to account for the acceptability of the plateaus in (10). The positive SSP condition can alternatively be expressed as a negative condition on syllabification as in (11). This will block superheavy syllables only if they show rise in sonority at their end. That is, only sonority reversals constitute true violations under the negative SSP condition.

3 SSP and OCP violations are always eliminated by epenthesis, whereas markedness violations may be eliminated either by epenthesis or assimilation, as will be discussed in the following sections.

(11) The Sonority Sequencing Principle: Negative Constraint
Between a postvocalic consonant and the right edge of a syllable, no sounds of higher sonority rank are permitted.

Conditions (7) and (11) are not equivalent. Condition (7) implies that only codas with falling sonority are well-formed thereby ruling out both sonority reversals and sonority plateaus. In contrast, condition (11) implies that only sonority reversals constitute a violation. Thus, syllables with coda clusters showing falling sonority or with equal sonority values are possible well-formed rhymes. This is a more desirable result since it is more compatible with the facts of PA. Many instances of sonority plateaus are acceptable in PA as the forms in (10) have shown. Such clusters are however monitored by other sequencing principles which assess their well-formedness. Thus, the negative SSP has nothing to say about sonority plateaus whose well-formedness is left for other principles to determine.

Both SSP formulations in (7) and (11) converge on predicting the derivability of complex CVCC syllables in PA if the coda cluster shows a decline in sonority while blocking the construction of complex syllables if the coda cluster shows a rise in sonority. Examining further data, however, demonstrates that this is not always the case. The forms in (12), for instance, satisfy the SSP requirement yet they fail to produce well-formed syllables.

(12) Sonorant+Obstruent (Guttural)

*manʕ	maniʕ	'prohibition'	*manħ	maniħ	'granting'
*balʕ	baliʕ	'swallowing'	*malħ	maliħ	'salt'
*ʔumʕ	ʔumuʕ	'funnel'	*ʔamħ	ʔamiħ	'wheat'
*samġ	samiġ	'glue'	*salX	saliX	'skinning'
*sɑlʔ	sɑliʔ	'boiling'	*ħarʔ	ħariʔ	'burning'

The codas in (12) consist of sonorant+obstruent sequences and the obstruent consonant in all these forms is a guttural. The term 'guttural' is used in traditional Arabic and Hebrew grammars to refer to the natural class containing dorsal segments of uvular, pharyngeal and laryngeal articulation /X/, /ġ/, /q/, /ħ/, /ʕ/, /h/ and/ʔ/. If we assume that gutturals are fricatives, i.e., obstruents, then the coda sequences in (12) do not violate the SSP and should be allowed contrary to data. On the other hand, if we concur with McCarthy's (1994) position that pharyngeals and laryngeals are sonorant consonants while uvulars are fricatives, this will lead to the prediction that the clusters [mġ] and [lX] are allowed whereas liquids and nasals followed by pharyngeal or laryngeal are not. Thus, the SSP predicts that all, or at least some coda consonant sequences in (12) should be well-formed. However, as is evident from the obligatory application of epenthesis, all gutturals regardless of their sonority value are preempted from occupying the second position in a coda cluster. Recall from the examples in (8) that sonorants may be followed by non-guttural obstruents of various places of articulation: Labial, [ʔalb] 'heart'; coronal, [dars] 'lesson', [ʕamd] 'premeditation'; and velar, [milk] 'property'. The class of gutturals, i.e., uvulars, pharyngeals and laryngeals, is the only class banned from sharing a node with a sonorant. These phonotactic facts corroborate McCarthy and Haddad's proposal of assigning a higher sonority rank to gutturals than regular fricatives, suggesting placing gutturals on a par with nasals. Therefore, the ill-formedness of the forms in (12) cannot be attributed to an SSP violation but rather to an OCP effect on sonority as will be discussed in Section 8.3.1.

The SSP would similarly allow liquid+nasal sequences as liquids have a higher sonority index than nasals according to all proposed sonority scales. Let us consider the status of such sequences in PA, as in (13).

(13) Liquid+Nasal

*ħilm	ħilim	'dream'	*ʕilm	ʕilim	'knowledge'
*furn	furun	'oven'	*ʔarn	ʔarin	'horn'
*farm	farim	'mincing'	*barm	barim	'rolling'

Liquid+nasal sequences trigger the application of epenthesis, indicating that either the sonority index of liquids and nasals is equivalent in PA, or that other constraints are at play restricting such sequences. I argue in Section 8.3.1 that all sonorant sequences are blocked regardless of their sonority index.

In summary, based on the data presented so far, the SSP correctly rules out sonority reversals or postvocalic sonority increase and correctly accounts for some acceptable sonorant-obstruent sequences. However, without the aid of other constraints, the SSP is not sufficient to account for all attested coda sequences as it runs into the problem of both over- and undergeneration. It overgenerates unattested sequences as in the liquid+nasal and sonorant+guttural examples, and undergenerates as it fails to account for acceptable obstruent sequences. For a descriptively adequate account of segment sequencing in PA codas, other sequencing constraints are needed to complement the SSP. These constraints are the focus of the next two sections.

8.3 The Role of the Obligatory Contour Principle

The Obligatory Contour Principle, henceforth the OCP, is a constraint on sequences of adjacent identical elements. This principle was proposed by Leben (1973) named by Goldsmith (1976), and defended in McCarthy (1979, 1981, 1986). Elements whose adjacency and identity trigger the OCP may be tone (Lebin 1973), segments (McCarthy 1979, 1981, 1986), or features (Mester and Itô 1989; McCarthy 1986; Borowsky 1986). Prosodic domain may be any prosodic constituent; the root (McCarthy 1981), the morpheme (Itô and Mester, 1986) or a subsyllabic constituent (McCarthy 1988).[4] The effect of the OCP ensures that a given domain may bear one and only one value for a feature or a set of features. This OCP effect is manifested in two ways: A feature may be allowed to spread onto more than one skeletal position, or the feature value is restricted to a single segment. One value of the relevant feature may appear on the appropriate melodic tier. The spreading or lack of spreading of this feature is considered to be a separate parameter of the theory (McCarthy 1986). In the following discussion I will show that spreading or lack of spreading within PA rhymes is not an independent parameter, but rather a direct consequence of assimilation.[5] In the subsections below, I discuss the role of the OCP in monitoring same-class sequences, beginning with sonority, manner, place then voicing.

8.3.1 OCP and Sonority

The SSP in (11) with its negative formulation allows the following sonorant sequences to appear in a single rhyme:[6] sequences with sonority decline,

4 Syllable constraints discussed in the literature can be more accurately called constraints on subsyllabic constituents. This is exemplified by the constraint on English onsets prohibiting segments of the same place features; e.g., *bw *pw *tl.

5 The OCP effect on the segment distribution within roots may be parametrized, however. Arabic roots, for instance, do not allow more than one labial segment despite the presence of place assimilation. Conversely, roots allow adjacent fricatives whereas syllables prohibit such sequences due to the absence of continuant assimilation in the language.

6 The discussion of sonorant sequences does not involve glides because glides in penultimate coda position merge with the preceding nucleus forming a long vowel by a rule of coalescence; e.g., /bayt/ > [beet] 'house', /yawm/ > [yoom] 'day'. The only instance in which a glide retains its feature [-syllabic] is when

liquid+nasal, or sonority plateau, liquid+liquid and nasal+nasal. It rules out sonority reversal, nasal+liquid. But as stated earlier, all sonorant sequences including those permitted by the SSP are precluded from codas in Palestinian. Some forms in (14) are repeated from (13) but the list covers the full range of sequencing possibilities:

(14) *Sonorant+Sonorant

*ħilm	ħilim	'dream'	*ʕilm	ʕilim	'knowledge'
*ħiml	ħimil	'load'	*naml	namil	'ant'
*ʔamn	ʔamin	'security'	*samn	samin	'ghee'
*furn	furun	'oven'	*barm	barim	'rolling'
*ʔamr	ʔamir	'command'	*ħumr	ħumur	'red-pl'

Unlike Lebanese which permits nasal-r but not nasal-l sequences, PA bans all sonorant sequences including those displaying the optimal sonority profile dictated by the SSP, e.g., liquid+nasal. The SSP by itself, then, is not sufficient to rule out these sequences. The preemption of sonorants in codas in the above forms can be expressed as an OCP-type well-formedness condition on codas prohibiting two adjacent coda segments with positive sonority values illustrated in (15). Since the OCP does not block obstruent sequences marked negatively for sonority, the proposed OCP constraint treats segmental features as univalent or privative, following earlier proposals by Avery and Rice (1989), Mester and Itô (1989), Steriade (1995) among others. Privative features are either present or absent, thus the OCP constraint in (15) targets adjacent sonorant sequences but has nothing to say about obstruent sequences many of which are allowed in PA.

(15) OCP Constraint on Sonorants

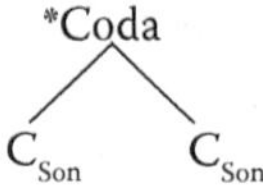

The OCP constraint in (15) will likewise rule out the sonorant+guttural sequences presented in (8) while allowing nasals and approximants to combine freely with other fricatives. Since gutturals enjoy a higher sonority index placing them with nasals with the voiced pharyngeal sonorant [ʕ] placed highest along with vocoids, then the OCP constraint is invoked to block adjunction of guttural to sonorant under one coda and epenthesis is

it is multiply linked to two positions, i.e., if it is a geminate; e.g., [ḍaww] 'light', [fayy] 'shade'. In these cases the linking constraint (Hayes 1986) is invoked to block coalescence from applying to geminate glides.

called in to rectify the violation, e.g., [maniʕ] *[manʕ] 'prohibition' as an example of sonority reversal and [samiġ] *[samġ] 'glue' as an example of sonority plateau.

8.3.2 OCP and Manner

The presence or absence of the manner feature 'continuant' determines the degree of coda clustering acceptability. Stop or [-Continuant] sequences may cluster under one coda node as shown by the forms in (16) but fricative sequences are subject to subsequent epenthesis as in (17):

(16) Stop+Stop

sabt	sabit	'Saturday'	ʕabd	ʕabid	'slave'
nabḍ	nabiḍ	'pulse'	wa?t	wa?it	'time'
Xabṭ	Xabiṭ	'pounding'	rabṭ	rabiṭ	'tying'

(17) *Fricative+Fricative

*lafẓ	lafiẓ	'pronunciation'	*nafX	nafiX	'blowing'
*mazž	maziž	'mixing'	*ʕafš	ʕafiš	'furniture'
*rafs	rafis	'kicking'	*ħažz	ħažiz	'reservation'

The prohibition against fricative but not stop clusters once again evidences the role of the OCP and the privative nature of segmental features. Adjacent coda segments identically marked by the feature [continuant] are ruled out by the OCP-manner and may not cluster under one coda node; however, stop sequences where the feature is absent escape the OCP prohibition as the identity requirement of the OCP is not met. The OCP constraint on continuancy is introduced in (18):

(18)

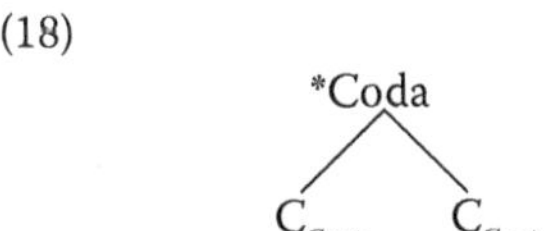

8.3.3 OCP and Place

Place features such as labial, coronal and dorsal do not violate the OCP if specified more than once in PA rhymes. Homorganic clusters, i.e., segments bearing the same value for place of articulation, may co-occur in a single rhyme.

(19) Homorganic clusters

zamb /zanb/	'guilt'	žamb /žanb/	'side'
ʕind	'with'	baŋk /bank/	'bank'

All the syllables in (19) terminate in a nasal followed by a homorganic obstruent. All these forms are the output of assimilation of the underlying alveolar nasal /n/ to the place of the following segment thus spreading the place feature of the trigger onto the place node of the target. There is thus one place feature node spreading to two roots as illustrated in (20). The OCP requirement of adjacency is not met; hence, the sequences are not ruled out. Following Hayes (1986), Goldsmith (1990), and Avery and Rice (1989) we maintain that coronal is the unmarked feature for place and is supplied later by a redundancy rule. Thus, the place node of the coronal nasal /n/ is underspecified and place assimilation spreads the place dependent feature of the trigger to the preceding target as in (20):

(20) Nasal-Place Assimilation

UR: /zanb/

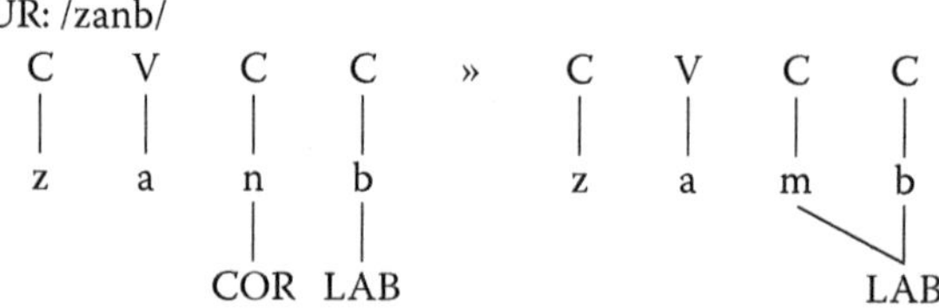

Once assimilation takes place, the partially assimilated structure becomes immune to epenthesis due to the line-crossing prohibition.[7]

(21) Epenthesis: *[zamib]

z a m i b

V LAB

As (21) shows, inserting an epenthetic vowel to the output of assimilation results in crossing another association line. Itô (1989: 234) proposes a prosodic theory of epenthesis whereby the appeal to line-crossing to block epenthesis in linked structures is rendered superfluous. She maintains that the line-crossing is perhaps not a viable explanation for geminate

7 In my dialect, assimilation is obligatory between nasals and following obstruents. In some PA dialects, however, assimilation is optional. If it fails to apply, epenthesis applies obligatorily yielding [zanib] and [žanib]. Epenthesis is triggered in these cases by a Markedness violation which prohibits adjacent coronal-labial sequences in one rhyme, as will be discussed in Section 8.4.

blockage because in non-concatenative morphology systems, vowels and consonants reside on separate tiers and association lines never cross when epenthesis takes place if the epenthetic vowel is on the vocalic tier. The answer to the second argument comes from underspecification whereby the rule of epenthesis provides a pure skeletal slot [V] whose melody is to be filled in by late redundancy rules. Insertion of a vocalic position cannot be blocked by line-crossing. As for the first argument, segregation of vowels and consonants is due to the morphemic status of the consonantal and vocalic tiers. In Semitic, vowels provide morphological information (voice, aspect) whereas consonants provide the core meaning of the word. Since epenthetic vowels are devoid of morphological information, there is no reason to believe that they reside on the vocalic tier solely by virtue of their being [+syllabic]. Furthermore, since epenthesis is post-lexical, it probably applies after tier conflation which merges the consonantal and vocalic tier into one. In this case, epenthesis does cross an association line as Itô correctly points out. As for the second argument, line-crossing is not a constraint on insertion, rather, it is a constraint on association. Inserting an epenthetic vowel slot is not blocked by line-crossing, but association of this slot with its melody is.

8.3.4 OCP and Voicing

Unlike sonorants and continuants, segments bearing the same value specification for the contrastive feature [voice] are not only tolerated but also preferred in PA rhymes:

(22) Voicing

a. Voiced+Voiced

nabḍ	'pulse'	nažd	'Najd'
ħizb	'political party'	waʕd	'promise'

b. Voiceless+Voiceless

waʔt	'time'	darast	'I studied'
zift	'tar'	ʔuXt	'sister'

The syllables in (22) which terminate in adjacent segments agreeing in voicing seem to be a violation of the OCP. Parallel to the argument constructed to explain the immunity of obstruent and stop sequences to OCP effect, we may argue that voiceless sequences are tolerated due to the privativity of the feature [voice]. But what about the acceptability of voiced sequences? The voiced clusters in the forms in (22) are not derived by assimilation and hence we cannot appeal to assimilation to produce linked feature matrices immune to the OCP as in the case of the homorganic clusters in (20). Hence, the feature [voice] is instantiated on two adjacent segments with the representation in (23).

(23)

[... V C_{Voi} C_{Voi}]$_{Coda}$

The question which these forms present concerns the discriminatory behavior of the OCP with respect to contrastive features. The OCP allows adjacent voiced but not adjacent sonorants or fricatives. To answer this question it should be noted that although the forms in (22) are not derived by assimilation, Voice Assimilation is operative elsewhere in the language. Voice Assimilation applies progressively or regressively to adjacent segments with opposite specification for voicing as exemplified by the forms below, all featuring the reflexive verbal form VII (traditionally, Arabic verb forms are numbered in roman numerals) derived by adding the infix -t- to the verb stem CVCVC. The infix acquires voicing if adjacent to a voiced stem segment as in (24).

(24) Progressive Voice Assimilation

/z-t-ahar/	[zdahar]	'flourish'
/z-t-aad/	[zdaad]	'increase'
/d-t-aʕa/	[ddaʕa]	'allege'

Voice assimilation also applies regressively within stems and in the resultative verbal form V derived by appending the prefix t- to the stem CVCCVC:

(25) Regressive Voice Assimilation

a. Within stem

/sġiir/	[zġiir]	'small'
/ma-sduud/	[mazduud]	'closed-psv.part.'
/yu-lfuẓ-u/	[yuluvẓu]	'3p-pronounce-pl'

b. Across morpheme boundary

/t-dallaʕ/	[(i)ddallaʕ]	'act coquettishly'
/t-dammar/	[ddammar]	'be demolished'
/t-žammad/	[džammad]	'be frozen'
/t-ḍaħħak/	[ḍḍaħħak]	'laugh'

Within Autosegmental Phonology, Assimilation is regarded as spreading of one feature onto two segments (Hayes 1986). According to this view assimilation spreads the feature [voice] from the trigger to the target which is unspecified for voice. If assimilation is capable of delinking a specification prior to spreading a feature in addition to filling in an already empty node it can apply vacuously to non-derived voiced segments thereby delinking one specification for voice and spreading an adjacent second as in (26).

(26) Vacuous Voice Assimilation

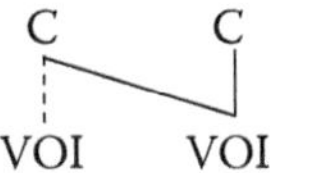

The multiply-linked structure in (26) is now transparent to the OCP because the adjacent identical sequences are now reduced to one.[8] In the case of adjacent fricative, no continuant assimilation is present in the language, hence, linked structures transparent to the OCP are non-derivable.[9] It is for this reasons that adjacent fricatives constitute an OCP violation in many languages (see Tserdanelis 2001 for Greek, and Borowsky 1986 for English). Consequently, adjacent fricatives are systematically broken up by Epenthesis.

In summary, the sensitivity of a feature to the OCP correlates inversely with its susceptibility to assimilation. Features which may be propagated by assimilation are always transparent to the OCP. Assimilation in our

8 The theory of spreading proposed in Avery and Rice (1989) holds that spreading occurs only if a target is present and that a feature node spreads to an empty node. Thus assimilation rules that do not trigger delinking as in (25) are ruled out by their analysis. There are cases of assimilation, however, which cannot be accounted for except by spreading following delinking. One such case is the total assimilation of the definite article /l/ to a following stem-initial coronal. According to their analysis /l/ has a supralaryngeal node dominating the feature [Spontaneous Voice].This node is proposed to distinguish sonorants from voiced obstruents. The node [SV] in turn dominates the ature [lateral]. This feature blocks assimilation to following sonorants (see their analysis of sonorant assimilation in Tubabatac; Avery and Rice 1989: section 2.4). In Arabic, however, the definite article assimilates in place not only to sonorants but also to obstruents: /l-naar/ = [nnaar] 'fire'; /l-taaž/ = [ttaaž] 'the crown'.

9 McCarthy (1988) cites cases of continuant spreading such as post or inter-vocalic spirantization in Spanish and Hebrew and defricativization of continuants before nasals in some English dialects, e.g., business = [bidnes]. All these cases, however, involve spreading of a redundant value of the feature [Cont]. In the case of spirantization, the feature [+Cont] which is a redundant value for vowels and the feature [−Cont] a redundant value for nasals are subject to spreading. I know of no case whereby assimilation spreads a contrastive value of the feature [Cont] from one segment to another. I assume that assimilation which rescues a representation from being ruled out by the OCP involves contrastive values only since the OCP itself is a constraint on contrastive feature values.

analysis may apply vacuously to segment sequences with identical feature values, as well as non-vacuously to segment sequences with distinct feature values. Non-vacuous assimilation spreads a specified feature node of the trigger onto an empty node present in the target. Vacuous assimilation on the other hand, delinks the feature node in the target prior to spreading an identically-specified feature of the trigger. This analysis explains why voiced and homorganic sequences are allowed in PA rhymes, whereas sonorants and fricatives are disallowed.

If a feature is non-assimilatory, i.e., it cannot spread by assimilation, then more than one instantiation of this feature in one domain will systematically create an OCP violation. It follows from this analysis that if voice and place assimilation is absent in a language, non-derived voiced and homorganic clusters as well as voiced and homorganic clusters derived by rules other than assimilation will be ruled out in that language.[10]

8.4 Markedness Constraint and Syllabic Well-Formedness

Two constraints have been discussed so far; the SSP which determines order of segments belonging to two different classes referred to in the Sonority Scale, and the OCP which governs the order of same-valued segments. There remain cases which cannot be accounted for under either constraint. These are the cases of obstruent sequences with distinct feature values. They cannot be explained under the SSP because they possess the same degree of sonority. Nor can they be accounted for by the OCP because their feature value specifications are not identical. Sequences of voiced and voiceless obstruents are examples of this case. When a rhyme terminates in obstruents distinct in voicing, syllabic well-formedness dictates that the voiced segment must constitute the penultimate coda consonant as in [sabt] 'Saturday' or [fuzt] 'I won.' However, if the order is reversed, epenthesis applies obligatorily as in (27).

10 A case in point is sequential voicing or Rendaku in Japanese where the initial voiceless segment of the second member of a compound becomes voiced. The rule is however blocked by an existing voiced obstruent, known as Lyman's Law. Itô and Mester (1986) analyse Lyman's Law as an OCP effect on the feature [voice] operating on both roots and surface forms. Voicing in Japanese is a dissimilatory rather than assimilatory feature, a cross-linguistic rarity (Kawahara and Zamma 2014:6).

(27) *Voiceless+Voiced

*nafḍ	nafiḍ	'dusting'	*rakḍ	rakiḍ	'running'
*ʕušb	ʕušub	'grass'	*lafẓ	lafiẓ	'pronunciation'
*masd	masid	'smoothing'	*rušd	rušud	'maturity'

Similarly, if a stop and fricative cluster in one rhyme, the fricative must precede the stop as in [zift] 'tar' and [mažd] 'glory' listed in earlier examples; otherwise epenthesis applies as in (28).

(28) *Stop+Fricative

*libs	libis	'clothes'	*Xubz	Xubuz/Xubiz	'bread'
*kitf	kitif	'shoulder'	*madġ	madiġ	'chewing'

A third type of ordering relation is imposed on segments differing in their place of articulation. If one of the coda segments happens to be a Coronal consonant, it always occupies the final position with the noncoronal placed postvocalically. The examples in (29) illustrate the ordering interaction of different places of articulation with coronal.

(29) Non-Coronal+Coronal

a. Labial+Coronal
   sabt 'Saturday' zift 'tar'
b. Uvular+Coronal
   waġd 'traitor' *ḍaġṭ 'pressure'
c. Pharyngeal/Laryngeal+Coronal
   waʕd 'promise' waʔt 'time'

If the order is reversed, epenthesis applies, as in (30).

(30) *Coronal+Non-Coronal

a. Coronal+Labial

*kizb	kizib	'lying'	*nadb	nadib	'mourning'
*kitf	kitif	'shoulder'	*ħadf	ħadif	'throwing'

b. Coronal+Velar/Uvular

*mask	masik	'holding'	*fatk	fatik	'killing'
*madġ	madiġ	'chewing'	*tibġ	tibiġ	'tobacco'

c. Coronal+Pharyngeal

*tusʕ	tusuʕ	'one ninth'	*waḍʕ	waḍiʕ	'situation'

If both consonants are non-coronal, epenthesis applies as well, as in (31).

(31) *Non-Coronal+Non-Coronal

*rubʕ	rubuʕ	'quarter'	*ħabk	ħabik	'weaving'
*saʔf	saʔif	'ceiling'	*Xafʔ	Xafiʔ	'beating (liquid)'

An optimal coda thus does not allow voiceless after voiced, stops after fricatives, or non-coronal after coronals. According to markedness theory, voiceless obstruents, stops and labials/velars are unmarked relative to their counterparts voiced obstruents, continuants and coronals respectively, relative markedness being determined on the basis of implicational universals governing phonological systems (Houlihan and Iverson 1979).

From these facts we infer that there is a constraint on codas in PA which stipulates that a penultimate coda consonant must be more marked than the final coda consonant. That is, marked segments occupy penultimate position, unmarked segments must be syllable-final. This constraint can be illustrated as in (32).

(32) Markedness Constraint

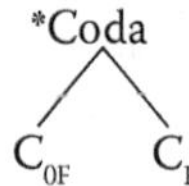

The markedness constraint in (32) stipulates that a segment marked for a certain feature may not follow another segment unmarked for the same feature within the same coda. This markedness constraint may appear too restrictive. Nevertheless, it correctly accounts for all the permissible coda segment combinations. Thus for coda consonants differing in both voicing and continuancy, four theoretically possible combinations may occur, listed in (33). The markedness constraint (32), however, allows only one combination, that of (33c):

(33) a. Voiceless fricative – voiced stop
b. Voiceless stop – voiced fricative
c. $Voiced fricative – voiceless stop
d. Voiced stop – voiceless fricative

As the $-sign indicates, only one possibility (33c) is permitted in PA rhymes. Adding the markedness constraint on place of articulation, we further conclude that the final voiceless stop must be a coronal.

8.5 How Sufficient is the SSP?

In order to account for the phonotactic constraints on PA codas, we have identified, in addition to the SSP, two important independently-motivated constraints, markedness and the OCP. A follow-up question that naturally presents itself at this point is whether OCP and markedness may be subsumed under the SSP.

The OCP as discussed in Section 8.3 blocks sonorant and continuant sequences while allowing obstruent and noncontinuant ones. A general sonority scale with positive formulation requiring a certain sonority distance between the first and second consonant in the cluster would rule out all obstruent sequences as the sonority distance is zero. As for sonorant sequences, it would mistakenly permit liquid+nasal sequences since they conform to the SSP. Conversely, overgeneration is the problem with the negative formulation of the SSP proposed in (11). Since this formulation blocks sonority reversals only, it will generate obstruent and sonorant sequences of all types unconditionally; again failing to account for PA syllabic phonotactic facts. The OCP, then, is a necessary constraint on coda sequences required to account for cases that fall through the SSP filter.

Markedness, on the other hand, regulates the same category sequences, i.e., obstruent sequences, with different specifications for place, voicing and manner. While Clements' general sonority scale with no subdivision is indeterminate about ordering, Jespersen's scale with class subdivisions assigning a higher sonority index to continuant over stops and voiced over voiceless segments would correctly predict only a few coda sequences: fricative+stop, voiced+voiceless. However, when it comes to place of articulation features not affecting the sonority index, the SSP fails to predict the ordering of labial and velar segments with respect to coronals and with respect to each other; hence, a markedness constraint is also necessary to account for the obligatory application of epenthesis when a coronal precedes a non-coronal or when the sequence contains non-coronal segments.

We may reverse the question and ask whether the SSP can be dispensed with allowing other constraints to assume its role. The answer again is negative. The SSP is needed to rule out sonority reversals, i.e., obstruent-sonorant codas. Such sequences cannot be blocked by the OCP given lack of identity. Neither can they be blocked by the markedness constraint proposed in (32) as markedness of sonorants and obstruents cannot be determined holistically. If markedness is determined on the basis of cross-linguistic frequency and L1 acquisition ordering, nasals are unmarked relative to fricatives, while /r/ is more marked; hence a markedness constraint cannot target the generalization that no obstruent may precede a sonorant in a single coda. In conclusion, this chapter has shown that phonotactic constraints on PA syllables require the collaboration of three constraints: the SSP, OCP and markedness, no one of which is reducible to another.

References

Avery, P. and Rice, K. (1989). Segmental structure and coronal underspecification. *Phonology*, 6, 179–200.

Borowsky, T. (1986). *Topics in the lexical phonology of English.* PhD dissertation, University of Massachusetts, Amherst.

Broselow, E. (1992). Parametric variation in Arabic dialect phonology. In E. Broselow, M. Eid and J. McCarthy (eds.), *Perspectives on Arabic linguistics IV* (pp. 7–46). Amsterdam and Philadelphia: John Benjamins.

Clements, G.N. (1990). The role of the sonority cycle in core syllabification. In M.E. Beckman and J. Kingston (eds.), *Papers in Laboratory Phonology I: Between the Grammar and Physics of Speech* (pp. 283–333). Cambridge: Cambridge University Press.

Farwaneh, S. (1995). *Directional effects in Arabic dialect syllable structure.* PhD dissertation, University of Utah.

Goldsmith, J. (1976). *Autosegmental phonology.* PhD dissertation, MIT.

Goldsmith, J. (1990). *Autosegmental and metrical phonology.* Oxford: Blackwell.

Haddad, G.F. (1984). Epenthesis and sonority in Lebanese Arabic. *Studies in the Linguistic Sciences*, 14, 57–88.

Harms, R. (1973). Some non-rules of English. Reproduced by the Indiana University Linguistics Club, Bloomington.

Hayes, B. (1986). Inalterability in CV phonology. *Language*, 6, 321–51.

Hooper, J.B. (1972). The syllable in phonological theory. *Language*, 48, 525–40.

Hooper, J.B. (1976). *An introduction to natural generative phonology.* New York: Academic Press.

Houlihan K. and Iverson, G. (1979). Functionally-constrained phonology. In D. Dinnsen (ed.), *Current approaches to phonological theory*, (pp. 50–73). Bloomington: Indiana University Press.

Itô, J. (1986). *Syllable theory in prosodic phonology.* PhD dissertation, University of Massachusetts, Amherst.

Itô, J. (1989). A prosodic theory of epenthesis. *Natural Language and Linguistic Theory*, 7, 217–59.

Itô, J. and Mester, A. (1986). The phonology of voicing in Japanese: theoretical consequences for morphological accessibility. *Linguistic Inquiry*, 17, 49–73.

Jespersen, O. (1904). *Lehrbuch der Phonetik.* Leipzig and Berlin: Teubner.

Kawahara, S. and Zamma, H. (2014). Generative treatments of Rendaku. New Brunswick, NJ: Rutgers Optimality Archives 1209.

Kenstowicz, M. (1986). Notes on syllable structure in three Arabic dialects. *Revue Quebecoise de Linguistique*, 16, 101–28.

Kiparsky, P. (2003). Syllables and moras in Arabic. In C. Féry and R. van de Vijver (eds.), *The syllable in optimality theory* (pp. 147–82). Cambridge: Cambridge University Press.

Ladefoged, P. (1982). *A course in phonetics*, 2nd edition. New York: Harcourt Brace.

Leben, W. (1973). *Suprasegmental phonology*. PhD dissertation, MIT. Distributed by Indiana University Linguistics Club.

McCarthy, J. (1979). *Formal problems in Semitic phonology and morphology*. PhD dissertation, MIT.

McCarthy, J. (1981). A prosodic theory of non-concatenative morphology. *Linguistic Inquiry*, 12, 373–418.

McCarthy, J. (1986). OCP effects: Gemination and antigemination. *Linguistic Inquiry*, 17, 207–63.

McCarthy, J. (1988). Feature geometry and dependency: a review. *Phonetica*, 45, 84–108.

McCarthy, J. (1991). Guttural phonology. In M. Eid and B. Comrie (eds.), *Perspectives on Arabic linguistics III* (pp. 63–92). Amsterdam and Philadelphia: John Benjamins.

McCarthy, J. (1994). The phonetics and phonology of Semitic pharyngeals. In P. Keating (ed.), *Phonological structure and phonetic form: Papers in laboratory phonology III* (pp. 191–233). Cambridge: Cambridge University Press.

Mester, A. and J. Itô. (1989). Feature predictability and underspecification: Palatal prosody in Japanese mimetics. *Language*, 65, 258–93.

Rubach, J. (1990). Final devoicing and cyclic syllabification in German. *Linguistic Inquiry*, 21, 79–94.

Selkirk, E. (1982). The Syllable. In H. van der Hulst and N. Smith (eds.), *The structure of phonological representations, Part II* (pp. 337–83). Dordrecht: Foris.

Selkirk, E. (1984). On the major class features and syllable theory. In M. Aronoff and R.T. Oehrle (eds.), *Language sound structure* (pp. 107–36). Cambridge, Mass.: MIT Press.

Sievers, E. (1881). *Grundzüge der Phonetik*. Leipzig: Breitkopf & Hartel.

Steriade, D. (1995). Complex onsets as single segments: The Mazateco pattern. In J. Cole and C. Kisseberth (eds.), *Perspectives in Phonology* (pp. 203–91). Stanford: CSLI.

Tserdanelis, G. (2001). A perceptual account of manner dissimilation in Greek. *Ohio State University Working Papers in Linguistics*, 55, 172–99.

Samira Farwaneh is an associate professor of Arabic language, linguistics and pedagogy at the School of Middle Eastern and North African Studies at the University of Arizona. Her research focuses on Semitic phonology, morphology and sociolinguistics, particularly diglossia, bilingualism and language and gender.

9
Exceptions to the SSP: Evidence from Ottawa for a Metatheoretical Approach

Marie Klopfenstein

9.1 Introduction

Ottawa is an Algonquian language spoken by an estimated 8,000 people from southern Ontario to northern Michigan. It is one of several dialects of Ojibwe, including Severn Ojibwe, Algonquin and Northwestern Ojibwe. The language is spoken in communities around Lake Huron and southern Ontario, right at the U.S.–Canada border. It can also found as far east as the Ottawa River. Ottawa is one of the many names in English for this particular language; others include Odawa, Chippewa, Ojibway, or even 'Indian', which is the preferred English term for many older speakers. Its speakers call the language *Nishnaabemwin*.

The Sonority Sequencing Principle (SSP) proposes that the syllable nucleus is the peak of sonority within the syllable, with progressively decreasing sonority values in the onset and coda, if present (Clements 1990; Selkirk 1984). While it is well known that languages like English and Russian also violate the SSP in some of their possible syllable structures, this chapter will examine Ottawa, a less commonly studied language, for any support it can lend to the various approaches that have been proposed to account for exceptions to the SSP.

Studies of sonority that have looked languages besides English include Dutch (Gerrits and Zumach 2006; Jongstra 2003), Hebrew (Ben-David 2006), Latin (Cser 2012), Norwegian (Kristoffersen and Simonsen 2006) and Spanish (Parker 2002); see also other chapters in this collection. It has been previously suggested that sonority is hardwired in the brain (Sussman 1984; Christman 1992a, b). If sonority really is universal, then data from a wide variety of languages representing many language families is needed.

To date, no Algonquin languages have been analysed using sonority theory. In this chapter, we will examine whether data from Ottawa follows the predictions of sonority theory and the SSP in particular. Several features of Ottawa, including vowel syncope and a complex system of inflectional morphology using prefixes and suffixes, allow for a variety of consonant clusters both syllable-initially and -finally. These and other data will be investigated for whether they follow the SSP and if not, which of the proposed approaches to SSP exceptions fits the data best.

9.2 A Brief Linguistic Description of Ottawa

Ottawa is actually spoken in several different communities spread over hundreds of miles, such as Walpole Island (unceded territory located on the border of Ontario, Canada and Michigan, United States) and Manitoulin Island (an island located in Lake Huron belonging to the province of Ontario). Each community uses a slightly different variety of the language, but these varieties are mutually intelligible and share vocabulary, pronunciation and grammatical features that set them apart from a larger, encompassing language group, Ojibwe (also sometimes written as Ojibway or Ojibwa) or *Anishnaabemowin* (Valentine 2001). This language group is one of the estimated 300 spoken at the time of European contact and is one of the few indigenous languages spoken by a relatively large number of individuals. Despite this, the language is considered endangered because it is spoken by an estimated less than 20,000 individuals out of an ethnic population of 60,000 ('Ottawa' n.d.). Most speakers of the language are adults and their numbers are declining, although language revitalization efforts are being made to teach the language in primary and secondary schools.

9.2.1 Ottawa's Sound Inventory

Traditionally, Ottawa has been described as having seven phonemic oral vowels. These include four long vowels and three short vowels, with varying phonetic realizations, as shown in Table 9.1. For purposes of understanding stress and the assignment of metrical feet in Ottawa, it is useful to group vowels into short and long categories. Therefore, the vowels are grouped accordingly below and organized by tongue position (Valentine 2001).

Table 9.1. Vowel inventory of Ottawa.

Long vowels			Short vowels		
Spelling	Phonetic values	Example words	Spelling	Phonetic values	Example words
/ii/	[iː]	*iidig* 'supposedly'	/i/	[ɪ]	*nini* 'man'
		niimi 'ANsg dances'			*mkizin* 'shoe'
		bzigwii 'ANsg moves, gets up'			*niiimi* 'ANsg dances'
/e/	[eː, ɛː, æː]	*emkwaan* 'spoon'			
		bezhig 'one'			
		miigwe 'ANsg gives things away'			
/aa/	[aː, ɑː]	*aakzi* 'ANsg is sick'	/a/	[ʌ]	*kajiish* 'wood-chuck, ground hog'
		maadaapi 'ANsg starts laughing'			*nmadbi* 'ANsg sits'
		maajaa 'ANsg goes away, moves'			*kina* 'all, every'
/oo/	[oː, uː]	*oodenaw* 'town'	/o/	[o, ʊ, ʌ]	*zosdam* 'ANsg coughs'
		doodooshaaboo 'milk'			*nokii* 'ANsg works'
		boozhoo 'hello'			*ngamo* 'ANsg sings'

Ottawa also has four nasal vowels, but their status as phonemes is unclear. Being found only in certain contexts may explain why some linguists have not explicitly listed them as separate phonemes (Rhodes 1993; Valentine 2001). Because Ottawa is a polysynthetic language, true minimal pairs contrasting oral and nasal vowels are difficult, if not impossible, to find. However, near minimal pairs are relatively easy to find for word-final vowels:

1a. *giigoonh* 'fish'	1b. *gegoo* 'anything, something'
2a. *bneshiinh* 'bird'.	2b. *Wemtigoozhii* 'Frenchman'
3a. *binoojiinh* 'child'	3b. *niijii* 'friend'
4a. *mzinhigewaanh* 'statue'	4b. *wiinwaa* 'them (animate)'

These pairs provide a strong argument for classifying nasal vowels as separate phonemes in the language, rather than allophones of oral vowels. In fact, Bloomfield (1957) considered these types of examples contrastive, stating that 'strong nasalization of a final long vowel occurs as a phonemic feature'. Finally, nasal vowels are represented orthographically by a vowel plus /n/ before /z/, /zh/, /s/, /sh/ and /y/.

Another context in which nasal vowels are found is in diminutive objects or in the diminutive form of an object. In the simplest terms the diminutive suffix is /-V̄s/, orthographically represented by *-ns* following a vowel. The diminutive suffix appears to be closely related to another noun ending called the 'contemptive': the nasal vowel represented by a following *-nh* in its written form. The contemptive is a suffix that can provide many subtle shades of meaning, such as 'vaguely negative or depreciative attitudes, such as "just an ordinary one," "of no great value," or "any old"' (Valentine 2001). The contemptive ending appears to be lexicalized in some instances with a more endearing connotation in words like 'child', 'old man', 'old woman' and many kinship terms. A few examples of contemptive and diminutive forms are shown in Table 9.2.

Ottawa has an inventory of approximately 17 consonants, as shown in Table 9.3. Orthographic representations of each sound are given in between

Table 9.2. Examples of contemptive and dimunitive forms.

Base form	Gloss of base form	Contemptive	Diminutive
daabaan	car	*daabaanenh*	*daabaanens*
ginii	rose	*giniinh*	*giniins*
nini	man	*niniinh*	*niniins*
mik	beaver	*mikoonh*	*mikoons*
sab	net	*sabiinh*	*sabiins*

Table 9.3. Consonant inventory of Ottawa with orthographic and phonetic realizations.

	Voicing	Bilabial	Dental/ Alveolar	Postalveolar/ Palatal	Velar	Glottal
Plosive	+v	/b/ [b]	/d/ [d]		/g/ [g]	
	-v	/p/ [p]	/t/ [t]		/k/ [k]	
Fricative	+v		/z/ [z]	/zh/ [ʒ]		
	-v		/s/ [s]	/sh/ [ʃ]		/h/ [ʔ, h]
Affricate	+v			/j/ [dʒ]		
	-v			/ch/ [tʃ]		
Nasal	+v	/m/ [m]	/n/ [n]			
Approximant	+v			/y/ [j]	/w/ [w]	

slashes and phonetic realizations are given between brackets. In the case of /h/, there are variations in productions depending on the phonetic environment, so both realizations are given. The sounds [f], [ɹ] and [l] can also be found in Ottawa, but only in loanwords from English (Rhodes 1993).

9.2.2 Syllable Structure and Stress

Authorities on Ottawa grammar and phonology like Piggott (1980), Rhodes (1993) and Valentine (2001) do not specify possible syllable shapes in the language. However, the syllable shapes shown in Table 9.4 can be attested.

Table 9.4. Syllable shapes in Ottawa.

Syllable shape	Example word	Gloss
V	*enh*	yes
CV	*maa*	here
CCV	*mshi*	yet
CVC	*mik*	beaver
CCVC	*ntam*	first
CCCVC	***mshkod**e*	prairie, plain, clearing

Like English, Ottawa has patterns of stressed and unstressed syllables. Metrically, Ottawa has feet consisting of two syllables, with the first syllable being weaker than the second, an example of which is shown in Figure 9.1.

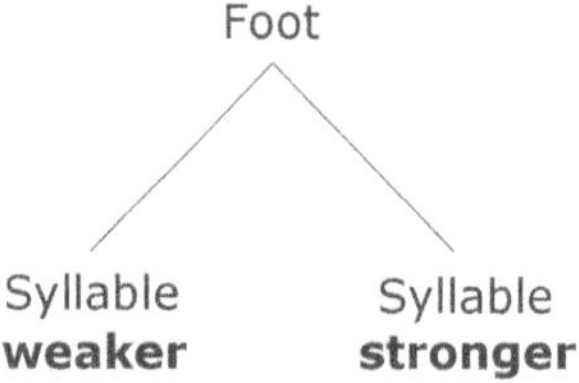

Figure 9.1. Foot patterning in Ottawa.

Ottawa also reduces vowels in weak syllables as part of the de-emphasis of these syllables. However, Ottawa speakers also may delete vowels completely, commonly referred to as vowel syncope, as part of the process of de-emphasis. This serves as a distinguishing feature of this dialect, as can be seen in the comparison in Figure 9.2 between Ottawa and Minnesota Ojibwe.

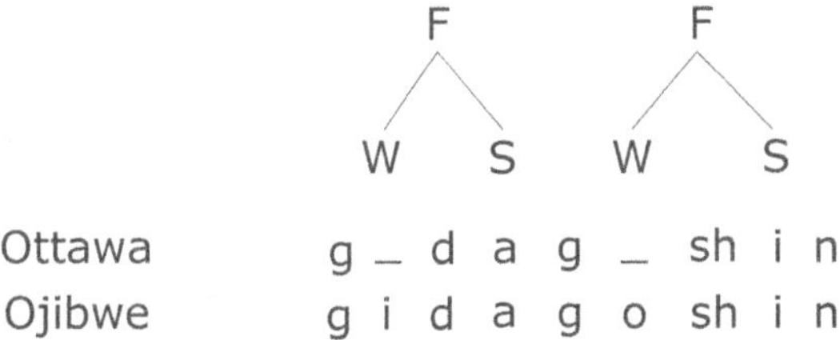

Figure 9.2. Vowel realization in Ottawa and Minnesota Ojibwe.

Feet are formed from the beginning of each word, proceeding to the end. The only exceptions to the iambic stress pattern of syllables occur when this assignment would cause the final syllable to be weak, which is not allowed in Ottawa. The final vowel of a word must always be strong, as shown in Figure 9.3. This means that syncopation is never seen word-finally and unusual syllable shapes due to vowel syncope alone do not occur.

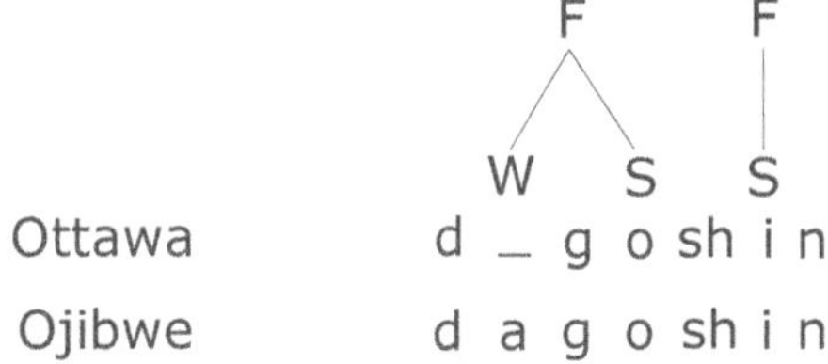

Figure 9.3. Stress on final vowels in Ottawa and Minnesota Ojibwe.

The final metrical stress rule in Ottawa is that long vowels can never occur in weak metrical positions; only short vowels can. This means that long vowels always receive some stress and do not undergo vowel syncope. If a long vowel occurs in a position that would normally be weak, a so-called defective foot with a strong single syllable is formed and footing resumes in the left to right pattern (Figure 9.4).

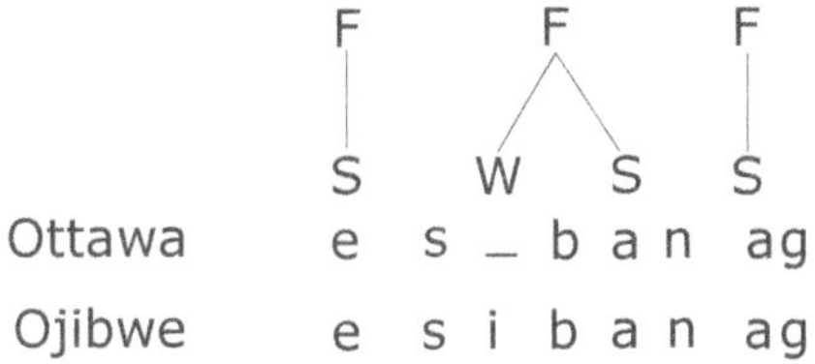

Figure 9.4. Defective feet in Ottawa and Minnesota Ojibwe.

As mentioned previously, long vowels always receive some stress. However, the strong syllable in the third foot counting back from the end of the word always receives the primary stress. All other strong syllables bear secondary stress. Because the writing system omits all weak vowels, even if only reduced to schwa, producing words with the correct primary stress is as simple as counting three vowels from the end. If a word has fewer than three feet, main stress is assigned to the foot farthest from the end of the word (Valentine 2001).

9.2.3 Ottawa Morphology

Ottawa is a polysynthetic language, meaning that its words can be composed of many morphemes. The language has both derivational and inflectional affixes that attach to word stems and compound words can form when word stems are combined. Ottawa's complex morphology united with vowel syncope can create some consonant clusters that violate predictions based on sonority theory, so we will briefly outline some of the morphology here.

Inflection is the modification of a word to express grammatical categories like tense, mood, person, number, gender, etc. Ottawa has a number of categories expressed via inflectional affixes, including person, number, tense, modality, evidentiality, negation and obviation. Ottawa derivational morphology forms words through a combination of roots and affixes, which then can be inflected via prefixes and suffixes (Valentine 2001). Because suffixes are typically a CV syllable shape and not subject to vowel syncope, we will focus on the prefixes that can provide the most insight on sonority.

There are a number of prefixes in Ottawa, including those that inflect for person and preverbs, which are words than can precede a verb and express tense, aspect or adverb-like meanings, and prenouns, which function much like English adjectives but are less common than preverbs. Since personal prefixes always are ordered first among prefixes, they are subjected to vowel syncope in Ottawa. Forms of personal prefixes are compared between Ottawa and other dialects of Ojibwe in Table 9.5.

Table 9.5. Forms of personal prefixes.

Person	Ojibwe	Ottawa
1st person prefix	ni-	n-
2nd person prefix	gi-	gi
3rd person prefix	o-	– (no form)

When the first or second person prefixes attach to a word (stem) that is consonant-initial, a cluster will result. These clusters may or may not follow predictions based on sonority theory, as we will examine below.

9.3 Application of Sonority Theory to Ottawa

The sonority scale from Ball, Müller and Rutter (2010) is given in Table 9.6 and was used for this analysis. The groups of sounds are listed in order of most sonorous (vowels) to least sonorous (plosives). In addition, sonority values adopted from Roca (1994) were assigned to each sound group. Sonority values provide an intuitive way to represent sharp rises or falls in sonority versus milder rises or falls.

Table 9.6. Sonority values of sound groups.

Vowels	low vowels high vowels	6
Glides		5
Liquids		4
Nasals		3
Fricatives	voiced fricatives voiceless fricatives	2
Plosives	voiced plosives voiceless plosives	1

In this section, we examine data from Ottawa in light of predictions based on the SSP, namely that there should be a rise in sonority towards the syllable nucleus, while the least sonorous segments are found at the extreme edges of onset or coda positions.

Table 9.7 gives examples of Ottawa words with consonant clusters in onset position that follow expectations of the SSP. These are just a few examples, but such examples are not difficult to find in Ottawa. There is a sharp rise in sonority with the segment closest to the syllable nucleus, which is due to a glide being in that position.

Table 9.7. Examples that adhere to the SSP.

Ottawa	Sonority values	Word class	Gloss
Dzhwegsidood	1–2–5	transitive verb with an inanimate object	spread s.t. out (of cloth)
Nwaatood	3–5	intransitive verb with an animate subject	be noisy
nwadkoneg	3–5	intransitive verb with an inanimate subject	catch fire
nwebid	3–5	intransitive verb with an animate subject	rest
nyaangim	3–5	adverb	until
nwezh	3–5	adverb	a long time
swesed	2–5	intransitive verb with an animate subject	splinter, splash, scatter
sweshkaad	2–5	intransitive verb with an animate subject	break up, disperse, be strewn
swii	2–5	adverb	but

It is also not difficult to find examples of consonant clusters in onsets that violate the SSP. Several examples are provided in Table 9.8.

These violations fall into two groups for the most part: fricative+stop consonant or nasal+obstruent consonant. Three of these examples have onset clusters of three consonants, yet still do not follow the SSP. The most extreme example is *mshkode,* which gets increasingly less sonorous towards the syllable nucleus. It is apparent that Ottawa has many consonant clusters that violate the SSP, so we need to consider how well various theoretical explanations fit these data.

Table 9.8. Examples that violate the SSP.

Ottawa	Sonority values	Word class	Gloss
mshkode	3–2–1	inanimate noun	prairie, plain, clearing
ndaajiiwaad	3–1	transitive verb with an animate object	beat s.t. for cooking
ndahbaan	3–1	inanimate noun	well, water hole
ngwaagan	3–1–5	inanimate noun	rainbow, trap, spider's web
nhishing	3–2	intransitive verb with an animate subject	adjust oneself in a lying position
nka	3–1	animate noun	Canada goose
nkaabaaw-dood	3–1	transitive verb with an inanimate object	dilute s.t., wet s.t.
nkwemog	3–1–5	intransitive verb with an inanimate subject	be a crossroads, the roads cross
nsaad	3–2	transitive verb with an animate object	destroy s.t., kill s.o., catch s.t., turn s.t. off
npaaj	3–1	preverb	incorrectly
npaadho-mod	3–1	intransitive verb with an animate subject	mispronounce something, say something wrong, misspeak
nsaabaaweg	3–2	intransitive verb with an inanimate subject	be wet
nshike	3–2	adverb	alone, by oneself
nsig	3–2	intransitive verb with an inanimate subject	be three [in number]
nswi	3–2	number	three
Nswi-giizhgad	3–2	inanimate noun	Wednesday
nzang	3–2	transitive verb with an inanimate object	boil s.t.
shkahaa	2–1	animate noun	new thing
shkib-boongi-isoons	2–1	animate noun	January (Little New-winter moon)
shkonjgan	2–1	inanimate noun	leftovers
shpaag	2–1	intransitive verb with an inanimate subject	be high
shpiming	2–1	adverb	above, in heaven, on high
spoging	2–1	intransitive verb with an inanimate subject	close up, heal up, be closed up, be healed up (of wounds)

9.3.1 Theoretical Explanations for SSP Violations Applied to Ottawa

Even though there is a strong tendency to follow the sonority scale in many languages, exceptions can be found. Phonologists have proposed various explanations for these exceptions. We will examine each of these proposals against the data from Ottawa in turn. The first type of explanation is metaphonological. Many different sonority scales have been proposed, some with slight variations. If a slightly different sonority scale is adopted, some of the sonority violations disappear. For example, using Clements' (1990) scale with all obstruent sounds classified as having the same, lowest sonority value, English /s/+stop consonant onset clusters (such as stop) no longer violate the SSP. Others (Ball 2016) have critiqued this approach, because the descriptive power of the sonority scale is weakened. Gradual rises or dips in sonority over onset and coda consonant clusters are lost if all obstruents have the same sonority level. This can be seen in words like 'left', which does not violate the SSP but would have a slight fall in sonority using the sonority scale included in this chapter. Another objection is that if we collapse obstruents into one sonority category, there is little justification to keep sonorants in separate categories. The collapse of sonorants into one category would leave us with only two sonority levels, which may account for much of the data but lacks richness in its description of possible consonant clusters across languages. It also does not follow the phonetic differences between the sounds, such as prolongability, which, it seems like, should play a part in a concept like sonority. If we apply a metaphonological approach to the sonority scale and Ottawa data, we find that even collapsing sonority categories does not exclude violations to the SSP. If all obstruents were placed in a single category with the lowest possible sonority value, it would eliminate violations like those onset clusters consisting of fricative+stop. However, many other violations would still remain, mostly in the form of nasal+obstruent sound(s) in onset consonant clusters. Therefore, a metaphological approach to explaining sonority violations does not work cross-linguistically.

Phonetic explanations have also been proposed for violations of the SSP like /s/+stop clusters in English. These explanations arise from the tendency of sounds to vary due to the context in which they are produced. For example, /t/ after /s/ in English is unaspirated and therefore differs from other realizations of /t/ in onset position, where it is aspirated. One could argue /t/ in a word like 'stop' is less sonorous than /t/ in 'top'. Similarly, /s/ in onset clusters may vary in duration from solo /s/

onsets, rendering it also different in sonority. Therefore, /s/+stop cluster in English may lack a rise in sonority as predicted by the SSP, but could have level sonority instead of an apparent fall in sonority as predicted by most sonority scales (Ball 2016).

This approach is appealing because it unites phonetic and phonological theory. However, there is no universal phonetic definition of sonority and this would introduce the need to define language-specific parameters for each language, rendering sonority less of a universal. Additionally, as a less studied language, there is a lack of phonetic data from Ottawa to create language-specific sonority values. Even with alternative sonority rankings based on finer phonetic detail, there still would be major SSP violations in Ottawa because of the language's tendency to have nasals at the beginning of onset consonant clusters.

English has /s/+stop combinations that violate the SSP, as mentioned earlier. Because this violation is restricted to /s/ clusters, several researchers have proposed that /s/+stop consonant combinations of sounds do not work as true clusters (Gierut 1999; Gussmann 2002). Instead, /s/ is described as an 'adjunct' and not part of the onset in a word like 'skate'. This explanation allows for the variety of /s/+stop sequences found in English within sonority theory, but can be criticized as a post hoc solution. Such a solution is also only necessary if one believes that sonority is hard-wired linguistically.

Like English, Ottawa also has /s/+stop sequences in onset position. However, we also saw that Ottawa can have combinations of voiceless fricatives and nasal sounds before stops in onset position, so an adjunct solution would have to apply to more than one sound to explain all possible violations to the SSP. In addition, Ottawa has a first person prefix that can create many SSP violating onsets. Proposing adjunct clusters in Ottawa would mean suggesting that person prefixes are adjuncts or somehow extrasyllabic, which prompts the question whether all prefixes should be adjuncts. As other prefixes do not violate SSP, this mechanism would introduce extra complexity to Ottawa's phonology that is not well-motivated.

Unfortunately, there are no studies on Ottawa acquisition that could shed more light on the various theories examined above. In English, there is support for adjunct segments from normal acquisition studies. Children often break up clusters in onset position with an epenthetic schwa, as in 'blue' [bəlu]. Interestingly, children tend to insert the schwa before /s/+stop clusters in English instead, e.g., 'stop' [əs.tɑp]. Cluster reduction is part of normal language acquisition and it would be interesting to observe how it occurs in Ottawa, especially given that certain consonants can convey important information, like the personal prefix system. Children may very well use epenthetic schwa in that case instead of eliding one or more segments.

Finally, there are some who take a metatheoretical approach and state that sonority is just a tendency and some languages will follow that tendency closer than others (Ball 2016). While this neatly explains all exceptions to the SSP, it is difficult to prove or disprove. In addition, the proposal that sonority is built in to a speaker's mental phonology is not possible if one adopts a metatheoretical stance. Despite this, a metatheoretical approach to sonority best fits with the data presented here. No other explanation can fittingly address the challenges posed to the SSP by the data from Ottawa.

9.4 Conclusion

To sum up, most theoretical approaches to clusters that violate the SSP do not work with Ottawa. Adjunct clusters cannot account for the variety of violations that Ottawa has. Metaphonological re-analysis of the sonority scale would also not fit with the data, due to the tendency for consonant clusters to begin with nasals, which are relatively sonorous consonants, in Ottawa. In addition, the existence of /n-/ as a first person prefix creates a very productive environment for SSP violations in onset clusters. Phonetic explanations at this stage also do not work, due to the extreme breaches of the SSP in Ottawa, although more phonetic research could lead to a refined sonority scale for the language. We must conclude that although a theory that does not make verifiable predictions is not very strong, the metatheoretical approach to sonority fits best with the data presented here.

Sonority principles, like any phonological principle, benefit from being applied to less commonly studied languages like Ottawa. Phonological theory equivocates at times about whether it reflects neurolinguistic aspects of human communication or is purely an abstraction. Without examination of a diverse selection of the world's languages, researchers cannot be sure they have found definitive conclusions to neurolinguistics hypotheses. Finally, studies of typical and atypical acquisition of consonant clusters in Ottawa or other Algonquin languages could also provide additional insights on sonority beyond what the data here show.

References

Ball, M.J. (2016). *Principles of clinical phonology: Theoretical approaches.* New York: Routledge.

Ball, M.J., Müller, N. and Rutter, B. (2010). *Phonology for communication disorders.* New York: Psychology Press.

Ben-David, A. (2006). On the acquisition of Hebrew #sC onsets. *Journal of Multilingual Communication Disorders*, 4, 205–17.

Bloomfield, L. (1957). *Eastern Ojibwa*. Ann Arbor: University of Michigan Press.

Christman, S.S. (1992a). Abstruse neologism formation: parallel processing revisited. *Clinical Linguistics and Phonetics*, 6, 65–76.

Christman, S.S. (1992b). Uncovering phonological regularity in neologisms: contributions of sonority theory. *Clinical Linguistics and Phonetics*, 6, 219–47.

Clements, G.N. (1990). The role of the sonority cycle in core syllabification. In J. Kingston and M. Beckman (eds.), *Papers in laboratory phonology 1: Between the grammar and the physics of speech* (pp. 283–333). Cambridge: Cambridge University Press.

Cser, A. (2012). The role of sonority in the phonology of Latin. In S. Parker (ed.), *The sonority controversy* (pp. 39–64). Boston: De Gruyter Mouton.

Gerrits, E. and Zumach, A. (2006). The acquisition of #sC-clusters in Dutch. *Journal of Multilingual Communication Disorders*, 4, 218–30.

Gierut, J.A. (1999). Syllable onsets: Clusters and adjuncts in acquisition. *Journal of Speech, Language and Hearing Research*, 42, 708–26.

Gussmann, E. (2002). *Phonology: Analysis and theory.* Cambridge: Cambridge University Press.

Jongstra, W. (2003). Variable and stable clusters: Variation in the realisation of consonant clusters. *Canadian Journal of Linguistics*, 38, 265–88.

Kristoffersen, K.E. and Simonsen, H.G. (2006). The acquisition of #sC clusters in Norwegian. *Journal of Multilingual Disorders*, 4, 231–41.

'Ottawa' (n.d.). In *Ethnologue: Languages of the World.* Retrieved from https://www.ethnologue.com/language/otw

Parker, S. (2002). *Quantifying the sonority hierarchy.* Doctoral dissertation, University of Massachusetts Amherst.

Piggott, G.L. (1980). *Aspects of Odawa morphophonemics: Outstanding dissertations in linguistics.* New York: Garland Publishing.

Roca, I. (1994). *Generative phonology.* London: Routledge.

Rhodes, R.A. (1993). *Eastern Ojibwa-Chippewa-Ottawa dictionary.* Berlin: Mouton de Gruyter.

Selkirk, E. (1984). On the major class features and syllable theory. In M. Aronoff and R. Oehrle (eds.), *Language Sound Structure: Studies in Phonology* (pp. 107–36). Cambridge, Mass.: MIT Press.

Sussman, H.M. (1984). A neuronal model for syllable representation. *Brain and Language*, 22, 167–77.

Valentine, J.R. (2001). *Nishnaabemwin reference grammar*. Toronto: University of Toronto Press.

Marie Klopfenstein is an Assistant Professor in the Speech Pathology and Audiology Program at Southern Illinois University Edwardsville. She has published work on sonority previously, including on cluster realizations in a child with phonological disorder. Her future research considerations include looking at the relationship between naturalness and intelligibility in speech disorders and the use of acoustically manipulated auditory feedback as facilitated by the use of apps with transgender voice services.

10 Parsing Salish Consonant Clusters[1]

Sonya Bird and Ewa Czaykowska-Higgins

10.1 Introduction

Salish languages are characterized by highly complex sound systems, with large consonantal inventories and complex clusters of consonants (Czaykowska-Higgins and Kinkade 1998). The Nxaʔamxcín word *snkɬxʷpáw̓stn* 'clothesline' (Czaykowska-Higgins and Willett 1997), for instance, illustrates an initial 6-consonant cluster containing a pre-vocalic sequence of 4 obstruents, and a post-vocalic 4-consonant cluster. Broadly speaking, research on the consonant sequences of Salish languages has largely focused on two sets of interconnected questions. The first set of questions involves descriptions of the consonant sequences themselves and determination of how those sequences can be simplified, either through insertion of schwas (e.g., Bianco 1996; Dyck 2004; Leonard 2007) or through consonant deletions (e.g., Blake 2000). The second set of questions builds on the description of phonotactics and the position of epenthetic vowels, in addition to considering prosodic morphological factors, in order to establish how complex consonant sequences are syllabified in Salish languages, whether syllabification is exhaustive, and if not,

1 We would like to acknowledge the late Elizabeth Davis who worked with Ewa Czaykowska in the 1990s and the Nxaʔamxcín speakers who worked with the late M. Dale Kinkade in the 1960s and '70s; our work would have been impossible if they had not shared their knowledge and expertise. We are grateful to the late Dale Kinkade for sharing his fieldnotes and for his mentorship. Thanks also to Ethan Dinnen who assisted us in coding the data. Thank you to K'saw's Ernest Brooks and the Nxaʔamxcín Language Program of Colville Confederated Tribes. This research has been permitted by the Colville Business Council of Colville Confederated Tribes (Resolution 2014-408), and supported by SSRHC.

how unsyllabified consonants might be prosodically licensed (e.g., Bagemihl 1991; Bates and Carlson 1992; Shaw 2002).

Descriptions of consonant sequences in all Salish languages highlight a significant distinction in the patterning of obstruent and resonant consonants,[2] and thus reveal that sonority distinctions play an interesting role in Salish phonotactics. Specifically, it has been claimed that Salish languages consistently favour obstruent-obstruent (OO) clusters, stem-initially and stem-finally, and that clusters containing resonant consonants (OR, RO or RR) tend to be less common in both positions. According to the markedness predictions made by the Sonority Sequencing Principle (SSP) (Selkirk 1984; Clements 1990), the best-formed syllable onsets should be those in which there is a rise in sonority, namely OR clusters, while the best-formed coda clusters should be those in which there is a fall in sonority, namely RO clusters. The fact that clusters conforming to the SSP in Salish languages appear to be comparatively less common, and that clusters that are more marked according to the SSP are more common, has been seen as a puzzle by Salish scholars and others, and has been taken by some as evidence that Salish languages do not have complex syllable margins. Of relevance to the current paper, Czaykowska-Higgins and Willett (1997) claim for Nxaʔamxcín that the only clusters allowed root-initially in Nxaʔamxcín are SSP-marked OO clusters and that all other clusters in this position surface with an intervening predictable schwa. As a result of this distribution, they conclude that Nxaʔamxcín does not have complex onsets of any kind; they then hypothesize that rather than being in a complex onset, the first consonant in an OO initial cluster is outside the simple CVC syllable template, and is moraically, rather than syllabically, licensed (following Bagemihl 1991).

Most other research focusing on the phonotactic and structural properties of consonant clusters in various Salish languages, like Czaykowska-Higgins and Willett (1997), has explored in some fashion Bagemihl's (1991) hypothesis that, in spite of the existence of long and complex consonant clusters, syllables in Salish languages are essentially quite simple (e.g., Bates and Carlson 1992; Bianco 1996; Blake 2000; Czaykowska-Higgins and Willett 1997; Dyck 2004; Matthewson 1994; Shaw 2002, 2008; Urbanczyk 2001). However, while the study of consonant clusters in Salish

2 In keeping with previous research on Nxaʔamxcín, and on other Salish languages, we primarily refer to sonorant consonants as 'resonants' or 'resonant consonants'. However, since authors like Flemming et al. (2008), Yun (2014), etc. use the term 'sonorant', we follow their usage when discussing their work.

languages has generated much scholarly work, apart from Shahin (2007) and Flemming, Ladefoged and Thomason (2008), there has been virtually no instrumental analysis of the pronunciation of these clusters. There is therefore little indication of what such analysis might or might not tell us about distinctions between obstruents and resonant consonants, about Sonority Sequencing, and/or about syllabification. In addition, the research on Salish clusters has not been placed in the larger context of research on cluster typologies (e.g., Morelli 1999, 2003; Kreitman 2006, 2012), or cue perceptibility (e.g., Fleischhacker 2001, 2005; Flemming 2008; Henke, Kaisse and Wright 2012; Fullwood 2014; Steriade 2001, 2008; Yun 2014), or on research about gestural (mis)timing and consonant clustering (e.g., Gick and Wilson 2006; Davidson 2006a, b; Chitoran, Goldstein and Byrd 2002; but see Parker 2011). Thus there is still much to be explored both in terms of understanding the phonetic properties of consonant sequences in Salish languages, and in terms of phonetic or phonological explanations for those phonetic properties.

The goal of this chapter therefore is to begin to fill in some of these gaps by providing a systematic acoustic study of consonant clusters in one particular Salish language: Nxaʔamxcín. Our starting point is an attempt to address two questions: (1) can we confirm instrumentally the auditory impressions that led Czaykowska-Higgins and Willett (1997, henceforth CH&W) to claim the occurrence of OO to the exclusion of other clusters in Nxaʔamxcín and (2) what, if anything, does our instrumental analysis tell us about the role played by the obstruent/resonant sonority distinction in determining how clusters are syllabified? Based on acoustic analysis of root-internal CC clusters, we build on CH&W's claims, showing that (1) OO clusters are indeed unique in never exhibiting schwa insertion, but that (2) syllable structure in Nxaʔamxcín is likely more complex than previously thought, and that OO clusters do not necessarily have special status with respect to syllabification.

The remainder of the chapter is structured as follows: Section 10.2 provides the context for the study, focusing in particular on the Salish literature; Section 10.3 presents the methodology used in this study; Section 10.4 summarizes the main results; Section 10.5 provides a discussion of these results, drawing from literature on syllable-based versus perception- and articulation-based accounts of cluster typology. Finally, Section 10.6 concludes by pointing to the next steps in elucidating the nature of Salish clusters and their role in syllable structure.

10.2 Preliminaries

The Salish language family consists of 23 distinct languages. Nxaʔamxcín itself is one of 7 languages from the Interior branch of the family, and was spoken historically in north-central Washington State, USA. The language has 4 varieties (Wenatchi, Moses-Columbia, Entiat and Chelan). There are currently approximately 3,500 tribal members descended from Nxaʔamxcín-speaking families living on the Colville Reservation, where their ancestors were confined by Presidential Executive Order in 1870. The Nxaʔamxcín Language Program has been active since the late 1990s, and is increasingly focusing on language revitalization. There is currently a single fluent speaker active in the Language Program.

The majority of the linguistic research on the language was carried out by the late M. Dale Kinkade, who worked with more than 20 speakers in the 1960s and 1970s. More recently (since the 1990s), Ewa Czaykowska-Higgins, Marie Louise Willett and Nancy Mattina have worked with speakers of the language and with members of the Nxaʔamxcín Language Program. The examples examined acoustically in this paper are from a recording of a story told by the late Elizabeth Davis to Czaykowska-Higgins (see Section 10.3). The database on which the initial research on Nxaʔamxcín clusters and syllables was carried out by CH&W in 1997 was primarily based on examples transcribed on Kinkade's file cards (based on his fieldnotes), supplemented by examples elicited by Czaykowska-Higgins and Willett. The speakers from Kinkade's corpus represented all the different varieties of the language; Elizabeth Davis was a speaker of the Moses variety from the snkáwsəxʷ.[3]

10.2.1 The Nxaʔamxcín Inventory

A typical Salish-language inventory has a small set of vowels and a large inventory of consonants (Czaykowska-Higgins and Kinkade 1998). Thus, the Nxaʔamxcín inventory in Figure 10.1 has labial, coronal, velar, uvular, pharyngeal and glottal consonants, plain and ejective stops, plain and glottalized resonant consonants, and a series of retracted as well as unretracted coronal consonants. The nasals, liquids, glides, voiced pharyngeal and glottals pattern together as resonants, distinct from the obstruent consonants.[4]

3 In Nxaʔamxcín orthography (see note 5): šnkáwšəxʷ.

4 Glottal stop is classed by many Salishanists as a resonant consonant, primarily because it often requires the presence of a preceding vowel (e.g., Willett and

	Labial	Coronal	Velar	Uvular	Pharyngeal	Glottal
Stop/ Affricate	p p̓	t t̓ c c̓ c̣	k k̓ kʷ k̓ʷ	q q̓ qʷ q'ʷ		ʔ
Fricative		s ṣ	x xʷ	x̣ x̣ʷ	ḥ ḥʷ	h
Lateral obstruent		ɬ ƛ'				
Nasal	m m̓	n n̓				
Liquid/ Glide		l l̓ y y̓ ḷ ḷ̓ r r̓	w w̓		ʕ ʕ̓ ʕʷ ʕ̓ʷ	

Figure 10.1. Nxaʔamxcín consonant inventory.[5]

The small vowel inventory (Figure 10.2) consists of 3 full vowels and their retracted counterparts, as well as the vowel schwa.

i ị   u ụ

ə ə̣

a ạ

Figure 10.2. Nxaʔamxcín vowel inventory.

The schwa vowel occupies a unique place in the phonologies of Salish languages and has been the subject of much discussion and study (e.g., Kinkade 1998; Blake 2000; Shaw 1996). For the most part, both the position in which a schwa appears, and its exact quality are predictable. Furthermore, surface schwas come from a variety of sources. In Nxaʔamxcín (1) schwas can be derived from full vowels in unstressed positions via reduction; (2)

Czaykowska-Higgins 1995; Flemming et al. 2008). In this chapter we treat it as a resonant but point out those cases where its behaviour differs from those of other resonant consonants.

5 Linguists working on Nxaʔamxcín (and Salish more generally) have used the North American Phonetic alphabet in transcriptions, while the Nxaʔamxcín Language Program uses an orthography based on the NAPA, with some modifications. For the sake of consistency with previously published research we use NAPA here. The NAPA diverges from the IPA as follows: [x̣]=IPA [χ] (NLP orthography: 'x̌'); [ḥ]=IPA [ħ]; [ƛ']=IPA [tɬ']; [y]=IPA [j], [ṣ, c̣, ḷ, ị, ụ, ə̣, ạ]=IPA [s̠, c̠, l̠, i̠, u̠, ə̠, a̠] (NLP orthography: 's, c, ll, ii, uu, əə, aa'; NAPA [s, c]=NLP orthography 's̆, č').

schwas can be underlying in a few historically-motivated environments; (3) schwas can be epenthesized into root morphemes to serve as carriers of primary stress in words where there are no full vowels (Czaykowska-Higgins 1993); (4) schwas can be inserted into clusters, where they surface unstressed, but where their position is predictable. In the last case, the inserted schwas have been claimed to be of two types: longer, epenthetic schwas and shorter, transitional (also termed excrescent or *svarabhakti*) schwas (CH&W; Willett and Czaykowska-Higgins 1995).

In our investigation of CC clusters, the fourth type of schwa is the most relevant: we are interested in establishing instrumentally where exactly schwas are inserted into underlying consonant clusters, and whether the inserted schwas are transitional elements or whether they are epenthetic. Transitional elements are not referenced by the phonology in any way, while epenthetic schwas should have some phonological status (see Hall 2006). In the next section, we turn to a summary of the claims that have been made on the basis of auditory descriptions regarding where schwas appear in Nxaʔamxcín words and whether they are epenthetic or transitional.

10.2.2 Consonant Sequences

In describing the phonotactic properties of Nxaʔamxcín consonant sequences, we follow CH&W and Willett and Czaykowska-Higgins (1995), who focus primarily on the properties of the approximately 1,500 root morphemes in a dataset based on Kinkade's fieldnotes. In this section we first discuss the general underlying and surface patterns of roots, and then turn to more fine-grained distinctions.

Underlying and Surface Root Shapes: Unlike prefixes and suffixes, roots in Nxaʔamxcín contain the whole range of consonants found in the inventory, and therefore provide the most extensive range of possible cluster types. The breakdown of these roots, in terms of type and token count, is provided in Table 10.1. The vast majority contain two underlying consonants (2C roots), with three (3C) or four (4C) consonant roots also occurring. The information provided in Table 10.1 includes the underlying representations of the roots, along with the surface forms they are claimed to have, based on auditory descriptions. As mentioned above, the counts are based on the examples of roots found in Kinkade's fieldnotes, supplemented by examples in the fieldnotes of CH&W. The schwas in the surface forms are assumed to be epenthetic rather than transitional elements. The sequences in **bold** are the underlying cluster types that we examine in this chapter.

Table 10.1. Underlying and surface forms of Nxaʔamxcín root morphemes.

	Underlying	Surface	Tokens of surface forms
2C roots	CVC	CVC	~550
	CC	CəC	~650
	CCV	**CCV**	2
		CəCV	4
	CVCV	CVCV	10
3C roots	CV**CC**	CV**CC**	216
	CCC	Cə**CC**	
	CV**CC**	CV**CəC**	93
	CCC	Cə**CəC**	
	CCVC	**CC**VC	19
		CəCVC	37
	CVCVC	CVCVC	15
	CV**CC**V	CV**CC**V	1
4C roots	**CCVCC**	**CCVCC**	4
		CəCVCC	4
		CCVCəC	0
		CəCVCəC	0
	CCCVC	Cə**CC**VC	3
	CV**CC**VC	CV**CC**VC	4
	CV**CCC**	CV**CC**əC	15
	CCCC	Cə**CCəC**	3

In this chapter, following CH&W, we have focused on examining the surface forms of potential clusters in 2C, 3C and 4C roots, but excluding the 650 √CC root cases, and C1C2 sequences in 3C √CCC roots and 4C √CCCC roots. The sequences we have chosen to examine are those in which the insertion of a schwa into an underlying cluster has the potential to be determined by considerations of syllable structure only, as opposed to considerations related to preferred root shapes.[6]

Root Clusters and Obstruent/Resonant Distinctions: If we look in more detail at underlying consonant sequences in Table 10.1, we see that the

6 Preferred root shapes are discussed in detail in Czaykowska-Higgins (1993, 1998) and CH&W.

distinction between obstruent and resonant consonants seems to play a significant role in how such sequences surface. Thus, according to CH&W's auditorily-based observations of the approximately 1,500 roots in the available corpus, 25 contain initial surface clusters, all of which are of the form OO (2 √CCV + 19 √CCVC + 4 √CCVCC) (1a). In contrast, potential OR (1b), RR (1c) or RO (1d) surface clusters are claimed always to surface with an intervening schwa vowel.

(1) Root-initial consonants[7]

		Underlying	Surface		
a.	OO	ptix̣ʷ	ptîx̣ʷ	spit	
		txʷul	txʷúl	house	
		ɬqʷut	ɬqʷút	willow	
		ɬx̣umx	ɬx̣úmx	child's voice changes	
		ƛ̓p̓at	ƛ̓p̓át	sack	
b.	OR	cnukʷ	cənúkʷ	syphilis	
		s-kʷlis	skʷəlîs	kinnickinnick berry	
		ṫway̓t	ṫuwáy̓t	cry hard	(ə→u/__w)
		ṫʕʷum	ṫaʕʷúm	small (sg.)	(ə→a/__ʕʷ)
c.	RR	mnak	mənák	excrement	
		mra	mərá	gather (plants, food)	
		ylam	yilám	run (pl.)	(ə→i/y__)
d.	RO	lkʷut	ləkʷút	far, long way	

According to the transcriptions provided in (1), OO clusters can include any combination of stops, fricatives or affricates; these have occasionally been transcribed with a tiny transitional schwa or with aspiration, reflecting the fact that initial stops in these environments in Nxaʔamxcín sound released. Thus, √*ptîx̣ʷ* 'spit' has been transcribed as [pʰtîx̣ʷ] and as [pᵊtîx̣ʷ] as well as as [ptîx̣ʷ].

In initial consonant sequences containing at least one R, a schwa is transcribed in the consonant sequence such that the schwa appears before the R in OR sequences, between the two Rs in RR sequences, and after the R in RO sequences. In RR and RO sequences the initial R can surface as a syllabic resonant consonant: thus, √*lkʷut* 'far', 'long way' has been transcribed as [l̩kʷút] as well as [ləkʷút]. In addition, initial glides may surface as vocalized segments – in examples from 'Crow's Daughter', discussed below, √*ylam* 'run (pl.)' surfaces in several tokens as [ilám]. In this chapter, we class nasal/liquid syllabification and glide vocalization together, considering them both to be instances of vocalization.

7 Examples are from CH&W (1997: 390, 392), apart from *yilám* 'run (pl.)', which is from the text 'x̣áʕx̣aʕ sṫámkaʔs'.

As far as root-final clusters are concerned, final OO clusters are claimed to surface with no intervening vowel (2a), final OR and RR sequences are generally claimed (see below) to surface with an intervening schwa (2b, c), and RO clusters are claimed to be systematically produced with a short (*svarabhakti*) schwa between R and O (2d) (CH&W 1997: 402).[8] In √CCC roots like √*mck*ʷ 'wild blackcaps', a schwa surfaces between the first and the second consonant in order to host primary stress, irrespective of what the final two consonants happen to be (2e).

(2) Root-final consonants[9]

		Underlying	Surface	
a.	OO	lip̓x̣ʷ	lip̓x̣ʷ	a type of rock formation
		tax̣s	táx̣s	start hauling
b.	OR	sapn	sápən	daughter-in-law
		mux̣ʷl̓	múx̣ʷəl̓	cradle-board
		sip̓y̓	sip̓iʔ	hide, buckskin, skin
c.	RR	t̓am̓n	t̓ám̓ən	mortar, iron bowl
		k-√tlm-s-cin	ktələmscin	send a message
		s-xʷ+√xʷl̓m	sxʷəxʷə́l̓əm	fool hen, spruce grouse
		t̓-√t̓aym̓-t	t̓t̓áyəm̓t	easy
d.	RO	s-n-√c̓lx̣ʷ-qin-m	snc̓əlᵊx̣ʷqinəm	whirlwind
		s-√wanx	swanᵊx	war dance, Nez Perce dance
		na-√ʔawt	naʔáwᵊt	behind
e.	OO	mckʷ	mə́ckʷ	wild blackcaps
		niʔ-√c̓pq	niʔc̓ə́pq	underbrush
		m̓ɬƛ̓ʷ	m̓ə́ɬƛ̓ʷ	blood
	RO	tmxʷ	tə́mxʷ	worn, ragged
	OR	s-c̓+c̓ƛ̓l̓	sc̓c̓ə́ƛ̓əl̓	cone
	RR	s-xʷ+xʷl̓m	sxʷəxʷə́l̓əm	fool hen; spruce grouse

As 2a and 2e suggest, OO clusters root-finally can contain any combination of stops, fricatives or affricates. Similarly, underlying OR, RR and RO sequences contain all possible combinations of O and R types. In cases where an R is final, the R may be pronounced as syllabic instead of being preceded by a schwa (e.g., √*t̓am̓n* 'mortar' has been transcribed as [t̓ám̓ən] or [t̓ám̓n̩]). If the R is a glide, R may surface as a corresponding vocalized vowel or, in the case of a glottalized R', as a vocalized vowel-ʔ sequence (e.g., √*ḥáw̓y* 'make, do' as [ḥáw̓i]); glide vocalization occurs in word-final position or preceding a C-initial suffix (e.g., ([ḥáw̓i-s],); preceding a V-initial or

8 Willett and Czaykowska-Higgins (1995) claim that the presence of schwa in RO# clusters is optional; the claims in CH&W are revised from the 1995 paper, based on more extensive analysis.

9 Examples are from CH&W (1997: 399–402 passim).

R-initial suffix, the glide often surfaces as a VG sequence (e.g., [ḥáw̓iy-əm]). As above, we assume nasal/liquid syllabification and glide vocalization to be instances of the same process of vocalization.

Finally, CH&W (1997: 404) claim that in cases of longer roots with medial clusters, a short transitional schwa can optionally appear between the two consonants. They also say that such a vowel appears most regularly when the medial cluster contains at least one resonant consonant (3).

(3) Root-medial consonants

	Underlying	Surface	
a. OO	pckl	pə́cᵊkəl	leaf
b. OR	q̓ʷutlʔ	q̓ʷútᵊlaʔ	race
c. RR	ʔinwil	ʔinᵊwil	yours
	tmnaỷ-m	təmᵊnáỷəm	corpse
d. RO	yamx̣ʷʔ	yamᵊx̣ʷaʔ	basket

To summarize (Table 10.2), auditory description suggests that sequences in which one or both of the underlying consonants is a resonant surface with an intervening schwa; if the resonant is root-final or root-initial, it may be syllabic, or if it is a glide, it may be vocalized. Furthermore, in the case of final RO sequences, or in the case of all medial sequences, the intervening segment is claimed to be a short transitional-like schwa, rather than an epenthetic vowel. Significantly, the only clusters that consistently surface in root-initial or root-final position without an inserted schwa are OO sequences; when the first of these obstruents is a stop, or when the stop is pre-pausal, it is claimed to surface with aspirated release.

Table 10.2. Summary: Auditorily-described surface forms of underlying clusters in roots.

	Underlying	Surface	Syllabification
Initial	OO	OO*	O.Ov
	OR	OəR	Oə.Rv
	RR	RəR or R̩R/VR (if R1 = glide)	Rə.Rv
	RO	RəO or R̩O/VR (if R1 = glide)	Rə.Ov
Final	OO	OO*	vO.O
	OR	OəR	v.OəR
	RR	RəR or RR̩/RV (if R2 = glide)	v.RəR
	RO	RᵊO	vRᵊ.O
Medial	CC	CᵊC	vCᵊ.Cv

* Cluster-initial stops are released.

In terms of syllabification, CH&W take the presence of inserted schwa as evidence of syllabification. Specifically, they assume that epenthetic schwa acts as a syllable nucleus where it occurs. In contrast, the short schwas claimed to appear in final RO clusters and in medial clusters are *not* taken to be syllable nuclei, but rather are analysed as occurring at, and therefore as indicating, syllable boundaries. Based on these assumptions (and combined with additional evidence from prosodic morphology), their analysis is that **no** clusters are tautosyllabic. This means, then, that syllables in Nxaʔamxcín are claimed to be restricted to the shapes Cv and CvC (where v = a full vowel or a schwa), as summarized in the last column of Table 10.2. What Table 10.2 shows is that in initial and final OO clusters, and in final RO clusters, the peripheral O is analysed as being extra-syllabic. As mentioned above, CH&W claim that this extra-syllabic O is moraically-licensed, in the sense of Bagemihl (1991); as such it would be incorporated into prosodic structure at the foot or word, but not at the syllabic level.

In addition to the moraic-licensing analysis, other analyses of OO clusters have been proposed for other Salish languages. Urbanczyk (2001) hypothesizes for Lushootseed that obstruents are onsets to syllables headed by voiceless schwas, while Shaw (2002, 2008) proposes that all consonants, including OO clusters in hən̓q̓əmin̓əm̓ are parsed into syllables. We return to these different analyses in Section 10.5.2 below.

10.2.3 The Phonetics of Consonant Clusters: Montana Salish and St'át'imcets

There are various auditorily-based descriptions of clusters of Salish languages which report observations similar, though not identical, to those made above in relation to Nxaʔamxcín clusters (e.g., Kuipers 1974; Thompson and Thompson 1992; van Eijk 1997); Shahin (2007) provides a preliminary acoustic analysis of clusters in St'át'imcets (see below). Here we briefly describe claims made in another paper, on the phonetic structures of Montana Salish (Flemming et al. 2008), a southern Interior Salish language like Nxaʔamxcín, which is spoken in Montana. Its inventory of segments closely resembles that of Nxaʔamxcín.

For our purposes, Flemming et al.'s (2008) most important observation is that Montana Salish exhibits a clearcut distinction between obstruent and sonorant (*l, m, n, w, j,* ʕ, ʕʷ and their glottalized counterparts) consonants. Long sequences of obstruents do surface (see 4a below) but, as they point out,

> [w]hile there is considerable freedom in combining consonants in a sequence, there are restrictions. The clearest to emerge ... is that sonorants and glottal stop generally do not follow obstruents in a cluster. They are usually separated by a vowel, although this appears to be optional in certain contexts.... The schwa vowel [ə] only occurs between a sonorant or a glottal stop and a preceding consonant so we can regard this vowel as epenthesized in order to break up these sequences. (p. 473)

Exceptions to the occurrence of [ə] include word-initial or medial sequences of [s]/affricate followed by a nasal which can surface with or without intervening [ə] (cf. 4b.i and 4b.ii), and lateral fricatives [ɬ] followed by a glottalized lateral sonorant [l̓] which appear without intervening [ə] (4b.iii). Additionally, although schwas are typically inserted into sonorant-sonorant clusters (4c.i), sonorants of identical type/place are not separated by vowels (4c.ii), and in sequences containing more than two sonorants there need not be vowels inserted preceding every sonorant (e.g., in 4b.i there is no intervening [ə] between [m] and [ˀn]; shown in bold italics). Finally, of interest is that nasals and laterals surface differently in word-initial position: nasals are typically preceded by a glottal stop and realized as syllabic (4d.i), while laterals are preceded by a glottal stop and short schwa in this position (4d.ii).

(4) Montana Salish clusters (relevant clusters in bold)

a.	#OO			**tʃɬkʷkʷt**əˀnéˀws	'a fat little belly'[10]
b.	#OR	(i)	#sn	**səˀn**ə***mˀn***é	'toilet'
		(ii)	#sn	**sn**éˀwt	'the wind'
		(iii)	#ɬˀl	**ɬˀl**ˀláq	'thin'
c.	#RR	(i)	#ˀmˀn	ˀ**məˀn**étʃ	'excrement, shit'
	RR	(ii)	_ll_	sqə**ll**ú	'tale'
d.	#RO	(i)	#nɬ	**ʔn̩ɬ**útskʷ	'soak'
		(ii)	#lˀl	**ʔəlˀ**láts	'red raspberry'

A final relevant observation from Flemming et al. (2008: 475) is that stops and ejectives are strongly released preceding other obstruents and pre-pausally. Release of stops in this position involves aspiration, although stops occurring prevocalically are not aspirated. If one puts all these different observations together (Table 10.3), what emerges is that, in Montana Salish, sonorants do not surface in clusters, while obstruents do. This result is in line with auditory observations made about Nxaʔamxcín (and other Salish languages as well).

10 In Flemming et al. (2008) glottalized resonants are transcribed with a raised glottal stop preceding the resonant. These transcriptions are in IPA.

Table 10.3. Montana Salish.

Underlying	Surface
OO	OO
OR	OəR (exception: #sR and #ɬˀl)
RR	RəR (exception: R_iR_i and RRR$_{\tilde{ɔ}}$ RəRR, ?RəRəR)
RO	RO (exception: #ʔN̩, #ʔəL)

In terms of the distribution of schwa, the key difference between the descriptions of Montana Salish and Nxaʔamxcín is that, according to Flemming et al. (2008), sonorants are almost always preceded by schwas, regardless of whether the sonorants are in an initial, medial or final cluster. In Nxaʔamxcín, in contrast, root-medial clusters are claimed to surface *only with transitional schwas,* even if the second consonant in the cluster is a resonant consonant. This apparent difference in the description of schwa's distribution in the two languages is due in part to differences in the data under consideration, and in part due to different conceptual approaches to the patterns observed. First, Flemming et al.'s description of schwa occurrence examines patterns throughout the whole word, while CH&W's description focuses primarily on schwa's occurrence in root morphemes. In fact though, both CH&W and Willett and Czaykowska-Higgins (1995) provide preliminary descriptions of schwa's occurrence in non-root environments, and from these preliminary descriptions it seems likely that Nxaʔamxcín is like Montana Salish (and the other Interior languages described in Kuipers 1974; van Eijk 1997; Shahin 2007; and Thompson and Thompson 1992) in allowing post-root resonant consonants to be preceded by schwas.

The fact that the descriptions of Nxaʔamxcín do not describe schwa's occurrence as being pre-resonant is due to the second, conceptual, difference between the descriptions of Montana Salish and Nxaʔamxcín. Specifically, Flemming et al.'s (2008) description refers simply to linear position ('preceding R'), while CH&W's work is informed and influenced by reference to abstract phonological structure (syllable structure). At the time the latter work was published, many accounts of consonant clustering made the assumption that phonotactics should be stated with reference to syllable structure, and that 'this syllable structure should be the same as that referred to by other arguably syllable-sensitive processes' (Blevins 2003: 377).

This conceptual difference between Flemming et al. (2008) and CH&W (1997) reflects a broader divide in approaches that linguists have taken in analysing the behaviour of consonant clusters: those that assume that phonotactic constraints are largely syllable-based (following Kahn 1976, for example) versus those focused on alternatives to syllable-based accounts of phonotactics. Flemming, et al. are influenced by the latter category of explanations, and in particular by those focusing on perceptual considerations (e.g., Steriade 1999, 2001, 2008; Fleischhacker 2001, 2005; Flemming 2008; Fullwood 2014), while, as mentioned, CH&W focus on syllabification considerations. For the most part, these two approaches have not explicitly converged in the literature so there is no consensus on the extent to which perceptual considerations might reflect syllable structures, or whether phonotactic and other phononological patterns should converge on one set of syllable structures (see Blevins 2003). As a result, there are different possible interpretations of the patterns observed in CC clusters in Salish.

As it turns out, discussions of Salish consonant clusters in the different conceptual models are based on very little by way of phonetic data on the actual realization of clusters. Indeed, while Flemming et al. (2008) provide a small number of spectrograms illustrating the lack of schwas in obstruent clusters, only one previous preliminary study (Shahin 2007) has attempted to systematically verify observations about how clusters surface through instrumental analysis. Shahin assumes a simple syllable analysis of St'át'imcets Salish, and examines acoustic tokens of words with CC clusters in word-initial, word-internal and word-final position in two varieties of the language. She distinguishes between excrescent schwas, with mean duration of 48 ms (standard deviation: 15), and epenthetic schwas, with mean duration of 71 ms (standard deviation: 23). She considers schwa occurrence and duration in OR, OO, RO and RR clusters, and claims that excrescent schwas occur very rarely in St'át'imcets data, surfacing most frequently between consonants in word-internal clusters. She also claims that there is 'frequent production of epenthetic schwa in consonant-resonant clusters' (p. 389). Two other papers co-authored by Shahin examine schwa properties independent of consonant clustering effects: Shahin and Blake (2004) claim that in St'át'imcets excrescent schwas have a mean duration of 28 ms, while epenthetic schwas, have a mean duration of 41 ms; Blake and Shahin (2008) claim that Sliammon excrescent schwa has a mean duration of 39 ms, while unstressed epenthetic schwa has a mean duration of 75–80 ms. Athough these studies show differences in the absolute duration of excrescent and epenthetic schwas, they do suggest that the two types of vowels are distinguished at least in part by durational differences.

If we are to evaluate conceptual approaches to clusters, it is crucial to understand the facts at hand. Clearly, there is still a great deal to explore in the study of Salish clusters, and it is this that we turn to next. Section 10.3

first lays out our methodology; then Section 10.4 reports results, guided by CH&W's description of the distribution of schwa in the realization of clusters in Nxaʔamxcín roots.

10.3 Methodology

The clusters analysed in this study were extracted from a 30-minute Nxaʔamxcín story entitled x̣áʕx̣aʕ sƛ̓ámkaʔs[11] 'Crow's Daughter', told in September 1990 by the late Elizabeth Davis to Ewa Czaykowska-Higgins. To make our results comparable with previous Nxaʔamxcín studies (in particular CH&W 1997), we focused primarily on CC clusters occurring within root morphemes. We also included in our analysis tokens of [imli] ('Emily'), containing a medial CC. Table 10.4 summarizes the 291 tokens that made up our dataset, by root type (note that in the case of CCVCC roots, two clusters are of interest, an initial and a final cluster).

Table 10.4. Clusters considered, by root type (target cluster in bold)

Position	Two-consonant roots		Three-consonant roots		Four/five-consonant roots		**Total by position**
Initial	**CC**V	5	**CC**VC	73	**CC**VCVC	2	81+7* = **88**
					CCVCCC	1	
Final			CV**CC**	108	CVCV**CC**	3	148 +7 = **155**
Final			Cə**CC**	37			
Both	–		–		**CC**V**CC**	14	
Medial	V**CC**V: [imli]	12	CV**CC**V	2	CV**CC**VC	34	**48**

* The additional 7 tokens in initial and final position come from the CCVCC roots.

Based on CH&W, clusters were categorized according to their component consonants: OO (obstruent-obstruent), OR (obstruent-resonant); RO (resonant-obstruent); RR (resonant-resonant). As we shall see below, finer grained distinctions among these general manner types were sometimes necessary. Sub-categories of obstruents included stops (T), fricatives (F), and affricates (A); sub-categories of resonants included glides (G), liquids (L), nasals (N), and pharyngeal/glottal segments (Gl). Table 10.5

11 In Nxaʔamxcín orthography: x̌áʕx̌aʕ šƛ̓ámkaʔš.

Table 10.5. Clusters available for analysis, by position.

Cluster	Initial		Medial		Final		**Total**
	Example	Number	Example	Number	Example	Number	
OO	√**kx**ap *chase*	34	√pi**sƛ̓**aʔ *big*	9	√ki**cx** *arrive*	41	**84**
OR	√**ɬw**am *go*	34	–	0	√ʔi**ɬn** *eat*	27	**61**
RO	–	0	√ya**mx̣ʷ**aʔ *basket*	21	√xə**lp** *daylight*	55	**76**
RR	√**yl**am *run*	20	√i**ml**i *Emily*	18	√ḥa**ẇy** *do*	32	**70**
Total		**88**		**48**		**155**	**291**

summarizes the clusters in our dataset, analysed in terms of position, cluster and position being the two primary factors under consideration.

As can be seen from Table 10.5, the number of clusters varies substantially across conditions. To some extent, the uneven number counts reflect distributional properties of different types of clusters in tri-consonantal roots alluded to above and discussed further below. These numbers also clearly reflect the recurrence of specific roots related to the content of the story. The most frequent roots were *√ʔiɬn* (final OR; 15 tokens), *√kicx* (final OO cluster; 13 tokens), *√imli* (medial RR; 12 tokens), *√q̓ʷmaɬ* (initial OR; 12 tokens), *√yamx̣ʷaʔ* (medial RO; 12 tokens), *√ḥaẇy* (final RR; 11 tokens), and *√ylam* (initial RR; 11 tokens). Except where noted otherwise, a maximum of 5 tokens per root were included in the analyses,[12] to avoid a single root skewing the results. For this reason, of the 291 tokens in our dataset, only 217 were analysed acoustically (see Appendix).

Clusters were located and labelled using the Textgrid function in Praat 5.4.04 (Boersma and Weenink 2014), and were coded for a number of predictor and outcomes variables. Predictor variables included: (a) cluster type: OO, OR, RO, RR; (b) position: root-initial, root-final, root-medial; (c) adjacent morphological context (initial and final clusters only): affix versus particle versus word boundary; (d) adjacent phonological context (initial

12 Tokens were excluded on the basis of environment and, when needed, proximity: multiple tokens occurring in similar environments were excluded, until a maximum of 5 was reached. When an additional strategy was needed, tokens that occurred very close to each other in the story were excluded. Tokens were *not* excluded based on realization; realization was unknown during the exclusion process.

and final clusters only): vowel, resonant, obstruent, glottal stop. Outcome variables included: (a) presence versus absence of schwa; (b) duration of schwa (when present); (c) duration of consonants within the cluster;[13] (d) whether a schwa occurred adjacent to the cluster, or outside of it. Cluster coding was extracted to a spreadsheet using a Praat script. Data analysis was conducted using R (R Core Team 2013).

10.4 Results: Distribution and Duration of Schwa

Before embarking on the data analysis proper, it is worth considering the distribution of the clusters at hand, as summarized in Table 10.5. This distribution provides a first indication of the phonological status of various cluster types. First, there are far more root-final clusters than there are clusters in other positions; in particular, root-final RO clusters are very common (55 tokens), considerably more so than their root-initial OR counterparts (34 tokens). Second, root-medial OR clusters and word-initial RO clusters are non-existent. Assuming that token counts represent markedness, at least to some degree, we can say that root-final RO clusters are the least marked, whereas root-initial RO and root-medial OR clusters are the most marked.

Sections 10.4.1 and 10.4.2 below present results relevant for the two research questions that we set out to answer through this work: the first focuses on the *distribution* of schwa in root-internal CC clusters, looking for instrumental support for CH&W's (1997) descriptions of the occurrence of schwa within clusters. The second considers the *duration* of schwa, when it occurs, as a clue to its phonological status, and consequently as a clue to the syllabification of the clusters in which it occurs.

10.4.1 Distribution of Schwa

Recall that the first goal of this study was to provide acoustic evidence for CH&W's description of schwa occurrence within clusters. In this chapter, the realization of clusters was judged based on auditory analysis and

13 In the case of stops and affricates, duration corresponded only to the release portion of the consonant.

visual inspection of the spectrogram and waveform of each token. In our coding system, we first distinguished three types of realization that led to the *lack* of a surface cluster: 'CC merger' was used for cases in which the consonants were merged, e.g., ***√m?amm*** > [m?a**m:**] (Figure 10.3); 'vocalized C' was used for cases in which one of the consonants was vocalized, e.g., ***√ylam*** > [**i**lam] (Figure 10.4); 'missing C' was used where there was no visual or auditory evidence of one of the consonants, e.g., ***√pa?xan*** > [pa**x**an] (Figure 10.5).

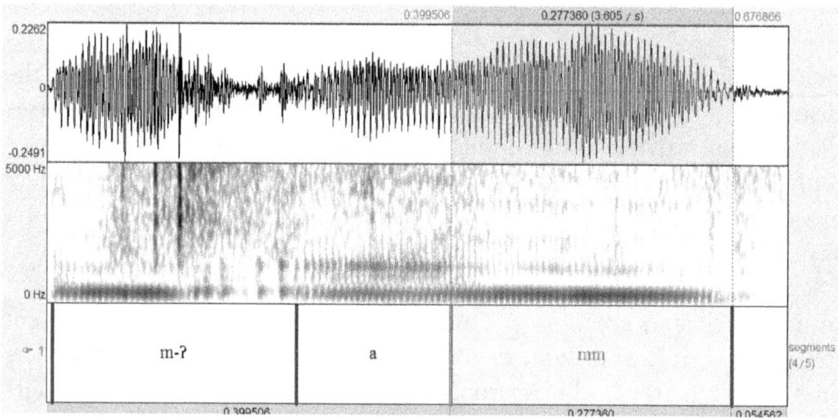

Figure 10.3. *√m?amm* > [m?am:]: 'CC merger' (final cluster).

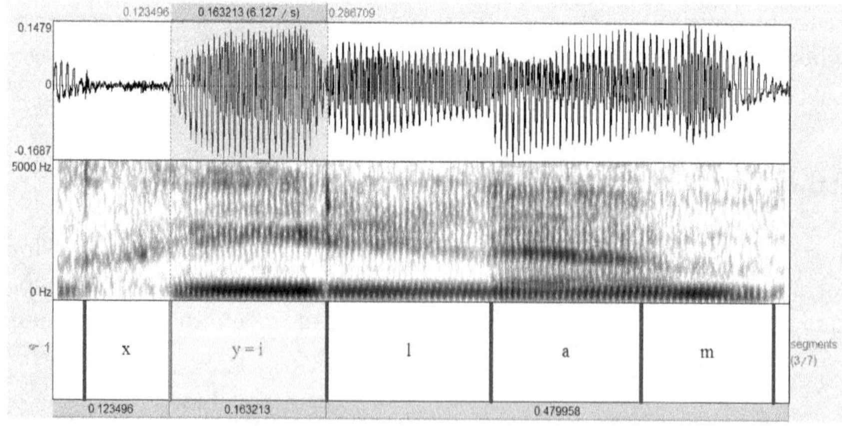

Figure 10.4. *√ylam* > [ilam] in *?ica kʷa?x √ylam*: 'C vocalization' (initial cluster).

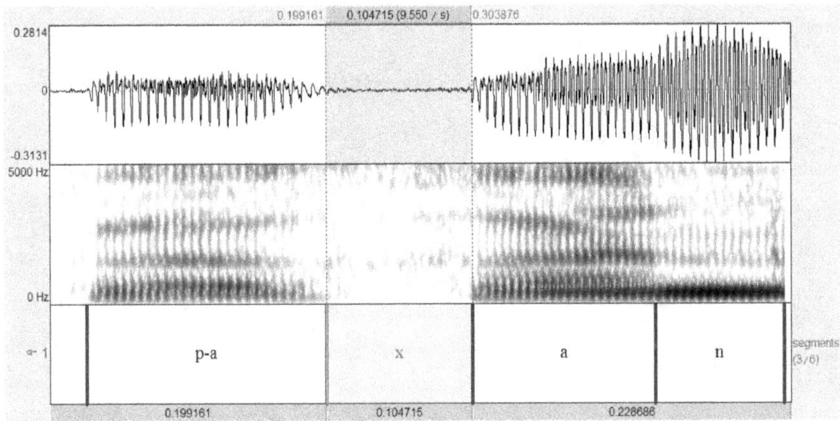

Figure 10.5. √*paʔxan* > [paxan]: 'missing C' (medial cluster).
Note the lack of irregular pitch pulses at the end of the vowel [a] preceding the cluster.

Cases which surfaced *with* clusters were categorized into three subtypes: 'voiced schwa' was used for cases in which there was a clear *voiced* (vocalic) element between the consonants, e.g., √*təɬm* > [təɬəm] (Figure 10.6); 'voiceless schwa' was used in a small number of cases, where there was a clear *voiceless* element between the consonants – this corresponded to frication which differed in spectral composition from that of preceding and following consonants, e.g., √*kicx* > [kici̥x] (Figure 10.7); finally, 'no schwa' was used where there was no clear transitional element between the consonants, either voiced or voiceless, e.g., √*yamx̣ʷaʔ* > [yamx̣ʷaʔ] (Figure 10.8).

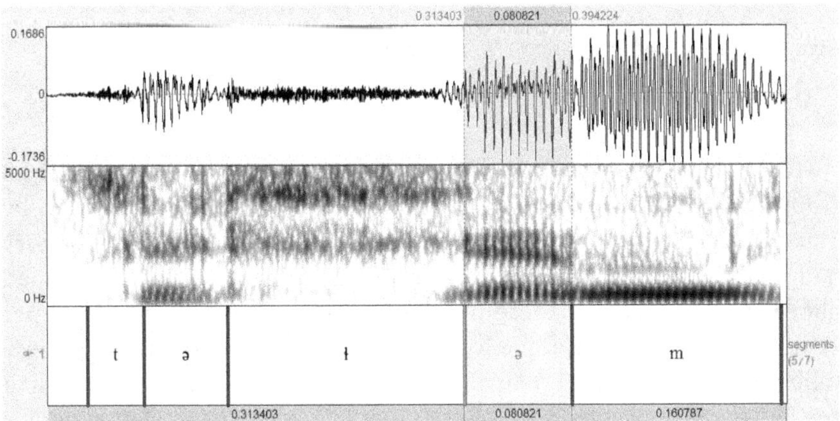

Figure 10.6. √*təɬm* > [təɬəm]: 'voiced schwa' (final cluster).

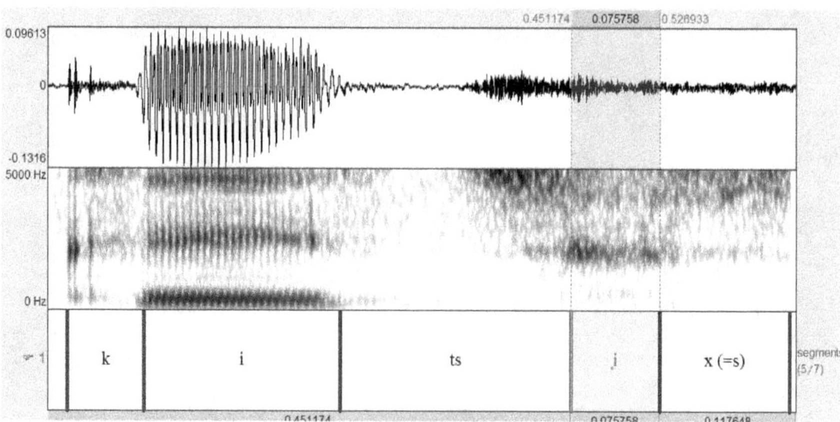

Figure 10.7. √*kicx* > [kici̥x]: 'voiceless schwa' (final cluster).

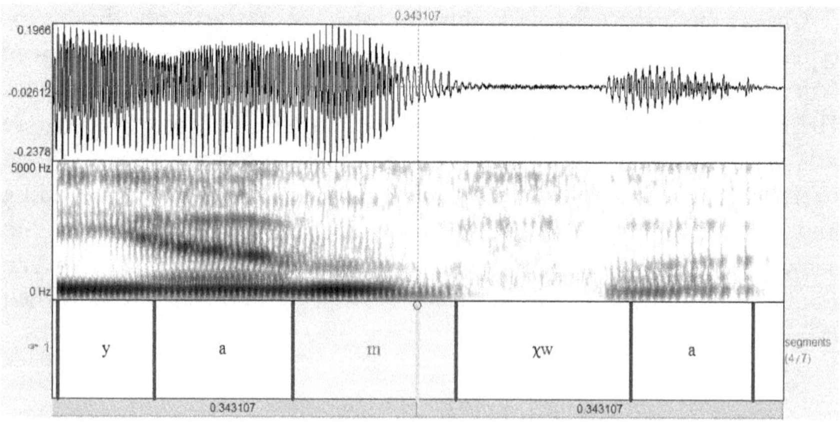

Figure 10.8. √*yamx̣ʷaʔ* > [yamx̣ʷaʔ]: 'no schwa' (medial cluster).

Tables 10.6 (root-initial position), 10.7 (root-final position) and 10.8 (root-medial position) provide raw token counts of each realization by cluster. To simplify presentation, in these tables the umbrella category 'No cluster' is used rather than the finer-grained categories described above. Also, recall that these numbers represent at most 5 tokens per root. This being the case, the total number of tokens presented in these tables is 217 (69 initial, 116 final and 32 medial), substantially fewer than the 291 tokens provided in Tables 10.1 and 10.2 above (see Appendix for token counts analysed per root).

Table 10.6. Cluster realization in root-initial position.

Cluster	No cluster	No schwa	Voiced schwa	Voiceless schwa	Total
OO	0	**25**	3	2	30
OR	3	1	**21**	0	25
RO	–	–	–	–	–
RR	**7**	4	3	0	14

Table 10.6 shows that, root-initially, OO clusters are generally realized without a voiced schwa between the consonants (25/30 tokens). In the three tokens that exhibit a voiced schwa, C1 is a labialized consonant: √***kʷ****tas* (2 tokens) and √***qʷ****tun*; possibly in these cases, schwa is related to the labialized release of C1.[14] OR clusters most often are realized with a voiced schwa (21/25 tokens). RR clusters vary in their production. The 'No cluster' tokens are all cases in which one consonant is vocalized, e.g., √***yl****am* > [**il**am]; the four 'No schwa' cases are tokens of √***mʔ****amm* preceded by the nominalizing prefix /s/, all of which are pronounced with a schwa between the prefix and the root rather than between the two consonants of the cluster: [s-ə**mʔ**am:] (*[s-**mə**ʔam:]); the three 'voiced schwa' tokens are in clusters consisting of a resonant (/l/ or /m/) followed by a glottal stop, cases that are somewhat difficult to analyse acoustically. Aside from the 'No schwa' RR cases, the realization of initial clusters generally supports CH&W's descriptions (see Table 10.2).

Table 10.7. Cluster realization in root-final position.

Cluster	No cluster	No schwa	Voiced schwa	Voiceless schwa	Total
OO	2	**24**	0	6	32
OR	3	0	**9**	0	12
RO	3	**36**	10	0	49
RR	**16**	0	7	0	23

As in initial clusters, root-final OO clusters generally do not exhibit schwas. Final clusters combining a resonant and an obstruent are realized somewhat differently from root-initial ones. In particular, one might expect root-final RO clusters to pattern similarly to root-initial OR clusters, since they are reflections of one another in terms of sonority (rising in initial OR; falling in final RO). However, whereas root-initial OR clusters are fairly consistently separated by a schwa (21/25 tokens; see Table 10.6), root-final

14 Note: other tokens of √**kʷ**tas and √**qʷ**tun do not exhibit a schwa; there is clearly variability in pronunciation in these cases.

RO clusters are most often *not* separated by schwa (36/49 tokens; see Table 10.7). Five of the clusters separated by a schwa are tokens of the root √*təṙq*, in which the cluster presents clear articulatory difficulties, thereby explaining the presence of a (transitional) schwa (cf. Gick and Wilson 2006). The sixth is √pu**ʔs**, with a glottal stop. This is another case where glottal stop presents particular difficulties in analysis: glottal stop is often followed by a short 'echo vowel',[15] a copy of the preceding vowel. In this case then, the occurrence of schwa is not surprising. The other four tokens are √*sawɬ*, √*pulx*, and two tokens of √*kʷanx*. There is no obvious reason why schwas would occur in these cases; in fact, it is the presence of schwa in specifically these cases that led CH&W to propose that final RO clusters do not form complex codas.[16] These four exceptions aside, RO clusters generally do not include schwa. RR clusters vary, just as they did root-initially. The 'No Cluster' cases include 5 tokens of adjacent /m/s in the root √*mʔa**mm***, which are always merged ([sə-mʔa**m:**]) and 11 tokens of clusters including a vocalized /y/, e.g., √*xʷu**ẇy*** > [xʷu**ẇi**]. The resonant /y/ is not always vocalized though; in particular, across tokens of √*ḥa**ẇy***, the realization seems to depend on the manner of articulation of the following segment, e.g., √*ḥa**ẇy-s*** > [ḥa**ẇis**] versus √*ḥa**ẇy-m*** > [ḥa**ẇiyəm**].[17] Of the 7 tokens that include a schwa, 3 are of the root √*ḥa**ẇy***; the remaining 4 include other combinations of resonants in the roots √*ʔaka**nm*** (2 tokens), √*ka**l̓m***, and √*kə**ṙm***. Overall then, our results support CH&W's description of final OO and RR clusters (although they do not talk about RR cluster merger at all). Where our findings diverge from their description is with respect to RO clusters, which in our examples do not generally exhibit a schwa.

Finally, Table 10.8 provides the results for root-medial clusters. OO clusters pattern as they do in initial and final position, although the variability found in initial and final position is missing in medial position: root-medially, they are systematically realized as 'No schwa' (7/7 tokens). Medial RO clusters pattern the same way that they do in final position: generally they surface without a schwa (9/14 tokens). Of the three that exhibit a schwa, two involve a glottal which, as discussed above, is often followed by an echo vowel (regardless of position): √*ka**ʔɬ**as* and √*pa**ʔx**an*; the third is a token of √*ya**mx̣ʷ**aʔ*, the realization of which is variable (in the other 4 tokens of this root, there is no schwa). Medial RR clusters are most often realized with a voiced schwa between them (10/11), unlike in root-initial and root-final position where they are more likely to vocalize.

15 This is a pattern found in various languages in the Salish family. See, for example, Jacobs (2012).

16 Shahin (2007) reports on a few such examples in St'át'imcets.

17 Note: [i] is the realization of schwa before [y].

Table 10.8. Cluster realization in root-medial position

Cluster	No cluster	No schwa	Voiced schwa	Voiceless schwa	Total
OO	0	7	0	0	7
OR	–	–	–	–	–
RO	2	**9**	3	0	14
RR	1	0	**10**	0	11

Following on the earlier research on Nxaʔamxcín syllable structure reported in Section 10.2, Czaykowska-Higgins (2002) observed that the occurrence of schwa in unstressed 2-consonant OO roots appears to depend on the first segment of the following suffix:[18] if the OO root-sequence is followed by an *obstruent*-initial suffix, a schwa is inserted into it (e.g., *√łċ = qin = aʔst-tn* [łəċqnáʔsn̥] 'salmon club'); if it is followed by a *vowel*-initial suffix, no schwa is inserted (e.g., *√łċ = alps = n* [łċálpsn̥] 'hit with a club'); if it is followed by a *resonant*-initial suffix, occurrence of schwa is variable (cf. *√łċ = min* [łċəmi̥n] 'a whip' versus *s-√tx = lup* [stxlúp] 'underblanket, undersheet'). If these observations are correct, then they point to the possibility that the surface realization of clusters depends on syllabification. Although we did not examine 2-C roots for this study, we did consider a parallel situation for 3-C roots, namely, what happens to root-final two-consonant OO sequences in different environments. Table 10.9 considers only root-final OO clusters followed by suffixes, focusing on the initial segment of the suffix (obstruent versus resonant versus vowel). Although there are comparatively few tokens in our dataset (only 17), it seems relatively clear that final OO clusters are never realized with a voiced schwa between the two obstruents, even when they are followed by a suffix-initial obstruent. This finding is not consistent with Czaykowska-Higgins' observations for OO roots,[19] and confirms our earlier findings (Table 10.6) that OO clusters tend not to be broken up by schwas, regardless of the following environment (but see Section 10.5 where we consider whether schwa surfaces *following* OO clusters).

18 See Shaw's (2002) extensive analysis of OO clusters in a related Coast Salish language.

19 There may be a structural reason related to constraints on root shapes for the difference in OO sequences in 2-C roots as opposed to OO sequences in final position of 3- or 4-C roots. Our findings suggests that it would be useful to examine OO clusters in roots with different numbers of Cs instrumentally to see whether Czaykowska-Higgins' (2002) description holds up under acoustic analysis.

Table 10.9. Realization of root-final OO clusters followed by suffixes with different initial segments.

Suffix-initial segment	No cluster	No schwa	Voiced schwa	Voiceless schwa	Total
Obstruent	0	**7**	0	2	9
Resonant	0	**5**	0	1	6
Vowel	0	**2**	0	0	2

Table 10.10 repeats the expected distribution of schwa across clusters from Table 10.2, and adds the observed patterns based on our data. In terms of distribution, what we see is that OO clusters do indeed have special status on the surface in that, while clusters involving at least one resonant (OR, RO, RR) are regularly realized with a schwa, OO clusters almost never are. As far as root-initial OR and their corresponding root-final RO sequences are concerned, our data show that whereas root-initial OR clusters generally exhibit a schwa (22/26 tokens with schwa), root-final RO clusters generally do not (10/49 tokens with schwa). This asymmetry has not been explicitly noted in CH&W's previous work on Nxaʔamxcín, although it is in fact compatible with their descriptions of schwa's durational properties (see Section 10.4.2 below). RR clusters generally pattern as predicted.

Table 10.10. Acoustic confirmation of claims summarized in Table 10.2.

	Underlying	Expected surface	Observed surface	Prediction met?
Initial	OO	OO*	OO*	Yes
	OR	OəR	OəR	Yes
	RR	RəR or R̩R/VR (if R1 = glide)	RəR, VR, əRR	Yes (with the addition of əRR, when preceded by prefix C)
	RO	RəO or R̩O/VR (if R1 = glide)	–	–
Final	OO	OO*	OO*	Yes
	OR	OəR	OəR	Yes
	RR	RəR or RR̩/RV (if R2 = glide)	RəR, RV, R:	Yes, mostly (no clear RR̩)
	RO	R^{ə}O	RO (RəO)	(No) (not many transitional schwas)
Medial	CC	C^{ə}C	CəC	Yes

* Cluster-initial stops are released.

10.4.2 Duration of Schwa

A close look at Table 10.10 shows that, in previous descriptions of Nxaʔamxcín, schwas have not all been treated as equal. In particular, root-final RO and all medial clusters are said to include short, transitional schwas in them (superscripted in Table 10.10), as opposed to the longer, epenthetic schwas that are claimed to occur in other clusters. In terms of syllabification, common assumptions in the Salish literature are that transitional or excrescent schwas appear due to low-level articulatory considerations, and that they do not have phonological status. In contrast, epenthetic schwas *do* have phonological status, serving as syllable nuclei. Thus, to answer our second question – how are clusters syllabified in Nxaʔamxcín – it is useful to consider schwa duration as well as distribution.

In compiling the duration results presented below, a number of tokens were excluded from the analysis: one token of the root √*ʔiɬn* (final OR cluster) and the root √*pulx* (final RO cluster) were excluded because they had unusually long schwas (152 ms and 86 ms respectively).[20] All five tokens of √*tər̓q* were also excluded, because these involve a clear articulatory conflict and therefore an extended transition (perceived as schwa). Finally, several tokens with glottal stop were excluded: the three initial RR tokens that had a schwa all included a glottal stop in C2 position; the schwas in these clusters had very different durations (46 ms, 88 ms and 109 ms), and the mean was thus not particularly meaningful. In addition, two of the three medial RO clusters also had a glottal stop as the R, and very long schwas (106 ms and 142 ms). In total then, 12 tokens were excluded from the analysis, leading to a total of 54 tokens, falling into 7 position~cluster pairs (Figure 10.9): final OR (8 tokens), final RO (4 tokens), final RR (7 tokens), initial OO (3 tokens), initial OR (21 tokens), medial RO (1 token), and medial RR (10 tokens).

Obviously, these number counts are very small and unevenly distributed across pairs, and we therefore deemed it inappropriate to conduct statistical analyses on the data. In addition, several key position~cluster pairs are missing, either because they do not contain schwas (final and medial OO clusters) or because we simply do not have available tokens to analyse in our dataset (intial RO, medial OR and initial RR clusters). Nonetheless, the patterns observed are telling. Overall, Figure 10.9 shows that the longest schwas occur in final OR and RR clusters (with mean durations of 51 and 55 ms respectively), clusters which, based on the Sonority Sequencing Principle, are likely not parsed as syllable codas. Schwas in initial OO

20 In the case of √*pulx*, schwa was also partially devoiced.

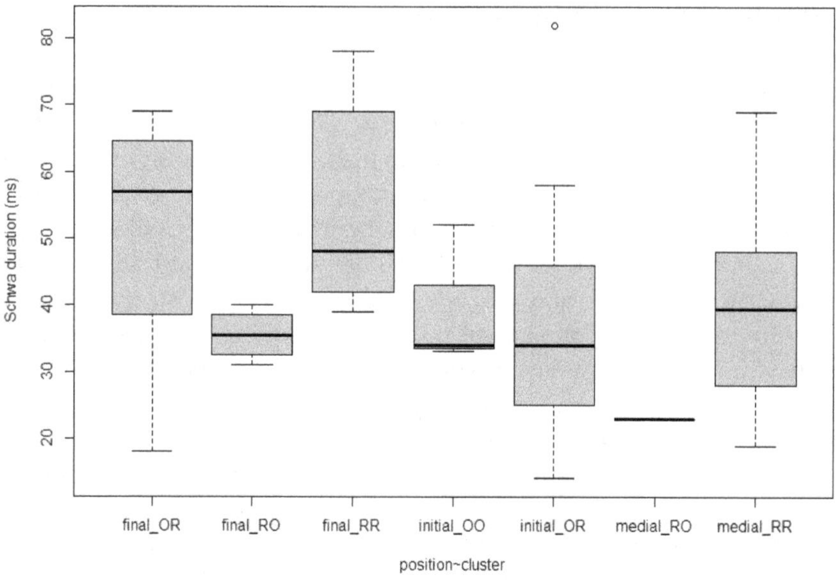

Figure 10.9. Schwa duration by position~cluster pairing.

(mean: 40 ms), initial OR (mean: 37 ms), final RO (mean: 36 ms), medial RO (single token: 23 ms), and medial RR (mean: 39 ms) clusters are shorter. If the differences between the longer and shorter schwas are meaningful, this suggests that schwas in final OR and final RR clusters are epenthetic (overall mean: 53 ms), whereas, when they do occur, schwas elsewhere are excrescent (overall mean: 37 ms). In particular, based on durational findings, the implication is that final RO clusters and initial OR clusters might not be heterosyllabic, contrary to previous claims.

10.4.3 Summary of Results

Our study of the distribution of schwa within root-internal CC clusters has shown two things: (1) in support of CH&W (1997) and Czaykowska-Higgins (2002), OOs do have special status, in the sense that they are the only type of cluster in which schwas do not tend to occur, and (2) building on both these works, root-initial OR and root-final RO clusters behave somewhat differently: schwas tend to occur in root-initial OR clusters, but do not tend to occur in root-final RO clusters, although when schwa does occur in either, it is approximately the same duration.

In more general terms, and in line with what Flemming et al. (2008) and others have said about Montana Salish, schwas occur preceding resonants much more frequently than they do preceding obstruents: in 59 per cent of clusters with R as their second member versus 13 per cent of clusters with O as their second member (see Table 10.11).

Table 10.11. Frequency of schwa occurrence preceding resonants versus obstruents.

Position	Preceding R (OR, RR)	Preceding O (OO, RO)
Initial	62% (24/39)	13% (4/31)
Final	46% (16/35)	13% (10/80)
Medial	91% (10/11)	14% (3/21)
Overall	**59% (50/85)**	**13% (17/132)**

In terms of duration, despite small and uneven token counts across positions, we have found a relatively clear split between the schwas that occur in final OR and RR clusters (53 ms overall) versus in clusters that appear elsewhere (37 ms overall). These two different schwas likely correspond to epenthetic versus excrescent schwa respectively, as their durational differences do resemble those previously described in the Salish literature (see results reported in the work of Shahin and Blake mentioned in Section 10.2).

In the remainder of this chapter, we consider the implications of the distribution and durational properties of schwa within root-internal CC clusters in terms of how they are syllabified, and offer possible alternative explanations in cases where syllable structure does not seem to fully account for the observed patterns.

10.5 Discussion

The results presented in Section 10.4 allow us to now address the research questions that we set out with: (1) Can we confirm instrumentally CH&W's (1997) descriptions of Nxaʔamxcín cluster realization? (2) Can we make any claims about the syllabification of these clusters, based on instrumental analysis? Sections 10.5.1 and 10.5.2 below provide a discussion of these two questions in turn, including the implications of our study for the Salish literature on cluster syllabification.

10.5.1 Evaluating Previous Claims about Nxaʔamxcín Clusters

The results of our instrumental analysis of Nxaʔamxcín clusters confirm that sonority plays a role in how clusters are pronounced in the language. However, our results are not entirely consistent with previous claims about Sonority Sequencing Principle violations in Nxaʔamxcín. We have shown that clusters containing two obstruents have a strong tendency to surface without any intervening vowel, both when the OO cluster occurs in root-initial position and when it occurs in root-final position. We have also shown that underlying RR clusters are always pronounced with some modification: either a schwa is inserted between the two Rs, or one of them becomes vocalized/syllabic (in #RR clusters, the first R is modified, while in RR# the second R is modified). Finally, we can say that #OR and RO# do not pattern the same way, at least in terms of the distribution of schwa, with many more cases of schwa in #OR clusters than in RO# clusters. Overall then, our data provide (a) instrumental confirmation that Nxaʔamxcín OO do not exhibit schwa insertion, and (b) evidence of subtle distinctions in the patterning of #OR versus OR# clusters with respect to schwa distribution (further discussed in Section 10.5.2).

The instrumental results discussed above also foreground the relevance to Nxaʔamxcín of the generalization, made by studies of other Salish languages, that one environment in which schwas are consistently inserted is preceding resonant consonants. This point is further reinforced when we examine the proportion of schwas occurring adjacent to, rather than inside, each cluster. Indeed, although the focus of this study was on schwa occurrence between consonants in a root-internal cluster, schwa also sometimes occurred preceding or following the root-cluster as a whole; for example *s-√qəl̓t-mixʷ* was realized [sqə**l̓t**əmixʷ], with a schwa after the consonants in the final [l̓t] cluster and before the following [mixʷ] suffix. Our findings show an interesting and relevant pattern here, summarized in Tables 10.12 and 10.13. With root-final clusters (Table 10.12), the manner of articulation of the segment following the cluster had a large effect on the likelihood of a schwa occurring adjacent to the cluster, in particular if the cluster was followed by a suffix (rather than a particle or word). Specifically, schwa often occurred preceding a suffix-initial resonant (22/28 cases), but rarely preceding any other consonants, regardless of morphology (particle/word versus sufffix).

With root-initial clusters (Table 10.13), the preceding segment did not have a clear effect on the likelihood of a schwa occurring adjacent to the

Table 10.12. Proportion of schwa occurrence following final clusters, by manner of following segment.

Following segment	Suffix	Particle/word	Total
Obstruent	2/25	2/16	4/41
Glottal stop*	–	–	–
Resonant	22/28	3/13	25/41

* Glottal stop is listed separately here; as mentioned above, it is classified as a resonant on phonological grounds, even though phonetically it is a stop consonant.

Table 10.13. Proportion of schwa occurrence preceding initial clusters, by manner of preceding segment.

Preceding segment	Prefix	Particle/word	Total
Obstruent	4/12	1/7	5/19
Glottal stop	0/5	0/2	0/7
Resonant	1/3	1/7	2/10
Vowel	4/11	0/15	4/26
Pause	0/1	0/7	0/8

cluster; in all cases, relatively few instances of schwa occurred between initial clusters and preceding segments.[21]

Further analysis of the data showed that whether or not schwa occurred preceding initial clusters depended primarily on the manner of articulation of the initial segment of the cluster: of the 14 initial RR clusters, 7 were preceded by a schwa, e.g., *s-√**m**ʔamm* > [sə**m**ʔam:] (mentioned in Section 10.4 above). This is in contrast to initial OO clusters, in which there was never a preceding schwa (0/30 cases) and OR clusters, in which a preceding schwa occurred rarely (4/25 cases).

Overall then, it seems that schwa is much more likely to occur preceding a resonant than preceding an obstruent, whether this resonant is part of the root cluster (Tables 10.6 and 10.7) or not (Table 10.12). This result is also not entirely consistent with Sonority Sequencing or with previous analyses of the realization of Nxaʔamxcín clusters, since it suggests that schwas are inserted into sequences where the second consonant is a resonant regardless of syllable structure (or morphological) considerations. This raises the questions, then, of whether syllabification plays a role at all in the realization of clusters, and of whether, in turn, the observed patterns

21 These findings support claims in Czaykowska-Higgins (1998) about phonological domains.

can tell us anything about syllabification. We turn to these questions in the next section.

10.5.2 The Role of Syllable Structure in the Distribution of Schwa

Table 10.14 (repeated from Table 10.2 above) summarizes CH&W's claims about how various clusters are syllabified in Nxaʔamxcín. In this section, we consider support for these claims, and more generally for the role of syllable structure in the parsing of clusters.

Table 14. Syllabifications proposed by CH&W (1997)

	Underlying	Syllabification
Initial	OO	O.Ov
	OR	Oə.Rv
	RR	Rə.Rv
	RO	Rə.Ov
Final	OO	vO.O
	OR	v.OəR
	RR	v.RəR
	RO	vRᵊ.O
Medial	CC	vCᵊ.Cv

A number of secondary findings reported above support the idea that syllable structure and syllabification preferences do have an important role to play in the distribution of schwas and concomitantly in the parsing of Nxaʔamxcín clusters. First, as we saw above, in C2 position in OR# and RR# clusters, the resonant /y/ usually vocalizes, but its surface realization seems to depend on the manner of articulation of the following segment. Recall that across tokens of *√ḥaw̓y*, for instance, /y/ vocalizes if the following segment is an obstruent, but not if it is a resonant (or a vowel), e.g., ***√ḥaw̓y-s*** > [ḥa**w̓is**] versus ***√ḥaw̓y-m*** > [ḥa**w̓yəm**].[22] Vocalization has long been viewed by phonologists as the result of a glide moving into a position

22 Transcriptions in Kinkade's and Czaykowska-Higgins' fieldnotes suggest a similar situation for C1 glides in #GR and #GO roots (i.e., G vocalizes if preceded by a consonant, but surfaces as Gv if preceded by a vowel). Similarly, the suffix -wa-'topical object marker' surfaces as [wá] when stressed, but as [u] when unstressed and interconsonantal. We do not exemplify these cases here because we do not have relevant examples in the text.

where it can be parsed as a syllable nucleus. Its existence in Nxaʔamxcín cluster parsing thus suggests some role for syllable structure.

Second, as already discussed, there are four 'No schwa' cases that are tokens of √*mʔamm* preceded by the nominalizing prefix /s/; all of these are pronounced with a schwa between the prefix and the root rather than between the two consonants of the cluster: [s-ə**mʔ**am:] (*[s-**mə**ʔam:]). If the insertion of schwas preceding resonants were simply governed by the presence of a resonant, then in cases of this kind, where there are two resonants in a row, one might expect two schwas: *[s-ə**m**əʔam:]. The fact that that is not the preferred parsing suggests again that structural considerations play a role in pronunciation such that the attested parse results in the construction of two simple CvC syllables.[23]

Third, in Section 10.4 we saw also that medial clusters generally have a relatively short schwa between them compared to the one found between consonants in final clusters. For example, schwas in medial RR clusters have a mean duration of 39 ms, while those in final RR and OR clusters have mean duration of 53 ms. This difference in duration suggests that the two C's in medial clusters are syllabified into separate syllables, and that the schwa in medial clusters is a transitional element. This is in contrast to final RR and OR clusters, which require an epenthetic schwa between them for structural reasons.

In addition to these secondary findings, the frequency counts that we laid out above lead to considerations of markedness and typology, and thus also to a consideration of the role of syllabification in Nxaʔamxcín consonant cluster parsing. Recall that CH&W's syllable analysis claimed that Nxaʔamxcín allows only simple onsets and codas. Their analysis predicts, therefore, two kinds of schwas: those that occur in positions where they can head a syllable (epenthetic) versus those that occur in positions that are between syllables (excrescent). Epenthetic vowels in turn should be longer than excrescent vowels. As Figure 10.9 shows, final OR and RR clusters have relatively longer schwas (53 ms) (there are no initial RO examples in our data). All other clusters (initial OR, final RO, medial RO and medial RR) have much shorter schwas (37 ms). Although these data must be taken as preliminary, assuming they are representative of a broader sampling, they have very clear implications for Nxaʔamxcín syllable structure since

23 Note that the initial s-'nominalizer' in this word is a prefix. The fact that its presence affects the position of schwa insertion suggests that this particular prefix may be in the same syllabification domain as roots, and that the domain of syllabification in Nxaʔamxcín may be as large as the word domain (Czaykowska-Higgins 1998).

they suggest that final OR and RR clusters are not tautosyllabic codas, but instead are broken up by an epenthetic schwa: OəR and RəR, as was claimed to be the case in CH&W. In contrast, all other clusters seem to have a different status, because they have smaller, excrescent schwas appearing within them. Note that this difference cannot be due to a final lengthening effect because, although final ROs can sometimes surface with schwas, the schwas in these cases are not long.

According to Kreitman (2006, 2012), OR onset clusters are cross-linguistically the most common, and the least marked, as predicted by the SSP, and their occurrence in a language is predicted by the existence of onset clusters of the other types: RO onsets are the most marked, followed by RR, OO and OR cases. As far as coda clusters are concerned, the results mirror those for onsets in the sense that the most common coda clusters are of the shape RO, followed by OO, RR and the least common OR codas (Pizzo 2009). These onset/coda typologies predict, then, that if a language has OO onsets it should also have OR onsets, and similarly, if it has OO codas, it should also have RO codas. RO and RR onsets, and OR and RR codas, are predicted to occur rarely. The typologies and implicational relationships predict that, if clustering effects reflect syllabification, then, since Nxaʔamxcín has OO clusters initially and finally, it should also have initial #OR clusters and final RO# clusters. What this suggests, therefore, is that Nxaʔamxcín may actually be a language that allows complex onsets of the two unmarked types #OR and #OO and complex codas of the two unmarked types #RO and OO#. To corroborate this, we first consider how OO clusters are syllabified in Nxaʔamxcín, and then turn to #OR and RO# cases.

Three analyses of OO syllabification have been proposed in the literature. As mentioned above, CH&W claim that the first O in initial #OO clusters and the second O in final OO# clusters is unsyllabified, and moraically licensed, in the sense of Bagemihl (1991); as such, it would be incorporated into prosodic structure at the foot or word, but not at the syllabic level.

Urbanczyk (2001) hypothesizes for Lushootseed that obstruents are onsets to syllables headed by voiceless schwas, and that voiced schwas occurring between obstruents and resonants are the result of pre-resonant voicing of the voiceless schwa. Shaw (2002) proposes that all consonants in hən̓q̓əmin̓əm̓ are parsed into syllables, and that OO clusters are complex onsets in root- and stem-initial positions.

It is likely impossible, based on the data at hand, to tease apart CH&W's and Shaw's (2002) analyses. To do this, we would need a more controlled study with triads, of the type described by Gafos and colleagues (e.g.,

Shaw, Gafos, Hoole and Zeroual 2011), where alignment to the V landmark is used to determine whether consonant clusters are tautosyllabic or heterosyllabic. However, our data suggest that we can at least rule out Urbanczyk's proposal by considering the release duration of stops in OO clusters. In Nxaʔamxcín, as in other Salish languages, when a stop occurs as the first consonant (C1) in a cluster, it is always released. It is this release of C1 that Urbanczyk (2001) has suggested might be equivalent to a voiceless schwa, and might act as a syllable nucleus, leading to the addition of a syllable: [Oə̥.O]. If this is the case, then in OO clusters (which don't have voiced schwas), one might expect the release of C1 to be equivalent in duration to an epenthetic schwa (53 ms in Nxaʔamxcín – see Figure 10.9).

Figure 10.10 compares the duration of plain (non-ejective, non-labialized) stops (merged across place of articulation) in stop-obstruent clusters without schwas (18 tokens, all stop-fricative) versus in stop-resonant clusters with schwas (6 tokens: 5 stop-glide tokens and 1 stop-nasal token),

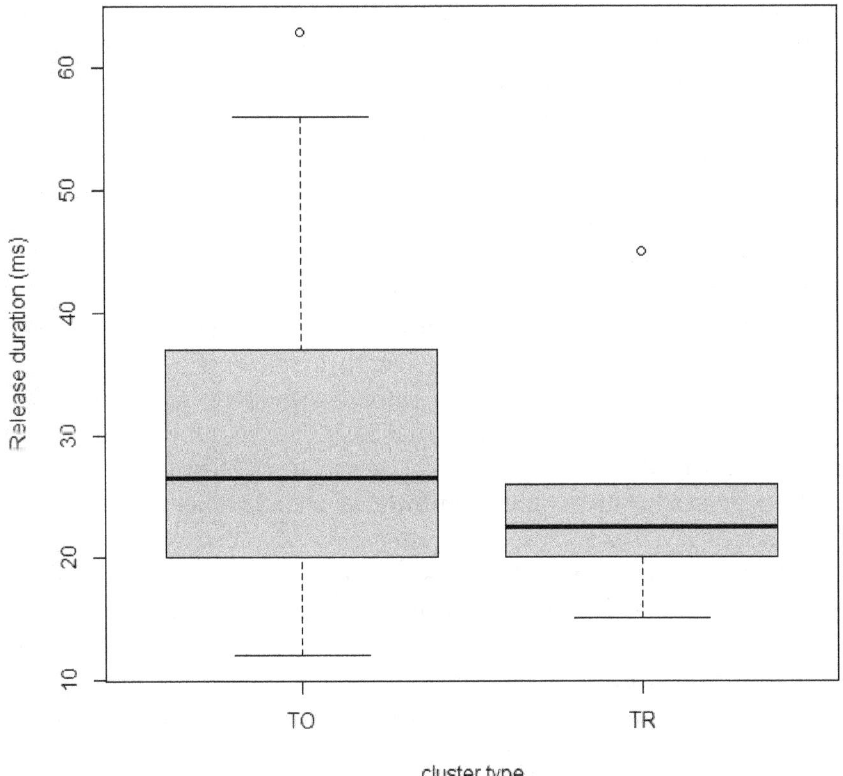

Figure 10.10. Stop releases in stop-O (without schwa) versus stop-R (with schwa) sequences.

merged across initial and final positions. Although very little data is available in our dataset, the patterns displayed in Figure 10.10 suggest two things: first, the average duration of the stop releases in stop-O clusters is longer (30 ms) than it is in stop-R clusters (25 ms). Second, even in stop-O clusters, the duration of the release is in the range of excrescent schwa rather than epenthetic schwa. In other words, even though stop releases are slightly longer preceding obstruents than resonants, they are not long enough to warrant analysing them as equivalent to an epenthetic schwa that provides a voiceless nucleus to an additional syllable.

What about the syllabification of initial OR and final RO clusters? Recall that #OR clusters are much more likely to include a schwa than are RO# clusters, suggesting that they are syllabified differently. It turns out though that when schwa *does* occur, whether it is in #OR or in RO# clusters, its duration is the same (37 ms versus 36 ms), and in the range of excrescent schwa (Figure 10.9). The implication is that, in fact, both of these clusters are tautosyllabic. Taking Kreitman's (2006, 2012) and Pizzo's (2009) work into consideration, we are led to the hypothesis that, contrary to the claims of CH&W, Nxaʔamxcín actually allows complex OO and OR onsets, and complex OO and RO codas. While our data do not allow us to prove this hypothesis beyond a doubt, our phonetic analysis certainly points us in this direction.

If OO and OR onsets, and OO and RO codas, are all well-formed in Nxaʔamxcín, why is it the case that schwa insertion occurs in some of these clusters more often than in others? Both articulatory and perceptual factor are likely at play. It is not surprising that schwa never appears within OO clusters: all obstruents in Nxaʔamxcín are voiceless; it would be highly unlikely to have a voiced schwa between two voiced segments unless it were for structural (syllabic) reasons, since this would require unnecessary articulatory (laryngeal) effort. #OR and RO# clusters on the other hand include a voiced R, and it is reasonable that the articulatory timing features of these clusters involves a short transitional period between the two consonants, perceived as a schwa (see further discussion below).

Perceptual considerations also likely contribute to schwa occurrence in #OR (and RO#) but not OO sequences. For example, based on the P-map hypothesis, Steriade (2001, 2008) has proposed that cluster modifications that involve smaller changes in perceptual cues are preferred to those which involve larger changes: this means that epenthesis is hypothesized to occur in those sequences in which its occurrence would result in a sequence that is perceptually relatively similar to the input sequence. The concept of perceptual similarity is used by Fleischhacker (2001, 2005) to account for the observation that, contrary to what the SSP would lead us to expect, unmarked OR onset clusters permit intrusion/epenthesis in loanword adaptation, whereas the more marked OO onset clusters do not. She argues that the asymmetry occurs because there is greater perceptual similarity between an OR cluster and its corresponding epenthesized OVR sequence, than there is between an OO cluster and its corresponding epenthesized OVO sequence. If we take perceptibility into consideration, the fact that #OR (and RO#) clusters are sometimes pronounced with a schwa in Nxaʔamxcín could be due not to constraints on or requirements of well-formed onsets (and codas) in Nxaʔamxcín, but rather to the fact that they are not explicitly prevented based on perceptual considerations.

As to why schwa occurs more frequently in #OR than in RO# clusters, the answer is less clear. Work on perceptibility effects has considered epenthesis (as well as deletion and assimilation) in different kinds of clusters, and has proposed various mechanisms, such as acoustic disjuncture (Yun 2014) or sonority angle (Fullwood 2014), to try to explain the observation that different types of clusters are affected by different simplification processes. In relation to Salish languages, Flemming has suggested that Montana Salish (and by association Nxaʔamxcín) is affected by a perceptual correlate related to absolute sonority, whereby all resonant consonants split into a schwa-resonant sequence through a process that he terms 'fission' (2008: 31). Flemming does not discuss what the phonetic basis might be for fission; it is possible that it results from articulatory timing effects such as those discussed in Gick, Campbell, Oh and Tamburri-Watt (2006) for liquids in different syllabic positions. In any case, both explanations based in perception, and articulatory timing explanations, seem like fruitful avenues to pursue in future work, particularly since there is an asymmetry in the position in which schwa occurs: in #OR cases, sequences exhibit schwa preceding R, whereas in RO# sequences, schwa (in the rare intances that it occurs) precedes O.

10.6 Conclusion

If the discussion in Section 10.5 is on the right track, then it has three significant implications for the understanding of Nxaʔamxcín consonant cluster parsing. First, it confirms that sonority distinctions play a major role in the parsing of consonant clusters in Nxaʔamxcín. Interestingly, though, it shows that rather than OO clusters being special, it is actually resonants that are special in Salish languages in terms of the distribution of schwa, in line with Flemming et al.'s (2008) claims about Montana Salish. Second, it suggests that, contrary to the hypotheses of CH&W, Nxaʔamxcín may allow complex onsets of the type OR and OO, and complex codas of the type RO and OO. Maximal syllables in Nxaʔamxcín might thus potentially be of the following shape: C1C2VC3C4, where C1C2 = OR or OO, and C3C4 = RO or OO. Third, it suggests that the parsing of clusters in Nxaʔamxcín, specifically in terms of where schwa does versus does not occur, is due to a complex combination and interaction of phonological constraints on syllable structure, perceptibility and articulatory timing effects.

As mentioned throughout this chapter, limitations due to the nature of our dataset mean that our findings, and consequently our interpretation of these findings, must be taken as preliminary. To the extent possible (given limited resources), future studies using more controlled datasets (e.g., triads like those used by Shaw et al. 2011) should be undertaken. These will undoubtedly further our understanding of how syllables are built in Salish languages, and more generally of how clusters are parsed cross-linguistically.

Appendix: Types and Tokens of Roots

Medial clusters	Token #	Initial clusters	Token #	Final clusters	Token #
kaʔɬás	2	c̓q̓ál	1	c̓uw̓y	2
p̓ísƛ̕’aʔ	5	c̓líx	1	hapy	1
paʔxán	2	cní	4	ḥaw̓y	5
síncaʔ	1	cqánaʔ	2	kál̓m	1
taʔlám	1	kʷnám	1	káɬx	1
t’ámkaʔ	1	k̓ʷtas	4	kámx	5
x̣əlwíʔ	2	kxáp	5	kər̓m	1
yámx̣ʷaʔ	5	lʔaw̓	1	kícx	5
ʔac̓x̣íl	2	ɬkáp	2	kínt	2
ʔímli	5	ɬwám	5	kʷánx	2
ʔincúl	2	mʔámm	5	luʔp	1
ʔinwí	1	mʔástm	1	ɬítk̓	2
ʔinca	1	mʔúm̓t	2	ɬət̓p	2
ʔinwíl	1	q̓ʷmáɬ	5	mʔamm	5
puʔlaʔ	1	qʷtún	2	mʔúm̓t	2
		slap	2	nált	2
		tw̓ít	5	naqs	2
		txác̓	3	núx̣ʷt	1
		txʷúl	5	p̓alk̓	1
		x̣lí	1	p̓uk̓ʷt	1
		xƛ̕’út	2	pulx	1
		x̣ʔít	1	puʔs	1
		ylám	4	qack	1
				qəl̓t	5
				q̓ʷáɬt	3
				sáwɬ	3
				súʔkʷ	2
				tər’q	5
				tínx	2
				wáʔx̣	1
				wə́nt	1
				x̣áct	2
				tə́ɬm	4
				x̣ə́lp	5
				x̣əlq	1
				x̣ʷuw̓y	5
				yáʕp	2
				y̓aw̓t	2
				ʔac̓x̣	2
				ʔakánm	2
				ʔiɬn	5
				ʔípn	1
				ʔítx	4
				ʔakást	1

References

Bagemihl, B. (1991). Syllable structure in Bella Coola. *Linguistic Inquiry*, 22(4): 589–646.

Bates, D. and Carlson, B.F. (1992). Simple syllables in Spokane Salish. *Linguistic Inquiry*, 23(4), 653–9.

Bianco,V. (1996). *The role of sonority in the prosody of Cowichan*. MA thesis, University of Victoria, Victoria, BC.

Blake, S. (2000). *On the distribution and representation of schwa in Sliammon (Salish): Descriptive and theoretical perspectives*. Doctoral dissertation, University of British Columbia, Vancouver.

Blake, S. and Shahin, K. (2008). On the phonetics of schwa in Sliammon (M. Comox Salish): Implications for the representations of Salish vowels. *Canadian Acoustics/Acoustique Canadienne*, 36(4), 42–3.

Blevins, J. (2003). The independent nature of phonotactic constraints: An alternative to syllable-based approaches. In C. Féry and R. van de Vijver (ds.), *The syllable in optimality theory* (pp. 375–404). Cambridge: Cambridge University Press.

Boersma, P. and Weenink, D. (2014). *Praat: Doing phonetics by computer*. http://www.fon.hum.uva.nl/praat/

Chitoran, I., Goldstein, L. and Byrd, D. (2002). Gestural overlap and recoverability: Articulatory evidence from Georgian. In C. Gussenhoven and N. Warner (eds.), *Laboratory phonology 7* (pp. 419–47). Cambridge: Cambridge University Press.

Clements, G.N. (1990). The role of the sonority cycle in core syllabification. In J. Kingston and M. Beckman (eds.), *Papers in Laboratory Phonology I* (pp. 283–333). Cambridge: Cambridge University Press.

Czaykowska-Higgins, E. (1993). Cyclicity and stress in Moses-Columbia Salish (Nxaʔamxcin). *Natural Language & Linguistic Theory*, 11(2), 197–278.

Czaykowska-Higgins, E. (1998). The morphological and phonological constituent structure of words in Moses-Columbia Salish (Nxaʔamxcín). In E. Czaykowska-Higgins and M.D. Kinkade (eds.), *Salish languages and linguistics: Theoretical and descriptive perspectives, Trends in linguistics, Studies and monographs 107* (pp. 153–96). Berlin/New York: Mouton de Gruyter.

Czaykowska-Higgins, E. (2002). Prefixes, roots, and domains in Nxaʔamxcín. Paper presented at Canadian Linguistics Association/Association Canadienne de Linguistique Conference, May 2002, Toronto, Ont.

Czaykowska-Higgins, E. and Kinkade, M.D. (1998). Salish languages and linguistics. In E. Czaykowska-Higgins and M.D. Kinkade (eds.), *Salish languages and linguistics: Theoretical and descriptive perspectives, Trends in linguistics, Studies and monographs 107* (pp. 1–68). Berlin/New York: Mouton de Gruyter.

Czaykowska-Higgins, E. and Willett, M.L. (1997). Simple syllables in Nxaʔamxcín. *International Journal of American Linguistics*, 63(3), 385–411.

Davidson, L. (2006a). Phonology, phonetics, or frequency: Influences on the production of nonnative sequences. *Journal of Phonetics*, 34, 10–37.

Davidson, L. (2006b). Phonotactics and articulatory coordination interact in phonology: Evidence from nonnative production. *Cognitive Science*, 30, 837–62.

Dyck, R. (2004). *Prosodic and morphological factors in Squamish (S<u>k</u>w<u>x</u>wú7mesh) stress assignment*. Doctoral dissertation, University of Victoria, Victoria, BC.

Fleischhacker, H. (2001). Cluster-dependent epenthesis asymmetries. In A. Albright and T. Cho (eds.), *Papers in phonology 5, UCLA working papers in linguistics* (pp. 71–116). University of California, Los Angeles.

Fleischhacker, H. (2005) *Similarity in phonology: Evidence from reduplication and loan adaptation*. Doctoral dissertation, University of California, Los Angeles.

Flemming, E. (2008). *Asymmetries between assimilation and epenthesis*. Unpublished manuscript, MIT, Cambridge, MA.

Flemming, E., Ladefoged, P. and Thomason, S. (2008). Phonetic structures of Montana Salish. *Journal of Phonetics*, 36(3), 465–91.

Fullwood, M.A. (2014). The perceptual dimensions of sonority-driven epenthesis. *Proceedings of the Annual Meeting on Phonology 2013 1* (1). doi: http://dx.doi.org/10.3765/amp.v1i1.14

Gick, B., Campbell F., Oh, S. and Tamburri-Watt, L. (2006). Towards universals in the gestural organization of syllables: A cross-linguistic study of liquids. *Journal of Phonetics*, 34(1), 49–72.

Gick, B. and Wilson, I. (2006). Excrescent schwa and vowel laxing: Cross-linguistic responses to conflicting articulatory targets. In L. Goldstein, D.H. Whalen and C.T. Best (eds.), *Laboratory phonology 8* (pp. 635–59). Cambridge: Cambridge University Press.

Hall, N. (2006). Cross-linguistic patterns of vowel intrusion. *Phonology*, 23(3), 387–429.

Henke, E., Kaisse, E.M. and Wright, R. (2012). Is the sonority sequencing principle an epiphenomenon. In S. Parker (ed.), *The sonority controversy* (pp. 65–99). Berlin/Boston: Walter de Gruyter.

Jacobs, P. (2012). Vowel harmony and schwa strengthening in S<u>k</u>w<u>x</u>wú7mesh. *Proceedings of the 47th International Conference on Salish and Neighbouring Languages: UBC working papers in linguistics 32* (99–146). University of British Columbia, Vancouver.

Kahn, D. (1976). *Syllable-based generalizations in English phonology* (Vol. 156). Bloomington: Indiana University Linguistics Club.

Kinkade, M.D. (1998). How much does a schwa weigh? In E. Czaykowska-Higgins and M.D. Kinkade (eds.), *Salish languages and linguistics: Theoretical and descriptive perspectives, Trends in linguistics, Studies and monographs 107* (197–217). Berlin/New York: Mouton de Gruyter.

Kreitman, R. (2006). Cluster buster: A typology of onset clusters. In J. Bunting, S. Desai, R. Peachy, C. Straughn and Z. Tomková (eds.), *Chicago Linguistic Society*, 42(1), 163–79.

Kreitman, R. (2012). On the relations between [sonorant] and [voice]. In P. Hoole (ed.), *Consonant clusters and structural complexity* (pp. 33–69). Berlin/Boston: Walter de Gruyter.

Kuipers, A.H. (1974). *The Shuswap language: Grammar, texts, dictionary*. The Hague: Mouton.

Leonard, J. (2007). A preliminary account of stress in SENĆOŦEN (Saanich/North Straits Salish). *Northwest Journal of Linguistics*, 1(4), 1–59. http://www.sfu.ca/nwjl/

Matthewson, L. (1994). Syllable structure in St'át'imcets. *Proceedings of the 1994 Annual Conference of the Canadian Linguistic Association/Association Canadienne de Linguistique* (381–92).

Morelli, F. (1999). *The phonotactics and phonology of obstruent clusters in optimality theory*. Doctoral dissertation, University of Maryland at College Park, Baltimore.

Morelli, F. (2003). The relative harmony of /s+ stop/ onsets: Obstruent clusters and the sonority sequencing principle. In C. Fery and R. van de Vijver (eds.), *The syllable in optimality theory* (pp. 356–71). Cambridge: Cambridge University Press.

Parker, A. (2011). It's that schwa again! Towards a typology of Salish schwa. *Proceedings of the 27th Northwest Linguistics Conference: Working Papers of the Linguistics Circle of the University of Victoria 21* (9–21). University of Victoria, Victoria. http://journals.uvic.ca/index.php/WPLC/issue/view/365

Pizzo, P. (2009). *A typology of sonority sequences in word-final consonant clusters*. Honors thesis, Emory University, Atlanta, GA.

R Core Team (2013). *R: A language and environment for statistical computing*. R Foundation for Statistical Computing, Vienna. http://www.R-project.org/

Selkirk, E. (1984). On the major class features and syllable theory. In M. Arnoff and R.T. Oehrle (eds.), *Language sound structures* (pp. 107–36). Cambridge, MA: MIT Press.

Shahin, K. (2007). An acoustic study of schwa production in two St'át'imcets varieties. *Proceedings of the 42nd International Conference on Salish and Neighbouring Languages: UBC Working Papers in Linguistics 20* (383–90). University of British Columbia, Vancouver.

Shahin K., and Blake, S. (2004). A phonetic study of schwa in St'át'imcets (Lillooet Salish). In D. Gerdts and L. Matthewson (eds.), *Studies in Salish linguistics in honor of M. Dale Kinkade: University of Montana Occasional Papers in Linguistics 17* (311–27). Missoula, MT: University of Montana.

Shaw, J., Gafos, A., Hoole, P. and Zeroual, C. (2011). Dynamic invariance in the phonetic expression of syllable structure: A case study of Moroccan Arabic consonant clusters. *Phonology*, 28, 455–90.

Shaw, P. (1996). *Headless and weightless syllables in Salish*. Paper presented at the University of British Columbia, Vancouver.

Shaw, P. (2002). On the edge: Obstruent clusters in Salish. *Proceedings of the 7th Workshop on Structure and Constituency in the Languages of the Americas: UBC Working Papers in Linguistics 10*. University of British Columbia, Vancouver.

Shaw, P. (2008). Constraints on the sequencing and syllabification of obstruents. Handout from CUNY Conference on the Syllable, City University of New York.

Steriade, D. (1999). Alternatives to syllable-based accounts of consonantal phonotactics. In O. Fujimura, B.D. Joseph and B. Palek (eds.), *Item order in language and speech* (pp. 205–45). Prague: Karolinum Press.

Steriade, D. (2001). Directional asymmetries in place assimilation. In E. Hume and K. Johnson (eds.), *The Role of speech perception in phonology* (pp. 219–50). New York: Academic Press.

Steriade, D. (2008). The phonology of perceptibility effects: The P-map and its consequences for constraint organization. In K. Hanson and S. Inkelas (eds.), *The nature of the word: Essays in honor of Paul Kiparsky* (pp. 151–80). Cambridge, MA: MIT Press.

Thompson, L.C. and Thompson, M.T. (1992). *The Thompson language. University of Montana Occasional Papers in Linguistics 8.* Missoula, MT: University of Montana.

Urbanczyk, S. (2001). *Patterns of reduplication in Lushootseed.* New York: Garland Publishing.

van Eijk, J. (1997). *The Lillooet language: Phonology, morphology, syntax.* Vancouver: UBC Press.

Willett, M.L. and Czaykowska-Higgins, E. (1995). Towards an analysis of syllable structure in Nxaʔamxcín. *Proceedings of the 30th International Conference on Salish and Neighbouring Languages* (pp. 114–26). University of Victoria, Victoria, BC.

Yun, S. (2014). The role of acoustic cues in nonnative cluster repairs. In R.E. Santana-LaBarge (ed.), *Proceedings of the 31st West Coast Conference on Formal Linguistics* (pp. 514–23). Somerville, MA: Cascadilla Proceedings Project.

Sonya Bird is an Associate Professor of Linguistics at the University of Victoria, British Columbia, Canada. Her research focuses on the phonetics of Salish and Dene languages of British Columbia, most recently the SENĆOŦEN dialect of North Straits Salish. Her work is primarily on the phonetic realization of articulatorily complex sounds and sequences of sounds, and on how this realization varies across speakers and languages. She has also recently expanded the scope of her work to second language acquisition of pronunciation in the context of language revitalization.

Ewa Czaykowska-Higgins (Linguistics, University of Victoria, British Columbia, Canada) has been a scholar of Salishan phonology and morphology for about 30 years, and has worked on both the Nxaʔamxčín and SENĆOŦEN Salish languages. Together with the late M. Dale Kinkade, she co-edited *Salish languages and linguistics* (1998). Her current research includes projects on phonological structure in Nxaʔamxčín and completion (with Colville Tribes' Nxaʔamxčín Language Program) of an online database and related print dictionary of Nxaʔamxčín legacy materials recorded in the 1960s and '70s by Dale Kinkade.

11
Sonority and Other Constraints in Gitksan Consonant Clusters[1]

Jason Brown

11.1 Introduction

While many languages of the world are limited in what kind of consonant clusters are tolerated by their phonologies, many other languages allow extensive clustering of consonants. Gitksan, an Interior Tsimshianic language of British Columbia, Canada, allows relatively extensive consonant clusters. This chapter outlines the phonotactics of Gitksan, with an eye to how sonority plays a role in constraining some clusters, but arguably does not play a role in prohibiting others.

Word-initial and word-final positions, which are the focus of the present study, yield many combinations of possible consonant sequences in the language. For example, in both word-initial and word-final bi-consonantal clusters, stops can be sequenced before fricatives, and they can even be sequenced before other stops. Fricatives exhibit a similar distribution, where they can be sequenced before both stops and other fricatives. Thus, there is prima facie evidence that any constraints on sonority sequencing in the language are lowly ranked. Curiously, however, there are relatively severe restrictions on sonorants. Sonorants cannot co-occur adjacent in a cluster, and while sonorant consonants can be sequenced after fricatives (i.e., fricative+sonorant) in syllable onsets, there is a gap corresponding to

1 Thanks are due to my primary Gitksan teachers, Barbara Sennott and the late Doreen Jensen. I am also grateful to the following individuals, who have provided input or discussion at some point in the development of this chapter: Henry Davis, Clarissa Forbes, Lisa Matthewson, Bruce Rigsby, Michael Schwan, and the Gitxsanimx Research Lab at the University of British Columbia. Much gratitude is due to Clarissa Forbes and Michael Schwan, who read and commented extensively on an earlier draft. An earlier exposition of these ideas is found in Brown (2009). All errors are my own.

stop+sonorant sequences. This gap extends beyond word-initial position: there are no stop+sonorant sequences present in the language (i.e., this type of sequence is missing in word-initial, word-medial and word-final positions, regardless of syllable affiliation of the consonants). This gap is unexpected, since fricative+sonorant sequences are tolerated by the language.

A sonority-based account of the obstruent-only clusters and the fricative+sonorant clusters is adequate, but such an account for stop+sonorant clusters fails, as fricatives are presumably either more sonorous, or equally sonorous as stops. Different versions of sonority-based approaches, such as the Syllable Contact Law (Murray and Venneman 1983; Venneman 1988) are likewise inadequate, as the restriction is evident in word-initial contexts where the consonants are tautosyllabic. An alternative approach to sonority is entertained for this gap, namely, one based in perceptual similarity (cf. Henke, Kaisse and Wright 2012), where it is the *perceptual distance*, rather than sonority distance, that is encoded in constraints on clustering.

This chapter is structured as follows: Section 11.2 lays out the general phonotactics of consonant clusters in the language, focusing on word-initial and word-final positions. This includes discussion of bi- and tri-consonantal clusters. This section also introduces the stop+sonorant consonant cluster gap. Section 11.3 attempts a preliminary analysis based on sonority and syllable structure, and a discussion is built around the challenges that Gitksan phonotactics pose for sonority-based theories. Section 11.4 outlines an alternative account which recasts some of the phonotactic patterns in terms of perceptual similarity. Section 11.5 deals with some lexical and morpho-syntactic exceptions, and Section 11.6 concludes.

11.2 Consonant Cluster Phonotactics

The consonant inventory of Gitksan is provided in Table 11.1 below, and is discussed in detail in Rigsby (1986), Brown (2008), and Brown, Davis, Schwan and Sennott (forthcoming).

As is evident, there are numerous obstruents in the inventory, including stops and fricatives at nearly all places of articulation, as well as glottalized[2] counterparts for the stops. The sonorant inventory is also relatively rich,

2 Given that stops exploiting the abstract feature [constricted glottis] are not ejective in all positions (Schwan 2013), the term 'glottalized' is employed here.

Table 11.1. Gitksan consonant inventory.

	Labial	Alveolar	Palatal	Pre-velar	Uvular	Glottal
Stop	p	t ts		k k^{w}	q	ʔ
Glottalized stop	p'	t' ts' tɬ'		k' k^{w}'	q'	
Fricative		s ɬ		x x^{w}	χ	h
Nasal	m m̓	n n̓				
Lateral approximant		l l̓				
Glide	w w̓		j j̓			

including nasals, lateral approximants, glides and glottalized versions of each of these.

This section aims to provide a catalogue of the consonant clusters in Gitksan. This includes an extended discussion of the word-initial clusters, but also of final clusters. The generalizations presented here are a summary of the observations made in Rigsby (1986) (some of these generalizations are also discussed to a lesser degree in Wickstrom 1974). The generalizations presented are as follows: first the general properties and restrictions of word-initial consonants are discussed, followed by both bi-consonantal and tri-consonantal word-initial consonant clusters. This is followed by the generalizations surrounding final consonant clusters, along with a summary of the phonotactic patterns.

11.2.1 Word-Initial Phonotactics

In his observations about word-initial segments, Rigsby (1986) notes that any consonant except /l̓/, /p'/, /x/, and /x^{w}/ can occur as a singleton word-initial consonant (though /p'/ occurs in initial position in the Western and Gitanyow dialects). The absence of the pre-velar fricatives falls out squarely from a generalized restriction in the language. There is a case of allophony whereby /x/ and /x^{w}/ alternate with the glides /j/ and /w/ when in intervocalic position, which is illustrated in (1) below.

(1) wa:x 'paddle' wa:jin 'your (SG) paddle'
$\quad$ mux^{w} 'ear' muwin 'your (SG) ear'

In this case, the restriction is one that generally holds in prevocalic position for these segments, and is not special to word-initial contexts. The absence of ejective /p'/ in word-initial position is more than likely due to its overall rarity in the lexicon. For instance, in the Gitksan Lexical

Database compiled by the author (cf. Brown 2008), there are a total of 6 instances of [p'] out of a number of 1601 entries (including morphemes and words). This contrasts with non-ejective /p/, where there are 48 instances word-initially (as the prevocalic allophone [b]). Thus, since /p'/ is rare to begin with, the non-existence of this particular segment in initial position is not surprising. The lack of /l̓/ in this position is curious, however, due to the high numbers of this segment in word-medial and final positions (31 total occurrences in the database, which is comparable to the other glottalized sonorants in non-word-initial position). There seems to be no principled reason[3] behind this gap at this point, as the glottalized nasals and glides are not restricted word-initially, so it will here be considered accidental (and not a systematic gap).

The properties of word-initial bi- and tri-consonantal clusters are outlined in the rest of this section.

Initial Bi-Consonantal Clusters: In terms of legal word-initial consonant clusters, according to Rigsby (1986), there can be either bi- or tri-consonantal clusters. Sonorants occur as rightmost members, as in (2):

(2)

Singleton initial		In a cluster	
laqs	'wash (one's body)'	χ**l**ilst	'to cough'
malk^w	'burn (up)'	s**m**ax	'meat, flesh, black bear'
ne:q	'hoof'	s**n**aχ	'thornberry'

Rigsby (1986) makes the observation that sonorants are always flanked by a vowel. Thus, there are no cases of sonorant+sonorant sequences, nor of sonorant+obstruent sequences in this position. Both of these restrictions are presumably due to the principle of Sonority Distance (Steriade 1982; Clements 1992), which demands that the sonority value between two segments in an onset rise a given amount, or simply to the Sonority Sequencing Principle, which demands that sonority rise in onsets. This will be expanded on below.

The inventory of all permissible word-initial bi-consonantal clusters in Gitksan is provided in (3) below, which is a summary of the generalizations provided by Rigsby (1986). It should be noted here that the stop+sonorant

3 Actually, Clarissa Forbes and Michael Schwan (personal communication) have suggested that the gap may in fact be due to a perceptual confusion with /n̓/ in intial position. Factors that support this view include variation between plain [n] and [l], as well as a possible sound change of /l̓/ > /n̓/. Evidence for this possible change is found in the Coast Tsimshian locative form /l̓i:/ and the Gitksan cognate /n̓i:/, and also the Coast Tsimshian word /l̓aχ/ (with the glottalized lateral in initial position) 'needle' and the Gitksan cognate /se:l̓aχ/.

sequence type is missing from this inventory. This will be discussed in more detail in Section 11.3.1.

(3) Inventory of permissible word-initial bi-consonantal clusters

a. Stop+Stop	pdo?o	'door'
	pts'ajtxʷ	'comb one's hair'
	tk'iɬxʷ	'child'
	tk'u	'around (PVB)'
	tq'a	'skin, hide'
b. Stop+Fricative	tχalpχ	'four (things, animals)'
	tχa:	'entirely, all'
c. Fricative+Stop	sgan	'pitch'
	sq'e:χxʷ	'dark'
	xba:w̓	'jaw'
	xʷdax	'be hungry'
	χdax	'eat with (someone)'
d. Fricative+Fricative	xsi:p	'(fine) sand'
	xʷsit	'fall, autumn'
	χɬa:ɬ	'red willow'
e. Fricative+Sonorant	smax	'meat, flesh, black bear'
	sm̓intsxʷ	'a winter game'
	sjan	'be tainted, affected'
	sj̓ un	'glacier'
f. Fricative+?	s?in	'bottom'
	χ?ana:x	'eat some bread'
g. Fricative+h	χhun	'eat some salmon'

Rigsby (1986) notes some manner restrictions that are present in word-initial bi-consonantal clusters. The first, which was mentioned above, is that the cluster must begin with an obstruent, namely a stop or a fricative. In addition to these manner restrictions exist place restrictions. Stops that are found in these clusters include /p/ or /t/. /p/ can participate in the following sequences: [pt-] [pts'-]. If the first member of the cluster is [t], it can precede either a dorsal glottalized stop, a dorsal fricative, or laryngeal [h],[4] but not plain stops. Plain dorsal stops [k], [kʷ] and [q] are absent in all initial clusters, and dorsal fricatives [x] [xʷ] are only followed by stops and non-dorsal fricatives.

4 Rigsby (1986) analyses the small set of aspirated stops in the language as either stop+/h/ sequences underlyingly, or as stop+/x/ sequences. In either case, the stops surface as aspirated, and not as a phonetic sequence of stop+[h]. The same is true for sequences with a glottal stop forming glottalized stops. This being the case, issues pertaining to the glottal consonants will largely be side-stepped in this chapter.

Initial Tri-Consonantal Clusters: As with the initial bi-consonantal clusters, there are manner restrictions with initial tri-consonantal clusters. Rigsby (1986) notes that tri-consonantal clusters almost always begin with fricatives; specifically the dorsal fricatives /x/ or /χ/. In addition, the second member is typically one of the coronal fricatives /s/ and /ɬ/. These clusters can have a stop, fricative, sonorant or glottal stop as the right-most member. The (limited) inventory of permissible word-initial tri-consonantal clusters in Gitksan is given in (4), where it can again be noted that stop+sonorant sequences are completely absent, just as in bi-consonantal clusters.

(4) Inventory of permissible word-initial tri-consonantal clusters

Fricative+Fricative+Stop	xsɢoːq	'be first'
Fricative+Fricative+Fricative	xsɬaw̓sxʷ	'undershirt'
Fricative+Fricative+Sonorant	χsmax	'eat meat'

11.2.2 Word-Final Phonotactics

Word-final clusters are similar to word-initial clusters in many respects: the presence of sonorants is limited to immediately postvocalic contexts, and there is a relatively free ordering of stops and fricatives. Any consonant can occur syllable-finally except for [h].

Final Bi-Consonantal Clusters: Words with final biconsonantal clusters include the types listed in (5).

(5) Final biconsonantal clusters[5]

Stop+Stop	dapt	'his, her liver'
Stop+Fricative	matx	'mountain goat'
Fricative+Stop	wist	'root'
Fricative+Fricative	diɬxʷ	'basket (woven from cedarbark)'
Sonorant+Stop	lalt	'snake'
Sonorant+Stop	sɢenx	'little finger'

It is worth noting that glottalized stops can also be sequenced before fricatives, or they can be syllable- or word-final. Sonorants can be followed

5 Given the restricted context of postvocalic position, the glottal stop appears to be acting as a glide. For instance, the sequences involving glottal stop that are permitted include: [ʔ]+Stop *lo'op* 'stone, rock', [ʔ]+Fricative *'mo'oxw* 'pus', and [ʔ]+Sonorant *mo'on* 'salt'. However, in each of these cases, there is an epenthetic vowel that appears between the glottal stop and following consonant. This is also the case for word-final glottal stops, which induce an epenthetic or possibly excrescent vowel: /pdoʔ/ 'door' surfaces as [pdoʔo]. These cases will be set aside.

by fricatives or by stops, and stops and fricatives can appear in either order: stop+fricative or fricative+stop.

Final Tri-Consonantal Clusters: The trisyllabic clusters are as listed in (6).

(6) Final trisyllabic clusters

Stop+Fricative+Stop	akst	'be wet (VI SG)'
Stop+Fricative+Fricative	da?aqɬx^w	'he can do it'
Fricative+Stop+Stop	χbiːstt	'his, her box'
Fricative+Fricative+Stop	diɬx^{w}t	'her basket'
Sonorant+Stop+Stop	ɢajtt	'his, her hat'
Sonorant+Stop+Fricative	haldawkx^w	'medicine'
Sonorant+Fricative+Stop	limxt	'his, her song'

The same restrictions apply to the sonorants (appearing only immediately postvocalically), and the same freedom of occurrence is observed with respect to the stops and fricatives. Given that there are numerous suffixes that involve only stops, or only fricatives (e.g., *-t* '3SG', *-tx^w* 'PASS', etc.), this increases the clustering with these consonants. The fact that stop+fricative sequences are possible again raises the issues around sonority, which will be addressed below.

Finally, Rigsby (1986) notes that there are some quadrisyllabic consonant clusters, all of which are polymorphemic, and where the same patterns can be observed as in (7).

(7) Final quadrisyllabic clusters

Stop+Fricative+Fricative+Stop	da?aqɬx^{w}t	'he can do it'
Sonorant+Fricative+Fricative+Stop	tq'al wilimɬx^{w}t	'his, her servant'

Word-medial clusters will not be a focus for this chapter, though given the rich clustering available for both word-initial and word-final position, this yields numerous theoretical possibilities. Thus, with these generalizations in hand, the discussion will move next to the structure of the Gitksan syllable, with an eye to determining the constraints on prohibited sequences.

11.3 Syllable Structure

The relevant phonotactic conditions outlined above can be summarized as follows:

(1) There are some prohibited sequences involving place of articulation
(2) Sonorants are always adjacent to a vowel
(3) Obstruent sequences are (relatively) unrestricted
(4) Stop+sonorant sequences are prohibited

The place of articulation constraints are expected on structural grounds, and are presumably not tied to sonority (Rice 1992); these constraints will therefore not be treated any further here. The sequencing of sonorants adjacent to a vowel is reducible to syllable structure effects, and will be discussed next. The free sequencing of obstruents is likewise a condition on sonority and syllable structure. It will be argued, however, that the stop+-sonorant gap in (4) is not conditioned by syllable structure, and is instead an independent constraint in the grammar.

Some preliminary comments about the structure of Gitksan syllables can be made here. There is little question that the CV demisyllable (in the sense of Clements 1990) constitutes an onset+nucleus sequence in the language. In cases of rising sonority, it seems clear that there are complex onsets. The existence of certain bi- and tri-syllabic clusters, including those that rise in sonority, however, indicates that these 'outer' consonants may be appendices, either parsed to a higher-level prosodic unit, or left unparsed entirely. Vaux and Wolfe (2009) present numerous pieces of evidence for the appendix cross-linguistically. Vaux and Wolfe cite the copying of reduplicative material as diagnostic for syllable-internal versus external structure. They present the case of Sanksrit (among others) to illustrate this point as shown in (8) (cf. Steriade 1982).

(8) Sanskrit reduplication
   a. du-droh- 'be hostile'
   b. si-ʂɳeh- 'be sticky'
   c. ti-ʂʈha- 'stand'

In (8), onsets that rise in sonority, such as (8a) and (8b), allow the first consonant to be copied. For clusters that fall in sonority, the first consonant is skipped in copying. This behaviour can be interpreted as the copying of the first consonant in syllable structure proper, with the fricative in (8c) falling outside of syllable structure. In Gitksan, reduplicative templates take the shapes CV, CVC or CVx-. There are few (rare) cases, however, of reduplication of a root beginning with a consonant cluster. Two of these forms, presented by Rigsby (1986), indicate that copying can target the 'outer' consonant, as in (9).

(9) Reduplication targets 'outer' consonants

tq'a	daχ-tq'a	'skin, hide'
sɢa n̓ist	six-sɢa n̓ist	'mountain'

Thus, while the evidence is limited, we will assume that the consonants in clusters are syllabified, and are neither appendices, nor degenerate syllables.[6]

In order to explain the phonotactics outlined above, some reference must be made to sonority. This work will assume the sonority hierarchy (10) as outlined in Clements (1990), where vowels are most sonorous, followed by glides, approximants, nasals and obstruents (though see Selkirk 1984, for further discussion of the hierarchy).

(10) obstruents < nasals < approximants < glides < vowels

Under this view, the stops and the fricatives are classed together as 'obstruents' with the same sonority value. Assuming that a sonority plateau is allowed in sequencing, then this accounts for the ordering of stops and fricatives; in other words, if we assume that all of the consonants are parsed into the syllable, then either stop+fricative or fricative+stop would be expected to occur if the stops and fricatives were of the same sonority value. This is consistent with Rubach and Booij's (1990) analysis of Polish, where there is a free ordering with respect to obstruents, resulting in substantial clusters of obstruents. Morelli (1999) claims that [s]+stop clusters are the unmarked forms, explaining why these structures show up with such frequency cross-linguistically; however, this isn't likely the case in Gitksan, where these clusters (as well as clusters with dorsal or lateral fricatives) are just as frequent as any others, and where stop+fricative can occur just as frequently.

Even with these under-articulated assumptions about sonority, there is still a problem inherent in the phonotactic generalizations on clustering in the language: the stop+sonorant prohibition. Since the stop+sonorant gap is prevalent in these initial clusters, this aspect of the phonology will be further explored below.

11.3.1 Challenges to Sonority-Based Approaches

A generalization that can be drawn about both the bi- and tri-consonantal clusters is that stop+sonorant sequences are not allowed as a permissible

6 This type of behaviour stands in contrast to that of the clitics, which do not participate in word-level phonological rules; see Section 11.5.2.

cluster. In fact, stop+sonorant sequences are lacking across the entire lexicon. There is no independent set of factors that will conspire to achieve this banned configuration.[7] The most promising area in this regard is affixation. For instance, stop-final stems could be suffixed with sonorant-initial suffixes. However, in these cases, epenthesis repairs these clusters (Rigsby 1986: 173; Forbes 2015), breaking up the cluster to form a new syllable, rather than inserting a vowel after the sonorant. Forbes (2015: 13) presents the following forms which illustrate that epenthesis rescues sonorants following stops (11), but epenthesis is not employed when two stops form a cluster, nor when a sonorant is followed by a stop (12).

(11)	/wak-n/	[wagɪn]	'your brother'
	/wil-n/	[wɪlɪn]	'your doing'
(12)	/wak-t/	[wakt]	'his/her brother'
	/wil-t/	[wɪlt]	'his/her doing'

While the obstruent+obstruent clusters can be accounted for by versions of the sonority hierarchy that do not differentiate stops from fricatives, or by approaches that allow for the free licensing and ordering of obstruents, the stop+sonorant gap poses a substantial challenge to any sonority-based account. The challenge that these sequences present will be outlined below, and some exceptional forms will be presented in the following section.

The stop+sonorant gap in consonant clusters is a peculiar one. One potential explanation could be based in something like the Sonority Sequencing Principle (cf. Clements 1990), which states that syllable peaks will be highest in sonority and syllable margins will be lowest, with the closer a consonant is to a peak, the higher the sonority (with sonority determined by a sonority hierarchy). Clements (1990) notes that large sonority differences are preferred in onsets, while small sonority differences are preferred in codas. It may be the case that in Gitksan, having a stop+sonorant sequence may be dispreferred to having a higher sonority rise, such as a stop+vowel sequence. The primary problem with stop-sonorant sequences is that whatever sonority restrictions that may be imposed in order to ban them will also inadvertently ban other well-formed (and existing) sequences. In other words, a sonority approach would require the grammar to consider stop+sonorant intrinsically worse than fricative+sonorant.

7 The only context that allows for a stop+sonorant sequence is found in a small set of function words that reduce postlexically. An example is the prospective aspect marker /dəm/, which surfaces either as [dɪm] or as [dm̩] in connected speech.

Given this sonority approach to word-initial clusters, the problem surrounding Gitksan immediately presents itself: Why would stop+sonorant be ruled out, and fricative+sonorant, with a smaller difference in sonority, be acceptable? Or, for that matter, under a more articulated version of the sonority hierarchy, where fricatives are more sonorous than stops, why would a sonority plateau (such as a fricative+fricative sequence), or even a sonority fall (such as a fricative+stop sequence) be tolerated more than a stop+sonorant sequence? Likewise, any attempt to account for the prohibition by means of the Syllable Contact Law, such that syllable codas must be higher in sonority than immediately adjacent onsets (i.e., to explain the lack of stop+sonorant sequences intervocalically) would likewise fail, as these structures are banned in word-initial position, where syllable contact is irrelevant. Thus, simple appeals to sonority cannot provide a solution to the problem that this prohibited sequence poses.

11.4 An Analysis Based in Perception

If the generalization above were to be translated into constraints, then this would yield a constraint as in (13), the grounding of which is left to be elucidated.

(13) *STOP-SON: Assign a violation for an ordered sequence of [-son, -cont]-[+son].

This raises the question of what the nature of this constraint is. Under this generalized scenario, *STOP-SON would need to dominate faithfulness, such as IDENT-IO, and quite possibly DEP-IO in order to induce the epenthesis effects in (11). The effects of *STOP-SON will be limited to the structure of lexical items. On the face of it, this constraint appears parochial; however, under orthodox assumptions in Optimality Theory, the constraint would also be presumed to be universal. But if the constraint is indeed universal, then are there should be other languages that satisfy the constraint; otherwise, it appears like a language-specific condition. It will be shown below that there is perceptual and cross-linguistic grounding for this constraint, a grounding which is divorced from sonority.

One promising possibility is that the stop+sonorant gap is due to perceptual factors. Following the general ideas laid out in Fleishhacker (2005), I entertain the idea that *similarity* is what is responsible for the gap. Fleishhacker claims that stop+sonorant clusters are oftentimes subject to skipping and intrusion in reduplication and loanword adaptation. The reasons for this are similarity with a base form and pressures from other phonotactic constraints. For example, Fleishhacker cites a hypothetical form *pa* sounding more like *pra* than *pira* in experimental contexts, and how in loanword adaptation, we tend to find *pa* substituted for *pra*, and not *pira*. This is supported by evidence from alliteration, loanword adaptation, reduplication,[8] puns, etc.

There appears to be further cross-linguistic support for the specific nature of this constraint. Seo (2003) reports that cross-linguistically, no language exhibits a pattern whereby liquid+stop sequences are repaired exclusively, while some languages will exhibit stop+liquid repairs (or both). The same does not hold for stop+nasal sequences (where the mirror image is equally likely). Seo claims that the underlying reason for this is the perceptibility of stops in pre-sonorant position:

> within the segment contact account, it is predicted that, in a given language, unreleased stop plus sonorant sequences will be more likely targets of phonological processes than sonorant plus released stop sequences since the perceptibility of unreleased stop consonants are relatively weak in this context. (2003: 71)

Thus, the constraint is justified on perceptual grounds, and the repairs are overlapped with the repairs on other clusters; i.e., the repairs are accidental, just like so many other 'accidents' that conspire to avoid this gap, leaving no hard evidence for the constraint (aside from the morpheme structure constraints and epenthesis facts).

As one final piece of evidence, there is also a phonetic counterpart to this approach, whereby Price (1980) has demonstrated that a lengthened [l] induces the perception of an epenthetic vowel. In that study, [bl-] onset sequences with a lengthened liquid resulted in [bəl...] percepts. With some durational modifications, these types of clusters appear to be relatively broken up by human speech perception.

If this overall analysis is correct for the stop+sonorant gap in Gitksan, where stop+sonorant sequences are more highly confusable with stop+vowel sequences, then this extends Fleishhacker's observations into the lexicon. In other words, this perceptual bias can serve as a morpheme structure constraint, since there is nothing in the theory to rule this out. This is in itself problematic, as the analysis depends on perceptual similarity between two forms, or two correspondents; however, Henke et al. (2012) take a similar approach to purported sonority effects, replacing

8 Incidentally, Fleishhacker (2005) cites reduplication in the related language Coast Tsimshian as evidence for this perceptual account.

them with perceptual effects. The important aspect to the study at hand is that the perceptual account is not based in sonority, and doesn't really mimic sonority, as is clear from the Gitksan data. Thus, it is an independent constraint, and one which is grounded in perceptual factors rather than acoustic ones.[9]

11.5 Complications Involving Stop+Sonorant Sequences

While the perceptual constraint approach accounts for the stop+sonorant gap, there are some further complications involving exceptions to this generalization. These are both lexical and morphosyntactic in nature, and will be outlined below.

11.5.1 Lexical Exceptions

There are to my knowledge two lexical exceptions to the stop+sonorant ban, both of which receive a straightforward analysis. One exception from Hindle and Rigsby (1973) is [liblеːt] 'priest' with the stop+sonorant sequence [bl] word-internally. This form is a loanword (ultimately from French), and is now archaic (though some researchers report that some current speakers know the word and pronounce it with a [p]). The other exception is [gloq], which can be loosely translated as 'shame'. Bruce Rigsby (personal communication) suggests that [gloq] may be derived from the form [tɬ'aq'], and perhaps ultimately from Coast Tsimshian [dloq']. Rigsby notes that [tɬ'aq'] has a nominal or deverbative sense, and signifies the inner lower lip, perhaps also the inner membrane of the lips and the eyelid and

9 It should also be noted that a purely sonority-based account would encounter difficulties in explaining the post-lexical sequences discussed in note 7, unless this phenomenon is relegated to a level of 'phonetic implementation' instead of a phonological surface form. In contrast, if a perceptual basis is assumed for the constraint, then this would likely yield a gradient grammatical constraint that would be readily violable in some surface forms and in some (postlexical) contexts. Furthermore, if for example the form of the prospective aspect marker sometimes surfaces as [dɪm], and sometimes as [dm̩], then this sidesteps perceptual confusability because the speaker could recover the underlying form of the sequence in normal tempo speech and in citation forms. This is a potential added advantage of the proposal that will be left for further investigation.

bottom cover (the pointing of the lower lip is a gesture of shame). Thus, reanalysis of the /tɬ’/ phoneme[10] (which is rare in the language) or a foreign [dl] sequence by more recent generations may have resulted in the present existence of the stop+sonorant sequence [gl].

Besides these genuine exceptions, there are many apparent exceptions to the stop+sonorant gap involving [gʷl] sequences, which are presented in (14) below. While these forms appear as such (in their corresponding orthographic forms) in Hindle and Rigsby (1973), the errata sheet to the dictionary lists all of the orthographic sequences involving <gwl> to <gwil>, and Rigsby (1986) indicates that [gʷi]~[gu] alternations should be spelled <gwi>. Most speakers pronounce these forms with a [u] (i.e. [gula] ‘blanket’); however, at least one fluent speaker pronounced the forms as in (14).

(14) [gʷla] ‘blanket’
[gʷne:qxʷ] ‘to be cold’
[gʷṅa] ‘to ask for, beg’
[gʷṅus] ‘newborn baby’

These are only apparent exceptions, and can be shown to have an underlying vowel intervening between the stop and sonorant. Evidence for this comes from the behaviour of these words under pluralization. One (relatively marginal) pluralization strategy in the language is an ablaut process whereby a short vowel becomes a long vowel. As it happens, almost all of the forms in (15) are pluralized using this strategy.

(15) singular plural
gʷla gʷi:la
gʷne:qxʷ gʷi:ne:qxʷ
gʷṅa gʷi:ṅa

Since the plural forms have a long vowel, it is reasonable to posit a short vowel in the singular forms. The examples in (15) indicate that the underlying representations of these words have a short [i] between the stop and sonorant, as in (16).

(16) /gʷila/ ‘blanket’
/gʷine:qxʷ/ ‘to be cold’
/gʷiṅa/ ‘to ask for, beg’
/gʷiṅus/ ‘newborn baby’

10 At least one speaker who pronounced the form as [gloq] has apparently also cited the form as [tɬ’oq], lending support to this point.

Furthermore, when consultants are asked to pronounce these words with a slower or monitored tempo, the vowel reappears. Thus, the forms in (14) are surface forms, and the stop+sonorant sequences are the result of a fast-speech vowel deletion. This is reminiscent of schwa deletion in English (Zwicky 1972; Hooper 1978; Davidson 2006), where the fast-speech deletion of a schwa results in surface consonant clusters that defy the general phonotactics of the language (for instance, derived initial stop-stop clusters like *pt-* from words like *potato*). Finally, the fact that these forms involve labialized pre-velar stops may not be an accident. As Anghelescu and Schwan (2013) point out, there is a curious empirical generalization governing syllable nuclei, whereby /xʷ/ is allowed as a nucleus, along with vowels, but where all other forms are not allowed.

Given this, these forms are not true exceptions to the generalization that stop+sonorant sequences are absent from the language. Some genuine exceptions will be presented next; exceptions that require a different analysis of prosodic structure. This includes the behaviour of clitics.

11.5.2 The Prosodic Structure of Clitics

One pocket of data that defies the general phonotactic pattern is the determinate marker clitic *t=*. This morpheme can appear proclitic to nominals in some positions, and enclitic to preceding predicates in others. Since this morpheme is made up of only a stop, this provides a ripe testing ground for whether it may be sequenced before a sonorant. Indeed, the clitic can appear preceding sonorants, as evidenced by the forms in (17) and (18).

(17) ***t=naa*** *ant gya'as Michael*
'Who saw Michael?'

(18) ***t=naahl*** *'witxwit*
'Who came?'

In addition, the same phenomenon appears whenever the determinate marker *t=* precedes a personal noun: *t=Nancy*, *t=Madeleine*, *t=Louise*, etc. These are prima facie exceptions to the stop+sonorant gap; however, there are peculiarities that are bound up with this clitic. The first is that it defies the process of prevocalic voicing of stops (Rigsby 1986; Rigsby and Ingram 1990; Brown et al. forthcoming), which is illustrated in (19).

(19) a.	/kup/	[gu**p**]	'to eat (intrans)'
	/kup-ət/	[gu.**b**ɪt]	'he/she ate it'
b.	/nəpip/	[nɪ.bɪ**p**]	'maternal uncle'
	/nəpip-ən/	[nɪ.bɪ.**b**ɪn]	'your (SG) maternal uncle'

There is good evidence that these clitics attach directly to the Prosodic Word, and are not a part of syllable structure proper. The evidence is that they defy the normal syllable structure constraints, they defy stop voicing, and they defy the normal clustering allowed in syllables. The result would be a representation as in (20) whereby *t=* falls outside of normal syllabification as an appendix (cf. Vaux and Wolfe 2009, for discussion).

(20) t[naːɬ]$_{\sigma}$...

As an appendix, the clitic would presumably attach directly to the Prosodic Word. This higher-level attachment would exempt the clitic from both stop voicing and the normal clustering phonotactics. Further evidence for this configuration comes in the mobility of the clitics in question, as they can be proclitic to some elements, or enclitic to others, depending on various conditions, as in (21) (example from Davis and Brown 2011: 53).

(21)	*Nee=dii=n*	*ga'a=hl*	***ligi=t***	*naa.*
	NEG=CNTR=1SG.I	see=CN	any=DM	who
	'I didn't see anyone.'			

Since these clitics are attached at the level of the Prosodic Word, and by extension, attach to the outside of the Prosodic Word, this allows for their ambi-directional mobility.[11]

Given these behaviours, the constraint *STOP-SON must be delimited to the domain of the syllable. The implication of this is that it is a grammatical/phonological constraint, and not simply a phonetic one.[12]

11.6 Conclusion

This chapter has explored the initial consonant clusters of Gitksan, where the discussion in Rigsby (1986) concerning the inventory of possible bi-consonantal and tri-consonantal clusters was summarized. It

11 I'm grateful to Clarissa Forbes for pointing this out.

12 Much the same can be said about the constraint on stop voicing, for the same reasons.

was shown that there is an unexpected gap in these word-initial clusters (and in consonant sequences generally in the language): stop+sonorant sequences are completely absent. It was shown that this gap presents a problem for sonority-based accounts of syllable structure and consonant clusters; however, if we assume, along with Seo, Fleishhaker, and Henke et al. that stop+sonorant clusters pose a perceptual problem, evidenced by this sequence being repaired in other languages, then this provides a natural account of the stop+sonorant gap in Gitksan. While much of the phonotactics can be attributed to sonority restrictions (including the pressure for sonorants to flank a vowel), this particular prohibition cannot be attributed to the same source.

Just as place features/restrictions are considered to be independent of sonority restrictions (Rice 1992), the condition on sonorant sequencing also appears to be an independent condition in the grammar. If we extract place effects and this major class effect, then we are left with a sonority system that is fairly well behaved, keeps sonorants adjacent to vowels, and allows for free ordering of obstruents.

References

Anghelescu, A. and Schwan, M. (2013). Nuclear consonants in Gitksan. Poster presented at the Canadian Linguistic Association Conference 2013, University of Victoria.

Brown, J. (2008). *Theoretical aspects of Gitksan phonology*. PhD dissertation, University of British Columbia.

Brown, J. (2009). An unexpected gap in Gitksan consonant cluster phonotactics. In C. Christodoulou and J. Lyon (eds.), *Proceedings of the international conference on Salish and neighboring languages* 43 (pp. 14–21). Vancouver: UBCWPL vol. 23.

Brown, J., Davis, H., Schwan, M. and Sennott, B. (forthcoming). Gitksan. *Journal of the International Phonetic Association*. http://journals.cambridge.org/action/displayAbstract?fromPage=online&aid=10210977&fulltextType=RA&fileId=S0025100315000432

Clements, G.N. (1990). The role of the sonority cycle in core syllabification. In J. Kingston and M.E. Beckman (eds.), *Papers in laboratory phonology I* (pp. 283–333). Cambridge: Cambridge University Press.

Clements, G.N. (1992). The sonority cycle and syllable organization. In W.U. Dressler, H.C. Luschützky, O. Pfeiffer, and J. Rennison (eds.), Phonologica 1988 (pp. 63–76). Cambridge: Cambridge University Press.

Davidson, L. (2006). Schwa elision in fast speech: segmental deletion or gestural overlap? *Phonetica*, 63, 79–112.

Davis, H. and Brown, J. (2011). On A'-dependencies in Gitksan. In J. Lyon and J. Dunham (eds.), *Papers for the 46th international conference on Salish and neighbouring languages* (pp. 43–80). Vancouver: UBCWPL vol. 30.

Fleishhacker, H. (2005). *Similarity in phonology: Evidence from reduplication and loan adaptation*. PhD dissertation, UCLA.

Forbes, C. (2015). Gitksan root stress: Phasal phonology and diachrony. Unpublished manuscript, University of Toronto.

Henke, E., Kaisse, E. and Wright, R. (2012). Is the sonority sequencing principle an epiphenomenon? In S. Parker (ed.), *The sonority controversy* (pp. 65–100). Berlin: Mouton de Gruyter.

Hindle, L. and Rigsby, B. (1973). A short practical dictionary of the Gitksan language. *Northwest Anthropological Research Notes*, 7, 1–60.

Hooper, J.B. (1978). Constraints on schwa-deletion in American English. In J. Fisiak (ed.), *Recent developments in historical phonology* (pp. 183–207). The Hague: Mouton.

Morelli, F. (1999). The phonotactics and phonology of obstruent clusters in optimality theory. PhD dissertation, University of Maryland.

Murray, R. and Vennemann, T. (1983). Sound change and syllable structure in Germanic phonology. *Language*, 59, 514–28.

Price, P.J. (1980). Sonority and syllabicity: Acoustic correlates of perception. *Phonetica*, 37, 327–43.

Rice, K. (1992). On deriving sonority: A structural account of sonority relationships. *Phonology*, 9, 61–99.

Rigsby, B. (1986). *Gitksan grammar*. Unpublished manuscript, University of Queensland.

Rigsby, B. and Ingram, J. (1990). Obstruent voicing and glottalic obstruents in Gitksan. *International Journal of American Linguistics*, 56, 251–63.

Rubach, J. and Booij, G. (1990). Syllable structure assignment in Polish. *Phonology*, 7, 121–58.

Schwan, M.D. (2013). Acoustic characteristics of glottalized obstruents in Gitksan. *Proceedings of Meetings on Acoustics*, 19, 060292.

Selkirk, E. (1984). On the major class features and syllable theory. In M. Aronoff and R. Oehrle (eds.), *Language sound structure: Studies in phonology* (pp. 107–36). Cambridge, MA: MIT Press.

Seo, M. (2003). *A segment contact account of the patterning of sonorants in consonant clusters*. PhD dissertation, Ohio State University.

Steriade, D. (1982). *Greek prosodies and the nature of syllabification*. PhD dissertation, MIT.

Vaux, B. and Wolfe, A. (2009). The appendix. In E. Raimy and C.E. Cairns (eds.), *Contemporary views on architecture and representations in phonology* (pp. 101–44). Cambridge, MA: MIT Press.

Vennemann, T. (1988). *Preference laws for syllable structure and the explanation of sound change: With special reference to German, Germanic, Italian, and Latin*. Berlin: Mouton de Gruyter.

Wickstrom, R. (1974). *A phonology of Gitksan, with emphasis on glottalization.* MA thesis, University of Victoria.

Zwicky, A. (1972). Note on a phonological hierarchy in English. In R. Stockwell and R. Macaulay (eds.), *Linguistic change and generative theory* (pp. 275–301). Bloomington: Indiana University Press.

Jason Brown is Senior Lecturer in Linguistics at the University of Auckland. He has been involved in language documentation research for many years, and has written at length on the Gitksan language, including his PhD dissertation *Theoretical aspects of Gitksan phonology*. His research is focused on phonological theory, and is concerned with segmental and prosodic phenomena, as well as the interaction between phonology, morphology and syntax.

12
Syllable Structure in Papiamentu and the Sonority Scale[1]

Yolanda Rivera-Castillo

12.1 Introduction

Papiamentu is a Creole language spoken in Curaçao, Aruba, Bonaire and Saba. Currently, Bonaire is under the jurisdiction of the Netherlands Antilles, while Aruba and Curacao are autonomous countries within the Kingdom of the Netherlands. Approximately 270,000 people speak Papiamentu (Ethnologue 2011). It originated in a situation of language contact between Iberian lexifiers and African languages (Joubert and Perl 2007; Holm 1988). It is currently in contact with Dutch (taught in schools), English (industry and tourism) and Spanish (migration), from which it borrowed a great number of lexemes (South American varieties). There is widespread multilingualism in these islands. According to the 2011 Census (Central Bureau of Statistics 2011, 2014), between 60 and 70 per cent of the population speaks Papiamentu as a first language in the ABC islands.

Papiamentu's syllable structure includes a large number of syllable types. Previous studies recognize six types in this language (Klein 2011: 182; Maurer 1998): V, CV, CVC, VC, CCV and CCVC. Following Levelt and van

1 I would like to thank the University of Puerto Rico for providing continuous support for the Papiamentu Project to conduct fieldwork and release time to work on the data analysis. Also, I would like to thank the University of Puerto Rico-Río Piedras for providing the hardware and the funding for RAs working on this project. I want to specially thank members of the team that gathered the data in Curaçao: Lucy Pickering, professor at Texas A&M-Commerce, Don Walicek, professor at the University of Puerto Rico, and Abigail Michel, linguist and native speaker of Papiamentu. Finally, I would like to thank my current research assistant, Camille Wagner, native speaker and linguist, for helping with the transcription and translation of sections of the data. Any errors or misinterpretations are my sole responsibility.

der Vijver (2004), this places Papiamentu in the Marked III class regarding syllable structure types. However, this language exhibits a larger number of types than the ones reported, including syllables with complex codas (CVCC), matching languages in the Marked IV type, like Dutch. There are words with complex codas that originate in different lexical sources: *accent* (English), 'accent'; and *Diaweps* (Spanish *día jueves*), 'Thursday'. Moreover, even words of Dutch origin, like *heft*, 'to join, to stitch' (from *hechten*), exhibit complex codas not attested in the source (Martinus 2004: 30).

More importantly, some complex onsets and codas in Papiamentu do not comply with the sonority scale, particularly clusters of /s/ plus a voiceless stop (sC, hereafter). If we take into account melodic features to analyse syllable structure, such description would challenge current hypotheses of sonority-based syllabic organization. In fact, Papiamentu complex onsets and codas consist of the least sonorous segments placed closer to the syllable nuclei: *skol*, *Diaweps*. This is attested even in cases in which the lexical sources have onsets and codas that comply with the sonority scale, indicating that these constitute system internal constraints on the phonotactic organization of melodic features, not exceptions.

This study describes syllable structure and melodic composition of onsets and codas in Curaçaoan Papiamentu. Examples of complex coda and onsets are retrieved from spontaneous speech samples including 19 speakers of the language. A phonetic description of codas and onsets that do not comply with sonority constraints is the core component of the data analysis.

In this chapter, we provide evidence that: (a) /s/ is not extrametrical in Papiamentu sC clusters; (b) /s/ constitutes a member of onsets in word-medial clusters; (c) there is no postlexical voicing of voiceless consonants in clusters of obstruents. Following Henke, Kaisse and Wright (2012), our findings indicate that phonotactic constraints based on melodic features provide a better description of Papiamentu consonant clusters than restrictions based on the sonority scale. This study also provides evidence that supports Klein's (2011) contention that Creoles can have a large set of syllable types.

The first section of this chapter (12.1) provides a description of the Papiamentu consonant system grounded on previous studies and some of our findings, and gives an account of the consonant clusters in onset and coda position. Section 12.2 summarizes the findings from the phonetic analysis of voice onset time for voiceless stops in sC clusters, and vowel duration before word-medial clusters. The last part of the analysis (Section 12.3) explains the issues related to the application of the sonority hierarchy in the description of these clusters, and provides an explanation to cluster organization in Papiamentu. In Section 12.4, we point out some repair strategies for sC clusters attested for Spanish-PA dominant bilinguals, and similar phenomena attested in Spanish and other Creoles. The last section (12.5) summarizes our conclusions.

12.1 The Papiamentu Consonant System

According to Munteanu (1996: 227), Papiamentu (PA) has 21 consonants, while Kouwenberg and Murray (1994: 8) propose that there are 24 consonants. On the other hand, Römer (1991: 43) describes 24 consonants (including glides and a velar nasal), and Birmingham (1971: 1) describes 22 (including glides but no palatal nasal). Despite these disagreements, it is evident that this language has a sizeable number of fricatives (5 consonants) and 5 approximants (see Table 12.1).

Table 12.1. Papiamentu's consonants.

	Labial	Labiodental	Dental	Alveolar	Palatal	Velar	Glottal
[−voiced, −cont]	p		t		tʃ	k	
[+voiced, −cont]	b		d		dʒ	g	
[+nasal, −cont]	m			n	ɲ		
[−voice, +cont]		f		s	ʃ		
[+voiced, +cont]		v		z	ʒ		
[+approx, +cont]	w		l	ɹ	j		h

Among approximants, one has a trill allophone ([ɹ]/[r]), and another has obstruents and Ø allophones ([h]/[x]/(Ø)). We describe /h/ as an approximant since our data (spectra) indicate that its formants mimic those of adjacent vowels.[2] Also, as indicated by Birmingham (1971: 21), a complete loss of /h/ is common in Papiamentu borrowings, as seen in (1).

2 As indicated by Ladefoged (1962: 107), for English: 'As the positions of the articulators during the sound [h] are the same as in the vowel which follows the [h], the frequency components in [h] sounds have similar relative amplitudes to those in vowels; but the complex wave has a smaller amplitude, and no fundamental frequency, since it is not generated by regular pulses from the vocal cords.' Ladefoged and Maddieson (1996: 325–6) describe /h/ and /ɦ/ as 'voiceless or breathy counterparts of the vowels that follow them [...] the shape of the vocal tract [...] is often that of the surrounding sounds [...]'.

(1) a. trabajo > trabow, 'work'
b. viejo > bjeu, 'old'
c. cangrejo > kangrew, 'crab'

Glottal /h/ never combines with other approximants (*hl, *hɹ). Only obstruents combine with approximants (/fɹ/, /pɹ/, /sl/). Also, /l/ is dental, as described by previous studies (Kouwenberg and Murray 1994: 8). The segment 'r' (/ɹ/) is clearly an approximant in word-initial position, as in the word *riba*, 'on top of', since F3 is very close to F2, if compared to any adjacent vowel, including back vowels. We classify /ɹ/ as an alveolar approximant since it has a trill allophone, and trills are typically alveolar. Additionally, regarding obstruents, PA's /t/ is non-strident since it is dental, like /d/ (Munteanu 1996: 227).[3] Also, we do not include /v/ as a phoneme, like previous descriptions, since it seems be an allophone of /f/, as indicated by Kouwenberg and Murray (1994: 8). It alternates with /f/ and /b/ in word initial position.

As for single consonants, all consonants in Table 12.1 can occur in syllable-initial position. In coda position, these must be either non-glottal sonorants or non-palatal voiceless obstruents: /l/, /ɹ/, /m/, /n/, /s/, /f/, /p/, /t/ and /k/. Single consonant onsets include segments that cannot constitute the first segment in clusters: nasals, the glottal approximant, liquids, and [– anterior] or [+voiced] sibilants. Section 12.1.1 below describes PA clusters in onset and coda position.

12.1.1 Consonant Clusters in Papiamentu

PA allows 23 different combinations of consonants in onset position and 20 in coda position. We exclude clusters with glides since these might constitute members of nuclei given the large number of diphthongs in the language (23, according to Maurer 1998: 148).

Complex onsets and codas are attested in many PA words (Birmingham 1971: 23; Kouwenberg and Murray 1994: 9–11; Martinus 2004: 30; Mansur 1991). Some of these sequences (underlined) violate sonority constraints, as seen in (2).

(2)	Source		Papiamentu
a.	Iberian:	día jueves	diaweps, 'Thursday'
b.	Iberian:	especialmente	specialmente, 'specially'
c.	English:	spark plug	sparkplug, 'sparkplug'
d.	Dutch:	hechten	heft, 'to join'

3 Sounds become more 'mate' the closer they are to the teeth, so Spanish /t/ is 'mate', not strident (Quilis 1988: 210).

Six sC sequences are possible, including those that violate sonority and those that do not: /s/+voiceless stop, like *splica*, 'explain'; and /s/+sonorant, like *smak*, 'flavour'. As in English and Dutch, sC clusters are attested in words of different origin: /sp/, /st/, /sk/, /sm/, /sn/ and /sl/ (Kouwenberg and Murray 1994: 10), as in (3).

(3)	Source		Papiamentu
	a. Iberian:	espera	spera, 'wait'
	b. Iberian:	estima	stima, 'to love'
	c. Iberian:	escapa	skapa, 'to escape'
	d. Dutch:	smaak	smak, 'flavor'
	e. Dutch:	sneetje	snechi, 'slice of bread'
	f. Dutch:	slag	sla, 'to blow'

Furthermore, PA allows clusters of up to three consonants in word-initial position. All of these start off with /s/ (Kouwenberg and Murray 1994: 10), as in (4).

(4) a. splika, sprùit
b. strepi, strategiko
c. sklavitut, skruf

There are some general restrictions on consonant position and clusters. For example, word-final obstruents must be voiceless, onsetless syllables are disfavoured, and obstruent plus central approximant (ɹ) onsets are unmarked in word-initial position. Diachronic data indicate consistent patterns for consonant features in the language. In the case of obstruents in coda position, borrowings in PA often exhibit final consonant devoicing (5a–f).

(5)	Source		Papiamentu
	a. absoluto	>	apsoluto, 'absolute'
	b. admirar	>	atmirá, 'to admire'
	c. observer	>	opservá, 'to observe'
	d. obvio	>	opvio, 'evident'
	e. virtud	>	virtut, 'goodness'
	f. ciudad	>	sudat, 'city'
	g. lagartija	>	lagadishi, 'lizard'
	h. gente	>	hende, 'people'
	i. monte	>	mondi, 'forest'

Voicing applies only in intervocalic position (5g) and to post sonorant consonants (5h–i) (Birmingham 1971: 17; Munteanu 1996). On the other hand, Munteanu (1996: 253) explains that, historically, PA has created new clusters by applying metathesis (6a–g), all of which result in obstruent+liquid combinations as in (6) (examples from Munteanu 1996; Martinus 2004: 174).

(6)	Source		Papiamentu
	a. tiburón	>	tribon, 'shark'
	b. estorbar	>	strobe/a, 'to hinder'
	c. dormir	>	drumi, 'to sleep'
	d. formiga	>	vruminga, ant'
	e. porfía	>	prufia, 'disagreement'
	f. ferment	>	promèntè, 'pepper'
	g. torcer	>	trose, 'to bend'

Actually, Elstak (1989: 496) indicates that 62.5 per cent of PA words have a CɹV cluster in initial position.[4] There is also a clear tendency to avoid word-initial onsetless syllables, which would explain why so many sC clusters emerged from words beginning with a vowel in the lexical sources [see (3), above]. In those cases, there is historical deletion (7a, b), prosthesis or metathesis (7c, d) (Munteanu 1996: 253):

(7)	Source		Papiamentu
	a. engañador	>	gañadó, 'deceiver'
	b. apretar	>	perta, 'to squeeze'
	c. olvidar	>	lubidá, 'to forget'
	d. ombligo	>	lombrishi, 'belly button'

Additionally, PA follows cross-linguistic restrictions on sequences of dental/alveolar stops and lateral consonants in onset position: *dl, *tl. Other unattested sequences include stops+nasals, which comply with the sonority hierarchy but are marked: /pn/, /pm/, /tn/, /tm/, /kn/, /km/. Another gap is the combination of /s/+voiced stops, which would not violate the version of the sonority hierarchy presented in Table 12.5, unlike the attested /s/+voiceless stops.

In coda position, the only clusters of obstruents allowed include voiceless stops and anterior voiceless fricatives (8a–c): /p/, /t/, /k/, /s/, f/. Obstruents can also follow sonorants in coda position (8d–h) (examples from Kouwenberg and Murray 1994: 11).

4 There a few cases in which metathesis eliminates a cluster or shifts its position but these are less common: temprano > trempan. However, the result is creating a Cɹ cluster in word initial position.

(8) a. diaweps
b. buks
c. kaft, test,
d. bals, mòrs, dams, stèns
e. wèrp, pòmp
f. vèlt, spart, karènt
g. spalk, hùrk, krènk
h. valf, durf

Kouwenberg and Murray (1994: 11) indicate that: 'Consonant clusters in the coda are more restricted than those in the onset.' Table 12.2 summarizes these combinations (based on Munteanu 1996 and Kouwenberg and Murray 1994, and examples from spontaneous speech data).

Table 12.2. PA combinations in onset and coda position.

Combination	C1 <	C2 <	C3	Examples
		ONSET		
[−cont] < [+voice, +approx]	/p/, /k/ /b/, /g/	/l/, /ɹ/		*produkshonan, kriminalidat, plaum, grandi, blanko, kla*
[−cont] < [+voice, +approx]	/t/, /d/	/ɹ/		*draai, trankil*
[−voice, +cont] < [+voice, +approx]	/f/	/l/, /ɹ/		*franko, refleshon*
[−voice, +cont] < [+voice, +approx]	/s/	/l/, /n/, /m/		*sla, snei, smak*
[−voice, +cont] < [−voice, −cont]	/s/	/p/, /t/, /k/		*spañó, stobá, skohe*
[−voice, +cont] < [−voice, -cont] < [+voice, +approx]	/s/	/p/, /k/, /t/	/l/, /ɹ/	*splika, sprùit, strea, sklabitut, skruf*
		CODA		
[+voice, +approx] < [−voice, −cont]	/l/, /ɹ/, /m/, /n/	/p/, /k/, /t/		*werp, pomp, spalk, crank, hurk, velt, beurt, tent*
[+voice, +approx] < [−voice, +cont]	/l/, /ɹ/	/f/		*valf, durf*
[−voice, +cont] < [−voice, −cont]	/f/, /s/	/t/		*soft, test*
[−voice, −cont] < [−voice, +cont]	/p/, /k/, /t/	/s/		*djaweps, buks, wals, mors, dams, stens, zoeits*
[+voice, +approx] < [−voice, +cont]	/l/, /ɹ/, /m/, /n/	/s/		*djaweps, buks, wals, mors, dams, stens, zoeits*

All the 20 combinations in the coda, except for some combinations of voiceless fricatives plus stops, have a corresponding combination in the onset (23 combinations). Among coda clusters, the following are missing in sonorant+voiceless stop sequences: /np/, /mk/, /mt/. However, the following combinations are possible: /mp/, /nk/, /nt/. Assimilation of nasals to the place of articulation of adjacent plosives explains this gap. In fact, the presence of nasals in the coda enhances audibility (Fairbanks 1958: 599).

We summarize the characteristics of PA onset and coda clusters in (9).

(9) a. Sonorants combine with obstruents, not with other sonorants.
  b. Two adjacent obstruents must be voiceless.
  c. Two adjacent obstruents must have different values for [±continuant]

In onset position, all sC clusters violate sonority. The same applies to codas (see Section 12.2.4, below).

In order to explain violations to the sonority scale in the case of sC clusters, some have resorted to extrametricality (Hall 2001). For example, Rialland (1994: 140–1) argues that /s/ in medial and word-initial clusters is always extrasyllabic in French. It is the case that glide formation is blocked after a cluster composed of an obstruent and a liquid (CL) but not after a single liquid (it is optional in these cases). Since glide formation is not blocked after clusters beginning with 's' (sC), Rialland argues that the 's' is extrasyllabic. However, the sC clusters in these examples include a voiceless stop or fricative that typically participate in palatalization (/k/, /t/ or /s/) before palatal vowels, which suggest that melodic restrictions might be playing a role in these cases.

Moreover, the main problem with extrasyllabicity is that the second consonant in sC clusters does not belong to a uniform set of segments across languages. In PA, sC clusters only allow a sonorant or a [−continuant] voiceless obstruent in second position. Therefore, the 'extrasyllabic' 's' would place language specific restrictions on the melodic composition of the following consonant. In fact, /s/ behaves as part of the onset.

In the following section (12.2.1), we provide phonetic evidence that /s/ in syllable-initial clusters is not extrametrical. For these clusters, we measured the voice onset time (VOT) for the stop in second position to determine whether the presence of /s/ affects VOT. If /s/ is extrasyllabic, then the stop should be in word-initial position and its VOT should not be different from that of word-initial plosives. However, we show that /s/ has an effect on the VOT of the following voiceless stop, suggesting that the plosive is not in syllable-initial position.

In word-medial position, we describe the duration of the vowel preceding /s/ and compare its duration to that of vowels in open syllables and to those before /s/ in word-final position. This chapter aims to provide evidence that word-medial sC clusters constitute onsets. The results suggest that 's' is not a coda of the preceding syllable but the initial segment of the following onset, such that a word like 'piska' has the following syllabic composition: pi.ska.

12.2 Phonetic Analysis

12.2.1 An Analysis of Papiamentu Clusters

The following sections describe the results of measuring VOT for voiceless stops and vowel duration as well in PA words. The author also conducted a visual inspection of glottal pulses (voicing) for PA obstruent clusters. The data sources are recordings of spontaneous speech samples conducted in 2004.

A team including Lucy Pickering (co-PI and professor at Texas A&M), Abigail Michel (linguist and native speaker collaborator), Don Walicek (professor at the University of Puerto Rico), and the author of this chapter, conducted fieldwork in the island of Curaçao. We recorded 10 hours of spontaneous speech samples[5] for 20 participants. At the University of Puerto Rico, the author segmented the samples into sentences with the assistance of Camille Wagner Rodríguez (research assistant), a native speaker of PA. The author identified clusters in onset and coda position for words attested in the data for 19 participants.[6]

5 We are aware of the problems associated with spontaneous speech data and VOT (Kessinger and Blumstein 1997: 144). However, a study of three languages by Kessinger and Blumstein (1997) has shown that there are asymmetries regarding the effect of speaking rate on the VOT of voiceless and voiced consonants. The asymmetries keep the consonants' VOT distinct enough for sound perception, with little overlap. Therefore, it is the phonemic, not the phonetic contrasts that matter (Kessinger and Blumstein 1997: 164): '[...] the results of this study suggest that even though there are clear context-dependent effects, the acoustic manifestations of the phonetic categories of speech are fundamentally very stable [...]'

6 One of the recordings was too noisy.

We compared VOT duration in onset position for sC clusters (#sC), word-initial (#C) and word-medial (stressed syllables: V'CV) voiceless plosives. For VOT duration, the author determined voicing lag duration measuring after the burst of the plosive (point zero) to the inception of vowel formants and/or glottal pulses. There were 270 items included, 90 items per consonant (/p/, /t/, /k/), 30 in syllable-initial position, 30 in word-medial position, and 30 after /s/. Different vowels followed the stops, and the author included a similar number of tokens per vowel. Since sC clusters are not as frequent as single consonants in onset position, we had to restrict our analysis to 30 tokens per stop.[7] The results were compared for each set of the same consonant to avoid the effect of the consonant intrinsic duration in its VOT. For example, /k/ showed longer VOT duration than /t/ in all cases, and /t/ a longer VOT duration than /p/ in almost all items. We expect voiceless stops in word-initial position to show longer VOT values than those following /s/. We assume that regarding the correlation between phonetics and phonology, this shows that /s/ is not extrametrical since it affects the plosive VOT values.

In the case of vowel duration, we compared the duration of /a/, /e/, /o/ and /u/, which are relatively stable in PA, in stressed open ('V.sC) and closed syllables ('VsCV and Vs#). We did not include /i/ since there was great variation in vowel duration. Closed syllables included /s/ as a coda, and some cases of /k/ before an sC cluster. We could not find sufficient examples of /i/ and /u/ before /s/ in final position to include this context in the statistical analysis. We measured vowels in words such as /ko<u>s</u>/ and /pɹo<u>s</u>tituʃon/, where /s/ might be in coda position. In word-medial position, we measured vowels in open syllables before a single /s/, as in /bo.<u>s</u>o.nan/. We included vowels before sets of three consonants as well: *e<u>k</u>s<u>p</u>erensia*. We compared items for the same stressed vowel in these contexts to avoid the effects of intrinsic duration and stress on measurements. Sixty measurements were completed for each item for a total of 240 items plus 20 cases of VksC, for a total of 260 items. If /s/ in word-medial sC clusters is a coda, then the vowel should be shorter than in open syllables. If /s/ is part of the following onset, /s/ should have no effect on the duration of the preceding vowel.

We compared the results using a One-Way ANOVA (analysis of variation), and a Tukey post-hoc test. As a result of this research, we confirmed the hypotheses in (10a) and (10b). We could not, however, confirm (10c).

7 Also, /sp/ clusters are less frequent than /sk/ clusters, which are less frequent than /st/ clusters.

(10) a. There are significant differences in VOT between word-initial and word-medial voiceless plosives, and voiceless plosives in sC sequences.
b. There are no significant differences in duration between vowels preceding an sC cluster in word-medial position and those in open syllables.
c. There are significant differences between vowels preceding an sC cluster in word-medial position and those preceding /s/ in final position.

Finally, we also conducted a visual inspection of glottal pulses in clusters of voiceless plosives and found that both consonants are voiceless in all cases. The discussion of results follows.

12.2.2 VOT for Voiceless Plosives

All consonants in PA showed a short lag for VOT values (Keating 1984), except for /k/ in mid word position. The results indicate that there are significant differences between plosives in initial position and those following /s/ as determined by one-way ANOVA, except in the case of /t/ and /st/. A Tukey Post-Hoc test indicates significant differences in duration for the following contexts: #k and #sk ($p = 0.001$); V'kV and #sk ($p = 0.000$); #p and #sp ($p = 0.002$); and V'pV and #sp ($p = 0.000$). On the other hand, /t/ and /st/ did not exhibit significant differences in their VOT values: #t and #st ($p = 0.113$); V'tV and #st ($p = 0.124$). Table 12.3 summarizes mean duration for /p/, /t/ and /k/ in all three positions: #sC, V.CV, and #CV.

Table 12.3. Mean VOT duration for /p/, /t/ and /k/ in milliseconds.

Consonant	#sC	V.'CV	#CV
/p/	10.00	18.25	15.85
/t/	22.53	22.69	29.00
/k/	16.08	42.61	33.23

These values indicate differences as large as 26.53 ms and as short as 0.16 ms. In English, previous studies indicate that speakers perceive a 20 ms difference in VOT if the consonants belong to different categories, such as voiced and voiceless stops (Sharma and Dorma 1999: 1082). Speakers would identify a consonant with a VOT ranging from 0–30 ms as voiced, and one with a VOT between 50–80 ms as voiceless (Sharma and Dorma 1999: 1079). The differences in VOT between single stops and those in sC clusters are not as sizeable in PA, except for the case of /sk/ and /k/ in mid word position. However, since we are measuring VOT for voiceless consonants only, we believe that these differences signal a distinction between consonants in syllable-initial and non-initial position, except in the case of /t/.

As shown, differences in the case of /t/ are less salient. We believe that this is due to similarities between /s/ and /t/ since both are anterior coronals, unlike combinations of /sk/ and /sp/. In the phonological analysis, we will show that /s/ and /t/ are the only consonants that can co-occur with other obstruents in coda position. We propose that similarities in place of articulation increase VOT duration for /t/ in /st/ clusters in order to highlight the presence of the voiceless stop in this cluster.

These results generally indicate that /s/ is not extrametrical but part of these clusters and, therefore, /s/ affects VOT duration. In languages genetically related to PA, such as Spanish, there is a much shorter lag for VOT values in voiceless stops (Lisker and Abramson 1964), and voicing starts before a voiced stop (negative values). We believe that this indicates that the PA system is different from the Spanish system but also different from the English system, in which there are greater numerical values for VOT.

12.2.3 Vowel Duration before a Coda

In the case of vowels preceding /s/, the results indicate that there are no significant differences in duration between vowels before sC clusters and those in open syllables: ('a.sC) and ('asCV) (p = *0 .983*); ('e.sC) and ('esCV) (p = *0.373*); ('o.sC) and ('osCV) (p = *0.214*); and ('u.sC) and ('usCV) (p = *1.00*). However, differences are not significant either for vowels before /s/ in word-medial position ('VsCV) versus those in closed syllables in final position ('Vs#): ('asCV) and ('as#) (p = *1.00*); ('esCV) and ('es#) (p = *0.986*); and ('osCV) and ('os#) (p = *0.985*). There are no significant differences in duration between vowels before a cluster of three consonants (*e<u>ksp</u>erensia*) and those before sC in word-medial position either: (p = *0.442*). In the case of /o/, there were many sequences of /os/ followed by a nasal (plural forms with *nan*). In these cases, there are near significant differences in duration between vowels preceding sC and sN clusters: (p = *0.054*).

One possible explanation for similarities between vowels in final position and those before sC clusters, is that vowels before voiceless consonants should have similar duration. Notice that near significant differences are attested when /n/ follows /s/, which produces spontaneous voicing in the preceding /s/. However, we should expect longer vowels before voiced consonants, not before their voiceless counterparts (Lisker 1974). Since most of the items included in the word-final category are monosyllabic, we believe that the presence of longer vowels in monosyllabic forms explains these results (Römer 1991).

However, we could not confirm whether voicing plays a role in vowel length or not since we found no examples of the voiced counterpart of /s/ – /z/ in coda position. Since /z/ is not distinctive in this position, and there is a general tendency in this language to devoice obstruents in the coda, we have no data to confirm differences in vowel duration before voiced and voiceless obstruents. Finally, duration is the main phonetic correlate of stress in this language (Rivera-Castillo and Pickering 2004), and since we chose only stressed syllables for measurements, vowels have similar duration given that stress distinctions are primary.

Mean durations, however, provide a complex scenario in which open syllables have shorter vowels than vowels preceding an sC cluster. The results are summarized in Table 12.4.

Table 12.4. Mean vowel duration for /a/, /e/, /o/ and /u/ in different positions (ms).

Vowel	VsCV	V.sV	Vs#	VksC	VsN
/a/	100.00	90.44	97.67		
/e/	106.33	78.44	100.56	74.78	
/o/	110.00	76.11	116.00		70.33
/u/	118.33	115.33			

In all four cases, the vowel is longer before an sC cluster than in open syllables. This runs contrary to placing /s/ in coda position for word-medial sC clusters. However, the results do not provide us conclusive evidence of coda membership.

12.2.4 Voicing and Consonant Clusters

We visually inspected glottal pulses in all clusters of voiceless obstruents in the data. In all cases, pulses stopped, unexceptionally, right at the end of the vowel preceding obstruents in coda position. For those clusters in the onset, pulses started along with vowel formants. Figure 12.1 shows the /stɹ/ sequence in word-initial position.

The initial cluster exhibits higher intensity for /s/ and a sharp drop at the inception of the voiceless stop /t/. Glottal pulses are absent from the first two consonants /st/ and start right after the inception of the approximant (/ɹ/). Coda obstruents are also voiceless (/ps/, /ts/, /ks/), as shown in Figure 12.2.

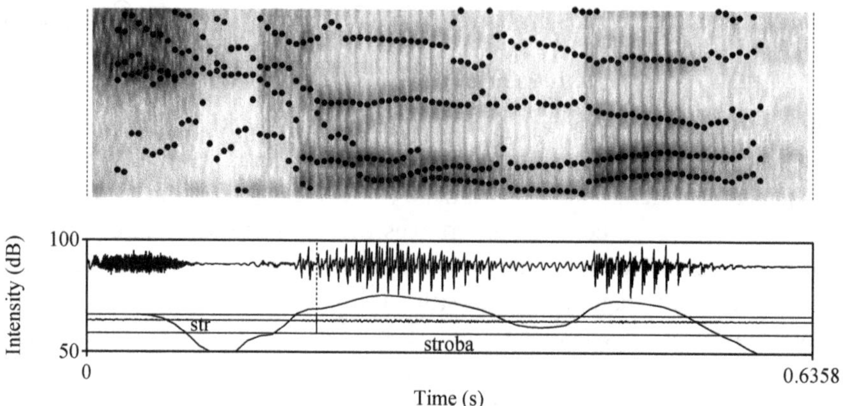

Figure 12.1. Word-initial /stɹ/ cluster for *stroba*, 'hamper'.

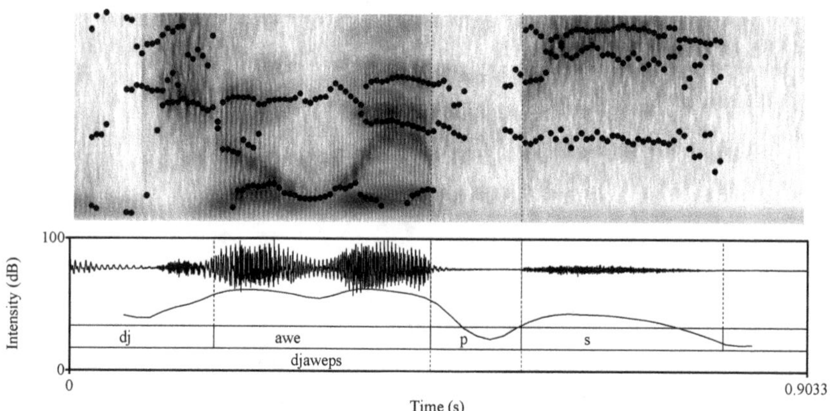

Figure 12.2. Coda /ps/ cluster in *djaweps*, 'Thursday'.

In both cases, intensity is higher for /s/ than for the consonant closer to the syllable nucleus. Both sequences should violate sonority restrictions.

12.2.5 Conclusions for the Phonetic Analysis

The phonetic evidence indicates that /s/ in sC sequences is not extrametrical in PA. Moreover, it also suggests that /s/ in sC medial sequences belongs to the onset of the following syllable. This militates against sonority-based restrictions, such as the Syllable Contact Law (Davis and Shin 1999), which describes the distribution of codas and onsets according to sonority restrictions in word-medial clusters.

Word-medial sC clusters create a sequence of falling instead of rising sonority in onset position. In fact, there are word-medial groups that cannot comply with sonority restrictions even if we apply the Syllable Contact Law, as in the case of the word *kapstòk*, 'hat': kaps.tok or kap.stok. In both syllabic distributions there is a group of consonants that violate sonority. Figure 12.3 shows that intensity falls at syllable edges and rises for /s/.

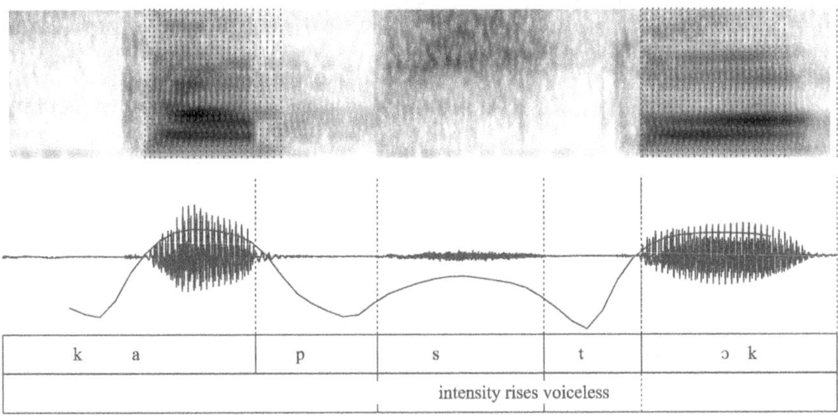

Figure 12.3. Word-medial /pst/ group for *kapstòk*, 'hat'.

These clusters exhibit an intensity peak between two syllables. Additionally, we have also provided evidence that clusters of obstruents must be voiceless in onset and coda positions.

Finally, these data suggest that sonority does not determine consonant phonotactics in PA. In the next section (12.3), we provide a phonological analysis of consonant cluster organization based on melodic properties rather than sonority. The first part describes problems with sonority in its application to PA data and alternatives to sonority-based analyses (Section 12.3.1). Sections 12.3.2–12.3.5 describe the melodic restrictions that constrain syllabic organization in this language.

12.3 Application of Sonority Analyses

12.3.1 Sonority and Melodic Restrictions

Analyses of syllable organization include approaches that resort to phonotactic constraints, as well as those based on sonority restrictions. Those resorting to phonotactic constraints assign relative saliency to specific phonetic properties or perceptual cues. Those coached in sonority describe the effect of increasing sonority from the syllable edges to its nucleus. Regarding the latter, Parker (2002: 7) proposes the 'Sonority Sequencing Principle' as stated in (11).

(11) a. In every syllable there is exactly one peak of sonority, contained in the nucleus.
b. Syllable margins exhibit a unidirectional sonority slope, rising towards the nucleus.

Parker proposes a universal sonority hierarchy (2002: 240), following similar scales originating in Whitney's (1981/1889) work, as seen in Table 12.5.

Table 12.5. Sonority hierarchy by Parker (2002).

low vowels	16
medial vowels (except /ə/)	15
high vowels (except /ɨ/)	14
/ə/	13
/ɨ/	12
glides	11
/r/	10
laterals	9
flaps	8
trills	7
nasals	6
/h/	5
voiced fricatives	4
voiced stops and affricates/voiceless fricatives	3
voiceless fricatives/voiced stops and affricates	2
voiceless stops and affricates	1

Regarding possible consonant clusters in PA, this scale has weak predictive power. Just in the onset, the sonority scale licenses only 15 combinations (out of 23) for PA's 22 consonants. In fact, it licenses 145 unattested combinations too (Table 12.6).

Out of 160 licensed combinations, only 9 per cent (15) of the cases predicted are attested in the language, while the scale does not rule out 145 (91 per cent) unattested combinations. Moreover, it rules out sequences

Table 12.6. Unattested combinations in onset position.

C1	C2
/p/, /t/, /k/, /tʃ/	/f/, /s/, /x/, /ʃ/, /b/, /d/, /g/, /dʒ/
	/z/, /ʒ/
	/h/
	/m/, /n/, /ɲ/
/f/, /x/, /h/, /ʃ/, /b/, /d/, /g/, /dʒ/	/z/, /ʒ/
	/h/
	/m/, /n/, /ɲ/
/x/, /h/, /ʃ/, /dʒ/, /tʃ/	/ɹ/, /l/
/d/, /t/	/l/
/s/	/z/, /ʒ/
	/h/
	/ɲ/
	/ɹ/
/z/, /ʒ/	/h/
	/m/, /n/, /ɲ/
/z/, /ʒ/	/ɹ/, /l/
/h/	/m/, /n/, /ɲ/
	/ɹ/, /l/
/m/, /n/, /ɲ/	/ɹ/, /l/
/l/	/ɹ/

allowed in the language, such as 8 combinations of /s/ in initial position followed by /p/, /t/, /k/ or by /p/, /k/+/l/ or /p/, /t/, /k/+/ɹ/. For such a small set of clusters (23), the scale is not sufficiently restrictive.

Parker (2002: 9) describes sC sequences as 'sonority reversals'. However, the non-reversed sequences – */ks/, */ps/ and */ts/ – are not attested in PA, and are infrequent cross-linguistically even though these follow sonority restrictions. On the contrary, /s/+voiceless stop clusters are commonly found in languages. Indeed, Morelli (2003) shows that, among groups of obstruents, the most frequent type is the combination of a fricative and a stop. Describing the sC cluster as a sonority reversal creates additional issues with s+plosive+liquid clusters. If only the sC sequence constitutes a reversal, there is no clear syllabic constituent associated with it.

Henke et al. (2012: 69) have pointed out that the scale over-generates and under-generates combinations: 'Another problem with sonority sequencing is its typological under- and over-generation. As for under-generation, it fails to predict typological common sonority plateaus, particularly word-initial sibilant+stop clusters, as in English [stɪk].'[8]

Another problem for the sonority scale is the fact that /tl/ and /dl/ clusters are cross-linguistically uncommon, even though these do not violate sonority restrictions (Ohala 1990, 1992; Harris 2006: 1486–7). However, the reversed order (which violates sonority: /ld/, /lt/) is favoured in the same languages in which /dl/ and /tl/ are not possible (Harris 2006: 1486). This restriction applies in PA, which has no /dl/ or /tl/ clusters. There are, however, no restrictions in PA against /bl/ or /pl/, which are comparable in sonority to /dl/ and /tl/.[9]

We believe that the issue with /dl/ and /tl/ clusters is 'modulation', or the requirement that the features of adjacent consonants should be sufficiently dissimilar. Autosegmental principles like the Obligatory Contour Principle (OCP) propose similar requirements. Ohala (1992: 321) indicates that there are constraints on the co-occurrence of labial vowels and labial consonants (bu, wu, pu) in English, Korean, Vietnamese, Zulu, Ronga, Tarascan and Urhobo. The same restrictions apply in the case of dental, alveolar, palatal consonants (acute consonants) and palatal vowels in Akha, Dagbani, Even, Gilyak and Wapishana: /dj/, /tʃi/. Some restrictions are linked to specific features more than to the sonority scale. For example, 'grave' plays a role in segment adjacency in Ewe (Duthie 1986: 354):

> The grave consonants (bilabial, rounded, labiodental; velar, glottal; labial velar) are followed by l in double realizing margins of syllables; while

8 We should add that it is not clear whether sonority is a prosodic or a segmental property. Sonority is an intriguing property since it does not pattern with other prosodic properties regarding anchoring, producing different levels of prominence between constituents, spreading or behaving independently of segmental positions, despite the syllable being a prosodic domain. Sonority relies on the ranking of individual segments while its effects are prosodic.

9 Additionally, Ohala (1992: 319–20) indicates that the definition of sonority is circular since the organization of segments according to increasing sonority is supported by syllabic organization while, at the same time, syllabic organization is explained by the sonority hierarchy. One of the most problematic aspects of this circular reasoning (that by itself is indefensible) is the case of ambisyllabic consonants, which might be parsed with the preceding or the following syllable. It is stress that determines their parsing, not sonority. If sonority is universal, it is problematic to explain why syllabification of word internal consonants is language specific.

	English	Spanish
(i)	bal.ance ['bæl.ənz]	ba.lan.ce [ba.'lan.se]
(ii)	ab.stract ['æb.strækt]	abs.trac.ción [abs.trak.'sion]

non-grave consonants (dental alveolar, palatal) are followed by ɹ. The two consonants which fall into neither group, being followed by neither l nor r, ɗ, n, which are allophones of each other and of r, as the latter occurs only in second margins.

In order to address these language specific restrictions, some have proposed a Minimum Sonority Distance (MSD) (Selkirk 1984), which requires that two adjacent segments have a minimal ranking distance in the sonority scale. The MSD should explain why certain combinations are possible while others are not.[10] For example, consonants in the /pɹ/ sequence have six levels of separation in the scale but those in /pn/ have only five. This would explain why the first combination is acceptable in PA but not the second one. However, the consonants in /fɹ/ are separated by the same number of steps in the scale as those in /pn/ but there are no restrictions against the former sequence in this language.

Identifying a phonetic correlate for sonority has also proven problematic. As stated by Henke et al. (2012: 68), intensity, claimed to be its strongest correlate (Parker 2002), does not correspond to the ranking in the scale: '[...] sibilant fricatives generate high intensity frication but still pattern as low sonority segments; and nasals have maximal oral constriction but relatively high sonority.' Notice that even those sC sequences that do not violate sonority restrictions, such as /s/+nasal clusters, exhibit a drop in intensity at the closure before the nasal consonant (Figure 12.4). This drop in intensity levels indicates that there is no smooth transition towards higher levels in the nuclei.

There are different alternatives to sonority that do not run into these problems. In fact, Henke et al. (2012: 78) propose that cue recovery predicts the types of combinations that are possible in segmental sequences. They state that the degree of constriction is a determining factor in syllable organization (ibid.: 74):

10 In fact, some propose that Optimality Theory (Prince and Smolensky 1993) can address some of the issues described above (Parker 2002: 10), since it 'provides an insightful answer to these dilemmas: all linguistically-significant generalizations (of which the SSP is clearly one) are universal in the sense that they are present in every language, but they are encoded as a series of ranked and violable constraints which potentially conflict with each other.' Therefore, sonority is a general (universal) constraint that can be subordinated to other constraints in the language. In OT, all constraints are universal indeed. Then, it seems that sonority might not play an important role in many languages since it can be ranked very low among constraints.

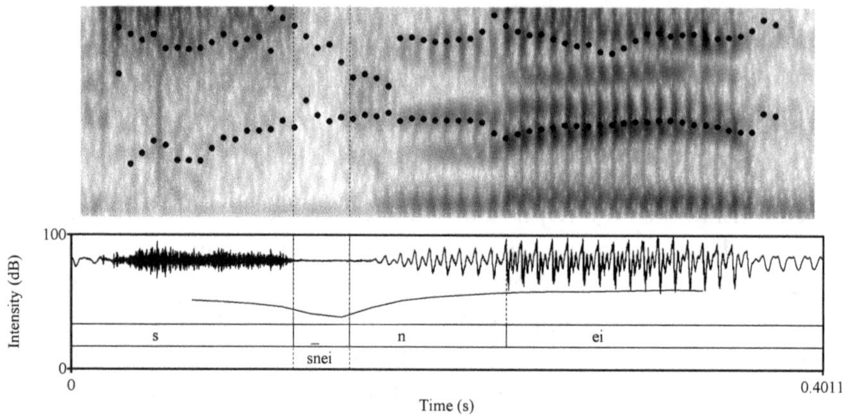

Figure 12.4. Drop in intensity at closure before nasal in *snei*, 'type of bean'.

> Coarsely speaking, ordering segments in terms of their degree of constriction from greatest constriction to greatest aperture, followed by increasing constriction after the aperture peak, ensures the greatest benefit from gestural overlap. Thus, without resorting to sonority itself or to syllable structure, the resulting sequencing of sounds looks very much like the traditional sonority sequence without some of its problem sounds (such as fricatives in general, and /s/ in particular): obstruents and nasals (full or nearly full occlusion of the vocal tract) > approximants (liquids > glides) > vowels.

Also, sounds with strong internal cues (like fricatives) provide more information on their features than those that depend on transitions (like stops). They propose the following preference scales for syllabic sequences in the coda (12a) and the onset (12b, c) (Henke et al. 2012: 79).

(12) a. CV > CVC [codas have strong transitional cues (glides or liquids), strong internal cues (nasals and fricatives), or nasal+oral stop place neutralized]
b. CV > CGV > CLV (L = liquid)
c. CV > SCV > FCV (F = fricative)

The most relevant preference scale for PA is 12c, which assigns sC clusters a preferred status over fricative+stop (FCV) clusters, including fricatives such as /f/, /ʃ/, /z/, /ʒ/. In PA, sC clusters are attested, while fC, ʃC, zC and ʒC clusters are not. Although these preference scales apply to PA, other language specific constraints are not addressed by these restrictions: (a) codas clusters must comply with constraints on segment voicing; (b) among liquids, only /l/ combines with /s/ in sC combinations; and (c) only two (/f/, /s/), from a set of six fricatives participate in onset clusters.

Given the fact that sonority has little predictive power in the case of PA consonant clusters, we conclude that other mechanisms must be constraining these combinations. We show below that melodic distinctions between obstruents, sonorants and approximants are key in the description of PA clusters. As shown below, we provide an account based on hierarchical relations between segmental features.

In the following sections, we account for PA onset and coda clusters by providing phonotactic constraints based on melodic properties. Manner, voice and place features are key components in these restrictions.

12.3.2 Phonotactic Constraints for Papiamentu Consonant Clusters

Ohala (1992: 319) proposes that the combination of segments is determined, not by rules but by melodic properties (see also Harris 2006). In fact, four features play a role in the composition of PA consonant clusters in onset and coda position: [±voiced] (voicing), [±continuant] (manner), [±distributed] and [±anterior] (place of articulation). There is 'local,' intersegmental evaluation of these properties, such that constraints license groups of adjacent consonants. Some restrictions license clusters, while others forbid clusters. Those constraints that forbid clusters place limits on the type of feature-values adjacent consonants can have.

We propose that constraints that are more specific, hard constraints (Bird, Coleman, Pierrehumbert and Scobbie 1992) instead of violable constraints, allow us to explain segment combinations in onset and coda position. Regarding features, we rely on features being organized hierarchically, in a Feature Hierarchy (Clements 2005). There are major features and minor features subordinated to these (Scobbie 1997: 40). Following Clements (2005), under major feature classes ([±consonantal] and [±sonorant]), there are oral/nasal distinctions and 'laryngeal' features (voicing). Subordinated to 'oral,' there are place ([±distributed], [±anterior]) and manner ([±continuant]) features, as in (13).

(13)

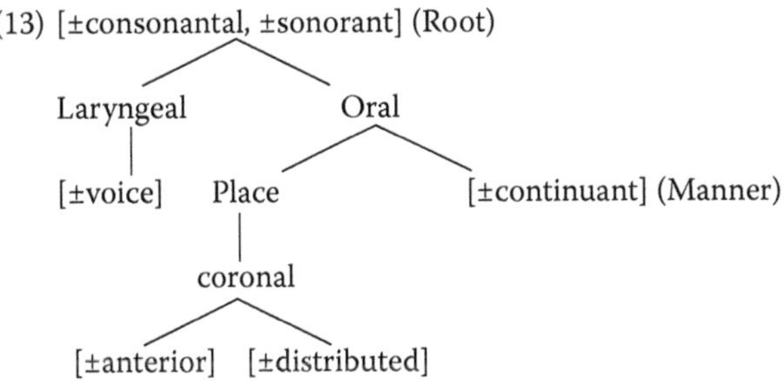

The constraints described in this chapter rely on relations between features in the feature hierarchy. There are three specific restrictions on melodic specifications that apply to both onset and coda clusters in PA [(9a–c), repeated below]:

(9) a. Sonorants combine with obstruents, not with other sonorants.
b. Two adjacent obstruents must be voiceless.
c. Two adjacent obstruents must have different values for [±continuant].

The restriction in (9a) licenses the most common cluster type in PA: obstruent+liquid. It also licenses some combinations in the coda: /mp/, /ɹp/, /lp/, /nk/, /ɹk/, /lk/, among others. The second restriction (9b) only licenses clusters of two obstruents with the same feature-value for voicing ([−voice]): */pb/, */kb/, */tb/, */fb/, among others. The third constraint (9c) restricts combinations of obstruents to groups of fricatives ([+continuant]) plus stops ([−continuant]): (a) in onsets, /sp/, /st/, /sk/; (b) in codas, /ft/, /st/, /ps/, /ks/, /ts/. It takes care of combinations between consonants in levels 1–4 of the sonority scale (Table 12.5) without excluding sC clusters. These restrictions do not filter some unattested clusters (/zl/, /dl, /tl/, stops+nasals, and /fp/, /fk/), but more specific ordering restrictions eliminate these groups, as shown below (Sections 12.3.3 and 12.3.4).

We represent the restrictions in 9a through 9c as precedence constraints and entailments ('<' for precedence;[11] comma for unordered combinations; → for entailment; ⇔ for mutual entailment; and * for forbidden sequences). Additionally, in order to describe these clusters in (14) and (15), we use the features [±consonantal] and [±sonorant] to distinguish obstruents from sonorants (Clements 2005).

(14) [+cons, −son] → obstruents

(15) [+cons, +son] → sonorants

The first restriction (9a) licenses combinations of two obstruents, an obstruent and a sonorant but not a combination of two sonorants (/ml/, /mn/, etc.), as shown in (16).

(16) *([+cons, +son] < [+cons, +son])

11 For the sake of representational simplicity, this paper assumes that ordering restrictions apply between segments. However, this is not intended as a segmental interpretation since there is feature overlap, and we follow proposals of a 'superweak segmental interpretation' (Coleman 1998: 43).

This language also requires that two obstruents ([+cons, -son]) in a cluster have the same value for [±voice] (see 9b above), as shown in (17).

(17) [+cons, −son] < [+cons, −son] ⇔ [+cons, −son] ⊃ [−voice]

This eliminates clusters such as /sb/, /fb/, among others. Third, two adjacent obstruents ([+cons, −son]) cannot have the same feature values under the 'Laryngeal' and 'Oral' nodes, so these cannot both be [−voice, −continuant] or [−voice, +continuant] as in (18).

(18) *([+cons, −son, −voice, ∝continuant], [+cons, −son, −voice, ∝continuant])

That means that a voiceless fricative ([−voice, +continuant]) can combine with a voiceless stop ([−voice, −continuant]) but not with another voiceless fricative ([−voice, +continuant]): /st/ or /ts/ but */sf/ or */fs/. The relation in the hierarchy for an */sf/ sequence is shown in (19).

(19)
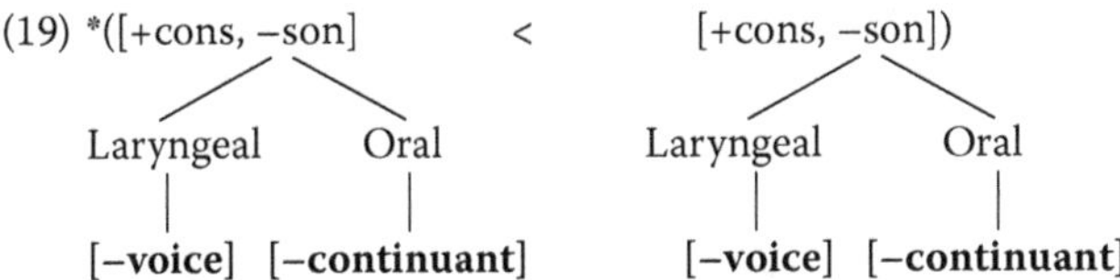

This constraint requires that adjacent sounds are different in their subordinate, minor features such that the combination complies with the Obligatory Contour Principle (OCP) and related constraints (Keer 1999). For these, we propose a general restriction on feature combination that should explain why some consonant combinations are not attested, as in (20).

(20) Identical Minor Feature-Value Constraint: Two adjacent segments may share one or more 'major' features (Laryngeal, Oral, Place), according to the feature hierarchy (Clements 2005), but these cannot share the same feature-values for more than one specific or minor feature in the same feature path.

This restriction conspires with licensing restrictions to render 23 onset clusters and 20 coda clusters in PA.

Finally, we need to state that obstruents and/or sonorants that combine in PA clusters must be non-palatal consonants (¬ [−anterior, +distributed]). This is a restriction on 'place of articulation' under the oral node. This applies to both onsets and codas as in (21).

(21) *([+cons, ±son, −anterior, +distributed], [+cons, ±son])

This limits the combinations of obstruents and sonorants to the following set: /p/, /t/, /k/, /b/, /d/, /g/, /f/, /s/, /z/+/m/, /n/, /l/, /ɹ/. This restriction excludes palatal consonants from clusters.

Other restrictions on place of articulation include those on combinations of coronal and dental obstruents with coronal and dental sonorants in onset position: */sɹ/, */dl/, */tl/. Combinations of /s/ (coronal) with /ɹ / (coronal) and /d/ and /t/ (dental) with /l/ (dental) in onsets are not attested in the PA data and previous descriptions do not provide evidence of these. These are described in Sections 12.3.3 and 12.3.4 with constraints that apply specifically to onset position and coda position.

12.3.3 Specific Constraints for Complex Onsets

There are 4 restrictions that apply to onsets, listed in (22).

(22) a. Only voiceless sibilants (/s/) precede [−continuant] obstruents (sC clusters).
b. Voiceless alveolar sibilants (/s/) cannot combine with alveolar approximants (/ɹ/).
c. Dental obstruents (/t/, /d/) cannot combine with dental sonorants (/l/).
d. Non-sibilant obstruents can precede liquids only (/pɹ/, /pl/, /kɹ/, /kl/, etc.).

The first constraint is a more specific version of the constraint in (19). As in (19), both are [−voice] (required for obstruents) and, therefore, cannot have the same value for [±continuant]. In the coda, other fricatives, like /f/, can combine with voiceless stops ([−continuant] obstruents). Finally, a formal version of (22a) follows in (23).

(23) $*([+\text{cons}, -\text{son}, -\text{strident}]_O < [+\text{cons}, -\text{son}]_O)$

In other words, only [+strident] obstruents (/s/) may precede another obstruent ([+cons, −son]). The second constraint (22b) is related to specific restrictions for place of articulation [describes sequences not excluded by (21), such as /sɹ/].

(24) $*([+\text{cons}, -\text{son}, +\text{ant}, -\text{dist}]_O < [+\text{cons}, +\text{son}, -\text{nasal}, +\text{ant}, -\text{dist}]_O)$

Both /s/ and /ɹ/ are [+anterior, −distributed], and their combination is restricted because their minor features are identical. Notice that anterior non-distributed nasal sounds can combine with /s/: /sn/. Similarly, the constraint in 22c, describes constraints for */dl/ and */tl/ clusters/ as in (25).

(25) *([+cons, –son, +ant, +dist]$_O$ < [+cons, +son, -nasal, +ant, +dist]$_O$)

Both /t/ and /l/ are [+anterior, +distributed], and their combination is restricted because their minor features are identical. Together, (24) and (25) are subsumed under a more general restriction in (26).

(26) *([+cons, -son, +ant, ∝dist]$_O$ < [+cons, +son, –nasal, +ant, ∝dist]$_O$)

In other words, if coronal sounds have the same feature value for [±anterior], these cannot have the same feature value for [±distributed], such as in the case of /dl/ and /tl/, as shown below in (27).

(27)

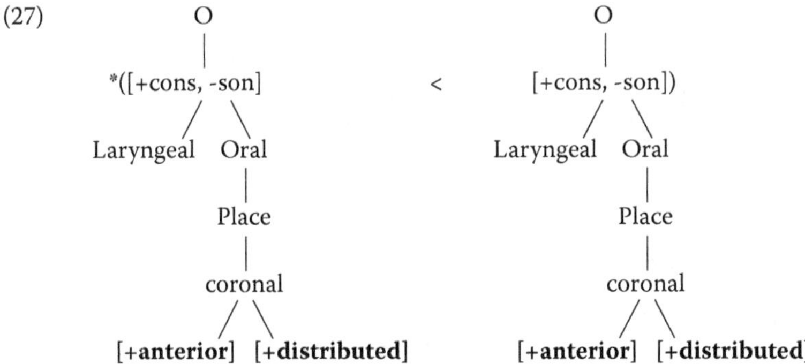

These have the same major feature (Place: coronal) and, therefore, cannot have the same feature values for two subordinate features [±anterior] and [±distributed].

The last restriction (22d) describes the most frequent onset cluster in PA, a voiceless obstruent plus a liquid: (/fl/, /fɹ/, /bɹ/, /bl/, /gl/, /gɹ/, /tɹ/, /dɹ/), as in (28).

(28) [+cons, –son, –strid]$_O$ < [+cons, +son]$_O$ ⇔ [+cons, +son] ⊃ [-nasal]

This requires that none of the consonants is a nasal sound, that both consonants have specifications under the Oral node. This constraint excludes sequences of stops+nasals, which comply with the sonority hierarchy but are unattested in PA: /pn/, /pm/, /pɲ/, /tn/, /tm/, /tɲ/, /kn/, /km/, /fn/, /fm/ and /fɲ/.

These restrictions, as well as those described in Section 12.3.4, are compatible with the general ones provided in Section 12.3.2.

12.3.4 Specific Constraints for Coda Clusters

Codas obey some specific restrictions as well, included in the 4 informal statements of (29).

(29) a. The last segment in a coda cluster is [−voice].
b. Sonorants precede non-palatal obstruents.
c. Only non-nasal sonorants precede non-sibilant fricatives.
d. Obstruents precede only anterior obstruents.

The first restriction in (29a) describes a property of the second segment in a coda cluster. It is subsumed to the restriction in (17), which requires clusters of obstruents to include only voiceless consonants. Finally, (29d) requires a constraint to license the following clusters in the coda: /ft/, /st/, /ps/, /ts/, and /ks/. However, in the coda, the final obstruent must be [−voice] even if preceded by a sonorant as in (30).

(30) $[+\text{cons}, \pm\text{son}]_C < [+\text{cons}, -\text{son}]_C \Leftrightarrow [+\text{cons}, -\text{son}]_C \supset [-\text{voice}]$

The specification '$[+\text{cons}, \pm\text{son}]_C$' indicates that first segment can be an obstruent ([+cons, -son]) or a sonorant ([+cons, +son]). The second segment must be a voiceless obstruent. This describes all final codas in Table 12.2.

The second restriction (29b) licenses most combinations attested: /m/, /n/, /ɲ/, /l/, /ɹ/+/p/, /t/, /k/, /f/, /s/. It also constitutes a specific version of the restriction in (21), which excludes palatals from these groups, as in (31).

(31) $*([+\text{cons}, +\text{son}]_C < [+\text{cons}, -\text{son}, -\text{anterior}, +\text{distributed}]_C)$

All voiced and/or palatal obstruents ([−anterior, +distributed]) are eliminated from these combinations by the constraints stated in (30) and (31). A more specific restriction disallows combinations of /f/ with nasals. As in the case of onsets [see (28)], nasal segments exhibit very specific restrictions and do not constitute clusters with non-strident fricative obstruents (/f/), as in (32).

(32) $[+\text{cons}, +\text{son}]_C < [+\text{cons}, -\text{son}, -\text{strident}, +\text{cont}]_C \Leftrightarrow [+\text{cons}, +\text{son}] \supset [-\text{nasal}]$

The set of obstruents that combine in coda position is also more restricted than the set selected by the general constraints, as in (32). If two obstruents combine, the second one must be an anterior coronal (s/ or /t/).

(33) $*([+\text{cons}, -\text{son}]_C \;<\; [+\text{cons}, -\text{son}, -\text{anterior}]_C)$

This licenses combinations of /f/, /s/+/t/ and /p/, /t/, /k/, /l/, /ɹ/, /m/, /n/+/s/ in coda position (see Table 12.2).

Finally, the restrictions on these clusters apply to onset and codas at word edges. A smaller set of clusters is attested in word medial position but these still follow the restrictions stated above. The most interesting case is the parsing of /s/ in sC clusters, which we discuss below.

12.3.5 Word-Medial Clusters

In Section 12.1, we stated that this chapter aims at determining whether sC medial clusters follow word-initial syllabification constraints. This is an important issue since these clusters violate sonority restrictions and we should find out whether the Syllable Contact Law (SCL) determines syllabification. For example, there are two possible syllabifications for the word 'piska', as we see in (34).

(34) a. pis.ka, 'fish'
     b. pi.ska

The parsing in 34a would result from applying the SCL since /s/ does not violate sonority as a coda; while 34b would violate the SCL by creating the sC sequence. As indicated before (Section 12.2.3), /s/ is not in coda position. Moreover, in combinations of three consonants, parsing is as in (35) (see Figure 12.5).

(35) ek.spe.ren.sia, 'experience'

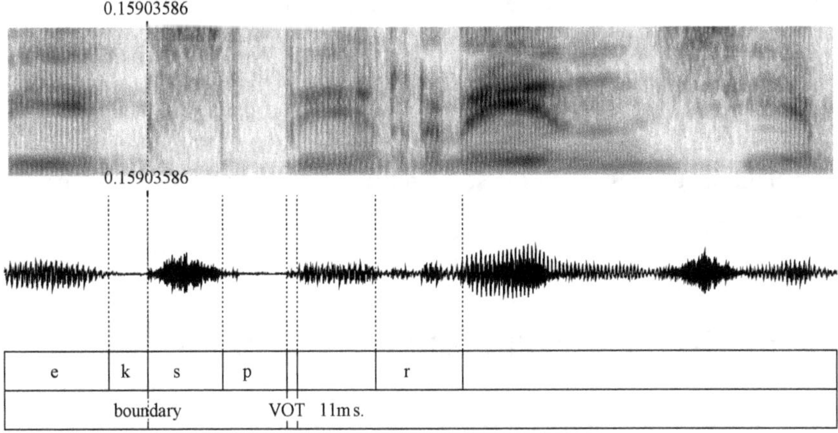

Figure 12.5. Word-initial syllable for *eksperimentá*, 'experienced'.

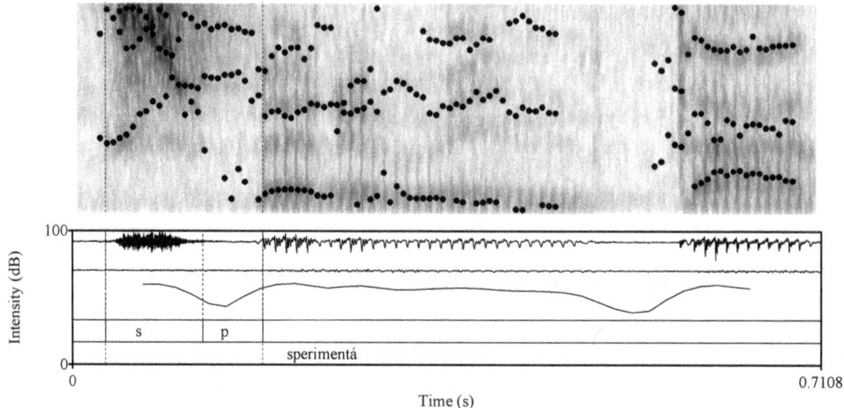

Figure 12.6. Aphesis in *sperimentá (eksperimentá)*, 'experience'.

In these cases, sonority is violated whether /s/ is a coda of the previous syllable or an onset of the second syllable. However, the preferred parsing includes /s/ with the onset. This is further supported by cases of aphesis in the data, in which speakers delete /ek/, not /eks/ (36) (see Figure 12.6).

(36) ek.spe.ri.men.ta → spe.ri.men.ta

Notice that there is deletion of the initial syllable, including the vowel and coda, consistent with a general dislike for onsetless syllables in the language (Section 12.1.2).

So, as in other languages, the set of consonant clusters allowed in word-medial position is a subset of the clusters attested in word-initial position. This includes clusters of obstruents and liquids, the same ones allowed in word-initial position. Additionally, clusters including /s/+nasal are not attested in medial position in the data we gathered.

Finally, unlike the PA dominant speakers we interviewed in Curaçao, Spanish/PA bilinguals exhibit the use of 'repair' strategies for /s/+voiceless obstruent sequences. The next section briefly describes previous work on these cases.

12.4 'Repair' Strategies and Papiamentu

Rivera-Castillo and Andre-Mather (2016) conducted a study of lexical borrowing in the case of four Aruban speakers, one of whom is a Spanish-PA bilingual. In the data, Rivera-Castillo and Mather found that in sC sequences, the speaker inserts a schwa before the sC sequence, as in (37).

(37) skol → əskol, 'school'

This schwa matches the first and second formant frequencies of preceding vowels, a feature that characterizes this vowel. This is attested only for one speaker in the study. The PA dominant bilinguals do not produce these forms.

Spanish has historically inserted a tense /e/ before 'impure' sC clusters. Lexical borrowing demonstrates this phenomenon as in (38).

(38) stress → estrés

In fact, some Creoles exhibit the same feature. PA, unlike other Portuguese-lexifier Creoles (Saramaccan, Príncipe Portuguese Creole, Angolar and Cape Verdean Creole), preserves sC clusters instead of applying repair strategies, such as vowel insertion or consonant deletion (Smith 1999; Avram 2008).[12]

Not all Creoles pattern the same way regarding these clusters. This shows that Creoles do not have the same set of syllable types or the same requirements on melodic composition for their clusters.

12.5 Conclusions

Constraints on feature value specifications for adjacent consonants determine the composition of PA's consonant clusters in onset and coda position. Given the low predictive power of the sonority scale and related constraints (Minimal Sonority Distance and Syllable Contact), the description

12 Similarly, other Creoles have sC sequences in word-initial position, such as Sranan. Armstrong Pedersen (2006) describes these sequences and argues that syllable composition is determined by stress position instead of sonority. He provides numerous examples of syllabic organization in word medial position for these clusters. As in English, stress placement determines if /s/ becomes the coda of a syllable preceding an sC cluster or part of the following onset. However, we have found no such correlation in PA. Since PA has tone and stress, further study of the relation between cluster organization and prominence is necessary.

provided in this chapter, based on feature hierarchies, offers a better explanation than mechanisms based on this scale.

As indicated before, we believe that these constraints correlate to perceptual cues but are based on phonological descriptions. As Reetz and Jongman (2009: 201) point out: '[...] most acoustic cues are highly *context-dependent.* [...] Demonstrations of the context-dependent nature of acoustic cues suggested that the invariance did not reside in the acoustic signal itself.'

This chapter contributes to understanding restrictions on syllable structure in PA and the role that feature co-occurrence restrictions have in limiting the set of possible syllables in this language.

References

Armstrong Pedersen, C. (2006). *Stress, sonority, and the syllable in Creoles and other languages.* PhD dissertation, University of Puerto Rico, San Juan.

Avram, A. (2008). The development of syllable structure in Cape Verdean Creole. *Bucarest Working Papers in Linguistics,* 1, 159–69.

Bird, S., Coleman, J., Pierrehumbert, J. and Scobbie, J. (1992). Declarative phonology. In A. Crochetière, J.C. Boulanger and C. Ouellon (eds.), *Proceedings of the XVth International Congress of Linguists, 9–14 August 1992.* Québec: Presses de l'Université Laval.

Birmingham, J.C. (1971). *The Papiamentu language of Curaçao.* PhD dissertation, University of Virginia.

Central Bureau of Statistics, Aruba (2011). *Language spoken at home.* Retrieved 23 February 2015. http://www.redatam.org/binabw/RpWebEngine.exe/Portal?&BASE=AUA2010

Central Bureau of Statistics, Netherlands (2014). *Statistics Netherlands: First language on Bonaire, Saba, and St. Eustatius.* Retrieved 23 February 2015. http://www.cbs.nl/en-GB/menu/themas/vrije-tijd-cultuur/publicaties/artikelen/archief/2014/2014-4225-wm.htm

Clements, G.N. (2005). Feature organization. In K. Brown (ed.), *The encyclopedia of language and linguistics,* Vol. 4 (pp. 433–41). Oxford: Elsevier.

Coleman, S. (1998). *Phonological representations: Their names, forms, and powers.* Cambridge: Cambridge University Press.

Davis, S. and Shin, S.-H. (1999). The syllable contact constraint in Korean: An optimality-theoretic analysis. *Journal of East Asian Linguistics,* 8, 285–312.

Duthie, A.S. (1986). Phonetic features. In K. Bogers, H. van der Hulst and M. Mous (eds.), *The phonological representation of suprasegmentals: Studies on African languages* (pp. 337–58). Dordrecht: Foris Publications.

Elstak, F.A. (1989). Metathesis in Papiamentu. In F. Martinus Arion (ed.), *Homenahe na Raul Römer* (pp. 39–49). Willmenstad, Curaçao: Instituto Linguistico Antillano.

Ethnologue (2011). Papiamentu. Retrieved 2011 from: https://www.ethnologue.com/language/pap

Fairbanks, G. (1958). Test of phonemic differentiation: The Rhyme Test. *The Journal of the Acoustical Society of America*, 30, 596–600.

Hall, T.A. (2001). The status of extrasyllabic consonants in English and German. *ZAS Papers in Linguistics*, 21, 89–117.

Harris, J. (2006). The phonology of being understood: Further arguments against sonority. *Lingua*, 116, 1483–94.

Henke, E., Kaisse E.M. and Wright, R. (2012). Is the sonority sequencing principle an epiphenomenon? In S. Parker (ed.), *The sonority controversy* (pp. 64–100). Berlin/Boston: Mouton de Gruyter.

Holm, J. (1988). *Pidgins and Creoles, Vol II: Reference Survey.* Cambridge: Cambridge University Press.

Joubert, S. and Perl, M. (2007). The Portuguese language on Curacao and its role in the formation of Papiamentu. *Journal of Caribbean Literatures*, 5, 43–60.

Keating, A. (1984). Phonetic and phonological representation of stop consonant voicing. *Language*, 60, 286–318.

Keer, E. W. (1999). *Geminates, the OCP, and the nature of* Con. PhD dissertation, New Jersey: Rutgers University.

Kessinger, R.H. and Blumstein, S.E. (1997). Effects of speaking rate on voice onset time in Thai, French, and English. *Journal of Phonetics*, 25, 143–68.

Klein, T.B. (2011). Typology of Creole phonology: Phoneme inventories and syllable templates. *Journal of Pidgin and Creole Languages*, 26, 155–93.

Kouwenberg, S. and Murray, E. (1994). *Papiamentu.* Languages of the World/materials 83. München/Newcastle: Lincom Europa.

Ladefoged, P. (1962). *Elements of acoustic phonetics.* Chicago: The University of Chicago Press.

Ladefoged, P. and Maddieson, I. (1996). *The sounds of the world's languages.* Oxford: Blackwell.

Levelt, C. and van der Vijver, R. (2004). Syllable types in cross-linguistic and developmental grammars. In R. Krager, J. Pater and W. Zonnefeld (eds.), *Constraints in phonological acquisition* (pp. 204–18). Cambridge: Cambridge University Press.

Lisker, L. (1974). On 'explaining' vowel duration variation. *Haskins Laboratories: Status Report on Speech Research*, 37/38, 225–32.

Lisker, L. and Abramson, A. (1964). A cross-language study of voicing. *Word*, 20, 384–422.

Mansur, J.M. (1991). *Diccionario Papiamento-Ingles/Ingles-Papiamento.* Orangestad, Aruba: Edicionan Clasico Diario.

Martinus, F. (2004). *The kiss of a slave: Papiamentu's West-Africa connections.* Curaçao: Fundasho Kas Di Kultura Kòrsou.

Maurer, P. (1998). El papiamento de Curaçao. In M. Perl and A. Schwegler (eds.), *América negra: Panorámica actual de los estudios lingüísticos sobre variedades hispanas, portuguesas y criollas* (pp. 139–217). Frankfurt/Madrid: Vervuert Iberoamericana.

Morelli, Frida. (2003). The relative harmony of s+stop onsets: Obstruent clusters and the sonority sequencing principle. In C. Féry and R. van de Vivjer (eds.), *The syllable in optimality theory* (pp. 356–71). Cambridge: Cambridge University Press.

Munteanu, D. (1996). *El papiamentu, lengua criolla hispánica*. Madrid: Editorial Gredos.

Ohala, J.J. (1990). There is no interface between phonology and phonetics: A personal view. *Journal of Phonetics*, 18, 153–71.

Ohala, J.J. (1992). Alternatives to the sonority hierarchy for explaining segmental sequential constraints. *Papers from the Parasession on the Syllable: Chicago Linguistics Society, 1992*, 319–38.

Parker, S. (2002). *Quantifying the Sonority Hierarchy.* PhD dissertation, University of Massachusetts-Amherst.

Prince, A. and Smolensky, P. (1993). Optimality theory: Constraint interaction in generative grammar. *Rutgers Optimality Archive; ROA-537-0802.*

Quilis, A. (1988). *Fonética acústica de la lengua española.* Madrid: Gredos.

Reetz, H. and Jongman, A. (2009). *Phonetics: Transcription, production, acoustics and perception.* Chichester: Wiley-Blackwell.

Rialland, A. (1994). The phonology and phonetics of extrasyllabicity in French. In P.A. Keating (ed.), *Phonological structure and phonetic form: Papers in laboratory phonology* (pp. 136–59). Cambridge: Cambridge University Press.

Rivera-Castillo, Y. and Andre-Mather, P. (2016). Codeswitching and borrowing in Aruban Papiamentu: The blurring of categories. In M. Rivera (ed.), *New perspectives in Spanish contact linguistics in the Americas.* Frankfurt/Madrid: Vervuert Iberoamericana.

Rivera-Castillo, Y. and Pickering, L. (2004). Tone and stress in Papiamentu: The contribution of a constraint-based analysis to the problem of Creole genesis. *Journal of Pidgin and Creole Languages*, 13, 297–334.

Römer, R.G. (1991). *Studies in Papiamentu phonology* (Caribbean Culture Studies). Amsterdam and Kingston: The University of Amsterdam.

Scobbie, J.M. (1997). *Autosegmental representation in a declarative constraint-based framework.* New York and London: Garland Publishing. Inc.

Selkirk, E. (1984). On the major class features and syllable theory. In M. Aronoff and R.T. Oehrle (eds.), *Language sound structure: Studies in phonology presented to Morris Hale by his teacher and students* (pp. 107–36). Cambridge, Massachusetts: MIT Press.

Sharma, A. and Dorma, M.F. (1999). Cortical auditory evoked potential correlates of categorical perception of voice onset time. *Journal of the Acoustical Society of America*, 106, 1078–83.

Smith, N. (1999). Pernambuco to Suriname 1654–1655: The Jewish slave controversy. In M. Huber and M. Parkvall (eds.), *Spreading the word: The issue of diffusion among the Atlantic Creoles* (pp. 251–98). London: University of Westminster Press.

Whitney, W.D. (1981/1889). *Sanskrit grammar, including both the classical language, and the older dialects, of Veda and Brahmana.* Cambridge, MA and London: Harvard University Press.

Yolanda Rivera-Castillo is a full professor at the University of Puerto Rico-Río Piedras in the PhD program in Creole languages and literature. Her main areas of research include Creole languages, prosodic systems and the Phonology-Syntax connection. Her research also comprises other areas of inquiry such as Caribbean Spanish phonology and historical linguistics. She is currently working on the creation of web-based corpora for different Creole languages, such as Papiamentu, Palenquero and Limonese.

13
A New Sonority Degree in the Realization of the Dental Affricates /ts dz/ in Italian

Chiara Meluzzi

13.1 Introduction

Detailed classifications of sonority (e.g., Roca 1994) categorize obstruents not only as separate manners (i.e., plosives, affricates, fricatives) but according to their voicing (voiceless versus voiced). Thus, a voiceless obstruent will be lower in sonority than a voiced one. In operationalizing the Sonority Sequencing Principle (Clements 1990), therefore, a binary distinction is available based on voice. In this chapter we claim that, at least in the Italian variety of Bolzano (South Tyrol, Italy), we need to consider a new sonority degree in the pronunciation of dental affricates.

Historically, South Tyrol is basically a German-speaking area, and it was united to Italy in 1918. An Italian community started to grow during the 1920s especially because of the Fascist politics of the so-called Italianization of South Tyrol. Italian speakers have come to Bolzano from all over Italy, and in particular from Veneto, Trentino, Campania (Naples) and Calabria. Nowadays, Bolzano has 102,869 inhabitants, among which 73 per cent are self-declared Italian-speaking, and only 26.29 per cent are German speaking. On the other hand, the population of South Tyrol is made up of 69.41 per cent German speakers and 26.06 per cent Italian speakers.[1]

This historical situation has three important consequences on the Italian variety. Firstly, the Italian community was not originally settled in South Tyrol: this means that there is no Italo-Romance dialect as substratum for

1 These data come from the last national census (see ASTAT 2012). Apart from German and Italian, the remaining part of the population is made up of Ladin speakers: Ladin is a rhaeto-romance language, which is mainly spoken in some valleys between the South Tyrol, Trentino and Veneto areas.

the Italian variety,[2] which constitutes a unique case in the Italian sociolinguistic situation (see also Berruto 1995). Secondly, the Italian community is very heterogeneous: since speakers came from different dialect areas, they spoke different Italian varieties, and in many cases also some Italo-Romance dialects, which came into contact in the town of Bolzano. Finally, South Tyrol remains a multilingual area, and the Italian community has always lived in contact, even if at different degrees, with the German varieties spoken by the other linguistic community. All these factors could have led to the creation of a new variety of Italian spoken in South Tyrol, but in particular in the main town Bolzano. However, the emergence of this new variety is only a hypothesis since until now there was a substantial lack of sociolinguistic studies on this variety. In recent years there has been a growing interest in sociolinguistic and sociophonetic issues concerning the languages spoken in South Tyrol, in particular from a contact linguistics perspective (e.g., Dal Negro 2013; Vietti 2012).

In this chapter, the focus will be on a very narrow topic within the main issue of linguistic variation in the Italian spoken in Bolzano. Indeed, the pronunciation of dental affricates shows a high degree of variability inside the Italian linguistic community, due to both historical and dialectological factors (see Section 13.2). The data were based on the first corpus of Italian of Bolzano, originally collected and annotated in Meluzzi (2013), and whose criteria are described in Section 13.3. These data are now part of the CItaBol (Corpus of Italian of Bolzano), partially available on the website of TLA (The Language Archive) iniative.

This study will follow a sociophonetic approach, in the sense indicated by Foulkes and Docherty (2006: 411), who clearly state that:

> [I]t (i.e., sociophonetics) refers to variable aspects of phonetic or phonological structure in which alternative forms correlate with social factors. These factors include most obviously those social categories which have been examined extensively by sociolinguists and dialectologists: speaker gender, age, ethnicity, social class, group affiliations, geographical origin, and speaking style. Correlation may be with more than one social category simultaneously, and variation may be observable within the repertoire of an individual speaker or across groups of speakers. In cases of sociophonetic variation, then, variable forms can be said to index some or other social category.

2 The label Italo-Romance dialect is defined in Cerruti (2011). On the sociolinguistic situation of Bolzano, and on dialects used by Italian speakers see also Meluzzi (2015a).

According to the sociophonetic approach, in the collection of the corpus many different linguistic and social variables have been taken into account (Section 13.3), as well as both discrete and continuous variables. Moreover, the attention devoted to the acoustic observation and annotation of each instance has allowed the analysis to highlight some interesting phenomena, not visible otherwise. One of these phenomena is indeed the emergence of a new sonority degree (Section 13.4), which is in between the typical voiced and voiceless affricates attested in literature. The analysis will concentrate on this phenomenon, by giving sociophonetic evidence of this distribution in the corpus, and then a possible explanation of the emergence of this new phone (Section 13.5). The final section of the chapter, then, discusses possible further perspectives of the research.

13.2 Italian Dental Affricates: Between Phonetics and Phonology

Generally speaking, dental affricates, and in particular voiced dental affricates, are rare phonemes: Maddieson (1984) calculated that the voiceless /ts/ is part of the phonology repertoire of only 95 of 317 languages, whereas the voiced /dz/ occurs in only 30 languages. As for the Romance family, only Rumanian uses the dental affricate /ts/, while in Spanish and French affricates evolved to fricatives (see Malmberg 1994).[3] Among the other European languages, it is worth remembering that the German phonological system acquired the two affricates /pf/ and /ts/ after the Second Germanic consonant shift (5th–7th centuries CE; see Wiese 2000). Finally, in Russian only the voiceless dental affricate is usually considered as a phoneme, whereas the voiced one is considered as an allophone (Jones and Ward 1969).

The Italian phonological system will thus be the only one among European languages which preserves the two dental affricates with a phonological status. However, the size of the Italian phonological repertoire is an issue of debate (see Calamai 2008), in particular concerning the sonority opposition between the two dental fricatives /s, z/, and the two dental affricates /ts, dz/. Historically speaking, dental affricates should be considered

3 On the presence of dental affricates in ancient French see also Bourciez and Bourciez (1967). Spanish also preserves a voiceless palatal affricate /tʃ/ (Buridant 2000), spectrographically analysed in Alvar (1999).

as different phonemes, since they originated from two different paths. In fact, the voiceless phoneme /ts/ derives from Latin words, in particular from the context with a dental occlusive and a palatal approximant (e.g., -TJ-), whereas the voiced phoneme /dz/ usually occurs in initial position in loanwords, mainly from German languages (e.g., *zaino* 'rucksack').[4] Nowadays, the two phonemes present few minimal pairs, which can basically be reduced to the single word *razza*, meaning a kind of fish (the *ray*) with the voiced phoneme, but *race* or *breeding* with the voiceless one.[5] Even though this opposition is presented as part of the Standard Italian repertoire, it is clearly preserved only in some Central varieties (i.e., Tuscan).[6]

As a matter of fact, Italian presents a great degree of areal variation, very well documented by many dialectologists (e.g., Rohlfs 1966; Canepari 1979; Loporcaro 2009). As for affricates, the main differences could be generally found between Northern and Southern varieties in intervocalic and post-sonorant position (basically after /n/ and /l/, but also after /r/). Northern varieties prefer voiceless realizations intervocalically and after liquids, but voiced realizations are attested after /r/ in Lombardy; on the other hand, the Southern varieties show more instances of voiced realizations in every context, but especially after sonorants. Moreover, some scholars have pointed out how it is possible to have an opposite distribution of the sonority contrast between the local dialect and the Italian variety, even if this issue has been mainly investigated for the Venetian area only (see Canepari 1979).

The high areal variability in realization of dental affricates makes them the perfect linguistic variable for a first sociolinguistic inquiry of the Italian of Bolzano. The Italian community is indeed composed of people from

4 For the diachronic origin of Italian dental affricates see also Celata (2004), who offers many examples, and Banniard (2008).

5 See also De Dominicis (1999), who discusses the low functional value of the sonority opposition between the two dental affricates.

6 From a sociolinguistic point of view, it is difficult to speak of the existence of a Standard Italian at the phonetic level. There are indeed manuals of the right (that is, standard) pronunciation (e.g., Canepari 1979), but the use of these manuals is actually limited to professional speakers such as actors or, in the past, TV-journalists. It is also very difficult to state if and to what extent normal speakers are aware of the existence of a norm for the pronunciation of Italian sounds. This makes it very difficult to conduct a proper Labovian sociolinguistic investigation on Italian, since first one must define the linguistic repertoire of a community and also the prestige values associated with the different languages in that repertoire. See also Berruto (1995), while Cerruti (2011) addresses the issue of the relationship between dialect and Italian varieties.

different dialectal areas, thus with different distribution of the sonority contrast of dental affricates in the various phonological contexts. By choosing this linguistic variety, it may be possible to observe how the linguistic system of the Italian community has been internally organized, and if there are certain values of prestige (both covert and overt) associated with certain realizations. The main hypothesis is that contact between different varieties will be reflected in the sociophonetic distribution of sonority according to one or more sociolinguistic variables. Indeed, it is logical to assume that the oldest speakers have preserved traces of the sonority opposition in their own variety or dialect, whereas the youngest speakers may show instances of the supposed reorganization of the system.

13.3 Building the Corpus: Problems and Perspectives

For the purpose of a wider analysis of the Italian spoken in Bolzano, a large corpus has been collected consisting of more than 43 hours of recordings with 42 speakers who performed different stylistic tasks, as described below. All speakers were previously informed that they would be recorded for a research work on the Italian community of Bolzano. A ZOOM H2 recorder with a SONY ECM-MS907 microphone was placed in front of the speaker in a reserved room at the Free University of Bolzano between October 2011 and May 2012.[7]

Participants were selected among the Italian linguistic group, criteria included that both parents were Italian speakers, and that they had to have been born in Bolzano or have lived in the city for the last 40 years.[8] The 42 speakers were stratified according to the main sociolinguistic variables of sex (23 males, 19 females),[9] age, and level of education, but the metadata

7 It is worth emphasizing that speakers believed that the study was on the community, not specifically on the language. For some very old speakers, however, it was necessary to record the interview at their homes, but this did not affect the quality of the recordings.

8 This distinction was necessary since the oldest speakers came to Bolzano during the Fascist period, and other speakers, especially from South Italy, arrived in South Tyrol during their childhood. For more details on the sociolinguistic profile of the Italian linguistic group, see Meluzzi (2015a).

9 In this chapter the label 'sex' will be preferred, since gender issues have not been addressed during the collection of the data. It is worth remembering that

collected also considered the district of residence in Bolzano, speakers' social class, parents' origins, and self-declared competence in one or more languages, also including Italo-Romance dialects. It is worth specifying that age does not correspond to the generation of immigration into South Tyrol, since speakers in their 40s may have either arrived in Bolzano during their childhood or been born in Bolzano, whereas younger speakers would always have been born in the town. Considering the sociolinguistic situation of South Tyrol, three age groups were identified: the first includes speakers older than 60 years, who were already in the town before the approval of the second statute of autonomy in 1972; the second group consists of speakers aged between 35 and 60 years, who entered schools after the reforms of 1972, and were also present during the tensions between the Italian and German linguistic groups in the 1980s. Finally, the youngest speakers were between 18 and 35 years old and, presumably, are the ones with the most contacts with the German language and group.

However, some issues have to be fully considered before we present our analysis. First, levels of education are not equally distributed among the three age groups: since 1962, compulsory schooling has been extended to 14 years of age (i.e., to Junior High), thus only the oldest participants may have the lowest degree of education. However, it is interesting to note that people older than 70 or 80 may also be graduates, in particular if they were teachers in the first Italian schools in South Tyrol, during or immediately after the Second World War. Secondly, it has been difficult to compute the variable of parents' origins, since in many cases father's and mother's origins were really different from a dialectological point of view (e.g., father from Calabria and mother from Veneto). Moreover, the high variability in parents' origins reflects the high areal variation inside the Italian-speaking group; the same happens for the self-declaration of knowledge of one or more languages other than Italian, including the Italo-Romance dialects. Thus, these variables cannot be used for a quantitative analysis of the data, like the one proposed in this chapter, even if they could be useful for more qualitative studies (e.g., Meluzzi 2015a).

As for the research protocol, each speaker was involved in several tasks in order to achieve stylistic variation in their speech: in Labov's (1972) terms, the recordings moved from a more informal task (free one-to-one interview with the researcher) to a more formal one (reading of words in isolation on a screen); 8 speakers were also involved in small dialogues by

---

in recent years, sociophonetic research has provided clear evidence of the need for a clear distinction between sex and gender, especially when dealing with phonetic analysis; for further reference to this subject, see Cheshire (2002).

using the map-task technique, and they also read a short novel.[10] The word list consists of real words and it presents all the phonemes of Italian in different phonological contexts, that is initial position (e.g., *zio* 'uncle'), singleton and geminate intervocalic position (e.g., *dazi* 'duties' and *pazzi* 'fools'), and post-sonorant position, which means after /m/, /n/, /r/ and /l/, whenever possible (e.g., *anziano* 'old man', *arzillo* 'lively', *alzare* 'to lift'). Among the 310 words, 66 contain a dental affricate in the aforementioned phonological contexts followed by the three corner vowels /i/, /a/, and /u/ or by middle vowels when there were no lexical items to fit that context.[11] In the case of multiple types for the same context, the words were selected that were lexically more frequent or with more probabilities of appearing during the interview: for instance, the word *Bolzano* fits the phonological context post-/l/ with a following tonic /a/, and also it would appear quite often during the interview, due to the sociolinguistic context and the aim of the interview. The word *razza,* which represents the only frequent phonological minimal pair, was presented in isolation, and also in the two nominal phrases *un cane di razza* 'a pedigree' (with an expected voiceless dental affricate /ts/) and *il pesce razza* 'the ray (fish)'(with an expected voiced phone /dz/).

More informal speech was obtained during the interview, when speakers were asked about their experiences living in Bolzano, and especially about their contacts with the German linguistic group. As a matter of fact, the aforementioned peculiar sociolinguistic context of South Tyrol created a high social bias for this question, which resulted in very emphatic speeches, full of pauses, reformulations, and in some cases also swearwords. If Labov (1972) used the 'danger of death' question to reach a more informal (i.e., closer to the vernacular) style, in our case the question was about the 'danger of life' in a multicultural town, which made speakers more concentrated on the topic of the talk than on the quality of their speech.

However, as has been pointed out by Di Paolo and Yaeger-Dror (2011), it is not easy to carry out a sociophonetic analysis which also deals with stylistic variation, since when the speech is more spontaneous, the recording may be not good enough for an acoustic phonetic analysis. This often

10 All these data are now part of the so-called CItaBol (Corpus of Italian of Bolzano), belonging to the Language Study Unit of the Free University of Bolzano. The corpus has been orthographically transcribed but the annotation is still in process.

11 Middle vowels were avoided, when possible, since they show a high degree of phonetic and phonological variation among different Italian dialects and regional varieties (see Calamai 2008).

happened in our recordings as well, since during the interview, and especially in the more emphatic parts, speakers tended to move away from the microphone or to tap on the table, thus resulting in tokens not usable for acoustic analysis. Concerning our phonetic variable, it is also worth noting that in spontaneous speech dental affricates are very rare, and mostly limited to some phonological contexts (i.e., the post-nasal as in the word *abbastanza* 'enough').

For these reasons, in this chapter the data analysed are taken only from the word list, which consisted of 4,244 tokens. In fact, this led to the emergence of some phonetic details, which are not always clearly detectable in spontaneous speech, mostly due to the aforementioned quality of some recordings. Moreover, using the word list means having the exact number of tokens for each participant, thus allowing the research to focus on the phonetic facts emerging during the acoustic analysis, and on the sociophonetic distribution of the phenomena in a more balanced corpus. Finally, after having discovered a pattern of variation, an analysis of stylistic variation was carried out in a case-study concerning a sub-group of speakers (see Section 13.4.2).

13.3.1 The Corpus: Transcription and Annotation

Before exploring the sociophonetic distribution of the data, each token was transcribed, annotated and then classified in a matrix for the analysis. A first orthographic transcription of the whole corpus was made in ELAN 4.8.1, by adding some extra labels concerning the use of language different than Italian (e.g., dialects, German), or peculiar voice qualities (e.g., whispering, shouting). As expected, none of these phenomena appear in the word list, since speakers repeated types mispronounced by mistake or if there was background noise in the recordings.

After the transcription, the 4,244 tokens were extracted and annotated in PRAAT (Boersma and Weenink 2013) following an annotation protocol specifically designed for this research (see also Meluzzi 2013: 65–77). In Figure 13.1 it is possible to see an example of the annotation with the three different tiers used in the analysis. The first tier considers the whole word which is orthographically transcribed, whereas the second tier isolates the dental affricate, whose right boundary was settled as being at the end of the fricative segment. In many cases, however, the end of the frication does not correspond to the immediate start of the following vowel, whereas the intensity only started to increase: this phase in between two

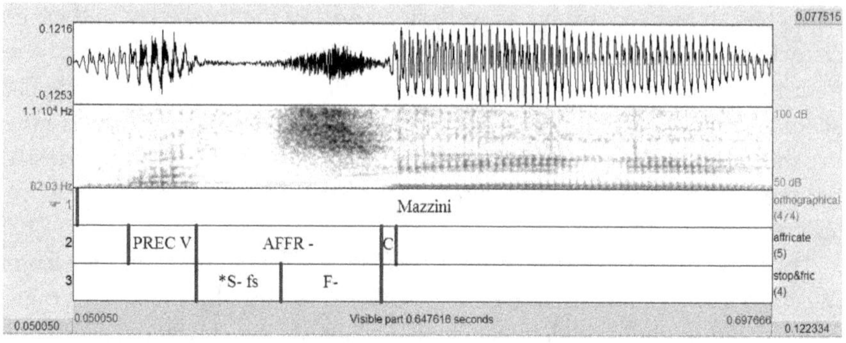

Figure 13.1. Example of the annotation of one token containing a dental affricate.

clearly delimited phones was labelled 'coarticulation' (CA), but not fully investigated yet.[12]

The placement of the left boundary is linked to the phonological context in which the dental affricate appears. At the beginning of the word, the boundary was placed at the beginning of the voicing bar for the voiced phones, whereas for the voiceless affricates it was decided to arbitrarily set the boundary at 50 ms before the main burst of the occlusive element, as has been done for the annotation of Italian plosives in previous studies (Crocco 2001). In intervocalic position, the affricate starts at the offset of the preceding vowel, that is when the F2 was no longer visible on the spectrogram (Cho and McQueen 2005); the preceding vowel was annotated as well, in order to check for a possible correlation with vowel duration between the two intervocalic contexts (see Meluzzi 2013: 110–12). Finally, in post-sonorant position the left boundary of the affricate is placed at the end of the preceding consonant, clearly detectable on both the spectrogram and the wave form.

In the third tier of annotation, the affricate was split between the plosive and the fricative part. The intermediate boundary was placed immediately after the burst (see also Foulkes, Docherty and Jones 2011), or, if the burst was not visible, at the beginning of the friction noise above 4,000–5,000 Hz (Giannini and Pettorino 1992). In this tier other phenomena were also

12 It is important to note that we use CA here as a mere label for a very complex phenomenon, investigated at length in the literature (e.g., Hardcastle and Hewlett 2006). A random survey of the corpus has revealed that this segment could show a very long duration in some speakers and in some words, thus allowing the hypothesis that it might have a sociophonetic value as well.

annotated: for instance, a special label was dedicated to the absence of the burst or, on the contrary, to the presence of multiple bursts, which seems to be an interesting characteristic of dental affricates in Bolzano.

However, in many cases the friction noise did not start immediately after the burst, but it was possible to isolate a sort of gap between the burst (or the multiple bursts) and the beginning of the characteristic fricative noise. It is also interesting to note that intensity may help in detecting this phenomenon, since it shows a drastic drop during this phase, before rapidly increasing again at the beginning of the proper frication. A similar phenomenon has been noted by Howell and Rosen (1983) for the English post-alveolar voiceless affricate /tʃ/, and for English dental plosives by Foulkes et al. (2011), who called this phase post-burst aperiodicity (PBA) with the label 'E'. A similar label was then used in our corpus, as is shown in Figure 13.2, which also represents the variation in the intensity.

It is worth noting that in our data the PBA showed a mean duration of 14–15 ms, and it does not seem to demonstrate sociophonetic variation, even if the presence or absence of this phenomenon shows a statistically significant distribution with respect to many linguistic and extralinguistic variables, in particular age and sex of the speakers.[13]

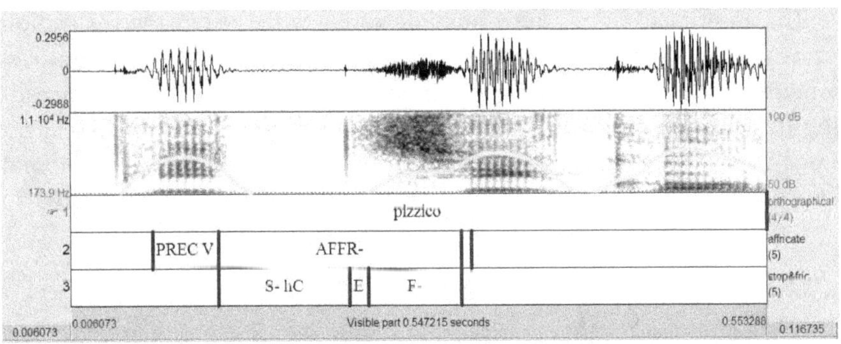

Figure 13.2. The presence of PBA (with intensity line) in the dental affricate of the word *pizzico* 'sting'.

13 In particular, PBA occurs more frequently in young and educated male speakers (see Meluzzi, 2013: 121–3).

13.4 A New Sonority Degree

With respect to the sonority of each token, the annotation criteria distinguished firstly between the voiced and voiceless affricates, with a '+' or a '–' added at the second tier (e.g., 'Affr–' indicates a voiceless production). However, during the manual annotation of the corpus, an interesting phenomenon emerged from the observation of the spectrograms: some dental affricates, in fact, presented a voicing distinction between the occlusive and the fricative part. This difference was clearly detectable on both the spectrogram, with the characteristic voicing band, and on the wave form, where the different periods of glottal activity could be easily counted. Since those cases did not seem to be isolated (i.e., related to peculiar features of one or two speakers), a new mark has been added on the second tier, thus distinguishing between voiced, voiceless and mixed (label 'mix') productions. On the third tier, the two parts of the affricates were also marked with respect to their sonority degree (i.e., voiced or voiceless). Figures 13.3 and 13.4 show two instances of mixed affricates as they occur in the production of two different speakers and in two different phonotactic contexts, with clear indications of voicing activity in the occlusive part on both the spectrogram and the wave form.

The identification of a new possible sonority degree in the realization of dental affricates was first viewed with scepticism for two reasons. As a matter of fact, these instances come from a very formal task (i.e., reading of words in isolation), thus supporting the view that these realizations were just the expression of hyper-articulated speech. A second and somehow opposite hypothesis was that mixed affricates were related to

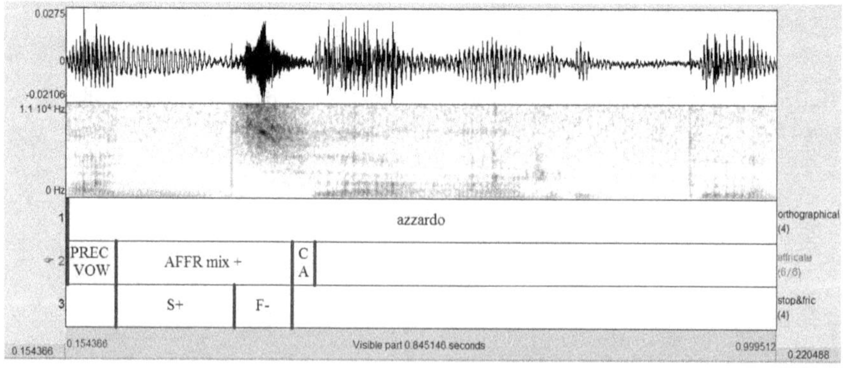

Figure 13.3. Mixed dental affricate in intervocalic geminate position (word *azzardo* 'risk').

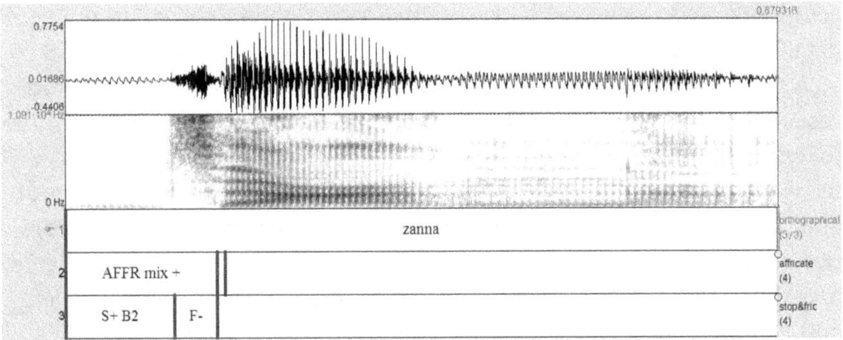

Figure 13.4. Mixed dental affricate in word-initial position (word *zanna* 'fang').

co-articulation, since they seemed more frequent in an inter-sonorant position (e.g., between vowels), and in elderly speakers, for whom minor articulatory control problems may be postulated (see, for instance, Gorham-Rowan and Laures-Gore 2006). However, at the end of the annotation, it was possible to study this phenomenon quantitatively with respect to both intra-linguistic and extra-linguistic factors: the analysis allows us to refute these first two conjectures in favour of a new one, that is, the emergence of a real new sonority degree for dental affricates in the Italian of Bolzano.

13.4.1 Sociophonetic Distribution of the Phenomenon

After the annotation, information about voicing, duration and place of articulation of each realized phone were organized into a matrix together with the sociolinguistic characteristics of the speaker (namely, sex, age group, district of residence, level of education, job, and mother's and father's origins). The duration was measured for both the whole affricate and for the plosive and fricative parts respectively, by using a PRAAT script created by Katherine Crosswhite and Mark Antoniu.[14] As for the place of articulation, it was measured on the central point of the fricative element, by extracting the four spectral moments, i.e., centre of gravity, standard deviation, skewness and kurtosis (Harrington 2013);[15] however, only the

14 The script is available on the PRAAT website: http://www. fon.hum.uva.nl/ praat/ (last accessed 10 June 2015).

15 For this analysis, a special script was devised at the Language Study Unit of the Free University of Bolzano. The script distinguished between voiceless and

centre of gravity appeared to be sensitive to sociophonetic variation in our data. The software used for the statistical analysis of the data was SPSS 20.

A look at the distribution of the voicing shows that mixed affricates represent about 25 per cent of the whole corpus, whereas 40 per cent of the tokens are realized as voiceless, and 35 per cent as fully voiced. This confirms the first impression of a non-isolated phenomenon, whose nature and origin have to be investigated with great attention. First, the distribution of these realizations in different phonotactic contexts was calculated, namely in word-initial position, in intervocalic position, both singleton and geminate, and finally after sonorants (/l/, /n/ and /r/). The results of this correlation are shown in Figure 13.5.

It is clear from the graph that the largest number of mixed affricates are found in intervocalic geminate position (e.g., *puzzare* 'to stink'), or after a sonorant (e.g., *garza* 'bandage'), which are the two contexts with the highest dialectal variability among Italian varieties (see Section 13.3). It does not seem a case that this variability is reflected in the distribution of voicing in dental affricates, with the emergence of this new degree of sonority. In particular in the post-sonorant context (Figure 13.6) it is possible to observe how mixed affricates emerge the most after /l/ and /n/. The most variable item is the Italian name of the town 'Bolzano', which is pronounced with a voiceless affricate in 33.8 per cent of the cases, with a voiced realization in 42.5 per cent of the cases and as mixed in 24.6 per cent. In the other items

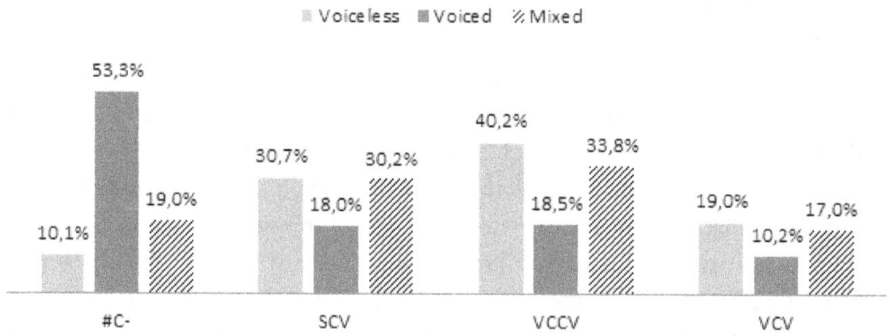

Figure 13.5. Distribution of voicing degree in different phonotactic contexts ($p < 0.001$, $\chi^2(6) = 789{,}65$).

voiced fricatives, and for the latter it applied a pass-band filter before extracting the values of the four spectral moments. The script worked on an FFT spectrum with a pre-emphasis of 6 db, and on a Hamming window of 20 ms, thus methodologically reproducing the work of Jongman et al. (2000).

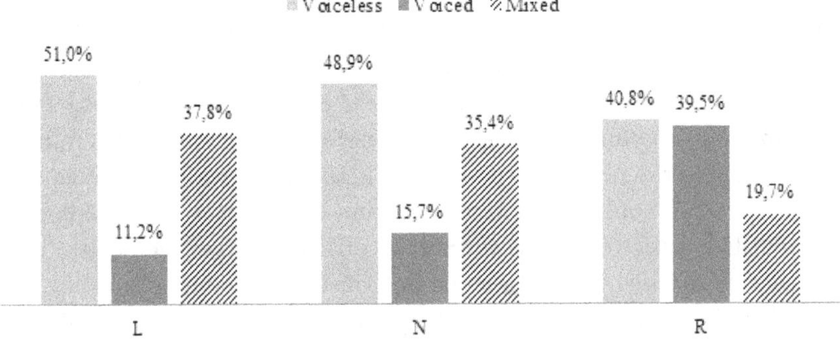

Figure 13.6. Distribution of sonority degree in post-sonorant context (SCV).

on the word lists, it is possible to notice that mixed affricates tend to occur in alternation with voiceless affricates, whereas when a high percentage of voiced realizations is preferred, the number of alternative realizations, including mixed affricates, is considerably lower. For instance, the post-nasal affricate in the word *zanzara* 'mosquito' is pronounced as voiced in 92.2 per cent of cases, whereas another common word like *anziano* 'old man' shows 54.7 per cent of voiceless realizations and 53.1 per cent of mixed affricates.

Concerning the other linguistic parameters, it is possible to note how mixed affricates have a mean duration in between voiced and voiceless phones, with the former showing the lowest values in all phonological contexts (see Table 13.1). The table does not show the word-initial context, since the annotation for this context set an arbitrary starting point at 50 ms before the burst for voiceless affricates (see Section 13.3.1). In post sonorant contexts, the mean duration of mixed affricates is close to that of totally voiceless phones, thus confirming the hypothesis, previously detected in the analysis of sonority, that this is the most interesting context. From the data it is also possible to note that all affricates in post-sonorant

Table 13.1. Mean duration (in ms) of dental affricates with respect to sonority degree and phonological context.

	SCV	VCCV	VCV	Mean duration
Voiceless	132.731	196.504	195.193	167.78
Mixed	131.376	186.072	180.765	153.20
Voiced	99.014	145.572	108.751	112.98
Total	124.259	182.692	171.561	–

context are shorter than in intervocalic contexts, as was also observed by Celata and Kaeppeli (2003) for another Italian variety. Moreover, the data show that there is not an opposition between the two intervocalic contexts for voiceless and mixed affricates, whereas the voiced realizations seem to maintain this phonological opposition between singleton and geminate.

Concerning the place of articulation, it has been previously stated that the analysis dealt only with the central point of the fricative element, thus a similarity between voiceless and mixed affricates was expected given the fact that mixed realizations are characterized by voicing only before the burst (i.e., in the occlusive part). However, the data in Table 13.2 show a different situation: while the mean values of the centre of gravity of mixed affricates are closer to voiceless than to voiced, a certain difference is maintained between the two phones. The main difference is again clearly visible between the post-sonorant and the intervocalic context.

Finally, it was observed that mixed affricates also frequently present the so-called post-burst aperiodicity, i.e., a separation between the occlusive and the fricative part. The post-burst occurs in 56 per cent of all mixed affricates, while it is present only in 48 per cent of voiceless realizations and in 47.3 per cent of voiced ones. Again, this phenomenon is more frequent in the post-sonorant phonological context (56.1 per cent of the cases).

When looking at sociolinguistic variables, interesting patterns of variation were found. The distribution of sonority among dental affricates statistically correlates with almost all the variables included in the corpus. More than statistical significance, variation in the realization of sonority follows an interesting sociolinguistic path, in particular for the mixed dental affricates.

First, with respect to the sex of the speaker it is clear that women tend to produce more mixed affricates than men do, with a difference of around 12 per cent; indeed, women realized mixed dental affricates in 32.7 per cent of the cases, whereas this percentage decreases to around 20.4 per cent for men. Men's realizations, on the other hand, are more polarized towards total voiceless or total voiced varieties, with 41.2 per cent of voiceless affricates and 38.4 per cent of voiced. These percentages are lower for

Table 13.2. Mean value of the centre of gravity (Hz) with respect to sonority degree and phonological context.

	#C-	SCV	VCCV	VCV	Total
Voiceless	7819.231	7895.784	8199.079	8253.631	8070.401
Mixed	8093.231	7503.798	7935.422	7689.570	7802.921
Voiced	8225.459	8243.109	7909.633	7862.489	8132.383

women with 37.9 per cent of voiceless realizations and 29.4 per cent of voiced realizations.[16]

A second correlation concerns the age of the speaker, with a pattern that could be summed up as: the younger the speaker the fewer the mixed affricates. In fact, mixed realizations are found in 31.3 per cent of the affricates produced by people older than 60 years, a percentage that constantly decreases in the other two age groups, going from 24.8 per cent in people aged between 35 and 60 years to 22.2 per cent in people aged between 18 and 35 years.[17] As for the other two sonority degrees, the youngest speakers show the highest value of total voiced dental affricates (38.3 per cent of the realizations within their age group), whereas voiceless affricates are preferred by people aged between 35 and 60 years (41.2 per cent of the realizations).

Combining these two variables, the results confirm the tendency already observed, as is shown in Table 13.3. It is possible to note that women always produce more mixed affricates than men, and that for both the sexes the percentages of these mixed realizations are lower in the youngest speakers than in the oldest ones. This shift is not very dramatic, but it is clearly visible in comparing the oldest and the youngest of the age groups.

Another interesting correlation concerns the distribution of sonority across different levels of education (Figure 13.7). The percentage of mixed affricates dramatically decreases from the 39.4 per cent of the lowest level of education (elementary school) to the 22 per cent recorded for graduates. This drop is also visible in the other levels, with 27.3 per cent of mixed

Table 13.3. Realization of dental affricates according to speakers' sex and age group ($p < 0.001$).

	Age group	Voiceless Aff.	Voiced Aff.	Mixed Aff.	Total
Women	60+ years	37.0%	25.4%	**37.6%**	100%
	35–60 years	38.9%	30.7%	**30.4%**	100%
	18–35 years	37.0%	31.4%	**31.6%**	100%
Men	60+ years	35.3%	41.2%	**23.5%**	100%
	35–60 years	42.4%	35.6%	**22.1%**	100%
	18–35 years	41.2%	43.1%	**15.7%**	100%

16 The correlation between sonority degree and sex of the speaker is statistically significant for $\chi^2(2)=79.67, p < 0.001$.

17 The correlation between sonority degree and age of the speaker is statistically significant for $\chi^2(2)=25.02, p < 0.001$

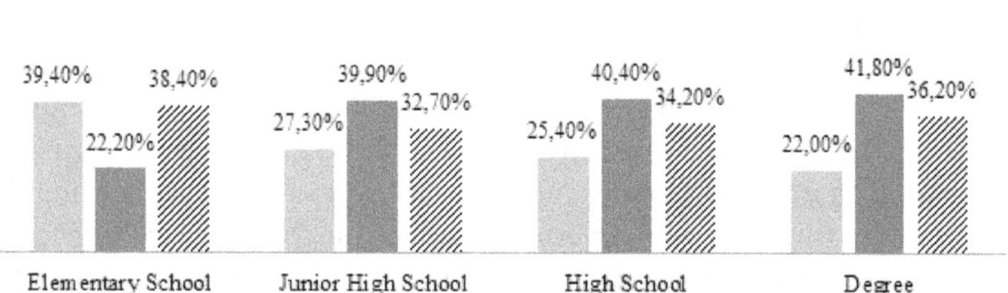

Figure 13.7. Realization of dental affricates in the different levels of education ($\chi^2(6)=40.45$, $p < 0.001$).

affricates shown by people with a junior high education, and 25.4 per cent in people with a high school degree. As it was for age, this situation could be simplified by the formula: the lower the education the higher the presence of mixed affricates.

A similar tendency was found for the correlation between mixed affricates production and social status of the speakers, although there is not a noticeable change with respect simply to speakers' social class.[18] Figure 13.8 shows the variation in sonority degree of dental affricates with respect to status, a complex variable which takes into account both level of education and job rank (Meluzzi 2013: 78). It is possible to notice how mixed

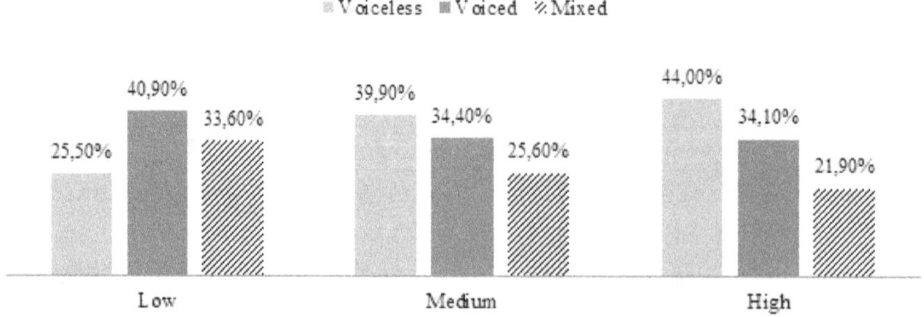

Figure 13.8. Realization of dental affricates in the three social status groups ($\chi^2(4)=37.75$, $p < 0.001$).

18 It is worth remembering that it is methodologically very difficult to apply the sociolinguistic concept of social class to our corpus. The notion of social class is mainly relevant for anglophone countries (see also Block 2013), but not for the Italian situation, in which social class seems to be determined more by level of education than by job position or possessions (see also Berruto 1980).

and voiced affricates characterize low social status, while their percentage noticeably decreases in the medium status group. Mixed affricates, then, show their lowest percentage of occurrence in the high status group.

Other correlations did not result in statistically significant findings: this happened in particular for multivariate analyses with subgroups of speakers selected, for instance, on the basis of sex and level of education. Moreover, other significant correlations did not show any interesting variation for the topic under discussion. For instance, with respect to the district of residence there is only a slight difference between mixed dental affricates produced by speakers in Italian districts (24.3 per cent) and the percentage used by speakers in German districts (28.3 per cent). Moreover, the two variables of parents' origins (i.e., father and mother) were not relevant, since they show a very high degree of variation, thus resulting in a difficulty in computing these variables in a quantitative analysis (see Section 13.3).

13.4.2 Formal and Informal Tasks: A Case-Study

The previous results were based on the productions recorded during the reading of the word list, that is in a very formal task. Thus, an intriguing question concerns the emergence of these mixed affricates (and other phenomena) in more informal speech, for instance during the interview or while reading a small number of tongue-twisters. As has been pointed out in Section 13.3, dental affricate phonemes are not very widespread in the Italian lexicon: in spontaneous speech, dental affricates are practically limited to a small number of words (e.g., *abbastanza* 'enough', *senza* 'without' or the name of the town 'Bolzano'), and to some phonological contexts such as post-sonorant or intervocalic (geminate), whereas it is impossible to have a real word-initial instance.

A small case-study on stylistic variation considered the productions of five speakers only, all belonging to the same family group, and differing in age, sex and level of education. The two women were aged 97 (019LR) and 31 (011StLG) respectively, and they both had a high school degree; the three men covered the three age groups and levels of education, with the father (037SaLG) having a junior high degree, the son (004SLG) a high school one, and the young cousin (018ALG) with an MA in architecture. This sub-corpus constituted about 4 hours of recording, among which were 2h 39m of free talk collected during the interview (see also Meluzzi 2015b). As for dental affricates, all speakers produced more than 20 instances of these phonemes, even if with major differences among them

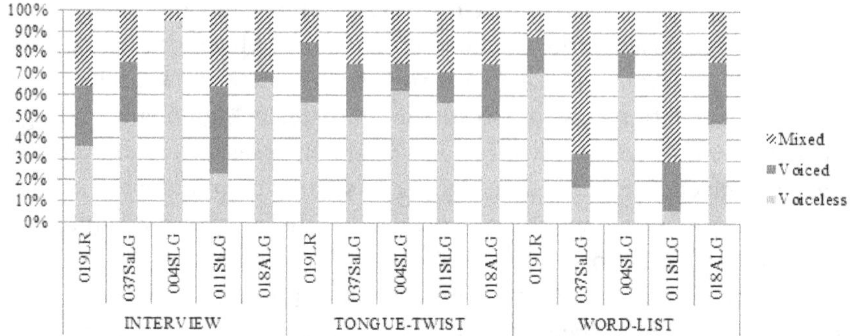

Figure 13.9. Sonority variation in the post-sonorant context in the LG family.

(e.g., 54 tokens from 011StLG, but only 21 from the grandmother 019LR). Moreover, as expected, only the post-sonorant context is well attested in the informal speech of all speakers. Figure 13.9 shows the distribution of sonority in the three different tasks for all the members of the family, limited to the post-sonorant context. Due to an insufficient amount of data, however, this correlation can be considered only as a qualitative picture, without any quantitative claims.

The graph shows that mixed affricates are attested in both formal and informal speech for all speakers, even if they are more frequent in the word list than in the interview. Interestingly, the youngest male speaker with the highest level of education (018ALG) shows an opposite pattern: the presence of mixed dental affricates in his production slightly decreases from the interview (28.5 per cent) to the tongue-twister (25 per cent) and finally to the word-list (23.5 per cent). As for the other family members, speakers with the largest amount of mixed realizations in the word-list are 011StLG (young female) and 037SaLG (old male educated up to junior high). During the interview, however, mixed affricates appear more frequently in the speech of the two women of the family (i.e., 019LR and 011StLG).

13.5 The Mixed Affricates: A Possible Explanation

The evidence of the existence of a new sonority degree in the realization of Italian dental affricates has already been provided during the acoustic analysis of the data, and the annotation of the corpus. The sociophonetic analysis then shows some patterns of variation that are particularly interesting, and that at least allow for a further hypothesis on the nature and origin of these phones.

As a matter of fact, the data do not confirm the initial conjectures that these realizations are due to some kind of hyper-articulation or co-articulation. Firstly, mixed affricates constitute one quarter of the whole corpus, and they statistically correlate with other linguistic and social variables. Secondly, the emergence of these phones does not seem to be related only to the possible hyper-articulated speech of the word-list. Mixed dental affricates have been found also in the informal speech of the interview of all the five members of the family analysed as a case-study. Moreover, these phones have been found for all speakers, thus refusing the hypothesis that this in-between sonority type is only found with people with deficits in the articulatory organs. For instance, in the family analysed it was noted how even the youngest man (018ALG) produced a noticeable number of mixed dental affricates in both word list style and informal interview.

But what are these mixed dental affricates? At the current state of our research it remains very difficult to answer this question. Phonetically speaking, these realizations could be easily considered as lenited phones, which have been frequently found in many languages, and also as a characteristic of some Italian varieties. Marotta (2008: 239) acoustically analyses lenited stops in the Centre-South of Italy, by showing the main spectral characteristics of such phones, that is:

> a slight voicing activity (...) at low frequency; the amplitude is less than that of the voice bar typical for plain voiced stops; VOT is not always present and the friction noise spans over a reduced frequency band; normally, no burst occurs; if present, it has a very little energy. Another acoustic feature is duration: lenited segments are longer than the corresponding voiced stops, but shorter than unlenited voiceless stops.

In our data, it has been noted how mixed affricates have a duration in-between voiceless and voiced phones, but more similar to the former than to the latter. However, the burst is usually clearly present in our data, and it also appears as multiple examples (multiple bursts). Moreover, it has been emphasized how mixed affricates tend to co-occur with another peculiar phenomenon, that is the gap between the occlusive and the fricative part of the affricate (post-burst aperiodicity, PBA). In our opinion, the presence of this gap speaks against the interpretation of mixed affricates as lenited consonants, since the introduction of this pause and the change in the sonority degree seems to indicate that the opposite process is going on. Thus, it seems more reasonable to consider these phones as in-between realizations, also with a characteristic sociophonetic distribution.

In fact, since they have not been documented elsewhere as far as we know, a second question concerns the possible origin of mixed dental affricates in the Italian variety spoken in Bolzano. The sociophonetic analysis has shown how mixed affricates appear more frequently in the speech of elderly people, women, and people with low status and low degree of education. On the contrary, young male speakers and speakers with a high degree of education tend to avoid mixed realizations, at least in more controlled speech, since the case study proved that even these speakers may use a high number of mixed affricates in casual speech.

This distribution may lead to the interpretation that mixed affricates are an old variant, which has emerged from the contact among different Italian varieties (and different Italo-Romance dialects as well). In fact, as noted, the distribution of sonority of dental affricates is particularly controversial within Italy, and in particular in some phonological contexts, such as post-sonorant and geminate intervocalic positions. In our data these contexts, and in particular post-nasal and post-liquid, show the highest frequencies of production of mixed affricates, thus confirming this interpretation. Putting it simply, when coming to Bolzano speakers had to deal with the variation in the distribution of sonority in dental affricates, a parameter highly variable and with no clear distributional laws: in this context, a new sonority degree has emerged as a variable of accommodation between conflicting systems. This is a known process which has already been attested in literature: for instance, Nocchi and Filipponio (2012) documented how a linguistic change in progress may led to the emergence of new interdialectal forms. A similar process may be seen in action for the Italian of Bolzano, which could be considered a real 'new town' in the sense indicated by Kerswill and Williams (2005), at least for how it concerns the Italian community.

13.6 Conclusions and Further Perspectives

This chapter has considered the emergence of a new sonority degree in Italian dental affricates as pronounced in the city of Bolzano. The peculiar characteristics of this Italian variety constitute the perfect research area for a sociophonetic investigation, especially in dealing with rare and variable phonemes such as dental affricates. Indeed, there is a great areal variation in the distribution of sonority in dental affricates, especially in post-sonorant and geminate intervocalic positions, among the different Italian varieties and Italo-Romance dialects. As many of these varieties came into contact in the town of Bolzano, a new sonority degree in dental affricates has emerged. This mixed affricate is acoustically characterized by voicing only in the occlusive part, whereas the fricative part is produced as voiceless. The sociophonetic distribution of this new sonority degree supports the claim that it is a contact-induced emergence in a situation of linguistic contact and of language change.

Many issues remain up to further investigations in this topic in order to improve our knowledge about this phenomenon. First, it seems necessary that a sociophonetic investigation be undertaken at the perceptual level too, in order to see if this new sonority degree is perceived by listeners, and if there is a prestige value associated with these realizations. Secondly, it would be interesting to verify the existence of similar phenomena for other variable phonemes, for instance for alveolar fricatives, which have already shown the possibility of intermediate phones with respect to sonority degree. This further research could be based on the already existing corpus, CItaBol (Corpus of Italian of Bolzano), in order to fully investigate the sociophonetic variation of the Italian variety of Bolzano.

References

ASTAT (2012). *Andamento e struttura della popolazione di Bolzano e dei suoi quartieri*. Bolzano: Città di Bolzano.

Alvar, D. (ed.) (1999). *Manual de dialectología hispánica. El Español de España*. Barcelona: Ariel.

Banniard, M. (2008). *Du latin aux langues romanes*. Paris: Armand Colin.

Berruto, G. (1980). *La variabilità sociale della lingua*. Torino: Loescher.

Berruto, G. (1995). *Fondamenti di sociolinguistica*. Roma: Laterza.

Block, D. (2013). *Social class in applied linguistics*. London: Routledge.

Boersma, P. and Weenink, D. (2013). *Praat: Doing phonetics by computer [Computer program]. Version 5.3.51*, retrieved 2 June 2013 from http://www.praat.org/.

Bourciez, E. and Bourciez, J. (1967). *Phonétique française. Étude historique*. Paris: Klincksieck.

Buridant, C. (2000). *Grammaire nouvelle de l'ancien français*. Paris: Sedes.

Calamai, S. (2008). *L'italiano: suoni e forme*. Roma: Carocci.

Canepari, L. (1979). *Italiano standard e pronunce regionali*. Padova: Cleup.

Celata, C. (2004). *Acquisizione e mutamento di categorie fonologiche. Le affricate in italiano*. Pavia: Franco Angeli.

Celata, C. and Kaeppeli, B. (2003). Affricazione e rafforzamento in italiano: alcuni dati sperimentali. *Quaderni del laboratorio di linguistica*, 4, 43–59.

Cerruti, M. (2011). Regional varieties of Italian in the linguistic repertoire, *International Journal of the Sociology of Language*, 210, 9–28.

Cheshire, J. (2002). Sex and gender in variationist research. In J.K. Chambers, P. Trudgill and N. Schilling-Estes (eds.), *The handbook of language variation and change* (pp. 423–43). London: Blackwell.

Cho, T. and McQueen, J.R. (2005). Prosodic influences on consonant production in Dutch: Effects of prosodic boundaries, phrasal accent and lexical stress. *Journal of Phonetics*, 33, 121–57.

Clements, G.N. (1990). The role of the sonority cycle in core syllabification. In J. Kingston and M. Beckman (eds.), *Papers in laboratory phonology 1: Between the grammar and the physics of speech* (pp. 283–333). Cambridge: Cambridge University Press.

Crocco, C. (2001). I corpora AVIP e CLIPS: il problema della codifica e della rappresentazione degli italiani regionali. In F. Fusco and C. Marcato (eds.), *Plurilinguismo. Contatti e culture* (pp. 151–64). Udine: Forum Editore.

Dal Negro, S. (2013). Dealing with bilingual corpora: Parts of speech distribution and bilingual patterns. *Revue française de linguistique appliquée*, XVIII/2, 15–28.

De Dominicis, A. (1999). *Fonologia comparata delle principali lingue europee moderne*. Bologna: Clueb.

Di Paolo, M. and Yaeger-Dror, M. (eds.) (2011). *Sociophonetics: A student's guide*. London/New York: Routledge.

Foulkes, P. and Docherty, G. (2006). The social life of phonetics and phonology. *Journal of Phonetics*, 34, 409–38.

Foulkes, P., Docherty, G. and Jones, M.J. (2011). Analyzing stops. In M. Di Paolo and M. Yaeger-Dror (eds.), *Sociophonetics: A student's guide* (pp. 58–71). London: Routledge.

Giannini, A. and Pettorino, M. (1992). *La fonetica sperimentale*. Napoli: Edizioni Scientifiche Italiane.

Gorham-Rowan, M.M. and Laures-Gore, J. (2006). Acoustic-perceptual correlates of voice quality in elderly men and women. *Journal of Communication Disorders*, 39, 171–84.

Hardcastle, W. and Hewlett, N. (2006). *Coarticulation: Theory, data, and techniques*. Cambridge: Cambridge University Press.

Harrington, J. (2013). Acoustic phonetics, in W.J. Hardcastle, J. Laver and F.E. Gibbon (eds.), *The handbook of phonetic sciences*, 2nd edition (pp. 81–129). London: Blackwell.

Howell, P. and Rosen, S. (1983). Production and perception of rise time in the voiceless affricate/fricative distinction. *Journal of the Acoustical Society of America*, 73, 976–84.

Jones, D. and Ward, D. (1969). *The phonetics of Russian*. Cambridge: Cambridge University Press.

Jongman, A., Wayland, R. and Wong, S. (2000). Acoustic characteristics of English fricatives, *Journal of the Acoustical Society of America*, 108, 1252–63.

Kerswill, P. and Williams, A. (2005). New towns and koineisation: Linguistic and social correlates, *Linguistics*, 43, 1023–48.

Labov, W. (1972). *Sociolinguistic patterns*. Philadelphia: University of Pennsylvania Press.

Loporcaro, M. (2009). *Profilo linguistico dei dialetti italiani*. Roma/Bari: Laterza.

Maddieson, J. (1984). *Patterns of sounds*. Cambridge: Cambridge University Press.

Malmberg, B. (1994). *Manuale di fonetica generale*. Bologna: Il Mulino.

Marotta, G. (2008). Lenition in Tuscan Italian (Gorgia Toscana). In J. Brandão de Carvalho, T. Scheer and P. Ségéral (eds.), *Lenition and fortition* (pp. 235–72). Berlin: Mouton de Gruyter.

Meluzzi, C. (2013). *Le affricate dentali nell'italiano di Bolzano. Un approccio socio-fonetico*. PhD thesis, University of Pavia / Free University of Bolzano.

Meluzzi, C. (2015a). Dialects and linguistic identity of Italian speakers in Bolzano. *Globe: A Journal of Language and Communication*, 1, 1–16.

Meluzzi, C. (2015b). La pronuncia delle affricate dentali di una famiglia Bolzanina. In E. Pirvu (ed.), *La lingua e la letteratura italiana in prospettiva sincronica e diacronica* (pp. 233–44). Atti del VI convegno italianistica dell'Università di Craiova, 19–20 settembre 2014.

Nocchi, N. and Filipponio, L. (2012). *Lo vuoi co[z]ì o co[s]ì? A sociophonetic study on sibilants in the regional Italian of Livorno (Tuscany)*. In S. Calamai, C. Celata and L. Ciucci (eds.), *Sociophonetics, at the crossroads of speech variation, processing and communication* (pp. 53–6). Pisa: Edizioni della Scuola Normale Superiore.

Roca, I. (1994). *Generative phonology*. London: Routledge.

Rohlfs, G. (1966). *Grammatica storica della lingua italiana e dei suoi dialetti, volume 2*. Torino: Einaudi.

Vietti, A. (2012). Language contact and sociophonetic variation. In S. Calamai, C. Celata and L. Ciucci (eds.), *Sociophonetics, at the crossroads of speech variation, processing and communication* (pp. 76–9). Pisa: Edizioni della Scuola Normale Superiore.

Wiese, R. (2000). *The phonology of German*. Oxford: Oxford University Press.

Chiara Meluzzi holds a post-doc in Phonetics at the Scuola Normale Superiore in Pisa (Italy). She completed her PhD in Linguistics at the University of Pavia and the Free University of Bolzano/Bozen (Italy) in 2014. Her main research focus is on sociolinguistics and related fields, in particular concerning Italian spoken and written varieties. For her PhD research, she collected a lot of data on the spoken Italian of Bolzano (South Tyrol), which constitutes the CITABOL corpus. She is now investigating Italian gemination and coarticulation with both acoustic and ultrasound techniques.

14
Sonority and Initial Consonant Mutation in the Celtic Languages

Martin J. Ball and Nicole Müller

14.1 Introduction

In this chapter we describe the characteristic of initial consonant mutation in Celtic languages, and investigate whether the patterns of sound changes that occur are in line with the predictions of sonority theory or not.

Sonority has been used as an explanation for syllable structure (via Clements' 1990 Sonority Sequencing Principle or SSP), and for phonotactics in general (via Clements' 1990 Sonority Dispersion Principle or SDP). The SSP predicts that a syllable onset will be lower in sonority than the nucleus (and, indeed, that the preferred syllable onset will be maximally lower in sonority producing a steep climb in sonority between the onset and the nucleus), whereas the syllable coda will be lower in sonority but preferably with a shallow fall in sonority rather than a steep one. The SDP predicts that, for example, neighbouring consonants in a cluster will preferably show larger (rather than smaller) distances in sonority ranking, and more or less equal spacing between the consonants and the following vowel in a cluster (using a typical 5-point ranking scale) (Parker 2012).

The differences in sonority between different speech sound groups is, unfortunately, not agreed on by phonologists (as seen in the different chapters in this collection). While it is universally agreed that vowels are the most sonorant sounds, and plosives the least, less agreement is found on how large groupings of sounds should be. Thus, vowels are usually all grouped together but Jespersen (1904), for example, divides vowels into three groups of high, mid and low. Obstruents are often all grouped together (Clements 1990), but may also be divided into plosives and fricatives (Blevins 1995), or into voiceless plosives, voiced plosives, voiceless fricatives and voiced fricatives (Burquest and Payne 1993). These differences clearly impact both the SSP and the SDP. For example, /s/ clusters (see Goad, this volume) breach the SSP if fricatives are separate from plosives, as the onset in an English word such as *speech* shows a fall in sonority from /s/ to /p/, followed by a rise from /p/ to /i/. However, if plosives and fricatives are classed together as obstruents, then /sp-/ produces a sonority plateau which, although not ideal, at least does not breach the SSP. Similarly, a combination of /pl-/ is preferable to a combination of /fl-/ under the SDP, but only if plosives and fricatives are in separate sonority groupings; if they are classed together as obstruents then the SDP cannot distinguish them.

In this chapter we adopt sonority rankings for each of the three Celtic languages that we investigate (Welsh, Breton, Irish) separately in the spirit of polysystemicity (see e.g., Firth 1948; Tench 1992; also Ball, Müller and Rutter 2008). The sonority ranks and ordering (from least to most sonorous) for Welsh are as follows: voiceless plosives, voiced plosives, voiceless fricatives, voiced fricatives, voiceless nasals, voiced nasals, voiceless liquids, voiced liquids, glides and vowels.[1] These categories are ranked from 1 (voiceless plosives) to 10 (vowels) in our description of syllable shapes and onset clusters in Welsh. For Breton, the ranks are as follows: voiceless plosives, voiced plosives, voiceless fricatives, voiced fricatives, nasals, liquids, glides, vowels, with values from 1 (voiceless plosives) to 8 (vowels). For Irish, we use the same ranks and ordering as for Breton with the exception of the glide category as we have treated glides as variants of voiced fricatives (as suggested by the mutation system). Thus the ranks are ordered from 1 (voiceless plosives) to 7 (vowels). We considered dividing each consonantal rank into a palatalized and velarized group, but as this distinction plays little part in initial consonant mutation this was not adopted for the present analysis.

14.2 Consonantal Systems of Welsh, Breton and Irish

The system of contrastive consonants in Welsh is shown in Table 14.1. The orthographic forms for the consonants are illustrated in Table 14.4. The transcription is based on Ball and Williams (2001).

1 As we will not be discussing affricates, we will not comment on how they should be characterized in terms of sonority. We will class Welsh /ɬ/ as a voiceless liquid, while recognizing that it could be argued that it should be included with the voiceless fricatives.

Table 14.1. Consonant system of Welsh.

	bilabial	labio-dental	dental	alveolar	post-alveolar	palatal	velar	glottal
vcls plos	p			t			k	
vcd plos	b			d			g	
vcls affric					tʃ			
vcd affric					dʒ			
vcls fric		f	θ	s	ʃ		x	h
vcd fric		v	ð	(z)				
vcls nasal	m̥^{h}			n̥^{h}			ŋ̊^{h}	
vcd nasal	m			n			ŋ	
vcls lat				ɬ				
vcd lat				l				
vcls trill				r̥^{h}				
vcd trill				r				
glide	w					j	w	

Note: the voiceless nasals are often considered to be clusters of nasal+/h/; /z/ is peripheral, occurring only in loans in the south, which are realized as /s/ in the north.

The system of contrastive consonants in Breton is shown in Table 14.2. The orthographic equivalents are illustrated in Table 14.5. See Press (2005) for a discussion of the fortis-lenis distinction in Breton and alternative ways of symbolizing the consonants. The transcription is based on Stephens (1993).

Table 14.2. Consonant system of Breton.

	bilabial	labio-dental	alveolar	post-alveolar	palatal	velar	labial velar	uvular	glottal
vcls plos	p		t			k			
vcd plos	b		d			g	g^{w}		
vcls fric		f	s	ʃ		x	x^{w}		h
vcd fric		v	z	ʒ					
vcd nasal	m		n		ɲ				
vcd lat			l		ʎ				
vcd trill			r					ʀ	
glide	ɥ				j, ɥ		w		

Note: The alveolar and uvular trills are alternative realizations for a single trill consonant. The orthographic *c'h* may have the following variants: [x], [ɣ] or [h]. The glides [w] and [ɥ] are generally deemed to be variants of a single unit.

The system of contrastive consonants in Irish is shown in Table 14.3. As palatalization versus velarization is contrastive in Irish, this distinction is shown in the table. Orthographic forms are found in Table 14.6.

Table 14.3. Consonant system of Irish.

	bilabial / labio-dental		dental / alveolar / post-alveolar		palatal / velar		glottal
	+pal	+vel	+pal	+vel	+pal	+vel	
vcls plos	pʲ	pˠ	tʲ	tˠ	c	k	
vcd plos	bʲ	bˠ	dʲ	dˠ	ɟ	ɡ	
vcls fric	fʲ	fˠ	ʃ	s	ç	x	h
vcd fric	vʲ	w, vˠ	ʒ	z	j, ʝ	ɣ	
vcd nasal	mʲ	mˠ	nʲ	nˠ	ɲ	ŋ	
vcd lat			lʲ	lˠ			
vcd tap/trill			rʲ, ɾʲ	rˠ, ɾˠ			

Note: [j] and [ʝ], and [w] and [vˠ] are variants of single units respectively; the tap and trill rhotics are also noncontrastive variants. Some dialects retain palatalized and velarized fortis laterals and fortis coronal nasals. The fortis examples are assumed to be longer and have greater tongue-palate contact. They are usually transcribed [Lʲ], [Lˠ], [Nʲ] and [Nˠ]. /ʒ/ and /z/ are restricted to loan words.

Phonetic transcriptions of Irish usually take one of two approaches. One approach (e.g., Hickey 2014) keeps the same symbol for most palatalized and velarized pairs of consonants using diacritics to distinguish each pair. An alternative approach (e.g., Ní Chasaide 1999) uses separate symbols where possible, restricting diacritics to those pairs where separate symbols are not appropriate. We adopt this latter view. Also, as noted in Table 14.3, the symbols /w/ and /j/ may both be realized with fricative variants and, for this reason, we exclude the category of glide from the chart. The palatalized oral and nasal coronal stops and lateral are usually dental, but for reasons of simplicity in transcription, we omit the nasal diacritic in these cases.

14.3 Syllable Onsets in Welsh, Breton and Irish

In this section we will consider possible onsets in Welsh, Breton and Irish excluding the effect of initial consonant mutation (ICM, see Section 14.4).

Thus, at this stage, we will exclude consonants that only occur through the application of the mutation system. All the Celtic languages allow vowel-initial syllables in word-initial position, but we exclude further consideration of these here.

14.3.1 Welsh

All consonants in Welsh can occur in syllable onset position except /ŋ/, /x/[2] and /ð/.[3] Czerniak (2015) notes that even these consonants do occur word-initially as mutation reflexes. Formerly, word-initial /l/ and /r/ were also only mutation reflexes, but borrowings and contracted forms have resulted in both these consonants being found in non-mutation environments. Sonority dispersion values (based on the classification in Section 14.1 above) vary from 1–10 for voiceless plosive singleton initials (e.g., *pen* 'head' /pɛn/), to 9–10 for glide initial words (e.g., *iaith* 'language' /jaɪθ/), with all possible dispersion values used except for 5–10, as the voiceless nasals do not occur word-initially except as mutation reflexes.

Onset clusters in Welsh may consist of two or three consonants; Czerniak (2015) notes that a few 4-consonant clusters are possible, and we return to discuss the analysis allowing this interpretation below. Awbery (1984) notes that 2-consonant clusters in onset position are restricted to obstruent+obstruent, or obstruent+sonorant. We illustrate these different types in (1) and (2) below, including the sonority dispersion values.[4]

(1) Obstruent+obstruent clusters

/sp-/	sbâr 'spare'	3–1
/st-/	stem 'steam'	3–1
/sk-/	sgôr 'score'	3–1

2 The velar fricative /x/ almost always appears word-initially only in /xw-/ clusters. A very few exceptions exist in colloquial speech, most notably /xi/ (*chi*, 'you' plural), which is a contracted form of literary *chwi*.

3 Native speakers may no longer feel that commonly occurring words such as *ddoe* ('yesterday') are, in fact, mutated, especially as the unmutated form *doe* occurs so rarely. However, time adverbs are subject to soft mutation, so technically *ddoe* is indeed a mutated form.

4 Some of the examples are our own, others are from Czerniak (2015). The latter source includes some clusters that are dialectal or colloquial, mostly based on Fynes-Clinton (1913). We have excluded several of these where we felt that they did not occur in mainstream colloquial speech of today. Clusters marked 'rare'

(2) Obstruent+sonorant clusters

/pn-/	pnawn 'afternoon'	1–6
/pl-/	plentyn 'child'	1–8
/pr-/	pryd 'time'	1–8
/pj-/	pioden 'magpie'	1–9
/bl-/	blas 'taste'	2–8
/br-/	brawd 'brother'	2–8
/bw-/	bwi 'buoy'	2–9
/tl-/	tlodi 'poverty'	1–8
/tr-/	tri 'three'	1–8
/dr-/	drwg 'bad'	2–8
/dj-/	diawl 'devil'	2–9
/dw-/	dweud 'to say'	2–9 (only found in this word and derivatives)
/kn-/	cnoi 'to chew'	1–6
/kl-/	cloch 'bell'	1–8
/kr-/	creu 'to create'	1–8
/kw-/	cwestiyn 'question'	1–9
/gn-/	gnawd 'custom(ary) '	2–6
/gl-/	glas 'blue'	2–8
/gr-/	grym 'strength'	2–8
/gw-/	gweld 'to see'	2–9
/fl-/	fflach 'flash'	3–8 (comparatively rare)
/fr-/	ffrâm 'frame'	3–8 (comparatively rare)
/vr-/	fri 'above'	4–8 (very rare)
/θr-/	thrôn 'throne'	3–8 (very rare)
/sm-/	smotyn 'spot'	3–6 (comparatively rare)
/sn-/	snisin 'snuff'	3–6 (comparatively rare)
/sl-/	sleisen 'slice'	3–8 (comparatively rare)
/xw-/	chwech 'six'	3–9

The /s-/ clusters in (1) above clearly break the SSP, but as many researchers have pointed out (see, for example, Goad, this volume), /s-/ clusters do seem to be a special case, and we will not discuss this point further here. The clusters in (2) follow the SSP, with sonority distances ranging from 8 down to 3.

In Welsh, 3-consonant clusters consist of two sub-groups: /s/+plosive+sonorant, and velar plosive+two sonorants. We exemplify these in (3) and (4).

---

are so judged against entries in *Geiriadur Prifiysgol Cymru* (Thomas, Bevan and Donovan 1967–2002); this does not necessarily imply that the example words are rare.

(3) /s/+plosive+sonorant clusters

/spl-/	sbloet '(an) exploit'	3–1–8
/spr-/	sbri 'fun'	3–1–8
/str-/	stryd 'street'	3–1–8
/skl-/	sglefrio 'to skate'	3–1–8
/skr-/	sgrechian 'to shriek'	3–1–8
/skw-/	sgwâr 'square'	3–1–9

(4) Clusters with velar plosive+two sonorants

/klj-/	cliaran 'term of reproach'	1–8–9 (dialect form from Fynes-Clinton 1913)
/krj-/	creadur 'creature'	1–8–9 (dialect form from Fynes-Clinton 1913)
/gwn-/	gwneud 'make, do'	2–9–6
/gwl-/	gwlad 'country'	2–9–8
/gwr-/	gwres 'heat'	2–9–8

The 3-consonant clusters in (3) are mostly derived either from borrowings, or from contractions of more literary forms starting with a vowel (e.g. *ysgrîn* → *'sgrin*). The clusters in (4) depend on an analysis where *cliaren* and *creadur* are deemed to have a semi-vowel /j/ in the onset rather than a vowel (these being dialect forms described a century ago in Fynes-Clinton 1913, that may no longer be used), or where /gw/ consists of two consonants rather than a labialized velar. We follow Czerniak (2015) in including these, but recognize that this is a matter of interpretation. Czerniak's analysis also permits a very few 4-consonant clusters. His example is [gwnjɑdrɑg] *gwniadwraig* 'sempstress'.

All the 3-consonant clusters break the SSP apart from the two starting with /k/. Although the cluster types in (3) are comparatively rare in terms of dictionary entries (Thomas, Bevan and Donovan 1967–2002), those in (4) are not; however, as noted, a different analysis would remove these latter from the list of 3-consonant clusters.

14.3.2 Breton

All consonants can appear in word-initial position with the exception of the palatal nasal and the palatal lateral. Sonority dispersion values (based on the classification in Section 14.1 above) vary from 1–8 for words such as *penn* 'head' /pɛn/, to 7–8 for words such as *yezh* 'language' /jɛz/. All possible dispersion values are used.

Onset clusters can be of two or three consonants. Two-consonant clusters are of two types: obstruent+obstruent, and obstruent+sonorant.

Three-consonant clusters are restricted to obstruent+obstruent+sonorant (/s/+plosive+liquid). The following examples are from Stephens (1993).

(5) Obstruent+obstruent clusters

/sp-/	sparfell 'sparrow-hawk'	3–1
/st-/	stank 'pond'	3–1
/sk-/	skuizh 'tired'	3–1

(6) Obstruent+sonorant clusters

/pl-/	pleg 'fold'	1–6
/pr-/	prim 'quick'	1–6
/bl-/	blejal 'to cry'	2–6
/br-/	bremañ 'now'	2–6
/tl-/	tleunv 'distaff'	1–6
/tr-/	tremen 'to pass'	1–6
/dl-/	dle 'debt'	2–6
/dr-/	dre 'through'	2–6
/kl-/	klask 'search'	1–6
/kr-/	kraoñ 'nut'	1–6
/gl-/	glas 'blue'	2–6
/gr-/	graet 'done'	2–6
/fl-/	flour 'smooth'	3–6
/fr-/	friko 'big meal'	3–6
/vr-/	fri 'nose'	4–6

Breton, as compared to Welsh, lacks glides in these clusters partly due to the usual classification of /kw-/ and /gw-/ in Breton as being labial-velars. Sonority distances in these clusters range from 5 to 2.

(7) /s/+plosive+liquid clusters

/spl-/	splann 'bright'	3–1–6
/spr-/	sprec'henn 'old horse'	3–1–6
/stl-/	stlabez 'rare'	3–1–6
/str-/	strollad 'group'	3–1–6
/skl-/	sklaer 'clear'	3–1–6
/skr-/	skrav 'stern'	3–1–6

As with the Welsh examples, the /s/+plosive+liquid clusters break the SSP, but as /s/ clusters in general have been discussed at length elsewhere we will not look at these further, as for neither Welsh nor Breton do they participate in ICM.

14.3.3 Irish

All Irish consonants can appear as singletons in word-initial position in non-mutatable contexts, except /rʲ/, the dorsal nasals and fricatives, and the voiced fricatives and glides. Sonority dispersion values (based on the classification in Section 14.1 above) vary from 1–7 for words such as *peann* 'pen' /pʲa:n/, to 7–8 for words such as *leon* 'lion' /lʲo:n/. Only five dispersion values are used; excluded is 4–7 (voiced fricative-vowel), except in a few loan words.

Examples of clusters are taken from Ní Chiosáin (1999) and our own data.[5] Both two and three member clusters are found and, with a few exceptions, the members of the cluster agree in terms of palatalization/velarization. Two-consonant clusters can be obstruent+obstruent, obstruent+sonorant or sonorant+sonorant.

(8) Obstruent+obstruent clusters

/spʲ-/	speal 'scythe'	3–1
/spˠ-/	sparán 'purse'	3–1
/ʃtʲ-/	stíl 'style'	3–1
stˠ-/	stoca 'stocking'	3–1
/ʃc-/	scéal 'story'	3–1
/sk-/	scadán 'herring'	3–1

(9) Obstruent+sonorant clusters

/pʲlʲ-/	pleidhce 'idiot'	1–6
/pʲrʲ-/	preab 'spring, jump'	1–6
/pˠlˠ-/	plúr 'flour'	1–6
/pˠrˠ-/	praiseach 'mess'	1–6
/bʲlʲ-/	bleán 'milking'	2–6
/bʲrʲ-/	breá 'fine'	2–6
/bˠlˠ-/	blúire 'bit, fragment'	2–6
/bˠrˠ-/	bróg 'shoe, boot'	2–6
/tʲrʲ-/	trí 'three'	1–6
/tˠnˠ-/	tnúth 'envy'	1–5
/tˠlˠ-/	tlus 'lies, falsehood'	1–6
/tˠrˠ-/	trá 'beach'	1–6
/dʲlʲ-/	dlí 'law'	2–6
/dʲrʲ-/	dream 'group'	2–6
/dˠlˠ-/	dlúth 'close, dense'	2–6
/dˠrˠ-/	draonán 'drizzle'	2–6
/cnʲ-/	cneasta 'honest, decent'	1–5

5 We have excluded four clusters that were in Ní Chiosáin (1999), as no exemplars were found. These are: /tʲnʲ-/, /tʲlʲ-/, /dʲnʲ-/ and /dˠnˠ-/.

/clʲ-/	clé 'left'	1–6
/crʲ-/	creid 'believe'	1–6
/knˠ-/	cnaipe 'button'	1–5
/klˠ-/	clú 'reputation'	1–6
/krˠ-/	croí 'heart'	1–6
/ɟn-/	gníomh 'doing, action'	2–5
/ɟlʲ-/	gléasra 'gear'	2–6
/ɟrʲ-/	greim 'grip, hold'	2–6
/gnˠ-/	gnáth 'usual'	2–5
/glˠ-/	glac 'take, accept'	2–6
/grˠ-/	grád 'grade, degree'	2–6
/ʃnʲ-/	sneachta 'snow'	3–5
/ʃlʲ-/	sliotar 'hurley ball'	3–6
/smʲ-/	sméara 'berries'	3–5
/smˠ-/	smaoinigh 'think'	3–5
/snˠ-/	snámh 'swim'	3–5
/slˠ-/	slán 'sound, healthy'	3–6
/srˠ-/	srón 'nose'	3–6

(10) Sonorant+sonorant cluster

/mˠnˠ-/	mná 'women'[6]	5–5

Three-consonant clusters consist of /sˠ/ or /ʃ/ plus a voiceless plosive and then a liquid.

(11) /s, ʃ/+plosive+liquid clusters

/spʲlʲ-/	spleách 'dependent'	3–1–6
/spˠlˠ-/	splanc 'flash'	3–1–6
/spʲrʲ-/	spreag 'inspire'	3–1–6
/spˠrˠ-/	spraoi 'fun'	3–1–6
/ʃtʲrʲ-/	stríoc 'streak'	3–1–6
/stˠrˠ-/	strus 'stress, strain'	3–1–6
/ʃclʲ-/	scliúchas 'rumpus'	3–1–6
/ʃcrʲ-/	scread 'scream'	3–1–6
/sklˠ-/	sclogaíl 'gasping'	3–1–6
/skrˠ-/	scrúdú 'examination'	3–1–6

All the /s/ and /ʃ/-initial clusters break the SSP except for those followed by sonorants. The clusters in (9) follow the SSP with sonority distances varying from 1–6 to 3–5. The cluster in (10) produces a sonority plateau of 5–5.

6 In most regional variants, this is either realized with an epenthetic vowel or with the /n/ changed to a rhotic.

The range of singleton and cluster onsets of these three languages is affected by the operation of initial consonant mutation. In the next section we look at this feature and how it operates in Welsh, Breton, and Irish.

14.4 Initial Consonant Mutation

The Celtic languages share the property of initial consonant mutation (ICM; see entries on specific languages in Ball and Müller 2009).[7] These mutations are phonological changes to the initial consonant of a word triggered by morphosyntactic contexts, rather than phonological ones (thus they are not sandhi phenomena). Thus, for example, the Welsh word *cath* ('cat' /kɑθ/) can appear with a voiced initial consonant as in *ei gath* ('his cat' /i gɑθ/); with a fricative-initial consonant as in *ei chath* ('her cat' /i xɑθ/); or with a nasal initial consonant as in *fy nghath* ('my cat' /ə ŋ̊ʰɑθ/); as well as in its unmutated form as in *eu cath* ('their cat' /i kɑθ/). Likewise, in Irish, *cat* ('cat' /katˠ/) can appear with an initial fricative consonant as in *mo chat* ('my cat' /mˠo xatˠ/), or with an initial voiced plosive as in *a gcat* ('their cat' /ə gatˠ/); as well as in its unmutated form as in *a cat* ('her cat' /ə katˠ/).

Table 14.4. Initial consonant mutations in Welsh.

Radical	Soft mutation	Nasal mutation	Aspirate mutation	Mixed mutation
p, /p/	b, /b/	mh, /m̥ʰ/	ff, /f/	ff, /f/
t, /t/	d, /d/	nh, /n̥ʰ/	th, /θ/	th, /θ/
c, /k/	g, /g/	ngh, /ŋ̊ʰ/	ch, /x/	ch, /x/
b, /b/	f, /v/	m, /m/	–	f, /v/
d, /d/	dd, /ð/	n, /n/	–	dd, /ð/
g, /g/	Ø	ng, /ŋ/	–	Ø
m, /m/	f, /v/	–	–	f, /v/
ll, /ɬ/	l, /l/	–	–	l, /l/
rh, /r̥ʰ/	r, /r/	–	–	r, /r/

7 We are aware that other languages demonstrate similar patterns, see, for example, discussion in Zimmer (2005), and a description of ICM in Fula in Arnott (1970).

Table 14.5. Initial consonant mutations in Breton.

Radical	Lenition	Spirantization	Provection	Mixed
p, /p/	b, /b/	v, /v/	–	–
t, /t/	d, /d/	z, /z/	–	–
k, /k/	g, /g/	c'h, /h/	–	–
b, /b/	v, /v/	–	p, /p/	v, /v/
d, /d/	z, /z/	–	t, /t/	t, /t/
g, /g/	c'h, /h/	–	k, /k/	c'h, /h/
gw, /gʷ/	w, /w/	–	kw, /kʷ/	w, /w/
m, /m/	v, /v/	–	–	v, /v/

Table 14.6. Initial consonant mutations in Irish.

Radical		Lenition		Eclipsis	
p	/pʲ/	ph	/fʲ/	bp	/bʲ/
	/pˠ/		/fˠ/		/bˠ/
t	/tʲ/	th	/h/	dt	/dʲ/
	/tˠ/		/h/		/dˠ/
c	/c/	ch	/ç/	gc	/ɟ/
	/k/		/x/		/g/
b	/bʲ/	bh	/vʲ/	mb	/mʲ/
	/bˠ/		/w/		/mˠ/
d	/dʲ/	dh	/j/	nd	/nʲ/
	/dˠ/		/ɣ/		/nˠ/
g	/ɟ/	gh	/j/	ng	/ɲ/
	/g/		/ɣ/		/ŋ/
m	/mʲ/	mh	/vʲ/		–
	/mˠ/		/w/		–
f	/fʲ/	fh	Ø	bhf	/vʲ/
	/fˠ/		Ø		/w/
s	/ʃ/	sh	/h/		–
	/s/		/h/		–

Note: The orthography distinguishes palatalized from velarized consonants via the choice of vowel letter for neighbouring vowels. As there are several vowel letters that can be employed for this, we have omitted these from the orthographic column.

Tables 14.4–14.6 illustrate the ICM systems of Welsh, Breton and Irish.[8] In each column, the orthographic form is given first, followed by a phonemic transcription.

The large number of morphosyntactic triggers of mutation in these languages need not be described here. However, full accounts of these for Welsh are available in Ball and Müller (1992) and Awbery (2005); for Breton in Press (2005) and Iosad (2014); and for Irish in Ó Baoill (2005) and Grijzenhout (1995). Nevertheless, we can note that these triggers include certain prepositions, conjunctions, numerals and possessive pronouns, all triggering ICM onto following words; determiners trigger mutation onto following nouns of specific gender and number; preverbal particles (such as negative or question particles) trigger mutation onto following verb forms; and adjectives may be mutated after nouns of certain gender and number. Mutation may also be used to mark case (e.g., direct object of an inflected verb in Welsh; genitive case in Irish in some circumstances) or marked word order (e.g., in Welsh).

14.5 The Effect of ICM on Onsets in Welsh, Breton and Irish

In this section we look at the effects on word-initial singleton and cluster phonotactics of the ICM systems of Welsh, Breton and Irish.

14.5.1 Welsh

The mutation systems described in Section 14.4 and illustrated in Table 14.4 expand the number of consonants that can occur as initial singletons. The voiceless nasals, /ð/ and /x/ are all found; the voiceless nasals as reflexes of the voiceless plosives via nasal mutation, /ð/ as the reflex of /d/ via soft mutation, and /x/ as a reflex of /k/ via aspirate mutation. This now permits a dispersion difference of 5–10. All three mutations reduce the

8 The Scottish Gaelic system is similar to that of Irish (see Gillies 2005). We exclude Cornish and Manx from this discussion partly due to the low number of speakers making it difficult to assess the vitality of ICM in these languages, and partly due to the similarity of their ICM systems to Breton and Irish respectively (see George 2005; Broderick 2005).

consonant-vowel sonority distance, apart from the soft mutation of /m/, where the distance increases.

The /s-/ clusters, as shown in (1) and (3) above, are unaffected by ICM, as /s/ is not a mutatable consonant in Welsh. The clusters in (2), however, mostly do start with mutatable consonants (those starting with plosives). The effect of soft mutation is to reduce the sonority dispersion score by 1 or 2 (e.g., radical /pl-/ changes to /bl-/; radical /bl-/ changes to /vl-/). Aspirate mutation also reduces the sonority distance between the members of the cluster, this time by 2: e.g., radical /pl-/ becomes /fl-/. Nasal mutation reduces the sonority distance by 4 (e.g., radical /pl-/ becomes /m̥ʰl-/, radical /bl-/ becomes /ml-/). Indeed, clusters such as /ml-/ and /nl-/ have a sonority dispersion score of only 1. The SDP posits an equal distance between C1, C2 and V in a 2-element cluster (but in terms of the typical 5-rank sonority scale). If we apply the 5-rank sonority scale to /blV/ clusters, we get a ranking of 1–3–5, while a /mlV/ cluster produces a ranking of 2–3–5. Further, the nasal mutation of the cluster /gwV/ would result in /ŋwV/, a 5-point ranking difference of 2–4–5.

In summary, ICM in Welsh reduces sonority distances in both singletons and clusters, but does not add to the number of clusters that already break the SSP.

14.5.2 Breton

Initial consonant mutations in Breton do not add to the possible singleton word-initial consonants. However, as in the case of Welsh, ICM often reduces the sonority distance between the word-initial consonant and following vowel, thus producing a less ideal sonority profile for the onset. Lenition reduces the sonority value of voiceless plosives by 1, and voiced plosives by 2, except in the case of /m/ which increases by 1. Lenition of /g/ and /gʷ/ are also exceptions; the former reduces by only 1, but the later by 4. Spirantization also reduces sonority distance between the consonant and vowel (by 2 or 3), while provection increases the sonority score by 1.

As with Welsh, /s/-initial clusters are unaffected by ICM. Plosive-initial clusters will see the same sonority score changes as just noted for singleton consonants thus, in most cases except for provection, reducing the distance between members of the cluster. As Breton lacks a nasal mutation, the greatly reduced sonority dispersion scores found with some mutated clusters in Welsh are not found. Nevertheless, a cluster such as /klV/ under spirantization yields /hlV/ – a change from 1–6–8 to 3–6–8 under our ranking (although under a 5-rank scale no difference would be recorded).

14.5.3 Irish

Initial consonant mutation permits those consonants not occurring word-initially in radical forms to appear (apart from /z/ and /ʒ/). Both lenition and eclipsis reduce the sonority rank of most of the affected consonants (using the scale for Irish described in Section 14.1 above). Lenited plosives and the labiodental fricatives reduce by 2 ranks, although lenited /s/ and /ʃ/ do not change rank and lenited /fʲ/ and /fˠ/ are deleted. Only lenited /m/ increases in rank, as seen also in Welsh and Breton. Eclipsis reduces voiceless plosives by 1 rank, and voiced plosives by 3 ranks.

In terms of the clusters, ICM produces a range of new types (even though singleton /s/-/ʃ/ is mutatable, 3-member clusters starting with these sounds are not mutated; thus there are no changes in 3-member clusters). Lenition produces the following new 2-member clusters: /fʲlʲ, fˠlˠ, fʲrʲ, fˠrˠ, vʲlʲ, wlˠ, vʲrʲ, wrˠ, hnʲ, hnˠ, hlʲ, hlˠ, hrʲ, hrˠ, çnʲ, xnˠ, çlʲ, xlˠ, çrʲ, xrˠ, jnʲ, ɣnˠ, jlʲ, ɣlˠ, jrʲ, ɣrˠ, wnˠ/. Eclipsis produces the following new 2-member clusters: /mʲlʲ, mˠlˠ, mʲrʲ, mˠrˠ, nʲlʲ, nˠlˠ, nʲrʲ, nˠrˠ, ɲlʲ, ŋlˠ, ɲrʲ, ŋrˠ/. Apart from reducing the sonority dispersion scores in most cases, these new clusters contain potential examples of sonority reversals: /wlˠ, wrˠ, jnʲ, jlʲ, wnˠ/. However, as noted earlier, we did not include a glide category for Irish, and have classed /w/ and /j/ among the voiced fricatives. Nevertheless, as Hickey (2014) notes, while fricative realizations of /w/ are most common before other consonants, glide variants are sometimes found; and we can note further that a glide realization of /j/ in these clusters is common. In such cases, and using the 5-rank scale, such clusters would score 4–3.

In summary, ICM in Irish, as with Welsh and Breton, reduces the sonority dispersion distance in both onset singletons and clusters. Further, a potential sonority reversal occurs in some 2-member clusters.

14.6 Conclusion

Initial consonant mutation is a pervasive feature of the modern Celtic languages. Comparing short texts across two of the languages, it becomes clear that mutations occur frequently. Take for example a recent article on higher education funding in the online version of the Welsh language newspaper *Y Cymro*:

> Yn ystod cyfarfod blynyddol Llys Prifysgol Bangor mynegwyd pryder dwys ynghylch y gostyngiad sylweddol yn y cyllid i brifysgolion yng

Nghyllideb ddrafft Llywodraeth Cymru ar gyfer 2016/17, a'r goblygiadau i economi a chymdeithas Cymru'n ehangach. Penderfynodd y Llys gefnogi swyddogion y Brifysgol yn eu hymdrechion i gynnal a chryfhau sefyllfa ariannol Addysg Uwch yng Nghymru, a Phrifysgol Bangor yn benodol.

(Retrieved from http://www.y-cymro.com/newyddion/c/x44/i/3188/desc/llys-prifysgol-bangor-yn-mynegi-pryder-dwys-ynghylch-toriadau-cyllid-arfaethedig-i-addysg-uwch-yng-nghymru/ 19 January 2016.)

During the annual meeting of the Bangor University Court strong concern was raised about the marked cuts in the grants to universities in the draft budget of the Welsh Government for 2016/17, and the implications for the economy and for society in Wales and beyond. The Court decided to support University officers in their attempts to maintain and strengthen the financial situation in Higher Education in Wales, and Bangor University especially.

In this passage, there is soft mutation on *dwys, gostyngiad, brifysgolion, ddrafft, gyfer, goblygiadau, gefnogi, Brifysgol, gynnal, benodol.* There is nasal mutation on *Nghyllideb* and *Nghymru,* and aspirate mutation on *chymdeithas, chryfhau* and *Phrifysgol.*

Similarly, a recent news item on the Irish site of RTÉ (the Irish national broadcaster) illustrates the frequent use of ICM:

Dúirt an tAire Stáit Joe McHugh go bhfuil Údarás na Gaeltachta ag súil go gcruthófar 500 post nua sa Ghaeltacht in 2016. Mar chuid de Phlean Gníomhaíochta Fostaíochta 2016 an Rialtais, d'fhógair an tAire Stáit inniu go bhfuil an Roinn Ealaíon, Oidhreachta agus Gaeltachta ag obair ar réimse gníomhartha a chuideos le cruthú fostaíochta sa Ghaeltacht. Ina theannta sin, dúirt an tAire Stáit McHugh go mbeidh forbairt an ionaid cuairteoirí ag Teach an Phiarsaigh san áireamh sa Chomóradh Stáit ar Éirí Amach 1916 agus go mbeidh an t-ionad seo tábhachtach do chruthú fostaíochta i gceantar Ros Muc i nGaeltacht Chonamara.

(Retrieved from http://www.rte.ie/news/nuacht/2016/0118/761128-suil-go/ 19 January 2016).

Minister of State Joe McHugh said that Údarás na Gaeltachta [Gaeltacht Development Office] expects to create 500 new jobs in the Gaeltacht in 2016. As part of the Government's 2016 Employment Action Plan, the Minister of State announced today that the Department of Arts, Heritage and the Gaeltacht will work on a range of actions which will assist job creation in the Gaeltacht. Furthermore, the Minister of State McHugh said that the development of the visitor centers at Pearse House would be included in the State Commemmoration of the 1916 Rising, and that this venue is important for employment creation in Ros Muc area in the Connemara Gaeltacht. [The *Gaeltacht* is the term used for the Irish-speaking areas within Ireland.]

Here, lenition is found on *Ghaeltacht, chuid, Phlean, fhógair, chuideos, theannta, Phiarsaigh, Chomóradh, chruthú, Chonamara;* eclipsis is found on *gcruthófar, bhfuil* (x 2), *mbeidh* (x 2), *gceantar,* and *nGaeltacht.*

Sonority theory would presumably predict that phonological changes should produce onset profiles that more closely approximate the ideal of the SSP. However, apart from provection (or hard mutation) in Breton – which itself is a less common ICM – nearly all the mutation processes in the Celtic languages reduce the sonority values of the consonants concerned, thus moving away from the predictions of the SSP. In this, the initial consonant mutations of the Celtic languages pose a challenge to sonority and its predictions.

References

Arnott, D.W. (1970). *The nominal and verbal systems of Fula.* Oxford: Oxford University Press.

Awbery, G. M. (1984). Phonotactic constraints in Welsh. In M.J. Ball and G.E. Jones (eds.), *Welsh phonology: Selected readings* (pp. 65–104). Cardiff: University of Wales Press.

Awbery, G.M. (2005). Welsh. In M.J. Ball and N. Müller (eds.), *The Celtic languages,* 2nd edition (2009, pp. 359–426). London: Routledge.

Ball, M.J. and Müller, N. (1992). *Mutation in Welsh.* London: Routledge.

Ball, M.J. and Müller, N. (eds.) (2009). *The Celtic languages,* 2nd edition. London: Routledge.

Ball, M.J., Müller, N. and Rutter, B. (2008). *Phonology for communication disorders.* Hove: Psychology Press.

Ball, M.J. and Williams, B. (2001). *Welsh phonetics.* New York: Edwin Mellen Press.

Blevins, J. (1995). The syllable in phonological theory. In J.A. Goldsmith (ed.), *The handbook of phonological theory* (pp. 206–44). Oxford: Blackwell.

Broderick, G. (2005). Manx. In M.J. Ball and N. Müller (eds.), *The Celtic languages,* 2nd edition (2009, pp. 305–56). London: Routledge.

Burquest, D. and Payne, D.L. (1993). *Phonological analysis: A functional analysis.* Dallas, TX: Summer Institute of Linguistics.

Clements, G.N. (1990). The role of the sonority cycle in core syllabification. In M.E. Beckman and J. Kingston (eds.), *Papers in laboratory phonology I: Between the grammar and physics of speech* (pp. 283–333). Cambridge: Cambridge University Press.

Czerniak, T. (2015). Word-initial clusters in Welsh: A typological analysis. In A. Bondaruk, A. Bloch-Rozmej, W. Malec, E. Mockrosz and S. Zdziebko (eds.), *Young minds vs. old questions in linguistics. Proceedings of the fourth Central European conference in linguistics for postgraduate students* (pp. 29–46). Lublin: The Institute of East-Central Europe, and The John Paul II Catholic University of Lublin.

Firth, J.R. (1948). Sounds and Prosodies. *Transactions of the Philological Society* 1948. 127–52.

Fynes-Clinton, O.H. (1913). *The Welsh vocabulary of the Bangor district.* London: Oxford University Press.

George, K. (2005). Cornish. In M.J. Ball and N. Müller (eds.), *The Celtic languages*, 2nd edition (2009, pp. 488–535). London: Routledge.

Gillies, W. (2005). Scottish Gaelic. In M.J. Ball and N. Müller (eds.), *The Celtic languages*, 2nd edition (2009, pp. 230–304). London: Routledge.

Grijzenhout, J. (1995). *Irish consonant mutation and phonological theory.* Doctoral dissertation, Utrecht University.

Hickey, R. (2014). *The sound structure of modern Irish.* Berlin: De Gruyter Mouton.

Jespersen, O. (1904). *Lehrbuch der Phonetik.* Leipzig and Berlin: Teubner.

Iosad, P. (2014). The phonology and morphosyntax of Breton mutation. *Lingue e linguaggio*, 13, 23–42.

Ní Chasaide, A. (1999). Irish. In IPA (eds.), *Handbook of the International Phonetic Association* (pp. 111–16). Cambridge: Cambridge University Press.

Ní Chiosáin, M. (1999). Syllables and phonotactics in Irish. In H. van der Hulst and N.A. Ritter (eds.), *The syllable: Views and facts* (pp. 551–75). Berlin: Mouton de Gruyter.

Ó Baoill, D. (2005). Irish. In M.J. Ball and N. Müller (eds.), *The Celtic languages*, 2nd edition (pp. 163–229). London: Routledge.

Parker, S. (2012). Sonority distance vs. sonority dispersion: A typological survey. In S. Parker (ed.), *The sonority controversy* (pp. 101–65). Berlin: De Gruyter.

Press, I. (2005). Breton. In M.J. Ball and N. Müller (eds.), *The Celtic languages*, 2nd edition (2009, pp. 427–87). London: Routledge.

Stephens, J. (1993). Breton. In M.J. Ball (ed.), *The Celtic languages*, 1st edition (pp. 349–409). London: Routledge.

Tench, P. (1992). From prosodic analysis to systemic phonology. In P. Tench (ed.), *Studies in systemic phonology* (pp. 1–18). London: Pinter.

Thomas, R.J., Bevan, G.A. and Donovan, P.J. (1967–2002). *Geiriadur prifysgol Cymru.* Cardiff: University of Wales Press.

Zimmer, S. (2005). The Celtic mutations: Some typological comparisons. In B. Smelik, R. Hofman, C. Hamans and D. Cram (eds.), *A companion in linguistics: A festschrift for Anders Ahlqvist on the occasion of his sixtieth birthday* (pp. 127–40). Nijmegen: Stichting Uitgeverij de Keltische Draak.

Martin J. Ball is Professor of Speech-Language Pathology (Clinical Linguistics and Phonetics) at Linköping University, Sweden. He is co-editor of the journal *Clinical Linguistics and Phonetics* (Taylor & Francis), and of the book series *Communication Disorders Across Languages* (Multilingual Matters). His main research interests include sociolinguistics, clinical phonetics and phonology, and the Celtic languages. He is an honorary Fellow of the Royal College of Speech and Language Therapists, and a Fellow of the Learned Society of Wales.

Nicole Müller is Professor of Speech-Language Pathology at Linköping University, Sweden; she will be taking up the position of Professor of Speech and Hearing Sciences at University College Cork, Ireland, early in 2017. Her areas of research interest include clinical linguistics, clinical discourse studies and pragmatics, age-related disorders of communication and cognition, multilingualism, and systemic functional linguistics. She is co-editor of the journal *Clinical Linguistics and Phonetics* and of the book series *Communication Disorders across Languages*.

15 Sonority in Acquisition: A Review

Jessica A. Barlow

15.1 Introduction

The goal of this chapter is to present an overview of research on the role of sonority in phonological acquisition. Any adequate theory of language must be able to account for and accurately predict the facts of the world's languages while also accounting for acquisition of those languages, as developing sound systems are instances of different possible human languages (Kager, Pater and Zonneveld 2004). Following from Ferguson and Garnica (1975), a linguistic framework must be able to account for learners' productions and the discrepancies between those productions and the target language. In addition, such a theory must be able to account for the range and variation that occurs within and across learners' sound systems, as well as the changes that occur over time as part of the acquisition process. Appealing to evidence from developing systems in order to understand sonority's role in phonological organization is important because it allows for the determination of the different ways that learners approach the target system. This allows for a comparison to phonological phenomena of fully developed systems to determine the similarities and differences that may exist. In turn, a better understanding of the full range of possible sound systems that may occur in human language is achieved. A cross-sectional evaluation of the world's languages allows for a typological investigation of possible sound systems; consideration of language change likewise illustrates how patterns may arise or be lost over time. With acquisition data, we are provided with a snapshot of a possible sound system at a given time and the opportunity to observe how it changes over a very short period of time.

The purpose of this chapter is to consider these criteria with respect to theoretical assumptions about sonority in the acquisition of syllable structure by adults and children, including children with speech delay. Converging evidence has pointed to the relevance and importance of sonority in phonological systems (Parker 2003, 2008, 2012b; Sprenger-Charolles and

Siegel 1997; Vroomen, van den Bosch and de Gelder 1998) and, as will be shown herein, that includes developing sound systems (cf. Harris 2006). The aim here is not to advance sonority-based frameworks as superior to or as uniquely and independently adequate in accounting for acquisition patterns; rather, it is considered in tandem with other theoretical accounts pertaining to phonotactic restrictions, asymmetries in syllable organization, as well as morphological features, in order to highlight the multiple factors that influence phonological acquisition specifically, and phonological organization more generally (see also Rahilly, this volume).

This chapter is organized as follows: First, general assumptions about the organization of the syllable and sonority's role in syllabification are considered. Next, common errors in phonological acquisition that pertain to syllable structure and sonority are discussed. Then, divergences from these common errors are considered in terms of variation within and across sound systems. Finally, the role of syllable structure and sonority is considered with respect to how developing sound systems change over time. The chapter concludes with a general discussion of how, in conjunction with other theoretical accounts, sonority can account for the facts of phonological acquisition.

15.1.1 Organization of the Syllable

Because the role of sonority in phonological systems is closely tied to syllable structure, we begin first with assumptions about syllable organization; however, as with the topic of sonority, a study of syllable structure and the organization of subsyllabic constituents is worthy of an entire volume (e.g., Bell and Hooper 1978; Clements and Keyser 1983; Féry and van de Vijver 2003). For expository purposes, the general onset-rhyme structure shown in (1) for the CCVCC word 'print' is adopted here (following Blevins 1995; Ewen and van der Hulst 2001; Fudge 1969; Halle and Vergnaud 1978; Pike and Pike 1947; Selkirk 1982), though there is quite some debate as to the exact makeup of the syllable template (Baertsch 2012; Broselow 1995; Hayes 1989; Hyman 1985; Zec 1995).

(1) Syllable template for the word 'print' ('σ' = syllable node)

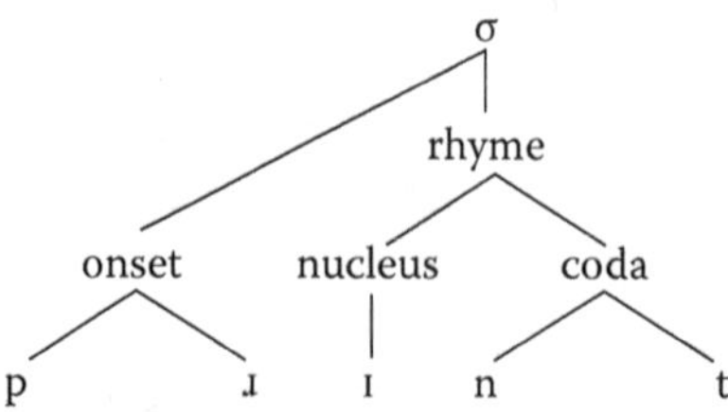

It is well established that languages vary with respect to the syllable types they allow, and this is attributed to the relative complexity of syllable types. Generally speaking, branching structure within the onset, rhyme, nucleus or coda is assumed to be relatively marked (Blevins 1995). All languages have CV (onset-nucleus) syllables, but not all languages allow other syllable structures. For instance, Finnish lacks complex onsets, Italian avoids complex nuclei, Fijian excludes codas and Spanish disallows complex codas. Finally, some languages, such as Hawaiian and Mba, allow only CV syllables (Blevins 1995; Maddieson 2013).

Additionally, it should also be noted that some researchers assume that postvocalic sonorants, such as [n] in (1) above, syllabify as part of a branching nucleus, rather than as part of a branching coda (Cairns and Feinstein 1982; den Ouden and Bastiaanse 2003). Others restrict that position to only off-glides of diphthongs (e.g., [aʊ] in 'round') and possibly liquids (e.g., [ɹ] in 'cart'), though this also depends on language-specific articulatory properties of the sounds in question, as well as phonotactics (Blevins 1995; Côté 2004; Harris 1994; Harris 1983; Hindson and Byrne 1997; MacKay 1978; Malsch and Fulcher 1989; Parker 2012b; Proctor and Walker 2012; Selkirk 1982; Stemberger 1983; Treiman 1984). Such differences in structural organization of the syllable are assumed to account for observed asymmetries in the patterning of postvocalic consonants, as will be illustrated below (see also Rahilly, this volume).

15.1.2 Sonority and the Sonority Sequencing Principle

Despite these differences, sonority plays a critical role in the organization of segments within the syllable. The most reliable acoustic correlate of sonority has been empirically established as intensity (Parker 2008, 2002). Accordingly, phonemes are ranked from most to least sonorous (most to least acoustic energy) as follows: vowels > glides > liquids > nasals > fricatives > stops (Hooper 1976; Selkirk 1984). Sound systems may make use of less or more detailed distinctions among these sound classes; for example, low vowels are more sonorous than mid or high vowels, and voiced obstruents are more sonorous than their voiceless counterparts (Blevins 1995; Clements 1990; Selkirk 1982). Generally, the Sonority Sequencing Principle (SSP; Clements 1990), also known as the Sonority Sequencing Generalization or the Sonority Dispersion Principle, requires that segments higher in sonority occur closer to the nucleus of the syllable, with the nucleus serving as the sonority peak. As per the SSP and core syllable structure, syllable onsets must rise maximally in sonority toward the peak and codas must drop minimally away from the peak or remain level (Clements 1990). Thus, preferred syllables have obstruent onsets ('strong' onsets), are open (CV), or are closed with a relatively unmarked sonorant coda, such as a nasal or liquid. When consonant clusters occur, those in the onset that maintain a steeper slope (that is, have a larger sonority distance) are preferred, while those in the coda may fall or remain level.

(2) Syllable template for the word 'sprints'

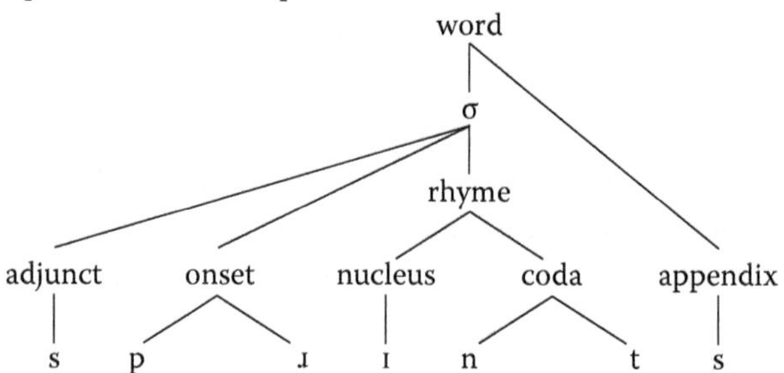

Consonant clusters that violate sonority sequencing (notably the /s/C and C/s/ clusters, among others) and/or exceed two segments may involve additional extrasyllabic structure. This has been proposed in part as an explanation for why languages appear to allow a larger variety of word-final clusters than they do word-internal syllable-final clusters; moreover, for many languages, final clusters do not carry syllable weight for stress assignment (Vaux and Wolfe 2009). As shown in (2), the *adjunct* (also referred to as an *appendix* or *prependix*) constituent is assumed to be a direct dependent of the syllable (Davis 1990; Ewen and van der Hulst 2001; Fikkert 1994; Kenstowicz 1994; Steriade 1982, 1988), though it is also proposed to be a *pre-margin* constituent within the onset (Cairns and Feinstein 1982). Similarly, the appendix at the end of the syllable has been proposed to syllabify as a direct dependent of the syllable (Borowsky 1989; Cairns and Feinstein 1982; Clements and Keyser 1983; den Ouden and Bastiaanse 2003; Fudge 1969; Fujimura and Lovins 1978; Grijzenhout 1998), or of the (prosodic) word, as shown for final [s] in (2) (Booij 1995; Ewen and van der Hulst 2001; Nathan 2008), or even as an onset to an empty syllable (Cyran 2008; Ewen and Botma 2009).[1] Still other accounts have been

1 Argument in favour of the appendix as a daughter of the word (rather than syllable) is based on the observation that appendices typically are filled by word-level morphological content. These are affixes that occur word-finally but not word-internally. Further support for this claim comes from the observation that many languages have stricter phonotactic restrictions on syllable edges

offered for /s/C and C/s/-type sequences, and they may furthermore vary across sound systems (Barlow 1997, 2001; Broselow 1987; Goad 2012, this volume; Kaye 1992; Selkirk 1984; Steriade 1994). Extrasyllabic constituents are assumed to be outside of the core syllable, and thus not part of the normal process of syllabification, nor must they follow the SSP (Selkirk 1982). Word-final obstruent+liquid clusters also occur in some languages and are assumed to form branching onsets to empty-headed syllables, given their similar behaviour to word-initial obstruent+liquid clusters (Dell 1995).

Just as languages vary in terms of whether or not they allow branching onsets or branching codas or even singleton codas, so do they vary with respect to the occurrence of extraprosodic structure just described. English and Dutch are assumed to allow both adjuncts and appendices, for instance (Ewen and van der Hulst 2001); Spanish allows neither (Harris 1983). As will be shown, these extraprosodic constituents figure prominently in the asymmetries observed in acquisition as well.

15.2 The Role of Sonority in Errors in Phonological Acquisition

In this section, errors in phonological acquisition are considered in terms of predictions about syllable structure and sonority. Errors that occur during the process of phonological acquisition reflect the influence of sonority. At the most basic level, it is apparent that errors tend to preserve much of the target structure, reflecting knowledge of the target form and its associated featural properties. Generally, obstruents are substituted for obstruents, and sonorants for sonorants, as observed in common phonological processes such as stopping, fronting and gliding (Ingram 1989; Locke 1983). In addition, children's errors on codas may be dependent on the sonority of the target form, such that obstruents may be omitted, but sonorants preserved. Moreover, sonority also influences children's truncation patterns in acquisition: Weak syllables with obstruent onsets are more likely to be preserved than those with sonorant onsets (Kehoe 1997, 2001). Yet, sonority's influence goes much further, and in a more gradient fashion, in the errors observed in acquisition. That is, specific predictions can be made with respect to the types of errors that occur in acquisition,

(Clements 1990; Kenstowicz 1994; Rubach and Booij 1990; Selkirk 1982). In languages such as English and Dutch, only coronal obstruents may occur in the appendix (Booij 1995; Borowsky 1989).

based on assumptions about syllable structure and sonority sequencing. We consider consonant singletons first, followed by initial, medial and final consonant clusters.

As mentioned, syllable complexity increases with branching structure within the onset and rhyme. Thus, CV syllables are preferred cross-linguistically, as reflected by the fact that all languages allow CV syllables, and some languages allow *only* CV syllables (Blevins 1995; Cairns and Feinstein 1982; Clements 1990; Greenberg 1965; Kaye and Lowenstamm 1981). This preference for simple syllable structure is likewise reflected in errors in phonological acquisition (Stoel-Gammon 1985; Velten 1943; Winitz and Irwin 1958). For instance, children's first utterances (in babbling and first words) are of CV shape (Demuth 1995a, b), and they continue to be the most frequent syllable type during the course of acquisition, as evidenced by the commonly occurring patterns of final consonant deletion and cluster reduction (Ingram 1989; Locke 1983). Similarly, research on adult second language (L2) acquisition has shown a preference for CV syllables among L2 learners. These learners exhibit repairs of epenthesis, prothesis and paragoge that yield CV forms; moreover, such repairs often cannot be attributed to native language (or L1) transfer or recoverability of the target structure (Broselow 1987; Broselow, Chen and Wang 1998; Carlisle 2001; Eckman 1981; Hansen 2001, 2004; Riney 1990; Ross 1994; Tarone 1980, 1972; Weinberger 1994).

15.2.1 Singletons

In acquisition, we see support for the SSP in the more frequent production of singleton obstruents as opposed to sonorants in the onset in children's acquisition of a variety of languages, including Dutch, English, Portuguese and Hebrew (Bat-El 2012; Fikkert 1994; Freitas 1996; Pater 1997). Relatedly, those children's sound systems that restrict the occurrence of obstruent stops tend to allow them in onset position and exclude them postvocalically. Note, however, the opposite pattern has been observed for fricatives (Dinnsen, Chin, Elbert and Powell 1990); such counterexamples to sonority predictions will be discussed further below.

A preference for low sonority onsets and high sonority codas also has been observed in L2 acquisition. For instance, vowel paragoge is more likely to occur following final obstruents than sonorants (Lee 1998); this is argued to be due to a preference for low sonority onsets, per the SSP, since the resulting repair creates a second CV syllable that is obstruent-initial. Similarly, L2 learners of English tend to show more errors on obstruent codas as compared to sonorant codas, even when the L1 allows both obstruents and sonorants in the coda (Baptista and da Silva Filho 2006; Eckman and Iverson 1994; Tropf 1987).

Although the research on L1 and L2 errors on onsets and codas shows support for the SSP, additional acquisition research shows a great deal of variation in terms of the apparent role that sonority has on the acquisition of syllables, particularly with respect to the coda. This will be elaborated on in the discussion of change over time, below. Next we consider the role of sonority in errors on consonant clusters.

15.2.2 Consonant Clusters

Much research in the last few decades has evaluated L1 and L2 acquisition of consonant clusters, with greater attention paid to word- and syllable-initial clusters than medial or final clusters. As mentioned above, consonant clusters are prone to simplification due to the cross-linguistic preference for CV syllables, particularly in developing systems (Locke 1983). The most common type of simplification pattern observed in child language is cluster reduction (e.g., 'tree' as [ti] and 'sand' as [sæn]) (Greenlee 1974; Ingram 1989; Locke 1983; Smit 1993), while for adult L2 learners, both epenthesis (e.g., 'tree' as [tiri]) and cluster reduction are common, with the former most often occurring for initial clusters, and the latter most often occurring for final clusters (Broselow 1987; Hancin-Bhatt and Bhatt 1997; Weinberger 1994). Children may also exhibit coalescence (e.g., 'swan' as [fɑn]), metathesis (e.g., Hebrew /bʁexa/ 'swimming pool' as [beʁxa]), and gemination (e.g., Cairene Arabic /ward/ 'flowers' as [wadd]), as well as epenthesis (particularly in later stages of development), alongside cluster reduction (Bloch 2011; Chin and Dinnsen, 1992; Demuth and Kehoe 2006; Greenlee 1974; Łukaszewicz 2007; Ragheb and Davis 2014; Smit 1993).

Initial Clusters: Recall that the SSP requires that onsets rise maximally towards the nucleus of the syllable, thereby creating a steep sonority slope. The preference for such structures is apparent in the most common type of cluster reduction pattern observed in L1 acquisition, commonly referred to as *sonority-based cluster reduction* (Pater and Barlow 2003). Specifically, across languages, onset clusters (both word-initial and word-medial) are most often reduced to the least sonorous segment, such that obstruents are selected in favour of sonorants (Barlow 1997, 2003; Bloch 2011; Fikkert 1994; Freitas 2003; Gnanadesikan 2004; Łukaszewicz, 2007; Núñez-Cedeño 2008; Ohala 1996, 1999; Pater and Barlow 2003). This is shown in (3) for (a) a typically-developing child, Amahl (Farris-Trimble 2014; Smith 1973), and (b) a child with phonological delay, KR (Barlow 2001).

(3) Sonority-based cluster reduction

a. Amahl (male, stages 2–11) (Farris-Trimble 2014; Smith 1973)

[b̥æŋkiː] 'blanket'	[b̥eːk] 'brake'	[g̊ɔk] 'clock'	[g̊aːvə] 'guava'
[g̊ɔt] 'cross'	[kaip] 'quite'	[d̥ɔp] 'drop'	[d̥ipt] 'tripped'
[g̊aːt] 'grass'	[d̥aif] 'twice'	[muːgiː] 'music'	[g̊uːt] 'cute'

b. KR (male, age 3;6) (Barlow, 2001)

[tɪn] 'twin'	[kin] 'queen'	[kut˺] 'cute'	[fu] 'few'
[peɪ] 'pray'	[gʌm] 'drum'	[go] 'grow'	[fowiŋ] 'throwing'
[bo] 'blow'	[kaɪm] 'climb'	[gʌv] 'glove'	[faɪ] 'fly'

Even in cases of coalescence, a less common repair strategy, an obstruent in the output form is typical, as with [fɪmɪn] 'swimming' or [fok] 'smoke' (Chin and Dinnsen 1992; Gnanadesikan 2004; Pater and Barlow 2003; Smith 1973). Moreover, substitution errors can also be attributed to the effects of the SSP, where clusters with a smaller sonority distance (thus, a shallow sonority profile) may undergo substitution to create a cluster with a large sonority distance, as with 'froggie' [pwagi] or 'tree' [twi], in the absence of such substitution patterns occurring on consonant singletons (Chin 1993, 1996; Kirk 2008).

This sonority-based account also explains the patterns of reduction for /s/+consonant clusters (hereafter, /s/C) for many children (Ben-David, Ezrati and Stulman 2010; Ohala 1999; Pater and Barlow 2003; Yavaş and Barlow 2006; Yavaş and McLeod 2010), but such clusters also show a great deal of variation with respect to acquisition and error patterns (Barlow 1997, 2001; Barlow and Dinnsen 1998; Farris-Trimble and Gierut 2008; Goad and Rose 2000). In fact, the patterning of /s/C clusters across languages and developing systems (Steriade 1982, 1988) has been of particular interest to researchers because they violate the SSP (in the case of /s/+stop clusters) and language-specific phonotactic restrictions (Barlow 1997, 2001; Barlow and Dinnsen 1998; Ben-David et al. 2010; Davis 1990; Goad 2011, 2012, this volume; Goad and Rose 2004; Ohala 1999; Pater and Barlow 2003; Yavaş 2014; Yavaş and Barlow 2006; Yavaş and McLeod 2010). In L1 acquisition, /s/+stop clusters are typically reduced to the less sonorous stop. However, children show very different patterns in reduction of /s/+sonorant clusters.

For instance, although some children reduce all /s/C clusters to the least sonorous singleton, as described above, other children, such as Amahl (Smith 1973) and KR (Barlow 2001) instead omit the /s/ in all forms, regardless of the sonority profile of the target cluster (Barlow 2001; Farris-Trimble 2014; Smith 1973). This is shown in (4).

(4) Reduction of /s/C clusters

a. Amahl (male, stages 6–14) (Farris-Trimble 2014; Smith 1973)

[wi:t] 'sweet' [li:p] 'sleep' [laitə] 'slicer' [maiu] 'smile'
[nif] 'sniff' [b̥aidə] 'spider' [d̥æp] 'stamp' [g̊in] 'skin'

b. KR (male, age 3;6) (Barlow 2001)

[wɪm] 'swim' [lipiŋ] 'sleeping' [mɛo^{ɫ}] 'smell' [no] 'snow'
[pũ] 'spoon' [kovi] 'stove' (dim.) [kaɪ] 'sky' [kawi] 'starry'

For both Amahl and KR, their omission of /s/ in /s/C clusters could be attributed to an independently occurring error pattern. For Amahl, /s/ was always replaced with a stop in all singleton contexts; for KR, initial /s/ was replaced by a velar stop, but occurred correctly in other singleton contexts. Thus, both children's sound systems showed a general avoidance of clusters and of (initial) /s/, and both employed an alternative strategy to deal with /s/+sonorant clusters because of the combined offense (a 'fell-swoop repair', to be discussed below; Farris-Trimble 2014).

Still other children may show the sonority-based pattern for /sn-/ and /sl-/, and coalescence to [f] for /sm-/ and /sw-/, showing faithfulness to labials in the input (Gnanadesikan 2004; Pater and Barlow 2003). However, in some cases, it is difficult to attribute the unusual behaviour of /s/C clusters to independent constraints. Consider KR's sound system at a later stage of development, shown in (5) (Barlow 2001). As stated, his omission of /s/ in /s/C clusters at age 3;6 was attributed to an independently-motivated error on singleton /s/. At age 3;11, /s/ has emerged in initial position, and now two-element /s/C clusters – all of them – occur target appropriately, as shown in (5a). At the same time, all other obstruent+sonorant clusters continue to be reduced to the least sonorous singleton, as shown in (5b).

(5) KR (male, age 3;11) (Barlow 2001)

a. /s/ clusters do not reduce

[swɪm] 'swim' [slipin] 'sleeping' [smeɪo] 'smell' [sno] 'snow'
[spun] 'spoon' [stovi] 'stove' (dim.) [skaɪ] 'sky' [stawi] 'starry'

b. Non /s/ clusters reduce to obstruent

[dɪn] 'twin' [kin] 'queen' [kut] 'cute' [fu] 'few'
[peɪ] 'pray' [dʌm] 'drum' [go] 'grow' [fowin] 'throwing'
[bo] 'blow' [gaɪm] 'climb' [gʌv] 'glove' [faɪ] 'fly'

c. Three-element clusters reduce to [s]+stop

[speɪ] 'spray' [stɔ] 'straw' [sku] 'screw' [skʊə] 'squirrel'

What would prevent /tw-/ from occurring correctly, when the more difficult /sw-/ is allowed to occur? Why would the child's sound system allow /sl-/ clusters, but not /fl-/? Because of the unusual behaviour of /s/C clusters in developing and fully-developed sound systems, many have argued that /s/C clusters, including those /s/+sonorant clusters, do not form branching onsets, and instead are represented with /s/ as the adjunct to the syllable, as in (2) above, or as some other structure that is distinct from branching onsets (Booij 1995; Fikkert 1994; Goad 2012; Kaye 1992; Pan and Chen 2008). (For a comprehensive discussion, see Goad, this volume.) In the case of KR, the assumption that all /s/C clusters were structurally distinct from branching onsets allowed for a systematic account of the differences between the cluster types; the account also correctly predicted how three-element clusters, which were assumed to include both types of structures, would be produced based on the behaviour of the independent structures, as shown in (5c). That is, for a target word such as 'spray' /spɹeɪ/, the branching onset portion of the cluster was reduced (/pɹ-/ as [p]), but the /s/ was retained, yielding [speɪ].

For other sound systems (developing or fully developed), it appears that the /s/+approximant clusters /sw-/ and /sl-/ behave differently from the /s/+nasal and /s/+stop clusters. This has led some researchers to assume that only the latter types of clusters are structurally different; yet, others assume that continuancy, rather than sonority, is relevant to the distinct patterning of these clusters (Enochson 2014; Gerrits and Zumach 2006; Yavaş 2006; Yavaş and Core 2006). Moreover, sound systems appear to vary with respect to how the /s/+nasal clusters pattern: In some systems they pattern with /s/+stop clusters; in others they pattern with other obstruent+sonorant clusters (Barlow 1997; Davis 1990; Goad 2011, 2012, this volume; Selkirk 1982; Steriade 1988).

Tautosyllabic and heterosyllabic word-medial clusters: Sonority is also implicated in the reduction of word-medial consonant clusters. Once again, such clusters typically are reduced so that the obstruent is retained, regardless of whether the cluster forms a tautosyllabic branching onset, as with 'zebra' [zi.bɹə], or a heterosyllabic cluster that spans the coda and following onset, as in 'window' [wɪn.doʊ], depicted in (6) below (Barlow 2003, 2005b, 2007a; Hansen 2004; Lleó and Prinz 1996; Ohala 1998, 1999).

(6) Syllable template for the word 'window' ('O' = onset, 'N' = nucleus, 'C' = coda, 'R' = rhyme)

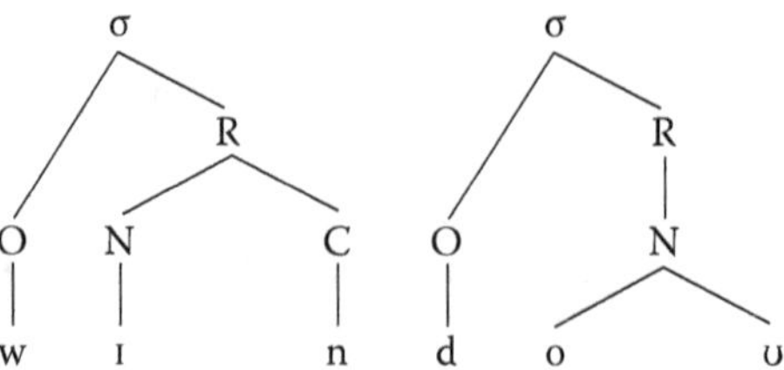

Errors on tautosyllabic and heterosyllabic two-element medial clusters can pattern independently and also can allow for correct predictions regarding how three-element medial clusters will surface. This is illustrated in (7) for a Mexican Spanish-speaking child with phonological delay (Barlow 2003, 2007a).

(7) SD1 (female, age 3;4): Initial and medial cluster reduction (Barlow 2003, 2007a)

a. Branching onsets do not reduce

/plato/ → [plato] 'plate' /bloke/ → [bloke] 'block' /brinka/ → [brika] 'jumps'
/tren/ → [tren] 'train' /krus/ → [krus] 'cross' /fresa/ → [freda] 'strawberry'
/ʧikles/ → [ʧikles] 'gum'

b. Heterosyllabic clusters reduce to least sonorous segment

/brin.ka/ → [brika] 'jumps' /xen.te/ → [exetes] 'people'
/len.gua/ → [legua] 'tongue' /gan.ʧo/ → [gaʧo] 'hook'
/del.fin/ → [ofi] 'dolphin' /tam.bor/ → [tabor] 'drum'

c. Three-element clusters reduce to branching onsets

/ʧan.klas/ → [ʧa.klas] 'sandals' /es.treja/ → [e.treja] 'star'

As shown in (7a), SD1 produces tautosyllabic branching onsets, but reduces heterosyllabic clusters, as in (7b). Three-element clusters, such as in *chanclas* /ʧan.klas/ 'sandals' or *estrella* /es.treja/ 'star' shown in (7c), which include a heterosyllabic cluster and a tautosyllabic cluster, reduce as would be predicted (Barlow 2003, 2007a). That is, the coda of the heterosyllabic cluster is deleted, and the branching onset remains intact.

Many heterosyllabic consonant clusters of fully-developed languages typically follow the Syllable Contact Law (SCL; Clements 1992; Davis 1998; Hooper 1976; Murray and Vennemann 1983; Parker 2003; S. Rose 2000; Vennemann 1988), which requires falling sonority across the syllable boundary. Because of this, one could also argue that the reduction pattern for heterosyllabic clusters shows a preference for preserving the segment in the onset as opposed to the coda (Beckman 1997, 1998; Rubach 2008), rather than any influence of sonority. Thus, if the majority of target medial clusters follow the SCL, then reduction to the least sonorous segment in fact may be attributable to some other feature, such as a simple avoidance of codas, or the need to preserve onsets or consonants that are otherwise considered prosodically strong (Blevins 1995; Prince and Smolensky 2004; Wilson 2001).

Ohala's (1998) study addressed this very issue, by comparing children's productions of medial clusters that varied with respect to sonority profile. Specifically, she compared stop+liquid clusters (e.g., [.bɹ] in 'zebra') versus liquid+stop clusters (e.g., [ɹ.p] in 'carpet), as well as stop+nasal (e.g., [k.n] in 'picnic') versus nasal+stop clusters (e.g., [n.k] in 'pinky'), and fricative+stop clusters (e.g., [s.k] in ‘biscuit’) versus stop+fricative clusters (e.g., [k.s] in ‘dachshund’). Notably, some of these clusters follow the SCL and are syllabified as complex onsets in English, some follow the SCL but are heterosyllabic, and some violate the SCL and are heterosyllabic. Across the cluster types, Ohala observed a preference for the less sonorous segment in the children’s reduction patterns. Thus, for ‘picnic’ and ‘dachshund’, the /k/ was retained, indicating that sonority, and not position within the syllable, most reliably predicted the reduction pattern.

Children may also exhibit compensatory lengthening as part of the medial cluster repair. Ota (2001) showed that young Japanese-speaking children reduced medial clusters and either lengthened the vowel (e.g., /panda/ ‘panda’ as [paːda]), geminated the consonant (e.g., /ombɯ/ ‘carry me!’ as [obbo]), or shortened the preceding vowel and lengthened the consonant (e.g., /keːki/ ‘cake’ as [kɪkkɪ]).

Final clusters: Final consonant clusters are much less straightforward than initial clusters and coda consonants when it comes to generalizing error patterns, in terms of sonority or otherwise. This is likely due to the assumed variety of possible structures that may occur in that context. Recall from the introduction that final clusters may comprise: (a) for languages with final obstruent+sonorant clusters, a branching onset to empty-headed syllables (e.g., European French *pauvre* ‘poor’ [pɔvʁ]); (b) a complex nucleus followed by a singleton consonant (e.g., ‘part’); (c) a branching coda (e.g., ‘pant’); or (d) a singleton coda followed by an appendix (e.g., ‘pats’). These different structures are illustrated in (8) below. The role of sonority in the reduction of final clusters therefore may depend on the structural representation. Indeed, structural differences are cited in accounts of asymmetries in the patterning of different types of final clusters in both developing and fully-developed systems, independent of sonority (Côté, 2004; Demuth and Kehoe 2006; Kirk and Demuth 2003, 2005; Ragheb and Davis 2014; Topbaş and Kopkallı-Yavuz 2008; Wiltshire 2006).

(8) Possible structures for final consonant clusters (‘A’ = appendix)

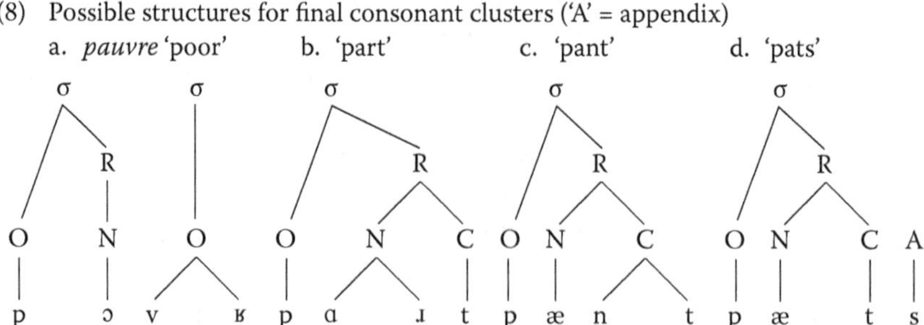

For final clusters that comprise branching onsets, as in (8a) above, the SSP predicts reduction to the least sonorous segment, as with word-initial and word-internal branching onset clusters; thus, *pauvre* 'poor' would be simplified to [pɔv]. Demuth and Kehoe (2006) observed patterns of cluster reduction to the least sonorous segment (as well as epenthesis) on final obstruent+liquid clusters in French-speaking children. In addition, some children showed reduction along with compensatory lengthening (gemination) of the retained consonant, as in /kɔfʁ/ 'chest' as [kɔfː] and /livʁ/ 'book' as [livː].

For those final clusters that span the nucleus and coda constituents, as in (8b) above, the SSP would favour omission of the less sonorous member of the nucleus, showing a preference for the more sonorous vowel, and the coda consonant would remain. Thus, 'part' would be simplified to [pɑt], with the result that the least sonorous segment of the cluster is retained. Topbaş and Kopkallı-Yavuz (2008) showed that Turkish-speaking children reduced sonorant+obstruent clusters to the sonorant and displayed a compensatory strategy of vowel lengthening as a means for preserving moraic structure. A similar compensatory strategy is argued to occur in the case of gemination of final clusters by children acquiring Cairene Arabic (Ragheb and Davis 2014). Refer to (9) for data reflecting these two compensatory strategies.

(9) Final cluster reduction and compensatory lengthening in acquisition

a. Turkish (Topbaş and Kopkallı-Yavuz 2008)[2]

/tyɾc/ → [tyːc] 'Turkish'	/ʃoɾt/ → [ʃoːt] 'shorts'	/kʌlp/ → [kaːp] 'heart'
/zʌɾf/ → [zʌːf] 'envelope'	/vintʃ/ → [viːtʃ] 'crane'	

b. Cairene Arabic (Ragheb and Davis 2014)

/ward/ → [wadd] 'flowers'	/bint/ → [bitt] 'girl'	/kalb/ → [kabb] 'dog'
/naml/ → [ʔall] 'ants'	/miʃtˤ/ → [ʔitt] 'I drank'	/ʔamħ/ → [ʔamm] 'wheat'

In contrast, for branching coda clusters, as in (8c), the SSP predicts that such clusters will reduce by preserving the *most* sonorous segment, following the assumption that sonorant codas are preferred to obstruent codas. This has been observed for both L1 and L2 learners of English; however, the findings are based on a small subset of the full range of possible final consonant clusters (Hansen 2001, 2004; Ohala 1999; Osburne 1996).

2 Note that, for the Turkish forms in particular, even nasals were omitted in these final clusters. As Topbaş and Kopkallı-Yavuz suggested, the behaviour of such forms suggests a closer affinity to the nucleus for sonorants, including the nasals, indicating all such forms patterned as in (8b). In other studies, the affiliation of nasals in the nucleus or coda has been shown to be indeterminate (Hindson and Byrne 1997).

Finally, for clusters that span the coda and appendix constituents, as in (8d) above, the role of sonority is unclear, as it is assumed that the SSP does not govern extrasyllabic constituents. It appears, however, that such clusters may be treated as structurally distinct, and moreover simpler. For instance, Kirk and Demuth (2003) noted that English-speaking children made metathesis errors that changed falling sonority /-sp/ to rising [-ps].[3] Similarly, in her study of Vietnamese L2 learners of English, Osburne (1996) found that clusters that violated the SSP were preserved more often than those that did not, and this was attributed to the presence of a grammatical morpheme in the offending cluster.

In contrast, L2 learners also have been reported to repair those final clusters that appear to be in violation of the SSP so that they surface with falling sonority (Carlisle 1991; Eckman 1987; Edwards 2006; Hansen 2004; Tropf 1987). For instance, in his study of Korean, Japanese, and Cantonese L2 English learners, Eckman (1987) found that three-element final clusters, as with 'clasped' /klæspt/, were typically reduced to [st] or [sp], to maintain falling sonority; rarely did [pt] occur. Interestingly, the fricative in such three-element clusters was more likely to be omitted when it marked grammatical information (as with [s] in 'opts' /ɔpts/ as [ɔpt]) than when it did not (e.g., 'waxed' /wækst/ as [wæks]), regardless of the sonority profile that obtained.

In fact, in English, clusters with a structure like that in (8d) commonly include grammatical morphemes, such as plural, third-person singular, or past tense. Because of this, cluster simplification patterns may be attributable to difficulty with morphological structure and/or the complex suprasegmental structure. Some research directly comparing phonetically similar mono- versus bimorphemic clusters suggests that such forms do not behave differently in children's acquisition of English (Kirk and Demuth

3 Children also employ metathesis as a strategy for dealing with marked syllable structure. For instance, Chin (1996) describes S36, an English-speaking child with phonological delay, who, in order to avoid final obstruents, creates onset clusters with rising sonority by moving the final consonant to the second position of the onset: [psæ] 'bath', [pʃæ] 'badge', [pʃɑɹ] 'sharp'. In contrast, Bloch (2011) describes two Hebrew-speaking children, RM and SR, who create codas in order to avoid branching onsets, by moving the more sonorous segment of the cluster to the coda: /skuteʁ/ as [kuθteʁ] 'scooter', /bʁexa/ as [beʁxa] 'swimming pool', /blondini/ as [boldini] 'blond'. Finally, Łukaszewicz (2007) describes a Polish-speaking child who alters word-medial stop+sonorant onset clusters via metathesis and substitution so that they conform to the SCL: /nudnɔ/ as [jun.dɔ] 'boring' (adv.), /dɔbra/ as [dɔmba] 'good' (fem.), /upadwa/ as [wupanda] 'she fell'.

2005; Klopfenstein and Ball 2010; Tolbert 2004), while other research indicates that such forms behave differently not only in acquisition but also fully-developed adult (L1) systems (Plag, Homann and Kunter 2013; Song, Demuth, Shattuck-Hufnagel and Ménard 2013). Nevertheless, children are known to make errors on grammatical morphemes and these are often impacted by phonological context, including sonority (Barlow and Pruitt-Lord 2014; Demuth 2014; Ettlinger and Zapf 2011; Riches 2015), though the specific impact of sonority is inconsistent across such studies. For L2 learners (both child and adult), inflectional morphemes are likewise often omitted (Blom and Paradis 2013; Moore and Marzano 1979; Politzer and Ramirez 1973).

Few studies have systematically compared performance on the different types of clusters that are proposed to be structurally different; instead, they are lumped together, and/or only a subset of the possible cluster types is evaluated (e.g., only sonorant+obstruent or obstruent+obstruent), often for methodological reasons (Eckman 1991; Kirk and Demuth 2005; Tolbert 2004). As a consequence, the findings from these studies are difficult to interpret in light of the above predictions. The lack of a comprehensive study of final clusters combined with their more variable patterning thus makes it difficult to make broad generalizations about the role of sonority in final cluster errors in L1 and L2 acquisition. Those studies that do evaluate multiple cluster types are revealing of the possible structural differences. For instance, Klopfenstein and Ball (2010) described a child who typically reduced final liquid+obstruent clusters to the obstruent, but (when reductions occurred) reduced fricative+stop clusters to the fricative, nasal+stop clusters to the nasal, and stop+fricative clusters to the fricative. One might argue that that the child's errors on liquid+obstruent clusters are consistent with predictions of the SSP, if such clusters are assumed to syllabify with the liquid in the nucleus. The behaviour of the fricative+stop and nasal+stop clusters would be consistent with SSP predictions for branching codas. Further, no matter what reduction strategy was exhibited, the stop+fricative clusters would not be in violation of the SSP if the fricative is in the appendix.

15.2.3 Summary of Cluster Reduction Patterns

To summarize, errors on clusters typically involve strategies that simplify the syllable structure and create low sonority onsets. In the case of initial and medial clusters, this pattern is particularly robust, with notable exceptions attributed to differing syllable structure. For final clusters, a general pattern of simplification is difficult to determine, likely due the heterogeneous nature of final clusters. We now consider additional, predictable variation that may occur within and across sound systems.

15.3 Variation within and across Sound Systems

Some of the more interesting research on the role of sonority in phonological acquisition pertains to predictions regarding variation, both within and across sound systems. That is, asymmetries in production can obtain within a given sound system, and individual differences are also observed in comparisons across sound systems.

We will consider how differences between children's sound systems occur in principled, systematic ways. In particular, the impact of co-occurring error patterns and other conspiracies that contribute to observed asymmetries in production will be discussed. In this section we focus primarily on error patterns associated with consonant clusters.

As discussed above, children's initial and medial clusters generally reduce to the least sonorous segment, and this is attributed to the SSP. Interestingly, this pattern can be subverted by other co-occurring segmental patterns, such as stopping or fronting. In (10) below, the cluster reduction strategies exhibited by two children with phonological delay are shown. These two children also exhibit an independent pattern of stopping of fricatives, and this error pattern impacts their cluster reduction strategies.

(10) Co-occurring stopping and fricative cluster reduction patterns

a. Subject 13 (male, age 4;8) (Barlow 1997):
Stop+sonorant and fricative+sonorant → stop

[tɪn] 'twin'	[kin] 'queen'	[bo] 'blow'	[gow] 'grow'
[bɔgo] 'froggie'	[baɪ] 'fly'	[tʌp] 'shrub'	[toʊ] 'throw'

b. LP65 (male, age 3;8) (Pater and Barlow 2003):
Stop+sonorant → stop, but fricative+sonorant → sonorant

[bɛd] 'bread'	[bʌʔ] 'brush'	[b̥ɪɾi] 'pretty'	[b̥aɪ] 'prize'
[wɛnd] 'friend'	[wʊːt] 'fruit'	[wi] 'three'	[woʊ] 'throw'
[wɪːn] 'swing'	[wɪəm] 'swim'	[niːd] 'sneeze'	[maɪjʊ] 'smile'

As stated, both children in (10) exhibited stopping patterns in their productions, but their errors on fricatives in clusters manifested in different ways. Subject 13 in (10a) reduced all fricative+sonorant clusters by deleting the sonorant and stopping the fricative, following the general sonority-based reduction pattern. LP65, in contrast, simply deleted the fricative in fricative+sonorant clusters, in which case the cluster is reduced to the *most* sonorous segment, as shown in (10b). This is an example of what Farris-Trimble (2014) describes as a fell-swoop repair: The grammar uses a stopping strategy for singleton fricatives, and the sonority-based cluster reduction strategy for stop+sonorant clusters, but uses a third strategy of deletion when the fricative occurs in a cluster (a double offence).

Similar patterns are observed for the co-occurrence of velar fronting and cluster reduction patterns. For instance, given a child who fronts all singleton dorsals with coronals (e.g., 'cup' as [tʌp]), the fronting pattern could apply in cluster contexts as well, as in the data shown in (11a) for Subject 25, a child with phonological delay. Alternatively, another fell-swoop repair of dorsal+sonorant clusters could occur, with deletion of the dorsal, as in the data shown in (11b) for LP65.[4]

(11) Co-occurring fronting and velar cluster reduction patterns

a. Subject 25 (male, age 4;10) (Barlow 1997):
Non-dorsal stop+sonorant and dorsal stop+sonorant → stop

[beɪ] 'play'	[bʌvʊ] 'brother'	[dihaʊs] 'treehouse'	[daɪv] 'drive'
[din] 'queen'	[dut] 'cute'	[dʌv] 'glove'	[daɪ] 'cry'

b. LP65 (male, age 3;8) (Pater and Barlow 2003):
Non-dorsal stop+sonorant → stop, but dorsal stop+sonorant → sonorant

[bɛd] 'bread'	[bʌʔ] 'brush'	[b̥ɪɾi] 'pretty'	[b̥aɪ] 'prize'
[jʌː] 'glove'	[joʊb] 'globe'	[jin] 'clean'	[joʊː] 'clothes'

Variation in cluster reduction patterns such as this has also been observed for medial and final clusters, particularly those involving nasals (Barlow 2003, 2005b, 2007a; Farris-Trimble 2014; Hernández-Chávez, Vogel and Clumeck 1975; Ingram 1989; Macken 1979; Velten 1943). For instance, Barlow (2003, 2005b, 2007a) described a Mexican Spanish-speaking child who reduced heterosyllabic nasal+voiceless obstruent clusters to the least sonorous segment, but reduced nasal+voiced obstruent clusters to the most sonorous segment, as depicted in (12a). A similar observation was made for Amahl's (Smith 1973) production of word-final nasal+consonant clusters. As Farris-Trimble (2014) notes, Amahl deleted nasals when followed by a voiceless obstruent; however, in nasal+voiced obstruent clusters, the obstruent was deleted, as shown in (12b). In each

4 As shown in (10b) and (11b), LP65's system displays an interaction between three processes: sonority-based cluster reduction, stopping and fronting. Refer to Pater and Barlow (2003) for a comprehensive account of this child's sound system within a constraint-based framework.

case, the divergence from the sonority pattern can be attributed to independently-motivated constraints against voiced obstruents.[5]

(12) Co-occurring constraints against clusters and voiced obstruents

a. SD2 (female, age 3;9) (Barlow 2007a): Medial clusters
Nasal+voiceless obstruent → obstruent, but nasal+voiced obstruent → nasal

/fɾente/ → [fete] 'forehead'	/kampana/ → [kapana] 'bell'
/bɾinka/ → [bika] 'jumps'	/pɾinsesa/ → [pisesa] 'princess'
/gɾande/ → [gane] 'big'	/bandeɾa/ → [βaneja] 'flag'
/lengua/ → [lenua] 'tongue'	/tamboɾito/ → [tamolito] 'drum' (dim.)

b. Amahl (male, stages 1–2) (Farris-Trimble 2014; Smith 1973): Final clusters
Nasal+voiceless obstruent → obstruent, but nasal+voiced obstruent → nasal

[ɛt] 'ant'	[d̥æp] 'stamp'	[b̥ʌp] 'bump'	[d̥ɛt] 'tent'
[g̊ik] 'drink'	[g̊ʌk] 'truck'	[ɛn] 'hand'	[mɛn] 'mend'
[d̥aun] 'round'	[ɔin] 'orange'		

More interesting divergences from the sonority pattern can occur that are attributed to co-occurring phonotactic (or markedness) constraints, and can be particularly revealing of what Pater and Barlow (2003) described as a *factorial typology* of possible cluster reduction patterns. In the case of fricative+sonorant clusters, Pater and Barlow predict that there is a fixed typology for how such clusters will surface, due to the effects of the SSP and fricative markedness: 'If a segment of a given sonority is chosen instead of the fricative then all segments of lesser sonority will also be chosen instead of the fricative' (2003: 499). Refer to (13) below for the complete factorial typology. For instance, as shown in (13a), if /s/ is omitted in /sw-/, then /s/ will also be omitted in /sl-/, /sn-/ and /st-/. In this particular case, the markedness of fricative /s/ is overriding the preference for low-sonority onsets, at least for the /s/+sonorant clusters. Moreover, /sw-/ could reduce to [s], as shown in (13b–d). However, if /s/ is omitted in /sl-/, as in (13b), then /s/ will also be omitted in /sn-/ and /st-/. In this case, the markedness of fricative /s/ is not apparent in the reduction of /sw-/, but is so for the remaining clusters.

(13) Typology of fricative+sonorant cluster reduction patterns (Pater and Barlow 2003)

a.	/sw-/ → [w]	/sl-/ → [l]	/sn-/ → [n]	/st-/ → [t]
b.	/sw-/ → [s]	/sl-/ → [l]	/sn-/ → [n]	/st-/ → [t]
c.	/sw-/ → [s]	/sl-/ → [s]	/sn-/ → [n]	/st-/ → [t]
d.	/sw-/ → [s]	/sl-/ → [s]	/sn-/ → [s]	/st-/ → [t]

5 Similar such patterns have been described for other children, and are also observed in adult connected speech, whereby a phrase such as 'send me' would be pronounced as [sɛ̃n mi], but 'sent me' as [sɛ̃t mi] (see also Greenlee and Ohala 1980).

The typology makes testable predictions about possible and impossible grammars,[6] and may explain the variation that occurs across studies with respect to the patterning of onset clusters (including /s/C clusters, despite the different structural representations that have been proposed for them), within and across languages (Ben-David 2006; Gerrits and Zumach 2006; Jongstra 2003; Kristoffersen and Simonsen 2006; Lleó and Prinz 1996; Yavaş 2006; Yavaş and Barlow 2006; Yavaş and Core 2006). In L2 acquisition, sonority affects repair patterns for initial /s/C clusters in a gradient fashion (Fleischhacker 2001; Goad 2012). Prothesis is more likely to occur for /s/+obstruent clusters (e.g., 'stop' as [ɛstɑp]), while anaptyxis is more likely to occur for /s/+liquid clusters (e.g., 'slop' as [sɛlɑp]), as is likewise observed for stop+sonorant clusters. /s/+nasal clusters fall within those two extremes (Carlisle 1991, 1997). Across these studies, the clusters that seem to be most variable in their patterning and which diverge from general predictions about how they will surface are the /s/+nasal clusters. It is possible that developing and fully-developed sound systems vary with respect to how /s/+nasal clusters are represented structurally (Barlow 1997).

To summarize, the general sonority-based cluster reduction pattern may be disrupted due to co-occurring error patterns that conspire against the offending form. In such cases, the grammar may employ a fell-swoop repair (Farris-Trimble 2014), resulting in omission of the least sonorous segment rather than the most sonorous segment. In other cases, the interruptions to the pattern may be attributed to independently-occurring markedness factors that manifest in very specific contexts. This latter phenomenon is often referred to as *emergence of the unmarked* in constraint-based theoretical frameworks (Gnanadesikan 2004; McCarthy and Prince 1994).

15.4 Change over Time

Thus far, we have considered sonority in terms of the types of errors that are observed in phonological acquisition. In this section, a consideration of the order of acquisition of syllable types is considered in light of predictions of the SSP. In general, developing systems are observed to progress from simple to more complex; that is, unmarked structures are present first and

6 Given the sonority hierarchy and the assumed role of other phonotactic constraints that restrict markedness in sound systems, other testable factorial typologies are predicted to occur (Barlow 2003, 2005b, 2007a).

more marked structure is acquired following positive input from the surrounding linguistic community (Barlow and Gierut 1999; Jakobson 1941; Smith 1973; Stampe 1969) or through language intervention or instruction (Gierut 2007). Of course, in the case of child or adult L2 learners, there is the grammar of the L1 that is already present that will also affect the course of acquisition of the L2; nevertheless, effects of Universal Grammar (of which the SSP is assumed to be a part), are still apparent (Eckman 2004). In this section, we consider the predictions of the SSP with respect to the order of acquisition of onsets, codas and clusters.

15.4.1 Sonority and the Emergence of Initial and Final Consonants

It should come as no surprise that CV syllables, which occur in all languages of the world (Greenberg 1978), are acquired before CVC, not to mention CCV(C) and CVCC (Demuth 1995b; Gnanadesikan 2004; Lleó and Prinz 1996), hence the common occurrence of errors on both codas and clusters (Carlisle 2001; Hancin-Bhatt and Bhatt 1997; Ingram 1989; Locke 1983). As stated, children produce obstruent onsets more frequently than sonorant onsets (Bat-El 2012; Fikkert 1994; Freitas 1996; Pater 1997), following from a cross-linguistic tendency for onsets to be strong (with low sonority) and to rise maximally to the nucleus, per the SSP (Steriade 1993).

Typological research also shows a cross-linguistic tendency to favour sonorants over obstruents in the coda, and evidence of an implicational relationship between the two types of coda has been observed for fully developed sounds systems (Blevins 1995; Clements 1990; Fonte 1996; Zamuner 2003). Thus, one would expect that coda sonorants should be acquired before coda obstruents. Interestingly, available research on L1 and L2 acquisition suggests that either obstruents or sonorants may be acquired first in final position, contrary to predictions of the SSP. Final sonorants have been observed to be more accurate for some adult L2 learners of English as well as Dutch-speaking adults with aphasia (den Ouden and Bastiaanse 2003; Eckman and Iverson 1994; Tropf 1987). Yet, final obstruents have been reported to emerge before final sonorants in not only English and Dutch, but also Hebrew and Catalan (Bat-El 2012; Fikkert 1994; Hansen 2001; Kehoe and Stoel-Gammon 2001; Prieto and Bosch-Baliarda 2006; Salidis and Johnson 1997), and individual differences are furthermore apparent (Stites, Demuth and Kirk 2003; Stoel-Gammon 1985).

In fact, there is more evidence to suggest that final obstruents emerge earlier than final sonorants. In Stoel-Gammon's (1985) longitudinal study of the phonetic inventories of English-speaking children, only one of the 34 children appeared to have acquired final sonorant consonants before final obstruents. Fourteen of the children acquired final obstruents (particularly fricatives) first, and for the remaining 18, no order of acquisition could be determined. Moreover, Stoel-Gammon observed that the occurrence of nasals in final position implied their occurrence in initial position, yet liquids showed the opposite pattern.

Hansen (2004) showed that Vietnamese-speaking L2 learners of English showed highest accuracy on nasals, voiceless fricatives and voiceless stops in final position; consonants that were more difficult thus included both sonorants (liquids) and other obstruents. Similarly, Fikkert (1994) reported the following order of acquisition of final consonants for a child learning Dutch: fricatives > stops > nasals > liquids. Prior to their acquisition, final sonorants were replaced with fricatives or omitted, especially in the case of liquids, due to their later acquisition in the segmental inventory. Fikkert also observed that sonorants were more likely to be omitted after long vowels as compared to short vowels. Based on this, Fikkert assumed that the child syllabified the sonorant into the nucleus, and this only could occur once the child allowed branching nuclei to occur. Thus, even in the case of singleton sonorants, Fikkert argued that sonorants (initially) are syllabified into the nucleus rather than the coda. Moreover, assuming that the rhyme is maximally bipositional, Fikkert claimed that, over time, the sonorant would move to the coda in order to allow for a long vowel followed by a consonant singleton or cluster. Although this explanation supported the observations Fikkert made for a child acquiring Dutch, they could not be corroborated with the facts of a study by Salidis and Johnson (1997), who found no difference between CVVC and CVC syllables in their longitudinal study of an English-speaking child.

Another explanation for the earlier acquisition of final obstruents is that they may not be codas at all, but rather word-final onsets to empty syllables (Goad and Brannen 2003; Harris and Gussmann 1998, 2002; Piggott 1999). Specifically, it is argued that some languages, particularly those like English that have a rich final consonant inventory, syllabify word-final obstruents as onsets to empty syllables, while sonorants syllabify as codas. Goad and Brannen (2003) cite word-final consonant release properties (vowel paragoge, aspiration, nasal release) in English-speaking children's early productions as evidence of this structural representation. This account is supported by the observation that final consonants pattern differently from word-internal codas in fully-developed and developing systems (Borràs-Comes and Prieto 2014; Echols and Newport 1992; Fikkert 1994; Freitas, Miguel and Hub Faria 2001; Harris 1994; Itô 1986; Kirk and Demuth 2006; Lleó, Kuchenbrandt, Kehoe and Trujillo 2003; Nuñez-Cedeño 2007; Piggott 1999; Y. Rose 2000).

Consider again SD1 (from (7) above) who omitted word-internal coda consonants (thereby reducing heterosyllabic clusters), as with /gan.ʧo/ 'hook' as [gaʧo], but accurately produced consonants at the end of many words, as shown for his accurate production of [tɾen] 'train' (Barlow 2003). Goad and Brannen (2003) suggest that acquisition proceeds in this way because final onsets are in fact the unmarked structure, and that children acquire final onsets prior to final codas, even if the adult language (in this case, Spanish) does not have word-final onsets. Because obstruent onsets are preferred to sonorant onsets, this would explain the earlier acquisition of final obstruents over sonorants for many children.

Taken together, the asymmetries observed in children's acquisition of final consonants once again may be attributed to differences in how such consonants are syllabified, rather than sonority per se; and these different structures are independently motivated by other production facts.

15.4.2 Sonority and the Emergence of Consonant Clusters

Recall that, per the sonority hierarchy and the SSP, languages that allow branching onset clusters with a shallow sonority slope (or small sonority distance) will also allow clusters with a steep sonority slope (or large sonority distance) (Davis 1990; Parker, 2012a; Steriade 1982). This implicational relationship has also been supported in L1 and L2 sound systems (Archibald 1998; Archibald and Vanderweide 1997; Berent, Harder and Lennertz 2011; Broselow and Finer 1991; Eckman and Iverson 1993; Hancin-Bhatt and Bhatt 1997; Petrič 2001; Smit 1993; Smit, Hand, Freilinger, Bernthal and Bird 1990; Smith, 1973; Yavaş and Barlow 2006; Yavaş and Core 2006).

Additional evidence in support of sonority and markedness in word-initial cluster acquisition comes from phonological treatment research for children with phonological delay. Specifically, treatment of those more marked clusters with a shallow sonority slope (or small sonority distance) was found to generalize to clusters with steep sonority slopes (large sonority distance) for children who produced consonant clusters in error (Anderson 2002; Barlow, 2005a; Elbert, Dinnsen and Powell 1984; Gierut 1999). In contrast, treatment of less marked clusters with a steeper sonority slope did not generalize to more marked clusters (Gierut 1999). Such findings add to our understanding of the role of the SSP in language generally and in acquisition specifically; they also inform best practice for children who have phonological delay.

Regarding medial clusters, the SSP and the SCL predict that heterosyllabic clusters with rising sonority would emerge prior to those with level or falling sonority. Martohardjono (1989) described a 3-year-old English-speaking child, Jenny, who allowed nasal+obstruent medial clusters to surface in her productions, but reduced any obstruent+obstruent clusters. Martohardjono claimed that the child's productions were constrained by the SCL, requiring rising sonority across the syllable boundary. While this may be so, it appears that this is not the only course of development. Barlow (2007a) described another 3-year-old Mexican Spanish-speaking child, Fabiola (Eblen 1982), who correctly produced sonorant+voiceless obstruent clusters and voiceless obstruent+voiceless obstruent clusters, but reduced all other medial clusters, including other clusters with rising sonority. Barlow also described a second child, Joaquín (Montes Giraldo 1971), who allowed all nasal+obstruent clusters to occur but reduced all other clusters (including others with rising sonority). Despite this variation, it appears that nasal+obstruent medial clusters are among the first to emerge, and may even serve as a substitute for other dispreferred clusters (Łukaszewicz 2007), despite cross-linguistic evidence that languages tend to avoid such clusters (Hayes 1999; Pater 1999, 2001).

Regarding final clusters, there is some evidence that branching coda clusters with a large sonority distance will emerge prior to those with a small sonority distance. This has been supported by some research on L2 learners of English (Eckman 1991; Hancin-Bhatt and Bhatt 1997; Hansen 2004). For instance, Eckman (1991) observed a general trend for L2 learners to acquire fricative+stop final clusters before stop+stop clusters, favouring falling sonority profile. Hansen (2004) observed that clusters with falling sonority, such as liquid+fricative and liquid+stop, emerged prior to clusters with level sonority, such as liquid+liquid or stop+stop; however, accuracy on singletons obscured the pattern in some cases. Given that the SSP prefers falling or level sonority for coda clusters, it is not clear why a steeper slope would be preferred in these developing sound systems.

Research findings on L1 acquisition of coda clusters are also less clear. Topbaş and Kopkallı-Yavuz (2008) found that Turkish-speaking children showed higher accuracy on nasal+obstruent final clusters as compared to liquid or flap+obstruent clusters, which have a steeper sonority slope. Further, although some studies point to earlier acquisition of final clusters with falling sonority (Ragheb and Davis 2014); others studies show that rising sonority clusters emerge first (Smith 1973). Once again, segmental and structural differences may play a role in this variation (Tolbert 2004; see below). The differences observed across children and studies may be due in part to the types of clusters that are specifically studied, and the possibility that cluster types may be structurally different, as discussed above. Once again, a systematic evaluation of the acquisition of different cluster types would allow for a determination of how such clusters are represented and in turn would aid in our understanding of how final consonant clusters emerge over time.

15.4.3 The Relationship between Codas, Initial Clusters and Final Clusters

There has been some attempt to determine if there is a universal order of acquisition of final singleton consonants, initial clusters and final clusters. For instance, some research has suggested that final clusters emerge prior to initial clusters (Kirk and Demuth 2003, 2005; Lleó and Prinz 1996; Templin 1957), which initially might be surprising if one considers that codas are typologically marked. Once again, the earlier emergence of final clusters may be due to the structural representation of the specific clusters that were evaluated in such studies. That is, sonorant+obstruent clusters might (initially) be represented with the sonorant in the nucleus; clusters with rising sonority might be represented with the second consonant in the appendix. Indeed, Kirk and Demuth (2005) compared /s/+nasal and /s/+stop initial clusters to stop+/s/ and nasal+/z/ final clusters, (at least some of) which are assumed to comprise structure outside of the core syllable, which was the authors' intention. Thus, it is still unclear whether branching codas would be acquired before branching onsets. Based on the available cross-linguistic typological facts (Blevins 1995), either order of emergence would be predicted to occur. Moreover, individual differences may be attributable to differences in how children analyse particular structures and organize them into specific subsyllabic constituents. In fact, individual differences in the order of initial and final clusters have been observed (Levelt, Schiller and Levelt 1999/2000). Given the range of possible syllable types that have been proposed to occur, as shown in (2) and (8), it may be difficult (perhaps inappropriate) to identify a specific order of acquisition for these structures. Though these issues appear to be beyond the scope of our discussion of sonority and the SSP, some researchers have suggested otherwise.

For instance, it has been proposed that codas and initial clusters are in an implicational relationship with one another, with codas (or coda+onset heterosyllabic sequences) serving as precursors to at least certain types of initial clusters (Vanderweide 1994, cited in Archibald 1998; Baertsch 2002; Baertsch and Davis 2003; Chambless 2006; Davis and Baertsch 2005; Kaye 1992; Pan and Chen 2008; Pan and Snyder 2004). Though in general the evidence suggests that heterosyllabic clusters and branching onsets emerge and pattern independently of one another (Barlow 2003, 2007a; Blevins 1995), there are nevertheless some interesting observations that can be made about the relationship between the coda and initial clusters, particularly in terms of sonority.

Baertsch (2002; Baertsch and Davis, 2003) proposed a more detailed organization of syllable structure in order to account for observed sonority-based relationships between segments in codas and onsets, as shown in (14). Baertsch proposed this structure, along with a *split-margin hierarchy* of sonority, in order to better capture the sonority profile of onsets and codas. Specifically, segments in the outside syllable margins (M_1) of the syllable are lowest in sonority, while the inside margins (M_2) are higher in sonority than M_1 segments, yet still lower in sonority than the nucleus or peak (P) of the syllable. Adapting Prince and Smolensky's (2004) constraint-based instantiation of the sonority hierarchy, Baertsch proposed that the sonority hierarchy be split for segments in M_1 and M_2. Specifically, the M_1 position would favour lower sonority consonants, and the M_2 position would favour higher sonority consonants, while the P position would favour the highest sonority segment overall (usually a vowel). Moreover, the onset position would favour M_1 singletons (with lower sonority), while the coda position would favour M_2 singletons. Thus, M_2 is optional in the onset (or absent in those languages disallowing branching onsets), and M_1 is optional in the coda (or absent in those languages disallowing branching codas).[7] This account thus better reflects the cross-linguistic preference for sonorants in the coda as opposed to obstruents, at least in fully-developed languages (Blevins 1995; Zamuner 2003).

7 Baertsch and Davis (2003) also entertain the possibility that languages may vary with respect to whether they require M_1 or M_2 singleton segments in the coda.

(14) Syllable template for the word 'print' ('σ' = syllable node)

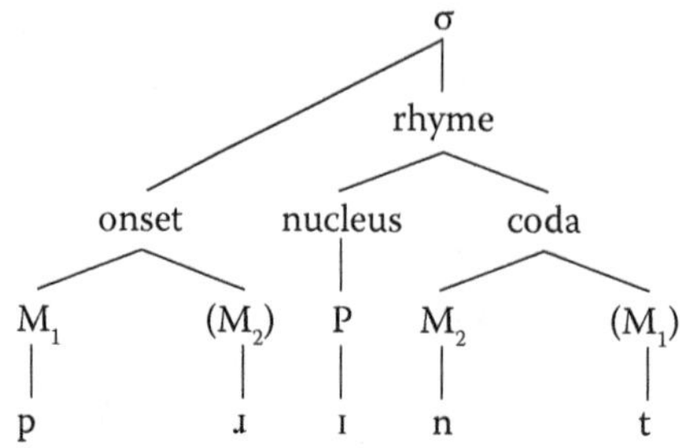

As per Baertsch's (2002; Baertsch and Davis 2003) account, since M_2 is optional in onsets, but required in codas, it is predicted that branching onsets cannot occur without coda consonants. In other words, codas must be prerequisites for branching onsets. Baertsch provides evidence from both developing and fully developed systems to illustrate this relationship, and also provides a principled explanation for why children may acquire liquids in branching onsets before onset singletons. Though there are documented languages that lack coda consonants but allow initial consonant clusters (Blevins 1995), Baertsch (2002) notes that the status of such clusters in those languages as branching onsets has been questioned by independent researchers (e.g., Pike and Pike 1947; Steriade 1994) who have proposed alternative accounts for those forms as complex segments, for example.

The predictions of the split-margin approach have been tested for English- and Spanish-speaking monolinguals and bilinguals in their acquisition of liquids and complex onsets (Barlow and Gierut 2008; Keffala, Barlow and Rose submitted). Though these studies showed that many children did acquire liquids in codas before branching onsets, there were sufficient numbers of children that did not follow this pattern that it cannot be assumed to be universal. Keffala et al. (submitted) argued that coda complexity, the preference for low sonority onsets and high sonority codas, as well as frequency effects served as better predictors of children's acquisition of liquids by position.

15.5 Other Factors that Contribute to Error and Acquisition Patterns

Not surprisingly, there are numerous other factors that have been identified as interfering with, obscuring or overriding the effect of sonority and the SSP on phonological patterns. Space limitations prevent a thorough discussion of any one of these factors, and so they are considered here as fodder for future investigations of phonological acquisition.

There may be language-specific factors that lead to differences in production patterns. For instance, in their study of cluster reduction patterns in children, Lleó and Prinz (1996) observed that German-speaking children tended to reduce to the first consonant (consistent with a sonority-based pattern of reduction), whereas Spanish-speaking children tended to reduce to the second consonant (contrary to findings by Barlow 2003, 2005b, 2007a). Lleó and Prinz attributed this to differences in directionality of syllable structure assignment for the respective languages.

Stress and other prominence factors have been observed to impact production patterns for codas and clusters (e.g., Borràs-Comes and Prieto 2014; Ohala 1998). For instance, though low sonority onsets are preferred cross-linguistically, this effect is less apparent in prosodically weak contexts, as evidenced by lenition patterns observed in both developing and fully-developed sound systems (Baković 1994; Barlow 2007b; Chela-Flores 1996; Hume and Odden 1996; Kirchner 1998). Moreover, Kirk and Demuth (2006) found that word length, word position and stress played a more important role than sonority in 2-year-old children's acquisition of coda consonants in English.

In addition, articulatory ease and the learner's existing segmental inventory can also interfere with the role of sonority on error rates as well as error types that affect codas and consonant clusters (Archibald 1998, 2003; Barlow 2001; Farris-Trimble 2014; Hancin-Bhatt 2000; Hancin-Bhatt and Bhatt 1997; Hansen 2004; Kirk and Demuth 2005; Osburne 1996; Tolbert 2004). For instance, Vietnamese L2 learners of English show different reduction patterns for final liquid+obstruent clusters: Those involving /l/ are reduced according to the SSP (preserving the /l/), while those involving /ɹ/ typically are reduced to the obstruent (deleting /ɹ/) because of segmental difficulty with /ɹ/ which is absent in the L1 (Hancin-Bhatt 2000; Hancin-Bhatt and Bhatt 1997; Hansen 2004; Osburne 1996). Similarly, Tolbert (2004) found that children's productions of target /-lf/ and /-lt/ final clusters were both less accurate than /-nt/ clusters; based on sonority distance, /-nt/ should have been intermediate to the two clusters for accuracy. Tolbert notes that this divergence from predictions of the SSP could be attributed to the children's existing phonetic inventories, which showed absence of or lower accuracy for singleton /l/.[8]

8 Alternatively, /-lf/ and /-lt/ may not be syllabified the same as /-nt/, as noted earlier.

For bilingual children, or child L2 learners, similar such cross-linguistic interactions (or transfer) may be observed. For instance, the smaller inventory of word-final codas and absence of coda clusters in Spanish has been shown to impact Spanish-English and Spanish-German bilinguals' acquisition of such forms in their other language (i.e., English or German), which has a larger inventory of those forms (Keffala, Barlow and Rose in press; Lleó et al. 2003). This has been shown to impact the acquisition of initial consonant clusters, of codas, as well as of liquid phonemes by context (Keffala et al. in press, submitted).

Frequency of occurrence of different types of phonological structure also has been identified as additional predictors of accuracy of production of codas and consonant clusters (Bat-El 2012; Keffala et al. in press, submitted; Leonard and Ritterman 1971; Ota and Green 2013; Polite 2008; Stites et al. 2003; Zamuner 2003; Zamuner, Gerken and Hammond 2005). For instance, Stites et al. (2003), in observing two separate paths for acquisition of sonorant versus obstruent codas, proposed that both sonority and frequency play a role in acquisition, influencing children to different degrees on an individual basis. A similar claim has been made for acquisition of sonorants and fricatives in Spanish (Nuñez-Cedeño 2007). A challenge for this account is finding a way to predict the degree to which children will be influenced by these two factors. Nevertheless, it is assumed that unmarked structures that are more frequent will be acquired at a faster rate and produced with less variability than those forms that are marked and/or less frequent (Keffala et al. in press, submitted).

15.6 Conclusion

Sonority is implicated in numerous patterns related to acquisition of syllable structure, in terms of the order in which properties are acquired as well as the types of errors that are observed. Nevertheless, sonority alone does not account for the facts of acquisition of syllable structure, nor should it be expected to do so. Other factors can and do interact with sonority to achieve effects that appear to be counterexamples to sonority-based explanations (see also Gouskova 2002). Apparent exceptions to the sonority pattern are often accounted for by independently-motivated, co-occurring phonotactic restrictions and different structural representations, as well as other independent factors. The impact of these additional factors work in tandem with the SSP to drive the complex process of acquiring and organizing a phonology as part of a larger linguistic system. A discussion of the role of sonority in phonological acquisition is impossible without also considering syllabic and subsyllabic structure. Indeed, this chapter focused heavily on syllable organization, addressing numerous different proposals regarding how singletons and clusters are represented, and ruling out few of them. That there may be multiple different ways that such forms could be organized within the syllable does not imply that the SSP is inadequate. These different structures were not proposed simply as a response to the fact that they pattern in ways that go against predictions of the SSP. Rather, such forms have been observed to be acquired in a different order, to be in violation of language-specific phonotactics, to pattern independently of other superficially similar forms, *and* also to go against predictions of SSP.

Acknowledgements

I would like to thank Daniel Dinnsen and Philip Combiths for comments on an earlier version of this manuscript. Aspects of the research presented here were supported by grants from the National Institutes of Health to Indiana University (DC01694), to San Diego State University (DC05754) and the American Speech-Language-Hearing Foundation.

References

Anderson, R.T. (2002). Onset clusters and the sonority sequencing principle in Spanish: A treatment efficacy study. In F. Windsor, M.L. Kelly and N. Hewitt (eds.), *Investigations in clinical phonetics and linguistics* (pp. 213–24). Mahwah, NJ: Erlbaum.

Archibald, J. (1998). Second language phonology, phonetics, and typology. *Studies in Second Language Acquisition*, 20, 189–212.

Archibald, J. (2003). Learning to parse second language consonant clusters. *Canadian Journal of Linguistics*, 48, 149–77.

Archibald, J. and Vanderweide, T. (1997). Second language syllable structure: Phonological government and typological universals. *Calgary Working Papers in Linguistics*, 19, 23–43.

Baertsch, K.S. (2002). *An optimality theoretic approach to syllable structure: The split margin hierarchy.* Doctoral dissertation, Indiana University, Bloomington.

Baertsch, K.S. (2012). Sonority and sonority-based relationships within American English monosyllabic words. In S. Parker (ed.), *The sonority controversy* (pp. 3–38). Boston: de Gruyter.

Baertsch, K.S. and Davis, S. (2003). The split margin approach to syllable structure. *ZAS Papers in Linguistics*, 32, 1–14.

Baković, E. (1994). Strong onsets and Spanish fortition. *MIT Working Papers in Linguistics*, 23, 21–39.

Baptista, B.O. and da Silva Filho, J.L.A. (2006). The influence of voicing and sonority relationships on the production of English final consonants. In B.O. Baptista and M.A. Watkins (eds.), *English with a Latin beat: Studies in Portuguese/Spanish-English interphonology* (pp. 73–90). Amsterdam and Philadelphia: John Benjamins.

Barlow, J.A. (1997). *A constraint-based account of syllable onsets: Evidence from developing systems.* Doctoral dissertation, Indiana University, Bloomington.

Barlow, J.A. (2001). The structure of /s/-sequences: Evidence from a disordered system. *Journal of Child Language*, 28, 291–324.

Barlow, J.A. (2003). Asymmetries in the acquisition of consonant clusters in Spanish. *Canadian Journal of Linguistics*, 48, 179–210.

Barlow, J.A. (2005a). Phonological change and the representation of consonant clusters in Spanish: A case study. *Clinical Linguistics and Phonetics*, 19, 659–79.

Barlow, J.A. (2005b). Sonority effects in the production of consonant clusters by Spanish-speaking children. In D. Eddington (ed.), *Selected Proceedings from the 6th Conference on the Acquisition of Spanish and Portuguese as First and Second Languages* (pp. 1–14). Somerville, MA: Cascadilla Proceedings Project. http://www.lingref.com/cpp/casp/6/index.html

Barlow, J.A. (2007a). Constraint conflict in the acquisition of tauto- and heterosyllabic clusters in Spanish. In F. Martínez-Gil and S. Colina (eds.), *Optimality-theoretic studies in Spanish phonology* (pp. 525–48). Philadelphia: John Benjamins.

Barlow, J.A. (2007b). Grandfather effects: A longitudinal case study of the phonological acquisition of intervocalic consonants in English. *Language Acquisition*, 14, 121–64.

Barlow, J.A. and Dinnsen, D.A. (1998). Asymmetrical cluster development in a disordered system. *Language Acquisition*, 7, 1–49.

Barlow, J.A. and Gierut, J.A. (1999). Optimality theory in phonological acquisition. *Journal of Speech, Language, and Hearing Research*, 42, 1482–98.

Barlow, J.A. and Gierut, J.A. (2008). A typological evaluation of the split margin approach to syllable structure in phonological acquisition. In D.A. Dinnsen and J.A. Gierut (eds.), *Optimality theory, phonological acquisition and disorders* (pp. 407–26). Sheffield: Equinox.

Barlow, J.A. and Pruitt-Lord, S.L. (2014). The role of phonological context in children's overt marking of '-s' in two dialects of American English. In A.W. Farris-Trimble and J.A. Barlow (eds.), *Perspectives on phonological theory and acquisition: Papers in honor of Daniel A. Dinnsen* (pp. 133–54). Philadelphia: John Benjamins.

Bat-El, O. (2012). The sonority dispersion principle in the acquisition of Hebrew word final codas. In S. Parker (ed.), *The sonority controversy* (pp. 319–44). Boston: de Gruyter.

Beckman, J. (1997). Positional faithfulness, positional neutralization, and Shona vowel harmony. *Phonology*, 14, 1–46.
Beckman, J. (1998). *Positional faithfulness.* Doctoral dissertation, University of Massachusetts, Amherst.
Bell, A. and Hooper, J.B. (eds.). (1978). *Syllables and segments.* Amsterdam: North-Holland.
Ben-David, A. (2006). On the acquisition of Hebrew #sC onsets. *Journal of Multilingual Communication Disorders*, 4, 205–17.
Ben-David, A., Ezrati, R. and Stulman, N. (2010). Acquisition of /s/-clusters in Hebrew-speaking children with phonological disorders. *Clinical Linguistics & Phonetics*, 24, 210–23.
Berent, I., Harder, K. and Lennertz, T. (2011). Phonological universals in early childhood: Evidence from sonority restrictions. *Language Acquisition*, 18, 281–93.
Blevins, J. (1995). The syllable in phonological theory. In J.A. Goldsmith (ed.), *The handbook of phonological theory* (pp. 206–44). Oxford: Blackwell.
Bloch, T. (2011). *Simplification strategies in the acquisition of consonant clusters in Hebrew.* Master's thesis, Tel-Aviv University.
Blom, E. and Paradis, J. (2013). Past tense production by English second language learners with and without language impairment. *Journal of Speech, Language, and Hearing Research*, 56, 281–94.
Booij, G. (1995). *The phonology of Dutch.* Oxford: Clarendon Press.
Borowsky, T. (1989). Structure preservation and the syllable coda in English. *Natural Language and Linguistic Theory*, 7, 145–66.
Borràs-Comes, J. and Prieto, P. (2014). The acquisition of coda consonants by Catalan and Spanish children: Effects of prominence and frequency of exposure, *Probus*, 26, 59.
Broselow, E. (1987). Non-obvious transfer: On predicting epenthesis errors. In G. Ioup and S.H. Weinberger (eds.), *Interlanguage phonology: The acquisition of a second language sound system* (pp. 292–304). Cambridge, MA: Newbury House.
Broselow, E. (1995). Skeletal positions and moras. In J.A. Goldsmith (ed.), *The handbook of phonological theory* (pp. 175–205). Cambridge, MA: Blackwell.
Broselow, E., Chen, S.-I. and Wang, C. (1998). The emergence of the unmarked in second language phonology. *Studies in Second Language Acquisition*, 20, 261–80.
Broselow, E. and Finer, D. (1991). Parameter setting in second language phonology and syntax. *Second Language Research*, 7, 35–59.
Cairns, C.E. and Feinstein, M.H. (1982). Markedness and the theory of syllable structure. *Linguistic Inquiry*, 13, 193–225.
Carlisle, R.S. (1991). The influence of environment on vowel epenthesis in Spanish/English interphonology. *Applied Linguistics*, 12, 76–95.
Carlisle, R.S. (1997). The modification of onsets in a markedness relationship: Testing the interlanguage structural conformity hypothesis. *Language Learning*, 47, 327–61.
Carlisle, R.S. (2001). Syllable structure universals and second language acquisition. *International Journal of English Studies*, 1, 1–19.

Chambless, D. (2006). *Asymmetries in the acquisition of consonant clusters.* PhD thesis, University of Massachusetts, Amherst.

Chela-Flores, B. (1996). Native language interference and the syllable structure in English: Fortition and lenition processes. *Lenguas Modernas*, 23, 181–90.

Chin, S.B. (1993). *The organization and specification of features in functionally disordered phonologies.* Doctoral dissertation, Indiana University, Bloomington.

Chin, S.B. (1996). The role of the sonority hierarchy in delayed phonological systems. In T.W. Powell (ed.), *Pathologies of speech and language: Contributions of clinical phonetics and linguistics* (pp. 109–17). New Orleans: International Clinical Phonetics and Linguistics Association.

Chin, S.B. and Dinnsen, D.A. (1992). Consonant clusters in disordered speech: Constraints and correspondence patterns. *Journal of Child Language*, 19, 259–85.

Clements, G.N. (1990). The role of the sonority cycle in core syllabification. In J. Kingston and M.E. Beckman (eds.), *Papers in laboratory phonology I: Between the grammar and physics of speech* (pp. 283–333). New York: Cambridge University Press.

Clements, G.N. (1992). The sonority cycle and syllable organization. In W.U. Dressler, H.C. Luschützky, O.E. Pfeiffer and J.R. Rennison (eds.), *Phonologica 1988: Proceedings of the 6th International Phonology Meeting* (pp. 63–76). Cambridge: Cambridge University Press.

Clements, G.N. and Keyser, S.J. (1983). *CV phonology: A generative theory of the syllable.* Cambridge, MA: MIT Press.

Côté, M.-H. (2004). Consonant cluster simplification in Québec French, *Probus*, 16, 151.

Cyran, E. (2008). Consonant clusters in strong and weak positions. In J. Brandão de Carvalho, T. Scheer and P. Ségéral (eds.), *Lenition and fortition* (pp. 447–81). Berlin: Mouton de Gruyter.

Davis, S. (1990). Italian onset structure and the distribution of il and lo. *Linguistics*, 28, 43–55.

Davis, S. (1998). Syllable contact in optimality theory. *Korean Journal of Linguistics*, 23, 181–211.

Davis, S. and Baertsch, K. (2005). The onset-coda connection and the case of Campidanian Sardinian. Paper presented at the Annual Meeting of the Linguistic Society of America, Oakland, CA.

Dell, F. (1995). Consonant clusters and phonological syllables in French. *Lingua*, 95, 5–26.

Demuth, K. (1995a). Markedness and the development of prosodic structure. In J. Beckman (ed.), *Proceedings of the North East Linguistic Society 25* (pp. 13–25). Amherst, MA: GLSA Publications.

Demuth, K. (1995b). Stages in the acquisition of prosodic structure. In E. Clark (ed.), *Proceedings of the 27th Child Language Research Forum* (pp. 39–48). Stanford, CA: CSLI Publications.

Demuth, K. (2014). Prosodic Licensing and the development of phonological and morphological representations. In A.W. Farris-Trimble and J.A. Barlow (eds.),

Perspectives on phonological theory and acquisition: Papers in honor of Daniel A. Dinnsen (pp. 11–24). Philadelphia: John Benjamins.

Demuth, K. and Kehoe, M. (2006). The acquisition of word-final clusters in French. *Catalan Journal of Linguistics*, 5, 59–81.

den Ouden, D.-B. and Bastiaanse, R. (2003). Syllable structure at different levels in the speech production process. In J. van de Weijer, V.J. van Heuven and H. van der Hulst (eds.), *The phonological spectrum, volume II: Suprasegmental structure* (pp. 81–107). Amsterdam: John Benjamins.

Dinnsen, D.A., Chin, S.B., Elbert, M. and Powell, T.W. (1990). Some constraints on functionally disordered phonologies: Phonetic inventories and phonotactics. *Journal of Speech and Hearing Research*, 33, 28–37.

Eblen, R. (1982). A study of the acquisition of fricatives by three-year-old children learning Mexican Spanish. *Language and Speech*, 25, 201–20.

Echols, C.H. and Newport, E.L. (1992). The role of stress and position in determining first words. *Language Acquisition*, 2, 189–220.

Eckman, F.R. (1981). On the naturalness of interlanguage phonological rules. *Language Learning*, 31, 195–216.

Eckman, F.R. (1987). The reduction of word-final consonant clusters in interlanguage. In A. James and J. Leather (eds.), *Sound patterns in second language acquisition* (pp. 143–62). Dordrecht, Holland: Foris.

Eckman, F.R. (1991). The structural conformity hypothesis and the acquisition of consonant clusters in the interlanguage of ESL learners. *Studies in Second Language Acquisition*, 13, 23–41.

Eckman, F.R. (2004). Universals, innateness, and explanation in second language acquisition. *Studies in Language*, 28, 682–703.

Eckman, F.R. and Iverson, G.K. (1993). Sonority and markedness among onset clusters in the interlanguage of ESL learners. *Second Language Research*, 9, 234–52.

Eckman, F.R. and Iverson, G. (1994). Pronunciation difficulties in ESL: Coda consonants in English interlanguage. In M. Yavaş (ed.), *First and second language phonology* (pp. 251–65). San Diego, CA: Singular.

Edwards, J.G.H. (2006). *Acquiring a non-native phonology: Linguistic constraints and social barriers*. New York: Continuum.

Elbert, M.F., Dinnsen, D.A. and Powell, T.W. (1984). On the prediction of phonologic generalization learning patterns. *Journal of Speech and Hearing Disorders*, 49, 309–17.

Enochson, K. (2014). The effect of continuance on the L2 production of onset clusters. In C.-Y. Chu, C.E. Coughlin, B.L. Prego, U. Minai and A. Tremblay (eds.), *Selected proceedings of the 5th Conference on Generative Approaches to Language Acquisition North America (GALANA 2012)* (pp. 1–9). Somerville, MA: Cascadilla.

Ettlinger, M. and Zapf, J. (2011). The role of phonology in children's acquisition of the plural. *Language Acquisition*, 18, 294–313.

Ewen, C. and Botma, B. (2009). Against rhymal adjuncts: The syllabic affiliation of English postvocalic consonants. In P. Backley and K. Nasukawa (eds.), *Strength relations in phonology* (pp. 221–50). Berlin: Mouton de Gruyter.

Ewen, C. and van der Hulst, H. (2001). *The phonological structure of words: An introduction.* New York, NY: Cambridge University Press.

Farris-Trimble, A.W. (2014). A faithfulness conspiracy: The selection of unfaithful mappings in Amahl's grammar. In A.W. Farris-Trimble and J.A. Barlow (eds.), *Perspectives on phonological theory and acquisition: Papers in honor of Daniel A. Dinnsen* (pp. 199–222). Philadelphia: John Benjamins.

Farris-Trimble, A.W. and Gierut, J.A. (2008). Gapped [s]-cluster inventories and stringency. In D.A. Dinnsen and J.A. Gierut (eds.), *Optimality theory, phonological acquisition and disorders* (pp. 377–406). London: Equinox.

Ferguson, C.A. and Garnica, O.K. (1975). Theories of phonological development. In E.H. Lenneberg and E. Lenneberg (eds.), *Foundations of language development* Vol. 1, (pp. 153–80). New York, NY: Academic Press.

Féry, C. and van de Vijver, R. (eds.) (2003). *The syllable in optimality theory.* Cambridge: Cambridge University Press.

Fikkert, P. (1994). *On the acquisition of prosodic structure.* The Hague: Holland Academic Graphics.

Fleischhacker, H. (2001). Cluster-dependent epenthesis asymmetries. In A. Albright and T. Cho (eds.), *Papers in phonology 5 (UCLA Working Papers in Linguistics 7)* (pp. 71–116). Los Angeles, CA: UCLA.

Fonte, I. (1996). *Restrictions on coda: An optimality theoretic account of phonotactics.* Doctoral dissertation, McGill University, Montreal.

Freitas, M.J. (1996). Onsets in early productions. In B. Bernhardt, J. Gilbert and D. Ingram (eds.), *Proceedings of the UBC international conference on phonological acquisition* (pp. 76–84). Somerville, MA: Cascadilla Press.

Freitas, M.J. (2003). The acquisition of onset clusters in European Portuguese. *Probus*, 15, 27–46.

Freitas, M.J., Miguel, M. and Hub Faria, I. (2001). Interaction between prosody and morphosyntax: Plurals within codas in the acquisition of European Portuguese. In J. Weissenborn and B. Höhle (eds.), *Approaches to bootstrapping: Phonological, lexical, syntactic, and neurophysiological aspects of early language acquisition* Vol. II (pp. 45–57). Amsterdam: John Benjamins.

Fudge, E.C. (1969). Syllables. *Journal of Linguistics*, 5, 253–86.

Fujimura, O. and Lovins, J. (1978). Syllables as concatenative phonetic units. In A. Bell and J.B. Hooper (eds.), *Syllables and segments* (pp. 107–20). Amsterdam: North-Holland.

Gerrits, E. and Zumach, A. (2006). The acquisition of ##sC-clusters in Dutch. *Journal of Multilingual Communication Disorders*, 4, 218–30.

Gierut, J.A. (1999). Syllable onsets: Clusters and adjuncts in acquisition. *Journal of Speech, Language, and Hearing Research*, 42, 708–26.

Gierut, J.A. (2007). Phonological complexity and language learnability. *American Journal of Speech-Language Pathology*, 16, 6–17.

Gnanadesikan, A.E. (2004). Markedness and faithfulness constraints in child phonology. In R. Kager, J. Pater and W. Zonneveld (eds.), *Constraints in Phonological Acquisition* (pp. 73–108). Cambridge: Cambridge University Press.

Goad, H. (2011). The representation of sC clusters. In M. van Oostendorp, C. Ewen, E. Hume and K. Rice (eds.), *The Blackwell companion to phonology* (pp. 898–923). Oxford: Wiley-Blackwell.

Goad, H. (2012). sC Clusters are (almost always) coda-initial. *The Linguistic Review*, 29, 335.

Goad, H. and Brannen, K. (2003). Phonetic evidence for phonological structure in syllabification. In J. van de Weijer, V. van Heuven and H. van der Hulst (eds.), *The phonological spectrum, Vol. II: Suprasegmental structure* (pp. 3–30). Amsterdam: John Benjamins.

Goad, H. and Rose, Y. (2000). Headedness versus sonority in cluster reduction. *Chicago Linguistic Society*, 36, 109–23.

Goad, H. and Rose, Y. (2004). Input elaboration, head faithfulness, and evidence for representation in the acquisition of left-edge clusters in West Germanic. In R. Kager, J. Pater and W. Zonneveld (eds.), *Constraints in phonological acquisition* (pp. 109–57). Cambridge: Cambridge University Press.

Gouskova, M. (2002). Exceptions to sonority generalizations. *Chicago Linguistic Society*, 38, 253–68.

Greenberg, J. (1965). Some generalizations concerning initial and final consonant sequences. *Linguistics*, 18, 5–34.

Greenberg, J.H. (ed.). (1978). *Universals of human language, Vol. 2: Phonology.* Stanford, CA: Stanford University Press.

Greenlee, M. (1974). Interacting processes in the child's acquisition of stop-liquid clusters. *Papers and Reports on Child Language Development*, 7, 85–100.

Greenlee, M. and Ohala, J.J. (1980). Phonetically motivated parallels between child phonology and historical sound change. *Language Sciences*, 2, 283–308.

Grijzenhout, J. (1998). The role of coronal specification in German and Dutch phonology and morphology. In W. Kehrein and R. Wiese (eds.), *Phonology and morphology of the Germanic languages* (pp. 27–50). Tübingen: Niemeyer.

Halle, M. and Vergnaud, J.-R. (1978). *Metrical structure in phonology.* Manuscript, Massachusetts Institute of Technology.

Hancin-Bhatt, B. (2000). Optimality in second language phonology: codas in Thai ESL. *Second Language Research*, 16, 201–32.

Hancin-Bhatt, B. and Bhatt, R.M. (1997). Optimal L2 syllables: Interaction of transfer and developmental effects. *Studies in Second Language Acquisition*, 19, 331–78.

Hansen, J.G. (2001). Linguistic constraints on the acquisition of English syllable codas by native speakers of Mandarin Chinese. *Applied Linguistics*, 22, 338–65.

Hansen, J.G. (2004). Developmental sequences in the acquisition of L2 syllable codas: A preliminary study. *Studies in Second Language Acquisition*, 26, 85–124.

Harris, J. (1994). *English sound structure.* Cambridge, MA: Blackwell.

Harris, J. (2006). The phonology of being understood: Further arguments against sonority. *Lingua*, 116, 1483–94.

Harris, J. and Gussmann, E. (1998). Final codas: Why the west was wrong. In E. Cyran (ed.), *Structure and interpretation in phonology: Studies in phonology* (pp. 139–62). Lublin: Folia.

Harris, J. and Gussmann, E. (2002). Word-final onsets. *UCL Working Papers in Linguistics*, 14, 1–41.

Harris, J.W. (1983). *Syllable structure and stress in Spanish*. Cambridge, MA: MIT Press.

Hayes, B. (1989). Compensatory lengthening in moraic phonology. *Linguistic Inquiry*, 20, 253–306.

Hayes, B. (1999). Phonological acquisition in optimality theory: The early stages. from Rutgers Optimality Archive, ROA-327, http://ruccs.rutgers.edu/roa.html

Hernández-Chávez, E., Vogel, I. and Clumeck, H. (1975). Rules, constraints and the simplicity criterion: An analysis based on the acquisition of nasals in Chicano Spanish. In C.A. Ferguson, L.M. Hyman and J.J. Ohala (eds.), *Nasálfest: Papers from a symposium on nasals and nasalization* (pp. 231–48). Stanford: Language Universals Project, Department of Linguistics, Stanford University.

Hindson, B.A. and Byrne, B. (1997). The status of final consonant clusters in English syllables: Evidence from children. *Journal of Experimental Child Psychology*, 64, 119–36.

Hooper, J. (1976). Word frequency in lexical diffusion and the source of morpho-phonological change. In W.M. Christie, Jr. (ed.), *Current progress in historical linguistics* (pp. 95–105). Amsterdam: North-Holland.

Hume, E. and Odden, D. (1996). Reconsidering [consonantal]. *Phonology*, 13, 345–76.

Hyman, L. (1985). *A theory of phonological weight*. Dordrecht, Netherlands: Foris.

Ingram, D. (1989). *First Language Acquisition*. Cambridge: Cambridge University Press.

Itô, J. (1986). *Syllable theory in prosodic phonology*. Doctoral dissertation, University of Massachusetts, Amherst.

Jakobson, R. (1941). *Kindersprache, Aphasie und Allgemeine Lautgesetze*. Uppsala: Almqvist & Wiksell.

Jongstra, W. (2003). Variable and stable clusters: Variation in the realisation of consonant clusters. *Canadian Journal of Linguistics*, 48, 265–88.

Kager, R., Pater, J. and Zonneveld, W. (2004). Introduction: Constraints in phonological acquisition. In R. Kager, J. Pater and W. Zonneveld (eds.), *Constraints in phonological acquisition* (pp. 1–53). Cambridge: Cambridge University Press.

Kaye, J. (1992). Do you believe in magic? The story of s+C sequences. *School of Oriental and African Studies Working Papers in Linguistics*, 2, 293–313.

Kaye, J.D. and Lowenstamm, J. (1981). Syllable structure and markedness theory. In A. Belletti, L. Brandi and L. Rizzi (eds.), *Theory of markedness in generative grammar: Proceedings of the 1979 GLOW conference* (pp. 287–315). Pisa, Italy: Scuola Normale Superiore di Pisa.

Keffala, B., Barlow, J.A. and Rose, S. (in press). Interaction in Spanish-English bilinguals' acquisition of syllable structure. *International Journal of Bilingualism*.

Keffala, B., Barlow, J.A. and Rose, S. (submitted). Markedness, frequency, and the positional acquisition of liquids.

Kehoe, M.M. (1997). Stress error patterns in English-speaking children's word productions. *Clinical Linguistics & Phonetics*, 11, 389–409.

Kehoe, M.M. (2001). Prosodic patterns in children's multisyllabic word productions. *Language, Speech, and Hearing Services in Schools*, 32, 284–94.

Kehoe, M.M. and Stoel-Gammon, C. (2001). Development of syllable structure in English-speaking children with particular reference to rhymes. *Journal of Child Language*, 28, 393–432.

Kenstowicz, M. (1994). *Phonology in generative grammar.* Cambridge, MA: Blackwell.

Kirchner, R. (1998). *An effort-based approach to consonant lenition.* Doctoral dissertation, UCLA, Los Angeles.

Kirk, C. (2008). Substitution errors in the production of word-initial and word-final consonant clusters. *Journal of Speech, Language, and Hearing Research*, 51, 35–48.

Kirk, C. and Demuth, K. (2003). Onset/coda asymmetries in the acquisition of clusters. In B. Beachley, A. Brown amd F. Conlin (eds.), *Proceedings of the Boston University conference on language development 27*, Vol. 2 (pp. 437–48). Somerville, MA: Cascadilla Press.

Kirk, C. and Demuth, K. (2005). Asymmetries in the acquisition of word-initial and word-final consonant clusters. *Journal of Child Language*, 32, 709–34.

Kirk, C. and Demuth, K. (2006). Accounting for variability in 2-year-olds' production of coda consonants. *Language Learning and Development*, 2, 97–118.

Klopfenstein, M. and Ball, M.J. (2010). An analysis of the sonority hypothesis and cluster realization in a child with phonological disorder. *Clinical Linguistics & Phonetics*, 24, 261–70.

Kristoffersen, K.E. and Simonsen, H.G. (2006). The acquisition of #sC clusters in Norwegian. *Journal of Multilingual Communication Disorders*, 4, 231–41.

Lee, P. (1998). Sonority-driven vowel epenthesis in L2 acquisition. *Language Research*, 34, 737–65.

Leonard, L.B. and Ritterman, S.I. (1971). Articulation of /s/ as a function of cluster and word frequency of occurrence. *Journal of Speech and Hearing Research*, 14, 476–85.

Levelt, C.C., Schiller, N.O. and Levelt, W.J. (1999/2000). The acquisition of syllable types. *Language Acquisition*, 8, 237–64.

Lleó, C., Kuchenbrandt, M., Kehoe, M. and Trujillo, C. (2003). Syllable final consonants in Spanish and German monolingual and bilingual acquisition. In N. Müller (ed.), *(In)vulnerable domains in multilingualism* (pp. 191–220). Philadelphia: John Benjamins.

Lleó, C. and Prinz, M. (1996). Consonant clusters in child phonology and the directionality of syllable structure assignment. *Journal of Child Language*, 23, 31–56.

Locke, J.L. (1983). *Phonological acquisition and change.* New York: Academic Press.

Łukaszewicz, B. (2007). Reduction in syllable onsets in the acquisition of Polish: Deletion, coalescence, metathesis and gemination. *Journal of Child Language*, 34, 53–82.

MacKay, D.J. (1978). Speech errors inside the syllable. In A. Bell and J.B. Hooper (eds.), *Syllables and segments* (pp. 201–12). Amsterdam: North-Holland.

Macken, M.A. (1979). Developmental reorganization of phonology: A hierarchy of basic units of acquisition. *Lingua*, 49, 11–49.

Maddieson, I. (2013). Syllable structure. In M.S. Dryer and M. Haspelmath (eds.), *World atlas of language structures online*. Leipzig: Max Planck Institute for Evolutionary Anthropology. Available online at http://wals.info/chapter/12, accessed on 8 June 2015.

Malsch, D.L. and Fulcher, R. (1989). Categorizing phonological segments: The inadequacy of the sonority hierarchy. In R. Corrigan, F. Eckman and M. Noonan (eds.), *Linguistic categorization* (pp. 69–80). Philadelphia: John Benjamins.

Martohardjono, G. (1989). The sonority cycle in the acquisition of phonology. *Papers and Reports in Child Language Development*, 28, 131–39.

McCarthy, J.J. and Prince, A.S. (1994). The emergence of the unmarked: Optimality in prosodic morphology. *Northeastern Linguistic Society*, 24, 333–79.

Montes Giraldo, J.J. (1971). Apropiación por el niño del sistema fonológico español. *Thesaurus*, 26, 322–46.

Moore, F.B. and Marzano, R.J. (1979). Common errors of Spanish speakers learning English. *Research in the Teaching of English*, 13, 161–7.

Murray, R. and Vennemann, T. (1983). Sound change and syllable structure in Germanic phonology. *Language*, 59, 514–28.

Nathan, G.S. (2008). *Phonology: A cognitive grammar introduction*. Philadelphia: John Benjamins.

Nuñez-Cedeño, R. (2007). The acquisition of Spanish codas: A frequency/sonority approach. *Hispania*, 90, 147–63.

Núñez-Cedeño, R. (2008). On the acquisition of Spanish onsets: A case study. *Southwest Journal of Linguistics*, 27, 77–106.

Ohala, D.K. (1996). *Cluster reduction and constraints in acquisition*. Doctoral dissertation, University of Arizona.

Ohala, D.K. (1998). Medial cluster reduction in early child speech. In E.V. Clark (ed.), *Proceedings from the annual child language research forum* (pp. 111–20). Stanford: Center Study for the Language and Information.

Ohala, D.K. (1999). The influence of sonority on children's cluster reductions. *Journal of Communication Disorders*, 32, 397–422.

Osburne, A.G. (1996). Final cluster reduction in English L2 speech: A case study of a Vietnamese speaker. *Applied Linguistics*, 17, 164–81.

Ota, M. (2001). Phonological theory and the development of prosodic structure: Evidence from child Japanese. *Annual Review of Language Acquisition*, 1, 65–118.

Ota, M. and Green, S.J. (2013). Input frequency and lexical variability in phonological development: a survival analysis of word-initial cluster production. *Journal of Child Language*, 40, 539–66.

Pan, N. and Chen, L. (2008). Onset clusters and coda-onset sequences in disordered speech: A government phonology analysis. *Asia Pacific Journal of Speech, Language and Hearing*, 11, 251–67.

Pan, N. and Snyder, W. (2004). Acquisition of /s/-initial clusters: A parametric approach. In A. Brugos, L. Micciulla and C.E. Smith (eds.), *Proceedings of the*

28th annual Boston University conference on language development (pp. 436–46). Somerville, MA: Cascadilla.

Parker, S. (2002). *Quantifying the sonority hierarchy.* Amherst, MA: GLSA, University of Massachusetts.

Parker, S. (2003). The psychological reality of sonority in English. *Word*, 54, 359–94.

Parker, S. (2008). Sound level protrusions as physical correlates of sonority. *Journal of Phonetics*, 36, 55–90.

Parker, S. (2012a). Sonority distance vs sonority dispersion: A typological survey. In S. Parker (ed.), *The sonority controversy* (pp. 101–66). Boston: de Gruyter.

Parker, S. (ed.). (2012b). *The sonority controversy.* Boston: de Gruyter.

Pater, J. (1997). Minimal violation and phonological development. *Language Acquisition*, 6, 201–53.

Pater, J. (1999). Austronesian nasal substitution and other NC̥ effects. In H. van der Hulst, R. Kager and W. Zonneveld (eds.), *The prosody morphology interface* (pp. 310–43). Cambridge: Cambridge University Press.

Pater, J. (2001). Austronesian nasal substitution revisited: What's wrong with *NC (and what's not). In L. Lombardi (ed.), *Segmental phonology in optimality theory: Constraints and representations* (pp. 159–82). Cambridge: Cambridge University Press.

Pater, J. and Barlow, J.A. (2003). Constraint conflict in cluster reduction. *Journal of Child Language*, 30, 487–526.

Petrič, T. (2001). Acquisition of marked consonant clusters in German as a foreign language. *Poznań Studies in Contemporary Linguistics*, 37, 157–86.

Piggott, G.L. (1999). The right edge of words. *The Linguistic Review*, 16, 143–85.

Pike, K.L. and Pike, E.V. (1947). Immediate constituents of Mazateco syllables. *International Journal of American Linguistics*, 13, 78–91.

Plag, I., Homann, J. and Kunter, G. (2013). *Homophony and morphology: The acoustics of word-final s in English.* Unpublished manuscript.

Polite, E.J. (2008). *The influence of frequency- and contextually-related factors on the use of regular noun plural -s by children with specific language impairment.* Doctoral dissertation, Purdue University, West Lafayette, IN.

Politzer, R.L. and Ramirez, A.G. (1973). An error analysis of the spoken English of Mexican-American pupils in a bilingual school and a monolingual school. *Language Learning*, 23(21), 39–62.

Prieto, P. and Bosch-Baliarda, M. (2006). The development of codas in Catalan. *Catalan Journal of Linguistics*, 5, 237–72.

Prince, A.S. and Smolensky, P. (2004). *Optimality theory: Constraint interaction in generative grammar.* Malden, MA: Blackwell.

Proctor, M. and Walker, R. (2012). Articulatory bases of sonority in English liquids. In S. Parker (ed.), *The sonority controversy* (pp. 289–316). Boston: de Gruyter.

Ragheb, M. and Davis, S. (2014). On the L1 development of final consonant clusters in Cairene Arabic. In R. Khamis-Dakwar and K. Froud (eds.), *Perspectives on Arabic linguistics XXVI* (pp. 263–81). Philadelphia: John Benjamins.

Riches, N. (2015). Past tense -ed omissions by children with specific language impairment: The role of sonority and phonotactics. *Clinical Linguistics and Phonetics*, 29, 482–97.

Riney, T. (1990). Age and open syllable preference in interlanguage phonology. In H. Burmeister and P. Rounds (eds.), *Variability in second language acquisition: Proceedings of the tenth meeting of the Second Language Research Forum* Vol. II (pp. 655–66). Eugene, OR: Department of Linguistics, University of Oregon.

Rose, S. (2000). Epenthesis positioning and syllable contact in Chaha. *Phonology*, 17, 397–425.

Rose, Y. (2000). *Headedness and prosodic licensing in the l1 acquisition of phonology.* Doctoral dissertation, McGill University, Montréal.

Ross, S. (1994). The ins and outs of paragoge and apocope in Japanese-English interphonology. *Second Language Research*, 10, 1–24.

Rubach, J. (2008). Prevocalic faithfulness. *Phonology*, 25, 433–68.

Rubach, J. and Booij, G. (1990). Edge of constituent effects in Polish. *Natural Language and Linguistic Theory*, 8, 428–63.

Salidis, J. and Johnson, J.S. (1997). The production of minimal words: A longitudinal case study of phonologial development. *Language Acquistion*, 6, 1–36.

Selkirk, E.O. (1982). The syllable. In H. van der Hulst and N. Smith (eds.), *The structure of phonological representations* Vol. 2 (pp. 337–83). Dordrecht, Netherlands: Foris.

Selkirk, E.O. (1984). On the major class features and syllable theory. In M. Aronoff and R.T. Oehrle (eds.), *Language sound structure: Studies in phonology presented to Morris Halle by his teacher and students* (pp. 107–36). Cambridge, MA: MIT Press.

Smit, A.B. (1993). Phonologic error distributions in the Iowa-Nebraska Articulation Norms Project: Word-initial consonant clusters. *Journal of Speech and Hearing Research*, 36, 931–47.

Smit, A.B., Hand, L., Freilinger, J.J., Bernthal, J.E. and Bird, A. (1990). The Iowa Articulation Norms Project and its Nebraska replication. *Journal of Speech and Hearing Disorders*, 55, 779–98.

Smith, N.V. (1973). *The acquisition of phonology: A case study.* Cambridge: Cambridge University Press.

Song, J.Y., Demuth, K., Shattuck-Hufnagel, S. and Ménard, L. (2013). The effects of coarticulation and morphological complexity on the production of English coda clusters: Acoustic and articulatory evidence from 2-year-olds and adults using ultrasound. *Journal of Phonetics*, 41, 281–95.

Sprenger-Charolles, L. and Siegel, L.S. (1997). A longitudinal study of the effects of syllabic structure on the development of reading and spelling skills in French. *Applied Psycholinguistics*, 18, 485–505.

Stampe, D. (1969). The acquisition of phonemic representation. In R.I. Binnick, A. Davidson, G.M. Green and J.L. Morgan (eds.), *Papers from CLS 5* (pp. 433–44). Chicago: Chicago Linguistic Society.

Stemberger, J.P. (1983). *Speech errors and theoretical phonology.* Bloomington, IN: Indiana University Linguistics Club.

Steriade, D. (1982). *Greek prosodies and the nature of syllabification.* Doctoral dissertation, Massachusetts Institute of Technology. Published by Garland Press, New York, 1990.

Steriade, D. (1988). Reduplication and syllable transfer in Sanskrit and elsewhere. *Phonology*, 5, 73–155.

Steriade, D. (1993). Closure, release and nasal contours. In M.A. Huffman and R.K. Krakow (eds.), *Phonetics and phonology, Vol. 5: Nasals, nasalization, and the velum* (pp. 401–70). San Diego, CA: Academic Press.

Steriade, D. (1994). Complex onsets as single segments: The Mazateco pattern. In J. Cole and C. Kisseberth (eds.), *Perspectives in phonology* (pp. 203–91). Stanford, CA: Center for the Study of Language and Information.

Stites, J., Demuth, K. and Kirk, C. (2003). Markedness vs. frequency effects in coda acquisition. In A. Brugos, L. Micciulla and C.E. Smith (eds.), *Proceedings of the 28th annual Boston University conference on language development* (pp. 565–76). Somerville, MA: Cascadilla.

Stoel-Gammon, C. (1985). Phonetic inventories, 15–24 months: A longitudinal study. *Journal of Speech and Hearing Research*, 28, 505–12.

Tarone, E.E. (1972). A suggested unit for interlingual identification in pronunciation. *TESOL Quarterly*, 6, 325–31.

Tarone, E.E. (1980). Some influences on the syllable structure of interlanguage phonology. *International Review of Applied Linguistics*, 18, 139–52.

Templin, M.C. (1957). *Certain language skills in children, their development and interrelationships (Institute of Child Welfare, Monograph Series 26).* Minneapolis, MN: University of Minnesota Press.

Tolbert, L.C. (2004). *Final cluster development in three and four-year-old children.* Doctoral dissertation, University of Nevada, Reno.

Topbaş, S. and Kopkallı-Yavuz, H. (2008). Reviewing sonority for word-final sonorant+obstruent consonant cluster development in Turkish. *Clinical Linguistics and Phonetics*, 22, 871–80.

Treiman, R. (1984). On the status of final consonant clusters in English syllables. *Journal of Verbal Learning and Verbal Behavior*, 23, 343–56.

Tropf, H. (1987). Sonority as a variability factor in second language phonology. In A. James and J. Leather (eds.), *Sound patterns in second language acquisition* (pp. 173–91). Providence, RI: Foris.

Vaux, B. and Wolfe, A. (2009). The appendix. In E. Raimy and C. Cairns (eds.), *Contemporary views on architecture and representations in phonology* (pp. 101–43). Cambridge, MA: MIT Press.

Velten, H.V. (1943). The growth of phonemic and lexical patterns in infant language. *Language*, 19, 281–92.

Vennemann, T. (1988). *Preference laws for syllable structure and the explanation of sound change: With special reference to German, Germanic, Italian and Latin.* New York: Mouton de Gruyter.

Vroomen, J., van den Bosch, A. and de Gelder, B. (1998). A connectionist model for bootstrap learning of syllabic structure. *Language and Cognitive Processes*, 13, 193–220.

Weinberger, S.H. (1994). Functional and phonetic constraints in second language phonology. In M. Yavaş (ed.), *First and second language phonology* (pp. 283–302). San Diego: Singular.

Wilson, C. (2001). Consonant cluster neutralisation and targeted constraints. *Phonology*, 18, 147–97.

Wiltshire, C.R. (2006). Word-final consonant and cluster acquisition in Indian English(es). In D. Bamman, T. Magnitskaia and C. Zaller (eds.), *Boston University Conference on language development 30 Online proceedings supplement.* http://www.bu.edu/linguistics/BUCLD/supp30.html

Winitz, H. and Irwin, O.C. (1958). Syllabic and phonetic structure of infants' early words. *Journal of Speech, Language, and Hearing Research*, 1, 250–6.

Yavaş, M. (2006). Sonority and the acquisition of #sC clusters. *Journal of Multilingual Communication Disorders*, 4, 159–68.

Yavaş, M. (2014). What guides children's acquisition of #sC clusters? A cross-linguistic account. In A.W. Farris-Trimble and J.A. Barlow (eds.), *Perspectives on phonological theory and development: In honor of Daniel A. Dinnsen* (pp. 115–32). Philadelphia: John Benjamins.

Yavaş, M. and Barlow, J.A. (2006). Acquisition of #sC clusters in Spanish-English bilingual children. *Journal of Multilingual Communication Disorders*, 4, 182–93.

Yavaş, M. and Core, C.W. (2006). Acquisition of #sC clusters in English speaking children. *Journal of Multilingual Communication Disorders*, 4, 169–81.

Yavaş, M. and McLeod, S. (2010). Acquisition of /s/ clusters in English-speaking children with phonological disorders. *Clinical Linguistics & Phonetics*, 24, 177–87.

Zamuner, T.S. (2003). *Input-based phonological acquisition.* New York: Routledge.

Zamuner, T.S., Gerken, L. and Hammond, M. (2005). The acquisition of phonology based on input: A closer look at the relation of cross-linguistic and child language data. *Lingua*, 115, 1403–26.

Zec, D. (1995). Sonority constraints on syllable structure. *Phonology*, 12, 85–129.

Jessica Barlow is Professor of Speech, Language, and Hearing Sciences at San Diego State University in California, USA. Her research focuses on phonological acquisition, phonological theory and phonological disorders, with an emphasis on English, Spanish and Spanish-English bilingualism. Most recently she has been focusing on morphophonology in acquisition. Her research has been published in such journals as *Bilingualism: Language & Cognition; Clinical Linguistics & Phonetics; Frontiers in Psychology; Journal of Speech, Language, and Hearing Research; Language Acquisition*; and *Lingua*. She is co-editor, with Ashley Farris-Trimble, of *Perspectives on phonological theory and acquisition: In honor of Daniel A. Dinnsen* (2014).

16 Acquisition of /s/ Clusters in a Greek-English Bilingual Child: Sonority or OCP?

Mehmet Yavaş and Elena Babatsouli

16.1 Introduction

This chapter reports on a longitudinal examination of the patterns in the acquisition of #sC clusters by a Greek-English bilingual child. The objective is to test the predictions of sonority based explanations and an opposing view espoused by the Obligatory Contour Principle.

In any discussion on the acquisition of consonant clusters, sonority plays an important role because the Sonority Sequencing Principle (hereafter SSP) states that in any syllable a segment constituting a sonority peak is preceded and/or followed by a sequence of segments with progressively decreasing sonority values. Therefore, the SSP is a significant force in languages and has been invoked in explaining various phenomena related to syllable phonotactics. Among these are Syllable Structure (Venneman 1972; Hooper 1976; Steriade 1990; Selkirk 1984; Prince and Smolensky 2004; Smolensky 2006; Zec 1995), and Syllable Markedness and Misperceptions (Berent, Lennertz and Smolensky 2011; Daland, Hayes, White, Garellek, Davis and Norrmann 2011). Sonority sequencing of consonants is also correlated with production accuracy in cluster acquisition and error types in typical first language phonological acquisition (Ohala 1999; Pater 2004; Barlow 2005; Yavaş, Ben-David, Gerrits, Kristoffersen and Simonsen 2008), second language phonology (Broselow and Finer 1991; Eckman and Iverson 1993; Broselow, Chen and Wang 1998; Broselow and Xu 2004; Carlisle 2006; Cardoso and Liakin 2009; Yavaş 2011), developmental phonological disorders (Gierut 1999; Barlow 2001; Yavaş 2010) as well as in aphasia (Romani and Calabrese 1998; Stenneken, Bastiaanse, Huber and Jacobs 2005; Romani and Galluzzi 2005; Miozzo and Buchwald 2013).

Sonority is related to the degree of opening of the articulators and to the relative prominence of one sound class versus another. As such, obstruents (stops, fricatives and affricates), nasals, liquids, glides and vowels constitute a scale of increasing sonority strength. It is commonly agreed on that the increase in sonority difference between the cluster members translates into their relative complexity (markedness). Firstly, clusters that have falling (negative) sonority (e.g., *skill* /skɪl/) are more marked than level-sonority clusters (e.g., Hebrew /ptiʧa/ 'opening') which, in turn, are more marked than rising sonority clusters (e.g., *blue* [blu]). The existence of a more marked cluster in a language implies the existence of a less marked cluster. Thus, if a language allows marked negative sonority clusters, it also allows level sonority and rising sonority clusters. Also, in rising sonority canonical clusters, the ones that have a smaller sonority distance are more complex (marked) than those with a greater difference. Accordingly, /fl/ (e.g., *fly*) which has a smaller sonority distance between its members is more marked than /pj/ (e.g., *pure*) which has a greater distance from C1 to C2. This is related to the minimal sonority distance principle. According to the Sonority account, syllable structures with least-marked sonority sequences are predicted to be acquired earlier in development than those with more-marked sequences (Clements 1990).

16.2 The Case of /s/ Clusters

In English, and some other Germanic languages such as Dutch and Norwegian, some #sC clusters (/sp/, /st/, sk/) are the only combinations that do not follow the SSP in that the sonority falls rather than rises from the first member to the second. There are other peculiarities of #sC clusters. For example, in English and Dutch, they violate the principle that prohibits homorganic clusters (/pw/, /bw/ are disallowed, but /st/, /sn/, /sl/ are not), and violate the generalization that disallows 'obstruent+obstruent' clusters (/kt/, /fp/ are disallowed, but /sp/, /sk/ are not). In addition, in English, 'obstruent+nasal' clusters are permitted only in #sC clusters (e.g., /sm/, /sn/). Such peculiarities have led some scholars to suggest a special 'adjunct' status for #sC clusters (Davis 1990; Fikkert 1994; Giegerich 1992; Kenstowicz 1994; Trommelen 1984). Under this view, the /s/ in #sC clusters are not syllabified directly under the onset position, but are a direct dependent of the syllable. Thus, we have two categories of cluster types: 'true clusters' (complex onsets), and 'adjunct clusters', as shown in figure 16.1.

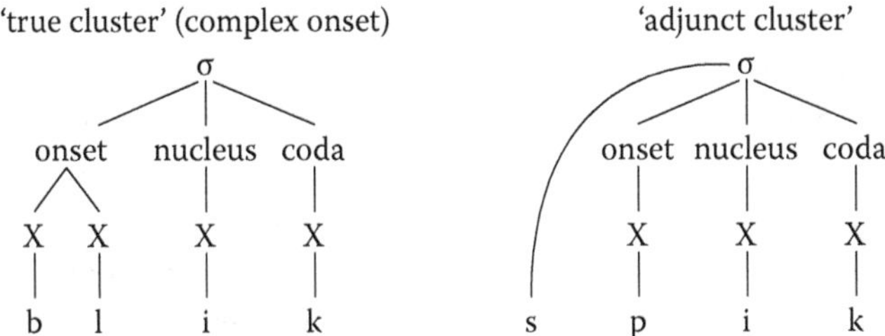

Figure 16.1. Metrical trees illustrating true and adjunct clusters.

There are, however, divergent views on which s-clusters should be treated as 'adjuncts'. For English, in general, only the negative sonority sequences (i.e., /s+stop/) are considered to have the 'adjunct' status. However, in some studies (Gierut 1999; Yavaş and Someillan 2005) /s+nasal/ sequences evoke the 'adjunct' status too. There is indeterminacy in other languages as well. In Dutch (Fikkert 1994) and German (Hall 1992) only /s~ʃ+stop/ sequences are treated as adjuncts, while in Italian (Davis 1990) /s+stop/, /s+nasal/ and /sl/ are treated similarly. No matter what sort of representational view is adopted, the Sonority account makes the predictions that the least marked /sw/ and /sl/ (i.e. '/s/+approximant') will be acquired earlier than the more marked '/s/+nasal' clusters, which are in turn predicted to be acquired earlier than the more marked '/s/+stop' clusters.

A number of cross-linguistic acquisition studies with typically developing children and children with phonological disorders revealed mixed results with respect to the predictions based on the SSP. In English (Yavaş and Core 2006; Yavaş and McLeod 2010), correct renditions supported markedness based on sonority distance between C1 and C2. In Dutch (Gerrits and Zumach 2006; Gerrits 2010) and Norwegian (Kristoffersen and Simonsen 2006), languages with similar cluster restrictions to English, however, there was no support for sonority based markedness. This was basically due to the less accurate renditions of the less marked '/s/+nasal' clusters than the more marked '/s/+stop' clusters. When we turn our attention to languages with more complex syllable structures (i.e., with multiple SSP-violating and level-sonority onsets) such as Hebrew (Ben-David 2006; Ben-David, Ezrati and Stuhlman 2010), Croatian (Mildner and Tomic 2010) and Polish (Yavaş and Marecka 2013), we also do not see any increase in production accuracy via sonority based markedness. An alternative view based on the continuancy of C2, however, seems to account for the patterns that are prevalent in the three Germanic languages, English, Dutch and Norwegian. Children's production accuracy is greater in '/s/+ [+continuant]' (i.e. /sl/, /sw/) than in '/s/+[−continuant]' (i.e., '/s/+stop' and '/s/+nasal'). However, for Hebrew, Croatian and Polish, an explanation based on the continuancy of C2 does not seem to work; the results in these languages are the opposite of those revealed by the three Germanic languages; '/s/+[−continuant]' targets enjoy better accuracy than those of '/s/+[+continuant]' targets.

Some studies in interlanguage phonologies have revealed similar results in that they show more correct productions of SSP-violating more marked '/s/+stop' and '/s/+nasal' targets than the less marked /sl/ (Abrahamsson 1999; Enochson 2014). Enochson suggests that this repeated binary split (i.e., '/s/+stop/nasal' versus '/s/+approximant') and seemingly contradictory results in studies can be explained with reference to the Obligatory Contour Principle (hereafter OCP) for continuance (Yip 1988). Simply stated, OCP is a principle for resistance to near identical segments, or a principle disfavouring identical sequences. Thus, clusters that violate OCP[continuant], (i.e., /sl/ and /sw/), are more marked (because there is no change in the value of [continuant]) from C1 to C2 than those that obey OCP[continuant] (i.e., '/s/+stop/nasal') by changing the value of [continuant]. Looked at this way, it will be expected that clusters that obey OCP[cont] will be produced correctly more often than those that violate OCP[cont].

Consequently, the two universals, markedness based on sonority distance and markedness based on OCP[cont], make opposite predictions about #sC productions.

16.3 #sC Clusters in Greek

There is a large number of #CC clusters in Greek (Setatos 1974; PAL 1995) of which 8 are /sC/→[sC] clusters (see Appendix). The following Greek /sC/ clusters are permitted both word-initially and word-medially (intervocalically): /sp/, /sf/, /st/, /sθ/, /sk/, /sx/ and /sk/→[sc]/ __ [i, e]; /sx/→[sç]/ __ [i, e]; /si/→[sç]/ __ [V]. Some of these either violate the SSP (/sp/, /st/, /sk/, [sc]) or stay with level-sonority sequencing between C_1 and C_2, i.e., /sf/, /sθ/, /sx/, [sç]. As for the OCP, the situation is reversed; the ones that violate the SSP are obeying the OCP[continuant], while the level-sonority targets violate it. With the exception of Greek word-initial /st/ in function words, e.g., *στο(ν)-'to the'* (singular-masculine) [sto(n)], *στη(ν)-'to the'* (singular-feminine) [sti(n)], *στις-'to the'* (plural-feminine) [stis], *στους-'to the'* (plural-masculine) [stus], etc., there are no monosyllabic #sC words in Greek.

Based on information found in a monolingual Greek normative study, PAL (1995), /sC/ clusters are acquired by 75 per cent of the children studied in the following order: [sp] < [st], [sk], [sc] < [sf] < [sx], starting with acquisition of [sp] in the age group 3;6–4;0 and ending with acquisition of [sx] sometime after age 6;0. Acquisition of [st], [sk], [sc] occurs between 4;0 and 4;6, while [sf] is reported acquired between 4;6 and 5;0. Data in Papadopoulou (2000) allow the following deduction: [st], [sc] < [sf], [sx], with age of acquisition of [st], [sc] < [sf] some six months earlier than those reported by PAL (1995). Acquisition of [sx] is reported between 4;1 and 4;6. Neither of these two studies provides information on acquisition of /sθ/ and allophone [sç] in Greek. For a table on the age of acquisition of Greek consonant clusters, see Mennen and Okalidou (2007). Sanoudaki (2007) studied Greek /sC/ clusters in 59 children using a non-word repetition task, finding greater accuracy in /sC/ cluster production than in that of other Greek clusters.

16.4 The Study

The longitudinal study reported here describes the acquisition patterns of /sC/ clusters that are found in a Greek-English bilingual child; our focus will be on the word-initial #sC clusters. Patterns in her correct productions as well as reductions are examined through the lenses of two competing accounts – sonority and OCP. There are 12 #sC clusters that are in focus: three of them are shared by the two languages (/sp/, /st/ and /sk/), four are English-specific (/sm/, /sn/, /sl/, /sw/), and five are Greek-specific (/sf/, /sk/→[sc], /sx/, /sx/→[sç]). Although /sθ/ is also permitted in Greek, it is not common; there is a lack of data on /sθ/ in the child's recorded speech which excludes it from the study.

16.4.1 Subject

The female child in this study was born and raised in Greece by native-Greek parents. Exposure to Greek in the ambient environment began at birth. Exposure to English started at age 1;0, when the child's mother consistently began communicating with her in fluent English. The onset of the child's recognizable speech (at 1;7 in Greek and 1;9 in English) accords with expected milestones in bilingual development (e.g., Brulard and Carr

2003), thus, entering the two-word stage (Ingram 1989) in English at 2;6. By age 2;7, there is stable enough speech production in both languages.

16.4.2 Data Collection

For the purpose of data collection, the child's utterances in both languages were digitally recorded at home with a hand-held Olympus WS11-311M during natural and unstructured routine interaction between mother and child. The recordings started when the child was at age 2;7 and run through age 4;0. The data in full utterances were phonetically transcribed in IPA and aligned to sound by the second author in a CLAN (MacWhinney 2000) database of 511 files (31,684 English utterances, 13,940 Greek ones), totaling 135 hours of recordings. An acoustic analysis was randomly performed on sC productions to ensure the reliability of transcription.

The files in the database include single-code utterances (SCUs), as well as mixed-code utterances (MCUs), since code-switching was typical in the child's speech and during the recordings, especially in the beginning months of the study. An investigation of the sC cluster production patterns with regard to possible effects of code-switching reveal no difference in reduction, substitution or acquisition patterns between SCUs and MCUs.

16.5 The Child's Consonantal System at 2;7

Information on the level of acquisition of consonants in singleton context and their dominant substitutions at the beginning of the study (at age 2;7) is provided here. Only those singletons in each language that are involved in the /sC/ clusters discussed in this study will be presented. So, the child's acquired consonants are:

/p, m, t, s/ in both languages; /n/ in English; /f, l/ in Greek (> 90 per cent)
/f, l/ in English; /n/ in Greek (> 80 per cent)
/z/ in Greek (> 75 per cent)

Non-acquired consonants are:

/k/ in both languages (at 5 per cent)
/z/, /w/ in English (at 67 and 15 per cent, respectively)
/x/, [c], [ç] in Greek (at 4, 4 and 9 per cent, respectively)

The child's consonant place markedness hierarchy for singleton consonants at 2;7 is:

LAB<COR<DORSAL.

The dominant substitutions of non-acquired consonants are:

/k/, [c]→[t]; /x/, [ç]→[ʃ, s]; /w/→[v]

16.6 Analysis

Data presentation for all clusters starts at age 2;7 and proceeds in subsequent months, if and as necessary, until conclusive observations can be made on reduction patterns and acquisition level per individual cluster. The targeted data in Greek are given in IPA representing adult surface rather than phonemic representations; orthographic forms and translations were deemed irrelevant, and thus omitted.

16.6.1 Clusters Shared by the Two Languages: /sp/, /st/, /sk/ (All SSP-Violating, but OCP[cont]-Obeying)

/sp/ at 2;7
Eng.: *speak* (1)→[**sp**]; *spoon* (6)→4[sp], 2[p]; *spaghetti* (1)→[p]
Grk.: spiti (5)→5[p]; spitaci (2)→2[p]; spiɾiðula (1)→1[p]; spɾoksis (3)→3[p]

The data at 2;7 provide conclusive information on the acquisition of /sp/ across the two languages. It is observed that in both languages, the [+cont] and thus the more sonorant member is reduced, when reduction occurs. Word-initial /sp/ is overall acquired in English monosyllabic words (there are no monosyllabic /sp/ words in Greek). In multisyllabic words, word-initial /sp/ is always reduced cross-linguistically. The reduction pattern /sp/→[p] occurs in all multisyllabic words, while rarely in monosyllabic words. By age 2;8, all word-initial /sp/ in monosyllabic words are produced correctly; there are several instances of [sp] word-initially in multisyllabic words, e.g., spiti, spitaci.

/st/ at 2;7

Eng.: *stay* (1)→[ts]; *steps* (2)→[**st**], [t]; *stir* (1)→[ts]; *story* (2)→2[**st**]; *strawberries* (1)→[ts]; *street* (1)→[**st**]; *stroller* (1)→[ts]

Grk.: stoma (1)→[**st**]; staglika (1)→[t]

The data at 2;7 provide information on the acquisition of /st/ across the two languages. It is observed that in both languages, the [+cont] and thus more sonorant member is deleted. Word-initial reduction persists as /st/→[t], e.g., at 2;8 *stones*→[t]. Unlike /sp/ that showed no substitution patterns, /st/ is affricated with metathesis, /st/→[ts], with the pattern being present across the two languages.

/sk/ at 2;7 through 2;10

Eng.: **2;7:** *school* (1)→[st]
2;8: *school* (6)→6st; *scratched* (1)→[t]; *sky* (1)→[st]
2;10: *school* (10)→10st; *scared* (1)→[st]; *scratch* (1)→[st]; *skirt* (2)→2st

Grk.: **2;7:** skamni (2)→[t],[0]
2;8: skaɾfaloso (1)→[t]; skoɾpizis (2)→[s], [st]; skoɾpisis (3)→[t], 2st; skotoθo (1)→[s]; skotoso (1)→[t]
2;10: skoɾpizis (5)→2[t], [st]; skotoso (6)→2[t], 4st; skotosume (1)→[k]

The reduction and acquisition patterns for /sk/ are based on data running from age 2;7 through 2;10. The child's languages seem to show somewhat different patterns. In English, which has all monosyllabic targets, the rendition is either correct or the affricate [ts], also a minor reduction to a [t], as [−cont] C2. Since /k/ is still not established, the fronting to [t] explains these patterns. In Greek, however, where the targets are not monosyllabic, we observe much more cluster reduction; these generally preserve the [−cont] C2 as [t], but there are a few cases of the retention of C1, /s/. The deletion of [+cont] C1 persists with age for all 3 clusters (/sp/, /st/, /sk/).

16.6.2 English-Specific Clusters: /sm/, /sn/ (SSP and OCP[cont]-Obeying) /sl/, /sw/ (SSP-Obeying, OCP[cont]-Violating)

/sm/ at 2;7 through 2;10

2;7: *small* (5)→5[**sm**]
2;8: *small* (2)→2[sm]
2;9: *small* (12)→12[sm]
2;10: *small* (14)→14[sm]; *smaller* (3)→3[sm]; *smiling* (1)→[sm]

(N.B: At 2;5 from diary notes: *small*→[m])

It is notable that, at least in monosyllabic contexts, /sm/ is acquired at age 2;7; multisyllabic contexts are not targeted. At 2;10, there is evidence that /sm/ is produced correctly in longer contexts, as well.

/sn/ at 2;7 through 2;9

2;7: *snail* (3)→[**sn**], [n], [ts]; *snot* (1)→[sn]
2;8: *snails* (2)→2[sn]
2;9: *snail* (6)→5[sn], [n]; *snot* (3)→2[sn], [zn]

Unlike s[LAB, +nasal], s[COR, +nasal] is not acquired at 2;7; the cluster is reduced to [−cont]: /sn/→[n], a pattern that persists and is still traced at 2;9.

/sl/ at 2;7 through 2;10

2;7: *sleep* (2)→2[s]
2;8: *sleep* (3)→3[s]; *sleeping* (3)→[s]
2;9: *sleep* (15)→[**sl**], 13[s], [t]; *sleeping* (11)→[**sl**], 10[s]; *sleepy* (1)→[s]; *'sleeped'* (1)→[s]
2;10: *sleep* (63)→16[sl], 39[s], [z], 2[l], [ts], [p], [pl], 2[tl]; *sleeps* (1)→[s]; *sleeping* (6)→6[s]; *slow* (1)→[sl]; *slowly* (1)→[s]

Unlike, [sm] and [sn], [sl] is not in the child's phonetic inventory at 2;7. It is always reduced to the least sonorant member in the sequence: [sl]→[s]. Thus, the s[+lateral] consonantal sequence is acquired after s[+nasal]. It should be noted that singleton /l/ in Greek is acquired at 2;7 at a criterion of over 75 per cent of correct production. However, this is not true in English because the lateral is involved in sC clusters. In other words, it's not articulatory ability that delays acquisition of /l/ in English, but the effect of the s[sonorant] sequence.

/sw/ at 2;7 through 3;3

2;7: *swings* (1)→[f];
2;8: *swing* (1)→[s]
2;10: *swim* (4)→2[s], 2[ts]; *swimming* (3)→3[s]; *swimsuit* (8)→8[s]; *swimsuits* (1)→[z]; *swing* (1)→[s]; *swings* (14)→10[s], 4[f]
3;2: *swallow* (1)→[f]; *swimming* (1)→[sl]; *swing* (2)→[s], [sl]; *swings* (3)→[s], 4[s]; *switch* (1)→[**sw**]
3;3: *sweater* (1)→[sɸ], *sweet* (2)→[s], [sf]; *swing* (9)→[sw], [s], [sf], 4[sl], [sm], [sʊ], reps: [tsl] [st], [t]; *swings* (4)→[s], 3[sl]; *swinging* (1)→[ts]

The analysis on the reduction and acquisition patterns for /sw/ is based on data running from age 2;7 through 3;3. For reductions, we see the retention of /s/ or the coalescence of /sw/ to a labial fricative [f] (i.e., the frication of /s/ and the labiality of /w/). At 2;10, reduction to /s/ is more prevalent. At 3;2, /sw/ slowly starts creeping in, while the other approximant, /l/, shows up in some substitutions as C2; nevertheless the flux continues. Unlike expectations based on monolingual English norms that report early acquisition of /w/ by age 3;0 (Smit, Hand, Freilinger, Bernthal and Bird 1990), the child's singleton /w/ is not acquired at the 75 per cent criterion before age 3;7. This may explain the delay in acquisition of /sw/. It is interesting, however, that in spite of the dissimilar levels of acquisition of singleton /l/ (mostly acquired at 2;7) and /w/ (not acquired until 3;7) in the child's system, there is significant delay in the acquisition of both s[+sonorant] clusters that involve them: /sl/ and /sw/.

16.6.3 Greek-Specific Clusters: /sf/, /sk/→/sc/, /sx/, /sx/→[sç]

/sf/ at 2;8 through 3;3

2;9: sfugaɾaci (2)→[f]
2;10: sfiga (2)→2[f]; sfugaɾaci (7)→7[f]; sfugaɾisis (3)→[f]; sfugaɾizmena (1)→[f]
3;1: sfixta (2)→2[f]; sfugaɾaci (3)→3[f]; sfugaɾi (1)→[s]; sfiɾixtɾa (3)→[0], 2[**sf**];
3;3: sfɾaʝiða (3)→2[sf], [sfɾ]; sfiɾixtɾa (2)→2[sf]

Unlike the consonant sequences discussed so far, there is level sonority sequencing between C_1 and C_2 in the following Greek-specific sC clusters discussed here: /sf/, /sx/→[sx], [sç]. They are also all OCP[cont] violating clusters. Because of level sonority, [PLACE] becomes the crucial factor in determining the reduction pattern in /sf/; thus, [LAB] is preserved: /sf/→[f]. Since /s/ is acquired earlier (2;7), the deletion of it cannot be attributed to any articulatory difficulty. First correct /sf/ production appears at 3;1 in a multisyllabic word, as only these are permitted in Greek. The cluster is acquired at 3;3, much earlier than monolingual Greek norms reporting acquisition after age 4;0.

Allophone /sk/→[sc] from 2;7 through 3;7

2;7: scepaso (2)→2[t]
2;9: scepasa (2)→[st], [ts]; scepases (1)→[st]; scepasis (1)→[st]; scepaso (7)→2[t], [s], 3st, [ts]; scepasto (2)→[st], [ts]; scia (3)→[**sc**], [st][ts]
2;10: scepasis (2)→2st; scepaso (2)→[t], [ts]; scilos (1)→[ts]; scilaci (1)→[ts]
3;0: scepase (1)→[st]; scepasis (3)→[sc], 2st; scepaso (1)→[st]; scepasto (2)→2st; scepastika (1)→[s]; scisume (1)→[ts]; scilaci (20)→[c], 18(st), [ts]; scilaca (3)→2(st), [ts]; scili (1)→[st]; sciʎa (2)→2(st)
3;7: scepasa (1)→[st]; scepaso (3)→3[sc], [sk]; scepasu (2)→2[sc]; scepasti (1) →[sc];scepastis (1)→[sc]; scilaci (6)→6[sc]; scilaca (4)→4(sc); scili (1)→[sc]

The reduction and acquisition patterns of /sk/ are somewhat mirrored in those of its allophone, [sc], although Greek words with /sk/ had more reductions to [t]. Reductions occur predominantly in multisyllabic words. Though both [+cont] and [−cont] members are deleted at initial stages, deletion of /s/, the [+cont] member, predominates later on. A first production is found at 3;0, while acquisition, at 3;7, is at about the same age as that of /sk/ and a little earlier than in monolingual norms (between 4;0 and 4;6). Similarly, [sc]→[st] is the dominant substitution.

/sx/ at 2;7 through 3;7

2;7: sxolio (3)→2[s], [ʃ]; sxoʎo (1)→[ʃ]
2;10: sxolio (13)→1[t], 7[s], [ʃ], 4st; sxoliko (4)→3[s], [st]
3;2: sxolio (1)→[**sx**], 3[s], 5st; sxoliu (1)→[s]
3;6: sxolio (5)→4st, [sk]
3;7: sxolio (4)→4[sk]

As in the case of /sf/, there is level sonority in /sx/ and its allophone [sç] discussed below. As a result, the least marked member, [COR], is preserved: /sx/→[s], [ʃ]. First correct /sx/ production appears at 3;2; the cluster is acquired after 3;10 which agrees with data reported in Papadopoulou (2000), though monolingual Greek norms report acquisition after age 6;0 (PAL 1995). The substitution patterns involve assimilation to [COR] or stopping of C_2: /sx/→[sk], [st], as less marked alternatives.

Allophone /sx/→[sç] at 2;7 through 3;10

2;7: nasça (1)→[s]
2;9: isça (1)→[st]
3;4: sçeðio (1)→[ts]
3;6: nasça (3)→3[s]
3;10: sçeðiaso (1)→[**sç**]; isça (2)→2[**sç**]

The analysis on the reduction and acquisition patterns for [sç] is based on data running from age 2;7 through 3;10. Acquisition of allophone [sç] follows the path of targeted /sx/. Reductions occur with a preference for least marked [COR], [sç]→[s]; as in /sf/ and /sx/, level sonority nulls distinction based on SSP. First productions appears at 3;10; this cluster is acquired later than /sx/. Normative studies provide no information on /sx/→[sç] acquisition for comparisons.

16.7 Discussion

There are differences in sC cluster acquisition and reduction patterns across the two languages based on the phonological structure of the clusters, and on the length of the word (monosyllabic or multi-syllabic).

Overall, the acquisition patterns show that 's+stop' and 's+nasal' (i.e., 's+[−continuant]') targets are correctly rendered earlier than others; we are excluding /sk/ from this discussion and judgement because of the late acquisition of singleton /k/. This pattern, obviously, cannot be accounted for through the SSP, because 's+stop' sequences are negative sonority clusters. However, all of these early clusters are OCP[continuant] obeying in that there is a change in the value of [continuant] when we move from C1 to C2. The earlier acquisition of these sequences is reminiscent of what has been found in other languages such as Hebrew, Croatian and Polish, which also have several SSP-violating, and level-sonority clusters.

With regard to sC acquisition level of [PLACE] in monosyllabic words, the following is found: /sm/</sp/</sn, st/</sl/</sk/</sw/ that may be represented as: s[LAB]<s[COR]<s[DOR]. This pattern, LABIAL<CORONAL <DORSAL, agrees with the markedness hierarchy observed for the child's acquisition of [PLACE] at age 2;7 and until complete acquisition at about age 4;0. It should also be noted that s[NASAL]<s[ORAL] or, more specifically, s[LAB, +nasal]<s[COR, +nasal], s[+oral]. The child has completely acquired /sm/ in English at 2;7, unlike monolingual English norms and despite the fact that /sm/→[sm] is not permitted in Greek in any position. This early level of acquisition of English /sm/ indicates that success in sC cluster acquisition is not affected by whether the sequence exists in both languages; it is systemic and independent of this.

With regard to Greek-specific /sf/ and /sx/→[sx], [sç] where there is level sonority sequencing between C_1 and C_2, reduction patterns exhibit different behavior; the focus shifts from SSP to [PLACE], i.e. [LAB] in the case of /sf/ and [DORSAL] in the case of /sx/; it appears that least marked is again the crucial factor. The systemic level of acquisition of singletons, idiosyncratic to the child or not, plays a significant role in the acquisition of sC clusters. Although the child's place markedness hierarchy for the acquisition of singleton consonants is: LAB<COR<DORSAL[−back]<DORSAL[+back], in the case of sC cluster acquisition it becomes: LAB<COR<DORSAL[±back, −cont], DORSAL[+back, −cont] <DORSAL[−back, +cont].

It is observed that the child's *sC performance* is not correlated to *frequency of occurrence* in the child's targeted speech. For example, while /sm/ is targeted in the child's speech considerably less frequently than /sp/ or

/st/, it performs much better than both of them in terms of correct production. Also, /sp/ is less frequent than /st/ but it performs better. The cases that reveal /sm/ earlier than /sn/, and /sp/ earlier than /st/ are suggestive of another OCP, this time related to [place]. Both /sm/ and /sp/ have changes in place of articulation as we move from C1 to C2, which is not the case for /sn/ and /st/. On the other hand, /sp/, /st/ are much more frequent than /sl/ and /sw/ and they perform much better. This is attributed to the OCP[continuant]-obeying nature of the former as opposed to the OCP [continuant]-violating in /sw/ and /sl/.

As for the patterns of reduction, our findings support the tendencies that are reported in several other languages. In 's+ stop' and 's+ nasal' targets, C2 is retained and C1, /s/, is deleted. While the deletion in the former (i.e., 's+stop') is in accordance with the 'retain the least sonorant' principle, it is contradictory for 's+nasal' targets, because the tendency is to retain the more sonorant C2, nasal, in the reductions. Thus, one more time, we need to bring in the continuancy of the C2 into the picture. The pattern can be described as follows: In the reduction of 's+[−cont]' clusters, the retained member is the [−cont] C2. In other targets (SSP-obeying, but OCP[cont] violating 's+[+continuant]), the situation is more complex. If the target is 's+approximant' (i.e., /sl, sw/), then it is more than likely that the less sonorant, /s/, will be retained. However, if both members of the clusters are fricatives (level-sonority), then [place] becomes crucial: for /sf/ the labial is retained, and for others the coronal, /s/, is retained.

16.8 Conclusions

The results of this longitudinal study on the acquisition patterns of #sC clusters by a Greek-English bilingual child give support to several findings reported in other languages. More specifically, it reconfirms the binary split in grouping of 's+stop' and 's+nasal' (i.e., 's+[−continuant]' together against '/s/+[+continuant]') sequences. To summarize, we can say the following: The pattern of sC cluster reductions in increasing order along the child's speech development are as follows: /sm/ < /sp/ < /st/ < /sk/→[sk, sc], /sx/→[sx, sç] < /sn/ < /sl/ < /sf/ < /sw/, which may be represented by: s[LAB, −cont] < s[COR, −cont], s[DOR] < s[CORONAL, +cont] < s[LAB, +cont] < s[−cons]. Notably, /sm/ is included at the beginning, although it showed no reductions. An examination of the relationship between *sC reduction* and *acquisition level* of the member consonants (in singleton context) shows that the amount of reduction in a cluster is not correlated to the level of acquisition of the consonants in singleton context. Although /s/ is acquired in singleton context, notably earlier than in both English and Greek monolingual norms, it is often the target of deletions in sC sequences. It is also interesting that reduction is more common in /sf/ than in all other sC clusters, except /sw/, considering that both /s/ and /f/ are acquired by the child in singleton contexts. The s[LAB, +cont] combination is marked because of the labiodental stricture required for /f/: there are more articulators actively involved in the production of [sf] than in all other sC combinations.

Finally, correctness in sC cluster production is a result of the interplay of the phonological nature of the cluster, and word length. Bilingual sC cluster acquisition is systemic and independent of whether a particular cluster is permitted by the phonotactics in the bilingual's other language. That is, the lack of a cluster in one of the languages is not inhibitory for early, successful acquisition of that cluster in the other language. sC articulatory ability is gradually built up from least to more marked, from shorter to longer words.

Appendix

Consonants in Greek

	Bilabial	Labiodental	Dental	Alveolar	Palatal	Velar
Stop	p b		t d		(c) (ɟ)	k g
Fricative		f v	θ ð	s z	(ç) (ʝ)	x ɣ
Affricate				ʦ ʣ		
Nasal	m		n		(ɲ)	(ŋ)
Liquid				ɾ l	(ʎ)	

Double Onsets in Greek

sp, st, sk, sc, sf, sç, pl, kl, fl, vl, ɣl, ft, xt, ps, ks, pɾ, bɾ, tɾ, dɾ, kɾ, fɾ, vɾ, ɣɾ, θɾ, ðɾ, pç, bʝ, tç, ðʝ, zm, zɣ, pn, kn, mn, xn, vɣ

References

Abrahamsson, N. (1999). Vowel epenthesis of / sC(C) / onsets in Spanish/Swedish interphonology: A longitudinal study. *Language Learning*, 49, 473–508.

Barlow, J.A. (2001). A preliminary typology of initial clusters in acquisition. *Clinical Linguistics and Phonetics*, 15, 9–13.

Barlow, J.A. (2005). Sonority effects in the production of consonant clusters by Spanish-speaking children. In D. Eddington (ed.), *Selected proceedings of the sixth conference on the acquisition of Spanish and Portuguese as a first and second language* (pp. 1–14). Somerville, MA: Cascadilla.

Ben-David, A. (2006). On the acquisition of Hebrew #sC onsets. *Journal of Multilingual Communication Disorders*, 4, 205–17.

Ben-David, A., Ezrati, R. and Stuhlman, N. (2010). Acquisition of /s/ clusters in Hebrew speaking children with phonological disorders. *Clinical Linguistics and Phonetics*, 24, 210–23.

Berent, I., Lennert, T. and Smolensky, P. (2011). Syllable markedness and misperceptions: It's a two-way street. In C.E. Cairns and E. Raimy (eds.), *Handbook of the syllable* (pp. 373–94). Boston, MA: Brill.

Broselow, E., Chen, S. and Wang, C. (1998). The emergence of the unmarked in second language phonology. *Studies in Second Language Acquisition*, 20, 261–80.

Broselow, E. and Finer, D. (1991). Parameter setting in second language phonology and syntax. *Second Language Research*, 7, 35–9.

Broselow, E. and Xu, Z. (2004). Differential difficulty in the acquisition of second language phonology. *International Journal of English Studies*, 4, 135–63.

Brulard, I. and Carr, P. (2003). French-English bilingual acquisition of phonology: One production system or two? *International Journal of Bilingualism*, 7, 177–202.

Cardoso, W. and Liakin, D. (2009). When input frequency patterns fail to drive learning: Evidence from Brazilian Portuguese English. In B. Baptista, A. Rauber and M. Watkins (eds.), *Recent research in second language phonetics/phonology: Perception and production* (pp. 174–202). Newcastle Upon Tyne: Cambridge Scholars.

Carlisle, R. (2006). The sonority cycle and the acquisition of complex onsets. In B. Baptista and M. Watkins (eds.), *English with Latin beat: Studies in Portuguese/Spanish-English interphonology* (pp. 105–38). Amsterdam: John Benjamins.

Clements, G.N. (1990). The role of sonority cycle in core syllabification. In J. Kingston and M.E. Beckman (eds.), *Papers in laboratory phonology 1: Between the grammar and physics of speech* (pp. 283–333). Cambridge: Cambridge University Press.

Daland, R., Hayes, B., White, J., Garellek, M., Davis, A., and Norrmann, I. (2011). Explaining sonority projection effects. *Phonology*, 28, 197–234.

Davis, S. (1990). Italian onset structure and the distribution of *il* and *lo*. *Linguistics*, 28, 43–55.

Eckman, F. and Iverson, G. (1993). Sonority and markedness among onset clusters in the interlanguage of ESL learners. *Second Language Research*, 9, 234–52.

Enochson, K. (2014). The effect of continuance on the L2 production of L2 clusters. In U. Munai Tremblay, C. Coughlin, C.-Y.Chu and B. Lopez-Prego (eds.), *Selected proceedings of the 5th conference on generative approaches to language acquisition – North America* (pp. 1–9). Somerville, MA: Cascadilla Press.

Fikkert, P. (1994). *On the acquisition of prosodic structure*. PhD dissertation, University of Leiden.

Gerrits, E. (2010). Acquisition of /s/ clusters in Dutch-speaking children with phonological disorders. *Clinical Linguistics and Phonetics*, 24, 199–209.

Gerrits, E. and Zumach, A. (2006). The acquisition of #sC clusters in Dutch. *Journal of Multilingual Communication Disorders*, 4, 218–30.

Giegerich, H.J. (1992). *English phonology*. Cambridge: Cambridge University Press.

Gierut, J. (1999). Syllable onsets: clusters and adjuncts in acquisition. *Journal of Speech, Language, and Hearing Research*, 42, 708–26.

Hall, T.A. (1992). *Syllable structure and syllable related processes in German*. Tübingen: Niemeyer.

Hooper, J. (1976). *An introduction to natural generative phonology*. New York: Academic Press.

Ingram, D. (1989). *First language acquisition: Method, description and explanation*. Cambridge: Cambridge University Press.

Kenstowicz, M. (1994). *Phonology in generative grammar*. Oxford: Blackwell.

Kristoffersen, K. and Simonsen, H. (2006). The acquisition of #sC clusters in Norwegian. *Journal of Multilingual Communication Disorders*, 4, 231–41.

MacWhinney, B. (2000). *The CHILDES project: Tools for analyzing talk*. Mahwah, NJ: Lawrence Erlbaum.

Mennen, I. and Okalidou, A. (2007). Greek speech acquisition. In S. McLeod (ed.), *The international guide to speech acquisition* (pp. 398–411). Clifton Park, NY: Thomson Delmar Learning.

Mildner, V. and Tomic, D. (2010). Acquisition of /s/-clusters in Croatian-speaking children with phonological disorders. *Clinical Linguistics and Phonetics*, 24, 224–38.

Miozzo, A. and Buchwald, A. (2013). On the nature of sonority in spoken word production: Evidence from neuropsychology. *Cognition*, 128, 287–301.

Ohala, D. (1999). The influence of sonority on children's cluster reductions. *Journal of Communication Disorders*, 32, 397–421.

PAL (Panhellenic Association of Logopaedics). (1995). *Assessment of phonetic and phonological development*. Athens: PAL (in Greek).

Papadopoulou, K. (2000). *Phonological acquisition of Modern Greek*. BSc Honors thesis, University of Newcastle upon Tyne, UK.

Pater, J. (2004). Bridging the gap between receptive and productive development with minimally violable constraints. In R. Kager, J. Pater and W. Zonneveld (eds.), *Constraints in phonological acquisition* (pp. 219–44). Cambridge: Cambridge University Press.

Prince, A. and Smolensky, P. (2004). *Optimality theory: Constraint interaction in generative grammar.* Oxford: Blackwell Publishing.

Romani, C. and Calabrese, A. (1998). Syllabic constraints on the phonological errors of an aphasic patient. *Brain and Language,* 64, 83–121.

Romani, C. and Galluzzi, C. (2005). Effects of syllabic complexity in predicting accuracy of repetition and direction of errors in patients with articulatory and phonological difficulties. *Cognitive Neuropsychology,* 22, 817–50.

Sanoudaki, E. (2007). Consonant clusters in the acquisition of Greek: The beginning of the word. *UCL Working Papers in Linguistics,* 19, 45–74.

Selkirk, E. (1984). On the major class features and syllable theory. In M. Aranoff and R.T. Oehrle (eds.), *Language sound structure: Studies in phonology presented to Morris Halle by his teacher and students* (pp. 107–36). Cambridge, MA: The MIT Press.

Setatos, M. (1974). *Phonology of Modern Greek.* Athens: Papazisis Publishers (in Greek).

Smit, A.B., Hand, L., Freilinger, J.J., Bernthal, J. and Bird, A. (1990). The Iowa Articulation Norms Project and its Nebraska replication. *Journal of Speech and Hearing Disorders,* 55, 779–98.

Smolensky, P. (2006). Optimality theory in phonology II: Markedness, feature domains, and local constraint conjunction. In P. Smolensky and G. Legendre (eds.), *The harmonic mind: From neural computation to optimality-theoretic grammar* (vol. 2, pp. 27–160). Cambridge, MA: The MIT Press.

Stenneken, P., Bastiaanse, R., Huber, W and Jacobs, A. (2005). Syllable structure and sonority in language inventory and aphasic neologisms. *Brain and Language,* 95, 280–92.

Steriade, D. (1990). Gestures and autosegments. In J. Kingston and M. Beckman (eds.), *Papers in laboratory phonology I* (pp. 382–97). Cambridge: Cambridge University Press.

Trommelen, M. (1984). *The syllable in Dutch: With special reference to diminutive formation.* Dordrecht: Foris Publications.

Venneman, T (1972). On the theory of syllabic phonology. *Linguistische Berichte,* 18, 1–18.

Yavaş, M. (2010). Sonority and the acquisition of /s/ clusters in children with phonological disorders. *Clinical Linguistics and Phonetics,* 24, 167–76.

Yavaş, M. (2011). The role of sonority in the acquisition of interlanguage coda clusters. In M. Wrembel, M. Kul and K. Dziubalska-Kolacyk (eds.), *Achievements and perspectives in SLA speech* (pp. 297–307). Bern: Peter Lang Verlag.

Yavaş, M., Ben-David, A., Gerrits, E., Kristoffersen, K. and Simonsen, H. (2008). Sonority and cross-linguistic acquisition of initial s-clusters. *Clinical Linguistics and Phonetics,* 22, 421–41.

Yavaş, M. and Core, C. (2006). Acquisition of #sC clusters in English-speaking children. *Journal of Multilingual Communication Disorders,* 4, 169–81.

Yavaş, M. and Marecka, M. (2013). Acquisition of /s/ clusters in Polish: Patterns in typical developments and in children with phonological disorders. *International Journal of Speech and Language Pathology,* 16, 132–41.

Yavaş, M. and McLeod, S. (2010). Acquisition of #sC onsets in English-speaking children with phonological disorders. *Clinical Linguistics and Phonetics*, 24, 177–87.

Yavaş, M. and Someillan, M. (2005). Patterns of acquisition of /s/ clusters. *Journal of Multilingual Communication Disorders*, 3, 50–5.

Yip, M. (1988). The obligatory contour principle and phonological rules: A loss of identity. *Linguistic Inquiry*, 19, 65–100.

Zec, D. (1995). Sonority constraints on syllable structure. *Phonology*, 12, 85–129.

Mehmet Yavaş is a Professor of Linguistics at Florida International University. He has published numerous articles on applied phonology and is the principal author of *Avaliacao Fonologica da Crianca*, a phonological assessment procedure for Brazilian Portuguese. His other publications include *Phonological disorders in children* (1991), *First and second language phonology* (1994), *Phonology: Development and disorders* (1998), *Unusual productions in phonology* (2014) and *Applied English phonology* (3rd edition 2015).

Elena Babatsouli is the Director of the Institute of Monolingual and Bilingual Speech in Chania, Greece. Her degrees on language and linguistics are from the University of London and the University of Crete. Elena's research is on normal and disordered speech with emphasis on the phonology of first and second language acquisition as well as early bilingual acquisition. She is the co-editor of the *Proceedings of the International Symposium on Monolingual and Bilingual Speech 2015*.

17 The Influence of Sonority on Cluster Acquisition by Egyptian Arabic Children Aged Two to Three Years

Mona Maamoun

17.1 Introduction

Understanding sonority is an essential factor in describing syllable structure and the patterns of cluster acquisition. According to Roca and Johnson (1999: 59) the term 'sonority' correlates with the degree and amount of airway constriction in the vocal tract associated with specific sounds. The degree of constriction in the oral cavity correlates with the amount of loudness and, thus, with the amount of sonority. In other words, as the degree of constriction increases, both the degrees of loudness and sonority decrease (Martz 2007: 19) and vice versa. There is a general agreement in the literature upon ranking vowels (which are produced with the least amount of constriction in the oral cavity) as the most sonorous sounds; on the other hand, stops (whose production requires a great degree of constriction) are of minimal sonority. The variation in the degree of oral constriction among different types of sounds led many linguists, such as Blevins (1995: 211), to represent the sonority of segments in a hierarchical scale which ranges from most sonorous to least sonorous in terms of manner of articulation as follows: vowels > glides > liquids > nasals > obstruents. Others such as Broselow and Finer (1991) provide another scale by dividing obstruents into stops and fricatives to refine the hierarchy as follows: vowels > glides > liquids > nasals > fricatives > stops. In order to formulate a more precise sonority hierarchy scale, voicing as an essential feature of sonority can be used. This leads to the following version of the sonority scale: vowels > glides > liquids > nasals > voiced fricatives > voiceless fricatives > voiced stops > voiceless stops. These sonority hierarchies govern the internal structure of syllables. It has been hypothesized for example by Clements (1990: 285), Giegerich (1992: 133) and Kenstowicz (1994: 254) that the distribution and sequencing of segments within syllables and across syllables could be described and explained with reference to a Sonority Sequencing Principle (SSP). This universal principle implies that the sonority of segments of a syllable starts low, rises as it approaches the peak, and then falls towards the end of the syllable in a mountain-like shape.

In order to test the reliability of the SSP, we need to measure the sonority distance between neighbouring sounds (especially between consonants in clusters), but we cannot do that without assigning values to each sound. Steriade's (1990) scale values are used to illustrate the sonority differences in onset position; this scale ranks from least to most sonorous as follows: voiceless stop (7), voiced stop (6), voiceless fricative (5), voiced fricative (4), nasals (3), liquids (2), glides (1) and vowels. In English onsets, the minimal sonority difference between clusters is 2, as in clusters of /sm/ and /sn/ (5 – 3 = 2), while the maximum is 6 as in clusters of /pj/ (7 – 1 = 6). However, the most common instance of SSP violation in English occurs in the case of onset clusters of the fricative /s/ followed by the stops /p, t, k/ whose sonority distance is the negative value –2 (5 – 7= –2).

Clusters of small and negative sonority distance values that violate the SSP are considered as marked clusters, as described by Steriade (1990), in Gierut and Champion (2001: 887). Rice (2007: 80) noted that the term 'marked' means the less natural, the more complicated, more specific, less frequent, and in some instances not essential. In addition, marked segments are acquired later, are lost early in language deficit, and are more difficult in articulation. The opposite characteristics identify the term 'unmarked'. Hence, clusters that obey the SSP are the unmarked simple ones that are acquired earlier, while those that violate the SSP are the marked, complex ones that are acquired later.

The SSP also applies to coda clusters in which the sonority value decreases after the nucleus till it reaches a minimum value in the coda position. Hogg and McCully (1987: 33) assigned sonority values which are appropriate for measuring the sonority distance between coda clusters as follows: low vowels (10), mid vowels (9), high vowels (8), rhotics (7), laterals (6), nasals (5), voiced fricatives (4), voiceless fricatives (3), voiced stops (2) and voiceless stops (1). Coda clusters of negative sonority distance values which violate SSP are the marked, complex ones which are acquired later. Clements (1990) notes that for English, at least, sonority falls in coda position are often less steep than the rises in onset position.

This was a brief review of the correlations between the formation of syllables and the SSP, cluster combinations and the SSP, markedness and the

SSP, and cluster acquisition and the SSP, with examples restricted to the English language. With regard to the constitution of clusters in Egyptian Colloquial Arabic (ECA), a question arises: do they follow the SSP or do they also show some violations that may influence Arabic cluster acquisition by normally developing Egyptian children? In the next section the reliability of the SSP as a phonological predictor of cluster formation in Egyptian Colloquial Arabic will be introduced. Next its role in the formulation of ECA clusters, within a brief review of the phonological system of ECA, will be described. Finally, the influence of the SSP on ECA cluster acquisition, which is the focus of the current study, will be examined.

17.2 The Sonority Sequencing Principle in Egyptian Colloquial Arabic Clusters

Very few studies on the role of the SSP in the formation of Arabic clusters exist; exceptions include one by Al Tamimi and Al Shboul (2013) which tests the influence of the SSP on the formation of coda clusters in Modern Standard Arabic (MSA). As far as ECA is concerned, very few studies to our knowledge have investigated whether the coda clusters of ECA are sonority-based or not. For example, Jany, Gordon, Nash and Takara (2007) tested the universality of the acoustic basis for the following sonority hierarchy: glides > liquids > nasals > obstruents in four languages including ECA. They found that the sonority hierarchy in Egyptian Arabic did not differ from the others.

17.2.1 Egyptian Colloquial Arabic

ECA is a spoken variety of Arabic; most often it reflects the spoken variety of Cairene Arabic. The phonological system of ECA has been described and investigated by many linguists such as Harrell (1957), Aboul-Fetouh (1969), Abdel-Massih (1975), Broselow (1976), Mitchell (1978), Gary and Gamal-Eldin (1982), Gaber (1986) and Watson (2002). These studies mostly agree upon the number of phonemes in the ECA phonemic inventory, including 27 consonant phonemes. However, they show slight differences in their description; for example, the specification of marginal phonemes and the identification of the place of articulation of consonants. Harrell (1957: 25–8) considered that the phonemes /q/ and /ʒ/ are the only marginal phonemes in the ECA phonological system. The /q/ occurs in a very limited number of words such as /qæ:hıræ/ 'Cairo' and /qʊrʔæ:n/ 'Holy Quran'. Otherwise, it turns into /ʔ/. The phoneme /ʒ/ occurs in loan words, those that were borrowed from other languages such as /gæræ:ʒ/ 'garage'. Watson (2002: 21) added to these two six more marginal phonemes, four emphatic phonemes /rˤ/, /bˤ/, /mˤ/, /lˤ/ and two loan phonemes /p/ and /v/.

In Watson's phonemic inventory, there is no uvular place of articulation included. In her inventory, /k/, /g/, /x/ and /ɣ/are grouped under the velar place of articulation where others assign the fricatives to the uvular category.

Table 17.1. The phonemic inventory of ECA adapted from Harrell (1957).

	Labial	Dental	Palatal	Velar	Uvular	Pharyngeal	Laryngeal
Stops	b	t tˤ d dˤ		k g	(q)		ʔ
Fricatives	f	s sˤ z zˤ	ʃ (ʒ)		χ ʁ	ħ ʕ	h
Trill		r					
Lateral		l					
Nasal	m	n					
Semivowels	w		j				

The vowel system of ECA is simpler in its structure than the Arabic consonant system as it is composed of five long vowel phonemes, /i:, e:, o:, u:, æ:/and three short vowels, /ı, ʊ, æ/. There are no short mid vowels. The long mid vowels /e:/ and /o:/ have been derived from Classical Arabic sequences /V+ semivowel/, /æ+j/ → /e:/, and /æ+w/ → /o:/.

Table 17.2. The vowel phonemes of ECA.

	Long	Short
High	/i:/ /u:/	/ı/ /ʊ/
Mid	/e:/ /o:/	
Low	/æ:/	/æ/

ECA syllables contain an obligatory onset, the nucleus and an optional coda. ECA exhibits a fairly limited range of syllable types; there are five syllable types as noted by Gamal-Eldin (1967: 12), Abdel-Massih (1975: 25) and Al Ani (1978: 117), namely: CV, CVC, CVV, CVVC and CVCC. CV and CVC count as short light syllables, while CVV, CVVC, CVCC are long, heavy syllables that take the primary stress. There is only one heavy syllable per word as highlighted by Ammar (2001: 154). ECA syllables are maximally bi-moraic. Syllables are not free in their distribution; there are some restrictions. For example, CV and CVC occur in all word positions, CVV occurs in pre-finals, and CVVC and CVCC occur only finally according to Gaber (1986: 15).

Table 17.3. Examples of the position of syllables within words.

fi	CV	inside
mæk.tæb	CVC.CVC	desk
kæ:.tɪb	CVV.cvc	author
kɪ.tæ:b	cv. CVVC	book
bæ:b	CVVC	door
/bæħr/	CVCC	sea

As shown in Table 17.3, the syllables CV, CVCC and CVVC can stand as separate monosyllabic words. The maximum number of syllables per word is seven; however, words of six and seven syllables are very rare. That is to say, our target syllabic structure in the current study, the doubly closed syllable CVCC, occurs only in word-final position of monosyllabic words.

17.2.2 Clusters in ECA

With regard to the clusters, it has been found that one of the constraints of the ECA phonological system is the non-occurrence of syllable-initial consonant clusters. Sequences of consonants occur only in final position with a maximum of two consonants. Harrell (1957: 31) described the occurrence of a consonant sequence in medial position across syllable boundaries and in junction positions of CVC.CV(C) as a type of cluster, but we will look only at coda clusters in this chapter. There are about nine permissible types of CC in coda position. In CVC1C2 where C1 is voiced obstruent, C2 could be either a voiceless obstruent, a voiced obstruent or a sonorant. When C1 is a voiceless obstruent, C2 could either be a voiceless obstruent, a voiced obstruent or a sonorant. If C1 is a sonorant, C2 could be a voiced obstruent, a voiceless obstruent or a sonorant. As languages change over time, some sequences of clusters that were mentioned by Harrell in the speech of his educated subjects no longer exist in the speech of educated Egyptians nowadays. According to the SSP, in coda clusters of CVC1C2, the sonority value is supposed to decrease after the vowel; the C1 value of sonority should be higher than that of the C2. In ECA this is not always the case as illustrated in the following charts (see Figures 17.1–17.3). Instances of sonority conformity (pure clusters) along with instances of sonority plateaus and sonority violations (reversal clusters) do occur in ECA coda clusters. In each chart, those clusters in the oval shape represent the ECA clusters violating sonority, the hexagon stands for the plateau and the square shape stands for the conforming types. The sonority scale adopted for the current study was developed by Giegerich (1992: 152) with the following values:

Semi-vowels (8) > /r/ (7) > /l/ (6) > nasals (5) > voiced fricatives (4) > voiceless fricatives (3) > voiced stops (2) > voiceless stop (1).

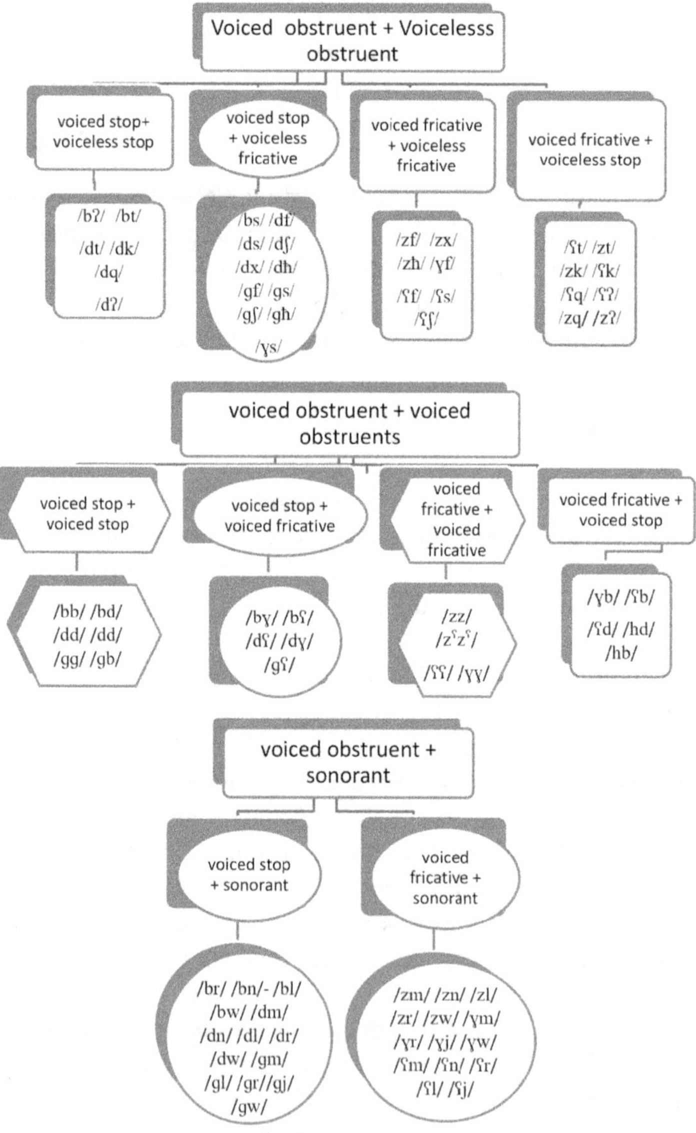

Figure 17.1. Clusters in which the first member is a voiced obstruent.

The sonority distance in ECA coda clusters of a voiced obstruent and a voiceless obstruent which conform to the SSP ranges from 1 to 3, while the sonority distance within such clusters that violate the SSP is –1. The sonority distance in ECA of conforming coda clusters of a voiced obstruent and a voiced obstruent is 2, while the sonority distance within such clusters that violate the SSP is –2. The sonority distance in ECA coda clusters that violate the SSP of a voiced stop and a sonorant ranges from –6 to –3, for clusters of a voiced fricative and a sonorant, the sonority distance ranges from –4 to –1.

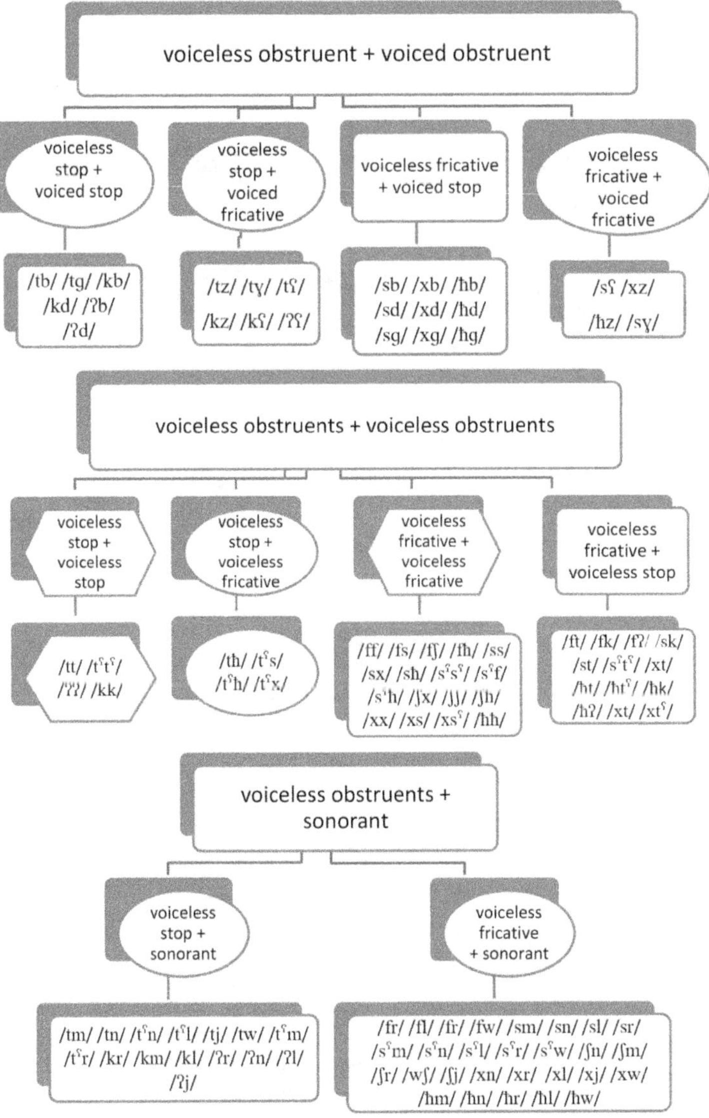

Figure 17.2. Clusters in which the first member is a voiceless obstruent.

The sonority distance within coda clusters that violate the SSP of a voiceless obstruent and a voiced obstruent ranges from –3 to –1, while the sonority distance within such clusters that conform to the SSP is 1. The sonority distance within coda clusters that violate the SSP of a voiceless obstruent and a voiceless obstruent is –2, while the sonority distance within the conforming clusters of this type is 2. The sonority distance within coda clusters that violate the SSP of a voiceless stop and a sonorant ranges from –7 to –4, while the sonority distance within clusters of a voiceless fricative and a sonorant ranges from –5 to –2.

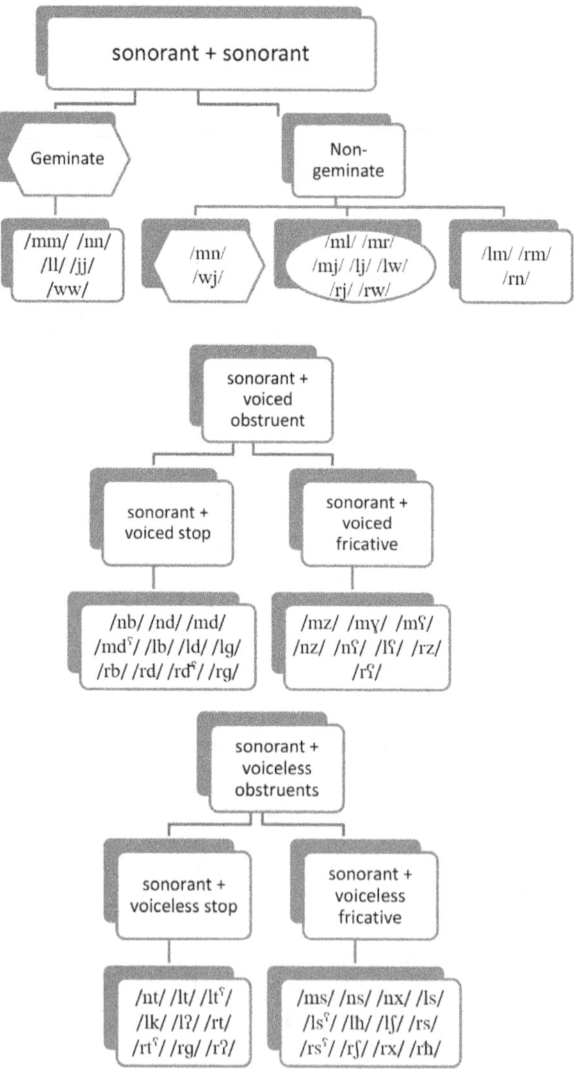

Figure 17.3. Clusters in which the first member is a sonorant.

The sonority distance within coda clusters that violate the SSP of non-geminate sonorants ranges from –3 to –1, while the sonority distance within conforming non-geminate sonorant clusters ranges from 1 to 2. The sonority distance within conforming coda clusters of a sonorant and a voiced stop ranges from 2 to 6, while the sonority distance within sonorant and voiced fricative clusters ranges from 1 to 4. The sonority distance within conforming coda clusters of a sonorant and a voiceless stop ranges from 4 to 7, while the sonority distance within a sonorant and voiceless fricative cluster ranges from 2 to 5.

It is observed from this review of ECA coda clusters that the SSP is not applicable to all ECA cluster types and that the sonority distances differ among clusters of different types. The minimal sonority distance, violating the SSP, appears among clusters of a voiceless stop and a sonorant (–7), and a voiced stop and a sonorant (–6). Hence, if the markedness concept is followed, and the results of previous studies on cluster acquisition are taken into account, these two types of clusters violating sonority will be ranked as the most difficult ones, and thus should be acquired later by children than other clusters.

17.3 The Current Study

This study investigates the influence of the SSP on the acquisition of ECA clusters in the speech of two- to three-year-old typically developing Egyptian children. The present study describes the way Egyptian children produce clusters in CVCC words. These words represent the three main types of coda clusters: clusters that obey and conform to the SSP, clusters that violate the SSP, and clusters with the same sonority values (plateau clusters). The results show different phonological error patterns exhibited by children in their production of each type of cluster. The results also demonstrate the types of cluster simplification phonological processes that the children produce in each type of word. From the results, a correlation between the SSP and cluster acquisition was noted. In addition, a correlation between markedness, sonority distance and cluster acquisition was detected. Further, treatment recommendations for developing an appropriate therapeutic programme for children with phonological disorders on developing consonant clusters are proposed.

17.3.1 Methods and Materials

Subjects: The subjects of the current study are 20 monolingual Egyptian children (10 girls and 10 boys) living in Alexandria. Their ages range from 2 to 3 years (mean age 2;4). They were divided into three age stages: stage 1 (2;0–2;4), stage 2 (2;5–2;9) and stage 3 (2;10–3;0). They were selected from three different nurseries; the teachers had noted that none of the children suffered from any physical, intellectual, behavioural or hearing impairment, and they do not have any history of speech and language disorders. The recording took place in the nurseries, apart from for three children who were recorded in their homes.

Speech Material and Elicitation Techniques: A word list was designed to elicit 63 monosyllabic CVCC words that were selected to cover the three sonority types under which the ECA clusters were grouped in the review above. Twenty-one CVCC words of CC sonority conformity, 21 CVCC words of CC sonority plateau and 21 CVCC words of CC sonority violation were included in the word list (see Appendix).

In order to elicit natural speech that reflects the real speech of the subjects, direct imitation was avoided. However, eliciting a speech sample from these young children without using direct imitation was very challenging and led to some restrictions on words selections, especially in the types and number of words. The words had to be familiar to the subjects, had to be represented by electronic cards, toys or real objects. Some words could not be represented by any of these; they are part of daily life routine and situations. Hence, three elicitation techniques were used to obtain data. The first was naming: electronic flash cards, interactive games, toys and real objects were used to elicit those familiar words that could be represented by cards. The second technique was indirect imitation which was used to elicit the less familiar words, and those which the child replaced with a synonym: for example, /lɪbs/ instead of /hɪduːm/ for the word 'cloth'. Finally, spontaneous speech (story-telling, free-play, answering questions) was used to overcome the young children's refusal to name specific pictures and to re-elicit these words in different contexts. Using toys and real objects in the naming procedure has many advantages: children at such a young age get bored very easily and very quickly; therefore, using toys decreases their likelihood of losing interest. Moreover, while playing, children do not concentrate on their speech. As such, they begin to produce speech which is more representative of their normal patterns. In addition to the recording, a live phonemic transcription was carried out during the elicitation.

17.3.2 Analysis

An ECA cluster analysis procedure was designed. This was composed of four columns: the first for the transcription of the target words, the second for the transcribed responses of the child, the third for the specification of the type of cluster simplification process, and the fourth for any notes (such as common error patterns occurring in the child's speech).

Live phonemic transcription by two well trained phoneticians (including the author) was undertaken. All the sessions were also recorded. Later the recordings of each subject were played back and a transcription was done to be compared with the live version acting as an intra-judge agreement strategy across the whole sample. Then they applied an inter-judge agreement strategy by a comparison between the two transcribers' results. The transcribers compared their transcriptions for each word for all the subjects. If there was total disagreement among the transcribers about any of the elicited items, another transcriber was invited as an external judge. If he agreed with one of the transcribers, this was considered as the target transcription. On the other hand, if he disagreed with the transcription of the two transcribers concerning any item, the three transcribers listened together to the target recordings. If they were not able to settle on a transcription from listening, they re-elicited the word from the subject. If they were unable to meet with the subject again, the doubtful items were eliminated from the sample (these were very few).

When a child gave a correct response, a check mark was added in the third column; if not, the type of phonological process was inserted beside the word in the third column. The percentage of correct responses under the three types of words in the speech of each child was computed. In order to be able to arrive at the percentage of occurrence of each process across the whole sample in each type of word, the percentage of each type of cluster simplification process in the speech of each child was computed first. This allowed the calculation of high scoring versus low scoring phonological processes in each type of cluster.

17.3.3 Results and Discussion

In the case of incorrect production of ECA coda clusters by the children in this study, the following phonological patterns were found:

1. Cluster assimilation
   (i) A more sonorant segment assimilates to a less sonorant one.
   (ii) The less sonorant segment assimilates to the more sonorant one.

2. Cluster substitution
   (i) A more sonorant segment is substituted by a less sonorant one as in lateralization, devoicing, and stopping.
   (ii) A less sonorant segment is substituted by a more sonorant one as in gliding.
   (iii) One segment is substituted by another one of a similar sonority value as in lisping and fronting of stops.
3. Cluster reduction
   (i) Deletion of the most sonorous segment and compensatory lengthening.
   (ii) Insertion of a short vowel to break the cluster (epenthesis).

Results for Clusters Conforming to the SSP: The percentages of the correct responses by each subject and the percentages of the different error patterns are illustrated in Tables 17.4–17.6.[1]

Table 17.4. Responses for words with clusters conforming to the SSP.

Name	Right	CC. ass1	CC. ass2	CC. sub	Gl	Lat	Lis1	Lis2	Fr1	Fr2	Dl	Ins	Dlt
A	25%	65%	0%	40%	5%	0%	0%	0%	0%	0%	0%	0%	17%
B	27%	47%	0%	33%	0%	0%	0%	0%	7%	0%	0%	0%	38%
C	19%	75%	0%	44%	0%	0%	0%	0%	0%	0%	6%	0%	33%
D	29%	36%	0%	36%	0%	7%	0%	0%	0%	0%	0%	7%	21%
E	27%	41%	0%	27%	18%	0%	0%	0%	5%	0%	0%	0%	8%
F	44%	33%	0%	11%	0%	0%	0%	0%	11%	0%	0%	0%	63%
G	22%	28%	0%	27%	6%	11%	0%	0%	6%	0%	0%	6%	25%
H	11%	61%	0%	39%	11%	0%	0%	0%	0%	0%	0%	6%	25%
I	29%	35%	0%	29%	0%	24%	0%	0%	6%	0%	0%	0%	29%
J	24%	57%	0%	33%	0%	10%	0%	0%	0%	14%	0%	0%	13%
K	26%	22%	4%	17%	0%	26%	0%	0%	0%	26%	0%	0%	4%
L	23%	36%	0%	18%	0%	18%	0%	18%	5%	0%	0%	0%	8%
M	17%	74%	4%	39%	0%	0%	0%	0%	4%	22%	0%	0%	4%
N	18%	59%	0%	50%	5%	9%	0%	0%	9%	5%	0%	0%	8%
O	30%	30%	5%	20%	0%	15%	5%	0%	5%	0%	0%	0%	17%
P	94%	0%	0%	6%	0%	0%	0%	0%	0%	0%	0%	0%	25%
Q	14%	52%	5%	10%	0%	14%	0%	0%	10%	0%	0%	0%	13%
R	41%	0%	6%	18%	0%	35%	0%	0%	0%	0%	0%	0%	29%
S	91%	0%	0%	0%	0%	0%	0%	0%	9%	0%	0%	0%	8%
T	23%	59%	5%	23%	9%	0%	0%	0%	0%	9%	0%	0%	8%

1 The key to the abbreviations in these and following tables is as follows:
CC.ass1: The more sonorous sound assimilates to the less sonorous
CC.ass2: The less sonorous sound assimilates to the more sonorous

Table 17.5. Percentage of cluster error patterns in clusters conforming to the SSP.

CC. ass1	CC. ass2	CC. sub	Gliding	Later	Lis1	Lis2	Fr1	Fr2	Dl	Ins
40.50%	1.45%	26.00%	2.70%	8.45%	0.25%	0.90%	3.85%	3.80%	0.30%	0.95%

Table 17.6. The cluster error patterns in clusters conforming to the SSP by age stage.

Age	CC. ass1	CC. ass2	CC. sub	Gliding	Later	Lis1	Lis2	Fr1	Fr2	Dl	Ins
2;0–2;4	55.60%	0.80%	32.40%	2.20%	4.80%	0.00%	0.00%	4.20%	4.40%	1.20%	1.20%
2;5–2;9	39.00%	1.90%	25.50%	2.00%	9.20%	0.50%	0.00%	3.70%	5.40%	0.00%	1.30%
2;10–3;0	28.40%	1.20%	20.60%	4.60%	10.60%	0.00%	3.60%	3.80%	0.00%	0.00%	0.00%

Results for the clusters conforming to the SSP show that only 2 children out of 20 produced correct responses in 90 per cent of the words. The correct responses for the rest of the subjects ranged from 10 to 40 per cent. This means that children at this age have not mastered the clusters that conform to the SSP. The different types of cluster error patterns occur in their speech at different percentages. Cluster assimilation occurred the most frequently: 40 per cent of the subjects assimilated the more sonorous segment to the less sonorous one. Cluster substitution was the second most frequently used process: 25 per cent of the subjects substituted the more sonorous segment with a less sonorous segment.

Results for Clusters Violating the SSP: Table 17.7 shows the realizations of the children for clusters that violate the SSP. Again, the percentages of correct responses by each subject and the percentages of the different error patterns are illustrated.

CC.sub: The more sonorous sound is substituted by the less sonorous sound, and vice-versa
Gl: Gliding
Lat/Later: Lateralization
Lis1: The substitution of /s/ by /t/
Lis2: The substitution of /z/ by /d/
Fr1: The substitution of /S/ by /s/
Fr2: The substitution of /k/ by /t/ - /g/ by /d/
Dl: The deletion of the most sonorous sound
Dlt: The deletion of the least sonorous sound
Ins: Vowel insertion

Table 17.7. Responses for words with clusters violating the SSP.

Name	Right	CC. ass1	CC. ass2	CC. sub	Gl	Lat	Lis1	Lis2	Fr1	Fr2	Dl	Ins	Dlt
A	20%	55%	5%	30%	0%	0%	0%	0%	0%	0%	0%	0%	5%
B	20%	50%	10%	0%	0%	20%	0%	0%	0%	0%	0%	0%	52%
C	0%	29%	29%	14%	0%	14%	0%	0%	0%	0%	0%	14%	67%
D	33%	0%	17%	17%	0%	25%	0%	0%	8%	0%	0%	0%	43%
E	6%	19%	13%	25%	19%	0%	0%	0%	0%	0%	0%	19%	24%
F	24%	29%	12%	35%	0%	0%	0%	0%	0%	0%	0%	0%	19%
G	28%	0%	17%	17%	0%	28%	0%	0%	6%	0%	0%	6%	14%
H	0%	15%	30%	30%	30%	0%	0%	0%	0%	0%	0%	0%	5%
I	44%	0%	0%	25%	0%	25%	0%	0%	0%	0%	0%	6%	24%
J	0%	25%	30%	35%	5%	10%	0%	0%	0%	0%	0%	0%	5%
K	15%	5%	30%	10%	0%	25%	0%	0%	0%	15%	0%	0%	5%
L	13%	13%	19%	19%	0%	25%	0%	0%	0%	0%	0%	13%	24%
M	0%	16%	32%	26%	0%	16%	0%	0%	0%	5%	0%	5%	10%
N	12%	12%	12%	47%	0%	29%	0%	0%	0%	0%	0%	6%	19%
O	35%	18%	18%	12%	0%	12%	0%	6%	0%	0%	0%	0%	19%
P	71%	0%	12%	6%	0%	6%	0%	0%	0%	0%	0%	6%	19%
Q	7%	7%	43%	7%	0%	29%	0%	0%	7%	0%	0%	0%	33%
R	54%	8%	8%	8%	0%	23%	0%	0%	0%	0%	0%	0%	38%
S	63%	0%	5%	0%	0%	16%	5%	5%	5%	0%	0%	0%	10%
T	13%	6%	25%	6%	5%	0%	0%	0%	0%	0%	0%	0%	24%

Table 17.8 shows the percentage occurrence of different error patterns for clusters that violate the SSP, and Table 17.9 displays these error patterns by the age grouping of the children.

Table 17.8. The cluster error patterns for clusters violating the SSP.

cc.ass1	cc.ass2	cc.sub	Gliding	Later	Lis1	Lis2	Fr1	Fr2	Dl	Ins
15.35%	18.35%	18.45%	2.95%	15.15%	0.25%	0.55%	1.30%	1.00%	0.00%	3.75%

Table 17.9. The cluster error patterns for clusters violating the SSP by age stage.

Age	cc.ass1	cc.ass2	cc.sub	Gliding	Later	Lis1	Lis2	Fr1	Fr2	Dl	Ins
2;0–2;4	17.80%	20.60%	26.00%	6.00%	11.00%	0.00%	0.00%	0.00%	1.00%	0.00%	5.00%
2;5–2;9	12.0%	21.40%	15.70%	1.00%	18.40%	0.00%	0.60%	2.10%	1.50%	0.00%	1.80%
2;10–3;0	19.00%	10.00%	16.40%	3.80%	12.80%	1.00%	1.00%	1.00%	0.00%	0.00%	6.40%

Results show that the correct responses for clusters violating the SSP were at 70 per cent in the speech of one subject, followed by 60 per cent in the speech of a second. The remaining 18 subjects' correct responses ranged from 10 per cent to 50 per cent. In clusters violating the SSP, the phonological error pattern of cluster assimilation (in which the less sonorous segment assimilates to the more sonorous one), and cluster substitution (in which the more sonorous segment is substituted by a less sonorous one) were the most frequently occurring. Cluster lateralization and cluster assimilation (in which the more sonorous segment assimilates to the less sonorous one) were the next most frequently used phonological patterns in the speech of the subjects.

Results for Sonority Plateau Clusters: Table 17.10 shows the realizations of the children for clusters that have sonority plateaus. As before, the percentages of correct responses by each subject and the percentages of the different error patterns are illustrated.

Table 17.10. Responses for words with sonority plateau clusters.

Name	Right	CC. ass1	CC. ass2	CC. sub	Gl	Lat	Lis1	Lis2	Fr1	Fr2	Dl	Ins	Dlt
A	67%	0%	0%	14%	0%	5%	10%	5%	0%	0%	0%	0%	0%
B	90%	0%	0%	5%	0%	5%	0%	0%	0%	0%	0%	0%	0%
C	94%	0%	0%	6%	0%	0%	0%	0%	0%	0%	0%	0%	14%
D	80%	0%	0%	15%	0%	5%	0%	0%	0%	0%	0%	0%	5%
E	85%	0%	0%	0%	10%	0%	0%	0%	10%	0%	0%	0%	5%
F	74%	0%	0%	21%	0%	0%	0%	0%	11%	0%	0%	0%	10%
G	85%	0%	0%	15%	0%	5%	0%	0%	0%	0%	0%	0%	5%
H	75%	0%	0%	20%	10%	0%	0%	0%	0%	0%	0%	0%	5%
I	58%	0%	0%	25%	0%	8%	0%	0%	17%	0%	0%	0%	4%
J	76%	0%	0%	10%	0%	5%	0%	0%	10%	0%	0%	0%	0%
K	90%	0%	0%	5%	0%	5%	0%	0%	0%	0%	0%	0%	0%
L	95%	0%	0%	0%	0%	5%	0%	0%	0%	0%	0%	0%	0%
M	67%	0%	0%	19%	0%	5%	0%	0%	10%	0%	0%	0%	0%
N	67%	0%	0%	29%	0%	5%	0%	0%	0%	0%	0%	0%	0%
O	68%	0%	0%	0%	0%	5%	26%	0%	0%	0%	0%	0%	10%
P	95%	0%	0%	0%	0%	0%	0%	5%	0%	0%	0%	0%	0%
Q	90%	0%	0%	0%	0%	0%	0%	0%	10%	0%	0%	0%	5%
R	100%	0%	0%	0%	0%	0%	0%	0%	0%	0%	0%	0%	0%
S	76%	0%	0%	0%	0%	0%	10%	5%	10%	0%	0%	0%	0%
T	90%	0%	0%	0%	10%	0%	0%	0%	0%	0%	0%	0%	0%

Table 17.11 shows the percentage occurrence of different error patterns for sonority plateau clusters, and Table 17.12 displays these error patterns by the age stages of the children.

Table 17.11. The cluster error patterns in sonority plateau clusters.

CC. ass1	CC. ass1	CC. sub	Gliding	Later	Lis1	Lis2	Fr1	Fr2	Dl	Ins
0.00%	0.00%	9.20%	1.50%	2.90%	2.30%	0.75%	3.90%	0.00%	0.00%	0.00%

Table 17.12. The cluster error patterns in plateau clusters by age stage.

Age	CC. ass1	CC. ass2	CC. sub	Gliding	Later	Lis1	Lis2	Fr1	Fr2	Dl	Ins
2;0–2;4	0.00%	0.00%	18.20%	2.00%	2.60%	0.00%	0.00%	7.60%	0.00%	0.00%	0.00%
2;5–2;9	0.00%	0.00%	7.90%	1.00%	3.50%	2.60%	0.50%	2.00%	0.00%	0.00%	0.00%
2;10–3;0	0.00%	0.00%	2.80%	2.00%	2.00%	4.00%	2.00%	4.00%	0.00%	0.00%	0.00%

Discussion of Results: From these results it is observed that the subjects scored the highest percentages of correct responses in clusters with sonority plateaus, followed by clusters that conform to the SSP (see Table 17.13). The highest number of incorrect responses occurred in clusters that violate the SSP. During the acquisition of the three types of cluster, the children showed different cluster production patterns. For example, clusters with a sonority plateau are the least challenging type as they are influenced by the devoicing of voiced obstruents, which is a common process during phonological acquisition. On the other hand, clusters that obey the SSP (conforming clusters) show error patterns in the form of cluster assimilation and cluster substitution in which the least sonorous segment is preserved. Examples include /kælb/ 'dog' realized as [kæbb], and /ʔɪrd/ 'monkey' realized as [ʔɪdd]. In contrast, clusters that violate the SSP (excluding /r/ and /l/) show the same types of error patterns, but this time the more sonorous segment is preserved. For example, /kɪtf/ 'shoulder' is realized as [kɪff], and /bætn/ 'stomach' as [bænn]. That means that Egyptian children follow the universal developmental pattern of keeping the least sonorous cluster member only, if the cluster follows the SSP, but in the case of reversal clusters the eliminated segment is the least sonorous. At this young age /r/ has its own specific restrictions as it is not influenced by the SSP. /r/ is the reduced cluster element in all three types of clusters as in /ʔɪrd/ 'monkey' realized as [ʔɪdd], and /ʔɪʃr/ 'peel' as [ʔɪʃʃ].

Table 17.13. Frequency of error patterns in clusters across the conforming, violating and plateau types.

Word	cc.ass1	cc.ass2	cc.sub	Gliding	Later	Lis1	Lis2	Fr1	Fr2	Dl	Ins
Conform	40.50%	1.45%	26.00%	2.70%	8.45%	0.25%	0.90%	3.85%	3.80%	0.30%	0.95%
Same	0.00%	0.00%	9.20%	1.50%	2.90%	2.30%	0.75%	3.90%	0.00%	0.00%	0.00%
Violate	15.35%	18.35%	18.45%	2.95%	15.15%	0.25%	0.55%	1.30%	1.00%	0.00%	3.75%

Hence the SSP and the sonority distance among cluster members are not the only factors that influence Egyptian children's cluster acquisition; developmental segmental error patterns also have an impact on the acquisition process. For example, the most common developmental phonological processes that occur at this age and which influence cluster production and must be taken into consideration while designing a treatment plan, are lateralization, gliding, devoicing, assimilation of liquids, sibilant deviation and fronting. Ammar and Morsi (2006) claimed that the most common phonological process at the age of 2;6 to 3 are devoicing, which lasts to 4 years, and /r/ deviation.

Regarding the effect of the sonority distance values among clusters, it is observed that clusters of zero distance are the easiest ones for children to produce. Clusters of minimal sonority distance (voiceless stop+sonorant /l/–/r/, and voiced stop+sonorant /l/–/r/) tend to be acquired after voiceless stop+sonorant /m/–/n/, and voiced stop+sonorant /m/–/n/.

17.4 Implications for Therapy

One cannot start working on coda clusters in Egyptian children with phonological disorders without taking into account two factors that are suggested by the results of the current study:

- First, the age of mastery of single phonemes by normally developing Egyptian children.
- Second, the sonority distances among clusters. It is recommended to start treatment with sequences of marked clusters with small sonority distances.

The more marked ECA coda clusters with low sonority distances across the three types of ECA clusters are:

- For CC codas that show sonority plateaus: the target clusters should be CVrr, then CVll, and then CVCC (where the clusters comprise voiced obstruents).
- For CC codas that conform to the SSP: therapists should start with /r/+obstruent, then /l/+obstruent (in both contexts start with stops then fricatives, and voiceless segments before the voiced ones).
- For CC codas that violate the SSP the sequence could be as follows:
  voiceless obstruent+/r/
  voiced obstruent+/r/
  voiced obstruent+/l/
  voiceless obstruent+/l/
  voiceless obstruent+/n/
  voiced obstruent+/n/
  voiceless obstruent+/m/
  voiced obstruent+/m/

17.5 Conclusion

The hypothesis of the reduction of the least sonorous cluster member cannot be generalized without reference to two basic factors: the first is the SSP status of the clusters. If the clusters conform to it, the hypothesis will be supported but if not, the hypothesis will be rejected. The other factor is the acquisition of the individual segments that make up the clusters. If the child has not mastered the singleton phoneme yet, it will be subject to reduction when it is in clusters regardless of its sonority profile.

Appendix: The Word List

No.	English orthographic gloss	Arabic transcribed word	No.	English orthographic gloss	Arabic transcribed word
Sonority Conform Clusters					
1	comb	mɪʃtˤ	11	flowers	wærd
2	cookie	kæħk	12	circus	sɪrk
3	under	tæħt	13	tower	bʊrg
4	sun	ʃæms	14	drawer	dʊrg
5	lash	rɪmʃ	15	lesson	dærs
6	candle	ʃæmʕ	16	aunt	tˤæntˤ
7	girl	bɪnt	17	salt	mælħ
8	cold	bærd	18	wire	sɪlk
9	after	bæʕd	19	ice	tælg
10	plants	zærʕ	20	sister	ʔʊxt
			21	dog	kælb
Clusters Violating Sonority					
1	cloths	lɪbs	11	food	ʔækl
2	morning	sʊbħ	12	leg	rɪgl
3	tammy	bˤatˤn	13	radish	fɪgl
4	shoulder	kɪtf	14	work	ʃʊʁl
5	train	ʔˤatˤr	15	full moon	bædr
6	rope	ħæbl	16	seeds	bɪzr
7	ear	wɪdn	17	rind	ʔɪʃr
8	lentil	ʕæds	18	sea	bˤaħr
9	hair	ʃˤaʕr	19	arrow	sæhm
10	chin	dæʔn	20	body	gɪsm
			21	tiger	nɪmr
Sonority Plateau Clusters					
1	bear	dɪbb	11	lettuce	xˤasˤsˤ
2	seeds	lɪbb	12	half	nʊsˤsˤ
3	food	mˤæmm	13	look	bʊsˤsˤ
4	meow	nɪww	14	rice	rʊzz

5	bark	hæww	15	nest	ʕɪʃʃ
6	put	ħʊtˤtˤ	16	face	wɪʃʃ
7	cheek	xædd	17	pain sound	ʔæjj
8	turn around	lɪff	18	vinegar	xæll
9	hot	ħærr	19	no	læʔʔ
10	finish	bæħħ	20	mouth	bʊʔʔ
			21	ducks	bˤætˤtˤ

References

Abdel-Massih, E. (1975). *An introduction of Egyptian Arabic.* Ann Arbor: University of Michigan Press.

Aboul-Fetouh, H. (1969). *A morphological study of Egyptian Colloquial Arabic.* The Hague: Mouton.

Al Ani, S. (1978). *Readings in Arabic linguistics: Phonetics and phonology.* Bloomington: Indiana University Press.

Al Tamimi, Y. and Al Shboul,Y. (2013). Is the phonotactics of the Arabic complex coda sonority-based? *Journal of King Saud University. Language and Translation*, 25, 21–33.

Ammar, W. (2001). Acquisition of syllabic structure in Egyptian Colloquial Arabic. In F. Windsor, M. Louise and N. Hewlett (eds.), *Investigations in clinical phonetics and linguistics* (pp. 153–60). London: Lawrence Erlbaum.

Ammar, W. and Morsi, R. (2006). Phonological development and disorders in Colloquial Egyptian Arabic. In Z. Hua and B. Dodd (eds.), *Phonological development and disorders in children: A multilingual perspective* (pp. 204–32). Bristol: Multilingual Matters.

Blevins, J. (1995). The syllable in phonological theory. In J.A. Goldsmith (ed.), *The handbook of phonological theory* (pp. 206–44). Oxford: Blackwell.

Broselow, E. (1976). *The phonology of Egyptian Arabic.* PhD dissertation, University of Massachussetts, Amherst.

Broselow, E. and Finer, D. (1991). Parameter setting in second language phonology and syntax. *Second Language Research*, 7, 35–59.

Clements, G. (1990). The role of the sonority cycle in core syllabification. In J. Kingston and M. Beckman (eds.), *Papers in laboratory phonology 1: Between the grammar and physics of speech* (pp. 283–333). Cambridge: Cambridge University Press.

Gaber, A. (1986). *The sounds of Arabic.* Giza : New Offset Printing Shop.

Gamal-Eldin, S. (1967). *A syntactic study of Egyptian Colloquial Arabic.* The Hague: Mouton.

Gary, J. and Gamal-Eldin, S. (1982). *Cairene Egyptian Colloquial Arabic.* Amsterdam: North Holland.

Giegerich, H. (1992). *English phonology: An introduction.* Cambridge: Cambridge University Press.

Gierut, J. and Champion, A. (2001). Syllable onsets II: Three-element clusters in phonological treatment. *Journal of Speech, Language, and Hearing Research*, 44, 886–904.

Harrel, R. (1957). *The phonology of Colloquial Egyptian Arabic* New York: American Council of Learned Societies.

Hogg, R. and McCully, C. (1987). *Metrical phonology: A course book.* Cambridge: Cambridge University Press.

Jany, C., Gordon, M., Nash, C. and Takara, N. (2007). How universal is the sonority hierarchy?: A cross linguistics acoustic study. In *Proceedings of the 16th International Congress of Phonetic Sciences* (pp. 1401–4). Saarbrücken, Germany, 6–10 August 2007.

Kenstowicz, M. (1994). *Phonology in generative grammar.* Oxford: Blackwell.

Martz, D. (2007). *Production of onset consonant clusters/sequences by adult Japanese learners of English.* Doctoral dissertation, Indiana University.

Mitchell, T.F. (1978). *An introduction to Egyptian Colloquial Arabic.* Oxford: Clarendon Press.

Rice, K. (2007). Markedness in phonology. In P. Lacy (ed.), *The Cambridge handbook of phonology.* (pp. 79–98). Cambridge: Cambridge University Press.

Roca, I. and Johnson, W. (1999). *A course in phonology.* Oxford: Blackwell.

Steriade, D. (1990). *Greek prosodies and the nature of syllabification* (Doctoral dissertation, Massachusetts Institute of Technology, 1982). New York: Garland Press.

Watson, J. (2002). *The phonology and morphology of Arabic.* Oxford: Oxford University Press.

Mona Maamoun is a lecturer in phonology in the Phonetics and Linguistics department of the University of Alexandria, Egypt. Mona's research interests are in clinical phonology, Arabic phonological acquisition (L1-L2) and the interrelationships between social factors and phonological variation. She received her PhD in phonology from Alexandria University in 2014. Currently, Mona's work focuses on the acquisition of Arabic as a second language and she lectures in Arabic phonetics and phonology at the Teaching Arabic as a Foreign Language Center, Alexandria University. 'The phonology of Egyptian children with Down syndrome' is her other ongoing research project, and she is the head of the clinical phonology programme of the Genetic Counseling Society, Egypt. Mona has presented many talks including one at the Jil Jadid Conference in Middle Eastern Languages and Literatures, Austin, Texas (2012), and most recently at the Hildesheim Conference, Germany (2014).

18 Sonority and Cluster Reduction in Typical and Atypical Phonological Development in Farsi

Froogh Shooshtaryzadeh

18.1 Introduction

An ongoing discussion in the literature is related to cluster development in children, which has been the focus of much research for a long time. These studies have mainly concentrated on the acquisition of onset clusters (e.g., Chin and Dinnsen 1992; Smit 1993; Ohala 1995; Barlow 1997, 2001; Gierut 1999; Gerken and Ohala 2000; Pater and Barlow 2002; Pater 2002; Kinney 2004; Vanderweide 2005; Gerlach 2010); nevertheless, the acquisition of coda clusters has also been considered in some studies (e.g., Braine 1976; Bernhardt 1990; Hindson and Byrne 1997; Kirk and Demuth 2003; Barlow 2005; Demuth and Kehoe 2006; Kirk 2008; Szreder 2011). A good number of the studies have assumed that sonority is the main motivation for cluster reduction (e.g., Chin and Dinnsen 1992; Smit 1993; Fikkert 1994; Demuth 1995; Gnanadesikan 2004; Ohala 1995; Barlow 1997; Bernhardt and Stemberger 1998; Gerken and Ohala 2000). Clements (1990) maintains that optimal syllables prefer a special sonority contour that comprises a sharp ascent in sonority from the initial consonant to the vowel with a minimal, or no, sonority descent. In line with Clements' assumption, the 'Sonority Hypothesis (SH)' (Ohala 1999) has predicted that children reduce word-initial and word-final clusters in a way that creates a maximal rise and minimal fall respectively in sonority. Sonority hierarchies are applied to predict which consonant is going to be deleted in cluster reduction. The sonority hierarchy employed in the present study is adopted from Burquest and Payne (1993).

- Relative Sonority of Phones:
  Vowel > Semivowel > Flaps > Laterals > Nasal > Voiced Fricatives > Voiceless Fricatives > Voiced Plosives > Voiceless Plosives

While findings from some studies on cluster reduction supported SH (e.g., Vasanta 2006), others have indicated that children adhere to SH in some reductions, but violate it in others (e.g., Wyllie-Smith, McLeod and Ball 2006). Some studies have also considered Ease of Articulation (EA) as the main motivation (e.g., Locke 1972; Braine 1976; Goodell and Studdert-Kennedy 1993; Kirk 2008; Szreder 2011), or as one of the effective factors (e.g., Pater 2002; Pater and Barlow 2003; Barlow 2005; Gerlach 2010) for reductions in clusters. The notion 'Ease of Articulation' is rooted in the idea that the pronunciation of some sounds and sound sequences is inherently easier than others. It has been taken into consideration both in studies related to changes in adult languages and in child language (e.g., Locke 1972, 1983; Menn 1978; Smit 1993; Archangeli and Pullyblank 1994; Hayes 1999; Harris and Lindsey 2000; Hayes, Kirchner and Steriade 2004; Shariatmadari 2006). Archangeli and Pullyblank (1994) and Hayes (1999) claim that ease of articulation is a major consideration and there should be constraints against everything that is articulatorily difficult to produce. Menn (1978) and Smit (1993) claimed that the segments which emerge sooner in child speech are (articulatorily) less marked than the segments that emerge later.

The idea has led to the 'Articulatory Ease Principle' (AEP) or 'Articulatory Ease Hypothesis' (AEH) which states clusters should be reduced to the articulatorily easier segments, which tend to be acquired sooner, and so emerge earlier in children's inventories in phonological development (Menn 1978; Smit 1993). Locke (1983) has proposed an order of acquisition for English consonants that is applied as a basis for the prediction of the consonant which is going to be deleted in cluster reduction in this language. The suggested *Order of Acquisition* for consonants is as follows:

- *Order of Acquisition* of consonants in English:
  n > m p h f w ŋ > t k b g s > j d > l r > ʃ ʧ ʤ >v > z ʒ > θ ð

In the above hierarchy, the consonants on the left side are articulatorily easier than the consonants on the right side. In the present study, this acquisition hierarchy is adopted from the order of acquisition of speech sounds suggested by Malayeri, Jafari and Ashayeri (2009) who surveyed the speech production of 593 Persian children in a cross-sectional study. This acquisition hierarchy shows several differences with the hierarchy reported for English, which can be due to some inbuilt differences between the two languages, such as differences in their consonant inventory. The order of acquisition for Farsi adopted from Malayeri et al. (2009) is as follows:

- *Order of Acquisition* of consonants in Farsi:
  b d m p > n h j > t k g > ʔ x ʤ > v s z ʃ l ʧ > q r > ʒ

So far, it has been observed that some studies suggest sonority and others suggest ease of articulation as the motivation for cluster reduction. However, a cross-linguistic study is necessary to uncover the main factors in cluster reduction and other cluster repairs. As a move towards achieving this goal, the present study considers cluster reduction in children acquiring Farsi as their first language.

18.2 Background to the Present Study

The present study is a qualitative cross-sectional study which focuses on cluster reduction and other cluster repairs in typically developing (henceforth TD) children and children with a phonological disorder (henceforth PD) acquiring Farsi as their first language. It aims to find out the role of sonority in the major and minor cluster modifications which occur during phonological development in Persian children.

Farsi (also called *Persian*) is an Iranian language in the Indo-Iranian branch of the Indo-European languages. Farsi has six vowel (/i, u, a, æ, e, o/) and 23 consonant (/b p t d g k q ʔ ʧ ʤ f v s z ʃ ʒ x h m n l r j/) phonemes. The consonants can be divided into six subgroups by manner of articulation: plosives /p b t d k g q ʔ/; fricatives /f v s z ʃ ʒ x h/; affricates /ʧ ʤ/; nasals /m, n/; liquids /l r/ and glide /j/. There are three types of syllable in Farsi: CV, CVC and CVCC, e.g., *ta* 'up to', *bar* 'load', *sang* 'stone' respectively. As the syllable structures indicate, clusters are only possible in word-final position (*coda cluster*) and in word-medial position (*abutting cluster*) but not in onsets. Abutting clusters are heterosyllabic, e.g., /dæm-paji/ 'slippery', while coda clusters are tautosyllabic, e.g., *sang* 'stone'.

18.3 Methodology and Data

18.3.1 Methodology

The participants in this cross-sectional study are 5 children diagnosed with the functional phonological disorder (PD), ranging in age from 4;6 to 6 years, and 5 typically developing children (TD) ranging in age from 2;6 to 4 years. The age difference between the two child groups is for the reason that a child is generally considered phonologically disordered if he/she continues to be unintelligible after 4 years of age, when typical children are usually intelligible to strangers (Adams, Byers Brown and Edwards 1997). Normally, children before this age, even if unintelligible, are not classified as PD. Consequently, this age range difference will tend to make the two groups more comparable. All the children are primarily monolingual and speak standard Farsi (Tehrani accent) in most domains and come from middle class families. The participants were selected after a check of their physical and mental health, considering all the candidates' medical profiles. Moreover, two types of questionnaire were administered to the candidates to access their family and health histories, and filled out by their parents. There were also interviews with parents and the related nursery school teachers. In addition, to select the members for the PD group, there were extra examinations of the candidates by a speech and hearing specialist, an audiometrist and a psychologist, who checked the children for their speech problems, their hearing ability and their cognitive abilities, respectively. These inquiries aimed to find out the children who were physically and mentally healthy and whose speech problem was only because of *functional/nonorganic phonological disorder*.

The phonological productions of the children participating in this study were tested through a linguistic task, namely a *Picture Naming Task*, which had been devised based on the requirements of the research and the features of the Farsi language. This task contains pictures of 132 recognizable objects which are designed to elicit the spontaneous production of 132 target words. The Picture Naming Task contains a good number of all types of clusters, which are mainly combinations of nasals, liquids, plosives and fricatives. In total, the task included 32 words with final clusters and 45 simple, complex and compound words with medial clusters.

18.3.2 Data

To collect data, the participants were first instructed in simple language how to answer the test. Then, the pictures were displayed to each child one by one and the child was asked to produce the name of the picture. The productions were recorded. Sometimes, data were collected from a child during two to three sessions, depending on his/her age and cooperation in answering the questions. The data were recorded by means of a solid state sound recorder (Samsung Voice Recorder *YPVP1*). The entire recording was done in a quiet place. In addition, there were 15–30 minutes of free recording for each child after providing motivation for speech through play and reading stories.

The recorded material was listened to carefully by three judges and was transcribed phonemically using the IPA. To determine reliability, the consensus method was used through taking the sound confirmed by at least two of three judges. After transcribing the data, the transcriptions were examined closely to find cases of cluster errors in the productions of the participants in this study.

18.4 Results and Discussion

Two types of clusters are introduced in the present study:

- Word-final or coda clusters (tautosyllabic)
- Word-medial or *abutting* cluster (heterosyllabic)

It should be recalled that initial (onset) clusters are not allowed in Farsi. Analysis of the data pertaining to word-medial and word-final clusters indicated different processes in clusters, such as cluster reduction, metathesis and voicing/devoicing which are presented and discussed below.

18.4.1 Word-Final Clusters

The children in this study exhibited considerably more errors in word-final clusters than word-medial clusters. The final clusters observed in this study are generally made up of the different combinations of plosives, nasals, fricatives and liquids. There are 28 final clusters in the test that make 28 potential contexts (PC) for each child for cluster modifications. Different types of error were observed in final clusters, such as: cluster deletion, cluster reduction, voicing/devoicing and metathesis. Cluster deletion and voicing/devoicing errors are not common in the production of either group.

Cluster reduction errors have the highest incidence in the data: PD children produced 100 errors (about 71 per cent of the PC) and TD children produced 42 errors (about 30 per cent of PC). The metathesis process also showed up in a few productions of final clusters in both the TD and PD groups. Though these errors are few (7 errors in the TD group and 4 errors in the PD group), their apparent relevance to sonority makes them noteworthy.

18.4.2 Abutting Clusters

The medial abutting clusters observed in the data contain combinations of liquid+obstruent/nasal, fricative+plosive/nasal, nasal+obstruent and fricative+fricative. In total, there are 45 abutting clusters in the Picture Naming task which make 45 PC for cluster repairs per child. The phonological processes observed in abutting clusters are cluster reduction, voicing/devoicing, metathesis, epenthesis and fusion. The last three processes are rare and can be ignored.

Cluster reduction is one of the major phonological processes which occurred in abutting clusters in both PD and TD groups. In total, PD children produced 52 and TD children 27 cluster reduction errors. Two types of voicing/devoicing errors are observed in abutting clusters in this study. In the majority of these errors, the first consonant in an abutting cluster is voiced or substituted with a voiced consonant, and the second one is devoiced or substituted with a voiceless consonant, so that the first segment is always voiced and the second one is voiceless; 33 errors of this type are observed in the PD group and 3 in the TD group. In other cases, both segments are produced with the same voicing feature, i.e., both segments are either voiced or voiceless. Ten cases of these errors are detected in the PD group and 2 cases in the TD group. Though voicing/devoicing errors are not normally discussed in the studies related to sonority and clusters, the special features observed in some of these errors make them worth mentioning in the present study. Tables 18.1 and 18.2 display the main repairs observed in medial and final clusters in PD and TD children in the present study with an example for each process.

Next, the processes introduced above will be examined more closely to find out the role of sonority or other factors in these processes.

Table 18.1. Cluster repairs in final clusters (Potential Context = 28 per child).

	PD	TD	Target	Production	Gloss
Cluster Reduction	100	42	/mobl/	[mob]	'sofa'
Metathesis	4	7	/sætl/	[sælt]	'bucket'

Table 18.2. Cluster repairs in abutting clusters (Potential Context = 45 per child)

	PD	TD	Target	Production	Gloss
Cluster Reduction	52	27	/zænbur/	[sæbu]	'bee'
Voicing/Devoicing	43	5	/lakpoʃt/	[labpoʃ]	'turtle'

18.4.3 Final Clusters

This section focuses on cluster reduction and metathesis in final clusters.

Cluster Reduction: Two types of cluster reduction were found in the PD and TD groups in this study. In the first type, all clusters are reduced to the segment that is easier to articulate according to the acquisition hierarchy in Farsi (adapted from Malayeri et al. 2009), irrespective of their sonority property or place in the cluster, as seen in the examples in Table 18.3.

Table 18.3. Reduction of coda clusters to articulatory easier segment.

	Target	Production	Gloss
1	/bærf/	[bæf]	'snow'
2	/deræxt/	[deræxt]	'tree'
3	/kerm/	[kem]	'worm'
4	/lamp/	[lap]	'light'
5	/qænd/	[qæt]	'cube sugar'
6	/qarʧ/	[qas]	'mushroom'
7	/qofl/	[qof]	'lock'
8	/sætl/	[sæt]	'bucket'
9	/ʧeʃm/	[ʧem]	'eye'
10	/zærd/	[zæt]	'yellow'
11	/ʔæbr/	[ʔæp]	'cloud'

In the second type, all clusters are reduced to their first segment, irrespective of their sonority property and ease of articulation, as seen in the examples in Table 18.4.

Table 18.4. Reduction of coda clusters to the first segment.

	Target	Production	Gloss
1	/deræxt/	[dedæx]	'tree'
2	/gævæzn/	[gævæz]	'deer'
3	/guʃt /	[guʃ]	'ear'
4	/qænd/	[qæn]	'sugar'
5	/sæng/	[sæn]	'stone'
6	/susk/	[sus]	'beetle'
7	/ʧeʃm/	[teʃ]	'eye'
8	/zærd/	[zær]	'yellow'
9	/ʔængoʃt/	[ængoʃ]	'finger'
10	/ʔæsb/	[ʔæs]	'horse'

None of these reduction types can be explained by SH because, though there are several errors in these two reduction patterns that can be categorized as errors motivated by sonority, the majority of them conflict with SH (99 from 134 reduction errors). Therefore, there should be motivations other than sonority that drive all these reductions in the developing phonologies investigated in this study. The scrutiny of errors reveals two main motives behind all the reductions in final clusters in this study, namely the *articulatory ease principle* (AEP) and the *continuity preservation property* (CPP). AEP has already been introduced in Section 18.1 and continuity preservation is the name given in the present study to 'the tendency to preserve the contiguity of the segments in the words during cluster reduction.' In this study, all cluster reduction errors can be explained by AEP and CPP. The first reduction pattern described above is consistent with AEP because the clusters are reduced to articulatorily easier segments, irrespective of their sonority property or their position in the clusters (e.g., [sæt], [zæt], [kem], [bæf] in Table 18.3). However, the second reduction pattern is consistent with CPP because the segment immediately after the vowel is always deleted, irrespective of its difficulty level or sonority property (e.g., [gævæz] and [teʃ] in Table 18.4). In the PD group, the majority of reduction errors (80 versus 30 errors) are compatible with AEP not CPP, while in the TD group, reduction errors are more compatible with CPP than AEP (26 versus 18 errors). It should be noticed that sometimes there can be an overlap of motivations in reduction errors (e.g., [qof] in Table 18.3). Figure 18.1 illustrates the amount of reduction errors in coda clusters motivated by AEP and CPP in each group participating in this study.

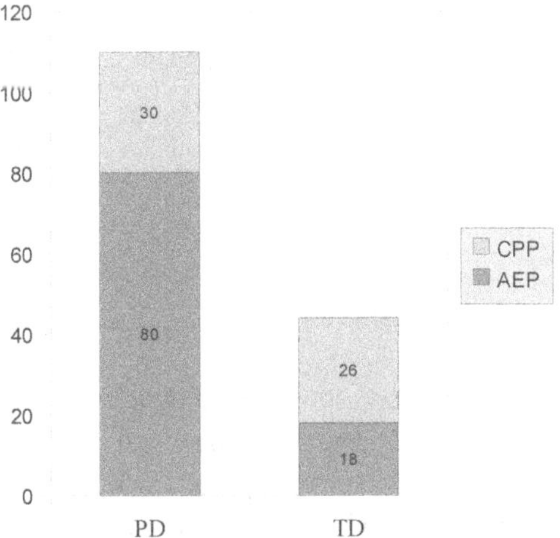

Figure 18.1. Reductions in coda clusters motivated by AEP and CPP in PD and TD children.

As displayed in Figure 18.1, AEP creates the most cluster reductions in PD children and CPP ranks in second place, while CPP generates the highest number of cluster reduction errors in TD children and AEP is in second place.

Metathesis: There are not many metathesis errors in final clusters; however, the special pattern observed in these errors makes them noteworthy. These errors are in agreement with the Sonority Sequencing Principle (SSP) that was introduced by Clements (1990). This principle declares phonemes with high sonority values are placed towards the centre of the syllable, while phonemes with low sonority values are located at the syllable margins. During metathesis, the clusters that conflict with the SSP are converted into clusters in agreement with it. So sonority appears to be the motivation behind the metatheses detected in final clusters in this study. Notably, in some examples, the children demonstrated different simplifications in the pronunciation of the same target words depending on whether they used metathesis or not. Apparently, when the clusters conflict with the SSP, it is hard for the children to produce them completely; therefore, they either reduce the clusters to a singleton that is usually an articulatory easier segment, or rearrange them through a metathesis process to become compatible with the SSP and then produce the word fully.

Table 18.5. Metathesis errors in some TD children.

Without metathesis			With metathesis		
Target	Production	Gloss	Target	Production	Gloss
/sætl/	[sæ**t**]	'bucket'	/sætl/	[sæ**lt**]	'bucket'
/mobl/	[mo**b**]	'sofa'	/mobl/	[mo**mb**]	'sofa'
/ʧætr/	[ʧæ**t**]	'umbrella'	/ʧætr/	[ʧæ**rt**]	'umbrella'
–	–	–	/ʔæbr/	[ʔæ**rb**]	'cloud'
–	–	–	/qofl/	[qo**lf**]	'lock'

18.4.4 Abutting Clusters

Unlike coda and onset clusters, abutting clusters are heterosyllabic. This phonotactic dissimilarity may lead to a difference in the motivation behind cluster repairs in abutting clusters compared with other types of clusters. To find out the real motivation behind the cluster repairs in abutting clusters, this study examines the cluster reduction and voicing/devoicing processes observed in the data.

Cluster Reduction: In our data, in almost all reduction errors, the first segment in the abutting cluster, i.e., the coda of the preceding syllable, is deleted and the second segment, i.e., the onset of the following syllable, is preserved, despite the articulatory ease of the segments or their sonority pattern. Table 18.6 presents some examples of cluster reduction in abutting clusters in the data.

Table 18.6. Cluster reduction in abutting clusters in PD and TD groups.

	Target	Production	Gloss
1	/ʃælvar/	[ʃævar]	'trousers'
2	/dærja/	[dæja]	'sea'
3	/jæxtʃal/	[dædʒal]	'refrigerator'
4	/sorsore/	[ʃosore]	'slide'
5	/tæxtexab/	[dæteqab]	'bed'
6	/tutfærængi/	[tufærændi]	'strawberry'
7	/xorma/	[ʔoma]	'date'
8	/zænbur/	[sæbu]	'bee'
9	/ʔæbru /	[ʔæbu]	'eyebrow'
10	/ʔængur/	[ʔæqur]	'grape'
11	/ʔænkæbut/	[ʔækæbut]	'spider'

As shown in Table 18.6, in examples 2 and 6 the first segments which are less sonorous than the second segments are deleted. In examples 1, 5 and 8 again the first segments, which this time are more sonorous than the second segment, are deleted. Moreover, in many cases such as examples 3, 10 and 11 the first segments are deleted though they are articulatorily easier than the second segments. Thus, abutting clusters are usually reduced to the second segment, irrespective of their sonority property or articulatory features. This reduction pattern converts the first CVC syllable involved in the creation of abutting clusters into the optimal syllable CV (Clements 1990). Because CV syllables are structurally less complicated than other syllable types, they are assumed as the most unmarked syllables in Optimality Theory (Prince and Smolensky 1993; McCarthy and Prince 1995). Therefore, converting a marked syllable into an optimal or the most unmarked syllable is the drive behind cluster reductions in abutting clusters in the present study.

Voicing versus Devoicing in Abutting Clusters: Though, generally, voicing and/or devoicing in the segments comprising a cluster have not been looked at in the studies related to clusters, the PD children participating in this study demonstrated a special pattern of voicing/devoicing errors in abutting clusters that makes it worth mentioning here. Abutting clusters are in word-medial position where, as noted in previous studies, the segments are likely to be voiced (Kirchner 1998; Keating, Cho, Fougeron and Hsu 2000; Lavoie 2001) because word-medial position is assumed to be a prosodically weak environment; hence, the obstruents produced in this environment are inclined to be of a shorter duration than those created in prosodically prominent environments and this gives rise to spontaneous voicing or a percept of voicing in this position. As some studies on child language have indicated, the occurrence of voicing errors in word-medial position is more prominent than other word positions (e.g., Viana 1984; Kim and Chin 2008). Minimization of articulatory effort is assumed as the primary motivating factor in the voicing process in word-medial contexts (Kim and Chin 2008). Child voicing errors in word-medial position occur either in an intervocalic environment or in assimilatory contexts. Voicing is also more expected in the syllable onset, while devoicing is normally expected in codas (e.g., Dinnsen 1996).

The PD children in the present study display special types of voicing/devoicing errors in abutting clusters that do not follow the general trend of voicing and/or devoicing in word-medial position. PD children illustrated this pattern in 26 errors from 33 errors that they produced regarding voicing or devoicing in abutting clusters. However, this type of error is rare in the TD group. Table 18.7 indicates some examples of these errors in the PD children.

Table 18.7. Examples of voicing/devoicing errors in abutting clusters in the PD children.

	Target	Production	Gloss
1	/bæstæni/	[bædtæni]	'ice cream'
2	/biskujit/	[biztuji]	'biscuit'
3	/boʃqab/	[pudtap]	'plate'
4	/jæxtʃal/	[tædtah]	'refrigerator'
5	/lakpoʃt/	[labpoʃ]	'turtle'
6	/mesvak/	[mebtak]	'toothbrush'
7	/tutfærængi/	[dudfæʔæki]	'strawberry'
8	/xæmirdændun/	[hæmitædtun]	'toothpaste'
9	/zænbur/	[dæbpur]	'bee'
10	/ʔængur/	[ʔædkul]	'grape'

As illustrated in Table 18.7, the first consonant of each cluster is converted into a voiced sound if it is voiceless (examples 1, 2 and 3) and the second consonant is converted into voiceless sound if it is voiced (examples 3, 6, 8, 9 and 10). Moreover, when the first consonant in a cluster is voiceless and the second one is voiced, the first consonant is voiced and the second devoiced; therefore, the same voiced+voiceless pattern is again followed in these medial clusters (examples 3 and 6). Recall that the first segment in medial clusters is the coda of the preceding syllable and the second segment is the onset of the following syllable, these productions do not fit the general tendency of codas to be devoiced and onsets to be voiced. Besides, the voicing+devoicing errors are not compatible with the AEP because devoicing increases the articulatory effort in this position. So, articulatory ease cannot be the motivation behind the strong trend which keeps the voiced+voiceless order in the abutting clusters in the PD group. Moreover, this process cannot be a kind of dissimilation because, though dissimilation can cause differentiation in adjacent consonants, it cannot create the same voicing/devoicing order in errors.

The sonority level of voiced and voiceless segments points to the main motivation behind these errors. As shown in the sonority hierarchy suggested by Burquest and Payne (1993) (see Section 18.1, above) and in the 'Margin Harmony Scale' introduced by Prince and Smolensky (1993), voiced obstruents are higher than voiceless obstruents in the sonority hierarchy, i.e., the voiced segments are more sonorous than the voiceless ones.

- Margin Harmony scale:
  Ons/*a* ≺ Ons/*y* ≺ Ons/*l* ≺ Ons/*n* ≺ Ons/z ≺ Ons/s ≺ Ons/*d* ≺ Ons/*t*

This means that the voiced+voiceless order of segments in abutting clusters creates a minimal descent from vowel to the end of the first syllable comprising the abutting cluster and a sharp ascent in sonority from the initial consonant to the vowel in the second syllable. Therefore, the PD children are trying to keep the preferred sonority contour stated in SSP (Clements 1990) in the related syllables through keeping a voiced+voiceless order in abutting clusters. This means that the motivation behind the voicing+devoicing errors in the PD group is arguably sonority. The preference of voiced+voiceless order in these abutting clusters also indicates that a falling (coda-like) sonority pattern is preferred in medial clusters to a plateau or rising (onset-like) sonority pattern.

18.4.5 Findings from Previous Studies

Clusters in onsets and codas: The analysis of the data pertaining to coda clusters in PD and TD children in this study has shown special reduction patterns that can be motivated by the Articulatory Ease Principle and Continuity Preservation Property. Bleile (2004) and Braine (1976) showed similar cluster reduction patterns in their studies on coda clusters. Fikkert (1994) also reported that in her study based on 12 children acquiring Dutch, coda clusters tended to reduce to obstruents. The reduction patterns observed in coda clusters are as follows:

Reduction patterns in the TD group:
(i) Liquid+Obstruent/ Nasal → Obstruent/ Nasal
(ii) Obstruent/ Nasal+Liquid → Obstruent/ Nasal
(iii) Plosive+Fricative → Plosive
(iv) Fricative+Plosive → Fricative
(v) Fricative+Nasal → Fricative

Reduction patterns in the PD group:
(i) Liquid+Obstruent/ Nasal → Obstruent/ Nasal
(ii) Obstruent/ Nasal+Liquid → Obstruent/ Nasal
(iii) Plosive+Fricative → Plosive
(iv) Fricative+Plosive → Plosive
(v) Nasal+Voiced plosive → Voiceless Plosive
(vi) Nasal+Voiced plosive → Nasal
(vii) Nasal+Voiceless plosive → Voiceless Plosive

As is indicated in the above patterns, the reduction of coda clusters in the present study does not demonstrate sonority as the motive behind coda cluster reductions, because, in spite of the prediction of SH, the produced coda clusters generally do not keep the most sonorous segment. As demonstrated above, except in pattern (iv) in the TD group and pattern (vi) in the PD group, in none of the coda cluster reductions can sonority be the motivation. In fact, the main motivations behind these cluster reductions are AEP and/or CPP because the clusters keep either the segments that are easier to articulate or the segments which are immediately after the vowel in the target word. Moreover, comparing patterns (iii) and (iv) indicates that the motivation behind pattern (iv) is also CPP, not sonority, because, though both clusters contain the same type of segments, i.e., fricative and plosive, a difference in the order of segments leads to different results in them, i.e., 'plosive' in pattern (iii) and 'fricative' in pattern (iv). The reduction of the cluster 'nasal+voiced plosive' to 'nasal' in pattern (vi) is also not related to sonority, though it may seem so at first glance. Comparing the cluster reductions in patterns (v) and (vi) reveals that the reduction in pattern (vi) is because of the voice feature in the plosives. Such reduction patterns are also detected in the previous studies (e.g., Smith 1973; Barlow 2005).

Unlike the present study and some other studies on coda clusters (Braine 1976; Bleile 2004; Fikkert 1994), many studies on onset clusters assume sonority as the motivation behind cluster reduction (e.g., Ohala 1995; Compton and Streeter 1977; Pater 1997; Gerken and Ohala 2000; Pater 2002; Barlow 2003, 2005; Gnanadesikan 2004; Kinney 2004; Gerlach 2010) because onset clusters are apparently reduced to the less sonorous segment as predicted by SH. Two types of cluster reductions are observed in onset clusters in these studies:

The first set of onset clusters is made of 'plosive+liquid', 'fricative+plosive' (Gnanadesikan 2004; Barlow 2005) and 'fricative+liquid' (Compton and Streeter 1977; Pater 1997; Barlow 2005). In all these cases, sonority is assumed as the cause of cluster reduction because the clusters are apparently reduced to the least sonorous segment:

(a) Plosive+Liquid → Plosive
(b) Fricative+Plosive → Plosive
(c) Fricative+Liquid → Fricative

Comparing these reduction patterns in onset clusters with the reduction patterns observed in coda clusters in previous studies (e.g., Braine 1976; Bleile 2004; Fikkert 1994) and in the present study indicate that reduction patterns in onset clusters are similar to reduction patterns in coda clusters; for example the patterns (a), (b) and (c) are similar to the patterns (i) and (ii) in the PD and TD groups. In addition (as with coda clusters) because all the preserved segments are articulatory easier than the reduced ones, all the reductions in the onset clusters type I also conform to AEP, as displayed below:

(a) Plosive+Liquid → Plosive
(b) Fricative+Plosive → Plosive
(c) Fricative+Liquid → Fricative

The second set of onset clusters is 'fricative+nasal', 'plosive+liquid' and 'fricative+liquid'. The reduction patterns in these clusters are assumed as exceptions in the related studies because they do not conform to SH. In all of these errors, the cluster is reduced to the second segment that is immediately before the vowel; therefore, it seems that the motivation behind these reduction patterns is also CPP.

(a) Fricative+nasal → nasal (Barlow 1997; Pater 1997)
(b) Plosive+liquid → [w] (Barlow 1997; Compton and Streeter 1977)
(c) Fricative+liquid → [w] (Barlow 1997)

While AEP and CPP can predict the reduction patterns observed in onset clusters in the previous studies, SH cannot predict the reduction patterns observed in coda clusters in this and similar studies. The similarity of reduction patterns in onset and coda clusters and that in both types of clusters (i.e., reductions are generally in conformity with AEP and CPP) leads to the conclusion that the major motive for reductions in both coda and onset clusters must be AEP and CPP, not sonority.

Abutting Clusters: The results obtained from the present study on abutting clusters also have some similarities to the results obtained by Barlow (2005) who studied cluster reduction in abutting clusters in three Spanish-speaking children. Two different reduction patterns are observed in abutting clusters in that study.

The first reduction pattern happened in nasal+plosive and liquid+ fricative clusters. In all these cases the most sonorous segment in the clusters was deleted. From these patterns Barlow (2005) concluded that sonority accounts for these reductions. Similar reductions were also observed in abutting clusters in the present study (Table 18.6) where the nasal+plosive and liquid+fricative clusters were reduced to nasal and fricative respectively. At first sight, one could conclude that sonority was the motive behind these reductions. However, there are other clusters like liquid+nasal/glide and plosive+fricative where liquid and plosive are deleted even though they are not the most sonorous segment in the cluster (e.g., *dærja*, 'sea', *tutfærængi*, 'strawberry', and *xorma*, 'date' in Table 18.6). Therefore, sonority cannot be the motivation behind these reduction patterns. A close examination of the reduction errors in heterosyllabic clusters in Barlow (2005) indicates that in all clusters, like the abutting clusters in the present study, the first segments were deleted. These segments are, in fact, the codas of the first syllables participating in the clusters. This point guides us to the main motivation behind these reductions, which is the production of optimal CV syllables rather than CVC or VC syllables. In Optimality Theory, the markedness constraints *CODA and ONS and faithfulness constraints MAX, defined in (1), account for the reduction pattern observed in the abutting clusters.

(1) *CODA: No codas (Prince and Smolensky 1993)
ONS: Every syllable has an onset (Prince and Smolensky 1993)
MAX: No deletion (McCarthy and Prince 1995)

*CODA and ONS constraints explain why reductions in abutting clusters usually happen in the first segment not in the second segment of the cluster, irrespective of their sonority pattern.

Tableau 1: /tutfæræŋgi/ → [tu.færæŋgi]

/tutfæræŋgi/ 'strawberry'	* **CODA**	**ONS**	**MAX**
a. [tut.færæŋgi]	*!		
b. ☞ [tu.færæŋgi]			*
c. [tut.æræŋgi]	*!	*!	
d. ☞ [tu.tæræŋgi]			*

In candidate d in tableau 1, the onset of the second syllable is deleted and the coda of the first syllable substitutes for the deleted onset through resyllabification. Therefore, this candidate satisfies both *CODA and ONS constraints and can be an optimal output. Then why was it not normally observed in the output of the children in this study? The faithfulness constraint ALIGN(R), defined in (2), answers this question.

(2) ALIGN(R): Align root morpheme boundaries with syllable boundaries at both edges (Yip 1994)

Tableau 2: Illustrative tableau for reduction in abutting clusters

/tutfæræŋgi/ 'strawberry'	* CODA	ALIGN(R)	ONS	MAX
a. [tut.færæŋgi]	*!			
b. ☞ [tu.færæŋgi]				*
c. [tut.æræŋgi]	*!		*!	
d. [tu.tæræŋgi]		*!		*

As displayed in tableau 2, candidate d is not the optimal output because, though it satisfies constraints *CODA and ONS, it violates ALIGN(R). Ranking of ALIGN(R) above ONS inhibits the emergence of candidate d in output.

The second type of reduction pattern is observed in nasal+voiced plosive clusters which are reduced to nasal. Such clusters are also observed in coda clusters in the present study, pattern (vi), and in other studies (e.g., Smith 1973). Though the reduction of nasal+voiced plosive to nasal in coda clusters can be attributed to sonority, the existence of the same reduction patterns in abutting clusters in Barlow (2005) confirms that sonority is not the motivation behind the reduction in any of these clusters, but in both of them the feature *voice* is the motive for the reduction of these clusters into nasal.

18.5 Conclusion

The evidence from this study reveals that the Articulatory Ease Principle (AEP) and Continuity Preservation Property (CPP) are the most plausible motivations behind the cluster reductions in the developing phonologies of Farsi-speaking children. Analysis of the data pertaining to (tautosyllabic) coda clusters in the PD and TD children acquiring Farsi has indicated that reductions in coda clusters in both groups are generally motivated by AEP and/or CPP, not sonority. However, the extent of influence of each of these factors is different in the PD and TD groups. Reduction in (heterosyllabic) abutting clusters is also decided by the place of segments in each cluster that originates from the tendency to produce an optimal syllable CV in developing phonologies.

Moreover, comparison of the results of this study on coda and abutting clusters with the results of some other studies on onset and abutting clusters puts doubt on the claim that the sonority pattern is the main motivation behind cluster reduction in onset clusters. The similarity observed in the reduction patterns of onset and coda clusters in different studies calls into question previous claims (e.g., Barlow 2005) regarding the influence of sonority on reduction in onset clusters, since the same types of reduction also happen in coda clusters that are incompatible with SH. Thus it seems that, like coda clusters, the reductions in onset clusters must be motivated by AEP or CPP and not by sonority.

While cluster reduction in coda and abutting clusters is not usually decided by the sonority pattern of the segments, processes such as metathesis in coda clusters and voicing/devoicing in abutting clusters appear to be mainly motivated by the sonority pattern of the segments in clusters. Therefore sonority has a role in some cluster repairs.

References

Adams, C., Byers Brown, B. and Edwards, M. (1997). *Developmental disorders of language*, 2nd edition. London: Whurr Publishers.

Archangeli, D. and Pulleyblank, D. (1994). *Grounded phonology*. Cambridge, Mass: MIT Press.

Barlow, J.A. (1997). *A Constraint-based account of syllable onsets: Evidence from developing systems*. PhD dissertation, Indiana University.

Barlow, J.A. (2001). The structure of /s/ sequences: Evidence from a disordered system. *Journal of Child Language*, 28, 291–324.

Barlow, J.A. (2003). Constraint conflict in cluster reduction. *Journal of Child Language*, 30, 487–526.

Barlow, J.A. (2005). Sonority effects in the production of consonant clusters by Spanish speaking children. In D. Eddington (ed.), *Selected proceedings of the 6th conference on the acquisition of Spanish and Portuguese as first and second languages* (pp. 1–14). Somerville, MA: Cascadilla Press.

Bernhardt, B. (1990). *Application of nonlinear phonological theory to intervention with six phonologically disordered children*. PhD dissertation, University of British Columbia.

Bernhardt, B. and Stemberger J.P. (1998). *Handbook of phonological development from the perspective of constraint–based nonlinear phonology*, San Diego: Academic Press.

Bleile, K.M. (2004). *Manual of articulation and phonological disorders: Infancy through adulthood*, Clifton Park, NY: Thomson Delmar Learning.

Braine, M.D.S. (1976). Review of N.V. Smith, *The acquisition of phonology: A case study*, 1973. *Language*, 52, 489–98.

Burquest, D. and Payne, D.L. (1993). *Phonological analysis: A functional analysis*. Dallas, TX: Summer Institute of Linguistics.

Chin, S.B. and Dinnsen D.A. (1992). Consonant clusters in disordered speech: Constraints and correspondence patterns. *Journal of Child Language*, 19, 259–85.

Clements, G. (1990). The role of the sonority cycle in core syllabification. In J. Kingston and M. Beckman (eds.), *Papers in laboratory phonology I: Between the grammar and physics of speech* (pp. 283–333). New York: Cambridge University Press.

Compton, A.J. and Streeter, M. (1977). Child phonology: Data collection and preliminary analyses. *Papers and Reports on Child Language Development*, 7, 99–109.

Demuth, K. (1995). Markedness and the development of prosodic structure. In J. Beckman (ed.), *Proceedings of the North East Linguistic Society*, 25, 13–25. Amherst, MA: GLSA, University of Massachusetts.

Demuth, K. and Kehoe, M. (2006). The acquisition of word-final clusters in French. *Journal of Catalan Linguistics*, 5, 59–81.

Dinnsen, D.A. (1996). Context–sensitive underspecification and the acquisition of phonemic contrasts. *Journal of Child Language*, 23, 57–79.

Fikkert, P. (1994). *On the acquisition of prosodic structure*. PhD dissertation, HIL dissertations 6, Leiden University. The Hague: Holland Academic Graphics.

Gerken, L. and Ohala, D. (2000). Language production in children. In L. Wheeldon (ed.), *Aspects of language production* (pp. 275–90). New York: Psychology Press.

Gerlach, S.R. (2010). *The acquisition of consonant feature sequences: Harmony, metathesis and deletion patterns in phonological development*. PhD dissertation, University of Minnesota.

Gierut, J.A. (1999). Syllable onset: Clusters and adjuncts in acquisition. *Journal of Speech, Language, and Hearing Research*, 42, 708–26.

Gnanadesikan, A. (2004). Markedness and faithfulness constraints in child phonology. In R. Kager, J. Pater and W. Zonneveld (eds.), *Constraints in phonological acquisition* (pp. 73–109). Cambridge: Cambridge University Press.

Goodell, E.W. and Studdert-Kennedy M. (1993). Acoustic evidence for the development of gestural coordination in the speech of 2-year-olds: A longitudinal study. *Journal of Speech and Hearing Research*, 33, 707–27.

Harris, J. and Lindsey G. (2000). Vowel patterns in mind and sound. In N. Burton-Roberts, P. Carr and G. Docherty (eds.), *Phonological knowledge: Conceptual and empirical issues* (pp. 185–205). Oxford: Oxford University Press.

Hayes, B. (1999). Phonetically driven phonology: The role of optimality and inductive grounding. In M. Darnell, E. Moravscik, M. Noonan, F. Newmeyer and K. Wheatley (eds.), *Functionalism and formalism in linguistics*, Vol. I: General papers (p. 242–85). Amsterdam: John Benjamins.

Hayes, B., Kirchner, R. and Steriade, D. (2004). *Phonetically based phonology*. Cambridge: Cambridge University Press.

Hindson, B.A. and Byrne, B. (1997). The status of final consonant clusters in English syllables: Evidence from children. *Journal of Experimental Child Psychology*, 64, 119–36.

Keating, P., Cho, T., Fougeron, C. and Hsu C.-S. (2000). Domain-initial articulatory strengthening in four languages. In J. Local, R. Ogden and R. Temple (eds.), *Papers in laboratory phonology* 6 (pp. 143–61). Cambridge: Cambridge University Press.

Kim, J. and Chin, S. B. (2008). Fortition and lenition patterns in the acquisition of obstruents by children with cochlear implants. *Clinical Linguistics and Phonetics*, 22, 233–51.

Kinney, J. (2004). *Common, uncommon, rare phonological disorders: An OT perspective*. MA dissertation, George Mason University, Fairfax, VA.

Kirchner, R. (1998). *An effort-based approach to consonant lenition*. PhD dissertation, University of California, Los Angeles.

Kirk, C. (2008). Substitution errors in the production of word-initial and word-final consonant clusters. *Journal of Speech, Language, and Hearing Research*, 51, 35–48.

Kirk, C. and Demuth, K. (2003). Onset/coda asymmetries in the acquisition of clusters. In B. Beachley, A. Brown and F. Conlin (eds.), *Proceedings of BUCLD 27* (pp. 437–48). Somerville, MA: Cascadilla Press.

Lavoie, L. (2001). *Consonant strength: Phonological patterns and phonetic manifestations*. New York: Garland.

Locke, J.L. (1972). Ease of articulation. *Journal of Speech and Hearing Research*, 15, 194–200.

Locke, J. L. (1983). *Phonological acquisition and change*. New York: Academic Press.

Malayeri, S., Jafari, Z. and Ashayeri, H. (2009). *Niyusha development assessment test*. Tehran: Shabak.

McCarthy, J. and Prince, A. (1995). Faithfulness and reduplicative identity. In J.N. Beckman, L.W. Dickey and S. Urbanczyk (eds.), *Papers in optimality theory:*

University of Massachusetts occasional papers in linguistics 18 (pp. 249–384). Amherst, MA: Graduate Linguistics Student Association.

Menn, L. (1978). Phonological units in beginning speech. In A. Bell and J.B. Hooper (eds.), *Syllables and segments* (pp. 157–72). Amsterdam: North-Holland.

Ohala, D. (1995). Sonority driven cluster reduction. In E. Clark (ed.), *Proceedings of the 27th annual child language forum* (pp. 217–26). Stanford, CA.: CSLI.

Ohala, D. (1999). The influence of sonority on children's cluster reductions. *Journal of Communication Disorders*, 32, 397–422.

Pater, J. (1997). Minimal violation and phonological development. *Language Acquisition*, 6, 201–53.

Pater, J. (2002). Form and substance in phonological development. In L. Mikkelsen and C. Potts (eds.), *WCCFL 21 Proceedings* (pp. 348–72). Somerville, MA: Cascadilla Press.

Pater, J. and Barlow, J. (2002). A typology of cluster reduction: Conflicts with sonority. In B. Skarabela, S. Fish and A.H.J. Do (eds.), *Proceedings of the 26th annual Boston University conference on language development* (pp. 533–44). Somerville, MA: Cascadilla Press.

Pater, J. and Barlow, J. (2003). Constraint conflict in cluster reduction. *Journal of Child Language*, 30, 487–526.

Prince, A. and Smolensky, P. (1993). *Optimality theory: Constraint interaction in generative grammar*. Oxford: Blackwell.

Shariatmadari, D. (2006). Sounds difficult? Why phonological theory needs 'ease of articulation'. *SOAS Working Papers in Linguistics*, 14, 207–26.

Smit, A. (1993). Phonologic error distributions in the Iowa-Nebraska Articulation Norms Project: Word-initial consonant clusters. *Journal of Speech and Hearing Research*, 36, 931–47.

Smith, N. (1973). *The acquisition of phonology: A case study*, New York: Cambridge University Press.

Szreder, M. (2011). The acquisition of consonant clusters in Polish: A case study. *York Papers in Linguistics Series* 2, 11, 88–102.

Vanderweide, T. (2005). A perceptual analysis of consonant cluster reduction. *Proceedings of the 2005 annual conference of the Canadian Linguistic Association*. Retrieved from http://westernlinguistics.ca/Publications/CLA-ACL/Vanderweide.pdf

Vasanta, D. (2006). Syllabic constraints in the phonological errors of children with pre-lingual hearing loss: A perspective from Telugu. In Z. Hua and B. Dodd (eds.), *Phonological development and disorders in children: A multilingual perspective* (pp. 179–203). Clevedon, England: Multilingual Matters.

Viana, M. (1984). *The acquisition of the phonology of Brazilian Portuguese with particular reference to stop consonants*. PhD dissertation, University of Reading (England).

Wyllie-Smith, L., McLeod, S. and Ball, M.J. (2006). Typically developing and speech impaired children's adherence to the sonority hypothesis. *Clinical Linguistics and Phonetics*, 20, 271–91.

Yip, M. (1994). *Phonological constraints, optimality, and phonetic realization in Cantonese*. Manuscript, Rutgers Optimality Archive.

Froogh Shooshtaryzadeh is an Assistant Professor of Psycholinguistics at Imam Khomeini International University, Iran. Since 2002, she has worked on language acquisition in adolescents and adults learning English and Persian as a second language with a focus on syntax. In 2008 she extended her research on language acquisition to first language and since then has worked on language acquisition in Persian children with typical and atypical language development, with a focus on phonology.

19
Sonority and Aphasia

Martin J. Ball, Nicole Müller and Chris Code

19.1 Introduction

19.1.1 Sonority

Traditionally speech sounds have been classified according to *sonority*, that is, the perceived loudness or clarity of the sound. This is usually correlated to the degree of obstruction within the supralaryngeal vocal tract (see, for example, the chapters by Rahilly and Barlow in this volume). Sonority has been used to explain both syllable structure in general, and the phonotactics of consonant clusters in particular. Clements (1990) describes a *Sonority Sequencing Principle* (SSP) which predicts that syllables should have low sonority onsets, high sonority nuclei, and codas that have a shallow fall in sonority rather than the steep climb preferred for onsets. Thus an obstruent onset is preferred to a sonorant one, and a sonorant coda is preferred over an obstruent one. Clements also discusses the *Sonority Dispersion Principle* (SDP) which describes the distance in sonority rank between neighbouring sound segments. So, for example, in an onset cluster, a combination of stop+liquid is to be preferred over stop+fricative as the liquid ranks part way between the stop and the vowel of the nucleus in most sonority rankings, whereas the fricative is closer to the plosive rank (or identical to it in some rankings).

These aspects of sonority have been examined in terms of natural language, and of typical and disordered phonological development (see many of the chapters in this collection), though comparatively few studies have looked at sonority in relation to the speech patterns found in acquired neurogenic disorders. In this chapter we review some of the studies that have been undertaken, and present some of our own data.

19.1.2 Neurogenic Disorders of Communication

There are various types of acquired neurogenic speech disorders, which affect speech in different ways. As described in Ball (2016), acquired speech disorders originating in neurological damage can be divided into three main types: aphasia (although only specific types of aphasia have implications for speech), apraxia of speech and dysarthria. We will look at aphasia in much more detail below, but will consider the other types briefly here.

Apraxia of speech (AoS) is a disorder at the phonetic planning and programming level. This means that people with apraxia of speech may be able to produce formulaic utterances with little problem, but their novel utterances demonstrate errors. The impairments include: slow speech rate, distortions to consonants and vowels, prosodic impairments and inconsistency in errors (Jacks and Robin 2010). Other features often noted are: difficulties initiating speech, articulatory searching and groping, perseverative errors, increasing errors with increasing word length and increasing articulatory complexity (Ball 2016).

Dysarthria is a neuromuscular disorder at the level of motor implementation, and various sub-types are recognized: flaccid, spastic, hypokinetic, hyperkinetic, ataxic and mixed (Duffy 2012). Different types of dysarthria affect the speech mechanism in different ways, and traditionally descriptions of these effects have taken a 'splintered view' looking separately at respiration, phonation, resonance, articulation and prosody (see Ball 2016, for an overview of these speech components and the effect on them of the different types of dysarthria).

Both AoS and dysarthria may be classed together as 'motor speech disorders' (Weismer 2006; Duffy 2012). Most of the effects on speech (but not all of them) would seem to be at the sub-phonemic level. In this case, it is arguable that the sonority principle does not apply (being a phonological principle). However, as several authors in this collection point out, it is also argued that sonority is in fact a reflection of articulation. Thus motor speech disorders are potentially of interest in the debate over the nature of sonority. We will look at a case of acquired motor speech disorder later in this chapter to see what light it can throw on the status of sonority theory.

The term aphasia covers a range of disruptions to language and/or speech. A widely used distinction is between fluent and non-fluent aphasia. Interestingly, both patterns may affect speech production. Non-fluent aphasia may manifest itself in slow, hesitant speech, and disruptions to both prosody and articulatory precision. However, this pattern is often found with concomitant apraxia of speech (see above), and so, arguably, is not relevant to a discussion of a phonological principle (though see Section 19.5 below).

Fluent aphasia also is characterized by speech impairments. In particular, phonemic (or literal) paraphasias may occur. These take the form of incorrect phoneme use,[1] or incorrect phoneme placement. An example might be /dæt/ for target 'cat'; there may also be transpositions of phonemes: *tevilision* for target 'television' (Brookshire 1997), and additions (e.g., *fafter* for target 'after', Buckingham 1989), among others.

As Code (2010) points out, these phonemic (or phonological) paraphasias, together with other types such as semantic (or verbal) paraphasias, can be considered a kind of *anomia* (word finding difficulties). The examples given in the previous paragraph contain just one phonemic paraphasia per word and so the target word is clear. However, if multiple paraphasias are in operation the target word will become obscured. In this case, *abstruse neologisms* or *nonwords* will be the result and it will become difficult to know where the boundaries between the speaker's intended words are located.

If a speaker produces mostly, or only, nonword paraphasic substitutions, their speech may be unintelligible, and classed as a type of *jargonaphasia*. Thus, we can consider the terms phonemic paraphasia and phonemic jargonaphasia as being at two ends of a continuum of phonological disruptions resulting from aphasia.

Cutting across this continuum is a classification concerned with the automaticity or otherwise of the speech produced by the person with aphasia. Thus, those who have global or Broca's aphasia may produce a type of automatic speech, which often consists of very few (often only one) recurring utterances. These utterances may be real words, or nonwords (lexical versus non-lexical speech automatisms).

In this chapter, we analyse data from various cases of aphasia and progressive speech deterioration that have been reported in the literature, and examine the effects in terms of sonority.

We will conclude by considering what the data from acquired neurogenic disorders tell us about the status of sonority, in particular the debate as to whether or not it is simply a tendency, or whether it is virtually invariant (and thus perhaps neurologically hard-wired). We will look in turn at paraphasias, jargonaphasia, real word and nonword speech automatisms,

1 For the sake of simplicity, we use the term 'phonemic' to indicate distinctions that potentially affect contrastivity. This is potentially problematic of course when looking at nonwords.

and motor speech disorders, before concluding by considering what the currently available evidence tells us about sonority and aphasia.

19.2 Paraphasias

19.2.1 Types of Paraphasia

Kohn, Melvold and Shipper (1998) describe three main types of paraphasia involving mispronunciations: formal, phonemic and neologistic. Not included in this classification are semantic (or verbal) paraphasias, where a semantically related word is used instead of the target (i.e., 'shoe' for 'foot').

Formal paraphasias involve the use of a real word of the language concerned, but not the intended word (e.g., 'fat' for target 'cat'). There is, however, a phonological similarity between the target and the realization, thus Kohn et al.'s (1998: 376) example of 'brook' for 'book.' As the resultant forms are words of the target language this type of paraphasia will not be considered further in this chapter as we are only concerned with disordered speech.

Phonemic paraphasias are realizations where the target word can be recognized but the form produced is not a real word of the language. Kohn et al. give the example of 'dook' for 'book' and term these forms 'pseudowords.'[2] These paraphasias can be subdivided into categories dependent on the type of error (e.g., deletion, addition, metathesis, substitution, etc.), and in terms of syllable effects (e.g., anticipatory, or perseverative errors). As we are concerned here with sonority effects, these classifications will not normally need to be referred to.

Neologistic paraphasias, on the other hand, result in nonwords (also termed neologisms). These nonwords can usually not be associated with an intended target unless there is specific help from the context of the utterance. Even so, repeated attempts at the same target may well result in very different nonword paraphasias. Examples from Rohrer, Rossor and Warren (2009) – where the target was known – include 'lobster' being realized as [dɛlkwɑɪ], and, when the assessment was repeated 7 months later, as [dʒuːn].[3]

2 Kohn et al. (1998) use a metric requiring at least 50% of the segments to be unchanged to distinguish a pseudoword from a nonword.

3 Transcriptions from the original.

19.2.2 Studies of Sonority Effects in Paraphasias

There have been a number of investigations of sonority effects in paraphasias since the 1990s. Some of these have mainly been interested in the predictions of the SSP and how well these are supported by the paraphasic data, whereas others have been concerned with how sonority effects inform theory building in aphasic speech production. We will look at a number of these studies in this section.

Van der Linde, Bastiaanse and Gilbers (1993) investigated phonemic paraphasias in their own and previously published data to analyse aspects of sonority in terms of the substitutions used. This was as part of an argument about then current models of phonology and the necessity of incorporating sonority into them. The data that they examined showed that the majority of substitutions were within the same sonority class (e.g. /fl-/ → [fr-]), with only about 17 per cent being between neighbouring classes, and a very small number crossing intervening classes. Of course, as with all studies of sonority, we need to know how the authors classify sonority. The maximalist approach of authors such as Jespersen (1904) has many more classes than the minimalist system of Clements (1990). Van der Linde et al. (1993) use a grouping whereby all obstruents are in a single class (obstruent-nasal-liquid-glide-vowel). This clearly disguises substitution patterns between stops and fricatives which may run counter to the expectations of sonority theory as originally understood (e.g., Jespersen 1904; Ladefoged 1975). Indeed, if we look at the authors' own data we find instances of stop to fricative changes, e.g.: /gr-/ → [xr-]. Along with these, there are changes that are counter to the expectations of the SSP even if using these broader sonority classes: /n-/ → [l-], /kn-/ → [kl-], [kr-]; as well as changes that the SSP would predict: /l-/ → [n-], /-l/ → [-n], /sl-/ → [sn-].

Bastiaanse, Gilbers and van der Linde (1994) return to sonority in acquired neurogenic speech disorders. In this study the authors are concerned with using sonority as a means of distinguishing between paraphasias produced by speakers with conduction aphasia as opposed to those with Broca's aphasia. They hypothesize that substitution errors involving sonority changes will occur in conduction aphasia but not in Broca's. They use the same sonority classification as van der Linde et al. (1993), thus collapsing the stop-fricative distinction (not to mention voicing distinction within those obstruent types). The authors stress the distinction between a sonority class change as opposed to a manner of articulation change by appealing to the notion of feature geometry (e.g., Roca and Johnson 1999), i.e., a sonority change, being higher up the feature tree, causes a cascade of other changes further down. However such an argument is of course based on a particular model of the atoms of phonological representation, a particular argument about the relations that hold between those atoms, and an assumption that abstract theoretical models of phonological organization have some kind of connection with psychological representations or neurological substrates (see arguments in Ball 2016). As with their previous study, reported above, the authors are only concerned with sonority substitutions (not with the direction of those changes). They conclude that their data show that sonority substitutions occur notably more frequently in conduction aphasia than in Broca's aphasia. The significance of this distinction, however, needs to be tempered by the fact that the minimalist sonority grouping deflates the number of cross-sonority group changes (and how many groups are crossed), and the lack of directionality means that the SSP is not tested in this study nor the previous one reviewed above.

Romani and Calabrese (1998) examine the SSP in aphasic speech via a single case study; indeed they criticize Bastiaanse et al. (1994) partly because these authors ignored direction of sonority change and whether the changes resulted in syllable types that fitted better with the predictions of the SSP. Like the previous studies, Romani and Calabrese use a minimal set of sonority classes where all obstruents are grouped together. They then use Clements' (1990) Sonority Dispersion Principle (SDP) to calculate sonority distances for specific onsets and onset clusters and for specific codas. They note that earlier studies by Buckingham (1986) and Béland, Caplan and Nespoulous (1990) both noted changes that aided agreement to the SSP and SDP in the speech of their clients with aphasia. In their own study the authors found that the errors made by their speaker tended to simplify complex onsets and through substitutions to maximize the SDP. However, not all the errors were one way, and there were also some (though few) substitutions that were classed as complications rather than simplifications.

Kohn et al. (1998) analysed the speech of two clients with fluent aphasia. Their primary interest was the situation of error patterns within feature geometry, and so the criticism we levelled at Bastiaanse et al. (1994) holds here too. Nevertheless, their data are interesting from the viewpoint of sonority too and, indeed, the authors do consider the sonority implications of their findings. Most of the changes of sonority they note are in accordance with the SSP, but a few produce changes that are in the opposite direction. Unfortunately, insufficient data are presented to see whether changes within the obstruent class were common and, if so, which direction these took. The authors conclude that their data support both the model of feature geometry that they use, and the SDP.

There have been fewer studies of sonority and paraphasias in recent years. A study by Biran and Friedmann (2005) looked briefly at sonority, although its main focus was how phonological errors in aphasia can be accounted for in psycholinguistic models of speech production. They investigated data from 9 Hebrew-speaking clients with anomia, who produced just over 200 paraphasias on a word naming task. In terms of sonority Biran and Friedmann conclude (2005: 606), 'Universal phonological rules were also kept in the errors: for example, all phonological errors preserved the sonority principle, and none of the phonological errors violated the sonority hierarchy within the syllable.'

Lastly, Miozzo and Buchwald (2013) used data from acquired neurogenic speech disorders to investigate whether sonority is a phonological or phonetic based feature. They analysed the spoken output of two clients; while both were classed as having fluent aphasia, one also exhibited signs of apraxia of speech. They therefore conclude that one disorder was mainly phonologically-based, while the other also had phonetic involvement (though see Ball 2016, for arguments against a binary division such as this). Miozzo and Buchwald (2013: 287) conclude that both clients showed the effects of sonority in the errors, and that thus, 'These findings indicate that the underlying principles governing sound structure that are captured by the notion of sonority play a role at both phonological and phonetic levels of processing.' Clearly, a study of just two speakers makes such a conclusion very tentative, and an investigation of more phonetic level impairments would presumably require clients with dysarthria as well as apraxia of speech. We return to such considerations later in this chapter.

19.2.3 Concluding Remarks

Studies of paraphasias have indicated that in the great majority of cases, errors have served to simplify syllable structure, or to promote better alignment to the SSP, or to maximize the SDP, or indeed all three. Nevertheless, most of the, admittedly few, studies reviewed here do acknowledge that some errors run counter to the predictions of sonority theory. If sonority is a tendency only (Ball 2016) then this creates no major problems. If it is hard-wired and resistant to neurological damage (see Section 19.3), then these counterexamples are problematic. Clearly, more data are needed. We noted earlier that jargonaphasia can be considered simply an extreme form of (neologistic) paraphasias; so we turn in the next section to consider what further evidence on the role of sonority in aphasia is available in the literature on jargonaphasia.

19.3 Jargonaphasia

19.3.1 Types of Jargonaphasia

Alajouanine's (1956) three categories of aphasic jargons essentially represent points on a continuum of comprehensibility: *paraphasic jargon* is grammatically intact language that contains semantic paraphasias; *asemantic jargon* represents largely intact syntax with neologisms; *undifferentiated jargon* consists of unintelligible sound sequences, often containing stereotypies and perseverations. Perecman and Brown (1985) use the terms *semantic, neologistic* and *phonemic* jargon, respectively. Aphasic jargon does not necessarily occur just in any one of these three categories, but 'mixed' output may be encountered. Jargon output tends to be fluent and connected, incomprehensible, and apparently unmonitored (Marshall 2006). A significant proportion of aphasic jargon is made up of nonword errors. Some of the published literature distinguishes between jargon that is related to an intended target (labelled phonemic or phonological paraphasias), versus jargon that is unrelated to the target (labelled neologisms) (Marshall 2006). We use the term *nonword* (following Marshall's usage) to denote any production that is not a recognizable word.

Some researchers have reported that nonword jargon essentially preserves the phonological system and structure of the premorbid language (including tendencies of frequency distributions), and that nonword jargon rarely contains segments not found in the premorbid language (see, e.g., Hanlon and Edmondson 1996, and Robson, Pring, Marshall and Chiat 2003, for English; Stenneken, Hoffman and Jacobs 2005, for German; also Marshall 2006, for further references). However, these findings are not without exception (e.g., Butterworth 1979; Perecman and Brown 1981; Peuser and Temp 1981; Cappa, Miozzo and Frugoni 1994). Nonword jargon may be perseverative, either in the form of total or so-called 'blended' perseverations (Moses, Nickels and Sheard 2004), or in a preference for syllable forms or segments that results in phonologically similar sequential output, or manifests across data samples (see Marshall 2006).

19.3.2 Jargonaphasia and Sonority

Several studies in the 1990s looked at jargonaphasia from the point of view of sonority theory. Christman (1992b) reviews the few previous studies of aphasia that have referred to sonority, and points out that many of them have invoked the notion as an explanation for the type of aphasic errors observed in the data. The studies support the idea that there is a hierarchy of syllable complexity, and that certain aspects of aphasic language breakdown may involve loss of control over more complex syllable structures.

Most previous studies have concentrated on utterances where the intended target was known, and so have been concerned with comparing intended and actual utterances. Christman notes that where the intended target is not clear, as with neologistic jargonaphasia which was the focus of her own study, then if neologisms do obey sonority constraints, 'then we may find that they are not constructed with phonological abandon, but rather with a certain degree of phonological regularity that can be captured at the level of syllabic organisation' (Christman 1992b: 225).

She further notes that such results would suggest that sonority is 'hardwired' in the brain, as proposed by Sussman (1984), in such a way that it survives extensive brain damage. Christman collected data from three English-speaking persons with jargonaphasia through both structured and unstructured language tasks. The transcribed language samples were then divided into four categories: contextually appropriate English words; semantic paraphasias (Christman did not include this second category in her sonority analysis); target related (containing 50 per cent or more of the phonemes of the intended target word); abstruse neologisms (containing less than 50 per cent of the phonemes of the target word and where no target word could be ascertained). All the selected utterances were divided into syllables, and then the syllables were divided into demisyllables (derived from work by Clements 1990: that is to say the onset and peak of a syllable made up one demisyllable, while the peak and coda made up the second; the syllable peak, therefore, appears in both demisyllables).

The three demisyllable databases were analysed in terms of their syllable patterns and sonority profiles, and compared to the three groupings. For both the target-related and abstruse neologisms, initial demisyllable shapes were predominantly CV, while for final demisyllables the most common pattern was VC, although V patterns were more common in embedded final demisyllables. These findings contrasted with those for English words where, although similar to the previous categories, other patterns scored relatively highly. For example in initial demisyllables, V patterns were quite common (these occurred in no more than 10 per cent of the neologism groups), and in final demisyllables VC and V types were more evenly balanced. The overwhelming majority of both CV and VC patterns in the neologistic speech had an obstruent in the C position. With the English words, obstruents were also the most common exponent of C in these patterns, although other types featured to a higher degree.

Christman comments that these results 'support the notion of sonority as (1) a hard-wired component of the language system, since its operation was not significantly impaired in phonological systems that have undergone serious impairment; (2) a mediator of phonological construction in all word forms, neologistic or otherwise; and (3) a useful metric in capturing the underlying phonological regularity of words that would otherwise appear to be somewhat randomly constructed' (Christman 1992b: 234).

Christman (1992a) applies the notion of sonority in jargonaphasia to models of syllable formation in theoretical phonology. The account is of interest, as Christman attempts to bring together more theoretical descriptions of syllable formation with more psycholinguistic models of speech production (a divide described in detail in Ball 2016). Christman (1994), on the other hand, returns to the data set of her 1992b study, and examines in detail the target related neologisms.[4] The analysis compared the actual productions with the target productions, and the demisyllables of both target and realization were scored for their sonority profiles. She found that errors were of three types: substitutions, omissions and additions. Whereas the first of these types generally produced segment strings that maintained or reduced sonority complexity, some of the omissions and additions increased sonority complexity. The view that syllable-initial sonority profiles should exhibit a steep rise in sonority is supported by these data. However, the view that syllable-final profiles should exhibit a shallow sonority fall or a sonority plateau, is not so supported. Most of the substitutions resulted in an obstruent being used instead of the target sound class (or a different obstruent for a target obstruent), and Christman argues that this is evidence of a default pattern for the selection of segments (i.e., to select obstruents) when normal speech production is impaired in aphasia. Although Christman continues to argue for some version of a hard-wired mechanism for sonority, it is interesting that this comparison study demonstrates only a strong tendency towards the SSP in these target neologisms, and that there were indeed exceptions both in syllable-initial and syllable-final positions.

More recently, Stenneken, Bastiaanse, Huber and Jacobs (2005) examined the syllable structure (in sonority terms) of the speech of a 59-year-old male German speaker with jargonaphasia, and compared it to sonority profiles for target German speech available in the literature. The speaker

4 It could be argued that this study is really about phonemic paraphasias rather than jargonaphasia. However, as we noted earlier, these two classifications are best thought of as being at two ends of a cline. As Christman's other work is concerned with jargonaphasia it was thought best to include this study here.

in this study showed a marked preference for obstruent singleton onsets (64 per cent compared to 50 per cent for the type analysis of the normal German database CELEX: Baayen, Piepenbrock and van Rijn 1993), and for syllable-finals without coda. Interestingly, the speaker with jargonaphasia produced a slightly greater percentage of syllable-initial clusters than was found in the normative database, but far fewer liquid singleton initials and approximately the same percentage of nasal singleton initials. This study, then, also shows evidence of a preference for obstruent-initial syllables in jargonaphasic speech.

In Müller and Mok (2012) the spoken output of a 78-year-old French-English bilingual woman from Louisiana with jargonaphasia was examined in detail. Her speech consisted virtually exclusively of nonword jargon, thus no target analysis was possible. One of the primary aims of this study was to compare the segmental and prosodic inventories of the speaker with the norms for both English and French. The data show a preference for canonical CV syllables (with 65.94 per cent of syllables beginning with a single consonant, and 63.94 per cent ending in a vowel), and also a preference for plosives and fricatives over other manners of articulation, which, taken together, point towards a weak preference for maximal sonority difference between onset and nucleus. On the other hand, no strong evidence for adherence to sonority as an organizing principle can be discerned overall: For example, 11 per cent of the speaker's onsets were two consonant clusters, and 23 per cent were vowel-initial; 36 per cent of syllable-finals were singleton consonants or two consonant clusters. Further, among the clusters were those that break the SSP albeit being normal for the target language(s): syllable-initial [st-, sj-, stɹ-], and syllable-final [-ts, -ks].[5] The speaker also produced one cluster that was not within the phonotactic possibilities of either target language: [df-]. This study suggests that notions that jargonaphasic speech will inevitably tend towards less complex sonority profiles may be too simplistic.

We will conclude this section by looking at two studies published in the 1980s: Perecman and Brown (1981), and Peuser and Temp (1981). The studies themselves do not address sonority, but they do provide a large

5 We are aware of course of the various proposals to bypass the SSP in regard to both initial and final [s] clusters; nevertheless, even if we accept these devices, we would assume that sonority theory would predict that simplification of syllable patterns (that might be expected in aphasia) would involve their removal. We leave to another time the discussion of whether adjuncts and appendices are convenient theoretical devices or have some psycholinguistic validity.

amount of data even though this is not subject to phonological analysis of the type described above.

Perecman and Brown (1981) report on K.S., a 74-year old German man (who became trilingual in German, Spanish and English) with jargonaphasia. They provide a large amount of phonetically transcribed data, and we will look at just a few utterances from part of a reading task. The transcriptions are as provided in the original (that is, with stressed syllables left unmarked), except for the correction of the wrong symbol for the voiced uvular fricative.

(1) [oɹadawsdɛnsdiʁst odɹadauskaniʁs oskandʌspəsvists] (target: 'truck'),
(2) [klopainəmiʁzajəstsastʃam] (target: 'try'),
(3) [baibɛʁsts sepaniʁsp saipɛniʁəs] (target: 'weak').
(Perecman and Brown 1981: 244)

Unfortunately, the authors did not indicate syllabification in their transcriptions (it is possible that this was too difficult to ascertain), so it is not always clear whether the speaker is using word internal clusters, or whether two abutting consonants are split across a syllable boundary. Nevertheless, apart from the sheer length of these nonwords, various segment strings run counter to the predictions of the SSP. For example, in (1), all three nonwords are vowel-initial, all end in coda clusters (in two cases of three consonants) and the final nonword ends in an [-sts] cluster, running counter to the SSP.[6] The nonword in (2), apart from its extreme complexity, also contains an [-sts-] string, and also an [-stʃ-] string. Of the nonwords in (3), the first two end in complex coda clusters: [-ʁsts], and [-ʁsp] respectively.

Peuser and Temp (1981) report on the jargonaphasic output of Mrs K., a 71-year-old German woman with jargonaphasia. The following items are from the recordings of a reading passage; this passage was read on several occasions, and (6–7) below were recorded two months after the time that (4–5) occurred.

(4) ['hintliːə]
(5) ['gɛgləvʊʃt]
(6) [gɛgvaltsi'mɪːjɔ]
(7) ['vɪkgvəgɪːr]
(Peuser and Temp 1981: 279)

6 The final [-ts] may well be an affricate phonetically, considering the target language contains such affricates. If we assume that affricates are located in a sonority class between stops and fricatives, however, this is still a breach of the SSP.

Nonword (4) contains a three-segment medial string (presumably [-nt.l-]); (5) a word-final [-ʃt] cluster, dispreferred under the SSP; (6) medial [-gv-] and [-lts-] strings (syllable boundaries unclear); and (7) a medial [-.gv-] cluster which is counter to German phonotactics, although being permitted by the SSP, but also counter to the Sonority Dispersion Principle.

19.3.3 Concluding Remarks

These excerpts illustrate that jargonaphasic data offers counterexamples to the Sonority Sequencing Principle, the Sonority Dispersion Principle, and to the phonotactic constraints of the target language. Together with the examples noted in Section 19.2 – also from a disruption at the level of phonological organization – this suggests that sonority might be better thought of as a tendency than as a phonological law. We turn in the next section to a consideration of speech automatisms.

19.4 Lexical and Non-Lexical Speech Automatisms

19.4.1 Introduction

A large proportion of global and Broca's aphasic speakers who have severe brain damage are left with both language and speech impairments. One of the symptoms of these types of aphasia is a kind of automatic speech, made up of stereotyped and involuntarily reiterative utterances (Blanken, Wallesch and Papagno 1990; Blanken 1991). A number of terms for automatic speech have been proposed, but recently researchers have agreed to use the general term *speech automatism*, although *recurrent* or *recurring utterances* may also be found, though this may be restricted to the non-lexical variety. Speech automatisms are highly stereotyped and repetitively used utterances that are produced without phonological control (Blanken, Dittman, Haas and Wallesch 1988). Typical examples are 'da-da-da', 'better, better' or 'wait a minute' (Code 1982, 1994). In general, we can describe speech automatisms as involuntary, stereotyped, repetitive and spontaneous speech which may be meaningful or non-meaningful.

The essential features of two major types of aphasic speech automatism have been identified (Code 1982, 1987, 1991; Wallesch 1990). These are *lexical* and *non-lexical speech automatisms.* Non-lexical speech automatisms are often made up of repeated concatenated CV syllables. Some selected examples of non-lexical recurring utterances (from Code 1982) are shown here: [bi bi], [ta ta], [wi wi wi], [du du du]. Lexical speech automatisms consist of recognizable words and are syntactically correct structures of the language concerned in the overwhelming majority of cases. With few exceptions, where such automatisms consist of multiple words, the initial words are stressed content words. Although it is not possible to be sure of the syntactic function of words in the samples in the literature, or even whether the words have a syntactic function, a classification of the words as if they were normally used shows that most initial words are nouns, pronouns or verbs. In normal conversational speech these are stressed lexical words, high in referential meaning (Code 1982; Blanken 1991; Blanken, Wallesch and Papagno 1990).

Speech automatisms in several languages have been studied. In particular, and in terms of sonority, studies have been undertaken on English, German and Cantonese. We report on these in the following subsections.

19.4.2 Non-Lexical Speech Automatisms in English and German

Code and Ball (1994) summarized the work on non-lexical speech automatisms in English and German. The two main collections of data accessed for this study were those reported for English (Code 1982), and for German (Blanken et al. 1990). The corpora for the study reported by Code and Ball (1994) were compiled through the inclusion of virtually all the forms reported in these two studies. This resulted in a total of 102 syllables for the English corpus, and 119 syllables for the German corpus. The analysis (based on Christman 1992b) required the division of all syllables into demisyllables: that is the onset and peak of a syllable are assigned to an initial demisyllable, and the peak and coda (of the same syllable) to a final demisyllable. Following Clements' (1990) observations on utterance final versus embedded final differences in sonority, all demisyllables were further divided into utterance peripheral (i.e. initial or final) and embedded (also initial and final), resulting in the four categories: utterance initial (UI), embedded initial (EI), utterance final (UF) and embedded final (EF). This study followed the transcriptions as published in Code (1982) and Blanken et al. (1990) to determine where the utterance boundary occurs.

For example, if an utterance is recorded as /do di do di/, we have assumed that the second /di/ represents the utterance final syllable. This means we assume that the speech automatism in this case was regularly /do di do di/. Demisyllable corpora were constructed from the English and German data. All demisyllables were assigned to a demisyllable context (UI, EI, UF, EF), syllable shape (CV, CCV, V, VC) and demisyllable sonority profile (OV, NV, VO, etc.).

Results showed firstly that the preferred syllable-initial sequence (both UI and EI) for both languages was CV. For English the figures showed that 69 per cent (UI) and 82 per cent (EI) of initial demisyllables were CV, with V the next most popular, and CCV in third position. For German, CV scored 87 per cent (UI) and 81 per cent (EI), with V second and CCV third for UI, and CCV second and V a close third in EI. For final demisyllables, both languages preferred V (English UF 86 per cent, EF 93 per cent; German UF 89 per cent, EF 98 per cent), with VC a distant second. Interestingly, the German data contained both a [-gn] and a [-bn] final cluster, both of which break the SSP, and German phonotactics.

In terms of the consonant classes, both languages showed a preference for obstruents in initial demisyllables, with nasal initials the second most popular class in CV initials. The obstruents were divided between plosives and fricatives, with the former more common than the latter. Very few initial clusters occurred, though the English data include a plosive plus liquid in EI position, and German some [ts] clusters in UI and EI positions (which are probably better analysed as affricates).

No examples were found of word-initial consonant clusters that adhered to the phonotactics of the language, but broke the rules of Sonority Theory. So, no instances of [sp- st- sk-] clusters in English, or [ʃp- ʃt-] clusters in German were found, for example (though see below for instances of embedded initial clusters). However, for both English and German there were instances of vowel-initial forms which are both counter to the universal preference for CV syllable onsets, and to the SSP requirement for onsets to rise in sonority. These include from Code (1982): [ibi ibi], [əzez əzez], and from Blanken et al. (1990) and Blanken and Marini (1997): [anana], [asa], [ede].

19.4.3 Lexical Speech Automatisms in English and German

The studies referred to earlier (Code 1982; Blanken et al. 1990; Blanken and Marini 1997) also included information on lexical speech automatisms in

English and German. The authors did not submit these data to phonological analysis, but it is clear that a variety of syllable types are in evidence including initial and final clusters. Interestingly, however, no examples of initial [s~ʃ]C clusters occurred with the exception of an EI [-.st-] cluster in the German data. Finally, one example of a [-ks] cluster in the German data would appear to be the only time the SSP is broached in this position.

19.4.4 Lexical Speech Automatisms in Cantonese

The English and German corpora are, of course, derived from closely related languages, and it is instructive to examine both non-lexical and lexical speech automatisms in a typologically and structurally different language. Cantonese, which is one of the main languages of China, is used mainly in the southern part of China, Hong Kong and Macau. It is a tonal language that uses six lexical tones (Li and Thompson 1987; although Fok 1979 argues for a nine tone analysis).

An investigation by Chung, Code and Ball 2004 explored whether the speech production of Cantonese aphasic speakers with lexical speech automatisms would be found to be similar to those described in non-tonal European languages. Hadano and Hamanaka (1997) have suggested that the production of speech automatisms with Japanese speakers with aphasia is similar to that of European languages; however, Japanese is unrelated to Chinese, and is not a tone language.

The first and last authors of this chapter undertook a preliminary phonological analysis of part of the corpus collected by Chung. Data on 16 patients were analysed. Seven of these used a single speech automatism, while nine used two different automatisms. Several patients had identical speech automatisms, and the total of different automatisms was 17. Some of these were single words, some contained two words, and two had three words; the total number of different words used was 33.[7] No segmental phonological errors were noted, and the transcriptions of the speech automatisms are given in Table 19.1. The transcriptions are given in both a broad phonemic version, and a narrow phonetic one.

7 If a word occurred as a singleton and also in a phrase, it was counted twice. If either the singleton or phrase was used by two or more subjects, it was counted only once.

Table 19.1. Cantonese lexical speech automatisms.

Subject	Literal translation	English equivalent	Phonemic transcription	Phonetic transcription
A	father	'father'	/pa pa/	[pʰa pʰa]
B	is person	'there is a person'	/jau jan/	[jau jɐn]
C	talk-not-out	'can't say'	/gɔŋ m̩ tsi/	[g̊ɔŋ m̩ tsʰɨ]
D, N	not-yes	'no'	/m̩ hai/	[m̩ hɐi]
E	ah-wai	personal name	/a wai/	[a wɐi]
F	yes	'yes'	/hai/	[hɐi]
F, G, I, J	oh	acknowledgement	/m̩/	[m̩]
G, I, J, N	no	'no'	/mou/	[mou]
H	yes	'yes'	/si/	[sɨ]
H	this+classifier	'this one'	/tsɛ gɔ/	[tsʰɛ g̊ɔ]
K	ah-oh	exclamation	/ai ja/	[ɐi ja]
L	anyway-is	'anyway'	/dzuŋ ˈdzi hai/	[d̥z̊uŋ ˈd̥z̊ɨ hɐi]
L	this+classifier	'this one'	/nei gɔ/	[nei g̊ɔ]
M	*not-is (ungrammatical)	'no'	/m̩ dzik hai/	[m̩ d̥z̊ɨk̚ hɐi]
O	that+classifier	'that one'	/gɔ gɔ/	[g̊ɔ g̊ɔ]
P	yes-particle	'really'	/hai a/	[hɐi a]
P	final particles	meaningless	/a a/	[a a]

Whereas Code and Ball (1994) analysed the data from English and German in terms of both syllable structure and phonotactics (especially of consonant clusters), the Cantonese data were restricted to a syllable structure investigation. This is because the language has a very simple phonological structure. The only syllable shapes to occur are V, CV, VC, CVC, and no consonant clusters are allowed (/ts/ and /dz/ are treated as affricates). It should also be noted that V can consist of vowels or syllabic nasals, that final consonants are restricted to /m, n, ŋ/ and to /p, t, k/,[8] and that the initial consonants are /p, t, k, kʷ, b, d, g, gʷ, ts, dz, m, n, ŋ, f, s, l, w, j, h/. Finally, we should note that words are mostly monosyllabic in Cantonese (Li and Thompson 1987).

The initial analysis undertaken was the syllable shape of each word in the data. The syllable shapes V, CV, CVC and VC occurred with frequencies shown in Table 19.2.

8 Phonetically, these are unreleased voiceless stops.

Table 19.2. Syllable shapes in the data.

Syllable shapes	No. of examples in data
V	9
CV	20
CVC	4
VC	0

General syllable theory, grounded in comparisons across natural language, would predict CV as common and VC as rare, and this is reflected in the results. To exploit the insights of Sonority Theory, the class of consonant occupying the C-slots was investigated. Table 19.3 shows the findings for CV syllables.

Table 19.3. Consonant-vowel combinations in the data.

Consonant-vowel combination	No. of examples in data
Plosive+vowel	9
Fricative+vowel	6
Nasal+vowel	2
Glide+vowel	3

This result is close to what Sonority Theory would predict: plosive+vowel most common, fricative+vowel next, then nasal+vowel and glide+vowel.

Examining the CVC syllables produces the results shown in Table 19.4, though it has to be borne in mind that there are very few examples.

Table 19.4. Consonant-vowel-consonant combinations in the data.

Consonant-vowel-consonant combinations	No. of examples in the data
Plosive+vowel+nasal	2
Plosive+vowel+plosive	1
Glide+vowel+nasal	1

These Cantonese data, despite the small number of tokens, support the proposition that Sonority Theory can predict syllable shape in speech automatisms, and so serves as extra evidence to that put forward in Code and Ball (1994), from a language of a very different type to that investigated in the earlier study.

19.4.5 Concluding Remarks

The data reported in this section are restricted to a small number of languages. Collections from many more are needed before we can state anything with certainty about the role of sonority in the production of speech automatisms. Unlike with paraphasias and jargonaphasia there appear to be almost no exceptions to the observation that nonword automatisms obey the SSP. On the other hand, these are usually so very simple it might be more useful to think of them as conforming to a very basic CV(CV) syllable structure where it is of course easy to conform to the SSP. Nevertheless, the results for English and German show there are some other syllable shapes, and there were some segment strings that had a smaller sonority distance than the preferred OV-. There were also a fair number of vowel-initial forms or vowel-only forms in the English, German, and Cantonese data.

19.5 Progressive Speech Deterioration

19.5.1 Introduction

It is arguable that motor speech disorders should not be included in an account of sonority and acquired neurogenic communication disorders, as sonority is a phonological property and motor speech disorders affect phonetic planning and phonetic implementation (see Ball 2016). However, claims made by Christman (1992b) and Sussman (1984) that sonority 'must also be "hard-wired" into the system, since it remains so resistant to disruption following neurological impairment' (Christman 1992b: 242) suggest that it can also be tested at the motor speech level. This is especially so since phonological entities such as sonority theory and principles such as the SSP cannot be totally abstract and must have arisen from phonetic causes.

Code and colleagues have described a case of progressive speech deterioration satisfying recent criteria for a diagnosis of progressive apraxia of speech (PAoS) (Duffy and Josephs 2012) in a series of publications (e.g., Code, Tree, Dawe, Kay, Ball and Edwards 2003; Ball, Code, Tree, Dawe and Kay 2004; Code, Müller, Tree and Ball 2006; Code, Tree and Dawe 2009; Code, Tree and Ball 2011; and Code, Ball and Tree 2013). The participant (CS) was a right-handed 63-year-old male at the time of data collection. He first noticed speech problems 8 years previously. He became unintelligible some 6 months after data collection, and almost mute, managing only the occasional utterance, a few months later still. Details of the various neurological examinations that were carried out are reported in Code et al. (2006) and Code et al. (2009), but we will concentrate here on the analyses of CS's speech.

Research suggests that progressive apraxia of speech (PAoS) may be significantly different from AoS from stroke. While single word production is relatively fluent in PAoS, connected speech is slow and distorted with syntactic errors, shorter utterances, lack of spontaneity and reduced complexity (Wilson, Henry, Besbris, Ogar, Dronkers, Jarrold et al. 2010; Patterson Graham, Lambon-Ralph and Hodges 2006; Sajjadi, Patterson, Tomek and Nestor 2012; Code, Ball and Tree 2013).

19.5.2 Speech Analyses

The analyses described in Ball et al. (2004) are based on a variety of verbal tasks, namely reading and repetition of increasingly complex English words, uttering sustained vowels in isolation, counting from 1 to 30, naming a series of pictures, reading a phonetically balanced passage (the Grandfather Passage: Darley, Aronson and Brown 1975), and a variety of diadochokinetic tasks. Responses to all these tasks were audio-recorded.

The analysis was undertaken using the PRAAT (Boersma and Weenink 2004) speech analysis software (version 4.0.26) running on a PC and much of the recorded material was also phonetically transcribed by the authors.

The main findings included a range of problems, for example intrusive schwa, devoicing voiced and voicing unvoiced fricatives and stops and loss of aspiration, some vowel distortions, anticipation of phones, increasing errors on repetition, but mainly additions. Unusual additions included the addition of labials preceding /r/-initial words, and [l]-following words ending in /u/. These patterns were for the most part variable, though the loss of aspiration became almost total in the recordings made in November 2002. Only a subset of the results are of interest in this chapter; thus, for example, we do not discuss slight distortions of vowels, sibilant noise spectra, or voicing and devoicing of fricatives.

Some of the results are amenable to phonological analysis (see also the phonological analyses of C.S. presented in Ball, Rutter and Code 2008). Of most interest to considerations of sonority are the following: denasalization, lateral addition and labial addition, and loss of aspiration. We will also look briefly at epenthetic schwa addition in clusters. (All the examples given in this section are taken from Ball et al. 2004.)

Examples of variable denasalization in C.S.'s speech include 'more' /mɔ/ → [bɔ], 'chin' /tʃɪn/ → [tʃɪd], and 'smoke' /sməʊk/ → [spəʊk]. These realizations are interesting from the viewpoint of the SSP. The denasalization in 'more' alters a nasal-vowel onset to a stop-vowel one, thus increasing the sonority slope to a steeper rise, as preferred by the SSP. However, the denasalization in 'chin', which also changes a nasal to a stop, but this time in the coda, produces a steeper sonority fall at the end of the syllable, which is not predicted by Clements' account of shallow falls or plateaux in this position. Finally, the denasalization in 'smoke' results in an [s]+stop onset, dispreferred in sonority theory and requiring ingenious devices proposed by theoretical phonologists to account for them.

The pattern of lateral addition is illustrated in the following examples: 'crew' /kru/ → [kɹuɫ], and 'screw' /skru/ → [skɹuɫ]. From a sonority viewpoint, the change from a plateau syllable end to a shallow sonority fall would seem to have few implications, as both patterns are deemed to fit the SSP (as noted in the previous paragraph). From the viewpoint of markedness, however, the change is from an unmarked no coda syllable to a more marked -VC pattern.

Labial addition is shown in the following examples: 'rap' /ræp/ → [bɹæp], [pɹæp], 'rig' /rɪg/ → [bɹɪg], 'ray' /reɪ/ → [pɹeɪ], [fɹeɪ], 'rue' /ru/ → [fɹuɫ] (this last also showing lateral addition). This addition pattern is also difficult to assess via sonority. On the one hand, the shallow sonority rise in the onset from liquid to vowel is changed to a steeper onset from stop to liquid to vowel. On the other hand, the simpler CV-onset has changed to a more complex CCV-onset.

Ball et al. (2004) report that the mean VOT values for word-initial fortis plosives in the earliest recordings made for their study was 65 ms, and for the lenis plosives was 24 ms. The same measures at the time of last recordings made some 6 months later (August 2002) were: fortis plosives 21 ms, lenis 18 ms. The change from aspirated to unaspirated plosives is an increase (albeit slight) in sonority, thus producing a sonority profile that is a little less steep. As many researchers do not distinguish between different types of obstruent when calculating sonority profiles, let alone between aspirated and unaspirated plosives, this difference is not of great importance in terms of the SSP. Nevertheless, it is an example where speech deterioration does not produce a pattern of simplification that would be predicted by the SSP.

Finally we can consider C.S.'s realizations of syllable shapes. As with the previous features, these patterns were variable. However, C.S. showed problems with both simple and complex codas, but much less so with complex onsets. Examples with simple codas include vowel addition: 'sag' [sægə], 'utmost' [ʌtəməʊst] (the latter illustrating the variable nature of the changes in that the complex final coda cluster is unaffected); and final consonant deletion: 'coat' [kəʊ], 'prig' [bɹɪə]. Complex codas showed cluster reduction, 'zest' [sɛs], 'bagged' [bæg]; epenthetic vowel usage, 'takes' [teɪkɪs]; and vowel addition 'kept' [kɛptə], 'slept' [slɛptə]. There are also instances of both vowel insertion and addition: 'apt' [æpətə], 'ripped' [ɹɪpətə]. C.S. used various deletion and addition patterns to simplify his codas towards an 'ideal' no-coda shape. He showed few problems, however, with complex onsets. Examples such as 'script' [skɹɪpətə] demonstrate both his abilities with three-consonant onset clusters and his problems with two-consonant coda clusters. The problems with codas but not with onsets appears to be connected with the irregular nature of the gradual speech deterioration that C.S. exhibited; sonority theory does not seem best placed to account for these changes, however.

19.5.3 Concluding Comments

The case reported above is not a typical example either of apraxia of speech from stroke or of dysarthria, but shares more with the former than the latter. So, it may well be useful to look briefly at some common patterns in the speech of dysarthria at the segmental level and how these would fit within the predictions of sonority theory.

Two of the most common features that affect segmental phonetics are articulatory imprecision and hypernasality (bear in mind that there are several types of dysarthria and these features vary in their frequency of occurrence according to these types). The realization of stops, for example, as fricatives or approximants (a common consequence of articulatory imprecision) will produce shallower sonority rises in syllable onset position (against the SSP), and the use of nasals instead of stops will do likewise. In syllable coda positions, however, these realizations will not breach the SSP assuming we follow Clements' argument concerning shallow or plateau codas.

That the same phonetic change can be both against the SSP and for it stongly suggests that sonority as often described in fact does not predict well disorders at the levels of phonetic planning and implementation, even if it does better with disorders at the level of phonological organization.

19.6 Conclusion

The topics reviewed above suggest that paraphasias (both phonemic and neologistic) have a strong tendency to adhere to the Sonority Sequencing Principle. Further, both real word and nonword speech automatisms also display this tendency.

However, the speech patterns described for PAoS in Section 19.5 above, and for dysarthria (brief comments in 19.5.3) do not show the same tendency and, indeed, some of these patterns run counter to the predictions of the SSP.

The implications are that if sonority does have a psycholinguistic reality, then its location (in terms of speech production) has to be at the organizational level of phonology, but not also at the levels of phonetic planning or implementation (thus supporting the conclusions of Miozzo and Buchwald 2013). However, we have also seen in this chapter (and indeed throughout the chapters of this collection) considerable variation in what are considered to be the sound classes that enter into a sequencing metric for sonority.

As can be seen from comparing the analyses we have reviewed in this chapter, and in comparing chapters in this book, there are a number of competing models of sonority classification. A maximalist approach taking into consideration both voicing contrasts and vowel height differences could potentially yield around 13 groups (assuming one wishes to eschew a separate sonority profile for each sound in a language). A minimalist approach could potentially be simply between obstruents and sonorants, or between obstruents, sonorant consonants and vowels. In practice, in the recent literature, there is a division between a simple $O < N < L < G < V$ model, and an $S < F < N < L < G < V$ one.[9] We have seen how the difference between these approaches can make a difference in the conclusion whether an utterance does or does not breach the SSP. Thus, realizing /gr-/ as [xr-] adheres to the Sonority Dispersion Principle under a minimalist model, but not under a more liberal interpretation of sonority groupings. Further, the [-.st-] and [-ks] clusters reported in the speech automatism data are unproblematic under a minimalist model, but break the SSP under any arrangement of sonority classes that differentiate between stops and fricatives. Clearly, unless or until phoneticians can demonstrate what sonority actually is, phonologists can adjust descriptions of it to suit the

9 Where O: obstruent; N: nasal; L: liquid; G: glide; V: vowel; S: stop; and F: fricative.

data they are analysing, and clinical phonologists may well fall into the trap described in Ball (2016) of equating a descriptive device with a psycho- or neurolinguistics characteristic.

These considerations allow us to revisit claims that sonority is hard-wired. As we saw, such claims come from the fact that sonority (in the form of the SSP) seems to survive brain damage. However, as Code and Ball (1994) point out, sonority seems to survive left hemispherectomy too. This suggests either that sonority is so basic that it is distributed widely across both hemispheres, or that the notion itself lacks explanatory power in that it aligns, perhaps, with a universal tendency to maximize speech sound perception and/or articulatory simplicity (see chapters in this collection for a range of possible explanations for the sonority effect). Under this latter view, then, sonority is an emergent feature, rather than a hard-wired one. This allows for exceptions to occur (as they do in both normal and disordered speech) without the need for complex architecture to account for them. It also allows for the non-operation of sonority at the motor level; as an emergent feature of phonological organization it can clearly be negated by impaired motor plans and motor implementation.

Further research on the speech aspects of acquired neurogenic disorders will doubtless shed further light on the role of sonority in such spoken output. Of special interest would be to look at disordered speech in some of the languages described in this collection where the SSP is definitely not adhered to. In the meantime, until we can ascertain what sonority actually is, it is difficult to see how we can definitively conclude whether it is a major factor in syllabification in language – either normal or disordered.

References

Alajouanine, T. (1956). Verbal realization in aphasia. *Brain*, 79, 1–28.

Ball, M.J. (2016). *Principles of clinical phonology.* London: Routledge.

Ball, M.J., Code, C., Tree, J., Dawe, K. and Kay, J. (2004). Phonetic and phonological analysis of progressive speech degeneration: A case study. *Clinical Linguistics and Phonetics*, 18, 447–62.

Ball, M.J., Rutter, B. and Code, C. (2008). Phonological analyses of a case of progressive speech degeneration. *Asia-Pacific Journal of Speech, Language and Hearing*, 11, 305–12.

Baayen, R.H., Piepenbrock, R. and van Rijn, H. (1993). *The CELEX Lexical Database* (CDROM). Philadelphia, PA: Linguistic Data Consortium, University of Pennsylvania.

Bastiaanse, R., Gilbers, D. and van der Linde, K. (1994). Sonority substitutions in Broca's and conduction aphasia. *Journal of Neurolinguistics*, 8, 247–55.

Béland, R., Caplan, D. and Nespoulous, J.-L. (1990). The role of abstract phonological representations in word production: Evidence from phonemic paraphasias. *Journal of Neurolinguistics*, 5, 125–64.

Biran, M. and Friedmann, N. (2005). From phonological paraphasias to the structure of the phonological output lexicon. *Language and Cognitive Processes*, 20, 589–616.

Blanken, G. (1991). The functional basis of speech automatisms (recurring utterances). *Aphasiology*, 5, 103–27.

Blanken, G., Dittmann, J., Haas, J.-C. and Wallesch, C.-W. (1988). Producing speech automatisms (recurring utterances): Looking for what is left. *Aphasiology*, 2, 545–56.

Blanken, G., and Marini, V. (1997). Where do lexical speech automatisms come from? *Journal of Neurolinguistics*, 10, 19–31.

Blanken, G., Wallesch, C.-W. and Papagno, C. (1990). Dissociations of language functions in aphasics with speech automatisms (recurring utterances). *Cortex*, 26, 41–63.

Boersma, P. and Weenink, D. (2004). Praat: Doing phonetics by computer [Computer program]. Version 4.0.26, retrieved 2004 from http://www.praat.org/

Brookshire, R.H. (1997). *Introduction to neurogenic communication disorders*. 5th edition. St. Louis, MO: Mosby.

Buckingham, H.W. (1986). The scan-copier mechanisms and the positional level of language production: Evidence from phonemic paraphasia. *Cognitive Science*, 10, 195–217.

Buckingham, H.W. (1989). Phonological paraphasia. In C.F. Code (ed.), *The characteristics of aphasia* (pp. 81–110). London: Taylor and Francis.

Butterworth, B. (1979). Hesitation and the production of verbal paraphasias and neologisms in jargon aphasia. *Brain and Language*, 8, 133–61.

Cappa, S., Miozzo, A. and Frugoni, M. (1994). Glossolalic jargon after a right hemisphere stroke in a patient with Wernicke's aphasia. *Aphasiology*, 8, 83–7.

Christman, S.S. (1992a). Abstruse neologism formation: parallel processing revisited. *Clinical Linguistics and Phonetics*, 6, 65–76.

Christman, S.S. (1992b). Uncovering phonological regularity in neologisms: Contributions of sonority theory. *Clinical Linguistics and Phonetics*, 6, 219–47.

Christman, S.S. (1994). Target-related neologism formation in jargonaphasia. *Brain and Language*, 46, 109–28.

Chung, K.K.H., Code, C.F. and Ball, M.J. (2004). Speech automatisms and recurring utterances from aphasic Cantonese speakers. *Journal of Multilingual Communication Disorders*, 2, 32–42.

Clements, G.N. (1990). The role of the sonority cycle in core syllabification. In J. Kingston and M. Beckman (eds.), *Papers in laboratory phonology I: Between the grammar and the physics of speech* (pp. 283–333). Cambridge University Press, Cambridge.

Code, C.F. (1982). Neurolinguistic analysis of recurrent utterances in aphasia. *Cortex*, 18, 141–52.

Code, C.F. (1987). *Language, aphasia and the right hemisphere*. Chichester: John Wiley.

Code, C.F. (1991). Speech automatisms and recurring utterances. In C.F. Code (ed.), *The characteristics of aphasia* (pp. 155–77). Hove: Lawrence Erlbaum Associates.

Code, C.F. (1994). Speech automatism production in aphasia. *Journal of Neurolinguistics*, 8, 135–48.

Code, C.F. (2010). Aphasia. In J. Damico, N. Müller and M.J. Ball (eds.), *The handbook of language and speech disorders* (pp. 317–36). Chichester: Wiley-Blackwell.

Code, C.F. and Ball, M.J. (1994). Syllabification in aphasic recurring utterances: contributions of sonority theory. *Journal of Neurolinguistics*, 8, 257–65.

Code, C.F., Ball, M.J. and Tree, J. (2013). The effects of initiation, termination and inhibition impairments on speech rate in a case of progressive nonfluent aphasia with progressive apraxia of speech with frontotemporal degeneration. *Journal of Neurolinguistics*, 26, 602–18.

Code, C.F., Müller, N., Tree, J.T. and Ball, M.J. (2006). Syntactic impairments can emerge later: Progressive agrammatic agraphia and syntactic comprehension impairment. *Aphasiology*, 20, 1035–58.

Code, C.F., Tree, J. and Ball, M.J. (2011). The influence of psycholinguistic variables on articulatory errors in naming in progressive motor speech degeneration. *Clinical Linguistics and Phonetics*, 25, 1074–80.

Code, C.F., Tree, J. and Dawe, K. (2009). Opportunities to say 'yes': Rare speech automatisms in a case of progressive nonfluent aphasia and apraxia. *Neurocase*, 15, 445–58.

Code, C.F., Tree, J.J., Dawe, K., Kay, J., Ball, M.J. and Edwards, M. (2003). A case of progressive speech deterioration with apraxias. (Proceedings of the BNS), *Neurocase*, 9, 448–9.

Darley, F.L., Aronson, A.E. and Brown, J.R. (1975*). Motor speech disorders*. 3rd edition. Philadelphia, PA: W.B. Saunders.

Duffy, J.R. (2012). *Motor speech disorders: Substrates, differential diagnosis and management*. 3rd edition. St. Louis, MO: Elsevier Mosby.

Duffy, J.R. and Josephs, K.A. (2012). The diagnosis and understanding of apraxia of speech: Why including neurodegenerative etiologies may be important. *Journal of Speech, Language, and Hearing Research*, 55, S1518–22.

Fok, A. (Chan, Y.Y.) (1979). The frequency of occurrence of speech sounds and tones in Cantonese. In M.R. Lord (ed.), *Hong Kong language papers* (pp.150–7). Hong Kong: Hong Kong University Press.

Hadano, K. and Hamanaka, T. (1997). Semistereotypic speech. *Aphasiology*, 11, 1117–25.

Hanlon, R.E. and Edmondson, J.E. (1996). Disconnected phonology: A linguistic analysis of phonemic jargon aphasia. *Brain and Language*, 55, 199–212.

Jacks, A. and Robin, D. (2010). Apraxia of speech. In J. Damico, N. Müller and M.J. Ball (eds.), *The handbook of language and speech disorders* (pp. 391–409). Chichester: Wiley-Blackwell.

Jespersen, O. (1904). *Lehrbuch der Phonetik.* Leipzig and Berlin: B.G. Teubner.

Kohn, S., Melvold, J. and Shipper, V. (1998). The preservation of sonority in the context of impaired lexical-phonological output. *Aphasiology*, 12, 375–98.

Ladefoged, P. (1975). *A course in phonetics.* New York: Harcourt, Brace, Jovanovich.

Li, C.N. and Thompson, S. (1987). Chinese. In B. Comrie (ed.), *The world's major languages* (pp. 811–33). London: Croom Helm.

Marshall, J. (2006). Jargon aphasia: What have we learned? *Aphasiology*, 20, 387–410.

Miozzo, M. and Buchwald, A. (2013). On the nature of sonority in spoken word production: Evidence from neuropsychology. *Cognition*, 128, 287–301.

Moses, M.S., Nickels, L.A. and Sheard, C. (2004). Disentangling the web: Neologistic perseverative errors in jargon aphasia. *Neurocase*, 10, 454–61.

Müller, N. and Mok, Z. (2012). Nonword jargon produced by a French-English bilingual. In M. Gitterman, M. Goral and L. Obler (eds.), *Aspects of multilingual aphasia* (pp. 224–41). Bristol: Multilingual Matters.

Patterson, K., Graham, N., Lambon-Ralph, M. and Hodges, J. (2006). Progressive non-fluent aphasia is not a progressive form of non-fluent (post-stroke) aphasia. *Aphasiology*, 20, 1018–34.

Perecman, E. and Brown, J.W. (1981). Phonemic jargon: A case report. In J.W. Brown (ed.), *Jargonaphasia.* (pp. 177–258). New York: Academic Press.

Perecman, E. and Brown, J.W. (1985). Ukeles, condessors, and fosetch. *Language Sciences*, 7, 177–214.

Peuser, G. and Temp, K. (1981). The evolution of jargonaphasia. In J.W. Brown (ed.), *Jargonaphasia.* (pp. 259–94). New York: Academic Press.

Robson, J., Pring, T., Marshall, J. and Chiat, S. (2003). Phoneme frequency effects in jargon aphasia: A phonological investigation of nonword errors. *Brain and Language*, 85, 109–24.

Roca, I. and Johnson, W. (1999). *A course in phonology.* Oxford, England: Blackwell.

Rohrer, J., Rossor, M. and Warren, J.D. (2009). Neologistic jargon aphasia and agraphia in primary progressive aphasia. *Journal of the Neurological Sciences*, 277, 155–9.

Romani, C. and Calabrese, A. (1998). Syllabic constraints in phonological errors of an aphasic patient. *Brain and Language*, 64, 83–121.

Sajjadi, S.A., Patterson, K., Tomek, M. and Nestor, P.J. (2012). Abnormalities of connected speech in the non-semantic variants of primary progressive aphasia. *Aphasiology*, 26, 1219–37.

Stenneken, P., Hoffman, M. and Jacobs, A.M., (2005). Patterns of phoneme and syllable frequency in jargon aphasia. *Brain and Language*, 95, 221–2.

Stenneken, P., Bastiaanse, R., Huber, W. and Jacobs, A.M. (2005). Syllable structure and sonority in language inventory and aphasic neologisms. *Brain and Language*, 95, 280–92.

Sussman, H. (1984). A neuronal model for syllable representation. *Brain and Language*, 22, 166–77.

van der Linde, K., Bastiaanse, R. and Gilbers, D.G. (1993). Sonority substitutions in language disorders. In F. Drijkoningen and K. Hengeveld (eds.), *Linguistics in the Netherlands 1993* (pp. 81–92). Amsterdam: John Benjamins.

Wallesch, C.-W. (1990). Repetitive verbal behaviour: Functional and neurological considerations. *Aphasiology*, 4, 133–54.

Weismer, G (2006). *Motor speech disorders.* San Diego, CA: Plural.

Wilson, S. M., Henry, M. L., Besbris, M., Ogar, J. M., Dronkers, N. F., Jarrold, W. et al. (2010). Connected speech production in three variants of primary progressive aphasia. *Brain*, 133, 2069–88.

Martin J. Ball is Professor of Speech-Language Pathology (Clinical Linguistics and Phonetics) at Linköping University, Sweden. He is co-editor of the journal *Clinical Linguistics and Phonetics* (Taylor & Francis), and the book series *Communication Disorders Across Languages* (Multilingual Matters). His main research interests include sociolinguistics, clinical phonetics and phonology, and the Celtic languages. He is an honorary Fellow of the Royal College of Speech and Language Therapists, and a Fellow of the Learned Society of Wales.

Nicole Müller is Professor of Speech-Language Pathology at Linköping University, Sweden; she will be taking up the position of Professor of Speech and Hearing Sciences at University College Cork, Ireland, early in 2017. Her areas of research interest include clinical linguistics, clinical discourse studies and pragmatics, age-related disorders of communication and cognition, multilingualism, and systemic functional linguistics. She is co-editor of the journal *Clinical Linguistics and Phonetics* and of the book series *Communication Disorders across Languages*.

Chris Code is Professorial Research Fellow in the School of Psychology at the University of Exeter, Foundation Professor of Communication Sciences and Disorders (Honorary) at the University of Sydney, and Visiting Professor at Linköping University. His research interests include the cognitive neuroscience of language and speech, psychosocial consequences of aphasia, aphasia and the evolution of language and speech, recovery and treatment of aphasia, and the public awareness of aphasia. He is co-founding Editor of the international journal *Aphasiology* (Psychology Press).

20 Motivating and Explaining the Structure of Segment Sequences

Mark J. Jones

20.1 Introduction

Sonority is widely portrayed as being the primary factor in determining which segment sequences are permitted within syllables; consequently, sonority plays a major role in how syllables are formed. The most sonorous segment occupies the obligatory nucleus of the syllable, which may then be called the (sonority) peak. Sonority rises from the onset of the syllable, if present, into the peak, and falls through the syllable into the coda, again if present.[1] A monosyllabic word therefore shows a rise-fall sonority profile (called the Sonority Cycle in Clements 1990). This view of sonority is widespread throughout phonology, but despite its prevalence and more than a hundred years of attention, a physical definition of sonority remains illusive and there is circularity in the construction of sonority hierarchies of segments. Furthermore, exceptions to the expected sonority profile appear in many syllables, and some sequences which conform to the rise-fall pattern are unexpectedly rare. Segment sequences which recur across languages may vary across syllable positions in different languages, suggesting that syllables themselves are irrelevant to segment sequencing preferences.[2] Even if sonority is accepted with no definition, considerable additional machinery is needed to drive syllabification, and the motivation for some

1 Some familiarity with theories of syllable structure is assumed here: an overview may be found in Blevins (1995). It is also assumed that there is no distinction between phonetic and phonological syllables (Hooper 1972), and that cross-linguistic tendencies should be explained by surface factors.

2 I use the term 'segment sequencing preferences' throughout rather than 'phonotactics', since phonotactics often seems implicitly restricted to consonant sequences, and the issues discussed here also involve consonant-vowel and vowel-consonant sequences.

of this machinery is disputed. Taken together, these criticisms seriously undermine the status of sonority as a driving force in determining what segment sequences are preferred across languages.

The aim of this chapter is to review the problems with sonority and to consider an alternative which has been proposed: acoustic-auditory recoverability. There is no novelty in arguing for an acoustic-auditory basis for observed cross-linguistic preferences in segment sequences, as the references in the section on acoustic-auditory recoverability show. However, previous advocates of acoustic-auditory recoverability have taken either a phonetic stance (e.g., Kawasaki 1982) or a phonological stance (e.g., Steriade 1999), and approached the issue of segment sequencing from a more acoustic (Kawasaki 1982) or a more auditory perspective (Wright 2004). This chapter aims at a synthesis of these views. An acoustic-auditory recoverability approach denies the syllable a role in motivating cross-linguistic preferences in segment sequencing, and that view is supported here. Nevertheless, arguments are presented to show that the syllable retains its importance as a unit of production and perception at the level of the individual, at least for speakers of some languages.

Section 20.2 below discusses problems with sonority and its role in syllabification. Section 20.3 examines different approaches to segment sequencing preferences within the framework of acoustic-auditory recoverability. Section 20.4 discusses the sources of cross-linguistic variation. Section 20.5 summarizes the arguments and evaluates the role that syllables play at a segmental level in speech production and speech perception.

20.2 The Problems with Sonority

Sonority exists to explain – some would say 'to describe' – recurring cross-linguistic patterns in segment organization, particularly in monosyllabic words or at word-margins. For example, in two unrelated languages like English and Lakhota, words may begin with sequences of a fricative plus lateral, e.g., English 'slow', Lakhota *sló* 'to be soft' (Ullrich 2011), but words in these languages may not begin with sequences of lateral plus fricative, e.g., [lso]. These sequencing preferences are not due to simple coincidence, since they are found across much wider samples of languages (e.g., Greenberg 1978). By analysing patterns within and across languages, a sonority hierarchy can be established, ranking segments in terms of their sequencing relative to the nucleus. A widely-used sonority hierarchy is given in (1), where sonority increases from left to right (i.e., as in syllable onset to syllable nucleus/sonority peak).

(1) Obstruent < Nasal < Liquid < Approximant < Vowel

The conventional account of the English and Lakhota words 'slow' and *sló* is that obstruents and laterals differ in sonority, and the less sonorous obstruents must be more peripheral than laterals to satisfy the rise-fall sonority profile of the syllable. A sequence like [lso] would run counter to the sonority hierarchy, and is for this reason dispreferred.

A major problem with sonority is the circularity in its usage (Ohala 1992: 320). In the absence of an independent definition, it is only the position of a segment relative to the syllable nucleus which determines the sonority value of that segment. If the sonority value of segments is then used to also 'explain' the position of the segment relative to the nucleus, a circular argument results, as in (2) below.

(2) [s] precedes [l] because [s] is less sonorous than [l], and [s] is less sonorous than [l] because [s] precedes [l].

In the absence of an independent definition of sonority, whatever that might be, the rank ordering of segments is not just based on circularity, but is in some cases unclear. The hierarchy in (1) is not the only sonority hierarchy to be proposed, and although the essential elements remain the same, variants typically differ in separating out and ranking fricatives and plosives, and in the level of detail within categories, i.e., whether voiced and voiceless fricatives should have the same rank, or open (low) and closed (high) vowels. Observation of some languages demonstrates that some segments may be ordered in more than one way relative to each other, e.g., English 'axe' with a final [ks] and 'ask' with a final [sk]. If sonority must fall through the coda, then the relationship between [k] and [s] in these words is problematic: neither appears to be more sonorous (i.e., more peripheral within the syllable) than the other. Here the segments appear to follow the sonority hierarchy in (1) and since both [s] and [k] can be final in the syllable, neither is more sonorous than the other – there is a sonority plateau, rather than a fall. Sonority plateaus have not received widespread acceptance, mainly because of the insistence on a rise-fall sonority profile across the syllable, a pattern which must itself be motivated and explained. Potential sonority plateaus have been analysed in other ways, as discussed below.

Most attempts to provide a physical basis for sonority focus on two aspects: (i) loudness (or its acoustic correlate in intensity) and (ii) vocal tract opening, particularly jaw height (e.g., Lindblom 1983). The two parameters of intensity and vocal tract opening are not completely independent, since in general a more open vocal tract results in a more efficient and therefore more intense transmission of sound energy. This relationship is not straightforward, however. As Keating (1983) notes, at very narrow constrictions of the vocal tract very intense high frequency aperiodic noise sources like frication in [s] can be produced. In any event, neither jaw height/constriction nor intensity present a lifeline for sonority. Constriction degree varies not just across manners but also across places of articulation (Keating 1983), complicating the sonority hierarchy. Intensity also varies within the traditional manner-based ranks of the sonority hierarchy, making the grouping of sounds within the ranks problematic. For example, sibilant fricatives like [s] and [ʃ] have much higher intensities than non-sibilant fricatives like [f] and [θ], and on the other hand, open vowels like [ɑ] and [a] are higher in intensity than [i] and [u] (this was recognized in Jespersen's version of the sonority hierarchy, see Clements 1990: 285). Indeed, [s] and [ʃ] may often be as intense as a vowel, giving rise to the classic problem that a word like 'stop' may have two intensity peaks, one for the [s] and one for the vowel.

Intensity poses a further problem for the sonority approach if surface segments, i.e., (allo)phones, are considered. The very idea of a physical basis for sonority in speech suggests that an abstract definition of manner classes at a phonemic level will not suffice. For example, the English word 'trip' is analysed phonemically as /trɪp/, and would be considered on this basis to fulfil the requirements for a rise-fall pattern in sonority since the word runs obstruent-liquid-vowel-obstruent. At the phonetic level, things become more complex. In terms of constriction degree, there may be no difference between the /r/ in 'trip' and the /r/ in 'drip', but the aerodynamic conditions and voicing are different. In 'trip', the wide abduction of the vocal folds at the release of the plosive results in a high volume-velocity of airflow during the /r/, creating a fricative realization. Figure 20.1 shows intensity curves for the words 'drip' (left) and 'trip' (right) from five repetitions of the words as produced by the author. The intensity curves for 'drip' show one peak in the vowel but there are two peaks in the intensity curves for 'trip', one for the fricative allophone of /r/ and one for the vowel; the devoicing of /r/ makes 'trip' effectively like a word with an initial [s]-plosive sequence like 'stop', a more infamous problem for sonority. Considering physical patterns in phonetics means that the attention must focus on the characteristics of the contextual realizations of those phonemes, i.e., the

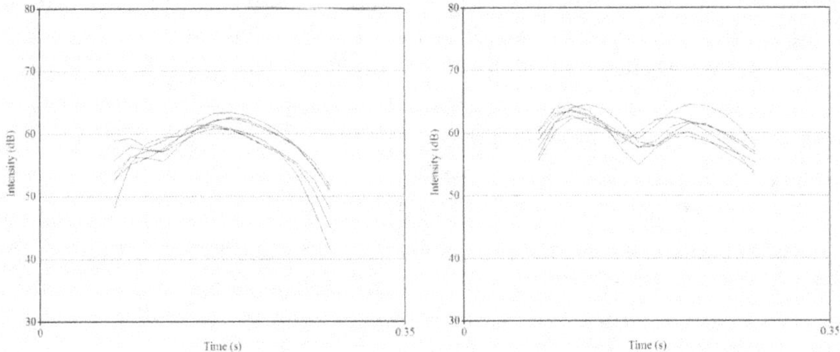

Figure 20.1. Intensity curves for five repetitions of the words 'drip' (left) and 'trip' (right) as produced by the author. The curves were generated in Praat from a 350 ms window left-aligned 55 ms before the plosive release in the waveform; as the VOT was longer in 'trip', the 350 ms intensity curves end before the closure for the final /p/. The 'drip' curves show a single peak, albeit with a less than smooth rise because of the plosive release. The 'trip' curves show two peaks of similar intensity, one for the fricated allophone of /r/ and one for the vowel.

allophones, rather than on broadly defined manner classes of phonemes (if a definition of manner is even possible in an abstract entity like a phoneme). Approaches to sonority which define it in terms of subsegmental Distinctive Features or structure (e.g., Rice 1992) merely relegate the explanation for cross-linguistic similarities in segment sequences to another (often equally disputed) area of investigation.

Two experimental approaches to sonority have attempted to investigate the characteristics segments show when their syllable position varies. Price (1980) used synthetic stimuli to investigate the percept of syllabicity (here taken to equate with degree of sonority, since the most syllabic element should be the most sonorous). She found that a change in segment intensity was not necessary to trigger the perception of originally monosyllabic words like 'prayed' and 'blow' as disyllables 'parade' and 'below'. In 'prayed' Price changed the duration of the /r/ and in 'blow' she changed the voice onset time (VOT) of the plosive. Neither duration nor VOT is considered a carrier of sonority: indeed, a longer VOT might even be seen as making the /b/ less sonorous in 'below' than in 'blow' because longer-lag VOTs are seen in voiceless aspirated plosives. In another study, Bell and Saka (1983) investigated the phonetic realization of clusters in Pashto, which has a series of cluster pairs at various points in the hierarchy, one of which is legally sonorous and the other has the reverse 'illegal' ordering of segments, e.g., legal [ml] in /mla/ 'friend (feminine singular)' versus illegal

[lm] in /lmar/ 'sun', or (at a different point in the hierarchy) legal [lw] in /lwaɻ/ 'coarse' versus illegal [wl] in /wlaɻ/ 'he went'. Bell and Saka found that amplitude increased gradually throughout all but one ([lm]) of the clusters investigated, suggesting that the rise-fall 'loudness' of a syllable is independent of the segment sequencing and that segments may vary as to their physical characteristics (cf. Laks 1995).

Phonologists have long recognized that sonority by itself cannot explain all the segmental patterns seen in syllables. On the one hand, there is the universal problem of VCV sequences, where the two vowels constitute sonority peaks and the consonant a trough in sonority. The sequence could be syllabified as VC.V (where . marks the syllable boundary), making the intervocalic consonant a coda to the first syllable, or as V.CV, making the consonant the onset to the second syllable. Two further possibilities exist: one in which the consonant is both coda and onset (i.e., ambisyllabic), and one in which the consonant is unsyllabified. The usual practice is to treat a word-medial intervocalic consonant as an onset, i.e. to maximize onsets and to syllabify VCV as V.CV. The maximization of onsets is not explained within the theory of sonority, since both VC and CV may function adequately to give the rise-fall pattern, but must be stipulated on the basis of the unmotivated cross-linguistic preference for CV structures and a general dispreference for or restrictions on VC units. Onset maximization may be defied, however, in cases where language-specific constraints come into play, and this leads to the other problem for sonority: cross-linguistic variation.

Cross-linguistic variation in sub-syllabic segment sequences runs counter to the idea of a universal sonority hierarchy, and it is not possible to vary sonority rankings across languages (or within languages, cf. /r/ in 'drip' versus 'trip' or the Pashto data above). Instead, languages may stipulate a minimum sonority distance between adjacent segments (the Dispersion Principle, Clements 1990: 302), so that, e.g., English may allow clusters of sounds separated by two places along the sonority hierarchy, whereas other languages may only allow clusters separated by one place. Once again, this stipulation requires further motivation, and it also rests on a proper and agreed conceptualization of the sonority hierarchy itself. Another way in which cross-linguistic variation in segment sequences may be accommodated is by using additional constraints on segments, e.g., place co-restrictions, or by allowing sonority to apply to segment sequences at some underlying level of analysis but not on the phonetic surface, effectively allowing troublesome segments to remain outside the syllable, or 'extrasyllabic'.

The extrasyllabic approach is the one often taken to deal with problem cases like the [s]-plosive onsets in English words like 'scar, skin, score'. Within a data-based approach and given the uncertainty over the sonority hierarchy, it might appear that [s] is less sonorous than the voiceless unaspirated [k] in such cases. In codas, however, both [s] and [k] may appear in either order, e.g., 'ask, axe', and also in bimorphemic forms such as 'packs', indicating that neither [s] nor [k] is more sonorous than the other. The extrasyllabic approach would exclude [s] from the level of 'core syllabification' in onsets in words like 'scar' and from codas in words like 'axe', with 'ask' having a legitimate coda. Even if the possibility of simply excluding problem cases is regarded as valid in itself, it should be clear how reliant such an approach is upon the idea of the sonority hierarchy and the unmotivated notion of the fall-rise pattern of sonority within syllables. Again, while this additional machinery may produce the correct results, it is unmotivated, however coherently it is applied within the framework of sonority itself.

There also exist a range of patterns which should be legally sonorous in onsets (as their mirror-images should be in codas, although Clements 1990: 300 claims that the sonority fall from the peak should be minimal) but which are nevertheless extremely rare. These patterns involve consonant-consonant sequences, such as [dl], [bm], [bw], [tj] as well as consonant-vowel sequences like [wu, ji]. The relative rarity of these patterns is usually explained using the place co-occurrence constraints or the versions of Clements' Dispersion Principle.

Finally, Blevins (2003) has shown that the same segment sequences are found across languages even if those languages vary in how the sequences are syllabified. For example, in both Klamath and Lithuanian, the voicing contrast appears in V-stop-sonorant-V sequences, even though in Klamath these sequences are syllabified as V.CCV, whereas in Lithuanian these sequences are syllabified VC.CV (Blevins 2003: 376–9). These cases and others demonstrate that sonority sequencing appears to apply with no regard for the syllable, and that the requirement for rise-fall sequences in sonority can be regarded instead as a characteristic of segments, regardless of the syllables to which the segments belong.

In sum, it can be seen that sonority faces several very real challenges to its suitability as a motivating factor in explaining segmental sequencing preferences and determining syllable structure. Aside from its lack of definition, and circularity, sonority by itself fails to explain the existence of some apparently 'illegal' sequences, while at the same time predicting other perfectly legal sequences which are in reality very rare. Sonority also fails to motivate the CV structure seen across almost all of the world's languages (see below), which must be stipulated to account for VCV patterns of syllabification. To deal with these problems, complex and problematic additional machinery is required, often with questionable independent motivation. Part of the problem, no doubt, is the insistence on the fall-rise sonority profile within syllables. This fall-rise profile is also unmotivated, and seems to be informed by partial preconceptions about the basis of sonority in loudness/intensity or articulatory openness/jaw height before such a basis is proven. An additional factor in problematizing sonority lies in the attempt to make sonority a vehicle to explain cross-linguistic parallels as well as accounting for language-specific differences. Sonority is forced into this position because its proponents adhere to the view that segment characteristics are universally defined. In light of these problems, it is hardly surprising that sonority fails, but rather more surprising that it persists as the current and most widespread approach to segment sequencing preferences.

What if there were one principle which could provide a testable and independently motivated explanation for all of these issues? Even if theory-internal arguments are accepted for place constraints, minimal ranking distances, extrasyllabicity and variation in the levels at which sonority applies, would it not make sense to unify a great many phenomena by recasting the notion of sonority, if possible, and by discarding it if not? There is one such principle: the principle of acoustic-auditory recoverability, and this will be the topic of the next section.

20.3 Acoustic-Auditory Recoverability

The acoustic-auditory recoverability approach can best be introduced by tackling two issues that sonority cannot address by itself: the problematic occurrence of the 'illegally sonorous' [st]-like sequences and the equally problematic rarity of sequences like [bw, ji, bm] which show sonority-legal 'rises'. As described above, sonority must invoke additional machinery to account for these exceptions. Acoustic-auditory recoverability explains both patterns in terms of the degree of modulation of the acoustic signal and the preservation of acoustic cues to segment identity. Both acoustic and auditory factors matter because acoustic events are processed in a non-linear way by the peripheral auditory system. For example, low frequency acoustic information is expanded in an auditory sense, while high frequency information is compressed, as shown by the Bark and ERB (equivalent rectangular bandwidth) scales (e.g., Johnson 2012: 82–99; for a brief overview of the relevant auditory theory, see Wright 2004: 42–6).

Figure 20.2 shows the words 'we' and 'ye' as produced by the author. The top panel shows the pressure waveform from the microphone, and below that is a time-aligned spectrogram. Below the spectrogram is a cochleagram, a visual representation of how the linear acoustic signal might be interpreted in a non-linear way by the peripheral auditory system, with the frequency bands here expressed in Bark. Spectrographically, the rise in F2 from the [w] into the [i] in the commonly-occurring [wi] sequence is very clear, whereas the absence of any similar spectral transitions in the cross-linguistically rare [ji] sequence is also apparent. Regarding the waveforms, the [ji] sequence does show more amplitude modulation as F2 strengthens into the vowel, but this is relatively minor, and a similar dip in amplitude – presumably due to an irrelevant source effect – can be seen part-way through the vowel in [wi] where it does not result in the percept of a change in segment. In the cochleagram, the higher frequencies are compressed while the lower frequencies are expanded, and here too the lack of modulation in the [ji] is clear. The [wi] sequence should therefore be robust and be effectively transmitted. The [ji] sequence, on the other hand, is likely to be misperceived as [i] (Ohala 1992: 323). Across languages, [ji] sequences appear to be dispreferred because they are prone to reanalysis and lost over time.

Figure 20.3 shows a similar waveform-spectrogram-cochleagram representation for the word 'star' produced by the author (non-rhotic accent). The large-scale spectral and amplitude changes are evident in both the spectrogram and in the waveform. The word begins with high-intensity high-frequency frication (aperiodicity) for the [s], there is then a period of near-silence apart from some weak excitation 5,000–6,000 Hz during the 'closure'[3] period for the [t], and then a transient as oral pressure is released, followed by a relatively short-lag Voice Onset Time and the appearance of a strong formant structure which dominates the frequency regions below 5,000 Hz. In the cochleagram, the non-linear effect of auditory processing is seen both in the compression of the frication and in the separation of F1 and F2 between 5 and 10 Bark in the vowel. The consonant sequence and the vowel occupy almost complementary frequency regions: [st] dominates the high frequencies, and [ɑ] dominates the low frequencies. The [st] sequence shows a very robust modulation of the signal relative to the vowel, and therefore it will be transmitted intact and preserved over time (Wright 2004: 50).

3 The presence of low-amplitude frication suggests that closure was incomplete – perhaps some medial grooving of the tongue for the [s] persisted into the [t] articulation.

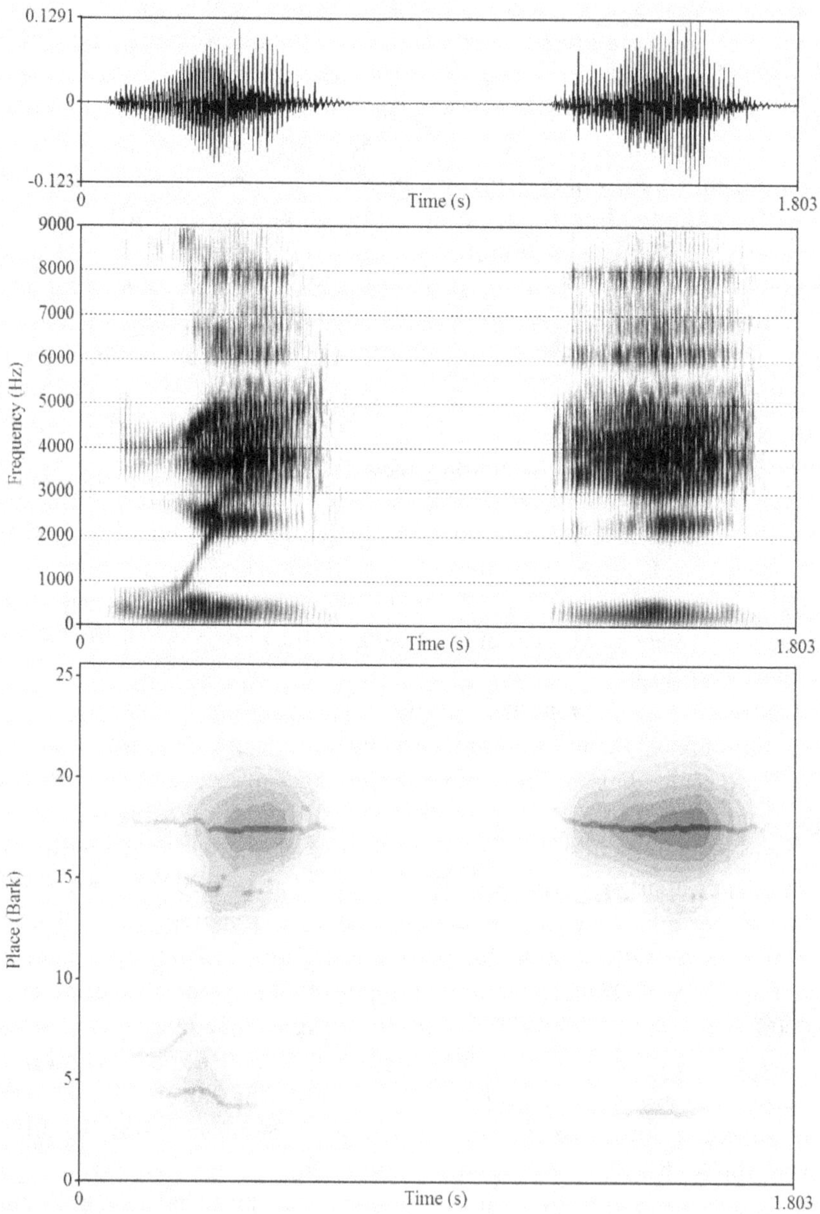

Figure 20.2. A waveform (top), spectrogram (middle), and cochleagram (bottom) of the words 'we' [wi] and 'ye' [ji] as spoken by the author, all generated in Praat (the spectrogram has a dynamic range of 30 dB/Hz with a maximum of 70 dB).

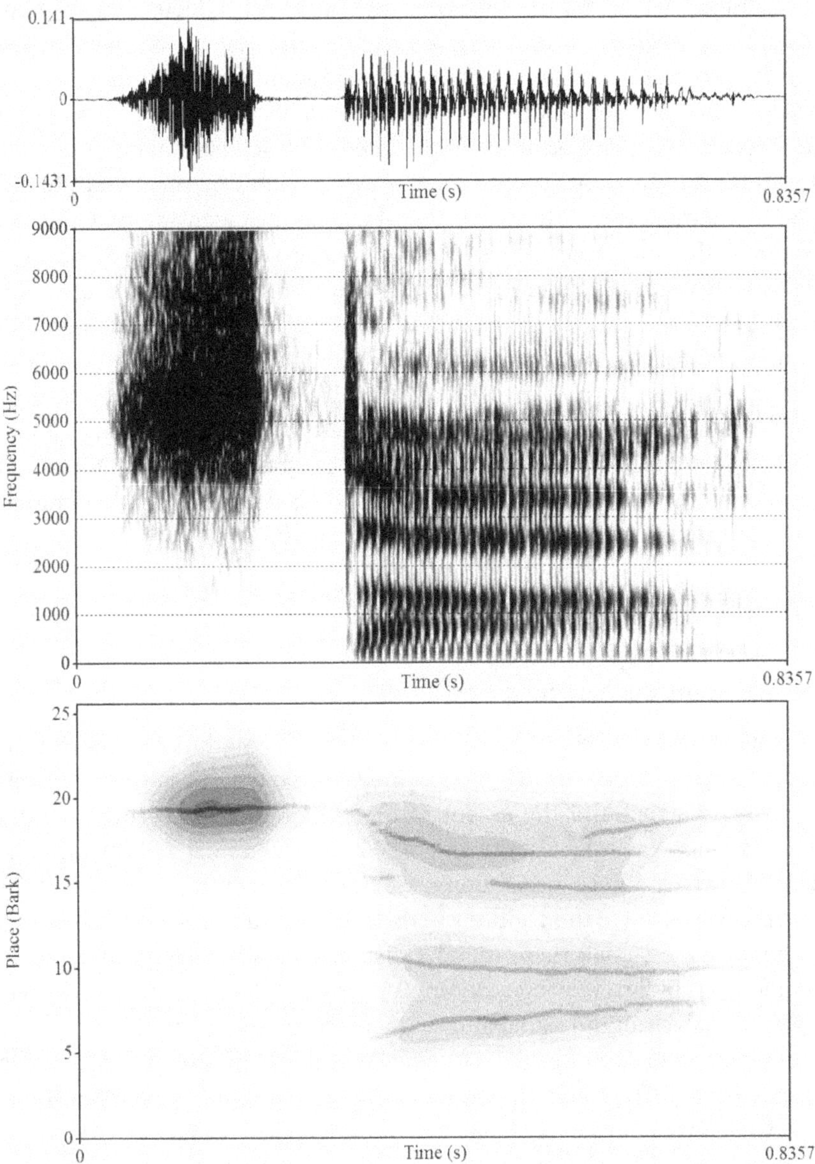

Figure 20.3. A waveform (top), spectrogram (middle), and cochleagram (bottom) of the word 'star' [stɑː] as spoken by the author, all generated in Praat (the spectrogram has a dynamic range of 30 dB/Hz with a maximum of 70 dB).

The idea of the robust encoding of speech as a factor in segment sequencing preferences is not new and is found elsewhere, even in the sonority literature. Clements (1990: 297) comments on the importance of perceptibility, as does Lindblom (1983) in his jaw-related approach to segment-sequencing, and Keating (1983) mentions acoustic parameters like F1 and high frequency spectral energy as correlates of vocal-tract openness. In a similar vein, Steriade (1999) talks about Licensing by Cue, and essentially the same approach is taken by Blevins (2003), though the idea of 'cue' here is vague. Hudson (1995) views the release as a relevant element. Harris (2006) also regards signal modulation as the primary determinant of segment sequencing preferences.

There is more to the acoustic-auditory recoverability approach than simple visual inspection of spectrograms, etc. Aspects of the signal can be picked out and changes or differences can be quantified. Ohala and Kawasaki-Fukumori (1997: 349) consider (at least) four acoustic parameters as the basis for robust encoding of the signal:

1. amplitude
2. periodicity
3. spectral shape
4. F0 (fundamental frequency)

Ohala and Kawasaki-Fukumori's parameters for modulation and robust encoding are all relatively concrete – they can be measured directly from the acoustic signal and the extent of inter-segmental differences can be quantified, as Kawaski (1982) and Kawasaki-Fukumori (1992) demonstrate. However, these parameters are not considered in the auditory dimension, and since the auditory system imposes a non-linear transform on the acoustic signal, there may be discrepancies between the acoustic and auditory effects. An acoustic-only approach is likely to present a conservative analysis of the signal and to underestimate most of the transition effects encountered rather than to overestimate them, except perhaps for the case of high-frequency spectral changes in sequences of sibilant fricatives, which are in any event very rare.

Wright (2004: 35) integrates this basically acoustic approach into a consideration of non-linear auditory characteristics relevant to the peripheral processing of the acoustic signal (following Bladon 1986; see also Greenberg 1996: 398–9) and gives the following list of parameters which in his view characterize a robust encoding of segments:

1. redundancy of cues
2. auditory impact

3. perceptual distance
4. resistance to environmental masking

Wright (2004: 50) reviews a number of common sequences in terms of his criteria. For example, sequences like CV, CGV (consonant-glide (approximant)-vowel) and CLV (consonant-liquid-vowel) will all result in a boost to the auditory nerve fibres, cue redundancy and significant perceptual distance between segments, and this is why they recur across languages. The Wright (2004) parameters are more difficult to quantify than the Ohala-Kawasaki parameters: cue redundancy and perceptual distance will be language-specific evaluations within a particular system (see below on cross-linguistic variation), and while auditory impact and resistance to environmental masking are more objective criteria, they are also not directly available in the acoustic signal itself. Wright's mixed approach shares some characteristics with sonority in that it attempts to represent both cross-linguistic patterns and language-specific patterns within the same framework. In essence, this is no bad thing: any patterns which persist in an individual language must be robustly transmitted. However, the difficulty of evaluating the impact of specific aspects of the signal and the likelihood of cross-linguistic variation in the appreciation of cues means that the Ohala-Kawasaki methodology must be considered not only more practical but more germane to the issue of cross-linguistic tendencies.

The use of multiple parameters echoes the views presented in Nathan (1989), Malsch and Fulcher (1989) and Clements (1990: 297–8), that sonority could also be defined in terms of more than one parameter, but the acoustic-auditory recoverability approach goes further in actually identifying measurable properties of the signal which could be examined, and in relating these to perceptual mechanisms and the successful transmission of speech in sound change. In utilizing insights from research into auditory processing, the primacy of onsets and CV units follows from the response of the auditory nerve (Wright 2004). The difficulties of perceiving codas could drive speakers towards articulatory organizations which allow minimal gestural overlap within coda consonants themselves, and extensive anticipatory coarticulation to maximize the availability of redundant cues (Ohala and Kawaski-Fukumori 1997; Wright 2004). In turn, recoverability of cues could motivate observed patterns of gestural organization in VC units (e.g., Krakow 1999; Nam, Goldstein and Saltzman 2009). However, auditory responses and acoustic modulation are, on the face of it, just as universal as the putative sonority hierarchy was intended to be. How then do cross-linguistic differences arise? The following section addresses this issue.

20.4 Cross-Linguistic Variation

Cross-linguistic patterns in segment sequencing provide the basis for generalizations but as is well-known, not all languages show the same patterns. Some languages, like Hawai'ian, have a strictly consonant-vowel structure whereas others allow complex sequences of consonants, and even words which lack overt vowels entirely, e.g., Bella Coola [qstχ] 'pull it off' (Bagemihl 1991: 592). To be taken seriously, any principles which claim to have universal roots, i.e., to be based on shared human aspects of speech production or speech perception or on innate grammatical structures, must also allow in a plausible and coherent way for exceptions and variation. This is as much a prerequisite for acoustic-auditory recoverability as it is for sonority. As set out above, sonority attempted to account for cross-linguistic variation by claiming constraints on sonority slopes, e.g., how many 'steps' between permitted tautosyllabic sequences, or by varying how different languages judged non-conforming segments to be extrasyllabic at an underlying level of representation, e.g., Hall (2002). These approaches were criticized as being otherwise unmotivated. How can cross-linguistic variation be accommodated within a theory based on acoustic transitions and the responses of the human auditory system?

Three sources of cross-linguistic variation in segment sequencing are identified here. The first concerns cross-linguistic variation in the acoustic transitions themselves. The second concerns differences across languages in the perceptual weighting of various acoustic events (cues). The third concerns an issue which has been hinted at in previous accounts: not all segment sequences are due to the direct operation of acoustic-auditory recoverability constraints. This latter point requires particularly careful consideration, since the exclusion of segment sequences from the principles of acoustic-auditory recoverability could be abused in a way similar to extrasyllabicity for simply purging the data of troublesome cases. Each of these ideas is discussed in turn. It is crucial to appreciate that these explanations are rooted in independent observations and that they are, in principle at least, testable in the laboratory.

The cross-linguistic comparison of languages involves the phone or segment – a unit of sound which is defined per the IPA in fairly gross articulatory-acoustic terms. A voiceless bilabial plosive [p], for example, is defined by a period of complete constriction to airflow at the lips with the velum raised and an absence of vocal fold vibration during the constriction phase. Other aspects of the sound – the duration of the constriction, the amplitude of the burst, the rate of vibration of the vocal folds at voice onset

– are immaterial to its classification as [p], in much the same way that two humans may differ in weight, height, skin and hair colour, etc. Within these gross categories there is therefore considerable room for phonetic variation. Some of this variation may be due to systematic differences in vocal tract morphology across sexes, races or age groups, or due to tangible and testable aerodynamic effects, say, altitude above sea-level and subglottal pressure (e.g., Jones 2013). Other aspects of variation may be systemic in nature, i.e., motivated by the need to contrast particular phones and not others within a language system. One example is of the relatively high amplitude in Ewe [f] compared with English [f]: Ewe contrasts [f] with a voiceless bilabial fricative [ɸ] and under systemic pressure to keep distinct, Ewe speakers produce [f] with a higher amplitude than [ɸ]-less English speakers do (Utman and Blumstein 1994). Other similar effects may be harder to explain but nevertheless exist: liquids show different patterns of F2 variation across accents (Carter and Local 2007; McDougall and Jones 2011), and semi-vowels have also been observed to show different patterns of formant structure and coarticulation across languages (Maddieson and Emmorey 1985). However these patterns are ultimately explained, the same transition between segments, e.g., [lja], may vary across languages. One source of cross-linguistic differences in segment sequencing preferences could be due to the fact that acoustic modulations may therefore vary in degree and temporal extent across languages for systemic (i.e., language-specific) reasons.

Perceptual differences are also a possible source of cross-linguistic variation. Any phone or segment is a complex articulatory event involving the coordination of numerous muscle groups and aerodynamic parameters. The result is itself a complex acoustic event, with multiple spectral changes depending not only on the segment itself but also on its precise context. Speakers of different languages can be hypothesized to use different cues for the same segment, and even to weight the same cues differently in terms of its perceptual importance. Speakers of a language with a strict CV structure may only need to attend to Voice Onset Time (VOT) to differentiate [p] from [pʰ], but in a language with more complex sequences including a voicing contrast, including plosives produced without audible release, VOT may be only one of a group of cues which are used to differentiate the same segments. Dalcher, Knight and Jones (2008) argued that F3 was differently weighted across British English and American English speakers in their perception of the [ɹ]-[w] contrast. Harnsberger (2001) showed that perceptual differences between the same nasal segments [m, n̪, n, ɳ, ɲ, ŋ] were structured very differently between speakers of different languages, suggesting that cue-weighting varied between languages. Even within languages, cue-weighting may vary for different listeners (Hazan and Boulakia 1993). Given the complexity of the acoustic signal and the need to process variation in cues across contexts, it is hardly surprising that variation occurs. It is therefore likely that some differences in segment sequencing constraints arise from differences in the perceptual flexibility and 'attentiveness' of listeners.

An explanation for language-specific effects in patterns arising outside the domain of acoustic-auditory recoverability constraints is the most troublesome source of cross-linguistic variation, and also the one that has received the least attention in previous accounts. Excluding patterns from consideration within the framework of acoustic-auditory recoverability may appear to be nothing more than a sleight of hand aimed at eliminating problem cases. For this reason, it must be invoked with care. One case involves the patterning of /j/ across English accents. In many accents of British English, /tj, dj, nj/ and even occasionally /lj/ are attested in onsets before /u/. In American English, the range of /Cj/ sequences is smaller, and /tj, dj/ and also /nj/ may be absent before /u/. In East Anglian English, the range of /Cj/ sequences is at its smallest, and /bj, pj/ are generally absent before /u/ (Wells 1982: 206–7, 330–1, 338–9, 412, 489, 496, 618; Cruttenden 2001: 212). The absence of /j/ in these cases seems ultimately to derive from the application of acoustic-auditory recoverability to sequences with a palatal or alveolopalatal component since this is the sequence which is absent across most accents. In this case, the high F2 of the palatal or alveolopalatal consonant preceding the /j/ could not be distinguished from the F2 of the /j/, analogous to the [ji] example above. This original pattern of /j/-loss has been extended first to sequences of alveolar+/j/, which may also be explicable in terms of the high F2 associated both with alveolars and with a [j], but its eventual persistence into contexts after non-lingual consonants like /b/ must be seen as a purely analogical extension. It is notable that the CV sequence /ju/ is still permitted in these accents, so the constraint appears to operate on /Cj/ sequences, not on /ju/. Another possible factor in variation across accents and the development of this pattern is the 'fronting' of /u/ from historical [u] with its very non-[j]-like low F2 to a more [ɨ]-like or even [i]-like realization with a higher F2 (Cruttenden 2001: 123; Harrington, Kleber and Reubold: 2011; Chládková and Hamann 2011). If the historical /u/ vowel had already fronted, this would make the [j] transitions from the preceding /Cj/ sequence even less distinct, even after /b/ etc. These dialect-specific features are obviously irrelevant to a wider theory of segment sequencing (although acoustic-auditory recoverability may have played a role in its origins), and conversely, a theory of segment sequencing need not apply to them.

The three sources of cross-linguistic variation discussed here are all compatible with the acoustic-auditory recoverability approach, and in each case they can be verified by phonetic analysis of data from speech production, by speech perception experiments, or looked at from a historical-comparative approach. Encoding and decoding segment sequences is a complex task, and since speech is behaviour rooted in physics and biology, some variation is expected. As Wright (2004) points out, redundancy enhances the robustness of the signal. What counts as redundant can obviously vary. An approach to segment sequencing which is rooted in the phonetic surface predicts variation, unlike the rigid sonority approach.

20.5 Syllables and Segment Sequences – What and Where?

The acoustic-auditory recoverability approach to segment sequencing works without reference to the syllable with its alleged rise-fall 'sonority cycle', as has been made clear by Ohala (1992, 1998, 2008), Ohala and Kawasaki (1997), Steriade (1999) in her idea of 'segmental autonomy', and Blevins (2003) in her string-based approach. Since there is no fall-rise, there is no peak; all that is needed is sufficient modulation between successive segments. The most extreme modulation is one between consonants and vowels (Wright 2004). The differing nature of these speech sounds results in transitions which are optimally robust for the auditory system to use.[4] Put another way, CV units are not about syllables – they are about segments.

This raises questions about the existence of syllables and whether the principles behind segment sequencing preferences should be located within an individual's grammar. Ohala (1998, 2008) makes the point that syllables are emergent units, although he recognizes elsewhere that they also provide a locus for prosodic information like stress and tone (Ohala

4 There may also be a role for cyclical movements of the mandible in both the ontogenetic and phylogenetic development of speech, as argued by MacNeilage (1998), Davis and MacNeilage (2002) and MacNeilage and Davis (2002), but Greenberg (1996) makes the point that the human auditory system differs little compared with other mammalian auditory systems whereas the human vocal tract is very different even from our closest non-human primate relatives – we can expect therefore that audition shaped speech production capabilities during the evolution of speech and language.

and Kawasaki 1984). Blevins (2003) shares the view that the syllable is an unnecessary unit for determining segmental sequences, but she also makes the case for syllables as multi-functional units. Vowels are useful units for prosodic information because they are ideal to carry the F0 modulations needed for tone and stress, so the two strands of what is traditionally viewed as syllable structure – prosody and phonotactics – align by accident, rather than by design. In some languages with weight-sensitive stress patterns, this alignment is closer than in others (e.g., Gordon 2004). Those languages which are argued to have no unambiguous need for syllables on prosodic grounds (Gokana: Hyman 2011) would also not require syllables on segmental grounds.

If segment sequencing arises externally to language through the filter of acoustic-auditory recoverability, there is no need for speakers to encode its principles in any kind of phonological representation. In some ways, this is parallel to sonority, since Clements (1990) and others attempted to derive sonority rankings of segments not through the use of some specific multivalued Distinctive Feature, but by viewing rankings as indirectly encoded in subsegmental structure. An attempt has been made to encode some aspects of acoustic-auditory recoverability in an Optimality Theoretic framework (see, e.g., Steriade 1999; Blevins 2003; Flemming 2004) and could work in approaches to subsegmental structure if acoustic-auditory factors were represented.

Even if these principles remain outside a speaker's cognitive representation of speech and language, language-specific patterns of segment sequences shape perceptual strategies and speech production routines. A growing knowledge of phonotactic regularities seems to play a role in child language acquisition. Infants quickly focus on perceptual cues which are relevant to the contrasts in the ambient language (e.g., Jusczyk and Luce 1994), and in mature speakers loanword adaptation sees a role for segmentation strategies that give preference to native patterns of cues (e.g., Adler 2006). It has even been argued that native-like segment sequencing patterns lead to the perceptual illusions of epenthetic vowels in the signal, even if such vowels were not physically present (Dupoux et al., 1999).[5] In

5 However, Kabak and Idsardi (2007) have suggested that the presence of these vowels does represent a role for the syllable in Korean. Their experiments used sequences of consonants which included legal codas but in illegal sequences, since the codas should have undergone manner assimilation, in addition to sequences that were simply illegal in all respects. Subjects' performance differed between these two conditions, suggesting a role for the syllable over and above simple parsing of segment sequences.

speech production, again, although there are cross-linguistic similarities in how some non-native sequences in loanwords are produced, presumably due to the shared capabilities of vocal tract structure, there are also patterns which reflect language-specific constraints. These constraints may arise in heavily routinized articulatory control strategies. For example, Davidson (2006, 2010) shows that in producing non-native sequences there are some aspects of articulation which seem due to shared human characteristics because they recur across speakers of different languages, but there are also language-specific patterns which arise from familiarity with producing certain sequences.

There is no need to posit a template or any other structure which requires the fall-rise pattern in sonority. Instead, sequences evolve where the transition is robust enough to be perceived, and this gives preference to onsets and CV structures in which the transitions are maximally distinct. Sequences like [st] persist – once they have evolved in the first place – because the sequence produces robust modulations, whereas sequences like [ji] or [bw] or [bm] are likely to be misperceived and reanalysed; again, once they have evolved. Vowels are not essential to this approach, and as languages like Bella Coola show, even quite complex sequences can persist with no need for vowels. The dispreference for VC units can be seen as the outcome of auditory pressure to perceive transitions with reference to following segments, and the less tightly coordinated and more coarticulated nature of any 'coda' consonants (e.g., Krakow 1999; Nam et al. 2009) can be viewed as the need to structure segmental overlap so that cues are maximally clear and redundant in view of these auditory predispositions. An acoustic-auditory approach can even be used to explain the apparent absence of supposedly universal CV units in some Australian languages (e.g., Sommer 1970): in those languages, the high prevalence of retroflex consonants with their heavily weighted VC cues (Steriade 1999) results in a perception and production preference for VC units (Tabain, Breen and Butcher 2004). Segui and Ferrand (2002) review some psycholinguistic evidence that suggests variable roles for syllable-units in lexical access and speech processing. The syllable may be an emergent unit which does not fulfil the same roles in every language, but once it exists for them, speakers do seem to make use of it.

20.6 Conclusions

Sonority has always been a problematic notion, and even accepting that it may be defined in terms of multiple parameters, it still requires a large amount of additional machinery to cope with cross-linguistically occurring segment sequences. Some of this machinery is relevant to language-specific patterns, but much of it is required to make sonority work across many languages. Even if this machinery and the assumptions behind it are accepted as valid, a single solution which does not require that machinery presents a more parsimonious account, and if that solution is testable and founded upon an independent basis, as the acoustic-auditory recoverability approach is, it becomes a strong contender to replace sonority as the determinant of segment sequencing preferences (phonotactics).

It is argued here that acoustic-auditory recoverability governs the diachronic selection of segment sequences such that robustly encoded sequences are transmitted effectively and persist while weakly encoded sequences are reanalysed. Syllables are not relevant here, and cross-linguistic variation, i.e., language-specific patterns, emerges because there are language-specific differences in implementation in order to distinguish system-internal contrasts, and because there are multiple cues at any segment transition so that speakers may not select the same cues (or weight them the same way) across languages. It is seen here as unnecessary to encode the principles of acoustic-auditory recoverability into the phonological representation, and even the concept of the syllable may be unnecessary in some languages. Nevertheless, just as there is more to syllables than just segment sequencing, so there is also more to segment sequencing than just syllables.

References

Adler, A.N. (2006). Faithfulness and perception in loanword adaptation: A case study from Hawaiian. *Lingua*, 116, 1024–45.

Bagemihl, B. (1991). Syllable structure in Bella Coola. *Linguistic Inquiry*, 22, 589–646.

Bell, A. and Saka, M.M. (1983). Reversed sonority in Pashto initial clusters. *Journal of Phonetics*, 11, 259–75.

Bladon, A. (1986). Phonetics for hearers. In G. McGregor (ed.), *Language for hearers* (pp. 1–24). Oxford: Pergamon Press.

Blevins, J. (1995). The syllable in phonological theory. In J. Goldsmith (ed.) *The handbook of phonological theory* (pp. 206–44). Oxford: Blackwell.

Blevins, J. (2003). The independent nature of phonotactic constraints: An alternative to syllable-based approaches. In C. Féry and R. van de Vijver (eds.), *The syllable in optimality theory* (pp. 375–403). Cambridge: Cambridge University Press.

Carter, P. and Local, J. (2007). F2 variation in Newcastle and Leeds English liquid systems. *Journal of the International Phonetic Association*, 37, 183–99.

Chládková, K. and Hamann S. (2011). High vowels in southern British English: /u/ fronting does not result in merger. *Proceedings of the XVIIth International Congress of Phonetic Sciences* (pp. 476–9). Hong Kong.

Clements, G.N. (1990). The role of the sonority cycle in core syllabification. In J. Kingston and M.E. Beckman (eds.), *Papers in laboratory phonology I: Between the grammar and physics of speech* (pp. 283–333). Cambridge: Cambridge University Press.

Cruttenden, A. (2001). *Gimson's pronunciation of English*. London: Arnold.

Dalcher, C.V., Knight, R-A. and Jones, M.J. (2008). Cue switching in the perception of approximants: Evidence from two English dialects. In *Penn working papers in linguistics, Volume 14.2: Selected papers from NWAV 36* (pp. 63–71).

Davidson, L. (2006). Phonotactics and articulatory coordination interact in phonology: Evidence from non-native production. *Cognitive Science*, 30, 837–862

Davidson, L. (2010). Phonetic bases of similarities in cross-language production: Evidence from English and Catalan. *Journal of Phonetics*, 38, 272–88.

Davis, B.L. and MacNeilage, P.F. (2002). The internal structure of the syllable. In T. Givón and B.F. Malle (eds.), *The evolution of language out of pre-language* (pp. 135–53). Amsterdam: John Benjamins.

Dupoux, E., Kakehi, K., Hirose, Y., Pallier, C. and Mehler, J. (1999). Epenthetic vowels in Japanese: A perceptual illusion? *Journal of Experimental Psychology: human perception and performance*, 25, 1568–78.

Flemming, E. (2004). Contrast and perceptual distinctiveness. In B. Hayes, R. Kirchner and D. Steriade (eds.), *Phonetically based phonology* (pp. 232–76). Cambridge: Cambridge University Press.

Gordon, M. (2004). Syllable weight. In B. Hayes, R. Kirchner and D. Steriade (eds.), *Phonetically based phonology* (pp. 277–312). Cambridge: Cambridge University Press.

Greenberg, J. (1978). Some generalizations concerning initial and final consonant clusters. In J. Greenberg (ed.), *Universals of human language, Vol. 2: Phonology* (pp. 243–79). Stanford: Stanford University Press.

Greenberg, S. (1996). Auditory processing of speech. In N. J. Lass (ed.), *Principles of experimental phonetics* (pp. 362–407). St Louis: Mosby.

Hall, T.A. (2002). Against extrasyllabic consonants in German and English. *Phonology*, 19, 33–75.

Harnsberger, J.D. (2001). The perception of Malayalam nasal consonants by Marathi, Punjabi, Tamil, Oriya, Bengali and American English listeners: A multidimensional scaling analysis. *Journal of Phonetics*, 29, 303–27.

Harrington, J., Kleber, F. and Reubold, U. (2011). The contributions of the lips and the tongue to the fronting of high back vowels in Standard Southern British English. *Journal of the International Phonetic Association*, 41, 137–56.

Harris, J. (2006). The phonology of being understood: Further arguments against sonority. *Lingua*, 116, 1483–94.

Hazan, V.L. and Boulakia, G. (1993). Perception and production of a voicing contrast by French-English bilinguals. *Language and Speech*, 36, 17–38.

Hooper, J. B. (1972). The syllable in phonological theory. *Language*, 48, 525–40.

Hudson, G. (1995). Consonant release and the syllable. *Linguistics*, 55, 655–72.

Hyman, L.M. (2011). Does Gokana really have no syllables? Or: What's so great about being universal. *Phonology*, 28, 55–85.

Johnson, K. (2012). *Acoustic and auditory phonetics*. Chichester: Wiley-Blackwell.

Jones, M.J. (2013). Phonetic universals and phonetic variation. In M.J. Jones and R.-A. Knight (eds.), *The Bloomsbury companion to phonetics* (pp. 140–54). London: Bloomsbury Ltd.

Jusczyk, P.W. and Luce, P.A. (1994). Infants' sensitivity to phonotactic patterns in the native language. *Journal of Memory and Language*, 33, 630–45.

Kabak, B. and Idsardi, W.J. (2007). Perceptual distortions in the adaptations of English consonant clusters: Syllable structure or consonant contact constraints? *Language and Speech*, 50, 23–52.

Kawasaki, H. (1982). *An acoustical basis for universal constraints on sound sequences*. PhD dissertation, University of California, Berkeley.

Kawasaki-Fukumori, H. (1992). An acoustical basis for universal phonotactic constraints. *Language and Speech*, 35, 73–86.

Keating, P. (1983). Comments on the jaw and syllable structure. *Journal of Phonetics*, 11, 401–6.

Krakow, R.A. (1999). Physiological organization of syllables: A review. *Journal of Phonetics*, 27, 23–54.

Laks, B. (1995). A connectionist account of French syllabification. *Lingua*, 95, 51–76.

Lindblom, B. (1983). Economy of speech gestures. In P.F. MacNeilage (ed.), *The production of speech* (pp. 217–45). New York: Springer.

MacNeilage, P.F. (1998). The frame/content theory of evolution of speech production. *Behavioral and Brain Sciences*, 21, 499–511.

MacNeilage, P.F. and Davis, B.L. (2002). On the origins of intersyllabic complexity. In T. Givón & B. F. Malle (Eds.), *The evolution of language out of pre-language* (pp. 155–70). Amsterdam: John Benjamins Publishing Company.

Maddieson, I. and Emmorey, K. (1985). Relationships between semivowels and vowels: Cross-linguistic investigations of acoustic difference and coarticulation. *Phonetica*, 42, 163–74.

Malsch, D.L. and Fulcher, R. (1989). Categorizing phonological segments: The inadequacy of the sonority hierarchy. In R. Corrigan, F. Eckman and M. Noonan (eds.), *Linguistic categorization* (pp. 69–80). Amsterdam: John Benjamins.

McDougall, K. and Jones, M.J. (2011). Liquid polarisation in Australian English. *Proceedings of the XVIIth International Congress of Phonetic Sciences* (pp. 1358–61). Hong Kong.

Nam, H., Goldstein, L. and Saltzman, E. (2009). Self-organization of syllable structure: A coupled oscillator model. In F. Pellegrino, E. Marisco and I. Chitoran (eds.), *Approaches to phonological complexity* (pp. 299–328). Berlin: Mouton de Gruyter.

Nathan, G.S. (1989). Preliminaries to a theory of phonological substance: The substance of sonority. In R. Corrigan, F. Eckman and M. Noonan (eds.), *Linguistic categorization* (pp. 55–67). Amsterdam: John Benjamins.

Ohala, J.J. (1992). Alternatives to the sonority hierarchy for explaining segmental sequential constraints. In *Papers on the parasession on the syllable* (pp. 319–38). Chicago: Chicago Linguistic Society.

Ohala, J.J. (1998). Content first, frame later. Comment on MacNeilage (1998). *Behavioral and Brain Sciences*, 21, 525–6.

Ohala, J.J. (2008). The emergent syllable. In B.L. Davis and K. Zajdó (eds.), *The syllable in speech production* (pp. 179–86). New York: Lawrence Erlbaum.

Ohala, J.J. and Kawasaki, H. (1984). Prosodic phonology and phonetics. *Phonology Yearbook 1*, 113–27.

Ohala, J.J. and Kawasaki-Fukumori, H. (1997). Alternatives to the sonority hierarchy for explaining segmental sequential constraints. In S. Eliasson and E.H. Jahr (eds.), *Language and its ecology* (pp. 343–65). Berlin: de Gruyter.

Price, P.J. (1980). Sonority and syllabicity: Acoustic correlates of perception. *Phonetica*, 37, 327–43.

Rice, K.D. (1992). On deriving sonority: A structural account of sonority relationships. *Phonology*, 9, 61–99.

Segui, J., and Ferrand, F. (2002). The role of the syllable in speech perception and production. In J. Durand and B. Laks (eds.), *Phonetics, phonology and cognition* (pp. 151–67). Oxford: Oxford University Press.

Sommer, B.A. (1970). An Australian language without CV syllables. *International Journal of American Linguistics*, 36, 57–8.

Steriade, D. (1999). Alternatives to syllable-based accounts of consonantal phonotactics. In O. Fujimura, B. Joseph and B. Palek (eds.), *Proceedings of LP 1998* (pp. 205–46). Prague: Karolinum Press.

Tabain, M., Breen, G. and Butcher, A. (2004). VC vs. CV syllables: A comparison of Aboriginal languages with English. *Journal of the International Phonetic Association*, 34, 175–200.

Ullrich, J.F. (2011). *New Lakota dictionary* (2nd edition). Bloomington, Indiana: Lakota Language Consortium.

Utman, J.A. and Blumstein, S.E. (1994). The influence of language on the acoustic properties of phonetic features: A study of the feature [strident] in Ewe and English. *Phonetica*, 51, 221–38.

Wells, J. C. (1982). *Accents of English*. Cambridge: Cambridge University Press.

Wright, R. (2004). A review of perceptual cues and cue robustness. In B. Hayes, R. Kirchner and D. Steriade (eds.), *Phonetically based phonology* 34–57. Cambridge: Cambridge University Press.

Mark J. Jones is Lecturer in Phonetics at City University London. He studied phonetics at the University of Cambridge and has taught phonetics at the universities of Cambridge, Manchester and York, and at the University College London. His main interest is in phonetic universals and phonetic sources of cross-linguistic variation. He is co-editor, together with Rachael-Anne Knight, of the *Bloomsbury companion to phonetics* (2013).

Index

www.ingramcontent.com/pod-product-compliance
Lightning Source LLC
LaVergne TN
LVHW021127110826
R19582500001B/R195825PG844660LVX00018B/33

* 9 7 8 1 7 8 1 7 9 2 2 7 8 *